BIRMINGHAM-SOUTHERN COLLEGE

50553001431359

Starling, Grover/Strategies for policy m
H97 .S75 1988 C.1 STACKS 1988

D1562978

H
97
.S75
1988

WITHDRAWN
FROM B'ham-Sou.
College Lib.

STRATEGIES
FOR
POLICY
MAKING

STRATEGIES FOR POLICY MAKING

WITHDRAWN FROM B'ham-Sou. College Lib.

Grover Starling

*Director, Center for the Management
of Advanced Technology*

*Professor, School of Business
and Public Administration*

University of Houston–Clear Lake

The Dorsey Press
Chicago, Illinois 60604

To my children,
Alexandra, Terry, and Gregory

© THE DORSEY PRESS, 1988

All rights reserved. No part of this publication may be
reproduced, stored in a retrieval system, or transmitted,
in any form or by any means, electronic, mechanical,
photocopying, recording, or otherwise, without the prior
written permission of the publisher.

Acquisitions editor: *Leo A. W. Wiegman*
Project editor: *Waivah Clement*
Production manager: *Charles J. Hess*
Cover designer: *Image House*
Compositor: *Arcata Graphics/Kingsport*
Typeface: *10/12 Palatino*
Printer: Arcata Graphics/Halliday

ISBN 0-256-05531-9

Library of Congress Catalog Card No. 87–72400

Printed in the United States of America

1 2 3 4 5 6 7 8 9 0 H 5 4 3 2 1 0 9 8

WITHDRAWN
FROM B'ham-Sou.
College Lib.

WITHDRAWN
FROM B'ham-Sou.
College Lib.

Preface

Once upon a time, a king sought training for royal children who would have to play chess as adults. He hired a wizard who developed a course based on checkers. Eventually, after examining the relationship of the training course to the chess problems he had in mind, the king became furious and had the poor wizard beheaded.

Today many seek training that will prepare them to make more intelligent decisions about public policy—that is, what the government should or should not do. Most people will make these decisions indirectly when they cast their vote for a candidate or for a proposition. A few will be more directly involved in the process as policymakers, policy analysts, or implementing officials. But, for both groups, my fairy tale raises a disturbing question: Are these men and women being trained to play checkers when the world's complexities demand a more rigorous course of study? Because most books on public policy base themselves on the unstated assumption that real-world problems can be fitted into the jurisdiction of a single academic department, I am forced to answer yes.

The economic approach, for instance attempts to provide answers to these questions. Who really benefits from a policy? Who pays for it? What is the ratio of benefits to costs? Often quite sophisticated quantitative tools and complex theories can be brought to bear on such questions. But these tools and theories alone are not enough; by themselves, they lead to a kind of hyperrationalistic view of public policy. By this awkward expression, I mean the naive notion that analysis itself sets the policy agenda and its directions; that well-done analysis is likely to be used. It may be neat to study the fifth derivative of the capital-asset pricing model, but we also need a sense of how things get done. Economists can tell us every specialized thing about the modern city we might want to ask except what we really want to know:

v

WITHDRAWN
FROM B'ham-Sou.
College Lib.

how do you put it all together to make the city livable, efficient, safe, and clean.

The political approach addresses a different set of questions. What is the process by which policy is formed? At what points can that process most easily be influenced? What values are at stake? What problems can arise when governments move beyond the formulation of policy to its implementation? These are all necessary questions, but by themselves they are not sufficient. A purely political approach to a public policy question—say, deregulation of natural gas—may tell us a lot, but it can also leave a lot unsaid. For example, a political approach will almost always ignore marginal cost pricing—a crucial concept in any meaningful discussion on the natural gas issue.

Several years ago, in an effort to help resolve some of these difficulties, I wrote *The Politics and Economics of Public Policy*. Its premise was that the most important factor affecting the analysis of public policy was politics and, conversely, that economic analysis could influence the play of power. Modifying John Keats's famous equation of beauty and truth, we might even say: Politics is economics, economics is politics, that is all ye know on earth, and all ye need to know. Well, I now know that was a vast oversimplification. Policy analysis is one of the most interdisciplinary of fields.

Awakening to this fact, some scholars have gravitated toward an issues approach to public policy. Unfortunately, that approach is geared more to categorizing and analyzing patches of knowledge—criminal justice, poverty, welfare, health, education, taxation, and so on—than to threading them together. Moreover, issues and priorities constantly change. What students of public policy really need is an approach that helps them develop a capacity for understanding that will be a continuing asset. Therefore, this book deals with concrete issues—but not as ends in themselves.

How then might we characterize our approach to public policy? In just five words: interdisciplinary, pragmatic, optimistic, international, and integrated. Regarding the first term, we can be brief. Whereas my earlier work merely yoked together politics and economics, this book also draws on psychology, history, cognitive science, systems analysis, and philosophy.

The pragmatism of the book is reflected in its title, *Strategies for Policy Making*. Our chief (though not exclusive) concern will be with those propositions, rules of thumb, concepts, and techniques that influence the actions of successful policy makers. What these strategies may lack in sophistication they more than make up for in their effectiveness. Let me explain.

Most decision makers are quite busy; they have to make decisions in a fairly short time and with limited information. As a former associate director for the Office of Management and Budget remarked, "You have to be able to make a big decision by three o'clock the same afternoon, even if you haven't had a chance to do all the homework you need." If you "spend two years studying something," a western governor once observed, "by the time you concluded it's a good thing to do, the best time for doing it may have passed."[1] Thus, relatively simple mathematical techniques are appropriate for analyzing problems when time is short and data limited. You can then focus on the concepts of analysis without getting bogged down in the details of complicated mathematics or modeling.

The book is also optimistic. Will Rogers said, "I don't make jokes— I just watch the government and report the facts." Decades later, pessimism about what government can do still rides tall in the saddle both in academe and in Washington. One distinguished scholar contends that our recent history of implementing public programs is a record of high aspirations with a dismal failure to deliver. "The age of design is over. . . . The time to modify objectives has come."[2] Meanwhile, in Washington, a tone of dogmatic disparagement of government's ability to perform has crept into policy debates. Conservatives suggest cuts in domestic programs because the-government-cannot-do-anything-right-anyway. Liberals declare that a proactive foreign policy is impossible because the-government-cannot-do-anything-right-anyway. Both are wrong. Government has played a large part in building the physical and intellectual capital of the country and foreign policy has had some remarkable successes. (Since 1945, democracy has slowly expanded and major wars have been avoided. In the sweep of history, these are no mean feats.)

Another characteristic of our approach is its international perspective. International and defense issues are, along with domestic issues, central research concerns, even though the field of policy analysis has tended to avoid the former. This avoidance is not without irony: Policy analysis owes a large methodological and intellectual debt to the early development of systems analysis and planning-programming-budgeting in the defense department. Furthermore, the links between domestic and international policies are too strong to ignore; one need only think of energy, technology, productivity, inflation and unemployment. Governors and mayors certainly recognize as much. Forty states now maintain offices in seventeen foreign nations to help forge trade agreements.[3] National security remains the federal government's highest responsibility. Finally, we must not forget that national security (especially the arms race) is a subject of intense discussion in dormitories and coffee

[1] Robert D. Behn and James W. Vaupel, "Teaching Analytical Thinking," *Policy Analysis* 2, no. 4 (Fall 1976), pp. 663–92.

[2] Aaron Wildavsky, *Speaking Truth to Power* (Boston: Little, Brown, 1979), p. 43.

[3] Michael H. Sherman, "Dateline Main Street: Local Foreign Policies," *Foreign Policy,* Winter 1986–87.

houses as well as in Washington. Why not bring the subject into the academic curriculum?

How can we discuss ways to bring the federal budget under control without considering defense expenditures? The essense of a policy analyst's job is to help order the nation's priorities. One cannot do that very well by ignoring, or acquiescing to, the Pentagon's budget requests.

The last characteristic that I wish to highlight is integration. Any subject so vast and eclectic demands it. Accordingly, the book consists of twelve tightly interwoven chapters. Chapters 1 and 2 provide the foundation for our inquiry. Chapter 1 provides several key definitions, presents the framework of the book, and briefly introduces fifteen core ideas. The second chapter sketches the institutional setting in which the policy process unfolds. Chapters 3 through 11 offer a detailed examination of the policy process and a look at how analysis can be used in it. The chapter titles tell the story: identifying the problem (Chapters 3 and 4); setting goals or strategy (Chapter 5); generating alternatives or options (Chapter 6); measuring costs, benefits, and risks (Chapters 7 and 8); getting the policy proposal adopted in the political arena (Chapter 9); implementing the policy (Chapter 10); and finally, evaluating it (Chapter 11). The last chapter explores normative or value questions that policy making raises.

Drawing on an extremely broad range of empirical knowledge that has been sifted, purified, and rearranged, *Strategies for Policy Making* will, I hope, generate some intellectual excitement. I have tried to keep it free of jargon, devoid of abstract theorizing, wide-ranging in application, yet with an intense analytical focus. In trespassing from one discipline to another, I have tried to perceive connections, and connections among connections, rather than grind out theorems and correlations. This is certainly not the only way to do social science, but I think it has a place.

Acknowledgment

These twelve chapters represent an effort to think about public policy in a rather different perspective, and because some are, to an extent, experimental and pioneering, I have doubtless fallen into errors of fact or logic. I may have stated as certainties propositions or rules that should be guarded or qualified. I am aware of such weaknesses, and I accept full responsibility for these failings.

That they are not more glaringly obvious is chiefly due to the exertions of reviewers and friends who saved me from a score of blunders. My heaviest debt is to Philip Whitbeck, who was responsible for my beginning to think about the application of policy analysis techniques to the needs of every public administrator. In a sense, neither this book nor its progenitor would have been written if it were not for him. Dennis Daley of the University of Mississippi, Larry Elowitz of Georgia College, and Eileen Von Ravenswaay of Michigan State University offered insightful suggestions throughout the project. I am obliged for advice on both technical and philosophical matters to Richard C. Allison and Roger E. Durant, both of the University of Houston–Clear Lake. It is also a pleasure to thank Betty Brott for secretarial work remarkable both in quality and amount. Finally, I wish to thank the University of Houston–Clear Lake for granting me faculty development leave. Much of the research for this book was made possible by that time.

Grover Starling

Contents[1]

List of Figures   xxi
List of Tables   xxiv

Chapter 1   Analysis for Action   1
  What Is Policy?   1
  What Is Analysis?   6
  The Policymaking Process   8
    Key elements in the policymaking process   8
    The interrelationship between policymaking and policy analysis   9
  Interdisciplinary Aspects of Policy Analysis   11
  Fifteen Core Ideas   13
    Idea 1:   Agenda setting   13
    Idea 2:   The use and abuse of history   14
    Idea 3:   The systems view   15
    Idea 4:   The fundamental theorem of welfare economics   16
    Idea 5:   Externalities: A justification for government action   17
    Idea 6:   The art of strategic thinking   18
    Idea 7:   The psychology of choice   20
    Idea 8:   Mapping the alternatives: The decision tree   21
    Idea 9:   The importance of marginal analysis   21
    Idea 10: True economic costs   22
    Idea 11: Discounting: The valuation of future consequences   24
    Idea 12: Pluralism, interdependence, and power dynamics   25
    Idea 13: The theory of nonmarket failures   26
    Idea 14: Output—not input—is the bottom line   29
    Idea 15: The ubiquity of ethics   29

---

[1] An asterisk (*) indicates material more suitable for advanced seniors and graduate students.

Chapter 2   Institutional Setting   35

  Key Participants   37
    Administration,   37
      The president   37
      Presidential staff   39
      Presidential appointments and issue networks   41
    Civil servants   45
    Capitol Hill   50
      The Intellectual origins of Congress' role in the adoption of policy   50
      Congressional resources   52
    The committee system   53
    The power of the purse   55
  *Think Tanks and policy intellectuals   57
    How are policy studies used?   58
    When will a policy study be used (and not just sought)?   60
    What are the pros and cons of using outside sources?   61
  Mass media   62
  A note on policymakers in state, urban, and institutional settings   64
    City councils and state legislatures   64
    The governing board   65
  A Model of Policy Issue Development   67
    Systemic and institutional agendas   68
    Sources of bias   69
    Countervailing factors   71
  Issue incubation and issue dissipation   75
  *The garbage can model: The theory   75
    *The garbage can model: Four case studies   77
    The Tax Reform Act of 1986   77
    Strategic defense initiative   79
    Industrial policy: A solution looking for a problem   80
    Acid rain: A problem in search of solution   81
  The Policy Process: A Wide-Angle View   82

Chapter 3   Diagnosis   87

  How Problems Capture Our Attention   87
  Sources of Error   92
    Organizational structure   92
    Ideology   94
    Ignorance and babel   95
    Noise   96
    Lag   98
      The big economic winners of the 1980s   98

Big mergers and the public interest   99
Shrinking nuclear arsenals   100
Avoidance   100
Masking problems   103
Pseudo-problems   105
*The lively art of problem representation   106
Proto-problems   107
Representing the poverty problem   110
The conservative view   110
Critique   111
National security   112
Unemployment   114
Gathering and analyzing the evidence   118
A brief note on statistics for policymakers   119
Measures of central tendency   119
Measures of dispersion   121
Survey research   123
Usefulness   123
Procedure   124
Analysis   124
Statistical pitfalls   125
Delphi technique   128
Consumer analysis   130
Indirect assessments   133
Correlation and causation   137
Relationships between attributes   137
The concept of correlation   139
An application   142
Causation   143
*The Power of Numbers   147

Chapter 4 Prognosis   154
The Naive Forecasting Manifesto   154
Models and Modeling   158
What is a model?   158
The growing use of models   159
Models and theory   160
Basics of model building   160
Initial stages of modeling   161
The dynamic behavior of the model   163
Heroin addiction: A case study in modeling   166
*Economic Models   169
Back to Eden   170

Marvelous markets 170
  Pareto optimality 171
The U.S. farm policy: An economic perspective 175
  Demand and supply of corn 176
  Putting it all together: Equilibrium 178
  The long-run U.S. farm problem 179
  The short-run U.S. farm problem 180
Government responses 183
  Price supports 183
  Governmental purchases, crop restrictions, and subsidies 184
Solving the problem 185
Trend Extrapolation 186
What trend extrapolation can do for policymakers 187
Distinguishing two types of changes 188
Straight-line trends 190
Fitted curves 193
Cycles 195
*A short discourse on the hazards of extrapolation 197
  The extrapolator's paradox 197
  Technical considerations 199
*Monitoring 201
Experts—A Fifth Forecasting Method 209
Expert panels 209
How expert are the experts? 211
Toward better forecasts 211
Concluding Observations 212

Chapter 5   Strategic Thinking 218
Prologue: Reflections on the Theory and Practice of Goal Setting 219
The case of Joan Claybrook 219
Developing goals 220
The Concept of Strategic Thinking 223
What it is 223
The grand strategy of Hannibal 223
The grand strategy of the North 226
Toward a Theory of Policy Design 229
Concentration 230
  Examples in foreign, domestic, and economic policy 231
  How not to concentrate: A White House perspective 233
  The concept of strategic factors 235
  Applications 238
Clarity 241

Changeability	245
Structuring flexibility	245
Paradox and tension in the design process	246
Challenge	248
Coordination	254
Consistency	257
Recapitulation	262
*The Use (and Abuse) of History in Policy Analysis	264
Putting problems in their historical context	265
Generational learning and prognosis	266
Perception and misperception	266
Implications	268
The momentum of historical experience	271
A final word of caution	271
What history teaches about goal setting	272
Economic history	272
Other lessons	274
One big lesson	275
Historical analogies and new options	277
The real purpose of analogy in policy analysis	278
*A Preview of the Next Three Chapters	280
Developing a range of alternatives	280
Screening the preliminary alternatives	281
Estimating the measurable consequences: Benefits, costs, and risks	282
Assessing provisional offerings	282
Determining the effect of constraints	283
Reassessing the ordering of the alternatives	284
Chapter 6 Options	289
Range of Government Action	290
Coercive actions	290
Noncoercive actions	291
Masterly inaction	293
Classifying Alternatives	296
Incremental	296
Branching	298
*Invention in Public Policy	301
Problems of definition	302
Applying the definition	306
Interpretation	307
Two recent examples of creativity: A proposal and a reality	311
The shared economy	311
Sharing sovereignty in Northern Ireland	312

Psychological Perspective on Choice 313
How psychological factors dictate choice 314
Bounded rationality 317
Heuristic search 319
  Selective search 320
  Satisficing 325
  Learning from experience 327
  Analogy 328
  Try something 331
  Means-ends analysis 332
  Decomposition 334
  Synectics 337
  Thought experiments 339
Groupthink 340
*Checking the Assessment 341

Chapter 7 Costs, Benefits, and Risks 349
Capturing All the Costs and Benefits 352
Real benefits and pecuniary effects 352
The direct and indirect categories 353
*Environmental programs: A case study in measuring costs
and benefits* 355
  Damage estimates 356
  Avoidance costs 357
  Abatement and transactions costs 358
Intangibles 359
Putting a value on life 360
Distributional Consideration 364
The distribution of benefits 364
The distribution of costs 366
Uncertainty and Risk 369
The quest for certainty 369
Risky business 374
  Star Wars 374
  Nuclear power 375
Risk in Perspective 376
Decision making under risk conditions 378
Subjective probabilities 381
The future of risk management 385
*Application: Offshore Oil Leasing Decision 387
The first principle 387
The second principle 388
The third principle 389

Chapter 8   Assessing Impacts   395
  Preliminaries: The Principal of Maximum Social Gain   395
    Cost-Benefit Analysis   398
    The discount factor   399
        Decision rules: Ratios versus absolutes   402
    Some illustrative examples   403
    Caveat   405
  Cost-Effectiveness Analysis   410
  Technology Assessment   418
    The problem defined: Unintended consequences   419
    The methodology of technology assessment   422
  Limits to Analysis   430

Chapter 9   The Political Factor   435
  The Nature of Politics   435
  Behavioral Models and Political Actions   439
    *Understanding movivations, beliefs, and roles   439
        Political psychology   440
        Inside the congressional mind   445
    Integrated political analysis technique (INPAT)   450
        Selecting participants   450
        Inventorying political resources   452
        Making rough calculations   453
  Institutionalism and Political Feasibility   456
  The Process of Pluralism   458
    Bargaining   460
        Conditions   460
        Consequences   461
    *A closer look at how the organized control policy   466
        Majoritarian politics   466
        Client politics   466
        Entrepreneurial politics   467
        Interest group politics   468
  The Foundations of Structural Analysis   468
    Politics as symbolic action   471
    Methods of symbolic action   475
  Public Choice Approach   478
    The problem of private goals   480
    *Voting   481
    *Coalition building: A laboratory experiment   484
    *Winner take less   486
  Managing the Process: A Synthesis   488
    Initiative   489

Gradualism   493
Coalitions   494

Chapter 10   Levers for Implementation   498
The Concept of Action Levers   498
  Types   498
  Exogenous elements   499
Design Levers   500
  Deinstitutionalization: A cautionary tale   501
  Additional comments on designing for implementation   504
    Why goals may sometimes need to be obscure   504
    Why less is better   505
Operating System Levers   506
  Start-up decisions   510
    The start-up period   510
    Learning curves   510
    Scheduling   514
  Public relations   518
  Contingency decisions   521
    What can the policy analysts do?   522
    Alternative scenario planning   524
  Incentive decisions   525
    The problem defined   525
    What to do   531
    Using CBA in incentive decisions   535
  *Pricing decisions   536
    Selling public services   540
    Marginal cost pricing   541
    Prices and behavior   543
Organizational Levers   549
  Simple versus complex organizations   549
  Contracting   550
  On being the right size   552
  *New and restructured institutions: A macroapproach to implementation   554
    The Constitution: Is it broke?   554
    Reshuffling and restructuring the executive branch   556
    Reform in Congress   559
    Crisis and reform in the federal court   560
Appendix 10–1   A Brief Note on a Vast Subject: Computers and
    Policy Analysis   562

Chapter 11   What Is Good Policy?   · 571
Seven Criteria   571
  Output (not *input*)   571
    Measuring outputs: Appalachian Regional Development Art   572

Measuring outputs: Military equipment readiness	573
Measuring outputs: The effect of Reaganomics	574
Side-effects	575
Efficiency	577
Strategy	579
Compliance	582
Justice and other normative standards	583
Intervention effect	584
Evaluation Methodologies	587
The Minneapolis domestic violence experiment	589
Purpose	589
Experiment design	590
Findings and policy implications	590
Field experiment: Workfare and project concern	591
Programs linking welfare to work	591
Evaluating desegregation	593
Case study versus sample survey: The causes and persistence of poverty	594
Auditing: How well OSHA saves lives in the workplace	596
Are the benefits of Head Start worth the cost?	598
Termination of Public Policy	599
Documentation and evaluation	600
Timing	600
Rate	600
Terminators and referees	600
Survival tactics	601
Weak points	601
Policies as Hypotheses	601
Chapter 12 Two Concepts of Ethics	606
The Ubiquity of Ethics in Policy Studies	607
The role of ideology in diagnosing the problem	607
Foreseeing consequences: A necessary condition for moral conduct	611
Playing fast and loose with the evidence	614
Soft theories paraded as hard facts	614
Ignore or "select" the data	615
Ethical issues during implementation	616
Tensions in evaluating policy	619
The forbidden experiment	619
Contemporary tensions	620
Economic Ethics	621
The "old" welfare economics: Utilitarianism	622
Jeremy Bentham	622
John Rawls's theory of justice	626

The new welfare economics: Pareto optimality   628
Applied welfare economics: Cost-benefit analysis revisited   631
Political Ethics   634
The Lincoln-Douglas debate reconsidered   634
Political debates today   636
Concept I   638
Concept II   639
Criteria of Choice   642
Learning from Lincoln   642
King and Kennan as exemplars   643
The link between virtue and policy   644
Appendix A   Compound Sum of $1   652
Appendix B   Present Value of $1   655
Appendix C   Practical Aspects of Managing and Performing Policy
Studies   657

Glossary   670

Index   687

LIST OF FIGURES

1–1	Linking policy, plan, and program	3
1–2	Universe of policies	4
1–3	Pathways between analysis and the policymaking process	10
2–1	Executive office of the president	40
2–2	A functional diagram of policy issue development	69
2–3	Hypothesized relationship between the systemic and institutional agendas	84
2–4	The life cycle concept applied to the environmental issue	85
3–1	Problem solving as pattern recognition: An example	97
3–2	Poverty rate among children under eighteen years and elderly sixty-five years or older (1970–1983)	102
3–3	How one problem can mask another: Two examples	103
3–4	How the Pentagon represents Soviet military power	113
3–5	Normal distribution	122
3–6	Trend in concentration of income	128
3–7	How to think about relationships between variables	138
3–8	Correlation of insurance coverage and hospital costs (hypothetical)	140
3–9	Health expenditures	152
4–1	A major purpose of forecasting: To narrow the range of uncertainty	157
4–2	A complete taxonomy of objectives for choosing an air pollution control program for a city	161
4–3	A model of fire department operations	162
4–4	Positive and negative relationships in model building	163
4–5	The Malthusian model	164
4–6	The Malthusian model redrawn	165
4–7	Critical flows in the heroin problem	167
4–8	Dynamic model of the heroin-using population	168
4–9	Demand and supply in the widget market	172
4–10	The signaling role of prices	174
4–11	Demand curve for corn (hypothetical)	177
4–12	Supply curve for corn (hypothetical)	178
4–13	Equilibrium in the corn market	180
4–14	Long-run U.S. farm problem	181
4–15	Short-term instability of farm prices	182
4–16	The rising cost of farm support	184
4–17	An economic model of three agricultural programs	185
4–18	Projected surplus in the social security trust fund (in billions of dollars)	189
4–19	Annual percentage change in U.S. gross national product, 1940–1985	190
4–20	Projecting female employment	191

4–21	S-curve	193
4–22	Time series showing secular trend and cyclical variation	195
4–23	Time series for incarceration	196
4–24	Extrapolating on a limited data base	199
4–25	Conceptualizing raw material supplies	214
5–1	Hannibal's theater of operations	225
5–2	Grand strategy of the North	228
5–3	Policy design framework	231
5–4	How four policies are connected	260
5–5	Conceptual environment/cost trade-off curve at a fixed level of energy production	261
6–1	Range of government actions	291
6–2	The creative process: Mozart and Beethoven compared	336
7–1	Estimating environmental damage costs	357
7–2	Typical preference curves	380
7–3	Decision tree for hurricane seeding	381
7–4	Typical probability distributions	382
7–5	Assessing the lower and upper quartiles	382
7–6	Cumulative distribution	384
7–7	Probability distribution of property damage	385
8–1	Representing social benefits	396
8–2	An optimal level of social benefits	397
8–3	Life cycle costs and benefits	398
8–4	Dollar benefits from the liquid metal fast breeder reactor with a 1993 introduction	402
8–5	Cancer program costs (estimated)	414
8–6	Deaths averted versus costs	415
8–7	Impact relevance tree for social impact analysis	426
9–1	Style orientations of political executives	441
9–2	Bargaining: Causes and consequences	461
9–3	How different policies tend to generate different politics	467
9–4	Four types of public policy	469
9–5	The voting paradox: A graphic representation	484
9–6	The positions of board members with respect to two goal dimensions	485
9–7	Using game theory to predict and explain political strategy	487
10–1	The probability of successful implementation as a function of participants	507
10–2	Sample pages of the code of federal regulations	511
10–3	Relationship among design, start-up, and steady state for four prototype programs—or why no one hits the ground running	513
10–4	An 80 percent learning curve	514
10–5	Cost curve for shuttle operations	515

10–6   Scheduling research and development of wind energy
        with PERT   516
10–7   The high cost of schedule changes   518
10–8   Pollyanna policy planning   525
10–9   The incentive problem   533
10–10   Marginal cost pricing   542
10–11   Cabinet structure with the addition of a department of
        science and technology   557
10–A1   A simple PERT network   564
10–A2   A simple PERT network continued   564
11–1   A simplified model of the dynamics of policy assessment   603
12–1   Okun's leaky-bucket experiment   612
12–2   Optimal distribution of income in a very simple society   623
12–3   Trade-off between equality and efficiency   625
12–4   Adam's indifference curve   629
12–5   Adam and Eve's indifference curves   630
12–6   An optimal distribution in Eden   630
12–7   The social economic pattern of a hypothetical city   650

LIST OF TABLES

2–1   Standing committees of the Congress   54
3–1   Surplus/Deficit as percentage of GNP for eighteen
       industrial market economies, 1983   110
3–2   Chicago Bears defensive team, standard deviation of the
       mean   122
3–3   Support of proposal to increase expenditures for public
       housing by income   125
3–4   Mean satisfaction rankings of service delivery by
       neighborhood   126
3–5   Standardized regression coefficients (beta weights)   141
3–6   Salaries paid and games won, 1985 season   143
3–7   Linear correlation: An illustrative example   144
4–1   Employment status of civilian women, 1950 to 1985
       (1,000s)   191
4–2   Least squares data table   192
4–3   Population growth and doubling time   194
4–4   Errors in population forecasts   200
5–1   Strategic factors for government success   237
5–2   The "top ten" strategic factors by level of government   239
5–3   Using strategic factors to get from problem definition to
       policy recommendation   242
5–4   Scope of goals for heroin addict policies   253
5–5   The U.S. future in space: Linking possible goals and
       objectives   258
5–6   Lessons from the American economic experience, 1963–1983   273
6–1   A tentative list of inventive public policies, 1949–1972   308
6–2   Sources of inventive policy, 1949–1972   309
6–3   Summary of rates of policy invention   311
6–4   Morphological analysis for personal transportation   318
7–1   Cost-benefit matrix   353
7–2   Cost-benefit matrix for the Satellite Solar Power System   362
7–3   Program benefits by age, income, region, and color of
       beneficiary   365
7–4   Annual expenditures per family on gasoline, by fifths of
       families ranked by money income   366
7–5   Tax hit list   367
7–6   Distribution of some costs and benefits in eleven
       programs, actual and proposed   270
8–1   A hypothetical cost-benefit analysis   403
8–2   Cost-benefit analysis of four power projects   404
8–3   Measuring the costs and benefits of the 55 mph speed
       limit: A critical appraisal   407
8–4   Ranking of countermeasures by decreasing cost
       effectiveness in present value dollars per total fatalities
       forestalled—ten-year total   412

8–5	Cancer control program: 1968–1972	413
9–1	ADA ideological rating and congressional vote on natural gas deregulation, 1976	447
9–2	Political feasibility analysis	451
9–3	The political feasibility of a city's criminal justice plan	453
10–1	Hypothetical marginal costs from the sale of marijuana by the state of Texas	543
11–1	Expected versus observed repeat violence over six months	590
12–1	Distribution of earnings	614

If we, the scholars, with our patient and unsensational labors, can help the statesmen to understand these basic truths—if we can help them to understand not only the dangers we face and the responsibility they bear for overcoming these dangers but also the constructive and hopeful possibilities that lie there to be opened up by wiser, more restrained, and more realistic policies—if we can do these things, then we will be richly repaid for our dedication and our persistence; for we will then have the satisfaction of knowing that scholarship, the highest work of the mind, has served, as it should, the highest interests of civilization.

George F. Kennon, 1982

Chapter 1

Analysis for Action

Imagine that you are czar of U.S. highways. Assume that a twenty mile per hour speed limit would reduce automobile-related deaths to virtually zero and that, for each ten miles per hour above this speed limit, the death toll rises by 10,000. What is a reasonable national speed limit?

After you successfully resolve that question, the president and Congress by acclamation make you Health Care Czar. Should a welfare recipient get $100,000 for a liver transplant or is the money better spent on medical checkups for needy kids? Should money go to keep a brain-damaged infant alive in intensive care or to provide prenatal guidance for low-income pregnant women? Should elderly people get heart bypass surgery at public expense?

Onward and upward—the president and Congress decide to give you *global* responsibilities. In many remote parts of the world, vast numbers of people die from famine, disease, and other generally predictable disasters. How much should the average American be willing to spend annually to reduce the number of these deaths?

These formidable questions all concern public policy—that is, what government should do. They are, of course, deadly serious questions. Furthermore, they are quite real, for today public decision makers must seek answers to just such questions as these. This is primarily a book about how such questions are analyzed. To put it a little more formally: Our aim is to suggest strategies for improving the quality of policy in any organization—federal agency, small city, large university, or even corporation.

WHAT IS POLICY?

While experts may quibble over exactly what constitutes a policy, most definitions boil down to this classic formulation: A policy is a

1

general statement of aims or goals. It is not quite the same thing as a plan, which is best thought of as specified means for achieving the goals of policy. Thus a policy is a kind of guide that delimits action; it is much more open-ended than a plan. A brief example might help clarify these terminological distinctions. The Public Health Service might put forward its policy for improving the health status of Americans. One of the goals might call for ultimately eliminating all forms of human cancer, but the Public Health Service does not give any specific deadline for achieving it. So it falls on the National Cancer Institute to outline a plan to attain that goal. The institute might, therefore, put forward the following objectives to serve as the strategy for cancer research efforts: reducing the ability of external agents, such as industrial chemicals, to produce cancer; enhancing the individual's resistance to the development of cancer, perhaps through vaccination; preventing body cells from becoming cancerous; preventing the growth of tumors from small groups of cells that have become malignant; conducting field studies to show the risks of cancer in large populations as an aid to improving prevention and cure; applying present knowledge to cure as many patients as possible; and, finally, stepping up efforts in patient rehabilitation. With each objective, we can, in turn, associate a wider range of programs and projects of the institute.

While there is hardly a consensus among public decision makers about what constitutes a policy, a plan, and a program, this should not be a license for us to use these terms inconsistently or synonymously. Figure 1–1 is an attempt to link these key terms, along with three others, in a logical fashion. While I shall endeavor to follow this usage throughout the book, it should be kept in mind that the linkage is an idealized one.

The term *policy*, as broadly defined above, applies to a wide range of human activities, and before we examine different types of public policies and their characteristics, it might be useful to consider briefly the universe of policies, to see just how broadly the term can be applied. As shown in Figure 1–2, policy can be considered, at one end of a broad spectrum, as being concerned with nations and international systems. The European Common Market Charter, signed in Rome in 1958, and the annual economic conferences of the U.S. president and the heads of other major industrialized nations are examples of policies with international scope. Of lesser scope are policies concerning a single nation. Such national policies may cover either the entire nation or only a part of it. An example of the former would be the Clean Air Act; an example of the latter, a policy of the Department of Transportation to solve the transportation problem of the northeast corridor from Boston to Washington, D.C.

Generally speaking, the policies of states, cities, institutions, and

Figure 1–1
Linking policy, plan, and program

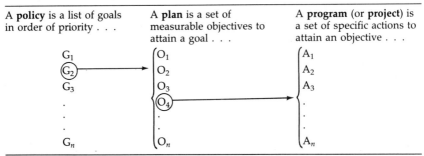

A **policy** is a list of goals in order of priority . . .	A **plan** is a set of measurable objectives to attain a goal . . .	A **program** (or **project**) is a set of specific actions to attain an objective . . .

A simple example will perhaps do much to clarify these terse terminological stipulations. Assume that the mayor of a city has among other goals an increase in the physical safety of the city's inhabitants and improvement in housing conditions. The mayor might then announce a policy that these goals, in the order stated, are to have priority over all other goals. A plan to implement this policy might specify the objectives of (1) reducing the rate of crimes of violence in the city, as well as the death rate from traffic accidents, by 25 percent, and (2) providing an additional 10,000 housing units. A program would spell out in detail the actions to be taken to achieve these objectives—for example, increasing the police force by 1,000 and providing city-backed, long-term loans to construction firms.

individuals would be somewhat narrower. The inclusion of individuals in our universe of policies should cause no puzzlement, since people do (either consciously or unconsciously) set goals for themselves.

Figure 1–2 also looks at the universe of policies in terms of specificity, since policies can be described at different levels of abstraction. These may range from broad guidelines to specific actions. The National Aeronautics and Space Act of 1958 provides an example of the former. In carrying out the policy of Congress, the agency's administration is told only that the activities in space should be devoted to peaceful purposes for the benefit of all mankind and that the functions of NASA are

> to conduct research for the solution of problems of flight within and outside the Earth's atmosphere and develop, construct, test, and operate aeronautical and space vehicles; conduct activities required for the exploration of space with manned and unmanned vehicles; arrange for the most effective utilization of the scientific and engineering resources of the United States with other nations engaged in aeronautical and space activities for peaceful purposes; and to provide for the wisest practicable and appropriate dissemination of information concerning NASA's activities and their results.

In contrast to these broad guidelines, President Carter's National Energy Plan set specific goals: reduction of the annual growth of U.S. energy demand to less than 2 percent; reduction of the level of oil imports to less than 6 million barrels per day; achievement of a 10

4

Figure 1–2
Universe of policies

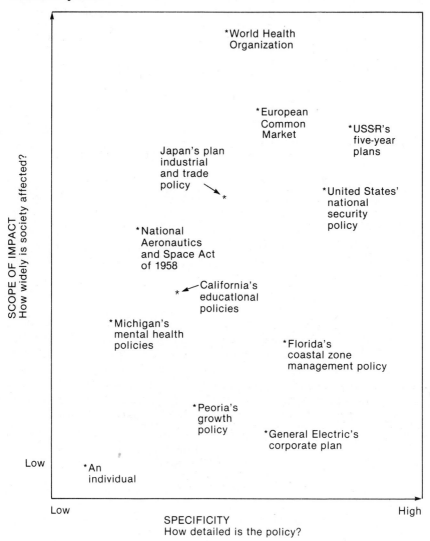

percent reduction in gasoline consumption; insulation of 90 percent of all U.S. homes and all new buildings; an increase in annual coal production to at least 400 million tons; and use of solar energy in more than 2.5 million homes.

Despite the wide applicability of the term policy, the focus of our inquiry will be chiefly on the subset of policies that we designate as public policies. But what are public policies? The special character of a public policy is that it is formulated, adopted, and implemented by what David Easton calls "the authorities" in a political system: those persons who "engage in the daily affairs of a political system," who are "recognized by most members of the system as having the responsibility of these matters," and whose actions are "accepted as binding most of the time by most of the members so long as they act within the limits of their roles"—that is, as "elders, paramount chiefs, executives, legislators, judges, administrators, councilors, monarchs, and the like."[1]

Public policies cover a wide and serious range of issues. Most of these issues can, however, be subsumed under one of the following sixteen groups:

National defense	Health
International affairs	Income security
Science, space, and technology	Law enforcement
Natural resources, environment, and energy	Government reorganization
	Civil rights
Agriculture	Economic control
Commerce and transportation	Taxation
Community and regional development .	Revenue sharing
Education, training, employment, and social sciences	

What this list fails to show, however, is how quickly policy issues can change. This is an important idea. Twenty years ago I doubt that energy would have appeared on so short a list; by 1978, its omission was inconceivable; by 1987, the president and some experts were questioning whether energy was still a priority issue. I leave it to the reader's own gifts of prophecy to say which issues will appear and disappear in the next ten years.

Given this flux, a broader system of classification might be helpful. In an important theoretical work, Theodore Lowi has developed a way of classifying domestic policies, according to their impact on society,

---

[1] David Easton, *A Systems Analysis of Political Life* (New York: John Wiley & Sons, 1965), p. 212. Note that Easton's definition of authorities extends to judges. Today the notion that judges always limit themselves to interpreting the law is more than suspect. When, for example, the U.S. Supreme Court, performing its assigned task of judicial review of legislative acts, laid down in *Brown* v. *The Board of Education* (1954) a new rule of law on school desegregation, it clearly did what Congress might have done—that is, make policy. The Supreme Court makes policy on many issues. Nevertheless, since this book views public policy chiefly from an administrative perspective, the judiciary's role as a source of public policy will not be emphasized.

into one of three "arenas"—distributive, regulatory, or redistributive.[2]

Distributive policies are governmental actions that convey tangible benefits to individuals, groups, or corporations. Distributive policies are synonymous with governmental subsidies or patronage. Included here are most contemporary public land and resource policies; rivers and harbors ("pork barrel") programs; defense procurement and research and development; labor, business, and agricultural "clientele" services; and the traditional tariff. These policies, in a sense, are not policies at all, but highly individualized decisions that only by accumulation can be called policies.

Regulatory policies are also specific and individual in their impact, though not quite to the extent that distributive policies are. Although the laws are stated in general terms ("Arrange the transportation system efficiently"; "Thou shalt not show favoritism in pricing"), the impact of regulatory decisions is clearly one of directly raising costs and/or reducing or expanding the alternatives of private individuals ("Get off the grass!" "Produce kosher if you advertise kosher!"). Regulatory policies are distinguishable from distributive policies in that the regulatory decision involves a *direct choice* as to who will be benefited and who will be deprived in the short run. Not all applicants for a single television channel or an overseas air route can be propitiated. But in making such decisions, agencies are establishing general rules; over time, and in the aggregate, these rules indicate a general policy direction.

Redistributive policies, the third type, involve a conscious attempt by the government to manipulate the allocation of wealth, property rights, or some other value among broad categories of private individuals in society. But the categories of impact, Lowi stresses, are much broader than those involved in regulatory policies. These issues, which include such matters as the income tax and various welfare programs, tend to be defined along class lines, the haves versus the have-nots.

Lowi's scheme of distributive, regulatory, and redistributive policies will prove a useful aid to our inquiry. In particular, it can increase our understanding of the politics associated with policymaking. But more on that later; now we need to couple the concept of public policy to that weighty word *analysis*.

WHAT IS ANALYSIS?

To many the word *analysis* conjures up an image of the laboratory replete with test tubes, retorts, centrifuges, and Bunsen burners. The

---

[2] Theodore Lowi, "American Business, Public Policy, Case Studies, and Political Theory," *World Politics*, July 1964, pp. 677–715. See also Lowi's *The End of Liberalism: The Second Republic of the United States* (New York: Norton, 1979).

image is not wholly inappropriate, for analysis forms the heart of much scientific research. The word itself comes from an ancient Greek word meaning "decompose," "break down," "separate the whole into component parts." Thus the German chemist Justus Liebig, by analyzing foodstuffs of every kind, came to the correct conclusion that the principal components of foods are proteins, fats, and carbohydrates. Given a complex whole such as the Clean Air Act, analysis seems to offer the best, perhaps the only, route to an adequate understanding of the subject.

Yet most of us are reluctant to submit our own problems, much less public policies, to such conscious and systematic decomposition. Apparently, we feel that problem solving and policymaking are natural talents that do not require intellectual strategies. Or perhaps we feel a little silly and self-conscious about organizing our thinking on paper. Whatever the reason, the human mind often does not work in an analytical fashion. Faced with complex problems involving uncertainty and trade-offs between important objectives, we tend to deny the existence of the uncertainty by establishing strong beliefs about the future. Similarly, we deny the existence of competing objectives and pursue them all, despite the contradictions.

To compensate for these cognitive tendencies, the self-discipline of analysis is required. As a kind of preview, we might at this point consider how basically we could do a quick analysis of a major public policy. Our line of attack, as illustrated below, is the epitome of analysis: what we have done is no more than write in an orderly way each of the components present in any policy issue.

Step 1: Defining the problem.
- Identify the specific need to be satisfied and indicate its magnitude.
- Isolate the causes of or major contributions to the problem.
- Identify how specific population groups (geographic, economic, racial, age, etc.) are affected.

Step 2: Stating goals and generating alternatives to achieve them.
- Identify the major goals and how they relate to the problem.
- Identify the alternative ways to achieve these goals.
- Evaluate the alternatives in terms of their benefits and costs.
- Identify the distribution of the impacts of each alternative in society.

Step 3: Using assumptions and limited information, assess the pros and cons of each alternative in terms of relevant criteria.

Step 4: Providing the implementation.
- Identify the organizations responsible for carrying out the policy.
- Identify the methods for evaluating the success of the policy.

THE POLICYMAKING PROCESS

One of the most fascinating things about public policy is how it is made. In this section, we will try to uncover the pattern that runs like a steel thread beneath the tangle of politics and complexity of modern government. With this done, we will be in a good position to show the relationship of the policy process to the special kind of research we call policy analysis; we will also understand better the relationship between policymakers and policy analysts. The resulting picture will provide the framework of the book.

Key elements in the policymaking process

Public policies must not be thought of as seashells, those osseous things with no apparent beginning or end. Public policies are kinetic; they are fragile. To see a document such as the 283 pages called the National Energy Plan is to see very little; only when the document is viewed within the context of the entire policymaking process does it become really meaningful. In recent years, describing this process has become a minor industry among political scientists. Fortunately, most of these descriptive models contain five common elements:

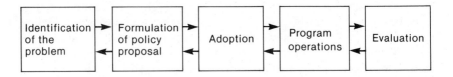

In simple terms, what the above schematic tells us is this. The identification of some problem (fuel shortage) or opportunity (moon landing) leads to the formulation of a policy. In the federal government this frequently, but certainly not always, occurs in the executive branch. The policy proposal, as we noted earlier, attempts to spell out in somewhat broad outline what should be done to mitigate the problem or realize the opportunity. Ideally, the proposal contains two major features: a listing of goals in order of priority and a statement of alternatives (or programs) to attain these goals. But things hardly end at this stage. Next, the proposal must be adopted or legitimated. In this stage of the process, the legislature, council, or board plays a central—indeed, decisive—role. Not only must these bodies give their authorization for the policy, after debate or modification, but they must also approve (appropriate) the funds necessary to attain the goals of the policy.

The Zulu expression *nala indaba* means "the talking is over." That expression might well be applied to the fourth stage of the policy process, because eventually action must be taken by specific individuals at specific times and places if the goals and objectives of a policy are ever to be attained. If the legislature, council, or board tended to be most conspicuous in the third stage, then surely the bureaucracy dominates here.

Not to be overlooked is the importance of the last stage, evaluation. Presumably, the participants in the policy process have established some criteria or measurement scales to help them determine the degree to which each alternative meets its objectives. The results of evaluation can then be fed back to earlier stages of the process, often leading to modifications in the original policy. Like some chemical reactions, the policy process is reversible at all stages (this is indicated in the above schematic by the use of two-directional arrows).

The interrelationship between policymaking and policy analysis

Thus far, this chapter has presented two key concepts—policy analysis and policymaking. Now the relationship between the two must be clarified. And in this clarification, we will begin to see the central thesis, the lodestar, of this work: policy analysis cannot be fully understood without also understanding the policymaking process.

In handbooks on Chinese traditional painting, a word of advice commonly given to the artist who wishes to learn to paint trees is to sketch them in winter, for then, in the absence of the confused and blurry effect of their leafy masses, their inner structure and specific character are best revealed. We can use this advice in trying to grasp the intricate relationship between the policymaking process and policy analysis. Figure 1–3, which shows that relationship in its stark nudity, is the result.

Essentially, Figure 1–3 reveals the specific points in the policy process at which a variety of analytical concepts, propositions, and techniques can provide direction to the thinking, choices, and administrative behavior of policymakers. The term *strategies* as used in the title of this book refers to those concepts, propositions, and techniques that have proven effective in helping people make better decisions about public policy. For convenience, I have grouped these strategies into chapters according to where in the policy process they most frequently apply. One should not infer from this arrangement, however, that a given concept, proposition, or technique can be applied to only one phase of the policymaking process. Quite the contrary; most strategies can be fruitfully applied at several junctures. For example, those who formulate a policy should give some thought to potential problems down the road, when the policy is being implemented. Therefore, most of the techniques in Chapter 10 apply to the policy formulation phase, as indicated by the connecting arrow in Figure 1–3. Examples could be multiplied and more arrows added, but it would make for a very messy figure.

Figure 1–3 applies to many types of organizations; it need not, and

Figure 1–3
Pathways between analysis and the policymaking process

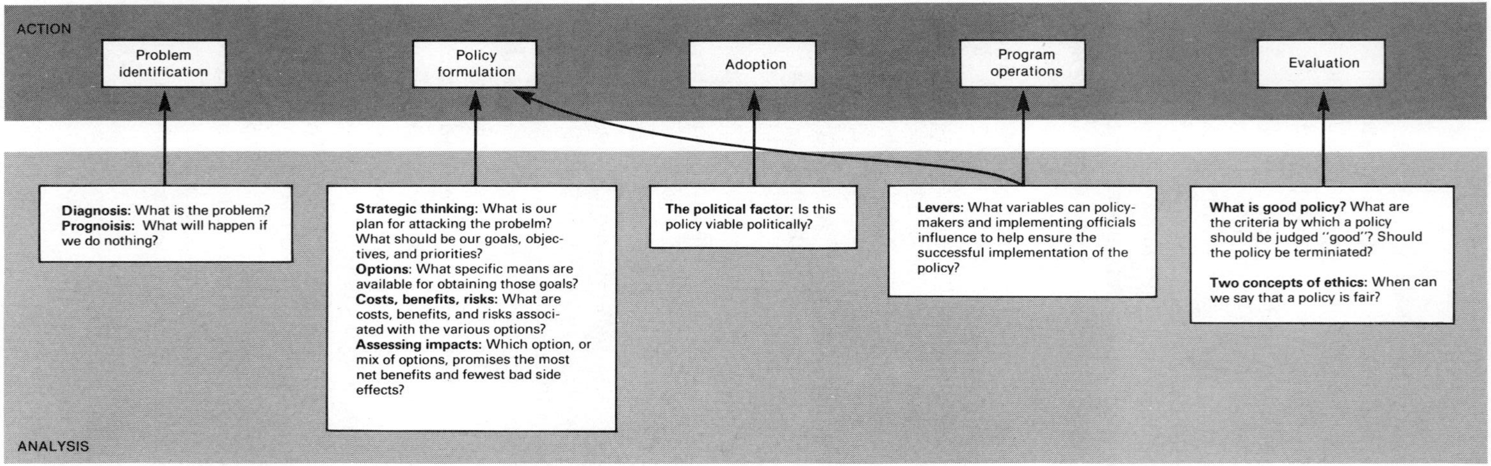

ACTION

| Problem identification | Policy formulation | Adoption | Program operations | Evaluation |

ANALYSIS

Diagnosis: What is the problem? **Prognosis:** What will happen if we do nothing?

Strategic thinking: What is our plan for attacking the probelm? What should be our goals, objectives, and priorities? **Options:** What specific means are available for obtaining those goals? **Costs, benefits, risks:** What are costs, benefits, and risks associated with the various options? **Assessing impacts:** Which option, or mix of options, promises the most net benefits and fewest bad side effects?

The political factor: Is this policy viable politically?

Levers: What variables can policy-makers and implementing officials influence to help ensure the successful implementation of the policy?

What is good policy? What are the criteria by which a policy should be judged "good"? Should the policy be terminiated?

Two concepts of ethics: When can we say that a policy is fair?

should not, be thought of exclusively in terms of the federal government. Hospital administrators, university presidents, mayors, police chiefs, and corporation executives all must (1) search out their organizations' needs and (2) formulate policies to deal with problems and opportunities. In both tasks, they will want the best advice available, and that of course is what the bottom half of Figure 1–3 provides. Further, these nongovernmental chief executive officers must have their major policies approved. But what is the analogue in their environment for the legislature? While I do not want to press the comparison too far, I think it is fair to say that major policy proposals for hospitals, universities, and corporations must generally go before a board of some type. In the case of a city manager or mayor, it is the council.

The decisive thing about Figure 1–3 is that the upper and lower halves are organically linked. Policymakers who focus only on the process travel too lightly. They will fail to detect the emergence of new issues and miss the long-term, multifarious consequences policies can have. Thus they must concern themselves with the netherworld of analysis. By the same token, the policy analysts cannot afford to ignore the play of politics, the world of action. They must not allow analysis to become an end in itself, as they spin out their analytical nets, like so many perverse spiders, oblivious to how and when their studies might be used. As one student of the subject has remarked:

> Policy analysts should direct attention toward public problems as they are anticipated or as they actually occur; analysts should recognize that policymakers confront issues which cannot be ignored or wished away. Accountable policymakers confront problems which are situational and real, not abstract or philosophical. The reputable policy analyst presents the decision maker with an analysis of feasible decision options and their costs and benefits. Should government intervene to solve a problem? How? How long? At what cost? Who will benefit? Is the solution satisfactory? At all levels of government the list of policy issues of this nature is long, changing, and complex.[3]

Because process and analysis are so tightly bound both in theory and practice, this book takes on a dual focus. We will not limit our inquiry to the quantitative and economic techniques of the analysts, nor spend all of our time in the political arena mesmerized by the wheeling and dealing. We will try, however, to obtain a clear, balanced picture of how analysis is used *in* the play of power.

INTERDISCIPLINARY ASPECTS OF POLICY ANALYSIS

Policy analysis is nothing more than the application of a variety of political and cognitive strategies to the formulation and implementation

---

[3] Norman Beckman, "Policy Analysis in Government: Alternatives to Muddling Through," *Public Administration Review* 37, no. 3 (May–June 1977), pp. 221–22.

12

of public policy. Policy analysis is a new field, but it has antecedents in the past. We should remember that by the time of Pericles (443–429 B.C.) rigorous policy debate was the norm. "We Athenians," he boasted, ". . . instead of looking on discussion as a stumbling block in the way to action, we think it an indispensable preliminary to any wise action at all."[4]

Policy analysis refuses capture by any single academic discipline. It is more concerned with broad policy issues than economics. For example, such issues as the trade-off between equity and efficiency in domestic policy, or between the navy and the army in defense policy, reflect the mixture of political, organizational, technological, and economic considerations that typically characterize policy analysis. With its emphasis on data collection and testing, policy analysis tends to be more quantitative, more statistical than political science or public administration.

A surprisingly large number of today's controversies can be understood if we view them as the result of too much reliance on a single discipline. In policy analysis one of the keys to judging expert testimony is to recognize the biases inherent in single-discipline answers. Excessive reliance on the humanities—excellent for illuminating normative issues— yields reports filled with such thought-stopping words as infinite, nonnegotiable, sacred, absolute, and sensitivity. Language is difficult enough itself, but with the aggressive popularity of cant words, we are like people coming from the dentist with our lips and tongues numbed by Novocain.

Pure quantification can also produce foolishness such as a price tag for human life based on the chemicals contained in a person's body. Consider the task of regulating automobile emission standards. The problem can be represented mathematically as follows: (1) the quantity of emissions is a function of the number of cars, how far they are driven, and their design cost; (2) the quality of air is a function of the level of emissions and of various geographical and meteorological parameters; and (3) effects on human health are a function of the quality of the air and the population exposed to it. An equation can be written in which health is the dependent variable and the cost of automobiles the independent variable. If a dollar value is assigned to health efforts, all the ingredients will be present for comparing the health benefits to the costs. But as Herbert A. Simon, a Nobel-laureate in economics, writes:

> It is only necessary to state the problem this way to show the preposterousness of attempting such calculations. Nevertheless, when the problem was pre-

---

[4] Thucydides, *The History of the Peloponnesian War*, trans. Richard Crawley (New York: Random House, 1951), Book 2, Chapter 6.

sented to the National Academy of Sciences—not because it was solvable, but because the Congress had to make a decision about emissions standards—the conceptual scheme . . . proved to be an excellent representation for organizing the subcommittees of experts who were asked to contribute their advice. . . . None of these committees was able to arrive at estimates that were believable in more than an order of magnitude.[5]

FIFTEEN CORE IDEAS

Many definitions of policy analysis have been proposed, but I prefer to avoid any attempt to define the field in a sentence or paragraph. Instead, this section will introduce you to policy analysis by letting the subject matter speak for itself.

Inevitably, we forget much of what we learn in a book. Don't bemoan this fact—everything is not equally important. Indeed, most fields of study really boil down to just a few core ideas. For physics, the list might run something like this: mechanics, thermodynamics, electromagnetism, relativity, and quantum mechanics. Every one of the myriad phenomena in the physical world that is understood is explained in terms of one or more of these five closely related theories. Biology offers us a staggeringly large collection of facts—perhaps more than any other science. Yet most biologists would probably agree that five large themes encompass the subject: the cell, evolution, genetics, development, and ecology.

In the same spirit, I have selected fifteen ideas from among the many contained in this book. Some will help you see beyond the headlines when you read a newspaper account of a public policy issue. Others will help you to make wiser decisions in your professional and personal life. All will provide a solid foundation for more advanced work in policy analysis.

I have organized my fifteen ideas roughly in the order in which they appear in the book. Since each of these ideas will be discussed in depth later, only a brief introduction will be attempted here.

Idea 1: Agenda setting

Not all problems that emerge in society generate policy responses. Before policymakers consider a problem, certain individuals or groups must get the issue placed on the *policy agenda*. No society actually has a physical list of issues with which it is most concerned, but members know that, at any given moment, a few issues are under serious consider-

---

[5] Herbert A. Simon, *The Sciences of the Artificial* (Cambridge, Mass.: MIT Press, 1981), pp. 167–68.

ation, while many others remain on the back burner—or even in total obscurity.

Success at getting on the agenda does not guarantee a policy response. In 1983, it seemed Democratic candidates would use the issue of "industrial policy" to challenge Ronald Reagan and provide a vision of economic revitalization through targeted governmental programs to promote U.S. industry. But the term soon vanished from the national agenda.

Although success at getting a problem on the agenda may not guarantee a solution, failure to do so guarantees the continued absence of a solution. Clearly, those who control the policy agenda have real political power.

For these reasons, then, agenda setting appears as our first core idea. We will devote much of the next chapter to examining it.

Idea 2: The use and abuse of history

One of the most surprising things about this revolutionary age is why the American people and their government are so often surprised by events. It was not conceivable, even in the midst of World War II, that Japan would attack Pearl Harbor and sink most of the U.S. Pacific fleet. Americans were surprised again when China sent a massive army across the Yalu River to meet General MacArthur's troops when they crossed the 38th parallel in Korea and approached the Chinese border. President Kennedy was not only surprised but humiliated by his bungled attempt to overthrow Castro with the Bay of Pigs invasion. President Johnson was sure that, while the Vietnamese communists had expelled the French from that country, they could not possibly hold out against the modern weapons of the United States. President Carter, a deeply religious man, was stunned and finally defeated by the Ayatollah Khomeini and his zealous followers, who defied the power of the United States and held its diplomats captive for over 400 days. President Reagan, who condemned Carter for his patience, was astonished by the destruction of his embassy and the murder of hundreds of U.S. Marines in Beirut.

One of the main reasons why Americans are constantly taken by surprise in a world they are trying to help is a collective lack of historical perspective. We will learn in Chapter 4 that the failure to understand history has caused troubles for domestic policy as well as foreign policy. Given this lamentable record, we ask in Chapter 4: What routine staff work might bring into view the historical evidence that has been overlooked?

We will also discuss the pitfalls of using history incorrectly. For example, the Ford administration was led into an unnecessary and politically damaging swine flu inoculation program by a poorly thought-out assumption that the flu outbreak in 1976 was analogous to the deadly influenza epidemic of 1918. Comparisons of Southeast Asia in the 1960s to Central Europe of the 1930s led the United States ever deeper into Vietnam. Similarly, comparisons of Central America of the 1980s to Southeast Asia in the 1960s are made by some in order to limit U.S. support of antigovernment forces in Nicaragua.

It is not enough to know a bit of history: using bad analogies and drawing erroneous conclusions can be worse than not considering history at all. Chapter 4 presents the case that careful analysis of the history of issues, individuals, and institutions can lead to better decisions—in business as well as in government.

Idea 3: The systems view

Some environmentalists might cite with approval the words of Francis Thompson, a turn-of-the-century poet: "Thou canst not stir a flower/ Without troubling a star." Beneath all the poetic hyperbole and environmental enthusiasm lies an important truth: Many things *are* interrelated.

Policy analysis seeks to produce information about the consequences of a proposed action. While we cannot predict the future, we can build *models* to tell us what the possibilities are based on various assumptions. ("If you do that, Mr. President, you will likely trigger the following chain of events. . . .")

The model may be no more than an image of the problem in the mind of the analyst or an elaborate simulation involving many analysts and high-speed computers. In either case, the model will rest on a *system view* of the situation. In other words, the model builders view society, or any part of it, as a system, that is, a set of elements in dynamic interaction, organized for a goal. Indeed, policy analysis itself might be defined as the search for a solution to a problem with the aid of the systems view.

In sum, the systems view, based on concepts of *dynamic feedback*, helps us see a little more clearly the nature of large, complex problems. A dynamic feedback system is an ongoing set of relationships in which the output of an action taken by one person or group eventually has an effect again on that person or group. The simplest example is the "hungry-eat causal-loop": "Being hungry causes me to eat" can be shown in a diagram like this:

Then comes the question of direction: a plus sign indicates positive feedback—the variable at the head of the arrow changes in the same direction as the variable at the tail of the arrow—and a minus sign, negative feedback. And finally, analysts determine the direction of the system as a whole, described as positive (a positive feedback loop is one that continues going in the same direction, eventually exploding) or negative with a plus or minus sign enclosed with a tiny arrow. Here are some examples:

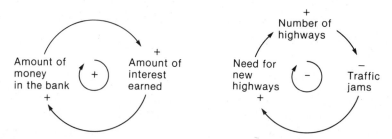

We will see in Chapter 4 (and elsewhere in this book) that the systems view can help us understand better the nature of a problem and avoid costly mistakes in the design of a solution.

Idea 4: The fundamental theorem of welfare economics

Policymakers must react to and assess a constant stream of proposals for government action. Given the enormous scope of activities undertaken by government, some kind of general framework is needed to organize thoughts about the desirability of various government actions. One such framework is *welfare economics,* the branch of economic theory concerned with the social desirability of alternative economic states. The framework allows us to distinguish those circumstances under which markets can be expected to perform well from those circumstances under which markets will fail to produce desirable results.

To understand welfare economics, one must first understand how markets work. In Chapter 4, we will consider a relatively complex one, but we'll keep it simple here. In this economy, there are only two people who consume two commodities with fixed supply. The two people are Adam and Eve, and the two commodities are apples (food) and fig leaves (clothing). When the market functions properly and resources shift in response to its signals, both Adam and Eve can be made better off. If two (or more) goods have different relative usefulness to two (or more) consumers, it is possible to improve the situation by a reallocation of goods between consumers without hurting anyone. Say that Adam starts off with the same number of apples and the same number of fig leaves that Eve starts off with. Say further that Adam values apples more than Eve does. Presumably, Adam and Eve could bargain until a point, an optimal point, is reached at which any further reallocation of apples and leaves would no longer make anyone better off.

Such an equilibrium is said to be *Pareto-optimal* only if there is no possible movement from it that could make everyone better off.[6] The Pareto criterion provides us with a basis for comparing alternative social states. Thus, state A is declared better than state B if someone is better off in state A and no one is worse off. If for a state A there is no state C that is declared better by the Pareto criterion, we call state A a Pareto-optimum. *Out of this notion emerges a prescription for policymakers: when choosing to make someone better off without making somebody else worse off the prescription is: Select a Pareto-optimum!*

The fundamental theorem of welfare economics holds that under certain ideal conditions, free competition, working through the price system, will produce a Pareto-optimum. This fundamental theorem, which Chapter 12 examines closely, need not imply a minimal government. The reason has to do with the fact that the "certain ideal conditions" required for its validity may not be satisfied by real-world markets. For an example of a situation in which markets fail and governments must act, look no further than the next core idea.

Idea 5: Externalities: A justification for government action

Suppose Adam had set up an apple press to make wine and that the waste products are dumped into a stream that flows into Eve's section of the Garden. Adam's private cost is less than the social cost because he does not have to pay for the water he uses (ruins). He has been able to externalize some of his costs. Hence, perfect market conditions do not exist, and the allocation of resources is inefficient.

Often free market transactions between buyer and seller affect uninvolved third parties. The utility company that supplies your electricity also produces pollutants that spoil the air. A farmer in Florida sprays his crops with toxic pesticides so that children in Chicago may have fresh fruit every day, but the poison may seep into the ground water and affect the health of nearby communities.

Such social costs are called externalities because they affect parties *external* to the economic transaction that causes them. These costs escape the market, that is to say, your electricity and grocery bills do not reflect the full costs of production. Moreover, neither the utility company nor

---

[6] Vilfredo Pareto (1848–1923) was an Italian economist and sociologist.

the citrus grower in a free market has any incentive to prevent pollution, since it behooves them to produce and sell as cheaply as possible.

The public policy implications of externalities should not be hard to grasp. Their existence provides a legitimate basis for government intervention into the economy—though the means and extent of that intervention may be the subject of vigorous political debate. Policy analysts must consider the *indirect* costs and benefits of programs and projects— not just the direct, easy-to-see, and easy-to-measure ones.

A related market failure concerns positive externalities or *public goods*. Some goods are consumed privately. When I wear my socks, no one can possibly wear them simultaneously. In contrast, public goods can be shared. When the lighthouse burns brightly it guides all ships, whether their owners help pay for the lighthouse or not. In using the lighthouse, people have an incentive to hide their true preferences. Suppose that it would be worthwhile for Captain Ahab to have the lighthouse operate. But he knows that once the beacon is lit, he can enjoy its services whether he paid or not. Therefore, he may claim that the lighthouse means nothing to him, hoping that he can get a free ride after other people pay. If there are enough captains like Ahab— and, unfortunately, there are—the lighthouse may not get built at all, even though its construction would clearly benefit all.

In sum, the market fails to force people to reveal their preferences for public goods, resulting in insufficient resources being devoted to them. Thus the free market is loaded in favor of such private goods as autos, soap, socks, deodorants, watches, refrigerators, and so forth, and against public goods like lighthouses, parks, police, museums, and public education. Because these public goods are considered desirable, if not essential, government provides for them either directly or indirectly (through subsidies and contracting).

Idea 6: The art of strategic thinking

At the start of his critical analysis of the Vietnam War, Harry G. Summers, Jr., gives this revealing anecdote:

> "You know you never defeated us on the battlefield," said the American colonel.
>
> The North Vietnamese colonel pondered this remark a moment. "That may be so," he replied, "but it is also irrelevant."[7]

Unlike the U.S. forces, the North Vietnamese had no big planning staffs, no elaborate, gold-plated planning processes. They seemed to

---

[7] Harry G. Summers, Jr., *On Strategy: A Critical Analysis of the Vietnam War* (Novato, Calif.: Presidio Press, 1982), p. 1.

lack the resources that would be needed to defeat a superpower. Yet despite these handicaps, year after year, they managed to move toward the conquest of South Vietnam.

How did they do it? The answer is easy. They may not have had a strategic planning staff of the best and the brightest, but they did have a strategist of great natural talent, Vo Nguyen Giap. He may never have taken a course or read a book on strategy, but he had an intuitive grasp of the basic elements of strategy:

1. What are we trying to do? That is, what are our objectives?
2. How are we going to do it?
3. Who is going to control it? That is, who is responsible?

The United States was able to move almost a million soldiers a year in and out of Vietnam, feed them, clothe them, house them, supply them, and sustain them better than any army had ever been sustained in the field. To project an army of that size halfway around the world was a *management* task of enormous magnitude. On the battlefield itself, the army was unbeatable. Yet, in the end, the North Vietnamese Army emerged victorious because it could satisfactorily answer the three questions above. Presidents Kennedy and Johnson, and their staffs of rational, by-the-numbers strategic and financial planners, could not.

The message in Idea 6, as you will have guessed by now, is that successful public policies require not just rigorous analysis, but also a particular state of mind. In what we will call the art of strategic thinking, insight and a clear vision of goals fuel a thought process that is basically creative and intuitive rather than rational. Strategists do not reject analysis; indeed, they could hardly do without it. But they use it only to stimulate the creative process, to test the ideas that emerge, or to work out their strategic implications. Great strategies, like great works of art or great scientific discoveries, call for technical mastery in working out an analysis of the problems, but originate in creative insight. Lincoln, who emerged as a master strategist during the Civil War, knew this well:

> The dogmas of the quiet past are inadequate to the stormy present. The occasion is piled high with difficulty, and we must rise to the occasion. As our case is new, so we must think anew and act anew.[8]

How can this kind of strategic thinking, with this inventive élan, be reproduced in government bureaucracy or corporate culture? I will address this question in Chapter 5. Although there is no secret formula for developing successful strategy, there are some specific concepts and

---

[8] Abraham Lincoln, *Second Annual Message to Congress* (December 1, 1862).

approaches that can help anyone develop a kind of mentality that comes up with sound strategic plans.

Idea 7: The psychology of choice

Consider the following problem.[9] Four cards are laid out as shown:

A	D	4	7

Each card has a letter on one side and a number on the other. You are then given this rule, whose truth you are expected to evaluate: If a card has a vowel on one side, then it has an even number on the other. You may turn over two, but only two, cards to determine whether the rule is correct. Which two would you pick?

If you are like 90 percent of the subjects (including many logicians) to whom the problem has been presented, you will pick the card with the vowel, for an odd number on the other side would invalidate the rule. Choosing the second card is more difficult. You will be tempted, like most subjects, to pick up the card with the even number *because the even number is mentioned in the statement of the problem*. But, in fact, it is irrelevant whether there is a vowel or consonant on the other side, since the rule does not actually take a stand on what must be opposite to even numbers. On the other hand, it is essential to pick up the card with the odd number on it. If that card has a consonant on it, the result is irrelevant. If, however, the card has a vowel on it, the rule in question is false for the rule says that the card *must* have an even number on it.

The results of this experiment and many more like it clearly challenge any notion that individuals are entirely logical, capable of applying the same modes of reasoning regardless of the specific information in the problem. Yet most theories of individual and organizational choice employ the concept of rationality, according to which individuals and organizations choose the best alternative. As we observed in Figure 1–3, such choices in the policymaking process require: (1) the generation of all possible alternatives, (2) assessment of the probabilities of all consequences of each, and (3) evaluation of each set of consequences for all relevant goals. These requirements, in light of what cognitive

---

[9] Amos Tversky and Daniel Kahnernan, "The Psychology of Preferences," *Scientific American* 246 (February 1982), pp. 160–74.

psychologists tell us, may assume powers of prescience and capacities for computation that just are not available.

I do not mean that policymaking is illogical or inexplicable. Rather, recognizing the limits of human capacity, in comparison with the complexities of the problems policymakers must face, helps the process. This recognition will alert us to the errors that might occur when we define a problem (Chapter 3). It also frees us to explore simplified models for choosing among alternatives (Chapter 6).

Idea 8: Mapping the alternatives: The decision tree

The last idea suggested that the rationality of policymakers is limited—or bounded—by their cognitive abilities. How can those limits or boundaries be pushed back? Idea 8 and the next three ideas suggest ways in which policymakers can upgrade their capacity to process and analyze information.

Almost any analysis can benefit from adopting the perspective of managerial economics, because it is about decisions. The underpinning of much managerial economics is the *decision tree,* a device that depicts alternative courses of action in situations fraught with uncertainty and risk. The decision tree provides a road map to help analysts pick their way through such situations. The method is particularly useful when analysts must decide on a course of action to be pursued, knowing that the consequences associated with the selection of any course of action will depend on future conditions and events. Decision trees have been used to address such diverse questions as whether to seed a hurricane, whether to build an airport, whether to develop a supersonic commercial aircraft, and whether to drill for oil.

Essentially, a decision tree is a flow diagram that reveals the logical structure of a problem that may be, and probably is, obscure to the human mind. In Chapter 7, we will examine the main elements that make up the tree and allow us to calculate the *expected monetary value* (EMV) of each course of action or "branch" in the tree.

Idea 9: The importance of marginal analysis

Many policy decisions are about a bit more of this or a bit less of that; we choose "at the margin." This powerful idea can best be explained by an example.

The pleasure or satisfaction we obtain from a good or service does not increase uniformly. The fourth slice of a pizza is not nearly as enjoyable as the first. Most government programs are the same; once a certain level of funding is reached, additional increments bring diminishing returns. Many pages in this book will be spent explaining and extolling the virtues of this type of analysis. (See especially Chapter 8.)

Margin means border or edge. Marginal analysis asks that we keep looking at rising expenditures at the border or edge. Yes, it is important to ask the total price of a military aircraft. But it is also important to know what more we get when we increase spending from $20 million to $21 million.

Idea 10: True economic costs

Economists say that the true costs of a project or program are not the dollars spent, but the value of what must be given up in order to fund it. These are called *opportunity costs* because they represent the opportunities the government must forgo to make the desired expenditure. No nation can have all the guns (weapons systems) and butter (social programs) it might wish. Eventually, trade-offs have to be made.

Let us reconsider the military aircraft example, applying to it this time the concept of opportunity costs. Below are a sample of trade-offs generated by the Reagan administration's proposed fiscal 1986 budget:

Navy (EA6B) airplane program for surveillance and communications jamming	= $2.18 billion =	Proposed cut in funds for mass transit systems
18 Navy F-14 jet fighters in 1986	= $1.2 billion =	1982–86 cuts in federal job training and in funds for public-service employment in New York City
The Stealth radar-evading bomber program	= $40.6 billion =	Mayor Koch's ten-year plan for repairing New York City's infrastructure
2B-1B intercontinental bombers	= $440 million =	Annual additional funds needed to restore acceptable maintenance of New York City's public schools
Half of the air force's 1986 heavy-transport (C-5B) airplane budget	= $1.2 billion =	Proposed 1986–88 cut in New York City medicaid funding, reducing medical services to the poor
One (F-16 jet fighter) antenna pulley puller tool; one antenna puller height gauge; one antenna hexagon wrench	= $42,287 =	Estimated cost of renovating an average five-room medium-income Manhattan West Side apartment

While this analysis nicely dramatizes the issue of defense spending, it might miss a couple of larger ones. *Point One:* The amount of money allocated for defense also must be measured against the military with which it is meant to cope and not just against domestic needs—however urgent these may be. It is illogical to urge cuts in defense appropriations on the grounds that there are higher priorities in social services. One may legitimately question whether the navy needs the EA6B, but the argument should be decided primarily on military, not social, criteria. Since defense expenditures are designed to meet concrete threats posed by foreign powers, they should not be treated as if they were wholly discretionary. Every country has an army on its soil, and the only choice citizens can exercise in the matter is to decide whether this army will be their own or someone else's.[10]

Point Two: Transfer of dollars between disparate programs is neither as smooth nor easy as the listing above implies. One million dollars taken away from a defense contractor might mean a lot of capital investment (plant and equipment) will go to waste. It also means a loss of x jobs in the defense industry and an increase of y jobs elsewhere in the economy (due, say, to more spending by welfare recipients and to increased government hiring to administer the program). I do not know exactly what x and y are, but I doubt that they are exactly equal. (Studies tend to show that spending on social programs generates more jobs than defense spending. Defense spending is very capital intensive and employs a relatively few highly trained people.)

For these reasons, a more promising application of the concept of opportunity cost would be intraprogram.

For example, in 1984, Dr. William DeVries sewed an artificial heart inside a patient. According to one estimate, the bill for that operation represented 790 days of hospital care, or full treatment for 113 patients for an average stay of one week. In terms of the poor, the comparisons look even worse. A liver transplant would finance a year's operation by a San Francisco inner-city clinic that provides 30,000 office visits in that time.[11]

One doctor, writing in *The New England Journal of Medicine*, sums up the dilemma:

> Because of our great and proper humanitarian desire to preserve life, we have difficulty desisting in our medical efforts, even when the probability of the patient's recovery approaches zero, and even when the costs in a futile attempt to save one life may consume resources that might save many. The costs of trying to preserve the life of one cirrhotic patient with bleeding esophageal varices might be used to treat and prevent alcoholism in many

---

[10] This line of analysis does not necessarily lead to higher defense expenditures; it could suggest even deeper cuts than the guns versus butter analysis seems to imply. See Grover Starling, "Evaluating Defense Programs in an Era of Rising Expenditures" in *Making and Managing Policy: Formulation, Analysis, Evaluation*, ed. by G. Ronald Gilbert (New York: Marcel Dekker, 1984), pp. 289–308.

[11] Estimate by Rina Spence, president of Emerson Hospital, Concord, Massachusetts. *Time* (December 10, 1984), p. 73.

persons. The cost of one heart transplant could support smoking-cessation programs, plasma-lipid-lowering diets, hypertension treatment, and physical-exercise programs for many. The cost of treating one premature newborn with respiratory-arrest syndrome could be used to provide nourishment for many expectant mothers, thus combating a major cause of prematurity.[12]

Idea 11: Discounting: The valuation of future consequences

To keep our discussion of the last three ideas simple, I have treated costs and benefits as if they were felt immediately. Yet I can think of no public policy for which this is true. Today's decisions have consequences that stretch well beyond tomorrow. Planting a hardwood forest may require substantial expenditure today, but will yield benefits many years in the future. Discounting allows us to compare future streams of benefits with future streams of costs. Then we can decide if the forest is really worth it—or a fusion power project—or a training program—or virtually any other undertaking.

Without getting bogged down in computations (we can save *that* for Chapter 8), the basic idea is: money has a time value. That sounds tricky, but it is not. A guarantee of $2,000 in three years is not the same as $2,000 in your hand at the moment. After all, you could go to your bank, deposit it, wait three years, and then receive the $2,000 *plus* interest. Thus, the present value of $2,000 in three years must be something *less* than $2,000.

Sound obvious? Not to Joseph Stalin and his fellow planners. Marx taught that labor—not capital—creates value, so there was no justification for paying interest rates to use money. State planners (rather than the market) would decide which industries would get scarce capital. The upshot of this zero-interest rate was planning blunders called *gigantomania*—the tendency to build huge plants, dams, and other installations. But big projects take a long time to complete. By the late 1950s, the planning bias for large-scale, distant-yield capital investments was apparent even to the party faithful. "We built [a 2,300,000-kilowatt hydroelectric station] in seven years" Chairman Khrushchev complained, "but with the same money we could have built in less time several thermal plants with a total capacity of 11,000,000 kilowatts." While the power from these plants would be more expensive, the plants could have supplied power to factories much earlier.[13]

---

[12] Cited in Richard D. Lamm, "Long Time Dying," *New Republic*, August 27, 1984, p. 21.

[13] Lawrence G. Hines, *Environmental Issues* (New York: W. W. Norton, 1973), pp. 123–24.

Idea 12: Pluralism, interdependence, and power dynamics

The picture of policy analysis that one gets from the last four ideas is one in which people use analytical economic tools to select alternatives to attain the goals of their policies. Getting the information needed to use these tools does not seem to be a problem. Nor does implementing the policies. It is a picture almost devoid of conflict, struggle, manipulation, antagonism, and the like. It is a very naive picture.

Idea 12 provides an alternative perspective—one that emphasizes the importance of the political factor. *Pluralism,* as I use the term, refers to the political struggle of groups inside and outside government that seek to have their interests prevail in the policy process. The Constitution (which fragments political power) and American society (which consists of a highly diverse people) sustain pluralism. *Interdependence* refers to the state in which two or more parties have power over each other because they are, to some degree, dependent on each other. This can be contrasted with a state of independence where parties have no power over each other, and with a state of unilateral dependence where one party has considerable power over another. Interdependence best characterizes the relationships found in the policy process in the United States. For example, the federal government depends on state and local officials for the implementation of many of its programs. While the former has no direct control over the latter, it can use indirect means, for example, persuasion and funding reductions, to encourage cooperation.

Pluralism and interdependence generally mean that agreement on what should be done, who should do it, and when it should be done is not easily or quickly achieved. Because of this interdependence, people will not be able to resolve these differences either by edict or by walking away. Under such circumstances, policymaking tends to be incremental; according to this view, most new public policies continue past government activities with only incremental (i.e., minor) modification. Besides encouraging *incrementalism,* interdependence also forces the participants in the policy process to look harder for ways to resolve disagreement.

Policymaking in a milieu of pluralism and interdependence requires (1) sufficient power to make up for the power gap inherent in leadership position and (2) the willingness to use that power to manage all the interdependence in as responsible a way as possible. We will see in Chapter 10 that the power needed by policymakers and implementing officials has many bases. One has already been suggested in Idea 1: controlling the agenda. We will also consider information or knowledge (e.g., who are all the relevant actors in this issue and what are their perspectives), good working relationships (with anyone on whom the success of the policy depends), credible track record (success breeds success), personal skills (e.g., in bargaining and conflict resolution), and material and symbolic resources (to use as rewards or withhold as sanctions).

An appreciation of the political factor and the reasons for its existence help policymakers be more patient with themselves and others as they try to get their plans adopted and then implemented. It can certainly help them put their successes and failures into a more realistic perspective.

Idea 13: The theory of nonmarket failures

In the debates between those who defend the market and those who wish to see more government intervention, the latter are at a theoretical advantage. As we suggested earlier (Ideas 4 and 5), economists have identified and elaborated a theory of market failures. But, until recently, there was no such explanation for the shortcomings of government intervention. While government programs do receive abundant criticism, much of it tends to be anecdotal and inconclusive.

Charles Wolf, Jr., of the Rand Corporation suggests a systematic explanation for why government programs do not work as well as expected and are difficult to evaluate. Because his explanation is patterned along the lines of the market failures, he calls his explanation a theory of nonmarket failures.[14]

Certain characteristics of government programs are fundamental to his theory. In the first place, because output (i.e., the real results intended, the bottom line) is relatively hard to measure, performance evaluation focuses on inputs. For example, health care should be evaluated not in terms of hospital beds or physicians per hundred thousand people, but in terms of infant mortality rates, overall age-adjusted death rates, and the incidence of acute rheumatic fever and measles. Likewise, educational programs should be evaluated not in terms of counselor per hundred thousand pupils or expenditure per capita, but in terms of reading levels. (See Idea 14.) Another important characteristic of government programs is the absence of competition, which might provide a benchmark by which to evaluate agency performance and an incentive for management excellence. Finally, the political process that creates public policies can also build in and help preserve inefficiencies. In that process, rewards accrue to policymakers who articulate and publicize problems and propose solutions rather than assuming responsibility for their implementation. Because of this reward structure, policy-

---

[14] Charles Wolf, Jr., "A Theory of Nonmarket Failures: Framework for Implementation Analysis," *The Journal of Law and Economics*, April 1979, pp. 107–40. Scholars like Wolf who are interested in the application of economic analysis to nonmarket decision making are often called public choice theorists. See James M. Buchanan and Gordon Tullock, *The Calculus of Consent* (Ann Arbor, Mich.: University of Michigan Press, 1962).

makers are often more interested in near-term consequences than in long-term consequences and in pleasing constituents rather than serving the national interest. We will briefly examine this phenomenon in the next chapter and again in Chapter 10.

Such characteristics of government programs lead to four specific types of failure.

1. Lacking direct performance indicators such as businesses have from consumer behavior and profits, public agencies tend to *develop their own private goals*. These are not necessarily consistent with the public interest. For example:

- Spend all your budget and, if possible, continue to expand it.
- Procure the most sophisticated (and expensive) technology. This internal goal is especially popular with hospitals and the armed services.
- Acquire and control information—even though other agencies might benefit enormously from it.

2. Since rewards frequently accrue in the political arena for getting policies on the agenda, many programs pursue infeasible or *inconsistent objectives*. The result: technically inefficient production and rising costs.

3. Government policies to correct market failures may generate *unintended consequences*. Because society is exceedingly complex and interrelated, and because the human mind has a finite capacity to understand it, unintended consequences abound. Consider these three examples:

- What could be more clear-cut than the Marine Mammals Protection Act of 1972? That law makes it illegal to hunt sea lions, seal, and sea otters—all staples of an adult shark's diet (that is s-h-a-r-k, as in *Jaws*). Because of the act, the food supply of the great white shark expanded and so did the number of great white sharks. Unintended consequence: according to records of the California Department of Fish and Game over the past thirty years, there have never been as many shark assaults off the U.S. coast as there were in the 1980s.

  What can be done about such unintended consequences as having American citizens disappear beneath the surface of the Pacific and re-emerge in the gaping mouths of twelve-foot sharks? The best answer has already been suggested (Idea 3): Everything in society, including the ecology, should be viewed as a system. Oceans, like urban communities, are not Tinkertoys that can be pulled apart and reassembled by policymakers. They are both living organisms, like flowers. They can be delicately pruned, but pulling them apart—engineering them—spells unintended consequences.

- What could be more straightforward than famine relief? Yet free food *weakens* the capacity of communities to respond to famine. In 1985, the *Economist* filed this report:

Countries have complex defense mechanisms against drought that local farmers know but international food bureaucrats and aid workers often do not. In the Sahel, when the cereal crops (millet, sorghum) fail, other farmers who produce tubers (cassava, yams) rush to sell their surplus to the cereal farmers. The distribution of cereal aid has severed that link. This year, tuber farmers have not been able to find so many customers; next year they might grow less.

Migration is another way in which farmers traditionally react to drought, moving their herds away from the brownest pastures. Now they go to the nearest relief camps instead. This is not laziness. It is a rational decision. Food brought in from outside has proved a reliable way of feeding their families. But it is creating food aid drones.[15]

- What could be more straightforward than rent control? The case seems clear: A shortage of vacant apartments, in a city like New York, leads to extortionate demands for higher rents. Moreover, regulating rents advances social justice—the poor gain from it while the rich lose. But the consequences of rent regulation are something quite unintended. Price regulation of any commodity makes it scarcer, driving up its real price. Rent regulation increases housing demand because it gives incumbent tenants a powerful incentive to stay put. It discourages them from moving to smaller apartments as their families shrink and from giving up their city space when they make a new home elsewhere. At the same time, regulation gives developers a good reason not to build or maintain rental housing. Together, increased housing demand and diminished supply naturally result in scarcity and high rents for vacant apartments—the situation it is supposed to remedy. The poor don't benefit more from regulation than the rich—the well-to-do move less often than the poor and get greater benefit from the ceiling that regulation places on rent increases. Furthermore, the dollar difference between regulated rents and unregulated rents is much greater in rich neighborhoods than in poor ones where there is often virtually no difference.

4. Many government programs generate *distributional inequities of power and influence* as well as wealth (as does a free market).

Public policy measures give authority to some that is exercised over others. Whether the authority is exercised by the social worker, the welfare-case administrator, the tariff commissioner, the utilities regulator, the securities examiner, or the bank investigator, power is intentionally and inescapably lodged with some and denied to others. The power may be exercised with scruple, compassion, and competence. It may be subject to checks and balances, on administrative procedures, on

---

[15] *The Economist* (July 26, 1985), p. 31.

the information media, and on other political and social institutions. Nevertheless, such redistribution of power provides opportunities for inequity and abuse.[16]

Idea 14: Output—*not* input—is the bottom line

In any agency charged with implementing a program, the tendency is to release information with numerous indicators of *inputs*. Obtaining information about *output*—that is, how well the agency is meeting program objectives—can be more like pulling teeth. Thus, a hospital will freely disclose figures on staffing ratios, capital equipment ratios, the proportion of certified physicians, the number of services provided, and other measures of input, but is reluctant to say how many of its patients get well or how many expire during their stay. Similarly, schools prefer reporting on the proportion of teachers with advanced degrees, the average per pupil expenditure, equipment per pupil, average class size, and so on rather than divulge how much scores on standardized tests have increased.

The analyst must not fall into this trap when evaluating the success of a program. Indicators of input resources should *not* be substituted for clear, accurate information about output. Ultimately, policies must be evaluated not by what they try to achieve, but by what they actually accomplish.

This book is chiefly about policy analysis—not policy or program evaluation. Yet these two topics are closely related. Unless policymakers have established clear goals and objectives, evaluators will be lost when it comes to addressing the question of whether a policy is good. Chapter 11 suggests several criteria for good policy; but in the long run, no criteria is more important than output.

Idea 15: The ubiquity of ethics

Moral considerations, questions about what we *ought* to do, are an integral part of policy analysis, although even the most experienced analyst may sometimes forget it. One former cabinet secretary even suggests that such considerations are more numerous than ever:

> Questions people once sought to have answered by prayer, issues once left for scientists to resolve in their laboratories, are now debated on the floor of Congress, by the brethren on the Supreme Court, thrown into the executive branch regulatory process, or demonstrated about. . . . In another age, these kinds of questions would have been fodder for Talmudic scholars,

---

[16] Wolf, "Nonmarket Failures," p. 27.

Jesuit priests, family doctors, and medical school students and professors. The peculiar and inescapable fact . . . is that these questions are intensely political as well.[17]

Nevertheless, many experienced practitioners of policy analysis may sometimes forget just how pervasive ethical considerations are.

At virtually every juncture in the policymaking process (Figure 1–3), the analysts must address questions about what they *ought* to do. What problem should they investigate, and which alternatives ought to be considered? (These choices will depend to a large degree on their own values.) What ought to be done to make the problem better, not worse? Should analysts be advocates? How should the equity standard be balanced with the need for efficiency? (We can seldom maximize both at the same time.) Are analysts hired guns for their clients, or should they serve the public interest first? In the formulation and implementation of public policy, how much public participation should there be? (Too much participation can mean that nothing gets done; too little means the technocrats run things.) As the foregoing questions suggest, ethics cannot be factored out of the analytical enterprise; the analyst may strive for objectivity, but must recognize that many subjective factors remain built into the process.

Well, why not let political institutions like Congress and the presidency resolve these issues? The answer is that we do not normally look to Congress for this kind of ethical resolution: the predominant role of that institution is not to weigh values, but to capture benefits for constituents. While the president presumably serves as the collective national representative, "a president who trafficked in sharply drawn value clarifications and trade-offs would be sawing off major constituencies at every turn of a trade-off."[18]

Moreover, there are several good reasons why some responsibility for examining hard choice and justifying policy decisions in ethical terms should be picked up by analysts, both inside and outside government. First, analysts are not directly subject to the intensive political pressures that confront the legislators and chief executives. Second, the expert is far more likely to have an ethos of neutral competence, of professional detachment. Third, because the analysts tend to work on a specific issue (health, defense, urban transportation, etc.) for many years (if not a lifetime), they have longer time horizons and a greater ability to put value conflicts in a historical perspective. In contrast, the time hori-

---

[17] Joseph A. Califano, Jr., *Governing America* (New York: Simon & Schuster, 1981), p. 209.

[18] Douglas T. Yates, Jr., "Hard Choices: Justifying Bureaucratic Decisions," in Joel L. Fleishman et al., *Public Duties: Moral Obligations of Government Officials* (Cambridge, Mass.: Harvard University Press, 1981), p. 46.

zons of political leaders might go no further than the next election. Fourth, because analysts tend to be more knowledgeable regarding the intricacies of an issue they are more likely to discover hidden ethical dilemmas.

Ethical analysis fits easily into my list of core ideas. If effective policy analysis requires attention to agendas, history, systems, welfare economics, externalities, strategic thinking, psychology, uncertainty, marginal analysis, opportunity costs, power dynamics, nonmarket failures, and output, it seems entirely appropriate that normative assessment take its place as a complement and corrective to economic, managerial, and political analysis.

The temptation is strong to regard ethical judgment as soft and subjective in comparison to the other fourteen ideas. But such a stereotype is surely mistaken, for we will see in Chapter 12 that ethical arguments can be as precise, as pointed, and often more powerful than those produced by other forms of analysis.[19]

Public policy is the means by which governments, for better or worse, affect our lives. In this opening chapter, public policy was defined as a broad course of action, designed toward some goal. Certainly most major legislative acts and executive orders would fall within the purview of this definition. But now I must reveal that this definition, though accurate, is a simplification, for public policy is not always so concrete. It may, for example, be no more than a guide to acting that influences government over long periods of time and that changes only incrementally (slowly). Or it can be thought of as a concept imposed on reality to help us make sense of the diverse effects of government action.

While these definitions may be too fuzzy for some, no one should have trouble seeing their verity. In a pluralistic society like America, where power is highly fragmented (Idea 12), many public officials are authorized to act for the community. But their decisions interact with and are buffeted by the pressure and perceptions of groups, cliques, and individuals—inside and outside government. Thus public policy-making in the United States unfolds on a large stage with a cast of thousands. Who then can be surprised to learn that public policies are not always explicitly defined before any government action occurs?

Chapter 2 identifies and tries to ascribe roles to the most significant actors in this drama. It will attempt to do more than just show how these characters make policy: its chief aim is to examine the interplay of the policy process and policy analysis. In it, I will attempt to show how the politics of the process constrains what analysis may ordain,

---

[19] Grover Starling, "New Issues in the Logic of Policy Analysis," *Policy Studies Review*, 5, 2 (November 1985), pp. 207–13.

and try to reveal what is too often hidden, namely, how politics and analysis can work in concert. Later, in Chapter 9, we will isolate and elaborate strategies that seem most likely to affect the policy process. These strategies may not always be methodologically the most elegant, but they are, I think, politically the most robust.

Of course, policymakers must know more than the principles of strategy. Like any good general, they must have a sense of when and where a particular strategy is apposite. It is no exaggeration to say that the beginning of wisdom in policymaking must be an appreciation of the institutional setting. Accordingly, the next chapter presents a quick overview of that setting followed by a more finely grained picture of the policy process than was given in this chapter.

FOR FURTHER REFLECTION

1. How would you answer the four questions posed at the start of this chapter? Which of the fifteen core ideas seem most helpful in your search for a solution?
2. Use the issue of illegal immigration to illustrate the policy analysis framework suggested on p. 7.
3. How might marginal analysis and opportunity cost be related?
4. Here is a simple exercise to see if you can think in terms of systems. One aspect of the oil crisis of the 1970s was the starting of a "vicious circle." Arab oil-producing countries agreed to raise the price of oil. The rise in oil prices meant that these countries made more money, so much more money that they could not spend it all. Realizing this, these countries decided to produce less oil. They knew that eventually their oil supply would run out and concluded that they might as well make it last as long as possible.

   Because less oil was being produced in the world and more oil was needed every day, a scarcity of oil developed. This scarcity of oil forced oil prices to go up even higher, continuing the vicious circle. Draw a feedback diagram showing this vicious circle. Label each arrow with either a + or −.
5. Explain each of the following statements in terms of one or more of the core ideas.
   a. The mindless stampede to protectionism against which the president warned at his news conference probably would be aimed mostly at Japan—but the Latin American debtor nations could well be among its major victims, with grim consequences for Latin democracy, hemispheric security, and the U.S. banking system.
   b. As the president considers a change in sugar import quotas, the United States needs to ask whether the current sugar program is in its national interest, not only because it brings on higher

consumer prices and inefficient agricultural practices, but perhaps more important, because it threatens the economies of nations that depend on sugar exports to survive.

c. The following statement was made in Congress by Representative Patricia Schroeder on February 7, 1986:

> One would have thought the Office of Management and Budget tight-wads could have located at least one Department of Defense program worthy of reform, termination, or cutting. In my thirteen years on the Armed Services Committee, I have seen evidence of many programs that are plagued by waste, fraud, and abuse.
>
> The central idea behind a budget is to list priorities and to institute discipline. This is a defense budget with no priorities and no discipline. It's a Twinkie defense. It's like a child loose in a pastry shop.
>
> Even if one swallows hook, line, and Trident, the Reagan-Weinberger sermon on the national security need for increased defense spending to meet the Soviet threat, the administration still ought to be able to reform, terminate, or cut those Department of Defense activities least useful to defending America in order to provide more money for those programs most useful to defending America.

d. General Motors has calculated that society spent $700 million a year to reduce carbon monoxide emissions from vehicles to fifteen grams per mile, thus prolonging 30,000 lives an average of one year, at a cost of $23,000 for each life.

To meet the 1981 standard of 3.4 grams per mile, the company estimated that it would cost $100 million in addition, and prolong twenty lives by one year, at an estimated cost of $25 million for each life.

Human lives are precious, which is why it is so sad to note another use of that money. It has been estimated that the installation of special cardiac-care units in ambulances could prevent 24,000 premature deaths each year at an average cost of $200 for each year of life. Thus, spending the $100 million for the special ambulances conceivably could save 500,000 lives a year.

e. According to *The New England Journal of Medicine* (May 1986), the nation's death rate from cancer rose from about 170 per 100,000 population in 1950 to 185 per 100,000 in 1982. These data, taken alone, provide no evidence that some thirty-five years of intense and growing efforts to improve the treatment of cancer have had much overall effect on the most fundamental measure of clinical outcome—death.

f. The following statement is by Dimitri K. Simes, a senior associate at the Carnegie Endowment for international peace:

> The National Security Council staff is rich in individuals whose love for conspiracy and devotion to the political fortunes of the president

34

are greater than their appreciation of the broad strategic context in which the United States has to function.

Henry Kissinger, when he was national security adviser, also strived in the world of conspiratorial intrigue. But he usually knew precisely what he wanted to accomplish and had a fair idea of what his counterparts were up to. His secret diplomacy vis-à-vis China was based on a careful calculation: The Peking leadership had sent definite signals regarding its willingness for reconciliation with Washington in the name of rivalry with Moscow. For the United States, the risks were negligible and potential benefits enormous.

The Reagan administration, on the other hand, dealt with uncertain partners in Iran in pursuit of even more uncertain objectives.

6. Education and health services can be provided by private enterprise on a fee basis. What is the rationale for government intervention in these areas? To what extent are education and health services public goods? In what ways can policy analysis help to shed light on proper public policy in these areas?

Chapter 2

Institutional Setting

Viewed on a weekday afternoon, K Street in Washington, D.C., looks like any other street in a business district: tall, no-nonsense buildings of glass and concrete overlooking young professionals hurrying about below. To get a sense of what is really going on, we must enter one of the buildings.

If you entered the building at 1627 K Street you would need to go no further than the elevator. There, posted in white letters on black background, you would read:

> Armour Food Company
> The Coca-Cola Company
> The Greyhound Corporation
> Richard Helms
> Institute of Scrap Iron and Steel
> Wilbur D. Mills
> National Newspaper Association
> Northern Illinois Gas Company

Now, go next door. The directory there announces:

> American Institute of Merchant Shipping
> American Recreation Coalition
> Council of American Flagship Operators
> Kerr McGee Corporation
> National Association for Milk Marketing Reform
> National Petroleum Council

In case you haven't guessed, you are in the kingdom of big-time lobbying. It is not a bad place to begin to understand the American policymaking system. According to our customary quantitative indicators, there can be little doubt that interest groups loom very large indeed in that system. In one recent survey, they were considered very important in fully one third of the interviews, and somewhat important in an additional 51 percent. This total of 84 percent compares to 94 percent for the administration and 91 percent for members of Congress, thus placing interest groups among the most discussed actors on the policymaking stage.[1]

Why are all these lobbies grouped together on K Street? You need walk south only a few hundred yards to find the answer, for there is the driving force of the whole system—the White House. Radiating southeast from that somewhat baroque building is Pennsylvania Avenue, which converges about a mile later into the Capitol.

Dominating the entire scene with its massive Renaissance domes, the Capitol was designed to assure citizens that representative government rested on a broad, solid foundation. Whether it assures the people on nearby K Street, I cannot say.

This quick tour of the policymaking system omits much that is important. I did not mention the presidential staff residing in the old Executive Office Building across the alley from the White House. Nor did I point out as you walked to Capitol Hill the four executive departments (Commerce, Labor, Treasury, and Justice) on your right. Nor did I say anything about the phalanxes of Congressional staff residing in the various office buildings that surround the Capitol. Nor did I recognize the fact that the policymaking system extends well beyond the Beltway that skirts the city—it includes the media, universities, think tanks, special panels and commissions, and the courts.

The literature about the policy system is enormous, and I do not wish to repeat its findings, theories, and arguments.[2] Still, a few critical questions are worth asking:

- What are the major sources of power in the system? How much of the participants' power flows from formal authority (constitutional and legal), and how much from political strategy?

---

[1] Based on 247 interviews with people inside and outside government concerned with health and transportation policy. John W. Kingdon, *Agendas, Alternatives, and Public Policies* (Boston: Little, Brown, 1984), p. 49.

[2] To mention only a few key works: James E. Anderson, *Public Policy Process* (New York: Harper & Row, 1984); J. Leiper Freeman, *The Political Process* (New York: Random House, 1965); Charles O. Jones, *An Introduction to the Study of Public Policy* (Boston: Brooks Cole, 1983); Theodore J. Lowi, *The End of Liberalism* (New York: W. W. Norton, 1969); Emmette S. Redford, *Democracy in the Administrative State* (New York: Oxford University Press, 1969); Randall B. Ripley and Grace Franklin, *Congress, the Bureaucracy, and Public Policy* (Chicago: Dorsey, 1980).

- What influence does analysis have? Can cold logic and computer print-outs change hearts and minds, or do they serve merely to shore-up the predetermined positions of the participants?
- Why do some issues get on the agenda while others slip quietly away? What are the dynamic relationships among participants, problems, solutions, and politics?

KEY PARTICIPANTS

This discussion of participants in the policy process is divided into the following parts:

I. Administration
    The president
    Presidential staff
    Presidential appointments and issue networks
II. Civil servants
III. Capitol Hill
    The intellectual origins of Congress' role in the adoption of policy
    Congressional resources
    The committee system
    The power of the purse
IV. Think tanks and policy intellectuals
    How are policy studies used?
    When will a policy study be used (and not just sought)?
    What are the pros and cons of using outside sources?
V. Mass media
VI. A note on policymakers in states, cities, and not-for-profit organizations
    City councils and state legislatures
    The governing board

Administration

The president. The logical place to begin is with the president, who can impose his leadership on the whole executive branch. Though the office has great prestige and formal powers, much of a president's real power depends on his ability to persuade—to convince others that he has the skill and will to use the advantages of office.[3] But these communication skills must be combined with a deft ability to pick his issues,

---

[3] The classic statement of this idea is Richard E. Neustadt, *Presidential Power* (New York: John Wiley & Sons, 1980). For a different view, see Richard M. Pious, *The American Presidency* (New York: Basic Books, 1979).

keep his opponents on the defensive, and thus dominate the policy agenda. Ronald Reagan provides a good example of how this is done.

His style of presidential leadership has seemed especially well adapted to the modern era. Before the legislative, electoral, and budget "reforms" of the 1970s, political success meant controlling Washington's levers of power, dominating the congressional leadership, and manipulating the executive branch. That was Lyndon Johnson's style; it was not Ronald Reagan's. In the new era, where political institutions are less subject to discipline and control, congressional leaders cannot always deliver the votes. House members, for instance, constitute 435 private fiefdoms.

So, unlike Johnson, Reagan did not even try to maintain control of Washington's governmental machinery. His strategy was to dominate the mass media and set the tone of debate on an issue-by-issue basis. When he could not, he tried for a compromise or continued the debate on his terms. Moreover, his ability to communicate directly with the voters was a factor that members of Congress had to consider. Even when Reagan was out of step with the voters on an issue, lawmakers feared that he could generate some kind of political retaliation if they opposed him.

Another factor was the president's steadfastness in rhetoric, a trait that most observers believe has contributed significantly to his popularity. He persevered in things he believed in and never failed to speak on their behalf. The result was twofold. First, it raised the threshold of victory for the opposition. When a trade bill to protect the textile industry appeared in 1985 in Congress amid growing protectionist sentiment, Reagan promptly threatened to veto it—and did so. If Reagan had gone for any kind of compromise, he would have ended up with a protectionist bill. Second, even when Reagan has supported unpopular causes, he has won some points with the public because of his strength of leadership.

Presidents occasionally appeal to departments or bureaus for support for their administrations' programs. The bureaucracy's support can ensure a policy victory, while their opposition, however subtle, can defeat policy initiatives. Conversely, each agency wants the president's support for its own budget, programs, and goals.

The pattern of control from the presidency down to bureau chiefs is crucial because it helps determine the extent to which bureau leaders feel compelled to support the administration when the political game gets tough. The more formal controls in this regard are:

Budgetary restrictions.

Clearance requirements for proposed legislation.

Staffing controls.

Departmental supervision and organization.

Restrictions on certain kinds of communication
from the bureau to groups outside the hierarchy.[4]

Another obvious source of control is the ability to dismiss bureau leaders. But presidents prefer not to draw attention to conflict with an agency because a protracted battle could dissipate the reserve of power needed for major policies.

Presidential staff. The president has a staff and a number of executive agencies to help him formulate and implement policy. Foremost among the agencies is the Executive Office of the President. This loose arrangement (see Figure 2–1) is analogous to a corporate presidential staff. Since almost every major objective of federal policy concerns several agencies, the job of the Executive Office has become one of coordinating their policies.

The White House Office includes the president's chief counsel, a press secretary, and special assistants. The members of the White House Office maintain communication with Congress, heads of other executive agencies, the public, and special interest groups. They are the president's main source of communication with the world outside the White House.

The Council of Economic Advisors (CEA), the Office of Special Trade Representative (OSTR), and the National Security Council (NSC) are also part of the White House Office since they advise the president on specific issues. Since its creation in 1946, CEA has been the most visible institution in the United States that is run by economists. While its influence has varied from administration to administration, the Council is concerned basically with how efficiently the economy operates. It has no outside clientele to please, unlike the economists in the Labor Department, Agriculture, or other agencies who will argue for their own agencies.

In the Reagan administration, the chairmanship of the CEA had little policymaking role. Power has shifted from the constituency-sensitive, often divided Cabinet officers toward the White House, the Federal Reserve Board, the State Department, and, above all, the Secretary of the Treasury. Early in Reagan's second term, the Treasury Secretary and the chief of staff of the White House formed a single Economic Policy Council to formulate positions on key economic issues. The EPC normally met twice a week in the Roosevelt Room in the East Wing of the White House, close to the Oval Office. At the end of an oblong table sat the "presenter," usually an assistant secretary and the chairman of an interagency "working group" appointed earlier to explore a policy proposal. The presenter would rise before the council to discuss the group's conclusions, on occasion a single proposal, more often a list

---

[4] Freeman, *The Political Process,* p. 35.

40

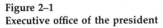

Figure 2–1
Executive office of the president

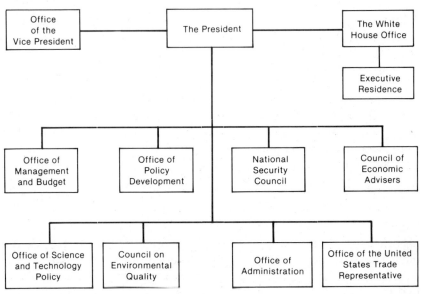

Source: *U.S. Government Manual, 1985*, p. 822.

of options for the council to weigh. With further refinement, the papers, usually of four or five pages, were dispatched to the president who then came to a meeting to talk them over. Usually he selected the council's choice among policy options, but on occasion he did not.[5] To define issues for domestic policy, the president established a similar forum, a Domestic Policy Council, chaired by the Attorney General.

The National Security Council (NSC), established by the National Security Act of 1947, advises the president with respect to the integration of domestic, foreign, and military policies relating to the national security. The NSC is chaired by the president. Its members are the vice president and the secretaries of State and Defense. The chairman of the Joint Chiefs of Staff is the statutory military adviser to the Council and the director of Central Intelligence is its intelligence adviser.

The NSC staff does not actually work for the Council. It works for the national security adviser to the president. But it is more than a personal staff. It is like a minigovernment, with sections for every region of the world, for military programs, arms control, intelligence, public diplomacy, and the like. Except for scandals like the Iranian arms deal

---

[5] Peter T. Kilborn, "How the Big Six Steer the Economy," *New York Times*, November 17, 1985.

in 1986–87, Security Council staff members are rarely mentioned in news articles or photographed. Nevertheless, they can be as powerful, or even more powerful, than assistant secretaries of State and Defense. In addition, their offices are among or close to those of the political operatives in the White House, and because of this, members of Congress and foreign leaders often use them as go-betweens rather than the departmental assistant secretaries. But of greater significance, NSC staff get to do two things beyond the reach of assistant secretaries. When a secretary of State or Defense sends a memorandum to the president, Council staff members write the short "cover memorandum" that summarizes and often characterizes what the Cabinet officer had to say. When the president is ready to make a decision, the staff members write the decision directive. In the Reagan administration, as with its predecessors, this was usually done without the directives even being seen beforehand by the Cabinet officers, let alone assistant secretaries.

Another major unit in the Executive Office is the Office of Management and Budget (OMB). A major intermediary between the president and the agencies and Congress, it assists the president in preparing the budget, evaluates programs, and reviews government rules and regulations (see boxed insert "Waiving the Rules"). For many years OMB has reviewed all legislative proposals bubbling up from the bureaucracy. Beginning in early 1981, all agencies were required to submit for OMB's approval all proposed regulations as well as all proposed legislation involving new programs or substantial changes in existing ones. This review procedure prevents agencies from bypassing the president.

Presidential appointments and issue networks. Political executives are men and women who supervise the bureaucracy. They include secretaries, under secretaries, assistant secretaries of the Cabinet, general councils, administrators and deputy administrators of agencies, and members of regulatory commissions and boards. They are, for the most part, presidential appointees who are expected to guide future policies and to direct the career staff (civil servants) in implementation of existing programs.

The tenure of most politically appointed executives is short. A typical term of office is two and one half to three and one half years; in contrast, the average length of service for the career staff is twenty-four years. It is easy to see why many political executives have difficulty redirecting agency goals.[6]

Increasingly, presidents have been appointing people with specialized credentials who are knowledgeable about complex policies to head bureaus, agencies, and departments. These people are often drawn from

---

[6] Hugh Heclo, *A Government of Strangers: Executive Politics in Washington* (Washington, D.C.: Brookings Institution, 1977).

Box 2–1
Waiving the rules

One evening last fall, five members of the Aspirin Foundation of America jumped in a cab to pay a hastily arranged call on a seemingly minor official of the White House's Office of Management and Budget.

They had a problem. After three years of medical studies, months of internal deliberations and a day-long public hearing, the Department of Health and Human Services was about to issue a regulation requiring a warning label on aspirin bottles.

The warning would say that aspirin had been linked to Reye's syndrome, a rare but often-fatal childhood illness, and that it shouldn't be given to children for flu or chicken pox without a doctor's approval.

As a result of this last-minute visit, the proposed regulation was never issued. It became one of more than 200 major proposed regulations that have been blocked by an efficient but secrecy-shrouded process of informal negotiations with industry that the Reagan administration has institutionalized as part of its effort to provide "regulatory relief."

James C. Miller III, chief architect of the Reagan deregulation effort, says he worries that fear of a backlash is making agency regulators skittish about further deregulation.

The problem, he says, began with the exposure of the Environmental Protection Agency's sometimes-intimate dealings with industry, and he fears it has spilled over into other agencies that deal with issues of public health and safety.

Miller argues that it is a lot tougher politically to remove a regulation than it is to impose or defend one.

Defense of agency's role

But Christopher DeMuth, the lawyer who currently runs the OMB's Office of Information and Regulatory Affairs, insists that the effort will continue and that "no future president will ever dismantle" the power given to the OMB to review most new government regulations.

The one thing that nearly everyone agrees about in this growing flap is that this power is not small.

"You go ahead and write the substance (of a given federal program), and I'll write the procedure and I'll shaft you every time," grumbles Rep. John D. Dingell, chairman of the House Energy and Commerce Committee, who says he will soon introduce a bill to regulate the deregulators. It would force OMB to disclose all contacts it makes with federal agencies and outside groups.

The aspirin case offers a glimpse of the informal, behind-the-scenes activity that can lead to the derailing of a major proposed federal rule. The power in this case was wielded by a slim, intense-looking man who sits behind an almost antiseptically clean desk and tries not to let a listener know whether he agrees with him.

Box 2–1 (*continued*)

He is James J. Tozzi, a veteran OMB bureaucrat, who sometimes functions as an informal court of last resort for people—usually representatives of big companies—who see themselves threatened by the prospect of a new federal regulation.

Executive Order 12291

Tozzi's real emergence as a behind-the-scenes power came in the early days of the Reagan administration, when Tozzi was named deputy OMB administrator for information and regulatory affairs and given a staff of 80—the largest in OMB—to carry out Executive Order 12291.

That order, signed by President Reagan, gave the OMB unprecedented power to review regulations of most government agencies. Under it, Tozzi could block regulations that didn't seem to make sense, or that didn't square with his cost-benefit analysis.

Many rules, both large and small, have been blocked as a result. Regulations recently returned to federal agencies for further study include: guidelines for operating rural health clinics; national standards for traffic-control devices; standards for the coating of soft-drink cans.

There has been relatively little public interest in the executive order, but Tozzi and his boss, Miller, have been besieged by an audience that is interested: lawyers and Washington representatives of major corporations.

To carry out his mandate, Tozzi sometimes found it helpful to talk with representatives of companies that would be affected by new regulations, so he set up a process that he calls "a modified black box."

Outsiders could argue for or against proposed rules, but they could see only Tozzi or his deputy, never his staff. The emphasis was on informal negotiations. Few, if any, records were kept.

Joseph M. White, chairman of the Aspirin Foundation, says he knew nothing of this until one day when he asked the foundation's lawyer if there wasn't something else they could do to stop the proposed labeling regulation.

The aspirin people had argued that the medical studies supporting it were faulty and that the rule would be widely misunderstood, costing the manufacturers some $100 million a year in unsold aspirin. Up to that point they had lost at every step of the way. The Food and Drug Administration and the HHS secretary had approved the rule. "It was going right along down the line," White says.

"Takes a lot of guts"

The lawyer arranged a meeting with Tozzi who, after some outside checking, agreed with the industry's argument. Tozzi then sent the rule back to the HHS department for further study.

"It is a wonderful thing that the government finally has a system to

---

Box 2–1 (*concluded*)

review these regulations," says White, who admires Tozzi "because it takes a lot of guts to stand up" and say "no" to a proposed rule.

Sidney Wolfe, director of Ralph Nader's Health Research Group, is apoplectic about Tozzi's role. "Everyone who was involved in this was outraged," argues Wolfe, who claims the delay will mean one hundred needless child deaths each year.

Wolfe, as it happens, was the man pushing the proposed rule all along. When the FDA was deliberating over internal reports about Reye's syndrome, Wolfe leaked them to the press. When HHS officials hesitated in backing the proposed rule, Wolfe sued them.

The Nader people didn't discover the real story of the regulatory about-face in the aspirin case until several months later, when Alan Morrison, the head of Nader's Public Citizen Litigation Group, happened to be talking with a friend: Jim Tozzi.

Morrison says he respects Tozzi as an honest man and a friend, but thinks that what he is doing is unconstitutional: "My view is that Jim Tozzi wasn't elected to run this country."

Source: Condensed from John J. Fialka, "Waiving the Rules: "Reaganites Find Plans for Deregulation Stall after EPA Revelations," *The Wall Street Journal*, June 6, 1983.

---

what Hugh Heclo calls "issue networks," a large group of people who share information about broad public policy issues (e.g., health care, nuclear power, gun control, consumer protection, and energy).[7] In the Reagan administration, Deputy Secretary of the Treasury Richard G. Darman and Secretary of the Navy John Lehman typified such leaders. They analyze and refine political strategies through which they (even when outside government) can shape public policy and determine government decisions. But whether inside or outside of the government, participants in an issue network usually operate from some institutional base: executive agencies, the legislature and its staff, private interest groups, foundations, state and local government units, universities, think tanks, and so forth.

Unlike the members of most special interest groups, network participants are motivated more by the substance of a public policy, even an ideological commitment to it, than any direct material benefits they may gain from it. They are like special interest groups in at least one

---

[7] Hugh Heclo, "Issue Networks and the Executive Establishment." In Anthony King, ed., *The New American Political System* (Washington, D.C.: American Enterprise Institute, 1978).

respect: they try to influence the policy process in many settings. Presidential appointees try to launch new policies from within the government, while outsiders testify at legislative hearings, work as consultants to government agencies, or publicize a particular issue.

Network participants are, if anything, expert in their fields of interest; and as the term *network* suggests, they work together and communicate frequently about their issue. While they may not always agree on what should be done, they do share a common vocabulary and knowledge base.

Issue networks were formed over the past twenty-five years partly in response to the tremendous growth in the scope of activity of the federal government, coupled with the virtual nonexpanding bureaucracy. Because of its small bureaucracy relative to the size of its spending and scope of activities, the federal government relies heavily on third parties (such as state and local governments, schools, hospitals, and social service agencies) for the administration of its programs. This strategy has enabled the federal government to avoid developing a vast bureaucracy, like those found in many European countries, but it has also complicated the relationship between administration and politics in Washington. Many policy concerns have been pushed out of the traditional power centers of the federal government and into the hands of numerous issue networks. Issue networks are likely to continue to overlay the existing governmental structure and provide both political parties with federal appointees.

Civil servants

The distinction between political appointees and career civil servants is sometimes blurry. An increasing proportion of the latter fill appointed executive positions, and there is little difference in social characteristics between the two groups. It is now widely recognized that high-level career officials participate in policymaking by assisting appointed officials in planning, implementing, defending, and changing agency programs. Both spend a considerable amount of time dealing with Congress.

Civil servants derive their political power from a number of sources. One is expertise. In a complex society, individuals who possess technical skills and information become major sources of influence and power. Since civil servants give full-time attention to specific problems or issues, they usually have an advantage over other participants in the policy process, such as political appointees and legislators.

Another important source of bureaucratic power is outside support. Virtually every bureaucracy administers some programs that someone has a vested interest in. A civil servant may be reluctant to openly fight a policy backed by the administration, but may oppose it quietly and indirectly by working with outside interest groups and friends in Congress. One student of bureaucracy has characterized this kind of covert opposition to official policy as guerrilla warfare rather than frontal assault.

> Career officials will confide their doubts about the wisdom of the policies being followed by their political superiors to friendly legislators or reporters, or they may alert pressure groups with which they have an intimate relationship that policy changes being contemplated by the administration in power are adverse to their interests. They thus convert disputes with political executives into conflicts between their superiors and outside organizations. In this way, they can pursue their objectives without jeopardy to the forms of bureaucratic life or the safety of their own position. Moreover, by avoiding an open break with their superior, they can continue to pass ammunition to a political executive's critics from the security of their intimate participation in the affairs and deliberations of the agency. In this surreptitious way, officials can incite political conflict in the outside world without risking their own safety by directly participating in the combat. Many of these tactics were used by career employees at the EPA in their struggles with political appointees during the early years of the Reagan administration.[8]

But such behavior is the exception rather than the rule. More often than not, political appointees and civil servants work out a mutual accommodation.

A more subtle source of power derives from the ability of civil servants to mold the views of other participants in the policy process. The way in which they present (or do not present) information cannot help but influence the way in which elected officials perceive an issue.

As Congress addresses more and more complex issues, it has been forced in many instances to grant more discretion and decision-making power to executive agencies. As a result, most of the rules and regulations that make legislation operational are written by civil servants. They interpret and implement the legislative intent by defining limitations, eliminating contradictions, and focusing strategy. For example, Congress created the Federal Communication Commission in 1932 with a brief piece of legislation giving the commission a mandate to regulate wireless communications in the "public interest, convenience, and necessity." Under this broad grant of authority, the FCC has written thousands of rules regulating the radio, television, and telecommunications industry.

But Congress has also put certain limits on agency policymaking.

---

[8] Francis E. Rourke, *Bureaucracy, Politics, and Public Policy* (Boston: Little, Brown, 1984), p. 129.

The Administrative Procedures Act (APA) of 1946 requires that agencies must, among other requirements, announce any proposed changes in regulation at least thirty days in advance, and they must give interested parties a chance to submit testimony and appear at a hearing to consider the new or revised rule.

In early 1986, the federal government began to take steps to ban asbestos, a widely used substance that experts say causes up to 12,000 cancer deaths annually in the United States. The decision was the culmination of more than six years of regulatory infighting within the government. Because the APA requires a step-by-step process for issuing rules, the ban did not take place instantly. The plan first had to be published in the *Federal Register*, the compendium of government regulatory and rulemaking proposals. Public hearings were scheduled starting three months after publications and public comment were submitted to the Environmental Protection Agency for ninety days after publication. This technique affords the administrator an opportunity to identify offending provisions, forecast administrative difficulties, and gain the consent of affected interests. It took about one year to complete public hearings and administrative review of the proposed asbestos rule.

The administrative practice of consulting or conferring with private interest groups frequently leads to establishment of advisory committees or commissions composed of these groups. In her analysis of the way in which social security policy developed in the United States, Martha Derthick shows the critical role advisory committees played whenever major changes were contemplated.[9]

Advisory committees help build political support for major changes in policy. The Reagan administration followed this strategy in 1982 when it established an advisory commission to draft proposals for reforming the Social Security Act. See the accompanying boxed insert for three more examples of how government uses commissions.

Commissions are usually asked to address broad public problems, like social security or Central America, that are not susceptible to easy solutions. They typically consist of distinguished members who represent diverse interests. They are expected to produce reports with near unanimity. Given these restraints, Paul E. Peterson of the Brookings Institution offers these observations about the inherent limitations of commissions. First, the report will not spell out the details of its proposals but state only broad, general objections. The report will tend to exaggerate the problem it addresses (all the better to attract attention) and to recommend changes that are beyond current technology and resources.

---

[9] Martha Derthick, *Policymaking for Social Security* (Washington, D.C.: Brookings Institution, 1979), pp. 89–109.

48

Box 2–2

Commission week: Americans tackle their problems

In the Washington headquarters of the President's Private Sector Survey on Cost Control, known as the Grace Commission, a staffer handed over a copy of his report embargoed until the next day. "Weren't you supposed to release this today?" I asked. "Yes," he sighed, "but the Kissinger Commission was already reporting today."

This was the quote of the week. It was a breathless week, an absolutely Adidas week, for all the pressies who had to cover public events in the nation's capital. Flashy shows abounded in politics foreign and domestic. But if one set of happenings dominated the tone of the procession, it was the back-to-back reports by several commissions appointed to help extricate us from long-running policy dilemmas.

The commissions certainly had competition for the limelight. Chinese Premier Zhao Ziyang won the East-meets-West incongruity award as he tootled around historic Williamsburg in a horse-drawn carriage. The United States re-established diplomatic relations with the Vatican, and Catholic and Protestant clergy debated the constitutional propriety of the act.

Still, the most arduous running track stretched among the offices, meeting rooms and briefing chambers of the three major commissions reporting this week.

The food assistance task force, better known as the hunger task force, went public first. This body had been appointed to cope with a typical political problem of advanced liberalism. The left "owned" the problem of hunger in America: It insisted that hunger was rampant among us, that the solution was money, and that anyone who said otherwise was in favor of starving babies. The Reagan administration needed moral and scientific permission to try to break the left's hammerlock.

The report that the task force staff drafted did indeed provide honest ammunition for a more skeptical view. It pointed out that we still have inadequate knowledge about the numbers of the hungry, and that the largest groups of the persistently hungry—the chronically homeless, the female-headed households and such—are those we can least easily keep well nourished just by anteing up more money.

But at the open meeting on Monday where the diverse group of public commissioners met to approve the draft, the time might just as well have been the McGovern era. The draft said it would be more efficient to decentralize the food stamp program, if states wanted to take it on. The commissioners from the enlightened business community protested. "No witness has come before us" talking specifically enough about the idea, one commissioner said in shocked tones. "The leveling effect of the present program might disappear," another manager voiced his objection. In the same way, the commissioners were all for administrative simplification,

Box 2–2 (*continued*)

but almost every time they came to a specific proposal they chickened out.

They need not have wasted so much time softening the report. When the document finally emerged, the hunger establishment still reacted as if the task force had proposed to starve the poor out of existence. All in all, the document marked a new pragmatism in our dealings with the hunger problem. But the resistance to taking its arguments seriously was fierce.

Likewise the Kissinger Commission was formed to tackle a paralyzing political problem caused by a liberalism nurtured in the 1960s. The administration wants to wage an active policy in Central America, but the dominant moral and intellectual authority in the field is still on the anti-interventionist left. The Kissinger report applied some serious weight against this orthodoxy.

The report allowed as how the underlying problems of Central America were socio-economic. But the document also insisted that there would be no political or economic progress in the region unless this country were permitted to help squash the troublemakers who are propped up by forces from outside.

A senior commission official briefed pundits on the report in the National Security Council conference room, which has three digital clocks high on one wall—the first labeled "Washington, D.C.," the second marked "GMT" for Greenwich Mean Time, and the third called "Beirut." Overwhelmingly, the press wanted to know about only one thing: whether the commission had assumed a morally correct position on human rights. The questions once more smacked of Vietnam: Who did the commission think should judge whether El Salvador was making acceptable human rights progress? Didn't Salvadoran authorities' connection with right-wing terrorism undermine the government? Were murderers preferable to Marxist-Leninists?

The same pattern has begun to appear even in the treatment of the Grace Commission. This group's recommendations vary in quality. But the report certainly recognizes that we have a major problem facing us in the management of modern liberalism.

And what have the preliminary stories about the commission dealt with? With the scandalous fact that someone decided to cut from the report the names of certain Congressmen who dip deeply into the pork barrel. To be sure, the pork barrel is a venerable, tacky, and expensive American phenomenon. But a lot of people on the receiving end of the Grace Commission report will use it to obscure just what the more central problem really is.

The commissions were of course diverse, but running through their ceremonies were a couple of significant lessons about the state of our

Box 2–2 (*concluded*)

policy thinking at the moment. One is that government does seem to be moving beyond the intellectual limitations and moral pieties that got fixed in our political universe twenty years ago. The other is that many people still have the desperate energy to drag us a considerable way backwards.

Source: Suzanne Garment, *The Wall Street Journal*, January 13, 1984.

The report will seldom call for institutional reform, because such proposals generate controversy.[10]

Capitol Hill

The U.S. Congress, as every schoolchild should know, consists of 100 senators and 435 representatives with diverse interests elected from the fifty states. Congress is the most visible participant in the policymaking process—its members must run for office, their actions on the floor and in hearings are televised, and their communication with constituencies continues.

Congress plays a four-fold role in the policy process: reformulation, adoption, appropriation, and implementation. We must not draw too sharp a distinction between reformulation and adoption. When the president has placed a proposal before Congress, Congress will itself modify the proposal before it becomes law; in that sense, reformulation and adoption are parallel activities. Thus, virtually all of the analytical concerns of Chapters 5 through 8 can be of interest to Congress as well as executive agencies.

Nor should we gloss over the profound significance of adoption in the U.S. political system. We can best see that significance by returning once again to the vital heart of things, the political tenets of U.S. government and the crucial role that these tenets provide for the legislature.

The intellectual origins of Congress' role in the adoption of policy. In 1690, John Locke put forward in his *Civil Government, Second Essay* several fundamental arguments for making the legislative body—not the executive or the courts—paramount in determining what activities government should undertake. First, the people (in a hypothetical state of nature

---

[10] Paul E. Peterson, "Did the Educational Commissions Say Anything?" *Brookings Review* 2 (Winter 1983), pp. 3–11. The presidential commission headed by former Attorney General William Rogers that investigated the space shuttle disaster appears to be a remarkable exception to Peterson's rule. See especially *Report of the Presidential Commission on the Space Shuttle Challenger Accident* (Washington D.C., Government Printing Office, June 6, 1986), pp. 198–201.

before the establishment of any government) had chosen to delegate their power to this body:

> The legislative cannot transfer the power of making laws to any other hands, for it being but a delegated power from the people, they who have it cannot pass it over to others. The people alone can appoint the form of the commonwealth, which is by constituting the legislative, and appointing in whose hands that shall be. And when the people have said, "We will submit, and be governed by laws made by such men, and in such forms," nobody else can say other men shall make laws for them; nor can they be bound by any laws but such as are enacted by those whom they have chosen and authorized to make laws for them. (Chap. 9)

Some today might find the state of nature argument mysterious at best, but Locke did not rest his entire case on it. He also argued that the legislature was less likely to do ill because it did not need to be as permanent or cohesive a body as the executive. Accordingly, supreme power—*the right to either approve or reject major policies*—should reside with it.

> The legislative power is that which has a right to direct how the force of the commonwealth shall be employed for preserving the community and the members of it. Because those laws which are constantly to be executed, and whose force is always to continue, may be made in a little time, therefore there is no need that the legislative should be always in being, not having always business to do. And because it may be too great temptation to human frailty, apt to grasp at power, for the same persons who have the power of making laws to have also in their hands the power to execute them, whereby they may exempt themselves from obedience to the laws they make, and suit the law, both in its making and execution, to their own private advantage, and thereby come to have a distinct interest from the rest of the community, contrary to the end of society and government. Therefore in well-ordered commonwealth, where the good of the whole is so considered as it ought, the legislative power is put into the hands of diverse persons who, duly assembled, have by themselves, or jointly with others, a power to make laws, which when they have done, being separated again, they are themselves subject to the laws they have made; which is a new and near tie upon them to take care that they make them for the public good. (Chap. 12)

In contrast, when the ultimate power is in a permanent, integrated body such as the bureaucracy or the presidency, there is a danger that "they will think themselves to have a distinct interest from the rest of the community, and so will be apt to increase their own riches and power by taking what they think fit from the people." (Chap. 11)

This line of thinking emerged, less than a hundred years later, in *The Federalist.* Madison, steeped in Locke, wrote unequivocally: "The idea of a national government involves in it, not only authority over the individual citizens, but an indefinite supremacy over all persons and things, so far as they are objects of lawful government. Among a people consolidated into one nation, this supremacy is completely rested in the national legislature" (no. 39). So, when policy analysts find themselves wishing to short-circuit the adoption stage, they might recall Article I of the Constitution, which follows the Locke-Madison line completely. They might also review Article V, the Catch-22 of the Constitution: Article V prohibits any changes to Article I, which gives supreme power to Congress, without approval by Congress.

Congressional resources. A couple of the reasons why members of Congress are important policymakers have already been suggested: constitutional authority and media access. Members also have the edge on the administration in terms of longevity. Secretaries of Agriculture, Defense, and Treasury come and go, but the chairmen of some committees seem to have been with us forever. Longevity in itself is not power; to the extent it allows a member of Congress to establish a wide range of connections in the government bureaucracy and with powerful interest groups as well as develop a certain level of expertise (especially the kind that lets one know the right questions to ask), it is.

Moreover, legislators are well situated in the information flow. They see and hear a wide range of studies, testimonies, leaks, interest-group pressures, and concerns from constituents. They are also able to draw on several important internal sources. For instance:

- *Congressional staff,* which increased dramatically in size during the 1970s, now numbers over 18,000. Most of this increase occurred not on the members' personal staffs but on committee staffs.

  Much of the back chamber maneuvering in Congress is governed by a code of silence only a little less sacred than the vow that bound the Arthurian knights. Among other things, the code maintains the fiction that members of Congress do all the work themselves. But, as any good lobbyist knows, much of the maneuvering and back-scratching—in short, bargaining—done by aides often occurs with only the sketchiest knowledge on the part of the senators and representatives involved.

  Congressional staff members exert great influence on their legislators because they control the information the legislators receive and they can specialize on a single issue. Staff members are often independently responsible for managing legislation and drafting many of the bills and resolutions that are introduced in Congress.

  Members of Congress must pass judgment on a wide gamut of issues, ranging from magnetohydrodynamics to the Daughters of the Confederacy patent renewal. That, not lassitude, probably explains why members allow staff aides to become influential. That too is why lobbyists—with their ability to cut through reams of bills and supporting documents with ten minutes of straightforward oral discussion—are necessary. Of course these presentations, though concise, are biased; but since the various sides usually come around to argue their case, there is a kind of rough balance. This is not always the case, especially when the benefits to one special interest are high and the cost to the rest of the citizenry is relatively low.

- *The Office of Technology Assessment* (OTA), created in 1972 as an arm of Congress, has the difficult assignment of trying to anticipate, understand, and describe how the world's new technologies will affect the people, environment, and institutions of the United States. In a world where dozens of powerful new chemicals, startling scientific discoveries, far-reaching computer systems, earth-shattering weapons, and potent drugs present difficult new social problems on almost a weekly basis, the challenge of this job is a major one. The problem is to keep the agency relevant to the political process, but to avoid partisan biases.

- *The Congressional Budget Office* (CBO) was created in 1972 to strengthen the hand of Congress in budget battles with the president. Located in the dingy former Federal Bureau of Investigation building, down the hill from the U.S. Capitol, the office generates economic forecasts, projections of federal spending and revenue estimates, and cost estimates of policy changes. And while it is still an infant among government agencies, the office has developed a reputation as an objective forecaster in the world of government, where numbers too often seem more a matter of politics than science.

- *The General Accounting Office* (GAO) audits expenditures and increasingly evaluates operations of agencies. In addition, GAO assists congressional committees in developing statements of legislative goals and analyzing federal agency programs.

The committee system. Congress works through committees and subcommittees. See Table 2–1. Almost all legislation begins the road to enactment in a subcommittee, and much of it dies there without being considered by either full chamber of Congress.

We can view much of the policymaking that occurs in subcommittees in terms of "iron triangles," whose three sides are made up of people from executive bureaus, subcommittee members, and interest groups. The congressional committees and their chairmen who form one side of the triangle operate, for the most part, independent of other members of Congress, congressional leadership, and party pressures. They often develop close relationships that cross party lines. The results are numerous minibureaucracies in Congress. Lobbyists and other interest-group leaders, which form another side of the triangle, are specialists in the areas for which they lobby, and one of their functions is to participate

Table 2–1
Standing committees of the Congress

House Committee	Senate Committee
Agriculture	Agriculture, Nutrition, and Forestry
Appropriations	Appropriations
Armed Services	Armed Services
Banking, Finance and Urban Affairs	Banking, Housing, and Urban Affairs
Budget	Budget
District of Columbia	Commerce, Science, and Transportation
Education and Labor	Energy and Natural Resources
Energy and Commerce	Environment and Public Works
Foreign Affairs	Finance
Government Operations	Foreign Relations
House Administration	Governmental Affairs
Interior and Insular Affairs	Judiciary
Judiciary	Labor and Human Resources
Merchant Marine and Fisheries	Rules and Administration
Post Office and Civil Service	Small Business
Public Works and Transportation	Veterans' Affairs
Rules	
Science and Technology	
Small Business	
Standards of Official Conduct	
Veterans' Affairs	
Ways and Means	

in deliberations between the bureaus and committees handling the policy decisions that affect their clients. The third side of the iron triangle is formed by bureau leaders whose ability to influence congressional committees is an important part of their power. They have several strategies for achieving their goals; they can anticipate the expectations of congressional committees and other groups, or play one committee off against another (for example, exploit the Senate appropriations committee's tendency to countermand decisions of its counterpart in the House). While committee hearings provide opportunities for all participants in a system to influence policymaking, bureau leaders and interest-group representatives are particularly adept at using hearings to build an impressive case for their side.[11]

Besides officially adopting or approving policy proposals and helping to reformulate the proposals, Congressional committees involve themselves in implementation and budgeting. Through its power of investigation and oversight and with the aid of its General Accounting Office, Congress reviews how well (or how poorly) the objectives of programs are being attained. Through its *power of the purse*, Congress determines how much money may be spent on a given program. Of the two roles—

---

[11] Freeman, *The Political Process.*

oversight and appropriation—the latter is easily the more important in the policy process.

The power of the purse. This power flows from Article I of the U.S. Constitution, which authorizes Congress "to lay and collect Taxes, Duties, Imports and Excises," and provides that "No Money shall be drawn from the Treasury, but in Consequence of Appropriations made by Law." Although those words were penned over two centuries ago, they continue to exercise a profound influence over the modern policy-maker who resides in the executive branch.

Arguably, budgeting is the single most important aspect of policy-making. As Aaron Wildavsky explains it:

> Budgeting is concerned with the translation of financial resources into human purposes. . . . Since funds are limited and have to be divided in one way or another, the budget becomes a mechanism for making choices among alternative expenditures. When the choices are coordinated so as to achieve desired goals, a budget may be called a plan. Should it include a detailed specification of how its objectives are to be achieved, a budget may serve as a plan of work for those who assume the task of implementing it. . . . If politics is regarded in part as conflict over whose preferences shall prevail in the determination of . . . policy, then the budget records the outcomes of this struggle.[12]

Prior to 1921, Congress itself prepared the budget piecemeal by enacting a series of laws that originated in the many committees involved in the highly decentralized process of authorizing expenditure, appropriating funds, and raising revenue. But no one was responsible for the budget as a whole. The chief executive's role consisted mainly of approving the revenue and appropriation bills, just as he approved any other piece of legislation.

In 1921, Congress changed all that. The Budgeting and Accounting Act placed responsibility for preparing the budget onto the president. The act established a Bureau of the Budget (later called the Office of Management and Budget) to assist the president in submitting *his* budget to Congress each January. In the past, executive agencies had submitted *their* budgetary requests directly to Congress. While Congress retained its authority to raise and spend funds, it would now begin its work from the president's budget. (The later 1980s found Congress willing to use President Reagan's budget, which contained deficits but no tax increases, as a point of departure. Indeed, the Democrats, who controlled Congress, derisively referred to the president's budget as Dead on Arrival.)

The annual budget the president submits applies to the next fiscal

---

[12] *The Politics of the Budgetary Process,* 3rd ed. (Boston: Little, Brown, 1979), pp. 1–2.

year (FY). Currently, the fiscal year runs from October 1 to September 30. The budget is named for the year in which it *ends*. Thus, the FY1988 budget applied to the twelve months from October 1, 1987 to September 30, 1988. The budget states how much government agencies will be authorized to spend for programs (their budget authority), how much they are expected to spend (called budget outlays or expenditures), and how much is expected in taxes and other revenues. For example, President Reagan's proposed FY1988 budget contained authority for expenditures of $1,099 billion, but it provided for spending (outlays) of only $1,024 billion. Reagan's budget anticipated receipts of $917 billion, leaving a deficit of $107 billion—the difference between receipts and outlays.

But the budget document contains more than numbers. It also explains individual spending programs in terms of national needs, agency missions, and basic programs. The budget cycle is *the* dominant management routine in government—whether federal, state, or local. In recent decades, public budgeting has become a high-level, sophisticated process for systematically identifying and analyzing policy choices. Many larger jurisdictions have adopted more elaborate processes for budget preparation involving a wider array of agency officials, including those associated with policy analysis.

The budget that the president submits to Congress each January represents the results of a process that began the previous spring under the supervision of OMB. At that time, OMB officials meet with the president to discuss the economic situation and his budgetary priorities. The OMB then sends broad economic guidelines to every agency and requests their initial projections of funds that will be needed for the next fiscal year. Based on these numbers, OMB prepares new guidelines and requests budgets based on them from agencies. By the fall, agencies submit their formal budgets to OMB. At this point, the political skills of public executives fighting for the goals of their policies become vital.[13] Political negotiations may extend into early winter, often to the moment the president's budget goes to the printer and then on to Congress.

Because one group of legislators in each house plans for revenues and many other groups plan for spending, no one is responsible for the budget as a whole. Congress has, however, added a new committee structure that addresses these problems. After bitter spending fights with President Nixon in the late 1960s and early 1970s, Congress finally

---

[13] While political skill is the subject of Chapter 9, we might note here that Aaron Wildavsky has identified several political tactics used by agencies to maintain or increase the amount of money available to their programs: creating and manipulating a client; placing potentially attractive programs in separate visible units; fulfilling expectations of potential supporters; doing favors that make friends; bargaining; adhering strictly to the rules of the game; shifting the blame for mistakes; and many more.

passed the Budget and Impoundment Control Act of 1974. That act fashioned a typically political solution to the problem that had frustrated previous attempts to change the budgeting procedure. All the tax and appropriations committees were retained, and new House and Senate Budget Committees were superimposed on the old committee structure. The Budget Committees supervised a new comprehensive budget review process, aided by the previously mentioned Congressional Budget Office. The CBO acquired a budgetary expertise equal to that of the president's OMB, so it could prepare credible alternative budgets for Congress. This process (or one very much like it) worked reasonably well for the first few years. Congress regained some capability to structure the budget as a whole, rather than merely alter pieces of it. But Congress encountered increasing difficulty in enacting its budget resolutions according to its own time-table. The problem became more severe under the Reagan administration.

Think tanks and policy intellectuals

An important source of policy ideas and policy advice are the think tanks, or research institutes, found in and around Washington, D.C., and the state capitols. Such research organizations provide the fodder for many speeches and legislative proposals. They are a permanent home for some policy analysts, and a way station for people who have served or wish to serve in the government.

Until recent years, the world of Washington think tanks revolved around a scholarly rivalry between the American Enterprise Institute and the venerable Brookings Institution, both of which are known for their academic, long-term studies of issues. Today, the two no longer have the field to themselves.

Since the mid-1970s, there has been a definite growth in the number of think tanks. Indeed, one of the newcomers, the twelve-year-old Heritage Foundation, which prides itself on fast analyses of current issues, has become the important new public-policy group. Clearly, the Heritage Foundation is no ordinary cloistered think tank. It claims that a full 60 percent of the more than 2,000 policy suggestions it made in 1980, when it issued *Mandate for Leadership* (a kind of conservative manifesto for Reagan's first term), have been at least partly supported by the administration. Among them were the 1981 tax cut, the idea of a subminimum wage for youths, and the proposed "Star Wars" space-based defense system.[14]

Think tanks also contribute to presidential campaigns and political

---

[14] Philip M. Boffey, "Heritage Foundation: Succession Obscurity," *New York Times,* November 17, 1985.

careers. Not long ago a presidential candidate could not become a serious contender unless he had written a book—or hired someone to ghostwrite one for him. Then, candidates needed a political action committee to spread funds around to help win the favor of other public officials. Now it seems that ideas are what matters. Accordingly, candidates in the late 1980s began setting up their own think tanks so they will have a staff to develop a detailed agenda and help establish themselves as candidates with ideas. Even the names of these policy foundations suggest a vision: Center for a New Democracy, Fund for an American Renaissance, and American Horizons. Presumably, ideas will give their campaigns a greater air of substance.

Universities may also serve as think tanks for government. In addition to many policy studies programs, specialized institutes such as the Institute for Research on Poverty at the University of Wisconsin, the Harvard-MIT Joint Center for Urban Studies, and the Regional Research Center of Princeton University develop policy ideas.

The work of outside policy analysts raises three questions for government policymakers: How exactly is policy research used in the policy process? Under what conditions is it likely to be used? What are the advantages of these external sources of policy studies over in-house research?

How are policy studies used?   Scholars investigating the role of policy analysis in the policymaking process have long acknowledged its use for strategic purposes, that is, to support a predetermined position. A case in point was the 1980 government study, *Global 2000 Report to the President*, which concluded that, if present trends continue, the world in the year 2000 will be more crowded, more polluted, less stable ecologically, and more vulnerable to disruptions than the world we live in now. The report supported important policy pronouncements of the Carter administration. Indeed, before it was completed, President Carter was discussing its conclusions with other world leaders at an economic summit held in Italy. The government distributed more than one million copies of the report. Two years later, with President Reagan in office, the Environmental Protection Agency asked critics of *Global 2000* to prepare a similar report. When the environmental movement learned of this plan, they began a campaign to prevent the project from being funded. EPA never came through with the funding.[15]

As one would expect, policymakers also use analysis substantively, that is, applied directly to policy decisions. According to one survey,

---

[15] Julian L. Simon and Herman Kahn, *The Resourceful Earth: A Response to Global 2000* (New York: Basil Blackwell, 1984), p. 37. For further discussion of strategic or political uses of analysis, see Carol Weiss, *Using Social Research in Public Policy Making* (Lexington, Mass.: D. C. Heath, 1977), pp. 1–22.

66 percent of policymakers interviewed rated researchers, academics, and consultants as being either "very" or "somewhat important" in the policymaking process.[16]

Congressional use of the Office of Technology Assessment's study of residential energy conservation provides a good example of the concrete, technical role of analysis. OTA staff provided Congress information on the number of houses and levels of insulation and reviewed drafts of the proposed legislation for increasing conservation in different economic sectors. Committee staff also frequently consulted OTA on the technical aspects of new energy conservation technology. The OTA was one of the primary documents Congress used.[17]

The third role is more indirect, though no less real. Policy analysis provides the conceptual language, the ruling models, the empirical examples (not evidence) that became the accepted assumptions for policymakers. Policy analysis, in this role, frames the debate. The most influential studies are those that manage to link a concept or theory to the practical needs and ideological predispositions of policymakers and politicians. As James Q. Wilson of Harvard University explains:

> At any given moment in history, an influential idea—and thus an influential intellectual—is one that provides a persuasive simplification of some policy question that is consistent with the particular mix of core values then held by the political elite. "Regulation" or "deregulation" have been such ideas; so also have "balanced budgets" versus "compensatory fiscal policy" and "integration" versus "affirmative action." Clarifying and making persuasive those ideas is largely a matter of argument and the careful use of analogies; rarely does this process involve matters of proof and evidence of the sort that is, in their scholarly as opposed to their public lives, supposed to be the particular skill and obligation of the intellectual in the *university*.[18]

In sum, what policy analysis chiefly brings to the policy process is *strategic* support for a predetermined view, *substantive* knowledge for program design, and *theoretical* concepts for framing the debate. The danger here is to dismiss the third role. Professor Wilson reminds us that theorizing is not the same as empty talk. "Good theory calls attention to obvious truths that were previously overlooked, finds crucial flaws in existing theories, and reinterprets solid evidence in a new light. And some theories, if adopted, will make us all better off. The problem is to know which ones."[19]

---

[16] Kingdon, *Agendas, Alternatives*, pp. 57–58.

[17] David Whiteman, "Reaffirming the Importance of Strategic Use," *Knowledge: Creation, Diffusion, Utilization* 6, no. 3 (March 1985), pp. 203–24.

[18] James Q. Wilson, "'Policy Intellectuals' and Public Policy," *Public Interest*, Summer 1981, p. 36.

[19] Ibid., p. 46.

When will a policy study be used (and not just sought)? A few years ago, Fred D. Baldwin suggested—tongue in cheek—a mathematical model "to predict the probable utilization of a report." The model is named Linked Indices for Assessing Relevance. "Because of its predictive accuracy, based on well-established theories of organizational behavior, LIAR has multiple uses for management decisions, including the evaluation of an evaluation division."[20]

In its simplest form, which requires the input of only six observations, the model is as follows:

$$P(U) = \frac{Z}{10}\left[\frac{X_1 + X_2}{2(Y_1 + Y_2 + Y_3)}\right]$$

where $P(U)$ is the probability that an evaluation report will be utilized, the Xs are incentives to utilization, the Ys are disincentives, and Z is an environmental constraint, with each variable given a weight from one to ten. Specifically:

X_1 = The importance of the subject matter of the evaluation to the management of the office which must act on the report.

X_2 = The clarity, precision, and technical quality of the evaluation report.

Y_1 = The technical difficulty of implementing the report.

Y_2 = Internal staff resistance to the report.

Y_3 = External political or other resistance to the report.

Z = The ability of the administrator nominally responsible for acting on the report to actually do so.

Though Baldwin is having a little fun with us—and perhaps analysts who may feel they do not get enough respect from policymakers—his list of incentives and disincentives is sound. I should like, however, to note one additional incentive and one disincentive. Let us call them X_3 and Y_4.

X_3 = The contribution the proposal will make to the reelection of the legislator. Perhaps the beginning of wisdom about Congress is to recognize the motivation of members to pursue policies that enhance their prospects for reelection. Certainly this helps explain why it might be difficult to expect members to vote for expensive projects such as the solar space power satellites that would not begin to return benefits (in this case, energy) for thirty years. One need not rush to an actuarial table to suspect that many of the members of Congress who voted for the solar

---

[20] Fred D. Baldwin, "Evaluating Evaluators," *Public Administration Review*, January–February 1972, pp. 49–53.

space power project would be dead when the voters began to enjoy the rewards of their representative's foresight. Conversely, the electoral connection goes a long way toward explaining why presidents find it exceedingly difficult to get congressmen to vote against the river and harbor projects of the Army Corps of Engineers—despite a plethora of studies showing that the costs exceed the benefits.

Y_4 = The degree to which the policy recommendations threaten the sponsoring organization. The report that recommends to the U.S. Air Force that missiles and drones can replace manned aircraft will probably be shredded, burned, and buried.

What are the pros and cons of using outside sources? Well, the advantages all seem, at first glance, clear enough. Outside advisers may be more objective because they are unhindered by the vested interests that are a product of the institutions in which the government official serves. Their objectivity and frankness may also be enhanced because they are not institutionally or politically dependent on political officials.

In contrast, in-house staff are too busy and may be too closely wedded to prevailing policy assumptions for truly imaginative or disinterested analysis. Henry A. Kissinger has cogently argued this view.[21] The administrative environment, according to Kissinger, offers little opportunity for creativity, and administrative skills are not always the same thing as executive skills. The administrator is preoccupied with building a smooth-running organization and with executing rather than creating policy. The demands for increased specialization encourage the development of administrative and technical skills and lead to excessive collection of facts and insufficient analysis of their significance. What passes for analysis is often performed by groups that seek a common denominator and consensus rather than a well-rounded point of view. The upshot of this situation can be a kind of "institutional self-deception": Top officials require facts and arguments to defend themselves against attack. Their subordinates and their staffs undertake to provide these to them. In order to serve their chiefs and to protect themselves, advisers and information sources inside the government tend to make their presentations in the most favorable light possible. The result, according to Kissinger, is that a kind of propitiatory optimism creeps into government reports and "what is taken to be true, therefore, is what it is politically desirable to believe."

The use of outside sources can help keep government bureaucracy lean. The advantages of lean staffs should be clear enough in light of the problems that have plagued White House operations in recent years.

---

[21] Henry Kissinger, *The Necessity of Choice* (New York: Harper & Row, 1960).

Despite an extensive inside network, presidents cannot be sure that their aides will support their policies or represent those policies from the presidential perspective. Size introduces serious managerial problems. Will the expanded staff unselectively flood the president with more information than he can assimilate? Will the staff attempt to shield their chief from unpleasant information and contacts and choke off certain alternative channels of information? On this last point, George Reedy, one of President Johnson's press secretaries, contended that the White House has a courtlike atmosphere that shields the president from reality and that Lyndon Johnson was a captive of this "inexorable White House mechanism."[22]

Nevertheless, using outside sources entails certain disadvantages. For example, when a government agency contracts with an outside group, policy must unavoidably be fragmented somewhat into doable pieces. Second, the number of truly first-rate research groups in a policy area (e.g., crime and energy) is severely limited; consequently, the same organization is called on again and again. Its decisions can soon become as predictable and even as stereotyped as those of the bureaucratic staff. Third, the ability of outside advisers can be hampered when effective consideration of a policy issue requires continuous, firsthand knowledge of classified data. Fourth, and perhaps most important, viewing a situation from a nongovernmental perspective, the outside analysts may not take the problems of implementing a policy into sufficient account. Unlike in-house analysts, they are not in a good position to influence effectively the carrying out of their recommendations.

Mass media

In the next section, we explore the first of the fifteen core ideas of this book: *agenda setting*, or the process by which problems get recognized. Conditions in society that are not recognized as problems never get on the agenda of government policymakers; those that are, do. Deciding what the problems will be is even more important than deciding what the solution will be.

The previously mentioned participants in policy process are usually forced to turn to the mass media to create, dramatize, and call attention to an issue. While the media may not always be able to determine how people view an issue, they certainly can determine what issue they will be viewing—and which they will not.

The mass media influences policymakers as well as citizens. When featuring a particular issue, the media asks policymakers to comment.

---

[22] George Reedy, *The Twilight of the Presidency* (New York: World, 1970).

This forces them to take a position; and since important people talk about the issue, it becomes even more important in the public's eye.

The media might deny its role in agenda setting, contending that it is like a mirror of society. There is much truth in this. Politicians, as I have already said, do use the media to get their message across. But the mirror simile carries us only so far. The media takes pride in the role it played in desegregation (by showing Congress, and the world, vivid photographs of police dogs attacking peaceful marchers), Watergate (by vigorously pursuing the trail of the cover-up), and Vietnam (by portraying the Tet Offensive as an American defeat).

The role of the media in the withdrawal of American forces in Vietnam tells us a lot about how the media operates. The mass media in general and television in particular have a bias toward good visuals. The gore of combat proved more sensational than the local warehouse fire. The aim was not to horrify, but to attract viewers. The networks are businesses that compete in the marketplace for viewers, and the size of their audience has a direct effect on their revenues and profitability.

For much the same reasons, the networks began exaggerating the importance of Reagan's meeting with General Secretary Gorbachev months before the meeting took place in Geneva in 1985. For example, one network graded General Secretary Gorbachev and President Reagan each morning on their performance the previous day. In what sounded more like a beauty contest than a superpower summit, they judged the leaders on the basis of initiative, style, substance, and public relations. Such an approach tended to trivialize the very events that the television reports were seeking to highlight.

The expressions "running with a hot item" and even "milking something for all it's worth" apply equally to domestic issues. In 1986, newspapers, news magazines, and the networks suddenly began reporting a "drug crisis." It was the perfect issue: sensational, colorful, gruesome, alarmist—with a veneer of social responsibility. Unfortunately, the statistics did not show that more people were taking drugs. To be sure, drug abuse was a major problem, but it was not as "pervasive and dangerous in its way as the plagues of medieval times" as *Newsweek* reported.

But these activities are somewhat in the nature of the medium. Getting back to the Vietnam example, we see more conscious forces at work. In early 1968, after five years of steady buildup, President Johnson still thought the war could be won. About this time CBS's television newsman Walter Cronkite broadcast a special report on the war, which Johnson watched. Cronkite concluded that the war was at a stalemate and victory was not possible. On hearing the Cronkite verdict, Johnson turned to his aides and said, "It's all over." Johnson was a great believer in public opinion polls and knew that a recent poll had shown that the American people trusted Cronkite more than any other American "to tell it like it is."[23]

A large capitol city like Washington can easily become a universe unto itself for the politicians and writers who reside there. Its quarrels and scandals consume their lives, as did the latest sensation in Rome in the sixteenth century and London in the eighteenth. "The man who is tired of London is tired of life," Dr. Johnson said, at exactly the moment England was losing the American colonies. What might be done about this all-consuming interest in Washingtonian politics? America might well be governed with more wisdom if its capitol could periodically be emptied and its inhabitants made to share the less exciting realities of state houses, city halls, and board rooms.

A note on policymakers in state, urban, and institutional settings

City councils and state legislatures. As Congress makes policy for the nation, councils make policy for the cities; that is, they choose among alternative courses for taxing people, spending money, and the like. The men and women who today serve on city councils vary so widely in income, education, occupation, and race, differ so sharply on philosophies of municipal government, and exercise such different powers and responsibilities that any attempt to describe a *typical* member should be brushed aside as fatuous.

But we do know a few things about how the composition and operations of councils can vary from jurisdiction to jurisdiction. For example, the use of ward or at-large elections affects the composition of councils. Ward elections tend to increase the representation of lower socioeconomic groups and minorities, whereas at-large elections increase the costs of elections and force all contenders to run before a constituency of the whole. Thus, under the at-large system, minority-group candidates in many cities must face a white majority; and even when minority-group candidates are successful, they are usually the more moderate ones. We also know that a council operating in the council-manager city is supposed to make policy but to leave questions dealing with administration to the city manager and his or her administrative agencies. Thus the council-manager of the city tries to separate policy and administration. In the strong mayor-council form of government, the initiative for policy is still more likely to come from the mayor than from the council, although the latter is not confined so narrowly as it is in the council-manager city.

The scope of the council's power is probably greatest in the weak-

---

[23] Austin Ranney, *Channels of Power: The Impact of Television on American Politics* (Washington, D.C.: American Enterprise Institute, 1983), pp. 4–5.

mayor system. Here the mayor must share power with other elected officials. The council, on the other hand, sometimes appoints officials, prepares the budget, and performs tasks that are considered administrative in other forms of government.

Finally, like all legislative bodies, the municipal council performs a representative function. Yet different council members will have different views about the proper role of the representative. And the formal structures of municipal government foster particular styles of representation. In the ward system, representation is likely to mean a narrow bricks-and-mortar orientation. Under this system, for example, members tend to look after their constituencies' desires for paved streets, parks, school facilities, and other tangible outputs of municipal government and are less likely to think in terms of the long-range public interest.

Since the process of policy adoption used by state legislatures closely parallels that used by Congress, little need be said about it. But despite the lack of respect that many citizens feel for state legislators, governors and members of the state bureaucracy fret many an hour over "this lower order of officeholder." To say the very least, it is essential that policy formulators understand how to get their bill adopted by the state legislature.

The governing board. In most organizations, top management is responsible to a governing board, at least some of whose members are not full-time employees of the organizations. In a corporation, of course, this is the board of directors. In nonprofit organizations, such as universities and many hospitals, it may be a board of trustees, a board of regents, or a "watchdog" committee. Boards usually approve or adopt programs and budgets proposed by management. They also take notice of the extent to which actual operations deviate from the approved policies.

The degree to which governing boards become involved in these matters varies. A considerable body of evidence indicates that boards of directors of many corporations take a quite perfunctory view of their responsibilities and essentially rubber-stamp the proposals of management. Still, boards generally act when they discover that the corporation is in trouble, for example, losing money.

Likewise, the governing board of a nonprofit organization has the responsibility of acting when the organization appears headed for trouble. But since there is no profit measure to monitor, this responsibility means that the board must spend a considerable amount of time studying the activities of the organization. Many governing boards do an inadequate job of this.

> There is not even a general recognition that this is the board's responsibility. In universities, for example, the following is widely quoted: "The function of a Board is to hire a president and then back him, period." In hospitals,

boards tend to be dominated by physicians, who are qualified to oversee the quality of care, but who may neither have the expertise, nor are willing to devote the time to check up on the effectiveness and efficiency of hospital management. In government organizations at all levels, auditors check on compliance with the statutory rules on spending, but very few overseeing agencies pay any attention to how well the management performs its functions. Although legislative committees look for headline-making sins, many committees do not have the staff or the inclination to arrive at an informed judgment on management.[24]

Consider one detailed analysis of 7,000 board actions recorded in the minutes of over one hundred meetings by nineteen trustee boards of public colleges and universities. The analysis showed that only 6 percent of the decisions were planning decisions. Most of the actions were routine decisions on administrative and operational matters, and about 25 percent of these actions were ratifications of decisions previously made by the administration.

If the board in a profit-oriented corporation presumably represents the interests of the stockholders and the legislature or council in a political jurisdiction presumably represents the citizens, then whom does the board in a nonprofit organization presumably represent? Well, it *should* represent a broader interest such as the public at large. But "when the board represents the interests of specific clients (such as physicians in hospitals), or of large donors (as is the case with some university boards), or bondholders (as is the case with many public authorities), it is unlikely that the public interest is adequately considered."[25]

In recent years, there has been some change in the "hands-off" attitude of governing boards.

There is much talk, and some action, about the necessity of board members spending more time on their job; of having regular visits to university campuses; of having meetings of the whole board, or of committees of the board, more often than quarterly; and in general of becoming better informed about what is going on. Boards are beginning to exchange information with other boards, so as to obtain a basis of comparing their own organizations with others. In part, this interest has been stimulated by the fact that an increasing number of boards have been sued, or threatened with suit, for not discharging their legal duties.[26]

Indeed, with respect to the policy process, the attitude is growing that the board should be actively involved in four activities:

---

[24] Robert N. Anthony and Regina E. Herzlinger, *Management Control of Nonprofit Organizations* (Homewood, Ill.: Richard D. Irwin, 1984), p. 67.
[25] Ibid., p. 68.
[26] Ibid.

Although the initiation and analysis of proposed new programs is the responsibility of the management, board members should be actively involved in at least the final stages of the process, so that the board can have an effective input before the proposal is placed before it formally for final decision.

Most of the budgetary process takes place within the organization. It is desirable that the board set general guidelines that govern the preparation of the budget and that a board committee review carefully the proposed budget before it is presented to the board for decision.

The board should receive reports of current performance, including both financial performance and also the quality of the services rendered. For the latter purpose, some mechanism that provides for communications from clients directly to the board is desirable. These communications should be analyzed so that danger signals are identified and appropriate questions asked of the administration.

From time to time, the board should initiate and participate in intensive reviews of the organization's activities as a whole or of important facets thereof. Some boards have staffs that do this work. Others hire outside consulting firms.[27]

Having described the major structural features of the policymaking system, the only question remaining concerns how they function *together*—that is, how do they convert ideas into public policy? While numerous suggestions were put forward regarding the contribution of each participant, we have yet to develop a coherent overview of the policy process.

A MODEL OF POLICY ISSUE DEVELOPMENT

How and why do dormant issues suddenly become transformed into highly salient political controversies? A few years ago a pair of political scientists, Roger W. Cobb and Charles D. Elder, set out to answer that question.[28] They began by noting three generally accepted but widely ignored observations about American political systems.

1. The distribution of influence and access in any political system has *inherent biases.* Consequently, it will operate to the advantage of some and the disadvantage of others.
2. The *range of issues and alternative solutions* that will be considered is restricted. All forms of political organizations have a bias in favor of some concerns and suppression of others. Some issues are, in

---

[27] Ibid.

[28] Roger W. Cobb and Charles D. Elder, "The Politics of Agenda Building," *Journal of Politics* 33, no. 4 (November 1971), pp. 892–915. See also Cobb and Elder's *Participation in American Politics: Dynamics of Agenda Building* (Baltimore, Md.: Johns Hopkins, 1983).

effect, organized out of the system. The popular balance of forces can change these priorities only slowly. In short, "there is a strong bias in favor of existing arrangement and agenda questions; and the legal machinery of that system is designed and operated to reinforce and defend that bias."

3. Thus, *prepolitical or predecision processes* play a critical role in determining which issues and alternatives are considered. Decision-making councils often do little more than "recognize, document, and legalize, if not legitimize, the momentary results of a continuing struggle of forces in society at large."

Figure 2–2 shows in some detail what occurs between the recognition of a problem (the subject of Chapters 3 and 4) and the formulation of a policy proposal (the subject of Chapters 5 through 8). More to the point, the figure help us answer a little better the question posed at the beginning of this section.

Systemic and institutional agendas

Cobb and Elder distinguish between *systemic* and *institutional agendas.* System agendas refer to all issues that are commonly perceived by members of the political community as meriting public attention and as involving matters within the legitimate jurisdiction of existing governmental authority. Every political system—national, state, and local—therefore has a systemic agenda. It is essentially a discussion agenda, a reflection of public concern.

Cobb and Elder define the institutional agenda as that set of items explicitly up for the active and serious consideration of authoritative decision makers. They distinguish between serious and "pseudoagenda items" to account for issues that get only vocal attention from decision makers. Once again, the precise identification of the agenda is no simple matter since one must establish criteria for determining what constitutes "active and serious consideration." But surely we can include here such formal expressions of agenda items as the State of the Union message, specific policy messages by the president, counterassessments by congressional party leaders, and major bills introduced into Congress.

In addition to these formal expressions of institutional agenda items, individual agencies and congressional committees have their own agendas.

Not all institutional agenda items reach the White House. Much research, definition, planning, and building support occurs within the labyrinthian structure of government. In fact, the really crucial agenda-setting processes for certain problems may occur deep within a department or congressional committee where specialists determine priorities and negotiate solutions.

Figure 2–2
A functional diagram of policy issue development

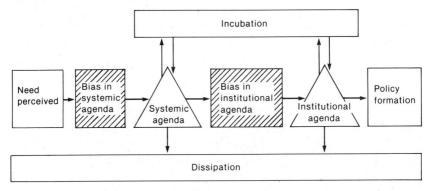

So—while determining what reaches the high levels of government is, in itself, an important task for studying agenda setting, analysis of what happens with regard to particular public problems and issues may well require extensive probing of the work plans and schedules of governmental subunits.[29]

Sources of bias

It is useful to think of the problem confronted by any newly formed or newly mobilized group as one of penetrating a screen of bias. Let us begin by considering the biases associated with the systemic agenda.

Almost irrespective of the particular issue, there is a bias against groups whose members lack status and community standing. "In other words, people without resources (e.g., lower-income groups) will have more difficulty attaining legitimacy than their higher-status counterparts. The antiwar movement, for example, initially promoted by student groups who traditionally have little political standing, received little public support until more socially prominent persons and groups entered the fray (e.g., business groups, military leaders, clergymen, and senators)."[30]

In addition, there are cultural constraints on the range of issues that are considered legitimate topics for governmental action.

The question of federal aid to education, for example, was long considered by many to be an inappropriate area for federal governmental action, a fact that precluded active and serious consideration of the merits of the issue for decades. Legitimizing issues that are considered to be outside the govern-

---

[29] Charles O. Jones, *An Introduction to the Study of Public Policy*, p. 41.
[30] Cobb and Elder, *Politics of Agenda Building*, pp. 909–10.

mental realm is difficult and will normally require an extended period of time. . . . The net effect of this is that new demands, particularly those of disadvantaged or deprived groups, are the least likely to receive attention on either the systemic agenda of controversy or the institutional agenda.[31]

There are equally consistent and identifiable biases that limit both the types of questions that will be considered and the groups and interests that will be heard on institutional agendas. One prominent source of such bias is the tendency of decision makers to give priority to "older items." These include items that previously reached the agenda but have either never been resolved or, having been resolved, are subject to periodic alteration. The recurrence of the medical care issue on the congressional agenda throughout the 1950s and early 1960s until its passage in 1965 is an illustration of the former; the history of social security legislation, of the latter. "Older items tend to dominate institutional agendas that are necessarily limited by time and the attention capacity of decision makers. The net effect is that it is very difficult to get new issues on the agenda."[32]

Decision makers themselves can be a source of bias, since an issue must command the support of at least some key decision makers to attain institutional agenda status. Political leaders, after all, are active participants in the agenda-building process, not simply impartial arbiters of disputes. "The great decisions a congressman must make are not so much those determining the position to take on individual bills, but rather decisions as to what kind of a congressman to be, what sorts of things to specialize in, how to allocate time, and how to project himself into a role of leadership."[33]

Being human, decision makers have a kind of selective attention. The issue of housing for the poor provides an excellent illustration of how the selective attention of decision makers operates. For the most part, federal public housing policy is based on very little information about the problem as defined by ghetto residents. As Nathan Glazer notes, we have only limited information about the effects of poor housing: "What is the effect of substandard and crowded housing on the families that live in it? Here we reach into the murkiest of sociological depths. I have indicated how culture-bound are our definitions of 'the standard' and 'the crowded.' We can find examples of entire societies living in housing that by our measures are substandard and crowded, and yet these conditions seem not to create a serious problem for family living." So, federal housing policy tends to concentrate on the problems

---

[31] Ibid.
[32] Ibid.
[33] Raymond Bauer, Ithiel DeSola Pool, and Lewis Anthony Dexter, *American Business and Public Policy* (Chicago: Aldine-Atherton, 1972), p. 220.

with which the decision makers are familiar. Glazer speaks of "the consistent bias in this country in favor of the owner-occupied, single-family, free-standing house, with a bit of land around it." Slums get the attention of reformers, writers, analysts; but "it is the single-family, owner-occupied home—getting it built, getting it financed, saving it from banks, reducing its cost, increasing its amenities—that has received the chief attention of elected officials, administrators, and the majority of the American people, perhaps even the poor among them." In contrast, housing efforts to aid the poor—public housing—have been relatively meager.[34]

Because decision makers have fairly direct control over what will appear on the institutional agenda, it follows that access to one or more key officials becomes quite important to political groups. The greater the ease of access, the more likely is the placement of demands on an agenda.

How a decision maker will respond to a group demand depends on several things. The decision maker may be indebted to or identified with a particular group. Some groups have more resources than others. Some groups as big business and agriculture are located so strategically in the social or economic structure of society that their interests cannot be ignored. And some groups, such as doctors and church leaders, are held in greater public esteem than others and thus can command greater access to decision makers.

Countervailing factors

At the same time that groups struggle to overcome these biases, certain factors can come into play that pull an issue forward, that help overcome the biases. What are these countervailing factors?

The media play an obvious role in bringing issues to the systemic agenda and increasing their chances of receiving consideration on institutional agendas. Other persons can acquire an audience and effectively publicize an issue simply by constantly appearing in the news. Ralph Nader, for example, has a ready-made constituency stemming from his many attacks on various business practices, and Carl Sagan has proven an effective national spokesman for parts of the scientific community.

As we saw earlier, certain kinds of policy analysis can be used as instruments in the play of power; that is, analysis can be used by a group to persuade, to reveal how a policy can serve the values of a given policymaker. We will have much more to say about this partisan

---

[34] Nathan Glazer, "Housing Problems and Housing Policies," *Public Interest*, Spring 1967, pp. 21–51.

use of analysis when we take a look at the strategies by which groups and some policymakers attempt to get their proposals adopted (Chapter 9). For the moment, however, we might consider a simple, generalized case of how analysis might be used to overcome biases of the institutional agenda.

One of the things that analysis can provide is a tabulation of many of the benefits and costs of a policy. But the significant thing about this exercise is that it usually discloses certain benefits—we call them indirect benefits—that are less than obvious but still quite revealing. Armed with information showing explicitly how a policy benefits a state, a district, or even a career, a group might be in a much stronger position to overcome the bias and solicit the cooperation of obstinate policymakers.

Analysis can also work in less obtrusive, more subtle ways; for example, by leading individuals within the bureaucracy and the legislature to accept the same conception of an issue.

> Patterns imposed on data can lead, ultimately, to evocative slogans—for example, the Need for a Sense of Community, the Weakening of the Family, Equality of Educational Opportunity, Advocacy, the Need for Income Redistribution. Such slogans and the metaphors that underlie them can provide a basis for harmonized action. Individuals influenced by a given conception emphasize it within their discretionary powers—here favoring a service or research project that seems in line with the conception, there adopting the conception as a criterion of quality for personnel selection, elsewhere allowing it to influence budget allocations. Thus, without an overt plan of cooperation, individuals distributed through the bureaucracy nevertheless make a particular conception of the problem a force in the system's pattern of action. Individual adherences are reinforced by more formal but secondary organizations of action: committees, interagency task forces, societies [associations with newsletters, etc.][35]

Another countervailing factor, which I term bureaucratic, is based on one of the predominant traits of U.S. government—fragmentation. That is, the U.S. government consists in not one but several sources of power. Interest groups have learned the tactical implications of the trait well: after failing to gain access to one branch, they try another, and if necessary, yet another. Thus the National Association for the Advancement of Colored People, having failed to overcome the bias of congressional and White House agendas in the first decade after World War II, turned to the courts with considerable effectiveness.

In this way, the agendas of bureaucracies provide groups with another alternative. Anthony Downs, drawing on studies in animal behavior,

---

[35] Martin Rein and Sheldon H. White, "Policy Research: Belief and Doubt," *Policy Analysis* 3, no. 2 (Spring 1977), pp. 237–72.

argues that bureaus engage in territorial struggle among themselves, each trying to establish a large enough territory to guarantee its survival. However, the struggle is not over geography but over "policy space."

> Territorial sensitivity has several important effects upon interbureau behavior. The first is expressed in the Law of Interorganizational Conflict: Every large organization is in partial conflict with every other social agent it deals with. Even if several agents are joint producers, the actions of each take place within the territory of the others; and every social agent is essentially a territorial imperialist to some extent. He seeks to expand the borders of his various zones in policy space, or at least to increase his degree of influence within each zone.[36]

The upshot of this territoriality is that agencies do have a certain receptivity to new issues—at least those that afford them an opportunity to expand within a policy space. These tendencies vary from agency to agency. Downs notes two extreme types. To minimize conflict, some bureaus narrow proposed action so that they affect fewer external agents. Downs labels this form of behavior the "shrinking violet syndrome."

In contrast, agencies may ignore other social agents and adopt new policies with alacrity. The farther a bureau is removed from direct responsibility for carrying out the actions proposed, the more likely it is to exhibit this "superman syndrome." For this reason, city planners are notorious for designing master plans that call for a variety of bold, new, and often quite unrealistic approaches. No matter: these supermen provide a hopeful alternative for groups that are unable to overcome the biases of legislators or administrators.

The last factor pulling a proposal forward onto the institutional agenda is perhaps the most important. Among political leaders—whether U.S. senators or small-town mayors—the search for issues is often vital to the advancement of political careers. Political careers (bureaucratic careers too, for that matter) are built on the capacity of individuals to seize an issue project or program early and become inextricably attached to it. As the policy becomes more important to the welfare of the polity, political fortunes escalate. In sum, I am saying that political leaders

---

[36] Anthony Downs, *Inside Bureaucracy* (Boston: Little, Brown, 1977), p. 216. Arnold J. Meltsner in "Political Feasibility and Policy Analysis," *Policy Analysis,* Winter 1975, p. 860, explains policy space this way: "Every political system contains a number of overlapping policy spaces. There is a health policy space, an education policy space, and a transportation policy space. The space is characterized by a stable set of actors whose specific policy preferences are ambiguous. Because of their continuing concern, certain actors and certain attentive publics dominate the policy space. No one can doubt that the American Medical Association, the Department of Health, Education, and Welfare, and the House Ways and Means Committee have something to say in the health policy space."

74

frequently have strong motives to be on the outlook for new issues—
even those put forward by groups that lack legitimacy.

Norman Mailer's observation made just after the 1968 Democratic
National Convention still holds true:

> Politics at national level can still be comprehended by politics-as-property.
> . . . Being a leading anti-Communist used to be an invaluable property for
> which there was much competition—Richard Nixon had once gotten in early
> on the equivalent of an Oklahoma landgrab by staking out whole territories
> of that property. "End the war in Vietnam," is a property to some, "Let
> no American blood be shed in vain," is obviously another. A politician picks
> and chooses among properties. If he is quick-witted, unscrupulous, and
> does not mind a life of constant anxiety, he will hasten—there is a great
> competition for things valuable in politics—to pick up properties wherever
> he can, even if they are rival holdings.[37]

Examples of the politics-as-property phenomenon abound. And the
following comment by Representative George P. Miller is, I think, indicative:

> I don't think that the damage being done to the environment is much worse
> today than it was five years ago. Yet nobody was concerned about it five
> years ago. People sat right at this table and told you some of the things
> you had to do to solve some of these problems. Then all of a sudden we
> get off on a good kick and it becomes quite a political issue. . . .
>
> About four years ago, Senator Jackson and I called a joint committee on
> the environment. Well we hardly got out of our meeting before a very persona-
> ble member of Congress, who is still here, I won't say anything, but a
> very impressive guy, was around organizing a committee on environment
> and asked me to serve on it. I had to write him a letter and tell him to
> take my name off it, because he didn't know what he was doing. He didn't
> know what he wanted to do other than that it was a good medium to get
> before the press. Now, isn't this part of the crisis, or of our troubles?[38]

More than one observer of American politics thinks that candidates
have become more sensitive to ideas in recent years as party discipline
became weaker. Richard Reeves, author and syndicated columnist,
writes:

> Ideas have always been important in campaigns, but in recent years they
> have often dominated elections, essentially replacing party identification as
> the banners under which candidates run. As the words "Republican" and
> "Democrat" have come to mean less to voters, and "conservative" and "lib-
> eral" labels have been rejected by candidates, politicians—particularly youn-

---

[37] Norman Mailer, *Miami and the Siege of Chicago* (New York: World, 1968), p. 147.
[38] U.S. Congress, House Committee on Appropriations, *Departments of Labor, and Health, Education, and Welfare, and Related Agencies Appropriation Bill, 1971* (Washington, D.C.: Government Printing Office, 1970).

ger ones—have tried to associate themselves not with traditional labels but with a set of ideas, usually presented as new.[39]

Issue incubation and issue dissipation

We have now discussed all of Figure 2–2 except for the top and bottom rectangles. The latter is fairly self-explanatory, simply serving to indicate that some issues, even if they get as far as the institutional agenda, can slowly fade away and eventually die. Like the hula hoop, we hear no more about them.

Other issues, however, do not die; instead they go through a kind of gestation. Nelson W. Polsby emphasizes the role of the legislature in this process.

> Many of our most important policy innovations take years from initiation to enactment. Surely the idea of medicare, to take an obvious example, was not "initiated" by the Johnson administration in the 89th Congress when proposals incorporating its main features had been part of the landscape since the early Truman administration. Medicare, like other great policy innovations, required incubation—a process in which men of Congress often play very significant roles. Incubation entails keeping a proposal alive while the problem to which it is addressed grows. Senators and (to a lesser extent) representatives contribute to incubation by proposing bills that they know will not pass, making speeches, making demands for data and for support . . . from interest groups favoring the proposal. Sometimes a sympathetic committee chairman can be persuaded to allow hearings on such a proposal. Hearings focus public attention, mobilize interest groups for and against, and provide an occasion for the airing of a proposal's technical justifications.[40]

The garbage can model: The theory

Although useful, Polsby's idea of issue incubation fails to tell us why some issues cease to incubate and begin to thrive. A model developed by Michael Cohen, James March, and Johan Olsen suggests an answer.[41]

Cohen and his colleagues see organizations as "organized anarchies." Flowing through organization or decision structures are four separate streams: problems, solutions, participants, and choice opportunities. Each of the streams has a life of its own. Thus participants generate

[39] Richard Reeves, "How New Ideas Shape Presidential Politics," *New York Times Magazine,* July 15, 1984, p. 28.
[40] Nelson Polsby, "Policy Analysis and Congress," *Public Policy,* 17 (Fall 1969), pp. 66–71.
[41] Michael D. Cohen, James G. March, and Johan P. Olsen, "A Garbage Can Model of Organizational Choice," *Administrative Science Quarterly* 17 (March 1972), pp. 1–25.

and debate solutions because they have some self-interest in doing so (e.g., keeping their job or expanding their unit). They drift in and out of decision making, carrying pet problems and solutions with them, looking for situations, or "choice opportunities," in which they might be aired.

Thus a choice opportunity is a kind of garbage can into which participants randomly dump various kinds of problems and solutions. Outcomes then are a function of the mix of garbage (problems, solutions, participants, and the participant's resources) in the can. For a problem to be resolved, the four separate streams must couple. Within the organization—which for our purposes, might be construed as the federal government itself—you must have a participant, who recognizes a problem, actually meeting with another participant who has a pet solution that he has been carrying about. Remember: The solution or policy proposal might have been developed independently, without any knowledge of the problem. Finally, participants, problems, and solution must be coupled with a political stream.

> Independently of problem recognition or the development of policy proposals, political events flow along according to their own dynamics and their own rules. Participants perceive swings in national mood, elections bring new administrations to power and new partisan or ideological distributions to Congress, and interest groups of various descriptions press (or fail to press) their demands on government.
>
> Developments in this political sphere are powerful agenda setters. A new administration, for instance, changes agendas all over town as it highlights its conceptions of problems and its proposals, and makes attention to subjects that are not among its high priorities much less likely. A national mood that is perceived to be profoundly conservative dampens attention to costly new initiatives, while a more tolerant national mood would allow for greater spending. The opposition of a powerful phalanx of interest groups makes it difficult—not impossible, but difficult—to contemplate some initiatives.[42]

In developing their garbage can model, Cohen, March, and Olsen used American colleges and universities as the prototype organized anarchy (make of that what you will). Does the model apply to the public policymaking process? More to the point, what *use* is the model?

Much about the model is obvious. After all you cannot have a policy proposal unless someone has a concrete solution to a real problem. Furthermore, I think that we can agree without too much argument, that the policy proposal must be politically feasible and that its advocates must sometimes be waiting for a window of opportunity to push it. The notion that a solution can actually *precede* a problem is much less

---

[42] Kingdon, *Agendas, Alternatives*, pp. 207–208.

obvious, however. So, too, is the notion that who the participants are—who is invited to the Monday morning meeting, or Saturday golf match, or cocktail party—determines whether a solution couples with a problem.

This picture does not look like rational decision making. John W. Kingdon of the University of Michigan explains the difference:

> People do not set about to solve problems here. More often, solutions search for problems. People work on problems only when a particular combination of problem, solution, and participants in a choice situation makes it possible. Nor do they go through a prescribed logical routine: defining the problem, canvassing the possible solutions, evaluating the alternatives in terms of their ability to solve the problem at the least cost. Rather, solutions and problems have equal status as separate streams in the system, and the popularity of a given solution at a given point in time often affects the problems that come up for consideration.[43]

Nor does the model necessarily resemble incremental decision making—which prefers only conservative, minimal departures from the status quo. Coupling of streams in a decision-making context can sometimes produce an abrupt change as a previously untried combination comes into play.

The Garbage can model: Four case studies

The Tax Reform Act of 1986. For more than two decades, reformers have called for a change in the U.S. tax system; specifically, they advocated a simpler code and fewer deductions (or loopholes). To get a flavor of that complexity, consider the last sentence of section 509(a) of the tax code: "For purposes of paragraph (3), an organization described in paragraph (2), shall be deemed to include an organization described in section 501(c)(4), (5), or (6), which would be described in paragraph (2) if it were an organization described in section 501(c)(3)."

Candidate Jimmy Carter adopted tax reform as a major presidential campaign issue in 1976, calling the tax system "a disgrace to the human race." As president, however, Carter failed in his efforts to effect tax reform, for two reasons. First, he had other priorities—such as energy legislation. In fact, Carter's energy specialists succeeded in enacting new tax breaks for energy conservation and the development of synthetic fuels. Second, he did not make his reform proposal sweeping or radical enough. This failure provides a good illustration of the serious limitations that a strategy of incremental change can have when applied to a long-entrenched governmental program.[44]

---

[43] Ibid., p. 91.

[44] Edward R. Kantowicz, "The Limits of Incrementalism: Carter's Efforts at Tax Reform," *Journal of Policy Analysis and Management* 4, no. 2 (Winter 1985), pp. 217–33.

Meanwhile, high inflation rates steadily pushed taxpayers into higher brackets even when their earnings rose less than prices. By 1980, polls showed that the public thought the income tax the least fair form of taxation. Tax evasion was on the rise. By 1980, the problem of the U.S. tax system was generally recognized.

The momentum for the solution of comprehensive tax reform began to grow. In the spring of 1982, Senator Bill Bradley and Representative Richard Gephardt proposed a code with low rates and few deductions. Soon afterwards, Representative Jack Kemp and Senator Robert W. Kasten introduced a Republican bill that embodied many of the same principles. Few observers gave these proposals much chance—the participants lacked the political influence. New participants would have to enter the fray.

President Reagan had advocated lower rates and a simpler system for years, but his 1983 State of the Union address contained only a single line about tax reform. Behind that brief mention was, however, a more serious interest encouraged by the president's friend, Secretary of State George Shultz. During a round of golf in Palm Springs, California, while the president was on vacation, Shultz mentioned academic studies about the advantages of a flat tax (that is, everyone pays the same rate).[45] Because he was interested in plausible ways to cut taxes further, Reagan decided to make brief mention of tax simplification in his State of the Union speech.

For a year, nothing much happened. But when time came to prepare his 1984 State of the Union address—which would set the themes for his re-election campaign—Reagan decided to announce that he was ordering Donald Regan, then Secretary of Treasury, to prepare tax reform recommendations. That directive was an effort to preempt the Democratic nominee, Walter Mondale, who Reagan's advisers thought might also propose tax reform. (He did not.)

After the election, the Treasury Department released its plan, which was similar to Senator Bradley's. At this point, Secretary Regan made an important modification in the "solution": He decided that the originally proposed individual tax rates—16 percent, 28 percent, and 37 percent—sounded "like a football signal" and changed them to the more easily remembered 15, 25, and 35.[46] The 35 percent rate became President Reagan's most important goal because it represented a cut by half of the 70 percent top rate that existed when he took office.

---

[45] This story is told in David A. Stockman, *The Triumph of Politics* (New York: Avon Books, 1987), pp. 251–67 and 282–83.

[46] Quoted in Jeffrey H. Birnbaum, "Tax Bill Saga," *The Wall Street Journal*, June 4, 1986.

In 1985, the political stream began to widen and comingle even more with the solution, which itself was becoming better defined. Citizens for Tax Justice had just released a list of 128 major corporations that paid no taxes at all and thereby increased considerable public indignation over tax laws. Meanwhile, Reagan was searching for a bold domestic initiative with which to begin his second term. His advisers thought tax reform might give the Republicans a permanent majority in the country by showing voters that the party was for the common man. This possibility, whether real or imagined, helped get the Democratic leadership in Congress behind the proposal.

Representative Dan Rostenkowski was among the first to recognize what some called the "dead cat syndrome": none of the major participants could afford politically to have tax reform die on their doorstep. At first, he could not get his Ways and Means Committee to move on the issue. Gephardt, a committee member, relates what happened next: "Danny called the members in, sat them down one by one, and said, 'This is it. Tax reform is going to go down, and we're going to get blamed for it.' "[47]

The Tax Reform Act of 1986 shows how four separate streams—problem, solution, participants, and politics—coupled to produce one of the few pieces of legislation that can truly be called historic. It affects nearly 100 million individuals and 3 million corporations that pay federal income taxes. And it reverses the whole direction that federal taxation had been following for decades.

Strategic defense initiative. In his Star Wars speech of March 23, 1983, President Reagan called on American scientists to find ways of rendering nuclear weapons "impotent and obsolete." A confluence of participants and ideas lay behind the speech, and a review of that history goes a long way toward illuminating the garbage can model.

Central to the story is Ronald Reagan himself. Even before assuming the presidency he had expressed strong interest in trying to defend the nation from enemy missiles. He recalls a tour of the North American Defense Command, a secret installation in a hollowed-out mountain in Colorado:

> They actually are tracking several thousand objects in space, meaning satellites of ours and everyone else's, even down to the point that they are tracking a glove lost by an astronaut. I think the thing that struck me was the irony that here, with this great technology of ours, we can do all of this, yet we cannot stop any of the weapons that are coming at us. I don't think there's been a time in history when there wasn't a defense against some kind of

---

[47] *Time*, August 25, 1986, p. 17.

thrust, even back in the old-fashioned days when we had coast artillery that would stop invading ships.[48]

But where was the solution? On November 14, 1980, the X-ray laser rumbled to life in a nuclear explosion beneath the Nevada desert. Some scientists thought this device could be the ultimate technological fix to the arms race. The nuclear X-ray laser would be based in space and use powerful beams to shoot down Soviet missiles. It would, they hoped, end the era of mutual assured destruction (MAD) doctrine—assuring the destruction of the Soviet Union, even after our absorbing a surprise first strike—and commence a period of assured survival.

In May 1981, George A. Keyworth, a nuclear scientist who was intimately familiar with the X-ray laser, was named the president's science adviser. Also in 1981, a group of influential scientists, industrialists, and generals began to meet at the Heritage Foundation, the conservative think tank mentioned earlier in the chapter, and to formulate a plan for creating a national system of defense. This group, along with Keyworth, had good access to Reagan and helped persuade Reagan to make his 1983 speech.[49]

Whatever factors led to the Star Wars speech, an irony of the story is that the X-ray laser solution, which helped bring it about, eventually fell out of official favor. The stress shifted to non-nuclear weapons to shoot down enemy missiles. A lingering question no one can answer is whether Star Wars would have happened in the absence of the X-ray laser.

Industrial policy: A solution looking for a problem.   Does the United States need a new industrial policy, directed by the federal government, to regain leadership as the fastest-growing economy among the world powers? This question was posed by many Democrats during 1983. Advocates said a policy was needed because of the American economy's poor performance in recent years. When its growth came to a halt in the 1979–83 period, the United States lost ground to Japan as the world leader in industrial expansion.

Stated generally, an industrial policy for the United States would use the federal government's money and authority to shape economic development. Advocates cite Japan's policy of targeting specific industries for favorable bank financing, tax incentives, research aid, and other benefits as an example of how government can direct growth.

A major argument for an American industrial policy is that one already

---

[48] Reagan quoted in Robert Scheer, *With Enough Shovels: Reagan, Bush, and Nuclear Weapons* (New York: Random House, 1982).

[49] William T. Broad, "Reagan's 'Star Wars' Bid: Many Ideas Converge," *New York Times*, March 4, 1985.

exists, the haphazard result of government tax, tariff, regulatory, and research-and-development policies. If these were coordinated into a coherent strategy, it is said, the United States could channel the flow of capital and labor to strengthen industries for competition with foreign business.

Among the opponents to an industrial policy is Charles L. Schultze, a former adviser to two Democratic presidents and now with the Brookings Institution. Schultze opposes any federal policy that seeks to direct the flow of capital to selected industries. Such a policy, he says, is not needed. Compared to most other countries, U.S. manufacturing did quite well in the 1970s. While the United States does have serious economic problems, the failure of the market to allocate investment in the right direction is not one of them.[50]

Another analyst at Brookings, Philip Trezise, labels as "mythology" the belief that the Japanese government and industry sit down and develop coherent policies to increase their export-market shares. In fact, Trezise says, the Japanese policymaking system is highly politicized, with most subsidies going to agriculture, the country's least-efficient industry, because that is where the vote is.[51]

Scholars contend the Japanese have had as many failures as successes in trying to manage development over the years. The Ministry of International Trade and Industry (MITI), the government's development agency, generally is credited with helping to build Japan's computer, semiconductor, and steel industries, among others. But MITI's efforts to promote the petrochemical, aluminum-refining, shipping, and commercial-aircraft industries are regarded as failures.

By 1986, the term *industrial policy* had largely vanished from political debate, partly because the subject had never merged with the political stream. Reagan and most other Republicans opposed a government-directed industrial policy on the ground that the marketplace allocates resources more efficiently, and the public seemed suspicious of anything that sounded like centralized economic planning.

Acid rain: A problem in search of a solution. A growing body of scientific research now indicates that acid rain is developing into a national problem, not simply a matter of concern to New England and New York's Adirondack Mountains. Data emerging from the expanding federal, state, academic, and private investigations are showing that wide areas of the country may be susceptible to damage and some

---

[50] See "Do We Need an Industrial Policy?" *Harper's*, February 1985, pp. 35–48.
[51] Philip H. Trezise, "Japanese Economic Success," *Cato Journal* 4, no. 2 (1984), pp. 545–48.

areas outside of the Northeast are already suffering harm, apparently in part as a result of acid rain.[52]

Recent studies indicate that many hundreds of lakes in the Rocky Mountain region may be in danger of acidification from the air pollution emitted by smelters in the Southwest and Mexico, posing a threat to fish and other aquatic life. National Park Service scientists at parks throughout the West are reporting periodic episodes of acid rain.

But even as the dimensions of the air-pollutant problem become more clearly defined, the solution is generally believed to be more elusive than previously thought. Researchers are finding that the atmospheric chemistry of air pollution, the physics of its movement through the atmosphere, and the chemical and biological impact of acid precipitation on the natural environment, form an intricate puzzle that may take years to untangle. Acid rain by itself is not now regarded as sole cause of forest decline in the eastern states, but it is considered a component of a complex "witches brew" of manmade pollutants. Among aspects of the problem that continue to elude understanding are the effects of acid rain on trees and soil. Questions about the terrestrial effects seem particularly "intractable" at this point.

In sum, government scientists are finding they have a long way to go before they are able to answer all the questions that policymakers say need to be answered before they can act on one of the most hotly debated of environmental problems. Some analysts think that more must be learned about the causes and effects of acid rain and other pollutants before a multibillion-dollar control program is mandated.

THE POLICY PROCESS: A WIDE-ANGLE VIEW

The basic question that Cobb and Elder raise with their discussion of agenda building, and the one that makes their work germane, is this: Where do issues of public policy come from? Or more specifically, How are issues created? Why do some controversies or incipient issues command the attention and concern of decision makers, while others do not? How is an issue placed on an agenda and who participates in the process of building it? These are the main questions that the foregoing discussion tried to answer.

But Cobb and Elder's inquiry goes even further: they offer an explanation, based on agenda building, of social conflict:

---

[52] Office of Technology Assessment, *Acid Rain and Transported Air Pollutants: Implications for Public Policy* (Washington, D.C.: Government Printing Office, June 1984); General Accounting Office, *An Analysis of Issues Concerning "Acid Rain"* RCED-85-13 (Washington, D.C.: Government Printing Office, December 1984).

Because of the inertia present in any system, institutional agendas will always lag to some extent behind the more general systemic agenda. This means that there will be traces of social conflict in even the most responsive and harmonious system. The extent of this lag will be magnified in periods of severe discontinuity such as depression, war, and technological change. If the lag becomes too great, the system will cease to function effectively and may even be destroyed. Thus, a corollary of our earlier proposition is that the viability of a polity is a direct function of its ability to cope with the lag between the two types of agendas and to keep the magnitude of the lag within tolerable limits.[53]

The idea might be viewed schematically as shown in Figure 2–3.

This proposition has a commonsense ring: it would seem that one can no more disagree with it than with the proposition that death is sad or that sex is less so. Or is this really the case? Does the temporal linkage built into the Cobb-Elder theory fit or do justice to the empirical data?

To find out, I examined five policy issues over time. Although these issues were not selected in a mathematically random fashion, I did establish a couple of criteria: First, they had to be drawn from a wide range of policy areas and, second, they had to be fairly recent, yet have already peaked in intensity. The issues selected were air pollution, civil rights, juvenile delinquency, poverty, and narcotic addiction.

The difficult methodological task was to operationalize the concepts of systemic and institutional agendas. As a rough approximation of the relative intensity of the former, I did a content analysis of the *Readers' Guide to Periodical Literature* for the years 1945–72 on each issue. As an equally rough approximation of the institutional agenda, I did a content analysis of the *Congressional Record* for the same years. My objective was to determine the year in which each issue peaked in terms of number of citations.[54] The results may be stated briefly: for all five issues, the systemic and institutional agendas peaked in the same year (air pollution, 1967; civil rights, 1964; juvenile delinquency, 1961; narcotic addiction, 1969; poverty, 1969). In other words, there was no apparent lag between the two agendas.

How might these surprising results be explained? One possibility has already been suggested: politics-as-property. In other words, once an issue has gained legitimacy in the systemic agenda, members of

---

[53] Cobb and Elder, *Politics of Agenda Building*, p. 906.

[54] In counting citations in the *Congressional Record*, I excluded entries under the subheadings "letters," "editorials," "articles," and "telegrams" on the ground that these were not as fine measures of institutional importance as items listed under the subheadings "bills," "resolutions," "remarks," "memorandums," "addresses," "statements," and "reports."

Figure 2–3
Hypothesized relationship between the systemic and institutional agendas

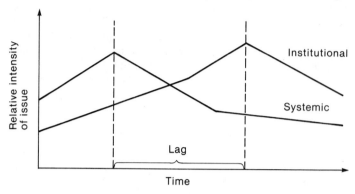

Congress have tremendous incentives to seize the issue and push it.

Another possibility centers on the notion that certain events "trigger" an intense flurry of activity both in the media—which are, I suspect, the best barometer of the systemic agenda—and among decision makers. The concept of triggering, however, is somewhat on the periphery of the Cobb-Elder model.

For this reason, it might be useful to think about the events leading up to policy formulation and adoption in terms of a life cycle. Figure 2–4 shows how the life cycle concept might be applied to that welter of events associated with the emergence of national environmental policy. Moreover, given the continuous infusion of new issues into the policy arena, I am inclined to think that the ultimate payoff of this broad framework is not so much to help policy analysts make sense of the past as to help them anticipate future—and as yet unknown—issues. As Alexander Leighton once said, "To the blind all things seem sudden."

As we saw early in this chapter, public policies are developed and implemented through institutions—the interest groups on K street or any street near a state capitol; presidents and their staffs; Congress and its staff; issues networks and executive bureaus; mass media; and state and local governments. In the final analysis, perhaps, it is the men and women who fill these institutions that really make policy, but institutions with their traditions, their cultures, their procedures profoundly shape those efforts. In any event, policy outside institutions seems inconceivable.

Indeed, as we saw in the later portions of this chapter, institutions play a crucial role in the process by which fledgling notions that something is wrong become transformed into mighty policy initiatives. For such notion to get on the systemic agenda, interest groups must become

Figure 2–4
The life-cycle concept applied to the environmental issue

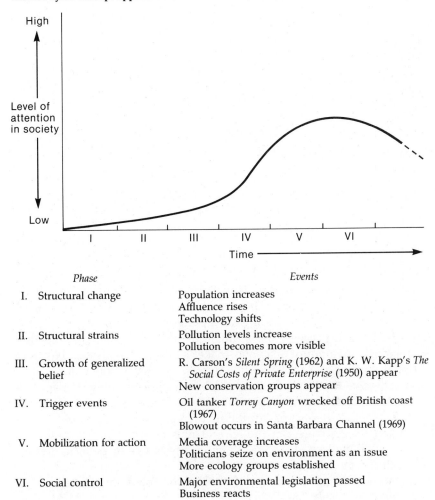

Phase	Events
I. Structural change	Population increases Affluence rises Technology shifts
II. Structural strains	Pollution levels increase Pollution becomes more visible
III. Growth of generalized belief	R. Carson's *Silent Spring* (1962) and K. W. Kapp's *The Social Costs of Private Enterprise* (1950) appear New conservation groups appear
IV. Trigger events	Oil tanker *Torrey Canyon* wrecked off British coast (1967) Blowout occurs in Santa Barbara Channel (1969)
V. Mobilization for action	Media coverage increases Politicians seize on environment as an issue More ecology groups established
VI. Social control	Major environmental legislation passed Business reacts

involved. For proposals to move onto the institutional agenda, policy-making bodies like executive agencies and legislative committees must be persuaded.

This journey from problem identification to formulation to adoption to implementation is, we know, erratic—even perilous. Viability depends not only on the inherent merits of the proposal but also on the predilections of the key players. As they initiate, confer, concur, coordinate, amend, delay, and veto, prospects for the unfolding policy wax and wane. But not to worry. Through it all, certain decisive points can be discerned. At the following points, policymakers must know how to act and have the will to do so:

- The diagnosis of the problem.
- The prognosis of the problem.
- The setting of goals.
- The generation of options.
- The estimation of costs, benefits, and risks.
- The assessment of impacts.
- The analysis of the policy's political feasibility.
- The search for implementation levers.
- The evaluation of results.

What strategies—intellectually incisive yet politically robust—are available to policymakers at each point? The next nine chapters address that question.

FOR FURTHER REFLECTION

1. In periods of severe budget constraint, inexpensive programs obviously come to the fore. Can you be more specific about the types of programs proposed during such periods?
2. In the budget process, the struggle to win the game can consume an inordinant amount of a policymaker's time and energy and distract him from his goal of contributing to public policy. Conversely, failure to recognize the importance of the budget process may damage the prospects of attaining those goals due to inadequate funding. What strategies can a policymaker follow to avoid these two traps?
3. Explain the garbage can model and illustrate it with recent issues and public policies. Can you think of any issues or policies that do not fit the model?
4. In the context of this chapter, explain the following passage from *To Empower People:* The Role of Mediating Structures in Public Policy, by Peter Berger and Richard John Neuhaus.

    Decentralization is limited to what can be done within governmental structures; we are concerned with the structures that stand between government and the individual. Nor, again, are we calling for a devolution of governmental responsibilities that would be tantamount to dismantling the welfare state. We aim rather at rethinking the institutional means by which government exercises its responsibilities. The idea is not to revoke the New Deal but to pursue its vision in ways more compatible with democratic governance.

Chapter 3

Diagnosis

The oldest scientific organization in Great Britain and one of the oldest in the world, the Royal Society ranks as the foremost organization of its kind. Its membership has always included leading scientists of the world. King Charles II once invited the members of the society to explain to him why a dead fish weighs more than the same fish alive. The scientists labored hard and offered him a number of ingenious explanations. He then pointed out that it does not.

I tell the story of King Charles's dead fish to drive home a very important point: Policy analysts must understand the problem clearly before they try to solve it. Indeed, more than one experienced practitioner has suggested that up to 50 percent of the analytical effort might be fruitfully devoted to specification of the problem.

The term *diagnosis* refers to this active process, which is ordinarily the forerunner of policy formulation. But policy formulation must also be based on an understanding of prognosis—that is, the outlook for the problem without a change in government action. These twin pillars of policy analysis are the subjects of this chapter and the next one.

HOW PROBLEMS CAPTURE OUR ATTENTION

The most straightforward way in which policymakers come to recognize that a problem might exist is by noting a significant *increase or decrease in a parameter* used to track some phenomenon. Many public policies mandate some data collection and these data are part of the feedback arrows shown in Figure 1–3 in Chapter 1.

Health care presents a problem mainly because the total spending on it in the United States grew an average of 12.7 percent a year from 1970 to 1983. More significantly, health care spending accounted for 6.1 percent of the gross national product in 1965 and its share grew to

10.6 percent in 1984.[1] At that rate, the nation would be spending nearly one fifth of GNP on health care by the turn of the century.

Other trends attract less notice. Only in the last few years have physicians and statisticians who analyze patterns of births in the United States concluded that the number of babies born with some physical or mental defect has doubled over the last twenty-five years. The origins of the development are far from clear, although theories about possible causes include increased cigarette smoking by women and improved medical techniques that allow people with disabilities to survive and pass the trait along. Experts think that it might be years or even a decade before the full effect of the increase can be determined because many cases of learning impairment are not identified until a child starts to school.[2]

Therefore, the recognition of ominous changes in a parameter does not automatically lead to a problem definition, much less a solution. Moreover, in other examples cited, policymakers must subjectively decide what is too much or too little. That is, reasonable men and women might disagree on what percentage of national wealth should be devoted to health care or what percentage of birth with cerebral palsy and mental retardation is "too much."

A second way in which policymakers realize that they may have a problem on their hands is the occurrence of *events*; these can be either dramatic or anecdotal.

The wreck of the oil tanker Torrey Canyon off the British coast in 1967 and the oil drilling blowout in the Santa Barbara Channel in 1969—both dramatic events—riveted attention of policymakers on environmental problems. The death of a star college basketball player in 1986 from an overdose of cocaine had a similar effect with respect to the drug problem.

The Reagan administration has been acutely sensitive to the persuasive power of anecdotes—stories about individuals that highlight a larger social problem or need. For example, many people with apparent disabilities were removed from the rolls of the social security disability program early in 1982–83 as federal officials interpreted the eligibility rules more strictly. But the administration loosened some of the rules after the case of Roy P. Benavidez came to public attention. Benavidez, a Vietnam War veteran, had received a Medal of Honor from Reagan, who commended him for "conspicuous gallantry." But as part of the drive to crack down on ineligibility, he was to be removed from the disability rolls until an administrative law judge acted favorably on his appeal.

---

[1] U.S. Health Care Financing Administration, *Health Care Financing Review*, Fall 1985.

[2] Richard D. Lyons, "Physical and Mental Disabilities in Newborns Doubled in 25 Years," *New York Times*, July 18, 1983.

His case, once public, seemed to illustrate a larger problem, which the administration then tried to solve by liberalizing program rules.

Sometimes problems appear when policymakers make *comparisons.* Another way to look at health care costs in the United States is to match them with those in other countries. Administrative costs (billing, accounting, marketing, planning) account for 18.3 percent of the money spent on hospital services in the United States. By comparison, hospitals in Canada have overhead costs of only 8 percent of their budgets.[3] Comparisons can help remove some of the subjectivity that surrounds the question of how much is too much.

Sometimes we can apply more than one comparison to a situation. Productivity measures how efficiently a country produces goods and services. We can regard productivity as a problem (1) in comparison with U.S. history, and (2) in comparison with U.S. trading partners.

Healthy productivity growth has eluded the United States ever since the 1950s and early 1960s, when output for every hour of work rose by 2.5 to 3 percent a year. The gains began to narrow in the mid-1960s, and since 1973, productivity growth has averaged less than 1 percent a year. That puts the United States into a weak position, not only historically, but also in comparison with hard-driving competitor nations like Japan and West Germany, where productivity gains have for years outpaced those in the United States. Though Americans still produce more per worker than workers in other countries, the gap is quickly closing.

The distinction between the two different productivity problems is useful because each has very different consequences for public welfare. The historical slowdown in productivity growth has aggravated inflation, made the financing of social problems more difficult, and held living standards almost level. On the other hand, the relatively slow growth in U.S. productivity compared to other countries has different consequences: it threatens the nation's ability to provide for national defense, causes painful shifts in jobs done by American workers, and requires constant costly restructuring of the composition of U.S. industry.

Perhaps the most dramatic example of a comparison that created a problem awareness occurred in 1957, when millions of Americans awoke one October morning to hear the first earth-orbiting satellite *Sputnik* beeping on their radios. It was Russian, not American. The conclusion

---

[3] David Himmelstein and Steffie Woolhandler, "Cost without Benefit: Administrative Waste in U.S. Health Care," *New England Journal of Medicine*, February 13, 1986, pp. 441–45. Much of the difference between the United States and Canada can be easily explained: Canada has a national health insurance system in which the government pays for and directs the delivery of health care. Such a system reduces costs by eliminating many redundant administrative activities. Hospitals, for example, have virtually no billing department.

seemed inescapable: the United States had fallen alarmingly behind the Soviet Union in science, technology, and education. Numerous public policy initiatives soon followed to stimulate research and development and to enhance education in science and engineering.

In addition to parameters, events, and comparisons, there is a fourth way in which we come to recognize problems: *changing the category*. Take the issue of urban transportation for the elderly and handicapped. Whether you categorize the issue as one of transportation policy or civil rights policy makes a difference. If you pick the latter, you will probably favor making regular urban transit systems fully accessible to handicapped persons; if you pick the former, you will favor providing supplementary demand-responsive services such as minivans for individuals who cannot use regular transit.[4]

Or take the issue of comparable worth. Some have called it the civil rights issue for the 1990s. Essentially, comparable worth means that different jobs with similar skill levels should be paid equally. Translated into practical terms it means that jobs like nurse and librarian should pay at least as much, if not more, than male-dominated jobs like plumber and truck driver. Note that comparable worth is not equal pay for equal work, that is, all telephone operators—male and female—must be paid the same; that has been the law of the land since 1963.

One might be less than enthusiastic about comparable worth as a civil rights issue. No one *forces* women into particular job categories. Anyway, these artificial barriers are already coming down, as more women become business executives, physicians, lawyers, and so on. But, if one views the issue as really one of need, his or her attitude might change. Historically, women were generally paid less because they would work for lower wages, since they had no urgent need for more money. Either they were married, or single and living with their parents, or doubling up with friends. Men, meanwhile, pressed for a "head of household" wage, which meant enough to support a family. Most of the jobs men have held were not more responsible or arcane than those held by women. (There is nothing intrinsically complicated about pouring molten steel that dictates high wages).

Today, not surprisingly, women who head households are following the path of their male predecessors. Younger women are increasingly taking hitherto male jobs, since that is where the money is. For older women on their own, however, this route is not so easy. Hence their call for "comparable worth," which is really another way of saying, as their fathers and husbands once did, that they need more money because

---

[4] Theodore H. Poister, "Federal Transportation Policy for the Elderly and Handicapped: Responsive to Real Needs?" *Public Administration Review*, January/February 1982, pp. 6–14.

it now falls on them to provide for their children as "the head of the household." A society that countenances widespread divorce should be prepared to relinquish a fair proportion of its income to the parents—mainly women—who are left with the children.

Let us now consider an example that is neither economic nor domestic: terrorism. Is an act of terrorism a criminal act or an act of war? If you categorize it as the latter, then certain alternatives open up: preemptive or retaliatory action and more aggressive monitoring of citizens' movements. It makes a difference.

Is the Sandinista government in Nicaragua an East-West issue or North-South? Georgie Anne Geyer, a syndicated columnist, puts it under the former heading and writes:

> The astonishing discovery in Grenada of five secret treaties with the Soviet Union, Cuba, and North Korea, along with large caches of arms and ammunition, present Americans with nagging questions of belief and denial.
>
> Let me suggest a theory: With the Cuban and Soviet presence in the Caribbean, we are dealing with an ambiguous intervention—something so incremental and creeping that we are largely incapable of defining or dealing with it. Look, first, at what we have found in Grenada:
>
> [T]he treaties . . . involve intricately tying a Marxist Grenada to the Eastern bloc. They show that the island was being indeed turned into a giant arsenal and training camp for use against other countries.
>
> Edward Gonzalez, Latin American specialist at the Rand Corporation in California, puts it this way: "The problem is that we are dealing with incremental threat situations that are not highly visible. At every stage, there is always a certain legitimacy to the acts. The Soviets get in, the Cubans get in. Our difficulty is in coping with the situations in the gray areas."
>
> In effect, the initiators of this new kind of warfare never pose a clear threat, they just keep enlarging their shadowy presence until it is too late for any great power to act. By that time, they are too deeply and intricately dug in. That is the real problem we are dealing with in Grenada—and in Nicaragua and El Salvador.[5]

Carlos Coronel Kautz was a Sandinista commander in the 1979 revolution, then a minister in the first Sandinista government. He later quit the government to fight with the anti-Sandinista rebel, Eden Pastora Gomez. Now living in exile in Costa Rica, he sees things differently than Geyer:

> The Sandinistas' quick seizure of power in 1979 completely changed the rules of the game between the United States and Nicaragua. . . .
>
> Victory in Nicaragua transformed the game because it rekindled the ances-

---

[5] Georgia Anne Geyer, "U.S. Facing Incremental Threat of More Hard-to-Define Warfare," *Houston Chronicle*, November 9, 1983.

tral concept of Latin American brotherhood. We Nicaraguans could feel the deep involvement of virtually all Latin Americans, and it gave us a new source of strength derived from our Latin American identity.

This sense of brotherhood gave meaning and order to what we call the southern half of the North-South relationship, specifically relations between the United States and Latin America. . . .

Nor does Cuban involvement today necessarily engage the East in a confrontational way. There is no reason why the situation in Nicaragua need drive the United States to confront the Soviet Union—and no reason why the Soviet Union should risk a confrontation there with the United States.

The trouble, of course, is that the Cuban involvement encourages the United States to see the Central American problem as a typical East-West conflict. This is a dangerous mistake, for what is happening here remains fundamentally a confrontation between North and South.[6]

So, categories do matter.

SOURCES OF ERROR

In analyzing the mistakes and false moves of policymakers trying to diagnose problems, I have identified nine sources of errors: organizational structure, ideology, ignorance, babel, noise, lag, avoidance, masking problems, and pseudo-problems.

Organizational structure

The information pathologies of overly hierarchical, overly specialized organizations are well known, but it is always disturbing to see them acted out. That information should be hidden and that requesting departments viewed as "enemies," is incompatible with effective problem identification. Harold Wilensky has identified at least four kinds of groups that are likely to restrict the flow of information in a bureaucracy.[7] The "time servers" (some agencies might call them "retired on the job") neither get much information in the first place nor have much motive for acquiring it. "Defensive cliques" restrict information to prevent change, because any change threatens their position. "Mutual-aid-and-comfort groups" have settled into a comfortable routine, and so they resent their more ambitious colleagues. Finally, "coalitions of the ambitious" would rather keep information in their own hands, to monopolize power.

Matching the motive and opportunity of subordinates to remain silent

[6] Carlos Coronel Kautz, "Nicaragua: No East-West Issue," *New York Times*, February 10, 1986.

[7] Harold L. Wilensky, *Organizational Intelligence: Knowledge and Policy in Government and Industry* (New York: Basic Books, 1967).

in a hierarchical structure are the superiors' motive and opportunity to close their ears to staff experts. "The common belief that staff experts should be on tap, not on top, functions to maintain line authority and reduce the status of staff. It acts as a self-fulfilling prophecy." Consequently, executives believe that the advice of low-status policy specialists, however good, can readily be discounted.

For purpose of early problem identification, the optimal shape of the hierarchy would be relatively flat (few ranks permit a speedier diffusion of more accurate information), with a bulge in the middle (more policy analysts who have information and more potential administrators motivated to command it). Whatever the shape of the hierarchy, however, to extract information about problems from those who have it typically requires bypassing the conventional chain of command. Techniques for doing this include team or project organizations, committees for communicating out of channels, machinery for investigation and inspection, and reliance on informed outsiders. Some presidents like Franklin Roosevelt used the last-named technique quite effectively; others like Jimmy Carter watched their presidency suffer because they ignored it.

Specialization within an organization can also interfere with effective problem definition. While it may be essential to efficient command of large-scale operations, specialization is "antithetical to the penetrating interpretation that bears on high policy; specialization and its concomitant, inter-unit rivalry, frequently block the sharing of accurate information." How many times after a disaster do we learn that no one went to the top executive because everyone thought someone else should or would go? Wilensky thinks that intelligence failures are greatest in organizations that specialize on the basis of geography (as opposed to problem, project, task, function, profession, or client). The reasons are not hard to see. "First, good intelligence cuts across arbitrary political boundaries; it is oriented toward problem, program, or discipline. . . . Second, . . . specialization overelaborates administrative apparatus and makes transfer of resources and information from one locality to another more difficult. It also spreads scarce technical staff too thin; attempts to duplicate staff services in every jurisdiction. . . ." [8]

One final organization feature ought to be noted: centralization. If policy analysts are lodged at the top, with too little accurate and relevant information, they may be too far out of touch and too overloaded to function effectively. If, on the other hand, analysts are scattered throughout many subunits, then too many officials and experts with too much specialized information may engage in the dysfunctional competition previously noted. In recognizing this dilemma, we should not lose sight

---

[8] Wilensky, *Organizational Intelligence,* p. 172.

of the fact there is a need for policy analysis skills at every point where important decisions are made. But the one decisive argument against this arrangement is costs.

Ideology

Ideology refers to the system of beliefs held by organizational members. Strobe Talbott in his *Deadly Gambits* (1985) gives us a vivid picture of how ideology affected the first Reagan administration's approach to arms control.[9] According to Talbott, a small group of men who had served in Reagan's earlier campaigns and in his gubernatorial administration in California assembled the top ranks of the Executive Branch. With little substantive interest in foreign policy, this group represented an ideological break with traditional Republican party concerns.

> The new President's views and those of his closest advisers on foreign policy tended to be simple, with more a touch of nostalgia for the good old days of global American predominance and the Cold War. They were less impressed than the leaders of previous administrations had been by the differences between Chinese and Soviet Communists, if they saw the Third World at all, it was an area of Manichean struggle between the superpowers; they had little understanding of, and even less patience with, Western Europe. . . .
>
> Thus both the initial and the eventual choices for the leadership of the agency in charge of arms control were men whose principal attraction in the eyes of the White House was their vigorous opposition to arms control as it had been practiced by the preceding three administrations.[10]

The danger is that ideology can become a filter or block to the voice of experience and concrete reality. The psychologist Festinger touched on this aspect of ideology when he put forth his theory of *cognitive dissonance*. Festinger argued that human beings find it hard to accept and hold in their minds several pieces of information that seem to contradict one another. We feel uncomfortable when we are expected to believe several things that do not fit together. Psychologists then say that we are suffering from cognitive dissonance. Their experiments show that people tend to reduce or abolish cognitive dissonance either by attempting to reconcile intellectually the seeming contradiction or, more often, by suppressing or forgetting the piece of information that does not fit.

Belief, he observed in his psychological examinations of religious groups, becomes not weaker but stronger when it is in greatest and most obvious conflict with reality. The nineteenth-century Millerites

---

[9] Strobe Talbott, *Deadly Gambits* (New York: Vintage Books, 1985), pp. 9, 11.
[10] Talbott, *Deadly Gambits*, p. 13.

(also known as Seventh-Day Adventists) predicted that the world would come to an end on March 21, 1844. Their number is estimated to have then been one hundred thousand. No such ending occurred, and Miller proclaimed a new date for the conflagration: October 22, 1844. In the interim the number of Millerites went up substantially, and when the second failure of prophecy was made evident, after thousands had sold or given away their material possessions, the number of communicants shot up impressively once more. The religion at the present time is among the fastest-growing in the world.[11] But cognitive dissonance occurs everywhere that ideologies are found. Belief hardens and chills into dogma.

Ignorance and babel

Ignorance of one's ignorance—not the lack of knowledge itself—is the third error. One of the most common manifestations of this error appears when the press reports ecological issues. There is widespread opinion within the scientific community and the chemical industry that one of the big difficulties in the formulation of environmental policy flows from journalism's failure to appreciate the language and methods of science. Moreover, reporters face deadlines and competition for hot stories.

Writers imbued with a crusading spirit often present exaggerated pictures of potential destruction of human and animal life from the use of pesticidal agents and food additives. Instead of clarity and under-standing, they inculcate in the mind of the public doubt and fear. Strong publicity may force public officials to act without data—Love Canal, Times Beach, dioxin, Agent Orange, chlorofluorocarbons and zone de-pletion, PCBs, etc.—and repent at leisure. "Once the scientific data are in—years later—so many people have invested in the wrong conclu-sion that they cannot afford to lose face by admitting they were wrong."[12]

Admittedly, environmental reporting is not an easy task; the problems are complex, the expert testimony voluminous. But if the problems are going to be correctly diagnosed, then journalist and policymaker alike will sometimes need to say, "I don't know." Dr. Johnson might be an excellent model. When asked by a lady why he defined "pastern" as the knee of a horse in his dictionary, Samuel Johnson replied, "Igno-rance, madame, pure ignorance."

Babel, the fourth source of error, refers to a confusion of messages that might waft across the desk of a government official. The U.S.

---

[11] Leon A. Festinger, *Theory of Cognitive Dissonance* (New York: Harper & Row, 1957).
[12] Geraldine Cox, "Risk Management: Panacea or Pandora's Box." *Governance,* Spring 1984.

ambassador in Botzanastan has received three hundred warnings of an imminent terrorist attack over the same number of days. Not surprisingly, he fails to heed the 301st and loses the east wing of the embassy. Babel therefore is just an old-fashioned way of saying that communications overload can prevent us from clearly seeing the real tions overload can prevent us from clearly seeing the real problem.

One of the best examples of this error is the energy issue of the early 1970s. Though the 1965 blackout on the East Coast was a sign that it was coming, not many experts interpreted the blackout that way. Actually, one could trace the signs, all largely ignored, as far back as the speeches of Theodore Roosevelt.

Clearly, then, the process of perceiving problems is a species of pattern recognition; it involves finding in events—or imposing on them—an order or structure. Yet perceptual obstacles prevent policy analysts from clearly perceiving either the problem itself or the information that is necessary to solve it. A good way to illustrate what I have been trying to say here is to have you look at a visual puzzle that requires you to detect meaning in the midst of apparent chaos. Can you tell what the illustration in Figure 3–1 represents?

Noise

Noise generally means any loud or disagreeable sound. But, in communications theory, the term means something else: noise is present when A knows what he wants to say but cannot predict what it will be when it reaches B.[13] The same original message can generate a variety of meanings because noise is added during the time of transmission and A can never be sure what will eventually reach B. Noise is a second communication. It introduces messages into the flow that neither A nor B can predict. Two or more messages interact with some mutual destruction.

Noise should be distinguished from babel. The latter term, we said, refers to the sheer volume of messages. Noise, on the other hand, can occur anytime one message blends with one or more other messages to cause confusion in the mind of the receiver.

In trying to understand the Nazis' problem in the 1930s, Walter Lippman, perhaps the most astute American journalist of this century, was remarkably wrong. The source of his error appears to be noise: The messages coming from Europe were getting mixed. Shortly after

---

[13] B. M. Johnson, *Communication: The Process of Organizing* (Boston: Allyn and Bacon, 1977). My own thinking on the subject draws, however, more from W. Ross Ashby, *An Introduction to Cybernetics* (New York: John Wiley & Sons, 1963), pp. 186–91. The classic in which those ideas were first developed is Claude E. Shannon and Warren Weaver, *The Mathematical Theory of Communications* (Urbana, Ill.: University of Illinois Press, 1949).

Figure 3-1
Problem solving as pattern recognition: An example

It's a Volkswagen, of course.

the infamous night in May 1933 when the Nazis made funeral pyres
of books written by Jews and "liberals," Lippmann warned in his column
that Hitler was preparing for war.

> A week later Lippmann again wrote about the Nazis. This time he analyzed
> a seemingly conciliatory speech in which Hitler claimed that Germany would
> not try to press its claims by force. Eager to believe that the dictator was
> now willing to moderate his revolutionary nationalism, to temper what
> Lippmann called the "ruthless injustice of the treatment meted out to the
> German Jews" and the barbarism of the book-burning orgy, he described
> the speech as a "genuinely statesmanlike address" that offered "evidence
> of good faith." Then he continued in phrases as remarkable in retrospect
> as they must have seemed at the time: "We have heard once more, through
> the fog and the din, the hysteria and the animal passions of a great revolution,
> the authentic voice of a genuinely civilized people." By this he meant that
> the Germans should not be judged simply by Nazi rantings or treated as
> permanent outcasts. Urging his readers to recognize the "dual nature of
> man," he maintained that "to deny today that Germany can speak as a
> civilized power because uncivilized things are being done in Germany is in
> itself a deep form of intolerance."[14]

---

[14] Ronald Steel, *Walter Lippmann and the American Century* (Boston: Little, Brown, 1980),
p. 331.

The noise implied here should not be confused with noises like static on a radio, because that kind of noise is a fixed distortion and can be filtered out if necessary. The noise being depicted here consists of messages that are valuable in their own right. Certainly no policymaker would want to have filtered out Hitler's "conciliatory" speech in 1933.

Lag

Let us now assume that a policymaker is in an open organization that is free of ideological biases. The messages he receives are simple and clear. Yet he still might err in problem analysis because of lag.

One does not turn a production-line sports car on a dime, nor do most of us discard our perception of reality overnight. Lag refers to the finite period of time that elapses between the moment we begin to receive new messages about a situation and the moment we begin to act in accordance with these new realities. New ideas, like new shoes, require some breaking in.

With which of the following statements do you agree?

1. The big economic winners in the 1980s have been people over sixty-five.
2. A merger of B. F. Goodrich and Uniroyal, the third and fourth largest tire manufacturers, would be economically helpful to the country.
3. The total destructive power of nuclear weapons in the world today is *less* than it was twenty years ago.

All these statements happen to be true, although the second is less factual than the first and third. If you are like most Americans, this requires a little getting used to.

The big economic winners of the 1980s. Contrary to popular impression, elderly Americans have become the big economic winners of the 1980s. As a group, families headed by a person sixty-five or over gained economic ground (up 9 percent) more rapidly than the college graduate (up 3 percent) or two-earner families (up zero). Nonelderly families overall lost 4 percent in the 1980–83 period. More generous social security benefits, better pension plans, and larger accumulated assets all contributed to the relative gains of older people.

At first look, it appears that despite progress, elderly families still have less total income than their younger counterparts. The typical nonelderly family with an income of $26,051 in 1983 got half again as much as the elderly family, which had a median income of $16,878. But elderly families are generally smaller than younger families. When adjusted for family size, the median income for elderly people reached 95 percent of the nonelderly. If an important noncash benefit, medicare, were counted, elderly families would be even closer—or perhaps higher.

The wealth, or property, owned by the elderly is much higher than it is in younger families: Among families where the husband is sixty-five or older, 88 percent own their own homes, most of which are paid for and in many cases are eligible for reduced taxes. In all then, less than 8 percent of married persons over sixty-five are below the poverty level, less than half the rate for the rest of the population.[15]

If anything is as powerful as an idea whose time has come, it is probably the mythology encrusting the idea whose time has passed. In the 1980s with budget deficits at record levels, President Reagan found himself forced to promise that, while almost everything else in the budget would be cut, not a penny would be cut from social security—not even from future benefits. There was a time, twenty or thirty years ago, when the elderly were, in fact, worse off as a group than younger people and were the subject of legitimate concern, but now policymakers need to consider the prospect that in thirty-five years the entire country is expected to have the same percentage of people over sixty-five as Florida does today.

Big mergers and the public interest. Neither the Department of Justice nor the Federal Trade Commission objected to the merger of Goodrich and Uniroyal or to similar big mergers. To many Americans, this is a curiously tolerant reaction by the government to increases in market share and company size that only recently would have been regarded as illegal. It reflects a growing recognition that the economic challenge has changed, that the route to growth is not through the atomistic firms of nineteenth-century economics, and that the imperfect market is often preferable to imperfect regulation.

The economic circumstances that face the United States today are radically different from the benevolent environment of the 1950s and early 60s. Powerful Japanese multinational companies are carving out dominant shares of rich Western markets; Europeans have built powerful positions in particular sectors such as heavy machinery, fine chemicals (West Germany), and shoes and fashion textiles (Italy); newly industrialized countries, such as Brazil and Israel, have built manufacturing sectors capable of export; Eastern Europe and the newest infant manufacturers provide an increasingly wide range of goods in the low end of the market. All find the American consumer an irresistible target. To survive this global competition, American companies need the low operating costs of large-scale operations and the resources for continual develop-

---

[15] *Economic Report of the President, 1985* (Washington, D.C.: Government Printing Office, 1984), pp. 159–86. According to Michael Harrington, "The welfare state in the United States is primarily for people over sixty-five, most of whom are not now, and for a long time have not been poor." *The New American Poverty* (Holt, Rinehart & Winston, 1984), p. 85.

ment that only regular profits can provide. This line of economic reasoning will take a while to find a place in the national psyche. When it does, the implications for antitrust policy will be far-reaching.

The size required to achieve the lowest possible costs may be very high relative to the national market. This seems to be true in steel, for example, where the Japanese have individual plants with capacity of more than 15 million tons. Moreover, there is considerable evidence that in many industries it is possible to manage costs so that they decline indefinitely as volume increases.[16]

Shrinking nuclear arsenals. Most people who can bring themselves to it, still think about nuclear strategy on the basis of what was true between 1945 and 1975. But due to the amazing increase in missile accuracy of recent years and the corresponding reduction in warhead yields, the real nature of deterrence today is drastically different than the public perceives. The Jonathan Schell scenario of massive exchanges against cities described in his widely read *Fate of the Earth* (1982) may be obsolete: Neither side would dare. A future war in Europe instead could start with a crippling Soviet nuclear strike against North Atlantic Treaty Organization conventional military objectives so precisely targeted that there would be little civilian damage, either directly or through subsequent fallout. In the past twenty years, the accuracy of Russian missiles has increased by a factor of ten, and American missiles, which were much more accurate to begin with, by a factor of five.

Both sides are rapidly shrinking their missiles' explosive force in order to be able to attack military targets without causing extensive collateral damage that would invite reprisals against cities. Specifically, the megatonnage of the U.S. missile arsenal has shrunk by about half since 1970 and by about three quarters since the late 1950s. According to General Pierre Gallois, the French air force officer who helped design that nation's independent nuclear force, it has become so dangerous—and indeed useless—to attack cities in the World War II style, that war once again may become professionalized, the way it was in the eighteenth century; uniformed forces versus uniformed forces, with the noncombatants on the sidelines.[17]

Avoidance

Policymakers consciously seek to avoid some problems because they are so discomforting. Again, nuclear weapons might serve to illustrate the point. In the 1950s and 1960s, many people did not want to think

---

[16] See Joseph L. Bower, *When Markets Quake* (New York: Harper & Row, 1986).

[17] Pierre Gallois and John Train, "When a Nuclear Strike Is Thinkable," *The Wall Street Journal*, March 22, 1984.

about the unthinkable. Indeed, when the late Herman Kahn dared to analyze the issue as objectively as possible, he was belittled as a "Dr. Strangelove." Arguably, this tendency to avoid the issue led to the simplistic policy of staying ahead through Mutual Assured Destruction (MAD), via endless reciprocal escalation between the United States and the Soviet Union. The world drifted into its current plight; it did not choose it.

Until recently, another carefully avoided problem was the plight of the black family. In 1965, in an address at Howard University, President Johnson declared, "Negroes are trapped in inherited, gateless poverty. The main cause of this predicament was the unstable black family."

At the time, few black children reached the age of eighteen having lived all their lives with both parents, and most black youngsters had received some form of public assistance. Unless efforts were made to strengthen the black family structure, Johnson asserted, other government measures would "never be enough to cut completely the circles of despair and deprivation." The speech was supposed to galvanize support for Johnson's war on poverty; instead, it created a furor.

Black community leaders said it diverted attention from the more important issues of discrimination. In the view of many blacks, Johnson and Daniel Patrick Moynihan, then an assistant secretary of Labor and author of the internal report on which the president's speech was based, were blaming the victims for their own distress. The furor over the so-called Moynihan report ended in a profound silence. One thing the controversy did was force scholars to shy away from sensitive issues surrounding black families.

Today there is a definite shift to talking about the issue openly and candidly. The growing mass of politically silent, poor youth in an affluent nation is described by some experts as a social revolution with unpredictable ramifications. "The United States today may be the first society in history where children are much worse off than adults," Moynihan, now a New York senator, says. See Figure 3–2. "It is time we realized we have a problem of significant social change unlike anything we have experienced in the past."

Moynihan, among others, sees the problem of poor children as a symptom of larger, ill-defined (but disturbing) changes in the American family and urban society. He recalls the 1965 uproar when the unmarried birthrate among blacks exceeded 20 percent. Today, that is the overall national rate. He notes studies that show that the stereotypical American family of working husband, nonworking wife, and children is now in the minority. "A majority of new American families forming today are single-parent families. By 1990 about half the kids coming of age will have lived in a one-parent family. A third of the kids born in 1980—one half in New York City—will spend part of their life on welfare.

Figure 3–2
Poverty rate among children under eighteen years and elderly sixty-five years or older (1970–1983)

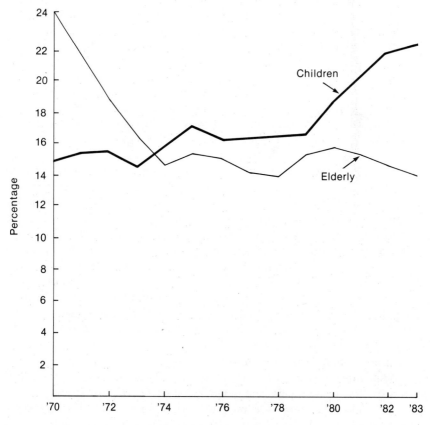

Source: U.S. Bureau of the Census, *Estimates of Poverty Including the Value of Noncash Benefits: 1984,* Technical Paper 55.

We don't know what all this means for the American family and the country. We don't know what's happening, let alone what to do about it."[18]

Only now are policy analysts beginning to seriously ask what all this means for the American family and the country. Having only recently decided to stop avoiding the problem, they will now have to try to understand what is happening. Only when, and if, that task is completed can they begin thinking about what to do. Avoidance has its costs.

---

[18] Interview with Daniel Patrick Moynihan, *New York Times,* October 20, 1985.

Figure 3–3
How one problem can mask another: Two examples

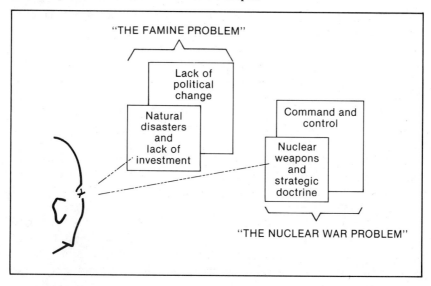

Masking problems

Certain problems that are fairly well defined and widely recognized do serve, in effect, to conceal other more important problems. These problems I call *masking problems*. For example, in trying to diagnose the famine in Africa or the risk of nuclear war, we may find ourselves in the position of the analyst in Figure 3–3.

A provocative primer on famine was published in 1984 by Earthscan, a group concerned with global development and environmental issues. The report decisively attributes the severity of the suffering that occurs amid droughts, floods, and other disasters to human practices and governmental policies, rather than to events such as shortages of water or the overflowing of river banks. Based on data compiled by the International Red Cross, the study asserts:

> Events called "natural disasters" are killing more and more people every year. Yet there is no evidence that the climatological mechanisms associated with droughts, floods, and cyclones are changing. . . . It is because people are changing their environment to make it more prone to some disasters, and are behaving so as to make themselves more vulnerable to those hazards.[19]

---

[19] Lloyd Timberlake, *Natural Disasters: Acts of God or Acts of Man?* Africa in Crises: The Causes, the Cures of Environmental Bankruptcy (Philadelphia: New Society Publications, 1986).

The Earthscan study declares that, in cases of "natural disaster," the kind of disaster relief currently being extended to Ethiopia and other African countries "may not be the most charitable, efficient, or most cost-effective means of alleviating human suffering." The study does not recommend political change, but it seems obvious that politics is at the heart of the misery besetting many Third World nations: the prevalence of the one-party state—"socialist" governmental model; the grotesque militarization of society and economy; the adoption of an urbanizing, high-tech, capital-intensive, high-prestige model of development that is often utterly inappropriate to local social, cultural, economic, and environmental conditions.

About the same time the Earthscan report appeared, a World Bank report also appeared flatly denying the widely held belief that sub-Saharan Africa has suffered more than other regions because of a lack of adequate investment. Rather, it shows that through the 1970s, sub-Saharan Africa "was not short of investment" compared to either its own record in the 1960s or the average of the lower-income South Asian countries. Like the Earthscan report, the World Bank document blames the region's decline on a combination of faulty economic and social policies. The bad economic policies range from overinvolvement by African governments in agriculture and business to excessive government subsidies and misspending on costly, badly planned "white elephant" projects.[20]

Although nuclear weapons and strategic policy attract increasing public concern, Paul Bracken of Yale offers an analysis that sweeps beyond the proposals—MX, freeze, and so on—on which the arms-building and arms-control debates have centered in recent years.[21] Bracken's contribution is to lay out the system of command and control of nuclear weapons that has been devised incrementally over the years, and to explore how it might work if an international crisis got out of hand and deterrence finally failed. His conclusion is that regardless of what weapons had been built and what "doctrines" conceived to guide their use, the actual organizational and human system of command and control is itself a source of danger and could easily break down and produce an uncommanded and uncontrolled war.

In short, if you are worried about war, you must worry first not about weapons inventories and doctrine, but about process and operations. Current Soviet-American agreements do not touch command and control. A freeze would leave in place the system that is so menacing

---

[20] World Bank, *Toward Sustained Development in Sub-Saharan Africa: A Joint Program of Action* (Washington, D.C.: World Bank, September 1984).

[21] Paul Bracken, *The Command and Control of Nuclear Forces* (New Haven, Conn.: Yale University Press, 1984).

now. So, too, would arms reductions. On the premise that war would be more likely to arise from the escalation of a crisis than from conscious policy, Bracken would work on what he calls nuclear "rules of the road"—to improve "command stability" and reduce the incentive for pre-emptive attack and blind escalation.

Pseudo-problems

Natural disasters, lack of investment, nuclear weapons, and strategic doctrine (e.g., Mutual Assured Destruction) are real problems that divert our attention from a greater one. But pseudo-problems are false problems in the sense that they cause no real harm. They may be discussed at great length and sometimes result in sweeping new legislation, but unlike droughts and ICBMs they have little potential for harm. Among the most durable and widespread pseudo-problems have been illegal immigration and illiteracy.

While not controlling one's own borders might be disconcerting, what impact does illegal immigration, in its current magnitude, have on the U.S. economy? That is, what is the net effect of illegal immigration? In a recent poll that question was asked of past presidents of the American Economic Association and those who have served on the president's Council of Economic Advisers. Result: 75 percent said that illegal immigrants have had a net "positive impact" on the U.S. economy, against 11 percent who said they have a "negative" effect.[22]

How big a problem is illiteracy in the United States? In its most simple definition, illiteracy means the inability to read or write a simple message. It is generally agreed that illiteracy in its strictest sense is low in the United States; the Census Bureau says about .5 percent of the adult population is illiterate. But then we come to another term: *functional illiteracy*, that is, a lack of basic reading and writing skills needed to perform productively in society. What does "perform productively" mean? Obviously, for many Americans, functional illiteracy separates them from much of society and limits their ability to make informed choices. But for others, the effects are not so severe. Literacy needs vary widely with the individual.

Two groups make up the bulk of those deficient in literacy skills: high school dropouts and immigrants. The illiteracy problem is particularly difficult to solve because illiterates are adults and, as much as some might wish, cannot be coerced into learning. Many illiterates are elderly, because they tend to have had less formal education. It may not be realistic to expect an adult who could not learn in elementary

---

[22] Stephen Moore, "Social Scientists' View on Immigrants and the U.S. Immigration Policy: A Postscript," *Annals*, AAPSS, 487 (September 1986), pp. 213–17.

and secondary school to go back to the same system believing that things are going to be different. Those who do choose to be trained are usually doing so for a practical purpose, such as getting a better job. But many jobs do not really require the skills a diploma implies; employers simply use it as a screening device.

Illiteracy is not necessarily totally incapacitating. Illiterates are not devoid of common sense. For help in paying bills and answering letters, they usually rely on a literate family member or friend. They work, raise families, and lead lives that are successful in their terms. Do we define a third-grade level reader who functions well on the job, raises children, and participates in church activities as functionally illiterate?

The interesting question, which I cannot answer, is why dubious or overdrawn generalizations about illegal immigration and illiteracy continue to circulate with little or no challenge. There is no surprise in those claims being made by, say, educational entrepreneurs who want more federal dollars "to solve the problem." The puzzle is why such fallacies persist for so long—especially when there are plenty of real problems around (such as the *technological* illiteracy of American executives).

THE LIVELY ART OF PROBLEM REPRESENTATION

As suggested by the preceding example of trade deficits, problems may be represented in different ways. In some representations, the problem may be easy to solve, while in others it may be difficult. Our choice of representation, then, can make a decisive difference in our search for a solution to a problem. One need only consider how much easier it is to solve arithmetic problems when Arabic numerals and place notation replace Roman numerals. Or consider the following problem:

> One morning, at sunrise, a monk begins to climb a mountain on a narrow path that wound around it. He climbed at varying rates of speed and made frequent stops. By sunset, he reached the top. The following morning at sunrise he began his desultory descent down the same trail. Show that there is a spot along the path that he will occupy on both trips at exactly the same time of day.

Success at solving this problem depends more on how you represent the problem—the freedom you feel to rearrange the material—than it does on your knowledge of algebra. The simplest solution is to imagine the monk walking up the hill, and then superimpose on this image one of the monk walking *down* the hill. Obviously the two figures *must* meet at the same point—regardless of what speed they walk or how often they stop.

To a degree, solving any problem simply means representing it in a way that makes the solution transparent. Unfortunately, we have only a sketchy and incomplete knowledge of the different ways in which policy problems can be represented. In this section, we will consider how problems of poverty, unemployment, and national defense can be represented. (No pseudo-problems in that trio.) But first I wish to introduce a concept that might prove useful in thinking about how to represent policy problems.

Proto-problems

Recently, John W. Kingdon of the University of Michigan said something very wise: "There is a difference between a condition and a problem. . . . Conditions become defined as problems when we come to believe that we should do something about them."[23] We are surrounded by conditions—bad weather, illnesses, pestilence, fanaticism, highway congestion, and dirty air. We may or may not choose to consider this set, or parts of it, a problem.

Schematically, we might show this transition from condition to problem as in the figure below:

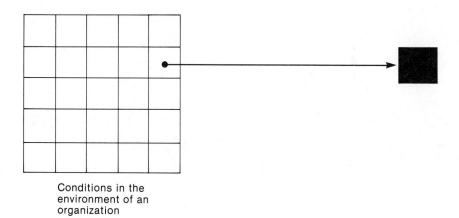

Conditions in the
environment of an
organization

The grid on the left represents the environment of an organization as a set of conditions; these may involve clients, the bond market, incidence of disease, or anything else relevant to the goals and objectives of the

---

[23] John W. Kingdon, *Agendas, Alternatives, and Public Policies* (Boston: Little, Brown, 1984), p. 115.

108

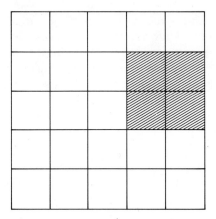

organization. The dark square to the right indicates that one condition has gone critical; it has become a problem.

But is this a useful way of looking at conditions in the environment of an organization? A condition does not become a problem suddenly, as when a light bulb burns out. If we survey our environment, we should be able to distinguish some conditions that are closer to problem status than others. These are represented by the cross-hatched areas in the figure above.

Therefore our original schematic might be redrawn as shown in this figure.

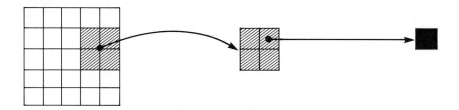

The cross-hatched squares are *proto-problems*. How does this concept facilitate the thinking about two well-publicized issues?

1. Communist regimes in the Third World are not the only threat to U.S. interest there. Preoccupation with these problems and lack of an adequate terminology has lead policymakers to either aggravate or ignore other conditions. Consider the distinction drawn between authoritarian and totalitarian governments. In contrast to totalitarian states, authoritarian regimes are said to be friendly to the United States and

at least potentially open to reform. In reality, authoritarianism could better be seen not as distinct from communism but as its precursor. Once assured of the unquestioning American support, authoritarian governments often become more removed from popular concerns and more reliant on the military, thus paving the way for communist organizers.

Henry A. Kissinger's years in the White House and the State Department are instructive. In 1972, a military coup blocked reform in El Salvador. Then, in 1972–73, Anastasio Somoza rewrote the Nicaraguan Constitution while Ferdinand E. Marcos rewrote that of the Philippines—both giving themselves the right to rule for life. But nowhere in Kissinger's memoirs is there any reference to these events.[24] Undoubtedly he believes that authoritarians such as Somoza and Marcos were "friends" in the struggle against communism and that no end is served by "destabilizing" them with demands for reform.

I submit that, with no terminology to clarify that Somoza and Marcos, if not problems, were at least worth special attention as proto-problems, Kissinger looked the other way. Thus, the seeds were sown of the fruit the United States would reap in Central America in the 1980s.

2.   The twelve-digit budget deficits that the federal government experienced through much of the 1980s may be another instance of a proto-problem. While quite a few experts claimed that annual deficits of this size would cause inflation and high interest rates and prevent economic recovery, experience contradicted their claim. Yet other experts, who doubted these claims all along, felt uneasy about simply ignoring deficits.

Only in the long run, if left unattended, do deficits present a threat. Massive annual deficits add to the national debt and that debt must be serviced though taxpayer revenues. Thus, deficits could divert increasing resources from the private sector where they would probably be used more efficiently and help raise the tax base and create jobs. But, in the short run, deficits were not necessarily a problem; indeed, by putting more money in Americans' hands, deficits increase the demand for goods and services and stimulate the economy.[25]

Deficits also illustrate the effect of problem representation. In comparison to a mortgage, $200 billion *is* a lot. An earnest politician might help us appreciate the gravity of the situation by telling us that a stack of 200 billion one dollar bills would reach to Pluto, or the Tarantula nebula, or some other dizzy height. But consider this: In 1983, in the

---

[24] Henry Kissinger, *White House Years* and *Years of Upheaval* (Boston: Little, Brown, 1982).

[25] For an argument that deficits have been *too small* in recent years, see Robert Eisner and Paul J. Pieper, "A New View of the Federal Debt and Budget Deficits," *American Economic Review*, March 1984, pp. 11–29.

110

midst of a severe recession, the U.S. deficit as a percentage of GNP was about the average of other industrial market economies (Table 3–1). Since then, the percentage has continued to shrink.

To better understand how representations are created and how they contribute to (or retard) the solution of problems, let us focus on some concrete issues.

Representing the poverty problem

The conservative view. The conservative view of the poverty problem might be stated as follows. First, the problem is not nearly as bad as usually rendered. The official figures, which show that some 14.4 percent of Americans are poor, are misleading because they ignore the substantial noncash benefits received by the group. Counting these additional benefits, and valuing them at market prices, reduces the official figure to 9.7 percent. In any case, the millions of Americans officially classified as poor are not for the most part stuck in poverty; instead, the group's members are constantly changing. Some are in young families just getting started; some are in older families that simply

Table 3–1
Surplus/Deficit as percentage of GNP for eighteen industrial market economies, 1983

	Percent
Norway	1.9
Switzerland	−0.3
Germany, Federal Republic	−2.0
Australia	−2.5
Finland	−3.0
France	−3.6
United Kingdom	−5.0
Belgium	−5.4
UNITED STATES	−6.1
Spain	−6.3
Canada	−6.5
Denmark	−7.5
Netherlands	−7.7
New Zealand	−9.5
Sweden	−10.1
Belgium	−12.9
Italy	−13.4
Ireland	−13.6

Source: Data from World Bank, *World Development Report, 1986* (New York: Oxford University Press, 1986), p. 223.

had a bad year. Scholarly studies suggest that about 60 percent of those entering poverty can expect to leave it within two years.[26]

The hard core of the problem, according to conservatives, is the poverty population whose members belong to female-headed households. This population, which showed no growth at all in the 1960s, has since been expanding steadily at an average rate of 4 percent and now totals over 12 million people. We have every reason to believe, conservatives argue, that this steady growth reflects the mistakes of the Great Society, whose enlarged benefits suddenly made government-supported dependency seem a plausible option to many young women. Nobody now knows how to spend government money in ways that will reverse this pathological process, and in general we cannot assume that spending more money will substantially shrink the poverty population. Indeed $80 billion or so that the federal government is already spending on means-tested benefit programs every year is more than enough to eliminate all poverty in the United States. These programs include Aid to Families with Dependent Children, medicaid, food stamps, rent subsidies, and certain social security payments. If all the benefits were converted to simple cash payments, and if all of the payments went exclusively to poor people, poverty would be instantly eliminated with about $25 billion to spare. But, of course, the politicians serving up the benefits have never really been concerned to limit them exclusively to poor people.

Tentatively, almost reluctantly, conservatives would conclude that changes in family structure, divorce, and parental attitudes are responsible for the squalid, disheartening picture presented by the statistics. They might quote psychologist Urie Bronfenbrenner, who said that the essential prerequisite for healthy human development is that "somebody has got to be crazy about the kid."[27]

Critique. Why count in-kind benefits at market rates if the poor themselves cannot use them efficiently? The head of one of those AFDC families might have more medical care than she really needs, but fewer food stamps than she wants; in the circumstances, she is clearly not getting full value out of her package of benefits. Once you start counting the cost of benefits as a recipient's "income," you get into the untenable

---

[26] See Greg J. Duncan et al., *Years of Poverty, Years of Plenty* (Ann Arbor, Mich.: Institute of Social Research University of Michigan, 1984). Unless otherwise noted, poverty figures cited in text are from U.S. Bureau of Census, *Current Population Report*, series P-60, No. 147 and 149; and *Estimates of Poverty Including the Value of Noncash Benefits: 1984*, Technical Paper 55.

[27] See Peter Uhlenberg and David Eggebeen, "The Declining Well-Being of American Adolescents," *Public Interest*, Winter 1986, pp. 25–38.

112

position of elevating people into the middle class just because their long and expensive illnesses generate huge medical bills.

Further, a good case could be made that the poverty population is, if anything, substantially undercounted. The undercount arises not only because many poor are simply missed in surveys, but also because the threshold of poverty might be set too high. There is, of course, an inescapable element of subjectivity in any definition of poverty; still, the case for a higher poverty threshold has some logic to it. When the present definition was first developed in the early 1950s, it reflected an assumption that food costs represented one third of a family's budget; hence the poverty level was put at three times the cost of an inexpensive but nutritionally adequate diet. Over the years, however, food has been a declining share of average family budgets, so you can make a case for a higher multiplier and, therefore, a higher poverty threshold.

The conservatives' claim that the people in poverty are constantly changing is a matter of perspective—or, if you will, how the problem is represented. Research finds that 48 percent of all women who receive AFDC are off the rolls within two years.[28] Now, consider exactly the same data, used to calculate another statistic: Of all women who were on AFDC at one time, 50 percent were in the midst of a cycle whereby they remained on it for eight or more years. For a typical year during the study, that translated into roughly 1.6 million families and more than 5 million people. Which view of the situation do you consider important?

Finally, the conservative view of poverty is hardly ground level. If they spent more time talking to the poor and living in their world, more hard-hearted conservatives might be discouraged from thinking that all the poor had it coming to them.[29]

National security

In his preface to *Soviet Military Power*, an annual report issued by the Department of Defense the secretary of defense could have quoted the words of the fat boy in *The Pickwick Papers:* "I wants to make your flesh creep." The purpose of this annual document is, quite obviously, to portray the Soviet armed forces in such a formidable light that the Pentagon has less difficulty in obtaining its budget request from Congress. An example from the report is shown in Figure 3–4.

Taking a closer look at the European match-up, the Soviet Union has 176 divisions, and NATO has 176 divisions. This seems very clear

[28] Duncan, et al., *Years of Poverty*, pp. 40–42.
[29] For some vivid portraits of poor people, see Michael Harrington, *The New American Poverty* (New York: Holt Rinehart & Winston, 1984).

Figure 3–4
How the Pentagon represents Soviet military power

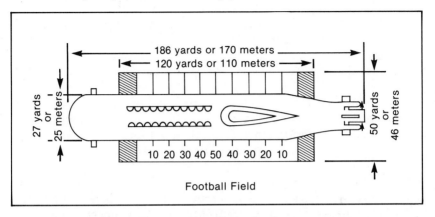

Football Field

In the early 1980s, the U.S. Department of Defense launched a new weapon to use in political battles on Capitol Hill: a magazine-style, full-color, red paperback report detailing the Soviets' armed might from foot soldiers to space lasers. Above is a new Soviet sub (Delta IV SSBN) capable of launching MIRVed SS-NX-23 ballistic missiles against land targets.

Source: U.S. Department of Defense, *Soviet Military Power, 1985* (Washington, D.C.: Government Printing Office, 1985).

cut. But before a Defense Department official can lean across the table at a congressional hearing to announce gravely that Soviet ground forces have a 2.0465 to 1 superiority over NATO's, a number of other factors must be considered:

- Soviet divisions tend to be smaller than those of NATO (when division equivalents are used the ratio is 115 to 108, or 1.06 to 1).

- Soviet divisions may be smaller, but they belong to one army under one central authority, whereas the Western total is split among the armies of the United States, Canada, Britain, Norway, Denmark, West Germany, Holland, France, Portugal, Italy, Greece, and Turkey—and the French divisions are not under alliance command and not necessarily available, the Greek divisions are of uncertain allegiance, and the American reserve forces must first be mobilized, then fitted out and updated in training, then transported across the ocean.

- Soviet allies such as Poland may not be steadfast in the event of a war.

- The NATO rule of thumb is that American, West German, and British divisions in action would be at least 40 percent more effective than their Russian counterparts. Israeli experts think that even this estimate is too modest; they would put the figure at better than 50 percent.[30]

In many respects the interpretation of national security needs is even more vexing than the preceding example of poverty. How much defense is enough? Are the Russians coming? Are they stronger?

Well, the Pentagon's answer runs something like this. The Soviet Union spends from 10 to 15 percent of its gross national product on defense, while the United States spends a paltry 6 to 8 percent. But this argument can cut the other way. As, I think, the case of agriculture, proves, American performance is much more effective than Russian performance: the United States gets a larger yield from a relatively smaller input.

How do you compare the Russian and American forces? The Russian military forces are twice as large as the American forces, but nearly half their divisions have been transferred to the Chinese front. How do you compare strategic weapons? The Russians have a lead in the number of missiles—2,400 to 1,600—and in the amount of explosive power in each warhead. But because of multiheaded missiles the United States has three times as many warheads as the Russians. The U.S. warheads are far more accurate, and accuracy counts more than sheer destructive power.

Even assuming that the foregoing difficulties could be resolved, the analysis would not go far enough, for military balance must be considered within a geopolitical context. In Western Europe, for example, the United States and its allies have a formidable force, including 850 planes and more than 1,250 tanks. The Warsaw Pact forces are larger—960 planes and 2,200 tanks. But the balance is probably evened out by the superiority of NATO weapons and the dubious loyalty of the Communist-bloc forces. In the Middle East and the Persian Gulf, the calculation is hard to make because it is not clear who is on what side. But the Soviet buildup in Syria and Iraq and the Persian Gulf is not to be lightly dismissed. And in north Asia only a trivial American force protects Japan and Korea. The Russians, with over forty divisions in the area, are clearly superior—even allowing for the Chinese forces.

Unemployment

People expect the Bureau of Labor Statistics (BLS) to tell them how many persons are unemployed in the United States.

---

[30] T. N. Dupuy, *Numbers, Predictions and War* (New York: Bobbs-Merrill, 1979).

Box 3–1
What is military capability and how is it measured?

DOD defines "military capability" as the ability to achieve a specified wartime objective—for example, win a battle or a war or destroy a target. Military capability is a broad term which cannot be readily quantified; therefore, DOD has divided capability into the following four subsets or pillars:

- *Readiness:* the ability of the military forces, units, weapon systems, or equipment to deliver the output for which they were designed (i.e., for a tank to move and shoot) in peacetime and at the outset of hostilities. Readiness is measured in terms of manning, equipping, and training the force and is defined to include the force's ability to mobilize, deploy, and employ without unacceptable delays.

- *Sustainability:* the staying power of military forces, or how long the forces can continue to fight. Sustainability involves the ability to resupply engaged forces during combat operations and is sometimes measured in terms of the estimated number of fighting days for which supplies are available.

- *Modernization:* the technical sophistication of forces, units, weapon systems, and equipment. Modernization can include new procurement and/or modifications, depending on the service. Assessments of modernization may compare new types of equipment with the items they replaced or may compare equipment in the U.S. inventory with that of potential adversary forces.

- *Force structure:* the numbers, size, and composition of units constituting the military forces. Force structure is usually described as numbers of divisions, ships, or wings.

The military services are not consistent in the items which are included under each of the four pillars, resulting in some difficulty in establishing clear-cut distinctions between them. For general discussions of military capability, readiness and sustainability are often discussed together, as are force structure and modernization. Developing tools which will measure current military capability, project future capability, and examine the potential impact of applying alternative levels of funding to a given military requirement is a very complex task.

Source: General Accounting Office, *Measuring Military Capability*, NSIAD-86-72 (Washington, D.C.: Government Printing Office, 1986), p. 7.

116

Lee M. Cohn, a Washington-based journalist, writes:

> Policymakers depend on BLS figures for guidance, and fluctuations of the statistics can decide elections. If the numbers are wrong, economic policies can go astray and voters can be misled.[31] But no formula can precisely fit everyone's idea about how to define and measure unemployment.

The BLS's method for measuring unemployment is to survey over 50,000 households monthly, categorizing each person as being *employed, unemployed,* or *not in the labor force.* The first category includes everybody currently working at a job—even part-time workers. The bureau also counts those temporarily laid off from a job to which they expect to return as employed. The remaining workers are asked whether they actively sought work during the previous week; if they did not, they are classified as "not in the labor force" rather than as unemployed. While this procedure might appear quite straightforward, consider the anomalies that result:

Bill Jones works forty hours a week and earns $240. Jack Smith averages only five hours weekly at odd jobs paying about $4 an hour, and his family barely scrapes by on welfare. The computers at BLS see no difference. Jones and Smith count equally in the official estimate of employed Americans.

Mary Jackson, a widow supporting three children, was laid off three months ago and is still job-hunting. Susan Whitaker, wife of a $100,000-a-year executive, wants to feel more independent, so she is looking for paid work. Susan's son, Tim, has registered with his college employment bureau for a Saturday job to earn money to buy gas for his car. BLS includes all three among the unemployed, without distinction.

Jim Dawson, a bachelor with simple needs, applied for an assembly-line job at a local factory four weeks ago and was offered a job as janitor, which he turned down. He has been taking life easy since then. Joe Jenkins looked for work unsuccessfully for more than two months and would still like a job, but he is so discouraged that he has quit looking. Dawson is listed as unemployed. Jenkins, by dropping out, has reduced total unemployment by one. He is classified as neither employed nor unemployed.

Grilling the BLS commissioner at a House Budget Committee hearing, one congressman objected to counting auto workers who receive generous unemployment benefits as jobless. Some of them in Ohio "were going to Florida and they weren't in too much of a hurry to get back in the wintertime to go to work," he said.

---

[31] Lee M. Cohn, "Counting the Jobless," *Washington Star,* May 25, 1977.

Box 3–2

Five myths about unemployment figures

Myth 1: Employment rises, unemployment always declines

The key word is *always*. The correct word is *often*, because sometimes the labor force will increase more than employment—because of new entrants attracted by improved job opportunities, population growth, statistical variability or other reasons—so unemployment will also rise.

Myth 2: Unemployment is involuntary

One definition of "voluntary" unemployment includes any unemployed person who will not accept a job unless it pays a higher wage than that person last received. Data shows that "voluntary" unemployment is not insignificant, amounting to about one third of all unemployed people with work experience. And unemployed people who "don't want to work" are not necessarily slothful, or any more slothful than the people who are employed. A person who is unemployed and doesn't want to work is one who doesn't want to work under certain conditions.

Myth 3: The lower the unemployment rate, the better

Certainly it is beneficial to reduce recession-level unemployment such as was experienced in 1982. But as economic expansion occurs and the labor market begins to tighten, the gains from additional jobs and economic growth diminish relative to the economic costs of rising inflation. There are differences of opinion among economists as to the lowest noninflationary rate of unemployment that is "safe" or "acceptable." For the current period most economists would probably say the rate is around 6 percent, although that figure could be reduced in the years ahead as the percentage of hard-to-employ young people in the population declines.

Myth 4: Nearly one out of every two black teenagers is unemployed

Despite all those references to black teenage unemployment rates approaching 50 percent, only one black teenager in ten is actually out of school, looking for work, and not finding it. Among both blacks and whites, teenagers accounting for the bulk of official unemployment are in school and looking only for part-time jobs.

Myth 5: Most of the unemployed are poor

Both in good times and bad in the last two decades the poverty rate for the unemployed (based on a cash income definition) has never been much

118

Box 3–2 (*concluded*)

more than one third. The poverty rate has not been higher both because of the availability of unemployment compensation and other cash benefits and because of the presence of other earners in households with an unemployed member.

Sources: Based on Herbert Stein, "Still at Work on Full Employment," *The Wall Street Journal*, February 13, 1986; Alfred Tella, "How to Be an Expert on Joblessness Figures," *New York Times*, July 18, 1983; and Ben J. Wattenberg, *The Good News Is the Bad News Is Wrong* (New York: Simon & Schuster, 1984).

Some critics say that BLS underestimates the magnitude of the problem, while other critics say that it actually overestimates it. How can this be? Many unemployed workers give up looking for jobs after a time. Why does the BLS not count these so-called discouraged workers as unemployed? Under the BLS, when people give up hope, official unemployment declines! (In 1984, the BLS estimated that about 1.5 million workers fell into this category.)

Those who maintain the BLS *overestimates* look at different figures. The unemployment rate of 1988, they argue, is not directly comparable to the unemployment rate of, say, 1960 simply because a larger fraction of all workers are young and women and these groups have always had relatively high unemployment rates. Another factor contributing to overestimation is the possibility that some would *say* that they are looking for work (and then be counted as unemployed) when they are not really interested in finding a job.

GATHERING AND ANALYZING THE EVIDENCE

These three examples—poverty, defense, and unemployment—serve, I hope, to destroy the notion that measurement of needs is a straightforward affair. Why, it may be asked, devote so much time to breaking this butterfly on a wheel? Answer: the problem of incompleteness or of bias in understanding a problem can lead to misleading, sometimes disastrous, conclusions. And the possibility is by no means confined to the three issues considered above.

Thus, it becomes essential that the intended users of the study, together with those persons responsible for the study, share a common understanding of the nature and scope of the issues at stake. A full and correct understanding of the nature of the problem will be aided by (1) considering its origin, if known; (2) reviewing legislative hearings, reports, and acts associated with it; (3) inquiring into the history of programs designed to deal with the problem; and (4) examining past analyses, evaluations, audits, and budget examinations of the same or related issues. Outlines and checklists can be helpful in this review.

The scope of a study depends both on the questions that it would be desirable to answer and on the availability of methods and data that will provide those answers. There is often a trade-off between the breadth of a study and the precision of the results. The planned scope should also consider the nature of the decisions that the study may affect. Similarly, an understanding is needed on the geographic coverage required (regional, state, local); on the areas, populations, individuals, or units to be included; and on the scope of coverage (how many individuals, approximately how much information from each, etc.).

Good, accurate data do not give answers to policy questions, but they do provide a basis for answers. The call for good information is not a call for the elimination of all subjectivity in policy analysis. The idea, rather, is simply this: we can be a little more comfortable with our policy decisions—regardless of how subjective they happen to be—when we know that our data base is as accurate as can be reasonably expected. The remainder of this section will explore specific ways in which that base—and hence our understanding of the problem—can be improved.

A brief note on statistics for policy analysis

First, let me state that readers with a basic understanding of statistics may safely proceed to the next subsection, Survey Research on p. 123.

Contrary to popular opinion, statistics is more than just data. We can define statistics as a body of methods for collecting, analyzing, interpreting, and presenting numerical data. The general purpose of statistics in the study of public policy is to furnish the analyst with the facts, in a convenient and summarized form, that will be the basis for wise recommendations.

Measures of central tendency. Once information is collected, it serves as the raw material for the statistician, who then analyzes and interprets the data.

One way to present data in a simple, easily understood way is to find the average. *Averages,* also called measures of central tendency, are numbers typical of a group of numbers or quantities. The term most often thought of as the average is the *mean,* the sum of all the items in the group, divided by the number of items in the group. For example, to find the mean weight of the Chicago Bears defensive team, which played in Super Bowl XX, one lists the positions together with their weights:

Position	Weight
RE	263
RT	308
LT	260
LE	267
OLB	225
MLB	228
OLB	232
RCB	187
LCB	188
SS	203
FS	196
Total	2,557

After totaling the weights, one divides the total by the number of defensive team members, so that the mean is

$$\frac{2,557}{11} = 232.4 \text{ pounds}$$

The advantages of the mean are ease of comprehension and speed of computation. One great disadvantage of the mean, however, is that it can be distorted by an extreme value at the high or low end. Obviously, additional methods of summarizing data are necessary.

When items or numbers are arranged from lowest to highest, the *median* is the midpoint, or the point at which half the numbers are above, half below. If the number of items is odd, the figure can be seen immediately. For example, rearranging the data on the Bears' defensive team it is apparent that the median is 228: There are five figures above it and five below. If there had been an even number—say the twenty-two players of both the defensive and offensive teams—the midpoint would be the mean of the two central figures.

Weight
187
188
196
203
225
228 ← Median
232
260
263
267
308

The median is easy to find and a great time-saver when items that are difficult to measure can be arranged in order of size. It also avoids the distortion caused by extreme values and is thus more typical of the data. In the study of the weights of the Chicago Bears, if the defensive right tackle's weight was 400 pounds instead of 308 pounds the median would not be affected.

The chief disadvantage of the median is that many people do not understand what it means. Moreover, it can sometimes be cumbersome to arrange items in order of size when there are many of them.

The *mode* is the number that occurs most often in any series of data or observations. The mode answers the question: "How frequently?" or "What is the usual size or amount?" For example, let us group the data on the weight of the Bears' defensive team as follows:

Class interval (pounds)	Number (frequency)	
185–210	4	← Mode
211–235	3	
236–260	1	
261–285	3	

Clearly, a slightly different picture emerges about the size of the Bears. As with the median, an advantage of the mode is that extreme values do not influence the average. The mode, however, should not be used when the total numbers of observation are this small. On the other hand, if one were interested in summarizing the weights of all players in the National Football League, the mode might be a useful measure.

Measures of dispersion. As useful as the various measures of central tendency are, they may present an incomplete picture of events; and this tends to destroy their usefulness. For example, given only the picture of the Bears defense that the mean, median, and mode provide, one might not expect to find one player over 300 pounds.

Measures of dispersion can, however, tell us how the individual items in a series are spread out. Two common measures of dispersion are described below.

The *range* is the difference between the low and high values in a series. The range of weights of the Chicago Bears was 120 pounds; the lightest player weighs 188 pounds and the heaviest weighs 308 pounds.

The statistical measure, *standard deviation* (σ), is a means for learning about all items in a distribution.

The basic approach to calculating standard deviation is to compare the mean with each item in the group to determine how far, "on an average," each item is from the mean. Table 3–2 shows the calculation

Table 3–2
Chicago Bears defensive team, standard deviation of the mean

Position	Weight (x)	Mean (x̄)	(x − x̄)	(x − x̄)²
RE	263	232	31	961
RT	308	232	76	5,776
LT	260	232	28	784
LE	267	232	35	1,225
OLB	225	232	7	49
MLB	228	232	4	16
OLB	232	232	–0–	–0–
RCB	187	232	45	2,025
LCB	188	232	44	1,936
SS	203	232	29	841
FS	196	232	36	1,296
				14,909

of the standard deviation of the mean weight of the Chicago Bears defensive team. What we have done is to take the difference between each player's weight *(x)* and the mean *(x̄)*, disregarding plus or minus signs because the values are later squared. The squared values *(x* minus *x̄)²* are totaled and divided by the number of items (11), and the square root is extracted. The standard deviation is $\sqrt{\dfrac{14,909}{11}}$ = 36.8 pounds.

When a large number of items are included in an analysis, they tend to follow a *normal distribution* such as shown in Figure 3–5. The center vertical line in the figure denotes the mean. This curve has a

Figure 3–5
Normal distribution

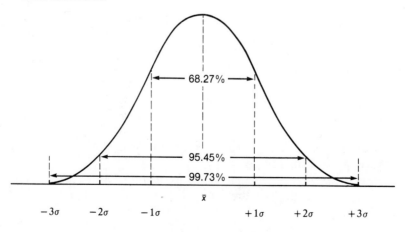

distinctively characteristic shape. We know, for example, that 68.27 percent of all the items in a normal distribution are included in an area ±1 standard deviation, that 94.45 percent are included in an area ±2 standard deviations, and that 99.73 percent are included in an area ±3 standard deviations. These relationships hold true no matter what the magnitude of the mean or standard deviation.

Survey research

In a democracy, policymakers must take into account what the people think about an issue. The most direct and potentially the most representative device for subjective assessment of citizen preferences is survey research. (Other devices to be considered include the Delphi technique and consumer analysis.)

Usefulness. Survey research can be used to reorient a policy to address citizen priorities or to set the boundaries within which policymakers act. Survey research, by eliciting citizen input, can help policymakers avert this tunnel vision, as the following story about a small Virginia town illustrates.

> The town manager and council members of this community felt they had a firm grasp on the service needs of area residents. These decision makers, as parents of school age children, were particularly enthusiastic about developing additional recreational facilities in the town. A swimming pool, tennis courts and possibly a golf course were planned. Alternative uses of available recreational funds suggested by several townspeople—such as the establishment of a crafts and recreation center in a former railway depot which had been deeded to the town—were not seriously considered. However, since a housing assessment survey of the community was planned, the town administrators decided to incorporate into the study an evaluation of public support for the proposed recreational facilities.
>
> The survey, a 20 percent random sample of all households in the town, precipitated reappraisal of the community's more pressing recreational priorities. While the majority of respondents stated that they and other family members would *never* use a pool (51 percent), golf course (69 percent), or tennis courts (57 percent), only 32 percent of the sample reported that they would never use the proposed recreational center. The survey also indicated that, not only would a center have a wider range of users than other proposed facilities, but that use would be more frequent. The decision makers, who believed they really "knew" their town, were astounded at the high proportion of retired residents living in the area. These individuals, having limited resources and little opportunity for social interaction, accounted for the differences in recreational priorities expressed through the community survey.[32]

---

[32] Gregory A. Daneke and Patricia Klobus-Edwards, "Survey Research for Public Administration," *Public Administration Review* 39 (September-October 1979), pp. 421–26.

Procedure. In designing a questionnaire to be mailed or a list of questions for interviewing, the researchers must avoid asking questions about complex issues for which citizens lack information. ("What do you think is the proper funding level for the Magneto Hydrodynamic Development Program?") Questions should also offer support ("Some people we spoke to said this, some said that, how do you feel?"). Avoid misleading or ambiguous questions ("How do you feel about honesty in government?"). Do not force or manipulate responses. (To show that a town really wants a new nuclear power plant, a utility might ask "How would you like your energy bill cut by a third?" and never mention the word nuclear.)

Many errors can be avoided—many bugs removed—if the research pretests the questionnaire on a small group of real respondents. Which brings me to the subject of sample size. The sample size depends on how much error is acceptable (±3 percent, for example) and the confidence interval (95 percent confident that the true answer is within 3 percent of the survey results).

Those surveyed should be selected randomly, that is, everyone in the targeted population has an equal chance of being selected. If a community has a relatively small minority population (e.g., recent Asian immigrants, aged, handicapped), it is possible that none of these individuals will be in the sample. To prevent this from happening, the researcher can *stratify* the population *before* selecting the sample. To stratify the population, the researcher divides it into subpopulations and selects from these.

Normally, a systematic cluster sample involving from 300 to 500 individuals will be sufficient for a community assessment. In the mid-1980s, the U.S. Census Bureau began quarterly surveys of American households in order to inform policymakers how many received direct benefits from the federal government (answer: one in three). For the survey, a sample of 36,000 households, chosen to be nationally representative, is used.

Analysis. Cross tabulations are frequency distributions of at least two categorical variables displayed in a tabular format such as Table 3–3. They enable comparison of group attitudes or behavior, as well as a statistical examination of the degree to which the variables influence each other.

A second method of analysis is a comparison of mean responses, categorized by group characteristics, to a series of related responses. This technique allows the researcher to determine needs both within and between groups. Table 3–4 illustrates how the technique can be used to differentiate between specific neighborhoods in a community. The mean rankings of services were calculated by neighborhood residence using a five-point scale with the following anchors:

1–very satisfied	2–satisfied	3–undecided	4–dissatisfied	5–very dissatisfied

Statistical pitfalls. Statistics tell some of the story, but not all of it. Averages, such as those appearing in Table 3–3, can blur the fact that the people that most frequently use recreational facilities might

Table 3–3
Support of proposal to increase expenditures for public housing by income

The data indicate that the support for public housing is significantly higher among low-income persons than among those of higher incomes. Generally speaking, since lower-income individuals seldom advocate programs and policies that suggest an increase in taxes, these findings point to an intensified level of perceived housing dissatisfaction within the low-income group in the sample.

Expenditure categories	Income categories		
	Low	Moderate	High
Spend more	47.6%	34.8%	29.3%
Spend same	38.7	47.2	21.7
Spend less	13.7	18.0	49.0

Significant at < .05 level
Gamma = −.35

The Gamma score (a statistic commonly used with nominal data) in Table 1 demonstrates that the negative relationship between the two variables is fairly strong and that discordant pairs predominate. In other words, low-income persons were more likely to respond "spend more," while high-income persons most often felt that administrators should spend less for public housing.

The statement means that the probability that the finding is accidental is less than .05, or one change in twenty. Many researchers have adopted $p = .05$ more or less as a cutoff point. Relationships with $p > .05$ (greater than .05) are usually called nonsignificant.

Source: Based on Gregory A. Daneke and Patricia Kobus-Edwards, "Survey Research for Public Administrators," *Public Administration Review* 39, September–October 1979, pp. 421–26.

Table 3-4
Mean satisfaction rankings of service delivery by neighborhood

Service type	Neighborhood		
	Maywood	Grayson	Oak Park
Police protection	4.43	2.95	1.53
Street maintenance	3.25	2.76	2.46
Quality of schools	3.83	3.02	4.48
Recreational facilities	3.87	2.45	2.05
Garbage collection	3.28	2.64	1.92

A comparison of the means with the first group indicates that Maywood residents are most concerned about the quality of their police protection. Dissatisfaction with recreational facilities and the quality of their schools are ranked second and third, indicating an ordering of need priorities.

Residents of Oak Park, on the other hand, appeared to be most concerned about the quality of schools in their area. Comparing means between neighborhoods illustrates relative differences in the overall dissatisfaction with the public services. Maywood residents generally gave a negative evaluation of the services which were analyzed as compared to Grayson and Oak Park residents. Only with respect to quality of schools was there some consistency in the responses between Maywood residents and the other two neighborhoods.

Source: Based on Daneke and Klobus-Edwards, "Survey Research for Public Administrators," pp. 421–26.

be highly satisfied with them. Or, to take a real rather than hypothetical example, overall poverty rates do not reveal dramatic changes in the composition of poverty: it has fallen sharply among the elderly, while it has soared among children. Specifically, the poverty rate in 1986 was about the same as it was in 1966—a little over 14 percent. But during the same period, poverty among the aged dropped from almost 30 percent to under 15 percent. Poverty among children reached a low point in 1969, then climbed rapidly and soared 38 percent in the past five years. Today, about 22 percent of America's children are considered poor.

Averages also hid the fact that within the black community a bifurcation, a pulling away process, has occurred. Some blacks did quite well after the beginning of the Great Society. Middle-aged black males narrowed the employment gap with whites throughout the 1960s. Black workers were narrowing the wage gap as well, especially in the upper brackets. By 1980, black males in professional and technical occupations were making 86 percent of the salary of their white counterparts and black females were making 98 percent, much closer to parity than they had been twenty years earlier. When additional factors are taken into account—differences in education, years of experience, and so on— some surveys find that the black-white income discrepancy nearly vanishes. But these agreeable generalizations hold true for only selected segments of the black population—namely, those who were at least in their middle twenties (the older the better) by the time the Great Society began and those of any age who got a good education and remained in the labor force.

Overall, the median income of black families was 56 percent of the median for white families in 1985. But black couples in which both partners had jobs came closer to their white counterparts. Median family income for such couples was 82 percent of the median for white couples in which husband and wife both worked. Structural differences between black and white families help explain the differences in income and poverty. Female-headed families account for 44 percent of all black families, but only 13 percent of white families.[33]

Despite the convenience and compactness of averages, the preceding examples should serve to remind us that data sometimes can be too aggregated; in such cases, to put it inelegantly, the analyst must deaggregate.

Another pitfall might be termed *freeze-frame statistics*. Take this frequently cited statistic: the richest 20 percent of Americans receive more income than the bottom 70 percent combined. And research finds that the trend is as flat as Lake Placid. Figure 3–6 shows how the richest and poorest have kept their relative shares of income almost constant since 1960. To make the case that free markets produce an unequal distribution of income, some deem no other data necessary.

But what if the people who constitute the top 20 percent and the bottom 20 percent are constantly changing, bubbling up and down rather than remaining frozen? According to the University of Michigan's Panel Study on Income Dynamics, from 1971 to 1978, about 52 percent of the families who started off in the top bracket shifted to a lower bracket, and 45 percent of those who started in the lowest bracket moved up. The overall conclusion: family-income mobility is "pervasive at all income levels."[34] Such movement (which overthrows conventional views of

---

[33] U.S. Bureau of Census, *Current Population Reports*, series P-60, No. 146.
[34] Duncan, et al., *Years of Poverty*, pp. 74–78.

128

Figure 3–6
Trend in concentration of income

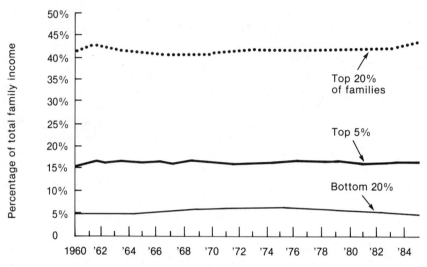

Source: U.S. Census Bureau, *Current Population Reports,* series P-60, No. 149.

income share) would be invisible to the freeze-frame statistics used to measure fairness.

Delphi technique

Participation, John Stuart Mill argued, is the first principle of democracy. Government officials, in other words, are not to make decisions in a vacuum.

Though it developed relatively late in Western political thought—principles of liberty and civil rights clearly precede it—citizen participation has surely proved a powerful doctrine: Western democracies, perhaps especially the United States, seem continually to be evolving new ways of letting citizens participate in the policy process: the Freedom of Information Act, sunshine laws, advisory committees, and so on. The trend has lagged somewhat but otherwise paralleled the trend toward the increasing professionalization of government service. Assuming that these trends hold, the second half of the twentieth century might be seen as a period during which bureaucracies and legislatures became more, not less, accessible to outside influences exercised by *citizens.* If this evolving concept of participation is to persist, it is essential that the public increasingly be provided in advance with the essential data on which basic decisions about public policy are made.

In this section we will consider another channel through which the needs of citizens can be assessed in order that policymakers can know the public's needs in advance.

Since 1966, much has been said and written about policy planning in health. At the core of all these discussions is the point that effective policy planning in this sector depends largely on an assessment of the health needs of the target population—be it a neighborhood, a community, a region, or a state. Despite such common acknowledgment of this point, very little attention is focused on methods for actually assessing health needs. In some cases, these needs are merely assumed to be known in advance; in others, the needs are identified on the basis of experience in the existing health care delivery components, or the perceptions of individuals involved in the delivery process, or estimates extracted from partial data collection. The Delphi technique, however, provides information from the people served.

But first: What is the Delphi technique? Forecasts by panels and committees—while usually better than forecasts by individual experts—are not without drawbacks. To overcome such problems, in the early 1960s, RAND researchers introduced the Delphi technique, designed to improve the use of expert opinion through polling based on three conditions. First, the experts do not know who is on the panel or, at the very least, do not know what predictions and critiques are associated with each individual. Second, the forecasts are structured so that respondents reply with a year of predicted occurrence (sometimes under different probabilities). The results are collated, and the median is computed. Some Delphi studies now also display extreme estimates (the highs and the lows) as well as the number of "nevers." And finally, the summation is returned to panel members who are urged to challenge or support predictions that fall very far away from the median and to make new predictions. The arguments and the new data are circulated; then counterarguments are circulated.

Why not apply this method of group consensus as a means of assessing health needs? In 1974, a ten-county region of central Texas with a population of about 600,000 was studied in this manner.[35] Because of the trial nature of the project, only a limited panel of 130 individuals was selected to participate.

The study itself consisted of a preliminary questionnaire round and three problem evaluation questionnaire rounds. The open-ended preliminary questionnaire was designed to elicit responses concerning the panelists' view on current and future health care problems in the region.

---

[35] Milton F. Schoeman and Mahajan Vijay, "Using the Delphi Technique to Assess Community Health Needs," *Technology Forecasting and Social Change* 10 (1977), pp. 203–10.

After a careful review of the variety of problems mentioned, nine were selected by the study staff as the most commonly considered, with a tenth added after the first round because of widespread interest. These problems were stated on the problem evaluation questionnaire as follows:

1. Underutilized and duplicated facilities and equipment.
2. Absence of effective preventive medical and dental health programs.
3. Lack of physicians (either shortage or poor geographic distribution).
4. Poor coordination of health-related social services (mental health, welfare, social security, public health, and education).
5. Lack of knowledge by the public of available health services and/ or how to gain access to these services.
6. Inaccessibility to health services due to location of facilities or lack of transportation.
7. High cost of health care.
8. Lack of personal concern and understanding of the patients by those who provide health services.
9. Inadequate emergency care.
10. Lack of health care personnel other than physicians (such as nurses and aides).

The evaluation questionnaire listing these problems was then sent to the panelists who were to assess the relative importance of the problems. Specifically, the panelists were asked to distribute one hundred points among the problems so as to reflect their order of priority and relative importance.

The results of the problem evaluation questionnaire were then analyzed: group averages and the range of responses given by the middle 50 percent of the panel) were computed. This information was then redistributed for two more rounds. Panelists whose responses fell outside of the middle 50 percent range were required to give reasons for their extreme opinions. A synthesis of these reasons was provided in the third round to assist the panelists in reconsidering and possibly revising their previous opinions. The study illustrated nicely an important trait of the Delphi technique: with iteration and feedback, the distribution of individual responses narrows.

Consumer analysis

Like the Delphi techniques, consumer analysis provides a more sophisticated approach to needs assessment than does the straightforward opinion survey. Consumer analysis premises that, after an organization has determined who its clients are, it will need to build up its understanding of these people. To do this, it must have a method of learning and monitoring the clients' needs. But a great many organizations and legislatures remain satisfied with simpleminded pictures of their clients' needs and wants. Too many public administrators and legislators assume that they can simply observe and intuit what their clients are like, what they want, how they see, and how they react.

In contrast, the market-oriented organization considers client research and analysis to be items of the highest priority. Indeed, it sees the client as the starting point for its thinking and policy planning. And it knows how to probe its clients' needs, perceptions, preferences, and satisfaction on a systematic and periodic basis.

Need measurement, however, is not an easy task. Philip Kotler of Northwestern University notes three major problems.[36] First, the concept of need is not well defined; it is used interchangeably with such terms as *want, desire,* and *demand.* For example:

> A patient in a hospital may want a doctor to visit her five times a day, the nurse to sit continuously at her bedside, the meals to be great, and the room to be large, single-occupied, attractive, and quiet. These represent an admixture of needs, wants, and desires. The hospital is not able to respond to all of her needs. It will try to distinguish between her "real" needs and her "trivial" needs.

Second, people are not always able to express their needs or wants clearly. Consider this example:

> A public housing commission recently decided to build new low-cost housing according to the ideas and wishes of the eventual users rather than the ideas of architects. After all, urban planners have been terribly wrong in the past about the type of housing that would meet the needs of the urban poor; many buildings have subsequently had to be torn down. The commission interviewed low-income families to learn their needs and desires with respect to how high the building should be, how many rooms each apartment should have, how big the kitchen should be, how the halls should look, and so on. To their surprise, they found that many of the families could not describe their ideal apartment or fell back on describing the housing in their past experience, which if taken literally, means rebuilding the same high-rise jungles they had before.

Third, it is difficult to assess the intensity of the different needs that people mention having. The Committee on National Priorities wanted to determine the relative importance to Americans of such values as clean air, safe streets, and stable prices. It found that respondents had great difficulty in rating the relative importance of these needs.

But Kotler has also noted three methods for learning the needs of

---

[36] Philip Kotler, *Marketing for Nonprofit Organizations* (Englewood Cliffs, N.J.: Prentice-Hall, 1975), pp. 128, 177, 178.

individuals: (1) they might be asked to describe their needs directly; (2) they might be asked to respond to vague material on which they will end up projecting their needs; (3) they might be given an experience with a real or prototypal gratification object to help them clarify their needs. Let us take a closer look at these three methods.

Marketing researchers use a variety of questioning techniques to assess client needs. They may conduct an interview with a single individual or lead a focused group discussion. They may use open-end questions (e.g., "What recreational facilities would you like to see added in the park?") to elicit opinions and clues as to the individual's needs and desires. Closed-end questions may also be included (e.g., "Rate each of the following city services on a scale of how much improvement is needed"). While open-end questions have the advantage of providing more insight than closed-end questions, they are more difficult to code and summarize.

Richard T. Coffing has proposed a client-need-analysis methodology that goes considerably beyond other methods based on direct questioning. The methodology requires the researcher to go through several steps. First, identify the decision maker who needs the client demand data—politician, health care provider, educational administrator, and so on. Then, identify the clients—users of services, employees, members, taxpayers, students, and so on. Next, identify the areas of interest to the decision maker. At this point, the researcher is ready to question a carefully chosen sample of clients about their needs. The objective is to have the clients determine and state their needs in the form of unambiguous statements about what they would like to see. The clients are asked to state their desires, to assign priorities, and to indicate what evidence would convince them that these desires are being met by the decision maker. A prepared statement of each client's needs is shown subsequently to the client who is asked to verify that the statement accurately reflects his or her desires. Coffing and his associates have applied this methodology to assessing the desires of the clients of the Veterans Administration.[37]

The direct questioning method assumes that clients are aware of their own needs and are willing to share the information with interviewers, but there are many issues about which clients may not know or want to share their true feelings. Kotler gives this example: high school students asked for more study periods when what they really wanted was less work. Thus, the needs that are verbalized may mask the real

---

[37] Richard T. Coffing, "Identifying Non-Market Client Demand for Services," Paper delivered at the 1973 annual meeting of the American Educational Research Association, New Orleans (February 25, 1973).

needs operating in the individual. If the organization responds to the verbalized needs, it might find that this still does not satisfy the clients.

Obviously, then, the organization must probe into the underlying motivational dynamics of its clients so that it can offer services that will meet real needs. A branch of consumer research called motivational research challenged the value of large-scale surveys that ask scores of superficial questions. Motivational research proposed instead that real knowledge of motivation would be better gained by interviewing a smaller sample of consumers in depth. The trained interviewer would involve the person in any one of a number of exercises that were designed to produce data that would be carefully analyzed to reveal the deeper needs and motives shaping consumers' attitudes toward the product. Box 3–3 describes four main techniques that were developed by psychologists and have been applied in motivational research.

A third method of probing consumer needs is to present a prototype of a possible solution to a need and let the client experience and respond to the solution. For example, many low-income families find it hard to articulate their wants with respect to new housing that might be designed for them. As a possible stimulus, they might be shown pictures of different room sizes and arrangements and asked to comment on what they like and dislike. Or they might be taken to model apartments. Their reactions can thus be analyzed.

Indirect assessments

Often, in making assessments, techniques such as sampling, Delphi, and consumer analysis are not feasible. For example, suppose that you wanted to know the number of heroin addicts in the South Bronx. Sampling would be difficult, since addicts are not always home, waiting eagerly to be interviewed by some social scientist. In addition, sample surveys may take too long when policymakers need immediate answers.

In such a situation, one has several options. One option is to simply avoid making any assessment or, more likely, to quote someone else's assessment (or guess). Another option is to make your own assessment by thinking about what you already know and about how you might adjust known but quite appropriate data. We call this *indirect assessment*. If the message of the preceding discussion was that people often think they know more than they actually know (and therefore should use such techniques as the sample survey), then the message of this discussion is that people sometimes really know more than they think they know.

The simplest application of indirect assessment is to use a single related uncertain quantity to assess another. For example, say that you wanted to know the amount a heroin addict spends on heroin in a

134

Box 3–3

Techniques of motivational research

1. *Word association.* Here subjects are asked to name the word that first comes to mind when each of a set of words is mentioned. The interviewer might start out by saying "tall," and a subject might respond "short." After a while, the interviewer might say "charity" and the subject might respond "guilt." By slipping in key words related to "the act of giving," the interviewer hopes to infer the associations that people make with giving to charity.

2. *Sentence completion.* Subjects are given a set of incomplete sentences and asked to finish them. One sentence might start: "The basic reason most people give to charity is _____." Another might start: "The main complaint people have about charity drives is _____." Sentence completion tests are very helpful in revealing people's attitudes and motivations. When a sentence is worded around the behavior of other people, subjects express their own feelings more freely because they are attributing those feelings to others.

3. *Picture completion* (called the Thematic Apperception Test, or TAT). Subjects are shown a vague picture and asked to make up a story about what they see. Or they may be shown a cartoon involving two people talking to each other, with one of the remarks deleted. A cartoon might show a volunteer fund raiser ringing a doorbell and stating, "We hope you can contribute $5 or more to skin disease research." Subjects are asked to fill in the words of the homeowner. If they say, for example, "I don't think you should tell me how much to give," this suggests something about their attitudes toward being told how much to give.

4. *Role playing.* Here one or more subjects are asked to act out a given role in a situation that is described in the briefest terms. For example, one subject may be asked to play the role of a successful business executive alumnus of a major university and the other the university president asking for a larger contribution. Through role playing, subjects project much of their needs and personality into the amorphous situation, thus providing useful clues on fund raising.

Source: Philip Kotler, *Marketing for Nonprofit Organizations* (Englewood Cliffs, N.J.: Prentice-Hall, 1975), p. 128.

---

year. It might be easiest to think first in terms of how much a heroin addict spends on heroin a day and then to multiply that number by 365.

Raiffa suggests a couple of ways of "thinking-up" a related uncertain quantity to assess.[38] The first is to assess in different units. Thus, instead

---

[38] Howard Raiffa, *Analysis for Decision Making* (Chicago: Encyclopedia Britannica, 1974).

of a number (e.g., the number of households that have been robbed in city Q), assess only a small proportion to determine the percentage that have been robbed and then multiply that percentage by the total number of households. The second is to assess an adjustment factor. Thus, to assess the percentage of annual housing construction that uses electric heating in Lansing, Michigan $(\tilde{y})$, look up the percentage of annual housing construction that uses electric heating in the United States (k) and then assess the ratio of $\tilde{y}/k$. (Note that we distinguish the assessed or estimated quantity by placing a tilde over the letter that represents it.) If this ratio is multiplied by k, you will have an estimate of the percentage of annual housing construction in Lansing that uses electricity for heating.

Suppose that you were asked to assess the number of dairy cows in the United States. Knowing very little about agriculture and having mislaid your World Almanac, how would you begin to find an answer? One strategy is indirect assessment using two or more related uncertain quantities. This is how it works:

To assess: $\tilde{y}$ = Number of dairy cows in United States
Given: k = Population of United States
Assess: $\tilde{x}_1$ = Milk consumption per person per day
$\tilde{x}_2$ = Ratio of production to consumption
$\tilde{x}_3$ = Milk production per cow
Then: $\tilde{y} = k\tilde{x}_1 (\tilde{x}_2/\tilde{x}_3)$

A frequently used strategy in indirect assessment is decomposition. The three standard methods of decomposition are (1) segmenting, (2) factoring, and (3) segmenting and factoring.

1. The objective in segmenting is to decompose an uncertain quantity into parts that can be *added* back together. For example:

To assess: $\tilde{y}$ = Total value of property stolen in a city
Assess: $\tilde{x}_1$ = Value stolen through shoplifting
$\tilde{x}_2$ = Value stolen through housebreaking
$\tilde{x}_3$ = Value stolen through holdups
$\tilde{x}_4$ = Value stolen through car thefts
$\tilde{x}_5$ = Value stolen through embezzlement
Then: $\tilde{y} = \tilde{x}_1 + \tilde{x}_2 + \tilde{x}_3 + \tilde{x}_4 + \tilde{x}_5$

2. In factoring, the objective is to decompose an uncertain quantity into parts that can be *multiplied* back together. The methodology with which the U.S. Geological Survey estimates oil reserves is a case in point:

To assess: $\tilde{y}$ = Amount of oil ultimately recoverable in the coterminous United States and the adjacent continental shelves

Assess: $\tilde{x}_1$ = Number of billion feet of exploratory drilling remaining
$\tilde{x}_2$ = Average billions of barrels of crude oil discovered
per billion feet drilled

Then: $\tilde{y} = \tilde{x}_1\tilde{x}_2$

3. Segmenting and factoring can be used in combination. The basic objective here is to assess the uncertain quantity for various parts of a population and then to calculate the weighted sum. For example:

To assess: $\tilde{y}$ = Proportion of Americans with sickle-cell anemia
Given: k_1 = Proportion of people age 0–19
k_2 = Proportion of people age 20–39
k_3 = Proportion of people over 40
Assess: $\tilde{x}_1$ = Proportion of people age 0–19 with sickle-cell
anemia
$\tilde{x}_2$ = Proportion of people age 20–39 with sickle-cell
anemia
$\tilde{x}_3$ = Proportion of people over 40 with sickle-cell
anemia

Then: $\tilde{y}$ = $k_1\tilde{x}_1 + k_2\tilde{x}_2 + k_3\tilde{x}_3$

Using segmenting and factoring should suggest other approaches for indirect assessment. Indeed, since there are several ways to assess the same uncertain quantity, it is sometimes best to proceed like a surveyor who takes several different sitings. Raiffa calls this approach, for obvious reasons, triangulation and suggests the following illustration of its application.

To assess $\tilde{y}$ = Number of heroin addicts in New York City
a. Assess: $\tilde{x}_1$ = Total value of addict crime (you can get this figure
by adjusting down the total crime cost)
$\tilde{x}_2$ = Average crime per addict (based on how much
money you think they need)
$\tilde{y}$ = $\tilde{x}_1\tilde{x}_2$
b. Given: k = Number of addicts on the narcotics register
Assess: $\tilde{x}$ = Proportion of addicts on the narcotics register
$\tilde{y}$ = $k/\tilde{x}$
c. Given: k = Number of addicts in jail (remember that the
police usually check prisoners for marks on
incarceration)
Assess: $\tilde{x}$ = Proportion of addicts in jail (one fourth? one
third?)
$\tilde{y}$ = $k/\tilde{x}$
d. Given: k_1 = Number of people in age category 1

Assess: $\bar{x}_1$ = Percentage of people in age category 1 who are
heroin addicts
$$\bar{y} = k_1\bar{x}_1 + k_2\bar{x}_2 + k_3\bar{x}_3$$

With these four sitings we should be able to have a tighter, more creditable estimate of the actual number of heroin addicts in New York City. Of course, when two or more sitings turn up roughly the same assessment, our confidence increases. Conversely, if we get widely disparate assessments, we might want to rethink our estimates and assumptions.

Correlation and causation

While sampling may provide valuable information, analysts often need to know more than the percentage of this or that; they need to know the *relationship* between two variables or among three or more. For example, do persons who have been in the Job Corps have a better employment record than their counterparts who have not? Does the cost of property destroyed in floods along a particular stretch of the Mississippi River increase with the amount of dredging? Analysts look for patterns in the relationship between the variables. Does the industrial injury rate go down as the number of inspections by the Occupational Safety and Health Administration goes up? Finally, analysts may want to search for a third, fourth, or more independent variable that might make the dependent variable rise or fall. The cost of collecting trash in a city has increased steadily over the last decade. What variables have most influenced cost?

Clearly, addressing these kinds of questions can lead policymakers to shift resources or to modify programs in significant ways. This section focuses on ways in which explanatory theories about public issues can be stated and tested by using descriptive statistical analysis.

Correlation is the tendency for two phenomena to vary together. If you measure the height of the Chicago Bears and how much they weigh, you will find that, on the average, the taller players are also the bigger players. That is a correlation; it *suggests* that height causes weight, but it does not prove it absolutely, for it deals only with averages. Some players who are tall are light (at least for professional football players), some who are short are heavy. The correlation shows only that height is *likely* to be connected with weight. As we will see later, many correlations exist that are not due to any causal connection between the two phenomena.

Relationships between attributes. Perhaps the most important point about correlation can be summarized in an eight-word question: "What do the other three boxes look like?" Now, let me explain what that

138

Figure 3–7
How to think about relationships between variables

	Patients with disease	Patients without disease
Patients with symptoms	37	33
Patients without symptoms	17	13

means. Suppose a physician has seen thirty-seven patients with a particular symptom who, on closer examination, are found to have a particular disease. Is it reasonable for the physician to conclude that there is a relationship between the symptom and the disease? Before the physician makes that inference, she should ask herself the eight-word question. If she did, she might come up with the 2×2 table shown in Figure 3–7.

The other three boxes are quite revealing. True, among people with the disease 68 percent, or thirty-seven out of fifty-four, had the symptom. But look at the right-hand column: among people *without* the disease 71 percent, or thirty-three out of forty-six, had the symptom. There is no variance of one factor when the other factor varies; that is, there is no correlation. The physician might also note that more people *without* the symptom were sick than well (seventeen as compared with thirteen).[39]

What causes crime? Crime inflicts so much harm on so many people every day that policymakers would certainly like a good answer to that perennial question. One widely held view among sociologists, jurists, and journalists is that social forces cause crime and that the individual is not fully to blame for his or her behavior. More than a handful of judges and legislators have said that we will never resolve the problem of crime without first addressing its roots in poverty and social injustice. Unfortunately, this view gets in the way of serious thought about alleviating the crime problem. The implication that the criminal is really a victim clouds the legitimacy of punishment. The focus on long-range social goals diverts attention from the limited steps that might make a worthwhile difference today.

---

[39] J. Smedslund, "The Concept of Correlation in Adults," *Scandanavian Journal of Psychology* 4 (1963), pp. 165–73. Cited in Morton Hunt, *The Universe Within* (New York: Simon & Schuster, 1982), pp. 185–86. For additional examples, see Grover Starling, "Three New Issues in the Logic of Policy Analysis" *Policy Studies Review* 5, 2 (November 1985), pp. 207–13.

By asking, in effect, "What do the other three boxes look like?" James Q. Wilson and Richard J. Herrnstein, both of Harvard, avoid this trap. In fact, they distill the case against social causation to one brief passage:

> During the 1960s one neighborhood in San Francisco had the lowest income, the highest unemployment rate, the highest proportion of families with incomes under $4,000 per year, the least educational attainment, the highest tuberculosis rate, and the highest proportion of substandard housing of any area of the city. That neighborhood was called Chinatown. Yet in 1965, there were only five persons of Chinese ancestry committed to prison in the entire state of California.[40]

Wilson and Herrnstein are aware that circumstances such as poverty affect human development. (Who is not?) But they insist on asking why circumstances affect different people so differently. "Many children may attend bad schools," they note, "but only a small minority become serious criminals. . . . Economic conditions may affect crime, but since crime rates were lower in the Great Depression than during the prosperous years of the 1960s, the effect is, at best, not obvious or simple."

To try to simplify the description of some of these relationships—between a symptom and a disease, between social conditions and crime—statisticians have adopted special terms. When high scores on one variable go with high scores on another, they are said to have a *positive association*. On the other hand, when high scores on one variable go with low scores on another, they are said to have a *negative association*, or you could say that they are *inversely related*.

The concept of correlation. When the relationships between the variables are linear (that is, they generally go up in a straight line when plotted on a graph) statisticians sometimes calculate a formula to express that line algebraically. Such a line is called a *regression line*, or *line of best fit*. In the next chapter, we will see how such a line can be used in forecasting.

Of course, real relationships do not fall neatly along straight lines. *Correlation coefficients* express how much difference there is between the general relationship expressed by the regression line, and the actual relationship between the two scores. For example, a policy analyst might compare the extent of insurance coverage in different states over a period of years and find a strong positive correlation between the extent of coverage and the price of hospital care. That is, hospital prices rise as more people are covered. In sum, the primary use of correlation analysis is to measure the strength of a relationship between variables—such as the relationships between the extent of insurance coverage and the

---

[40] James Q. Wilson and Richard J. Herrnstein, *Crime and Human Nature* (New York: Simon & Schuster, 1985), p. 459.

140

Figure 3–8
Correlation of insurance coverage and hospital costs (hypothetical)

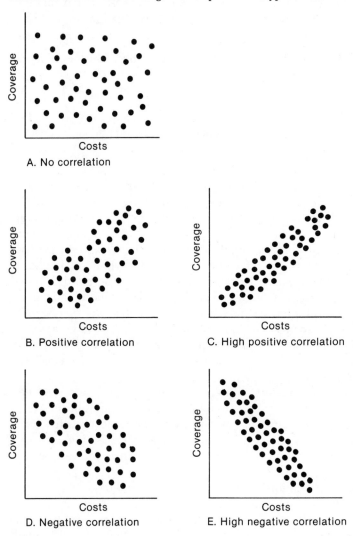

A. No correlation

B. Positive correlation

C. High positive correlation

D. Negative correlation

E. High negative correlation

price of hospital care. When the analyst plots the data, several relationships might appear. The scatter diagrams in Figure 3–8, where each dot might represent a state, show five hypothetical possibilities.

A coefficient of linear correlation, r, can be derived for each of the five sets of data in Figure 3–8. The strength of the relationship is determined by the effect any change in one variable (e.g., insurance coverage) has on the other (e.g., hospital costs). In the figure, 3–8A, r is very

Table 3-5
Standardized regression coefficients (beta weights) showing variance in the level of use and satisfaction with recreational services by selected sociodemographic factors

Sociodemographic factors	Recreational facilities assessment	
	Use	Satisfaction
Age of head of household	−.35	.12
Family income	.19	−.05
Length of residence	.02	.21
Number of family members	.28	.02

Source: Based on Daneke and Kobus-Edwards, "Survey Research for Public Administrators," pp. 421–26. *Public Administration Review* (September–October 1979).

close to zero. In Figure 3–8C and 3–8E, *r* approaches +1 and −1, respectively. Only if the data fell on a straight line, slanting either to the left (indicating a negative association) or to the right (indicating a positive one) would *r* be exactly 1.

The basic principles of regression may be applied to the analysis of community survey discussed earlier (see Tables 3–3 and 3–4). Through the examination of regression coefficients, regression enables the researcher to assess the contribution of a specific independent variable to the variation in a dependent variable. Suppose, for example, policymakers are interested in learning which characteristics of citizens are most likely to explain the use of and satisfaction with the various community services. Table 3–5 shows how the technique can be used. By examining the relative differences between the regression coefficients for age of the head of household, income, length of residence in the locality, and number of family members, the researcher can estimate which group characteristics best explain use of and satisfaction with recreational services. Of the four variables selected, age is the best predictor of whether community recreational services are used. A negative coefficient indicates that, the younger the head of household, the higher the use level. Length of residence has a negligible influence on service utilization.

Statisticians have a useful way to express the regularity of such patterns. It is called "explaining the variance," which simply means that one can calculate the percentage of variance that is accounted for by the hypothesized "causes" being considered. (In our example, the "causes" are sociodemographic factors.) If a factor can explain 100 percent of the variance, then the researcher can "predict" the use and satisfaction levels for every citizen. If a factor explains none of the variance, then the researcher might as well guess at random.

In this instance, only one variable—the length of residence—explains more than 20 percent of the variance in satisfaction of those respondents who used the services. This figure is not too bad. Social scientists have been known to buy a round of drinks when they can explain just 30 percent of the variance.

An application. The calculation of r involves fairly elementary mathematics, but the number of operations required can often make the process long and laborious. Fortunately, this is no longer true thanks to the wide availability of desktop statistical calculators and microcomputers which make the calculation of r simple. Nonetheless, it is important to see the mechanics of this operation. Among other things it will provide the basis for an important forecasting technique to be presented in the next chapter, least-square trend estimation.

We will need to work with concrete data, so let us pick a couple of subjects virtually everyone is interested in—salaries and baseball. Table 3–6 shows the average salaries paid by major league baseball teams in 1985 and the number of games won in the 1985 regular season.[41] The computation of r is illustrated in Table 3–7 with the above data modified for ease of compilation.

We have not shown a strong relationship between the two variables. But, if we had, we would not be through. Two crucial methodological questions would remain—one concerns *significance,* the other *validity.*

Significance deals with the question of whether the observed results are very likely to be different from chance. Say that we wanted to see if there was an association between party affiliation and sex. In a sample of eight, we found that four men were Democrats and four women were Republicans. This is a strong relationship indeed. But is it significant? I would be inclined to think it was just chance. But, if the sample were of 800 and the same proportions held—all men being Democrats, all women Republicans—I would no longer be able to attribute this to mere chance. Therefore, statisticians should test for significance. (How this is done is beyond the scope of this discussion.)

Validity deals with the question of whether the relationship is really what the researcher thinks it is. Validity also refers to whether data were gathered properly. Salaries of baseball players might be suspect since owners might understate the figures in order to keep wage demands from other players down. Validity can also refer to whether the relationship would hold for a future set of data.

---

[41] Data on salaries from *New York Times* (December 4, 1985); data on team records from *The World Almanac & Book of Facts 1986* (New York: Newspaper Enterprise Association, 1985), pp. 878 and 881.

Table 3–6
Salaries paid and games won, 1985 season

Team	Average salary	Games won 1985
Yankees	$546,364	97
Atlanta	540,988	66
Baltimore	438,256	83
California	433,818	90
Milwaukee	430,843	71
Los Angeles	424,273	95
Chicago Cubs	413,765	77
Detroit	406,755	84
San Diego	400,497	83
Philadelphia	399,728	75
Pittsburgh	392,271	57
Mets	389,365	98
Boston	386,597	81
St. Louis	386,505	101
Toronto	385,995	99
Kansas City	368,469	91
Houston	366,250	83
Oakland	352,004	77
Chicago White Sox	348,488	85
Cincinnati	336,786	89
San Francisco	320,370	62
Montreal	315,328	84
Minnesota	258,039	77
Texas	257,573	62
Cleveland	219,879	60
Seattle	169,694	74

Causation. A statistical correlation between two variables does not necessarily demonstrate a *causal relationship* between them. For example, if we note time and time again a larger number of fire trucks around the bigger fires, are we to conclude that the number of fire engines (X) determines the fire damage (Y)?

While it may be easy to recognize that fire engine–fire damage relationships are spurious and that the size of the fire (C) drives both X and Y, in other situations the identification of such spurious relationships might be more difficult. Take, for example, cancer research. Some psychotherapists believe that the cancer victim usually has a psychological orientation that increases the chances of getting cancer. In evaluating this hypothesis, it is essential to consider the possibility that between an emotional imbalance (X) and a malignant tumor (Y), some intervening factor (C)—such as a hormonal disturbance—might exist.

When trying to infer causation from correlation, the policy analyst needs to be aware of five types of relationships besides X→Y (X causes change in Y).

Table 3–7
Linear correlation: An illustrative example

Salaries (X) (in thousands of dollars)	X^2	Wins (Y)	Y^2	XY
546	298,116	97	9,409	52,962
541	292,681	66	4,356	35,706
438	191,844	83	6,889	36,354
434	188,356	90	8,100	39,060
431	185,761	71	5,041	30,601
424	179,776	95	9,025	40,280
414	171,396	77	5,929	31,878
407	165,649	84	7,056	34,188
400	160,000	83	6,889	33,200
400	160,000	75	5,625	30,000
392	153,664	57	3,249	22,344
389	151,321	98	9,604	38,122
386	148,996	81	6,561	31,266
386	148,996	101	10,201	38,986
386	148,996	99	9,801	38,214
368	135,424	91	8,281	33,488
366	133,956	83	6,889	30,378
352	123,904	77	5,929	27,104
348	121,104	85	7,225	29,580
337	113,569	89	7,921	29,993
320	102,400	62	3,844	19,840
315	99,225	84	7,056	26,460
258	66,564	77	5,929	19,866
258	66,564	62	3,844	15,996
220	48,400	60	3,600	13,200
169	28,561	74	5,476	12,506
9,405	3,687,223	2,101	173,729	768,052

$$r = \frac{n(\Sigma\, xy) - (\Sigma\, x)\,(\Sigma\, y)}{\sqrt{n(\Sigma\, x^2) - (\Sigma\, x)^2} \cdot \sqrt{n(\Sigma\, y^2) - (\Sigma\, y)^2}}$$

$$r = .24$$

The first we have already seen in the fire truck example: X is spuriously related to Y. The possibility is illustrated in the following equation:

A slight variation of this relationship is illustrated by the following equation:

Consider the relationship between welfare benefits *(X)* and poverty *(Y)*, state by state, between 1969 and 1979.[42] In this period, the ten states that spent the least on AFDC experienced a decline in their poverty rates, but only four of the ten states that spent the most experienced a reduction in their poverty rates. I suspect there is more to the story than meets the eye. Except for Arizona, all the states that spent the least were in the South. The 1970s was a time of relative prosperity for the South, especially the oil-producing states; for the North, it was a time of transition as old industrial plants closed and new high-technology industries struggled to get started. I submit therefore that region was an important variable in the equation.

A second possibility is that *C* intervenes between *X* and *Y*. The president's efforts *(X)* to encourage toxic waste cleanup may seem to elicit subsequent public compliance *(Y)* even though how well he persuades state and local officials to comply *(C)* may be the intervening relationship. Symbolically:

$$X \rightarrow C \rightarrow Y$$

For years, women have been outliving men. Scholarly articles have suggested that women, not men, were really the stronger sex. Some researchers speculated that women were inherently stronger because of genetic characteristics. Some said higher estrogen levels help protect women from cardiovascular disease, the leading killer—thus they live longer. Some said more men were dying because of job stress. In short, it was gender *(X)* that explained longevity *(Y)*. But more recent research finds that all those studies missed the point; gender did not have a *direct* link to longevity. Gender did relate to smoking, however, as men tend to smoke more than women. If we control for smoking by calculating life expectancies solely among lifelong nonsmokers, the life expectancy tables between men and women are virtually identical. In fact, in some age groups, men actually have a longer life expectancy.

A third possibility is that *C* comes before *X* and *Y* and is not related to *X* or *Y* but conditions the effect of *X* or *Y*. For example, attitudes *(C)* may be a prior condition for a graduate of a work force training program getting a job. Symbolically:

---

[42] See U.S. Social Security Administration, *Social Security Bulletin,* June issues, 1969 to 1979.

$$C \rightarrow X \rightarrow Y$$

In the United States, a handful of elite universities and service academies produce a disproportionate number of influential people. Should we explain the success of the graduates on the quality of those four years, or on the selection process these institutions follow? (The only sure way to know is to order the next freshman classes at Elite U. to attend State U. instead, and then see how many still manage to become successful political leaders, National Academy of Science members, corporate executives, and generals. (Not a likely experiment.)

A fourth possibility is that Y is actually driving X. Symbolically:

$$X \leftarrow Y$$

To illustrate, let us return to the issue of what causes crime. The view that society is at fault often involves unproven assumptions about which way causality runs. Did these young men become criminals because they live in a high-crime neighborhood, or is it a high-crime neighborhood because so many people like them live there? Youthful criminals are often unemployed, but does the unemployment cause the crime—or does crime get in the way of employment? "Suppose some people find that crime is more profitable than working, even though jobs at decent wages are available," Wilson and Herrnstein write. "They would tell government agencies they are unemployed when in fact they are working at crime."[43]

Lastly, we come to one of the most harmful mistakes a policymaker can make: to infer that certain actions produced a desired result, when the result was due simply to the normal tendency of events to regress from the unusual to the usual or due *entirely* to some other factor. The mistake is an ancient one: it is the one that says that if Y follows X, then X has caused Y. (Also known by its Latin name: *Post hoc, ergo propter hoc*, "After this, therefore because of this.")

In his *Losing Ground* (1984), Charles Murray points out that unemployment among young blacks soared the moment that the social programs of President Lyndon Johnson's Great Society began in the mid-1960s.[44] While I am willing to concede that the Great Society programs may have had some of the disincentives Murray notes, the more important cause, it seems to me, was not these programs but the start of stagflation (i.e., slow or no growth coupled with high inflation). This was coupled with industrial transition in the North and other economic ills that hit the less stable, secondary segments of the American economy (where

---

[43] Wilson and Herrnstein, *Crime and Human Nature*, p. 318.

[44] Charles Murray, *Losing Ground: American Social Policy, 1950–1980* (New York: Basic Books, 1984).

many blacks worked) earlier and much harder than the stable, primary—and white-dominated—segments.

Here is a more recent example of the *post hoc, ergo propter hoc* fallacy. In his 1986 State of the Union Message, President Reagan correctly observed that Scholastic Aptitude Test (SAT) scores began to dramatically rise in 1981 (the first year of his administration), but his implication that those increases were a consequence of his administration's policies is uncorroborated by reliable evidence. The only systematic research that I know of that might help explain such a rise focuses on family size and birth order. More specifically, an only child is exposed primarily to his parents' well-developed vocabularies and adult decision processes. This type of environment facilitates the child's mental growth. In contrast, a child with five older siblings is exposed primarily to immature individuals, whose vocabularies, intellectual processes, and approaches to life's uncertainties are mostly undeveloped. Thus, on the average, large family size is related to poorer intellectual growth in children. Because the SAT is usually taken by seventeen-year-olds, we would expect increases in SAT scores since 1980 to correspond to decreases in average family size beginning in 1963. One need only look at U.S. census data from the 1960s to see how true this correspondence is.[45]

THE POWER OF NUMBERS

The last half of this chapter has been concerned largely with numbers, as will later chapters. The reason for this focus should be made clear. From body counts in Vietnam to economic forecasts in the 1980s, the power of numbers in policy debates has been noted by bureaucrats, lobbyists, members of Congress, and presidents, all of whom struggle to come up with the best numbers to make their cases. Numbers are the tools policymakers use to buttress their views. The secret is not to be fooled by them.

Numbers often set the boundaries of policy debates and sometimes determine the outcome. One side of the House of Representatives supports the administration's contention that a 13.5 percent increase in military spending is essential, while the other side argues that a mere 3.5 percent would be adequate. Both sides formally agree somewhere in between. The administration argues that its economic programs have reduced inflation and thereby assisted the poor. Congressional opponents charge that because of these policies, the poor suffer a net annual loss of $280. Debates go on.

Whether at a congressional hearing, agency meeting, or dinner party,

[45] See Robert Zajonc, "Family Configuration and Intelligence," *Science* 192 (April 16, 1976), pp. 227–36.

persons with the numbers tend to set the tone of the discussion and their figures have to be debunked before their arguments can be refuted. Some observers think that the Pentagon wins most battles against the State Department because it comes up with the numbers, while the State Department is more amorphous, less given to exactitude.

When someone says, "Did you know that there are 27 percent more something than last year?", we must be alert to the *fallacy of misplaced concreteness*, to the notion that numbers can be manufactured to convey an aura of spurious exactitude. Policymakers and analysts must be skillful at using numbers, but they must also recognize how slippery some of them are.

Herbert Kaufman, a political scientist formerly with the Brookings Institution, recalls how a cabinet secretary was once asked to estimate the cost of a proposed change in social security. He put the figures at $600 million to $700 million. The committee chairman asked for a more specific figure, and the witness promised to return with one the next day. The secretary left the hearing room, had lunch, saw a movie, enjoyed dinner, watched television, and came in the next morning with a precise figure: $627.3 million. The chairman was pleased.[46]

Not long ago, I recall hearing on the radio that the Washington-based Community for Creative Non-Violence (CCNV), an advocacy group for the homeless, claimed that there were 2.2 million homeless in 1980 (the time of the last census). Knowing that the population of Kansas was roughly that size, I tried to conjure the image of the entire population of that state—man, woman, and child—sleeping on park benches in our dozen largest cities. It just did not make sense. So I tried a different tack. The population of the United States in 1980 was 226 million, 110 million of whom were employed and therefore unlikely to be homeless. That leaves 116 million Americans, many of whom were spouses of employed Americans or retirees drawing social security. Of these, 67 million were seventeen years old or younger. For purposes of estimation, I assumed that the vast majority of the under-seventeen population were at home or in school. That leaves 49 million Americans that fit the general description of the homeless: an unemployed adult. Since the CCNV had focused on the urban homeless, and I knew that 74 percent of Americans live in urban areas, I adjusted the 49 million downward to 36 million. Now the original estimate could be put in some perspective: 6 percent of unemployed adult Americans living in urban areas supposedly were on the streets. As this simple paper and pencil exercise shows, you do not need sophisticated research techniques to see that the 2.2 million figure is preposterous. Only through repetition has it become conventional wisdom.

To conclude, if you are going to use a number, you should know

---

[46] Quoted in *New York Times*, June 5, 1984.

where it comes from, how reliable it is, and whether it means what it seems to mean. The garbage-in, garbage-out (GIGO) problem has been with us a long time. As the great British economist Sir Josiah Smith once put it: "the Government [is] very keen on amassing statistics. They collect them, add them, raise them to the *n*th power, take the cube root, and prepare wonderful diagrams. But you must never forget that every one of these figures comes in the first instance from the village watchman, who just puts down what he damn well pleases."[47]

FOR FURTHER REFLECTION

1. A few years ago, the National Collegiate Athletic Association (NCAA) adopted new requirements for freshman participation in varsity sports. "Proposition 48" ruled that no first-year student could compete in intercollegiate athletics unless he or she achieved both a "C" average in a high school core curriculum and a combined score of 700 (out of a possible 1600) on the Scholastic Aptitude Test. What was the problem the NCAA was trying to address? How else might the problem have been defined?

2. Using indirect assessment, estimate *(a)* the area of Mexico and *(b)* the numbers of people who would benefit from expenditures to make mass transit accessible to handicapped people.

3. Policymakers tend to neglect geography almost as much as history when trying to understand a problem. Iran, Nicaragua and South Africa are three nations that profoundly concern policymakers and all Americans. Discuss the problems each country presents Washington from a *geopolitical* standpoint.

4. In *Beyond Belief: The American Press and the Coming of the Holocaust* (1985), Deborah E. Lipstadt cites examples of how the most horrifying news about Nazi enormities were tucked away on inside pages of American papers. In December 1942, for example, when the *Chicago Tribune* covered a major report in which Nazi-occupied Poland was described as "one vast center for murdering Jews," the paper put the story on page eighteen next to a marriage announcement. The previous month the *New York Times* had run a story about a statement from a member of the Polish National Council that a million Polish Jews had already been killed. It appeared on page sixteen, next to a report on the hijacking of a truckload of coffee in New Jersey. Such editorial decisions were the norm, not the exception, and there was relatively little improvement until the very end of the war. How do you account for this excessive skepticism?

---

[47] Quoted in Robert J. Samuelson, "The Joy of Statistics," *Newsweek*, November 4, 1985, p. 55.

5. Discuss possible limitations in the following statistics:
   a. The average family in the United States was better off financially in 1985 than in 1980.
   b. Government average payment to a farm in 1984 was $3,621.
   c. There were thirty-seven rapes per one hundred thousand population in 1984.
   d. In Georgia, defendants who kill white victims were eleven times more likely to be sentenced to death than those who killed blacks.
   e. Black family income, in constant 1980 dollars, declined by 4 percent from 1970 to 1980; the ratio of black median family income to white went from .61 to .58.
   f. In the 1950s only about 33 percent of all cancer patients survived five years. Now it is 50 percent.
6. Assume that you have operable lung cancer and must choose between two treatments—surgery and radiation therapy. Of one hundred people having surgery, ten die during the operation, thirty-two (including those original ten) are dead after one year, and sixty-six after five years. Of one hundred people having radiation therapy, none die during treatment, twenty-three are dead after one year and seventy-eight after five years. Which treatment would you prefer? What principle do you think this question illustrates?
7. How would you define poverty? Does poverty have a cause?
8. A certain town is served by two hospitals. In the larger hospital about forty-five babies are born each day; fifteen babies are born each day in the smaller hospital. Although the overall proportion of boys is about 50 percent, the actual proportion at either hospital may be greater or less than 50 percent on any day. At the end of a year, which hospital will have the greater number of days on which more than 60 percent of the babies born were boys?
   a. The large hospital.
   b. The small hospital.
   c. Neither—the number of days will be about the same (within 5 percent of each other).
   What statistical principle does this question illustrate?
9. Assume that you wanted data from your community regarding population, housing, school enrollment, income, employment, crime, transportation, and taxes. Where would you look?
10. Assume that you have asked your local librarian and several key public officials for help in finding the data asked for in question 9. They give you extensive files, bibliographies, and reports on each subject, but the data may not always be directly relevant to the task you need the information for. Are you correct in assuming that more information will improve your judgment as to what the

true conditions are likely to be? Circle one: Yes, No, or Not necessarily.

11. Imagine an urn filled with white balls and black balls. You know that two thirds of the balls are one color and one third are the other, but you do not know which color predominates. One blindfolded person plunges a hand into the urn and comes up with three black balls and one white ball. Another uses both hands and comes up with fourteen black balls and ten white balls. Both samples suggest that black balls are more numerous. Which sample provides the more convincing evidence?

12. For the data below, answer the following questions:
    a. Which pair is more strongly correlated (Y,X) or (Y,Z)?
    b. For which pair should the fraction of variance explained be largest?
    c. What trick might you employ to improve the correlation for the worse of the pairs?

Y	X	Z
2	12	1
4	14	4
6	16	9
8	18	16
10	20	25

13. After Ronald Reagan's election in 1980 a two-pronged attack was made on rising health costs. The first came from the business community, which pays for about a third of all health-care expenditures through employer-paid health insurance premiums. It sought to control the rise in its premiums by forcing employees to share a greater proportion of their health-care bills at point of consumption, and by encouraging them to join Preferred Provider Organizations (PPOs) or Health Maintenance Organizations (HMOs). Under a PPO, a business firm (and/or its insurance carrier) seeks price concessions from a limited set of doctors and hospitals who render care on a fee-for-service basis.

The second cost-containment effort was made in the federal medicare program for the aged. In 1983, that program abandoned its erstwhile policy of reimbursing each hospital for the full costs of treating medicare patients in favor of a phased transition toward compensating individual hospitals according to a schedule of flat fees for some 500 distinct Diagnostically Related Groupings of medical cases (DRGs).

Has the problem of rising health-care costs been alleviated? A comparison of growth rates in health expenditures in nominal dollars (dark line) and constant 1985 dollars (dotted line) is given in Figure 3–9. What insights do these data provide?

152

Figure 3–9
Health expenditures

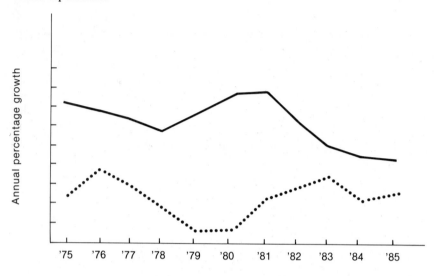

14. The politics of criminology mirror the politics of crime. Any complete
account of why people commit crimes must include two elements:
a description of how criminals differ from noncriminals and an explanation of how they got that way. In most cases, however, conservative criminologists emphasize the psychological differences between
criminals and noncriminals, while liberals emphasize the social circumstances that produce these psychological differences. Indeed,
extreme liberals sometimes argue that there are no stable psychological differences between criminals and the rest of us, and that criminals are just ordinary people who find themselves in especially
trying or tempting circumstances. The extreme conservative position, in contrast, seems to be that social circumstances have nothing
to do with crime; some people are just born rotten. A survey of
criminal convictions among Danish males adopted by nonrelatives
who have never been convicted of a crime is provided below. What
insights do these data provide?

	Convictions per one hundred adoptees	Actual number of adoptees
Natural parents had:		
no convictions	33	2,492
one conviction	42	574
two convictions	54	233
three or more convictions	80	419
All adoptees	41	3,718

Source: Estimated from data in Sarnoff A. Mednick, William F. Gabrielli, and Barry Hutchings, "Genetic Influences in Criminal Convictions: Evidence from an Adoption Cohort," *Science*, May 25, 1984, pp. 891–94.

15. By 1980, fully 45 percent of married women with children under six were employed, and the proportions were even higher for other categories of women of working age (overall, 60 percent of women work outside the home). The trend began as long ago as 1890, but it accelerated threefold after 1950. What were the causes of this trend?

16. What concept does the following excerpt from *Business Week* (July 25, 1983) illustrate:

> In fact, the rising average age of Americans virtually guarantees that the United States will continue to demand more medical care. And the advent of modern, high-cost medical techniques means that care is going to cost more.
>
> That raises extremely difficult moral and ethical questions, "including whether Americans want to pay $50,000 to $100,000 for care of an eighty-five-year-old patient whose quality of life is gone," observes Dr. Harvey B. Karsh, a doctor of internal medicine in Denver. People are unwilling to talk about such issues, he maintains. But "someone soon is going to have to make some decisions."

17. Foreign investment in the United States, which has risen sharply since 1980, has caused anxiety among many Americans. How real is this problem?

Chapter 4

Prognosis

THE NAIVE FORECASTING MANIFESTO

This chapter is about the future or, more precisely, how analysts forecast the probable course of problems and policies. It builds on four assumptions that should be made clear from the start.

The first is that *forecasting is not prophecy*. The techniques described in this chapter seek to discern the future in today's trends and conditions. The trick is to know where to look.

There is at least one dependable (though not perfect) crystal ball for inspecting America's future. It is a powerful one, helping policymakers answer important questions like the following: When will policymakers have to think about building schools—or closing them? Will the crime rate keep on veering downward? Will there be a decline in the number of volunteers for the military, creating pressure for a draft? Answers to those questions, and many more, can be extracted from a single, simple source—the population by years of age. There's nothing speculative about that crystal ball, it is not based on projections, but on people already born.

If you know how many Americans are now eight years old, you have a good idea how many will be of college age in 1994. If you know how many women are now twenty-two, you can estimate how many births are likely in 1989. Thinking about such variations confirms Yogi Berra's view: You can observe a lot by watching. It is also possible to forecast—not divine—events such as famine in Africa. Just *observe* the dynamics of the process. A series of survival thresholds are crossed before a community leaves home and is classified as famine victims. These thresholds give fairly reliable early warning.

First year: the family lives off the surpluses of previous good years.

Second year: the men and older boys range further afield selling their labor in the surrounding nondrought areas.

Third and fourth years: people are selling off their livestock.

Fifth and sixth years: household goods and family possessions are sold.

Seventh and eighth years: personal possessions and jewelry are sold.

Toward the end of the decade: when all possessions have been sold, the community sets off to the nearest better-off area in search of food and wages.

The community settles: food prices increase because of the extra strain on food resources; conversely, in the now saturated labor market supply exceeds demand and wages fall.

Finally: the enlarged community falls prey to hunger and is forced to move; thus, small pockets of hunger merge and grow until eventually the government, or the world's news media, declares that there is a famine across a whole region.[1]

If this sequence of survival mechanisms could be identified early (say in the first two or three years) and remedial action taken through modest development aid (seeds, hoes, pumps), the famine could be prevented or at least minimized.

The second assumption of this chapter is that *forecasting should avoid crisis-mongering*. Even the best minds can be seduced by the possibility of some future catastrophe. In 1865, William S. Jevons, an economist, wrote *The Coal Question* to express his fear that British industrial growth would halt because the country's coal reserves were running out. Yet, well over a century later, Britain still has enough coal to protect the industry and the jobs of more than 100,000 miners against competition from imports. Jevons also forecast that the price of coal would rise as it became scarcer. Instead, the real price of coal in Britain rose hardly at all between the 1870s and the early 1970s. Jevons failed to anticipate fully the development of substitutes for coal, of new engines, and of other technologies that made more economical use of fuel.[2]

The dire population forecasts of Thomas Malthus are better known. In 1803 he warned that population would always continue to increase sufficiently to hold real wages at low levels unless young men and women delayed marriage and had fewer children. Yet, for most of the following 150 years, real wages in Britain increased despite a rapid

---

[1] Brian W. Walker, "When Famine Gives Early Clues," *New York Times*, March 2, 1985.

[2] Charles Maurice and Charles W. Smithson, *The Doomsday Myth: 10,000 Years of Economic Crisis* (Palo Alto, Calif.: Hoover Institution Press, 1984).

growth in population and a lowering of the average age at marriage. Malthus failed to foresee the continuous advances in technology after the Industrial Revolution and the desire for small families in modern economies.

The fact that outstanding thinkers like Jevons and Malthus could not foresee future developments any better should have taught modern forecasters a lesson. But sober judgments seldom compete successfully for attention with crisis-mongering, and in the 1960s and 1970s, the spirit of Malthus spoke again in numerous forecasts of runaway world population growth that would destroy the environment and economic development. The ghost of Jevons presided over the fear that the world would run out of fossil fuels. Many voices warned also of an environmental crisis, a nuclear crisis, and an urban crisis.

The available evidence is not kind to these forecasts. Estimates made in the 1960s of future world population growth have already been revised downward substantially as China, India, and other developing countries have reduced their birthrates. Some developed countries have begun to worry about families that are too small and about birthrates that are below the level necessary to prevent declines in their population. The apparent shortage of fossil fuels merely reflected the high prices received by OPEC. These prices induced both conservation in fuel use and the discovery of alternative supplies that have seriously weakened the oil cartel and temporarily ended concerns about an energy squeeze.

The third assumption is not unrelated to the second. *The accuracy of a forecast is inversely proportional to the square of its timeframe.* This means that as we try to peer farther into the darkness of the future the accuracy of our forecast drops off sharply. See Figure 4–1.

This limitation is not all bad. If we had perfect knowledge of the future, we might find ourselves so overwhelmed in trying to plan for the crises of today that we would simply give up. But even if we could act, we would still be unable to foresee and calculate the consequences of our actions for more than a year or two.

Therefore, we should not try to see too far ahead. But what is "too far"? To answer that, we must remember why we are concerned with the future: because securing a satisfactory future may require actions in the present. "Any interest in the future that goes beyond this call for present action has to be charged to pure curiosity. It belongs to our recreational rather than our working day."[3]

The fourth assumption is best expressed in the engineering acronym KISS (*Keep It Simple, Stupid*). As we career toward that magic year 2001,

---

[3] Herbert A. Simon, *The Sciences of the Artificial* (Cambridge, Mass.: MIT Press, 1981), p. 184.

Figure 4–1
A major purpose of forecasting: To narrow the range of uncertainty

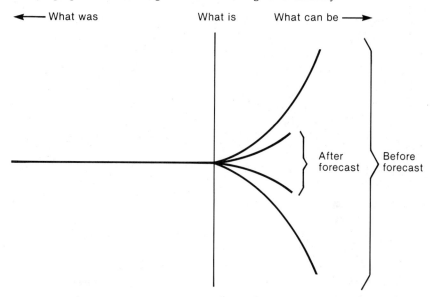

interest in forecasting has grown. With that growth has come increasingly sophisticated techniques like the following:

- *Catastrophe theory:* A methodology to forecast trends where small changes in one variable produce large changes—a catastrophe—in another variable. Examples are economic depression and political revolution.

- *Econometric models:* Systems of equations estimated from past data that are used to forecast economic variables such as GNP, unemployment, and changes in price level. Using highly sophisticated statistical techniques and containing over 200 equations, large econometric models are also used to forecast the effects on the economy of alternative government policies—for example, to estimate the effects of the Tax Reform Act of 1986 on GNP and unemployment.

- *Cross-impact matrix:* A table that lists potentially related events along row and column headings to assess how the occurrence of one event will affect (cross-impact) the likelihood of another.

- *Input-output matrix:* A table that shows the interdependencies between consuming and producing units in society. The numbers entered in the cells of the table express the proportion of one unit's output to another unit's uses. Thus, input-output analysis could show the economic impact of a decline in auto sales on the glass and the leather industries.

Judiciously used by qualified people, techniques like these and others can make important contributions to the forecasting enterprise. But they are costly, time-consuming, and often too clever by a half. As every armchair quarterback knows, good blocking and tackling—not complex playbooks—get teams to the Superbowl. Accordingly, this chapter stresses the forecasting fundamentals:

  I. Models and modeling
 II. Economic models
III. Trend extrapolation
        Structural change
        Cyclic change
 IV. Monitoring
  V. Using experts

MODELS AND MODELING

The concept of modeling is fundamental to policy analysis and, for reasons that will soon be apparent, is linked inextricably to our third core idea, the systems view. In light of the fact that models appear at all stages of policymaking, it is appropriate that we begin this chapter by reviewing the experience in modeling in various fields and unifying those elements of the modeling process that appear most relevant to policy analysis.

What is a model?

A model is a *simplified* representation of some part of reality. Because society is too complex to copy exactly and because much of the complexity is irrelevant to the policymaker's purpose, the essence of a model is simplification. For example, you do not have to specify the color of the carpet in every house in a community in order to develop a land-use planning model for it. On the other hand, the model must have a level of complexity sufficient for the uses to which models are put— namely, to enhance prediction and to facilitate understanding. If you do study the performance of the economy, a model that ignores international trade is probably too simple to do either very well.

There is then a definite link between understanding and prediction. When we can identify functional relations or cause-effect relations between events, we can then construct better models to predict the occurrence of future events, and in some cases we can cause the occurrence of future events through the control of key variables.

The idea of modeling is hardly new. Ancient astronomers had models of the universe they saw, Roman engineers probably modeled their aqueducts, and medieval architects their cathedrals. Of particular historical interest is Sir Issac Newton's inverse-square model of gravitation. In this model, each mass throughout the universe attracts every other mass. The force of attraction between two masses, M_1 and M_2, increases in direct proportion to their product, and decreases in proportion to the square of their distance d. In the language of mathematics, this can be stated in this form

$$F = c \frac{M_1 M_2}{d^2}$$

in which F is the force of attraction, and c is a constant. To Newton, this equation was a model that explained many phenomena and served as the frame for understanding and predicting such diverse events as free fall of objects, tides, motions of planets, and oscillation of a pendulum. Each of these events, it is important to note, becomes understandable only when put in the larger frame of gravity.

Similarly, when we claim to understand a person's behavior on a particular occasion, we mean that we view it as part of a more complex pattern of behavior, a larger frame, that characterizes this person or people in general. Indeed, we might even say that understanding of any phenomenon—falling apples, a person's hostile behavior, or some social issue—stops when we cannot find a frame for the idea or event that we wish to understand. We understand an event or a problem only when we identify it as part of a larger frame.

The growing use of models. In recent years, the recognition has grown, certainly among students of public policy, that models can be applied to more than physical systems. Why this growth? First, the manipulation of people, organizations, and communities is now frowned on and often outlawed. Moreover, large-scale social experimentation can be quite expensive.

Second, the amount of uncertainty with which policymakers must deal has increased considerably. To the extent that models enhance prediction and facilitate understanding, they help lower the level of uncertainty and the number of costly errors.

Third, the ability to build models that are good representations of all kinds of phenomena has improved since World War II, when the government invested heavily in operations research work aimed at tackling logistical problems. Computer capabilities have also increased dramatically. Most new models in policy analysis owe their strength to the interaction between these methodological improvements and computer developments.

Models and theory. Webster's defines theory as a formulation of apparent relationships of certain observed phenomena (e.g., force of attraction and distance) that have been verified to some degree. How then are theory and models related? The short answer is *intimately.* Model building *supports* the development of theory.

But there are subtle differences between a model and a theory. A model is a simplified representation; a theory is a broad, systematic explanation. Furthermore, theory is generalized to include all specific cases, whereas models seldom include more than a few specific situations. A general community of experts determines the acceptability of a theory, whereas a particular group of analysts or organization decides on the acceptance of its own models. However, analysts should always prefer models with a strong foundation in theory.

Basics of model building

From the preceding discussion, it should be clear that a model is not the real thing—it is an abstract representation of reality. The representation may emphasize form and content. For example, the taxonomical model signifies more than a list of relevant variables; at its most basic level, it is an ordered list. In the biological sciences, we have this well-known hierarchical arrangement.

Kingdom
  Phylum
    Class
      Order
        Family
          Genus
            Species

Let us consider the taxonomy of objectives for choosing an air pollution control program for a city (Figure 4–2). It is a map or catalog that allows us to structure the decision problem. This includes identifying all objectives and selecting, for each of these, a measure of effectiveness that can be used to indicate the degree to which the objective is met.

Rather than emphasize form and content (like Figure 4–2), a model may emphasize functions and operations for serving a purpose. Suppose a team of analysts wanted to help a fire department improve its policies and programs. By building a model of fire department operations (Figure 4–3), the team would have a better sense of where to focus their research.

Whether they emphasize form and content (like Figure 4–2) or functions and operations (Figure 4–3), models evolve, that is, they change as new understanding is gained, and old models give way to new ones

Figure 4–2
A complete taxonomy of objectives for choosing an air pollution control program for a city

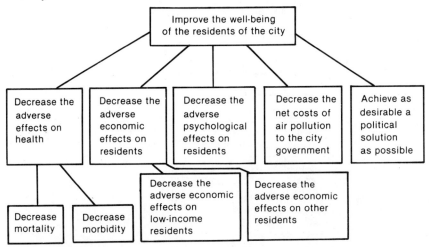

that are more useful and productive in achieving the purpose for which they were constructed in the first place.

Initial stages of modeling. The modeling process at the early stage consists of these fundamental steps. First is to establish the purpose of the model (e.g., "To better understand the state's persistent housing shortage," or "To predict the relationship between actual population size and population carrying capacity of the world by the year 2100"). Next is to determine the elements that appear relevant to that purpose. Then elements are aggregated or chunked together by virtue of the strong connection between them. Suppose, for example, one were trying to model a state's housing problem. Condition, location, environment, tenantry, and cost might be aggregated into a chunk called "Existing Housing Stock." Similarly, social and psychological factors, purchasing power, and tenant preferences might be chunked as "Tenant Characteristics."

This process of modeling permits decomposing the model into smaller parts and enhances the analyst's ability to deal with complexity. The weakly linked parts are studied separately and then the completed model is synthesized from the constituent parts. Complexity is a function of the number of links between elements—not the number of elements. Even in extremely sophisticated models purporting to predict the future of world population, only five chunks or aggregated elements appear:

Population

Capital

Food

162

Figure 4–3
A model of fire department operations

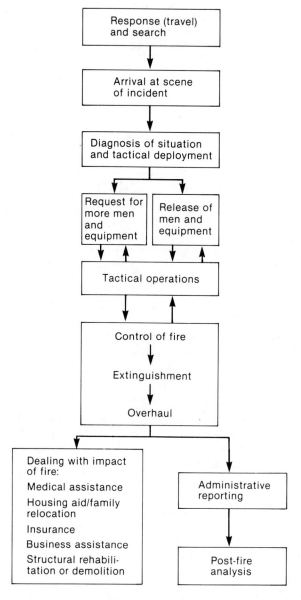

Source: Adopted from Edward H. Blum, *Urban Fire Protection: Studies of the Operations of New York City Fire Department* R-681 (New York: New York City-Rand Institute, 1971), p. 107.

Natural resources

Pollution

The dynamic behavior of the model. Regardless of its complexity, the dynamic behavior of every model depends, in the final analysis, on two kinds of relationships—positive and negative. To better understand these relationships, let us more closely consider food and world population.

Two major variables measure world growth: industrial capital and population. Investment *positively* affects industrial capital (factories, machines, vehicles, equipment), but depreciation (through obsolescence, and wear and tear on machines and equipment) *negatively* affects it (Figure 4–4A). Population, meanwhile, is positively influenced by the birth rate and negatively by the death rate (Figure 4–4B). If the flow

Figure 4–4
Positive and negative relationships in model building

(A)

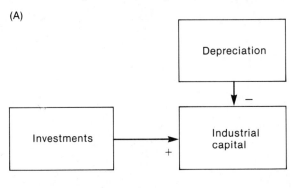

(B)

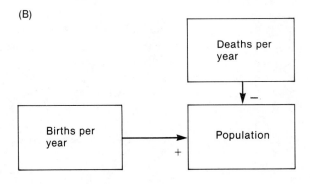

164

Figure 4-5
The Malthusian model

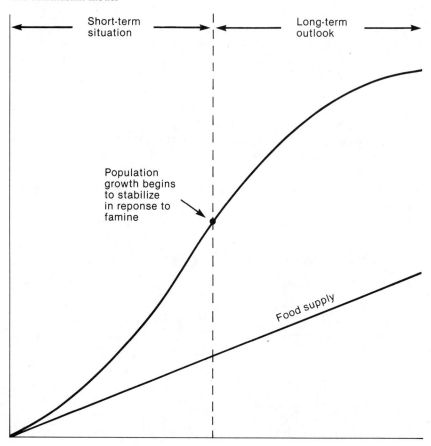

of investment is equal to the flow of depreciation, or if births equal deaths, a state of dynamic equilibrium is achieved—a stationary (not static) state called zero growth.

What will happen then when several flow and state variables interact? Consider a simple model, the well-known Malthusian model.[4] World resources of food grow at a constant rate, that is, a linear, arithmetic progression, while world population grows at a rate that is itself a function of population, that is, a nonlinear, geometric progression. Thus,

---

[4] Thomas Robert Malthus (1766–1834) was an English economist, sociologist, and pioneer in modern population study.

Figure 4–6
The Malthusian model redrawn

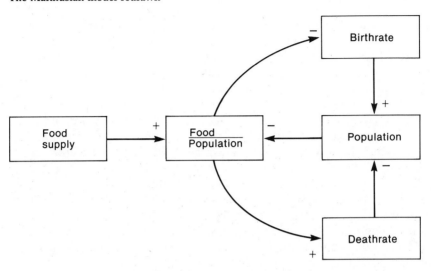

as the left side of Figure 4–5 indicates, the food supply increases at a constant rate, while the population increases at an accelerating rate. The decisive variable becomes the quantity of food available to each individual (Figure 4–6). A decrease in this variable leads to famine and eventually an increase in deaths per year. The population growth curve stabilizes in an S-curve, which is typical of growth limited by outside factors, as the right side of Figure 4–5 indicates.

Equations corresponding to the various relationships between variables can be programmed on a computer in order to verify the validity of certain hypotheses: What would happen if the birth rate doubled? If it were reduced by half? If food production doubled or tripled due to technological innovation? The present example is of only limited interest because it is such a rudimentary model; in the presence of several hundred variables, however, the simulation can achieve valuable results. Instead of modifying one variable at a time, it uses a computer to simultaneously set in motion groups of variables in order to produce a real life situation. A simulation can also be used to give in real time the answers to different decisions. Examples of the application of simulation are found in many areas of public policy: *ecology*—effects of atmospheric pollutants, concentration of pollutants in the food chain; *city planning*—growth of cities, appearance of slums, automobile traffic; and *social problems*—growth of aged population, housing shortages, and drug addiction.

Heroin addiction: A case study in modeling

To better illustrate the construction and use of a model, we will consider a model of the heroin problem developed by Mark H. Moore.[5] The beauty of this model is that it allows us to concentrate on small components without losing sight of how these components fit together to make the larger problem. Ideally, the model will: (1) suggest simple terms for summarizing and comparing the effects of different policies; (2) identify the major, distinct components of the problem that can be attacked by government intervention; (3) facilitate the sorting of policy instruments into subsets that attack the same component of the problem; (4) alert us to interdependence among attacks directed at different components; and (5) explicitly introduce the dynamics that cause the size and character of the problem to change over time.

Let us begin by asking what factors determine the number of users. Well, as a first cut at an answer, we can say that the number of users is determined by the rate *into* and *out of* the population of users. Each of these two rates can be broken down into several flows, which are shown in Figure 4–7.

A careful study of Figure 4–7 leads to an important insight: small changes in the relative size of these flows can lead to surprisingly large differences in the number of users. And the insight has policy implications: each of these flows might be an important target of government programs and policies. "In general, the government's objectives should be to expand flows out of the population and reduce flows into the population. The obvious exception is the objective to reduce the rate at which users die: deaths among users constitute a major cost of the heroin problem and signal the failure of government programs."[6]

Another critical question for the modeler is, What factors influence the behavior and condition of the user? While the user's level of heroin consumption is undoubtedly a major factor influencing behavior and condition, it would be wrong to assume that the use of the drug, in and of itself, accounts completely for the user's state. A number of other influencing factors could be present: the habits, skills, and attitudes that shaped the user's life before he or she went on heroin; the set of opportunities accessible to the user; the user's participation in supervised programs; and finally, the prohibition of the manufacture, distribution, and possession of heroin.

Figure 4–8 is a dynamic model of the heroin-using population that comprehends most of the factors just discussed. It is a powerful means

---

[5] Mark H. Moore, "Anatomy of the Heroin Problem: An Exercise in Problem Definition," *Policy Analysis* 2, 4 (Fall 1976), p. 659.

[6] Ibid.

Figure 4–7
Critical flows in the heroin problem

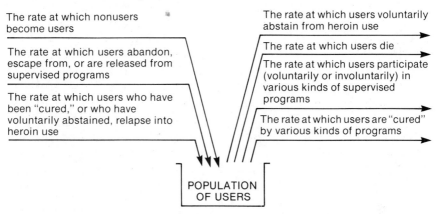

by which we can organize our analysis of the heroin problem. Moore's
discussion of it is incisive and worth quoting at length:

> The factors determining the number of users are straightforwardly repre-
> sented by the arrows connecting the various states in the model. You can
> visualize the government's objectives as contracting the arrows into the popu-
> lation and expanding the arrows (but not the death arrow) out of the popula-
> tion.
>
> The factors influencing the behavior and condition of users are represented
> much less straightforwardly. Indeed, two of the major factors (the set of
> opportunities and the prohibition of heroin) are not explicitly represented
> at all. Perhaps the easiest way to think of these factors in terms of the
> diagram would be to imagine a box drawn around the entire system, with
> these factors influencing that box.
>
> The influence of levels of heroin consumption and the pre-addiction life-
> style of users is captured by distinguishing among eight different types of
> users. These types represent different combinations of heroin consumption
> and pre-addiction life-style. The government's objective is to increase the
> proportion of users who have relatively good life-styles (for example, matur-
> ing-out users and conformists) and to reduce the proportion who have rela-
> tively poor life-styles (for example, burned-out users, hustlers, and drug
> dependents).
>
> The diagram captures the influence of supervised programs by distinguish-
> ing between users participating in these programs and users on the street.
> The government's objectives in this area are to increase the number of users
> in supervised programs, increase the numbers in specific kinds of supervised
> programs, and exploit the comparative advantages of programs in treating
> special types of users.
>
> The failure of the figure to represent the prohibition policy and the set
> of opportunities available to users is dangerous to the extent that we are

168

Figure 4–8
Dynamic model of the heroin-using population

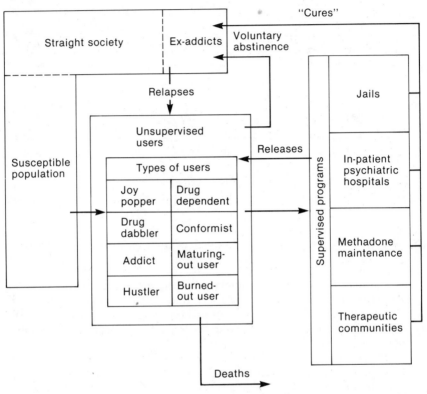

Source: Mark H. Moore, "Anatomy of the Heroin Problem: An Exercise in Problem Definition," *Policy Analysis* 2, 4 (Fall 1976), p. 659.

led to ignore the possibility of improving heroin policy by manipulating these factors. The danger is particularly grave because both factors influence not only the users' behavior but also their number. Consequently, in any analysis of the problem, one should take care to consider the impact of these factors and the potential for manipulating them.[7]

Models are used widely in policy analysis. Though the above discussion applied models in order to understand a problem, their application to other phases of policy analysis, such as selecting alternatives, should be obvious. For this reason, we will have occasion to take up many other types of models later in this book.

[7] Ibid.

ECONOMIC MODELS

The field of economics has developed an important set of theories in the form of models of markets. Like other models, markets have two functions: to enhance prediction and to facilitate understanding. By showing a variety of cause-effect relationships, they improve the policymaker's ability to assess the economic consequences of changes in public policy and to appreciate the policy implication of economic trends and events.

But the economic models of various markets also have a prescriptive function. It is rooted in Adam Smith's (1723–1790) concept of invisible hand:

> Every individual necessarily labors to render the annual revenue of the society as great as he can. He generally indeed neither intends to promote the public interest, nor knows how much he is promoting it. . . . He intends only his own gain, and he is in this, as in many other cases, led by an invisible hand to promote an end which was no part of his intention. . . . By pursuing his own interest he frequently promotes that of the society more effectually than when he really intends to promote it. I have never known much good done by those who affected to trade for the public good.[8]

In effect, Smith places the burden of proof on those who recommend government intervention in a free market. If the market works correctly, then the material needs of consumers are probably being satisfied better than any public policy could satisfy them. But Smith also identified types of market failures in which citizen preferences and public interest are not served. In those cases, even a conservative thinker like Smith would prescribe government action.

This section sketches the basic outlines of economic market models. Since not all market structures can be presented, our presentation will have to be parsimonious. We begin with the idea of free exchange, an idea on which the free market model builds. This is not a bad place to begin, for it takes us back to Eden. (You will recall, I hope, the fig leaves and apples that Adam and Eve were swapping in Chapter 1.) Then we will consider, in very general terms, how modern markets work, and why economists who have followed Adam Smith think that markets are such good things. We will also note, as Smith himself noted, four specific ways in which markets can fail. The major portion of this section concerns however U.S. agriculture policy. Can the market model help policymakers understand the farm problem? Can it help them predict the consequence of various policy initiatives? We will see shortly.

---

[8] *Wealth of Nations,* bk IV, ch. 2.

Back to Eden

Say that Adam and Eve each have modest supplies of both apples and fig leaves, but that Eve prefers fig leaves whereas Adam prefers apples. That is, the relative usefulness of fig leaves as compared with apples is greater for Eve than for Adam. If Eve were to get fewer apples but more fig leaves, while Adam got more apples and fewer fig leaves, both could benefit as a result of this allocation.

The relative usefulness of small increases (or decreases) of various goods to a consumer is called the *marginal substitution* of one good for another. Suppose Eve is willing to give up just four pounds of her supply of apples if she could get in their place another basket of fig leaves. (Of course, she would be even more willing to get a basket of leaves at the sacrifice of less than four pounds of apples, but she is not willing to give up more than four pounds for another basket of leaves.) The marginal substitution of fig leaves (for apples) is four because one basket of leaves can be substituted for four pounds of apples. The substitution of apples (for fig leaves) is the inverse of this, namely, one fourth, since a pound of apples is substitutable for only one fourth of a basketful of fig leaves.

Adam, on the other hand, being more fond of apples, is willing to give up a basket of fig leaves for only one additional pound of apples. *Clearly a reallocation of fig leaves and apples between Adam and Eve could benefit both.* Eve can give up four pounds of apples for an additional basket of fig leaves without being any worse off. This additional basket of fig leaves could be obtained from Adam who could provide it for only one of the four pounds of apples that Eve would give up and still be no worse off than in the beginning. This will leave three pounds of apples as a pure surplus that could be divided between Adam and Eve and thus *make both of them better off than before.*

Marvelous markets

Of course, the simplest way to judge what Smith said about the virtues of the market is to compare the world's capitalist economies with its centrally planned ones (the United States to Russia, Japan to China, West Germany to East Germany, South Korea to North Korea, etc.). The comparison shows not just that the market economies have achieved, over a period, higher living standards but also that they run much more smoothly. Whereas the Russian shopper spends his time trudging from queue to queue, often having to buy what he wants from an illegal black-market trader, the American finds amply stocked shelves wherever he goes.

Evidently, markets are much better than bureaucrats at finding out what people want, and then providing it. Why? Markets, in effect, process two kinds of information: first, information about what people want; second, information about the economic costs of meeting those wants. Then they send out signals that guide producers in deciding what and how much to make and also guide consumers in deciding what and how much to buy. All this happens simultaneously for thousands of producers, millions of consumers, and billions of different transactions.

Such is the complexity that underlies the familiar diagram of supply and demand curves. That diagram, which we will get to presently, gives pride of place to prices. Constantly, prices signal producers and consumers and ensure that the actions of both mesh. The demand curve says that the quantity of a good demanded will fall as it gets dearer. The supply curve says that the amount supplied will rise as it gets dearer. There must therefore be a price, P in Figure 4–9, at which the amounts demanded and supplied are equal.

To understand the signaling role of prices, ask what happens if the demand for widgets suddenly falls at every price—as it might, for example, if a cheaper substitute came on the market. See Box 4–1. This fall in demand is also illustrated in Figure 4–10 as a downward shift in the demand curve from D_1 to D_2.

If allowed to, the price of widgets will move to bring supply and demand back into balance. Producers will start to offer their widgets for less, to avoid unwanted stocks. As the price falls, consumers will want more widgets. Eventually, at a price of P_2 in Figure 4–10, demand and supply will be back in balance at Q_2 widgets.

Pareto optimality. A fully competitive market system is, as economists are fond of saying, "optimal." Vilfredo Pareto defined the idea early this century. He showed that, on certain assumptions, a free-market economy will allocate resources in such an efficient way that it is then impossible to make somebody better off without making somebody else worse off. Economists call such an allocation Pareto optimal.

So, the invisible hand of the market has skills that go beyond mere technical efficiency (i.e., avoiding surpluses and shortages). Markets also have a quasi-ethical claim to be allowed to do their work; the model is prescriptive.

Since Pareto, economists have argued about the application of the master's theories. One strand of the debate says that his test for optimality is useless as a guide to the virtues of markets. The biggest drawback of his rule, critics say, is that it regards an increase in the average level of welfare (however large) as a shift away from optimality if even one person (however trivially) is made worse off than before. To cope with this absurdity, economists came up with welfare criteria that allow for the possibility of compensation. For example, a reallocation of resources could count as an improvement in society's overall well-being

172

Figure 4–9
Demand and supply in the widget market

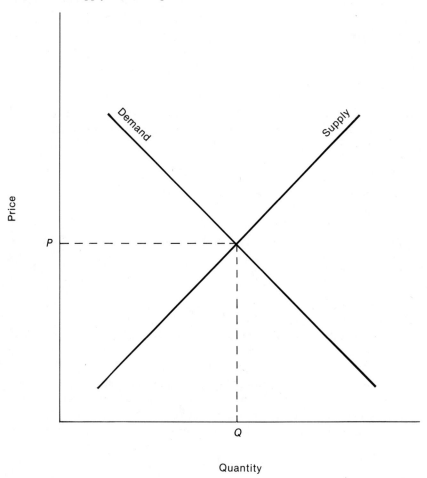

Quantity

if it increased output by so much that the gainers could compensate the losers, leaving the losers no worse off than before, and leaving themselves better off.

Another attack on Pareto's praise of markets goes deeper, arguing that his conditions for optimality are so severe, so hard to obtain that the idea is irrelevant. The most important of these conditions is that producers should be in perfect competition. If some companies have enough market power to affect the price, then the allocation of resources will generally be inefficient. An extreme form of such market power is a *monopoly*—only one seller in the market for a given commodity. In

---

Box 4–1

The great whale oil shortage, or why market forces call the tune in the long run

In the early 1970s the world seemed to be running out of oil. Consumption exceeded production, and known reserves were dwindling. The industrial economies appeared to be doomed.

But when the oil shortage led to higher energy prices, production and consumption patterns changed. Consumers installed insulation, lowered thermostats, and bought smaller cars. As energy prices rose faster than labor and capital costs, manufacturers switched to fuel-efficient production processes. By the early 1980s, U.S. oil consumption was falling, oil production was rising, and the shortage turned into a surplus.

This is a classic example of the market at work. The market economy will adjust to any resource shortage and eventually come back stronger than ever.

Consider, for instance, the great whale-oil shortage. Prior to the Civil War, whale oil was America's prime lubricant and illuminant. But as the prewar economy expanded, demand for whale oil rose and oil prices soared. More whalers put to sea, but the catch declined as the whales were hunted to near extinction. Between 1846 and 1856, a period of relative price stability, the price of whale oil jumped 143 percent.

Rising oil prices spurred entrepreneurs to look for a suitable substitute. By the mid-1850s "rock oil" petroleum was being used as an illuminant and lubricant, but no one knew how to get it out of the ground in sufficient quantities. Seepages were drained and wells were dug, but supplies remained inadequate. In 1857, however, the newly formed Seneca Oil Company hired Edwin L. Drake to drill for oil near Titusville, Pennsylvania. On August 27, 1859, Drake's well came in. Within two and one-half years, the ensuing oil rush cut the price of petroleum from ten dollars a barrel to ten cents—less than the price of whale oil. The crisis was over; the switch from whale oil to petroleum triggered America's greatest economic expansion.

Source: Based on Charles Maurice and Charles W. Smithson, *The Doomsday Myth: 2,000 Years of Economic Crisis* (Palo Alto, Calif.: Hoover Institute Press, 1984).

---

situations where monopolies are desirable—for example, supplying electricity to a community—the case for government regulation is usually persuasive.

Perfect competition, therefore, requires many buyers and sellers and that firms must have free entry to, and exit from, the industry; and that buyers and sellers have full information about the market—both as it is now, and as it will be in the future. A perfectly working market

Figure 4–10
The signaling role of prices

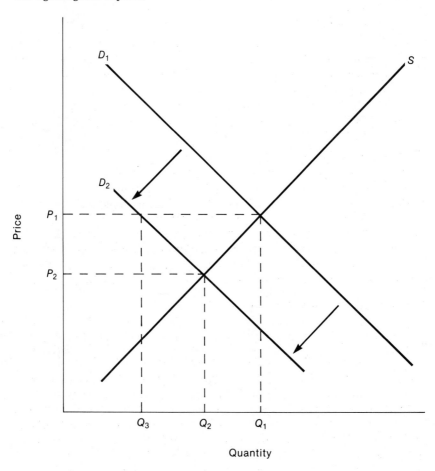

(1) Demand (D_1) falls but . . .
(2) The price remains stuck at P_1.
(3) Therefore, there is a surplus ($Q_1 - Q_2$).
(4) Faced with this surplus, producers are forced to drop their price from P_1 to P_2.
(5) This delights the consumers who now increase the quantity purchased from Q_3 to Q_2.
(6) Supply and demand are now in balance.

assumes that information on existing prices is somehow spread around at no cost, so that everyone can find the best (lowest) price. But shopping around requires time and expertise. (Is this car a lemon?) Thus, individuals will not have the kind of information they need to make the right economic decisions, and inefficient patterns of allocation will emerge. Because *imperfect information* is a day-to-day reality, we have, among other things, legislation requiring companies to meet health and safety standards and provide product information.

Besides imperfect competition and information, two more hurdles, both noted in Chapter 1 (Core Idea 5), block the path to Pareto optimality. Free markets, operating without any government regulation, tend to produce a variety of negative externalities; pollution being merely one nasty example. And, while the private sector operating in a free market can produce public goods such as education (e.g., Eton and Yale), police protection (e.g., Brinks and Pinkerton), health care (e.g., Humana and Hospital Corporation of America), and even national defense (just check want ads in *Soldier of Fortune*), these positive externalities tend to be undersupplied. That is to say, a free market will not supply them at a level that is optimal for the community at large.

In sum, the fundamental theorem of welfare economics (Core Idea 4) says strive for a Pareto optimum. Stripped of jargon, the prescription is this: The free market puts the burden of proof on advocates of government intervention, but market failures put another burden on the advocates of free enterprises to show why this monopoly or that deceptive ad or those sulfur dioxide emissions or these illiterate children do not require government action.

Now let us see how well the market model enhances prediction, facilitates understanding, and prescribes action in one especially nettlesome policy area.

The U.S. farm policy: An economic perspective

In July 1985 the Live Aid concert for African famine relief demonstrated the power of show business talent to tap America's generosity. No surprise, then, that it was followed a couple of months later by a Farm Aid concert, a similar affair to raise money for struggling farmers.

The exuberance and good feeling created by these events, however, blurs some important distinctions. Feeding starving children is the kind of straightforward challenge that charity can address effectively. Even an obtuse Ethiopian government could not utterly frustrate the effort. Helping American farmers is far more complex. Farm Aid cannot deliver the kind of salvation some farmers want.

The concert of country and rock performers raised about $10 million, far less than the organizers hoped and a tiny fraction (.00047 percent) of farm debt—which exceeds $210 billion. The organizers, however, justified the concert as a means of attracting public attention. But to what purpose? Charity to relieve victims of drought, flood, or earthquake seems wholly appropriate; the causes of the catastrophes are beyond the power of man to prevent. In sharp contrast, the nation's farm problem is the result of all-too-human politics and economics.

The choices are real and painful. Even if the farmers' debts were refinanced on manageable terms, the structural problems of American agriculture—overcapacity and overproduction—would remain. A compassionate national policy would seek to ease the transition from farming to other occupations for those who must make it. *But inevitably, the American farm sector must shrink.* Unfortunately, Farm Aid raised hopes that this winnowing can be avoided. If Willie Nelson had just applied Economics 101, he would have known that it cannot be avoided.

Demand and supply of corn. The demand and supply model shows how the price and output of a commodity are determined in a competitive market. What factors influence an individual's decision to consume a certain good? To make the problem concrete, let us consider the specific case of corn. A moment's reflection suggests that at least four factors affect the amount of corn and corn-derived products that an individual will want to use during a year.

1. *Price.* As price goes up, the quantity demanded goes down.
2. *Income.* The effect of income on demand is not as simple as price. At higher incomes, people may purchase more corn, but they may also consume less, perhaps spending their money on lobster.
3. *Prices of related goods.* Suppose the price of sugar goes up. If people can substitute corn syrup for sugar (candy companies certainly can) this increase in the price of sugar will increase the amount of corn people wish to consume.
4. *Tastes.* The extent to which people like something will affect the amount they demand. Presumably, more corn is demanded in Mexican-American communities because of dietary preferences.

While a wide variety of things affects demand, economists find it useful to focus on the relationship between the quantity of a commodity demanded and the price. The demand curve (Figure 4–11) shows the relation between the market price of a good and the quantity demanded. The horizontal axis measures bushels of corn per year in a particular market and the price per bushel is measured on the vertical. Thus, for example, if the price is $2.29 per bushel, people are willing to consume 750 bushels; when the price is only $1.38 (as it was in the early 1970s), they are willing to consume 1,225 bushels. The downward slope of the demand curve reflects the reasonable assumption that when the price goes up, the quantity demanded goes down.

The demand curve, then, tells us people's "willingness to pay," because it shows the maximum price that people would pay for a given quantity. For example, when people purchase 750 bushels per year, they value it at $2.29 per bushel. At any price above $2.29, they would not willingly consume 750 bushels per year. If for some reason people

Figure 4–11
Demand curve for corn (hypothetical)

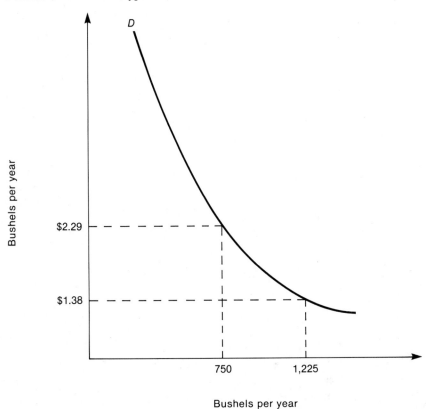

Bushels per year

were able to obtain 750 bushels at a price below $2.29, this would be a "bargain."

Now consider the factors that determine the quantity of a good that a farmer will *supply* to a market. Three are readily apparent:

1. *Price.* Generally, the higher the price per bushel, the greater the quantity that profit-minded farmers will supply.
2. *Price of inputs.* Corn producers have to use inputs to produce corn— labor, machinery, fuel, fertilizer, etc. If their input costs go up, then the amount of corn that they can profitably supply at a given price declines.
3. *Conditions of production.* Technological improvements increase supply. Weather is also important for corn.

Economists are especially interested in the relationship between the price and the quantity of a commodity supplied. The supply curve

178

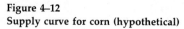

Figure 4–12
Supply curve for corn (hypothetical)

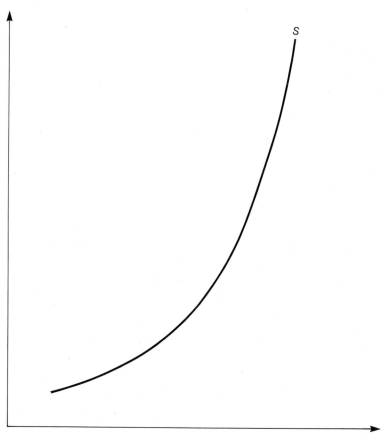

Bushels per year

relates price to the amount of a good that producers will supply during
a given period of time.

Figure 4–12 depicts a supply curve for corn. Its upward slope reflects
the assumption that the higher the price, the greater the quantity supplied.

Putting it all together: Equilibrium. The demand and supply curves
provide answers to questions such as:

- If the price of corn is $2 per bushel, then how much will consumers
  be willing to purchase?
- If the price is $1.75 per bushel, then how much will farmers supply?

Neither Figure 4–11 nor Figure 4–12 by itself tells us what the actual price and quantity will be, but together they do. So, in Figure 4–13, we superimpose our demand curve on our supply curve. We want to find the price and output at which there is an equilibrium—that is, a situation that will tend to be maintained unless there is an underlying change in the system.

Suppose the price is P_1 dollars per bushel. At this price, the quantity demanded is Q_1, and quantity supplied Q_2. Obviously, we have a problem: Price P_1 cannot be maintained because farmers want to supply more corn than consumers will purchase. This excess supply, or surplus, pushes down the price (as suggested by the arrows).

Now consider price P_2. At this price, the quantity of corn demanded (Q_3) exceeds the quantity supplied (Q_4). Because there is an excess demand for corn, or shortage, we expect the price to rise.

Thus, any price at which the quantity supplied and quantity demanded are unequal cannot be equilibrium. In Figure 4–13, quantity demanded equals quantity supplied at P_e. The associated output level is Q_e bushels per year. Unless something else in the system changes, this price and output combination will continue year after year. It is an equilibrium.

The long-run U.S. farm problem. Historically, a number of long- and short-run problems have plagued American agriculture. Until the 1970s, the long-run problem was excess capacity and low income returns to farmers. The reason, in a nutshell, was that growth in demand for food products failed to keep up with the growth of agriculture's productive capacity.

Although per capita income in the United States increased substantially since the turn of the century, the per capita demand for food has gone up much less in proportion. By contrast, the growth in agricultural productivity (output per acre) has been brisk, due to mechanization, land management programs, pesticides, higher quality seeds and fertilizers, and better breeding and care of livestock. Since these advances were not accompanied by any real reductions in farm land use, capacity had to increase.

Figure 4–14 illustrates the results. The demand curve shifts to the right over time as a result of increasing incomes, international trade, and population. But, because of rapid increases in farm productivity, the increase in supply is much greater than the increase in demand. As a result, farm prices fall relative to the price of other goods and services and farm income improves little, if at all.

But the picture changed in the 1970s. A rising world population and improved capability of some developing countries to buy food caused the growth in demand to exceed growth in supply. Consequently, *real* food prices increased and per capita incomes of farmers averaged 90

180

Figure 4–13
Equilibrium in the corn market

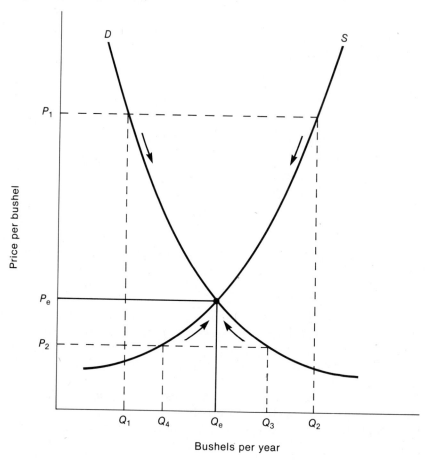

Bushels per year

percent of those earned by the nonfarm population (up sharply from the 60 to 65 percent figure of the preceding twenty-five years). What did this rise in agricultural exports mean in terms of Figure 4–14? The demand curve over the course of the 1970s increased by more than the supply curve, raising *real* food prices and farm incomes.

The short-run U.S. farm problem. In most industries, the growing increases and technology discussed above would be welcomed. If an electronics firm can slash its price for microwave ovens and VCRs because of lower manufacturing cost, then it will sell more and its income will go up. Unfortunately for the agricultural industry, consumers do not increase their food purchases very much when farm prices fall. Economists have a way of expressing this phenomenon: The *price elasticity*

Figure 4–14
Long-run U.S. farm problem

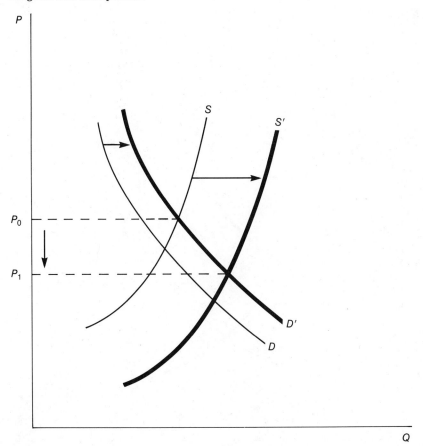

of food demand is low. Consequently, abundant harvests (rightward shifts of the supply curve) can lead to sharply lower prices and a *decline* in total revenues.

The *income elasticity* of food demand is also low. As incomes increase, people tend to buy more goods and services, but they do not buy much more food. Hence, neither lower prices nor higher incomes significantly increase the quantity of food demanded.[9]

---

[9] Price elasticity and income elasticity may be calculated. Formally stated, price elasticity of demand is the percentage change in quantity demanded divided by the percentage change in price. Income elasticity of demand is the percentage change in quantity demanded divided by the percentage change in income. See Chapter 10.

Figure 4–15
Short-term instability of farm prices

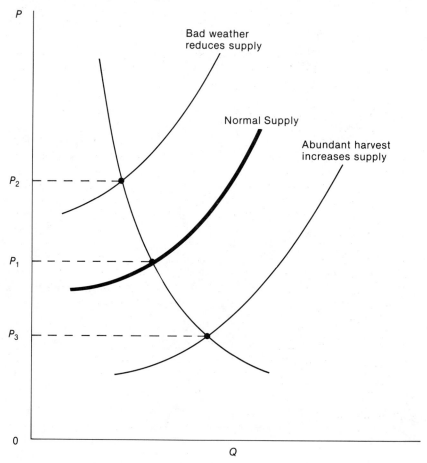

The low elasticity of demand helps explain the short-run problem of agriculture: price instability. Because the demand for and supply of food have such a low elasticity, small changes in either demand or supply lead to very large changes in prices—and thus incomes. Unpredictable changes in the weather can cause sharp variations in supply in the United States, while changes in weather overseas can cause variations in demand for American exports.

Figure 4–15 illustrates these natural price swings. Notice how the price of corn jumps from P_1 to P_2 when bad weather reduces the harvest. If good weather follows, prices may fall to P_3. Thus, a bushel of corn sold for $1.45 in 1970, went up to $3.36 in 1975, dropped to $2.99 in

1979, was up to $3.41 the next year, dropped to $2.91 in 1982, but bounced up the following year. So it goes.

No single farmer can avoid the boom-or-bust movement of prices. Even a corn farmer who has mastered Economics 101 has little choice but to plant more corn when prices are high. If he does not, prices will fall anyway because his production decisions do not affect market prices.

Government responses

Congress has responded to these problems with a variety of programs. Most seek to raise and stabilize prices; others seek to reduce the costs of production. More recently, the federal government has also provided direct income support to farmers. During the 1984 presidential campaign, Reagan bragged that net farm cash income would reach a record level of over $42 billion that year. There was an irony in this: an ostensibly free-market administration unabashedly boasting that a major industry was on welfare in an amount roughly equal to five sixths of its net profits (Figure 4–16).

Price supports. Price supports have always been the primary focus of U.S. farm policy. As early as 1926, Congress decreed that farm products should sell at a "fair" price. By fair, Congress meant a price higher than the market equilibrium. Unfortunately, since above-equilibrium prices would create a market surplus (recall Figure 4–13), President Calvin Coolidge vetoed this legislation both times Congress passed it.

But, as we know from Chapter 2, policy proposals tend to resurface. The notion of fair prices became the cornerstone of the Agricultural Adjustment Act of 1933. The objective of this act was to restore the farm-nonfarm price relationship of 1909–14. Congress regarded that relationship fair, and it became known as parity. "One hundred percent parity" means that the ratio of prices received to costs are today the same as they were in the 1910–14 period (which, incidently, was the heyday of agriculture). It means that if four bushels of corn bought one pair of shoes in 1910–14, then it should buy the same pair of shoes today. Although the concept of 100 percent parity has not been embraced by government for all goods, the milk lobby has obtained it. In other goods, the government has almost always stepped in to support agricultural prices whenever the parity ratio fell too low.

American agricultural policies are a cruel joke. Sugar prices are pegged at four times world prices. The dairy program drives cheese prices to double world price levels. The consequences of these price support policies are not good. A surplus of agricultural products emerges and the incentive for resources to shift out of agriculture diminishes. Since the supply of food over time has a tendency to rise more rapidly than

184

Figure 4–16
The rising cost of farm support

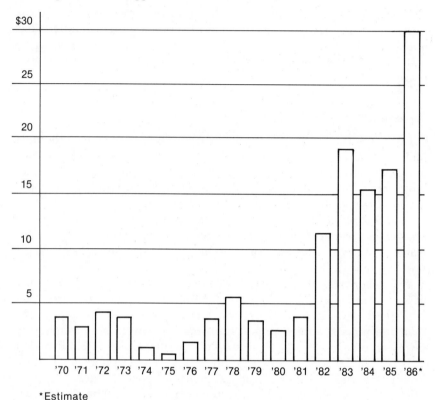

*Estimate

Source: U.S. Department of Agriculture, *Agricultural Statistics*, 1986.

demand, the free market would have dictated a decline in agricultural prices relative to other goods and services. Government interference has prevented the American people from enjoying these benefits.

Governmental purchases, crop restrictions, and subsidies. To maintain prices at this artificially high level, government has used three programs. First, government can simply purchase the surplus at the predetermined support price. The aim is to support farm income by supporting price (Figure 4–17A). What happens to this surplus after the government buys it? Some of it is given as foreign aid and some of it is used in school lunch programs, but much of it just rots in storage.

So, policymakers decided to experiment with crop restrictions. The government would guarantee a support price only if farmers will cut back their production. By shifting the supply curve to the left, policymakers hoped to reduce the size of the surplus (Figure 4–17B).

Figure 4–17
An economic model of three agricultural programs

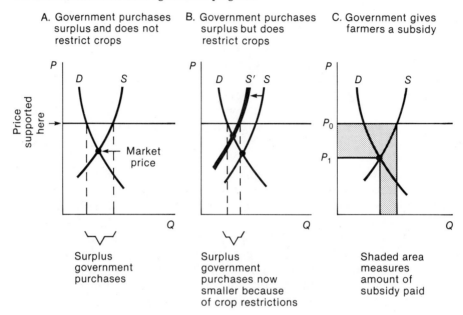

A. Government purchases surplus and does not restrict crops

B. Government purchases surplus but does restrict crops

C. Government gives farmers a subsidy

Surplus government purchases

Surplus government purchases now smaller because of crop restrictions

Shaded area measures amount of subsidy paid

In 1973, with passage of the Agriculture and Consumer Protection Act, policymakers took a third and quite different tack. Now government would set a "target price." Whenever the market price fell below it, government would provide farmers with a direct subsidy equal to the difference between the target price and the market price. The intersection of the demand and supply curves (P_1 in Figure 4–17C) determines the market price—so, in one sense, the consumer is "protected." The target price is P_0. The government subsidy *per bushel* equals P_1P_0; the amount of the government subsidy equals the shaded area in Figure 4–17C. Guess who pays that subsidy?

Solving the problem

With existing farm programs, costs to taxpayers have soared, while crop exports and farm income have fallen. Yet, most members of Congress favor perpetuating these programs or making them even worse, by imposing mandatory production controls over millions of farmers.

The farm recession of the mid-1980s stemmed largely from the 1981 Farm Bill that presupposed (1) world demand for American crops would continue to expand as it had in the 1970s, and (2) Congress could set price support whenever it chose. But foreign demand dropped as it became cheaper to buy elsewhere. When it became obvious that price supports were too high, the Reagan administration responded with the $10 billion Payment In Kind Program (PIK), which paid farmers not to grow crops. By slashing its production, the United States hoped to boost world prices, but this action only encouraged foreigners to plow more land, which both further reduced America's share and kept world grain prices down.

American agriculture is also depressed partly because of government-sponsored cheap credit. In the past, whenever farming was on the verge of shrinking to a reasonable size, Congress rushed in with more easy money. The result was soaring land values and continual overproduction.

Many Americans favor an agriculture policy designed to protect the small-sized, full-time family farmer. But there is no way for farm income support programs to be both equitable and effective. If federal aid is to reduce crop sizes significantly, it must also go to big farmers who do not need the money. Small farmers do not produce a large enough share of the harvest to make a difference.

The best thing for the future of U.S. agriculture would be gradual deregulation and for much of the farmland brought into production during the booming 1970s to be retired. The result would shake out a lot of medium-size farmers. But it should not be beyond the nation's capacity to ease their transition into nonfarm employment. This may seem unkind to farmers, but the alternative is for taxpayers to perpetually pay farmers not to farm.

Furthermore, policymakers should recognize the existence of world markets. If American crop price supports were reduced to between 75 and 80 percent of world markets, this would dampen prices and make it too expensive for European countries to continue their large subsidies to their farmers. That event would clearly be good for American farmers. After a few hard years of deregulation, they could recapture the lost export market.

TREND EXTRAPOLATION

One of the most widely used forecasting techniques is trend extrapolation, or as it is sometimes called, the lost-horse method. The technique involves the assumption that future events will continue along an established path; in other words, past patterns of behavior prevail sufficiently to justify using historical patterns to forecast the future. In much the same way, a farmer seeks a lost horse: the farmer proceeds to the spot where it was last seen and then searches in the direction it was heading.

More formally, trend extrapolation is a family of quantitative forecasting techniques, all of which depend on extending, or extrapolating, time-series data in accord with specified, usually mathematical, rules. The extrapolations constitute the forecast.

Trend extrapolation is generally easy to do. Once appropriate time-series data are plotted, the rhythm of the curve is often self-evident. In some cases, all that is required to extrapolate is a ruler, a black thread, or a French curve. For more complex situations, analysts unfamiliar with statistical mathematics will need help. Very often this help is readily available in the form of computer programs for curve fitting.

What trend extrapolation can do for policymakers

If a city transit authority is about to spend several billion dollars to build a rail system, it might want to know whether ridership will increase by a sufficient amount to justify this expense. The U.S. Geological Survey might want to know what the water needs of the country will be by the end of this century. Another doubling of usage suggests a whole series of actions today: greater reuse of water, more limits on pollution, control of urban and suburban development, and so forth. And just about every public official should want to know how many older Americans there will be in the coming decades. Let us look at some numbers and see why.

Currently, 27 percent of the federal budget is spent on the aged—compared with only 2 percent in 1940. The Population Reference Bureau projects that by the year 2025 people over sixty-five will absorb half of all federal outlays.[10] Not only that, there will be fewer younger people to pay all those bills. By 2025, every 1,000 Americans aged eighteen through sixty-four will be called on to support 333 of their seniors—close to double the current load. Expenditures on older citizens fall under two major headings: (1) social security pensions and (2) physicians' and hospital charges under medicare and medicaid. I will focus on the latter first, if only because medical charges are growing at a faster rate.

In 1967, when medicare began in earnest, the program spent twenty-two cents for every dollar paid in pensions; by 1983 it was spending ratio had grown to thirty-eight cents. At that rate, by the year 2005 medicare outlays for older people will be larger than social security outlays.[11] Because of increasing life spans, more older people will develop diseases that would not have appeared had they died earlier of more conventional causes. The National Cancer Institute estimates that

---

[10] Population Reference Bureau, *Death and Taxes: The Public Policy Impact of Living Longer* (Washington, D.C., 1984).

[11] Barbara Torrey, "Guns vs. Canes: The Fiscal Impact of an Aging Population," *American Economic Review*, May 1982.

by the year 2030 the country will have twice as many cancer cases, with most of the increment coming from aged citizens.[12] Obviously, these people will have to be treated at not-insignificant costs. These trends pose difficult questions for policymakers. And the fact that Americans see themselves as living in the richest nation in the world, where no person should be denied whatever treatments are available, make them even more difficult.

Trends in social security pose a somewhat different challenge. For the next forty years, the social security cash benefit programs are *too well funded*. The current balance in the social security trust fund is only about $27 billion, but the surplus is projected at least to exceed one trillion dollars before the year 2000. Continuing to rise, it will peak at $20 trillion in the 2040s. See Figure 4–18. Will politicians be able to resist spending these surplus funds that will not be needed for nearly forty years? Furthermore, how does government invest $20 trillion without violating traditional boundaries between the public and private sectors? Under current law, the treasury secretary invests cash balances in U.S. Treasury securities. But in the near future there will not be enough Treasury debt to purchase. What then? Right now the New York Stock Exchange has a market value of less than 3 trillion dollars. Do we really want cabinet officers deciding what companies the federal government will take over, in effect, by buying controlling interests?

Distinguishing two types of changes

In this section, we will deal with two types of change: structural and cyclic. The distinction is crucial.[13]

- *Structural change* is a fundamental transformation of some activity from a previous state. Usually the transformation occurs because of some trend—that is, the rise or decline over time in amount or size. The result is a change in the essential quality, or structure, of the activity or institution. For example, the population density and growing congestion of a city require a new transit system; the doubling of water usage requires control of urban development; expenditures on and for older citizens require another overhaul of the social security system and a drastic change in eligibility standards for medicare and medicaid.

---

[12] Dwight Janerich, "Forecasting Cancer Trends to Optimized Control Statistics," *Journal of the National Cancer Institute*, June 1984.

[13] Leon Martel, formerly of the Hudson Institute, draws this useful distinction in his *Mastering Change* (New York: Simon & Schuster, 1986). Typically, structural changes occur in areas such as technology, education, population, work, income, and attitudes. Changes in the business conditions, demand and supply of goods, organizational behavior, and social behavior are usually cyclic.

Figure 4–18
Projected surplus in the social security trust fund (in billions of dollars)

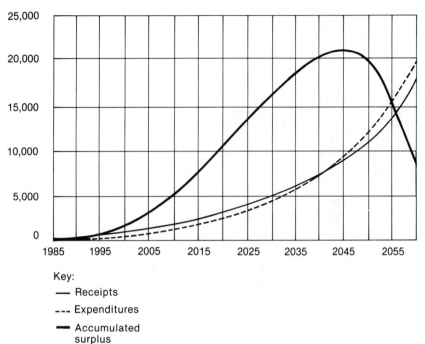

Key:
— Receipts
--- Expenditures
— Accumulated
surplus

Source: Alternative II-B Social Security Administration Forecast of May 23, 1983.

The point about structural change is this—just as the change is permanent, so too must be the adjustment to it.

- *Cyclic change,* on the other hand, is temporary change in a certain measure or condition from a level or state to which it is likely to return later. Over time, cyclic changes follow a discernible pattern in their fluctuations, returning regularly to prior states. They usually do not cause any alterations in structure or basic policy, and because their durations are limited, adjustment to them is usually either temporary or unwise.

Figure 4–19 charts the annual percentage change in gross national product (the sum of the money values of all final goods and services produced by the economy in a year). During periods of decline, with unemployment relatively high, political pressures build to launch public works programs to create jobs. Unfortunately, it is highly unlikely that such programs will have any significant impact on reducing the unemployment rate. Indeed, it may even increase joblessness. The

Figure 4–19
Annual percentage change in U.S. gross national product, 1940–1985

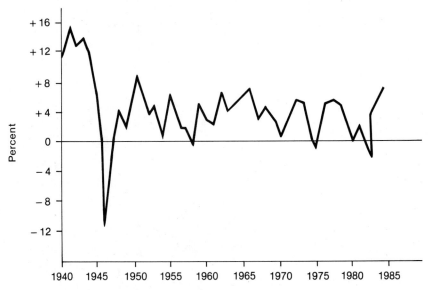

Source: *Economic Report of the President, 1986*, p. 255.

principal problem is that business cycles can seldom—if ever—be identified until they have substantially run their course. Consequently,
federal jobs programs invariably are not enacted or implemented until
the recession is virtually, or even entirely, over. This is particularly
so because politicians are inclined to react to the unemployment rate,
which lags behind the business cycle, rather than to changes in real
GNP growth.

Straight-line trends

Let us begin with an easy one. A straight-line trend will be drawn
from the data shown in Table 4–1. Among the various patterns that
can be plotted from time-series data, the straight line is the one that
shows the trend of the time series with no abrupt changes in direction.
A straight line on arithmetic or linear graph paper represents a *constant
amount of change* per unit of time. The first straight-line trend will be
drawn by the freehand method—simply drawing a straight line through
the data, using sight and judgment. Figure 4–20 shows the data plotted
and a freehand straight line drawn through the data points.

The freehand method is subjective, and it is not recommended for
use when a high degree of accuracy is desired. Fortunately, a number

Table 4–1
Employment status of civilian women,
1950 to 1985 (1,000s)

1950	17,795
1955	20,154
1960	22,516
1965	25,952
1970	31,233
1975	36,981
1980	44,934
1985	50,891

Source: *Statistical Abstract of the U.S., 1987,*
p. 382.

of alternatives to the freehand method are available. We might consider
one—the *least squares method*. The least squares method is a convenient
and simple device for obtaining an objective fit of a straight line to a
series of data. It allows us to accurately calculate the values for a and
b in the trend equation $y = a + bx$. In computing a trend by the least

Figure 4–20
Projecting female employment

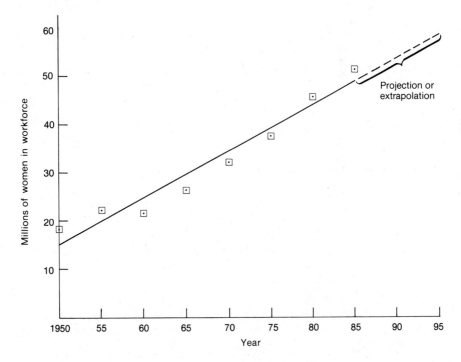

192

Table 4–2
Least squares data table

(1) Year	(2) x	(3) y	(4) x^2	(5) xy
1950	10	17.8	100	178
1955	15	20.2	225	303
1960	20	22.5	400	450
1965	25	26.0	625	650
1970	30	31.2	900	936
1975	35	37.0	1,225	1,295
1980	40	44.9	1,600	1,796
1985	45	50.9	2,025	2,290
$n = 8$	$\Sigma x = 220$	$\Sigma y = 250.5$	$\Sigma x^2 = 7,100$	$\Sigma xy = 7,898$

squares method, one can often simplify the data like those in Table 4–1. Note that Table 4–2 uses 10 rather than 1950, 15 rather than 1955, etc. The population figures have been converted to millions. Thus we can work with 17.8 rather than 17,795,000; 20.2 rather than 20,154,000; etc. The procedure is as follows:

1. Square the x's and total the products to obtain Σx^2. (See column 4 of Table 4–2.)
2. Total the original values of the y variable to obtain Σy. (See column 3 of Table 4–2.)
3. Multiply x by y for each year and sum up these products to obtain Σxy. (See column 5 of Table 4–2.)
4. We now have the quantities to compute the values of b and a:

$$b = \frac{n\,\Sigma xy - \Sigma x\,\Sigma y}{n\Sigma x^2 - (\Sigma x)^2}$$
$$= \frac{(8)\,(7,898) - (220)\,(250.5)}{(8)\,(7,100) - (220)\,(220)} = .96$$
$$a = \frac{\Sigma y - b\,\Sigma x}{n}$$
$$= \frac{(250.5) - (.96)\,(220)}{8} = 4.87$$

5. Write the equation of the trend line by substituting the results obtained in step 5.

$$y_t = a + bx = 4.87 + .96x$$

But our interest in trend analysis is not confined to determining the growth pattern of a series in the past: we are primarily concerned with forecasting the future. To forecast trend values, we use the equation

Figure 4–21
S-curve

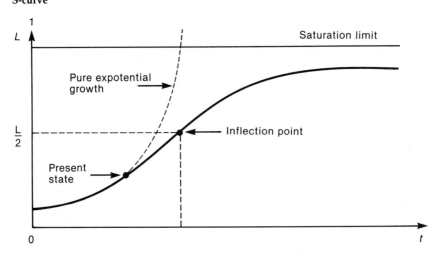

found in step 5. For example, if we want to forecast the trend values for the year 2000 in the example considered, we first note that 2000 is sixty years later than the origin. The value of x is therefore sixty, and we solve the established trend equation to determine y.

$$y_{2000} = a + bx = 4.87 + .96(60) = 62.57 \text{ million}$$

We may then state that, under the assumption that the same trend factors that produced the trend equation for 1950 to 1985 will remain operative, in the workforce will include 62,570,000 women in the year 2000.

Fitted curves

The trend discussed above progressed more or less arithmetically. In such cases, in which the series changes by equal amounts during each time period, the methods used were appropriate. In many cases in the study of public policy, however, we deal with variables that grow more rapidly in later time periods than in earlier ones. World population is a prime example of this type of growth, which we call *exponential*. Such trends have a plot similar to the dashed line in Figure 4–21.

The concept of doubling time—or how long it takes the parameter (e.g., population) to double—is one of the keys to understanding this kind of growth. Actually, in the case of population growth, only a small change in the growth rate can cause the base of people to double

Table 4–3
Population growth and doubling time

Nature of growth	Annual percentage of growth	Approximate doubling time (years)
Slow	0.1	700
Moderate	0.5	140
Rapid	1.0	70
Very rapid	1.5	47
	2.0	35
	2.5	28
Explosive	3.0	23
	3.5	20
	4.0	18

much more quickly (see Table 4–3). The approximate number of years it takes to double a population is the number 70 divided by the annual growth rate.

A method of forecasting population or any other exponential trends (e.g., the number of telephones in service) may have already occurred to anyone who has ever pondered the growth of bank savings. Namely, find the rate of change and then multiply that percentage change for the required number of years by, say, the current population. In other words, investors could figure the growth of population in exactly the same way that they calculate the growth of saving—by using the compound interest formula:

$$A_n = P(1 + i)^n$$

where n is the number of years, i is the interest rate, P is the number of dollars deposited, and A is the number of dollars after n periods.

Essentially the same formula can be applied to make estimates of future populations. Let us consider the case of Kenya, the fastest growing country in the world. The population rate for Kenya is about 4 percent. Kenya's 1983 population was about 18.5 million. To forecast its population in the year 2000, we would just solve the following modified compound interest equation:

$$
\begin{aligned}
\text{Population in 2000} &= \text{1983 population} \times (1 + \text{Growth rate})^{17} \\
&= 18,500,000 \times (1.04)^{17} \\
&= 18,500,000 \times 1.95 \\
&= 36,075,000
\end{aligned}
$$

An equally important growth curve in the analysis of public policy is the S-curve. As shown in Figure 4–21, the S-curve is actually exponential growth subject to a saturation limit. This makes good sense, for not all growth can go on indefinitely. Since plotting S-curves by the least squares method is a little more involved mathematically, we will not consider it here.

Cycles

Trend curves like those considered so far are sometimes called monotonic, because their chief characteristic is a long-run increase or decrease. But some parameters oscillate over time; that is, they increase and decrease in the short term, while showing a long-term decrease or increase. For example, in Figure 4–22 we see four increases and three decreases in the short term, while the long-term trend is increasing.

These oscillating functions form the mathematical tool for all cycle theories. In the United States one speaks of a farm cycle whose classical example is found in the Old Testament, in chapter 41 of Genesis: Pharaoh's dream of the seven fat years and the seven lean years. There are also biocycles, such as the eight-year cycle of the salmon. The Canadian Railroad supposedly has had a freight boom every 9.18 months, forty-eight times in succession. Even without choosing such far-fetched examples, it is evident that many kinds of development, especially economic, occur in cycles. Although this is common knowledge, many policy analysts do not take account of the characteristic shape of a cyclic function.

Figure 4–22
Time series showing secular trend and cyclical variation

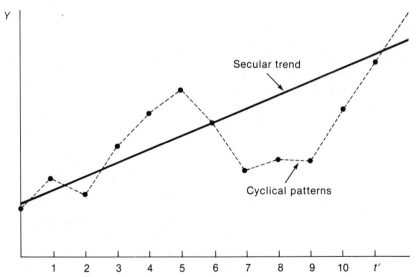

Figure 4–23
Time series for incarceration

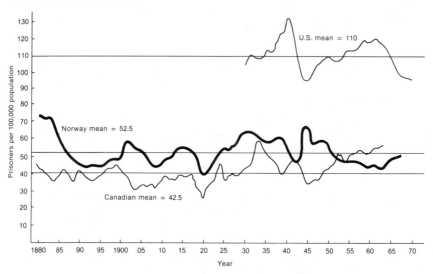

Source: Alfred Blumstein and Daniel Nagin, "On Optimum Use of Incarceration for Crime Control," mimeographed, October 1976.

Since the use of oscillating functions is less applicable to public policy, with the important exception of economic policy, than to business policy (where seasonal variation is a major concern), we will consider only one example of a time series.

Imprisonment for crime control—unlike many crime rates—does not follow a trend; rather, it is cyclic. Alfred Blumstein and Daniel Nagin maintain that this pattern is due, in part, to the fact that a society can only deliver a fixed (and thus limited) amount of punishment. Based on studies in the United States, Norway, and Canada, they report a long-term trendlessness in imprisonment rates that seems to give strong support to this contention (see Figure 4–23). But what are the policy implications of this finding?

These stable levels of imprisonment may arise simply from constraints on available resources or, more fundamentally, from considerations of societal homeostasis. For example, if too large a portion of society is punished for being criminally deviant, they may well represent a serious threat to the stability of that society, and so exert an effective pressure to restrain the imprisonment rate. Alternatively, if too few are punished, the basic identifying values of the society will not be adequately articulated and reinforced, and pressure will develop to increase the rate of punishment. If such a homeostatic phenomenon prevails, changes in aggregate social behavior may result in adjustments in the standards or thresholds that define punishable behavior and in the level of punishment delivered, so that roughly a constant proportion of the population is always being punished. While we would certainly not argue that the constant imprisonment rate proportion that has been observed immutably fixes prison population, it does suggest that major changes are not easily attained, and that the characteristic imprisonment rate can be treated as a constraint on the amount of imprisonment a society can deliver. . . .

Even without invoking such fundamental speculations, the number of people who can be imprisoned is constrained, at least in the short run, simply by the physical capacity of prisons. Increases in prison capacity require legislative commitment to construction; development of construction plans, solicitations, and contracts; and the long process of the construction itself; and all this must be done in the face of an effective constituency that is opposed to any such expansion of capacity. Thus, even when the imprisonment rate is viewed as a policy variable, significant changes from current levels will be extremely limited and slow, and so imprisonment rates can still reasonably be treated as a constraining factor on the more immediate sanction variables.[14]

Thus, by demonstrating that the imprisonment rate is stable, the analysis tends to show that a number of prescriptions for imprisonment policy are pretty much beside the point. To argue for or against incarceration and certain absolute levels may be less fruitful than focusing analysis on how to allocate a fixed prison resource.

A short discourse on the hazards of extrapolation

The extrapolator's paradox. As interest in the future has grown, so too has the popularity of taking existing trends and making instant predictions. In the late 1960s, the number of articles and the amount of scholarly research predicting the spread of the counterculture—at the expense of middle class values—became astonishingly large. Journalists, commentators, and scholars had looked out their windows, seen a trend, and made a roughly correct (mathematically) extrapolation. By the mid-1970s, Andy Warhol, the late pop artist, offered this ironic assessment of how accurate these predictions proved:

> The amazing thing is that we have turned back the clock in this country. When I go out and stand on a street corner, everything and everybody looks just like they did in 1959. It's like eighteen years just disappeared. The people look exactly like they did before the hippies came in. Everybody's back to short hair and suits and ties. The hippie look is out. Even in Los

---

[14] Alfred Blumstein and Daniel Nagin, "On the Optimum Use of Incarceration for Crime Control." Mimeographed, October 1976.

Angeles, really beautiful restaurants are back in style, and people dress well.[15]

But, on reflection, the problem of naive forecasting is neither peculiar to the late 1960s nor limited to second-order intellects. As one of Tom Stoppard's characters in *Travesties* says:

> Marx got it wrong. He got it wrong for good reasons, but he got it wrong just the same. And twice over. In the first place he was the victim of a historical accident, and in the second place his materialism made a monkey out of him, and of his theory. . . . The historical accident could have happened to anybody. By bad luck he encountered the capitalist system at its most deceptive period. The industrial revolution had crowded the people into slums and enslaved them in factories, but it had not yet begun to bring them the benefits of an industrialized society. Marx looked about him and saw that the system depended on a wretched army of wage slaves. He drew the lesson that the wealth of the capitalist was the counterpart to the poverty of the worker and had in fact been stolen from the worker in the form of unpaid labour. He thought that was how the whole thing worked. The false assumption was itself added to a false premise. This premise was that people were a sensational kind of material object and would behave predictably in a material world. Marx predicted that they would behave according to their class. But they didn't. Deprived, self-interested, bitter, or greedy, as the case may be, they showed streaks of superior intelligence, superior strength, superior morality. . . . Legislation, unions, share capital, consumer power—in all kinds of ways and for all kinds of reasons, the classes moved closer together instead of further apart. The critical moment never came. It receded. The tide must have turned at about the time when *Das Kapital* after eighteen years of hard labour was finally coming off the press.[16]

What we have here I like to call the "extrapolator's paradox": the more sensitive analysts are to change, the less likely they are to successfully predict it. The paradox is probably best explained with the earlier example of the counterculture movement of the late 1960s. While many authorities extrapolated freely from the counterculture movement to predict what the late 1970s would be like, almost none of these individuals had been able in the *early* 1960s able to predict what would come in the *late* 1960s. Why? They looked outside; saw a square culture (one that appeared to be getting squarer); studied and wrote about it (witness *The Organization Man* and *The Man in the Gray Flannel Suit*); and naturally assumed more of the same in the future. The sequence is precisely the one that obtained in the late 1960s, with works like *The Greening of*

---

[15] Interview with Andy Warhol, *U.S. News & World Report*, June 27, 1977, pp. 57–58.
[16] Tom Stoppard, *Travesties* (New York: Grove Press, 1975), p. 38.

Figure 4–24
Extrapolating on a limited data base

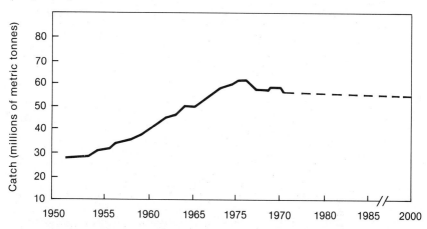

Source: Adapted from Julian L. Simon and Herman Kahn, *The Resourceful Earth: A Response to Global 2000* (London: Basil Blackwell, 1984), p. 28.

America and *The Making of a Counter-Culture* gliding easily into the slots that had been occupied by the previously cited works.

Technical considerations. Besides paradox, those who analyzed trends need to keep a few more technical things in mind. Below we will consider (1) the limits of the data base, (2) reliability of extrapolation, (3) the span and accuracy of forecasts, and (4) inappropriate assumptions.

Data base limitations refer to the fact that information on many key variables has been recorded for periods that are too brief to permit clear analysis of trends. Worse, data for different periods may not in fact be comparable, although they may be presented as such. Definitions and standards of data acquisition and recording vary greatly from time to time, place to place, and situation to situation; accordingly, the challenge of comparability of data is often severe.

The 1980 *Global 2000 Report to the President* tended to heavily weigh a few recent observations rather than look at long-term trends. For example, the report extrapolated continued stagnation in world fish catch because it only looked at the last few years' data leading up to 1975 (See Figure 4–24). Data for the years since 1975 indicate that the long-run trend toward a larger catch has resumed (17.3 percent for 1975–81). This should have been expected based on the overall trend in the series (note rise between 1950 and 1970).[17]

---

[17] Julian L. Simon and Herman Kahn, *Resourceful Earth* (London: Basil Blackwell, 1984), p. 27.

200

Table 4-4
Errors in population forecasts

Forecasting method	Average error in percent	
	10-year forecast (percent)	20-year forecast (percent)
Graphic extrapolation of past population growth	34.9	61.8
Projections based on exponential growth pattern	33.0	61.0
Projections based on linear growth pattern	14.2	18.8
Projections based on ratio of area to projected population of region	9.3	15.6
Projections based on S-shaped growth pattern	8.8	10.6

Source: Based on F. E. McJunkin, "Population Forecasting by Sanitary Engineers," *Journal of the Sanitary Engineering Division*, ASCE, 90, Proc. Paper 3993 (August 1964), pp. 31–58.

The reliability of trend extrapolation also involves the issue of technical competency. A forced-fitting of data points to a preconceived curve may conceal more than it reveals. Insufficient tests of statistical significance may suggest important correlations where none actually exist or may obscure the fundamental relationships sought.

Time spans vary enormously from application to application. The U.S. Census Bureau, for example, regularly projects population trends for 50-year periods. By contrast, few econometricians care to project economic trends farther than five years in advance. The nature of the topic under study also helps determine appropriate time spans. Long-term demographic trends, for example, may develop over many years before they are detected. By contrast, trends in, say, securities markets may develop dramatically over a few days or weeks because securities trading is a fast-moving, volatile enterprise.

Differences in accuracy among extrapolation techniques can be very great. To illustrate, Table 4-4 shows errors in population forecasts using various methods. In this particular case, the costs of the methods are so similar that one would normally select the one having the least error.

A major problem in the *Global 2000 Report* cited above was that it assumed that human beings take no action to avert tragedy. The authors forgot that human beings can innovate to alter the carrying capacity of their environment. Someone making this error in 1900 might have predicted that the United States would never be able to sustain 200 million people because there would not be enough land to pasture each person's horse.

Transit planners in many major cities share an unfortunate history of vastly overestimating the number of people who will actually ride expensive rail systems once they are built. It is not their forecasting models that are wrong so much as the assumptions they feed into them. One of the more notorious examples of mistaken assumptions is the Miami Metrorail system:

- Miami planners *assumed* that the city's central business district would grow at a much higher rate than it did, and assumed in the late 1970s that the price of gasoline would rise rapidly. Instead, the Florida city's downtown growth was marginal, and gasoline prices fell.

- Miami Metrorail planners *assumed* downtown parking to remain a problem that would encourage train riders, but the Miami Parking Authority built more parking space.

- Miami's transit planners *assumed* the cost of a ride at a certain amount, with no charge for transfers. But Miami ran into financial trouble and began charging for transfers as well as for parking at Park & Ride lots—a definite deterrent to riders.

MONITORING

Trend extrapolation works best when the data base goes back a number of years and the significant parameters are readily quantifiable. But some trends, though important, do not meet those conditions; they are too new, too amorphous. See Box 4–2.

In cases such as these, the analyst might want to turn to *monitoring*. As was discussed in Chapter 2, issues have a life cycle; therefore, it may be possible to monitor this development so as to react wisely in the future. Most problems are visible in society long before they begin to have a substantial effect. It should be possible to monitor the environment to detect the coming, the progress, and the consequences of potential problems. *Monitoring* is based on assessing ongoing events. It includes two main activities: searching the environment for signals that may be forerunners of significant change and identifying possible governmental actions if these signals are not spurious and if the trends they suggest continue. But monitoring includes much more than scanning traditional library references. It may require scanning fringe media and underground presses, unpublished notes and speeches, newsletters, and poll data; attending technical conferences; and building networks.

Having determined the important data and events to monitor, the analyst should then set up a data collection system. For each potential signal identified, the analyst should try to answer at least two questions. What is the probability (high, medium, low) that the trend will eventually become a full-blown problem and not dissipate? How significant (high, medium, low) is the problem to my organization? Clearly those trends that score high on both counts merit particular watching. Continual review and analysis, as well as comparison with other signals, will eventually lead to discarding some possibilities. It may lead to the estab-

Box 4–2
Fifteen trends worth tracking

The list of fifteen problems below is the result of a National Science Foundation search for future problems. It includes not those critical problems that are widely known (e.g., food, energy, and environment) but those important problems that are not getting adequate attention and which might be appropriate for monitoring. A very brief statement for each problem is provided. What policies and programs, if any, do each suggest?

1. Limits to the management of large, complex systems

The power to create large, complex systems (economic, political, social) does not automatically confer the power to effectively control such systems. There is growing evidence that we have aggregated small, comprehensible systems into supersystems that are very difficult to manage at all, let alone in a democratic, participatory fashion. Further, large, complex systems tend toward conditions of relatively low performance as they become more incomprehensible and less amenable to democratic control. There is a tradeoff between reduced efficiency and increased capacity for survival through many levels of backup systems. Large, complex systems also tend to become increasingly vulnerable to disruption at key points as a consequence of increasing levels of interdependence. They also demand an ever higher level of self-discipline on the part of individuals.

2. The social impact of the changing role of women

Increasingly, women are entering the work force. Equal opportunity laws and changing mores suggest that many will eventually assume senior positions in government and business. Moreover, they will do so without having to adapt to male behavioral norms. As the number of women in these positions increases dramatically, the nature of the institutions will probably change in response. In the long term, the change should prove productive and beneficial. During the transition, however, internal problems, resembling those of a clash of cultures, can be anticipated. Institutional effectiveness may suffer a short-term decline while the problems are resolved.

3. Loss of cultural diversity

The emergence of one interdependent world economy linked by rapid communications and transportation is leading to homogenization of world culture. The resulting standardization would allow greater economic efficiency and greater political and social stability. However, a culturally unified world might be less adaptable and less creative than a culturally heterogenous one. It is well known that a complex ecology (e.g., a tropical rain-forest) has greater potential for survival and is more stable than a simple ecology (e.g., monoculture). Moreover, our rich mix of cultural systems is worth preserving because such systems have intrinsic worth

Box 4–2 (*continued*)

and may also contribute understanding essential to the solution of human problems.

4. Teenage alcoholism

Heavy consumption of alcohol among adolescents (13–18 years of age) is now at about 25 percent. This extension of adult drinking patterns into youth groups indicates that the present serious problem of high alcohol consumption endemic in the United States may grow worse. Further, teenage alcoholism contributes to the problem of juvenile crime.

5. Police alienation from the populace

New technology is having an unanticipated effect on the nature of U.S. law enforcement activities. The demand has been for technological augmentation and extension of each officer's capabilities. The economic pressures that necessitate increasing the area of his coverage, the speed of his response, and the level of force he employs have increased the social distance between the officer and the citizens he serves. Alienation of police officers from all segments of our society is such that police forces are regarded in some places as an army of occupation.

6. The sociocultural impact of media

Rather than direct experiences in the real world, an increasing proportion of people's life experiences are vicarious through the media. Consequently, their perception of social reality may be distorted, and their judgment may be more susceptible to intentional and unintentional manipulation. They may also tend to withdraw from direct political and social participation.

7. The social implications of changing family forms

During the past decade, the United States has seen a drastic increase in the divorce rate and in the number of single-parent families. Traditionally, we have expected the products of broken homes to exhibit undesirable social behavior. If true, society can expect increased delinquency, alienation, and mental illness. Perhaps as significant is a growing acceptance of the nonpermanent marriage and nonrelated family groups, which undercut older expectations of permanence and family stability. This will have impact on the whole range of social, economic, and legal institutions designed for the nuclear family (parents and children).

8. Weapons technology and the right to bear arms

In the past, certain weapons (explosives and machine guns) have been excluded by law from inclusion in the constitutional right to bear arms. However, new weapons technology, resulting from military research and the public's demand for better anticriminal weapons, is already beginning

Box 4–2 (*continued*)

to strain existing laws. Weapons such as electric-shock Tasers and tranquil-
izer guns are already widely available. Terrorists may begin to use plastic
weapons that cannot be detected at security. Controlling this proliferation
of new weapons is difficult because of a perceived growing gap between
the arms allowed the private citizen and the arms used by the police
and military.

9. Cumulative effects of pollution

As new industrial processes are developed and new products are manufactured, the number and quantity of new chemical compounds released
into the environment have increased dramatically. The effects of these
compounds on human health and personality and on the stability of the
ecosystem may be unknowable for years or even generations. The large
number of such new compounds (estimated at about 5,000 per year) makes
it almost impossible to establish an acceptable testing program, which is
the necessary first step in determining potential deleterious effects. Monitoring of pollutants, understanding how they reach man and his environment, characterizing their interactions with other chemicals, and assessing
their potential for inducing low-level, long-term effects are beyond our
present capabilities.

10. The potential use and misuse of "consciousness technologies"

Various consciousness technologies constitute an applied science that
draws on medicine, physics, psychology, neurophysiology, and parapsy-
chology. Research is revealing the potential impacts of these technologies
upon humankind—both for good and for ill. Whether they present a
considerable opportunity or a considerable problem depends on their
diffusion and application.

11. Social effects of redefining legal liability

Increasing complexity, interdependence, and scale of action in society
have increased the potential liability for decisions of individuals and organizations, while permitting lines of responsibility to blur. Legal devices to
avoid responsibility tend to reduce the legitimacy of existing institutions
and to reinforce loss of trust and confidence in institutions and the professions. Loss of trust and confidence, in turn, has been reflected in increasing
resort to the courts to seek redress for real or imagined grievances. Consequently, entrepreneurial and professional risk-taking has become far more
hazardous.

12. Loss of political and social cohesion

There seems to be a decline in political and social cohesion—the sense
of shared purpose that provides the balance between individual desires
and the general well-being. This decline seems to result from a number

---

Box 4–2 (*concluded*)

of forces including high mobility; erosion of communities; the replacement of the extended family with the nuclear family; an inward turning on personal goals resulting from a sense of individual powerlessness in a mass society; and the growth in effectiveness of interest group politics. The consequence of this loss is the undermining of the efficacy and legitimacy of society's basic institutions.

13. Vulnerability of water supplies

The development of highly toxic chemicals and bacteriological substances and the increasing availability of powerful radiological materials pose a clear and present danger. Their accidental or deliberate introduction into public water supply systems would have disastrous results. The complexity of modern water supply systems and the vast population they serve exacerbate the problem.

14. Advanced microcomputers and rights to privacy

The development of powerful microcomputers, combined with improved semiconductor memories, will make possible inexpensive and highly sophisticated individual surveillance and the maintenance of vast numbers of data banks. Individuals will find it impossible to know who is keeping dossiers on them and what information is in those dossiers. Privacy and other personal rights will be threatened as this technology develops.

15. Chronic unemployment

Contrary to many predictions, fundamental changes in the economic situation (e.g., environmental and other constraints to economic growth, and basic long-term capital shortage) present the possibility of chronic unemployment. Various analyses indicate high degrees of hidden unemployment at present, and more in the future. Various societal full-employment bills in Congress betray awareness of the problem. Inaccurate identification of the long-term nature of the new unemployment could result in expensive attempts to resolve the problem with the wrong approaches.

Source: Based on the National Science Foundation's *Assessment of Future National and International Problems*, vol. 1 (Washington, D.C.: Government Printing Office, February 1977).

---

lishment of others (and eventual crystallization of the true direction or major impact) or to the total discard of this particular signal. It should be apparent that new possible signals are constantly emerging and should be continually introduced into the analysis.

To illustrate how useful a monitoring system can be in practice, consider the accompanying insert on issues management by corporations.

Box 4–3
Public policy analysis in corporations

In February 1981, many business executives were still gleeful over Ronald Reagan's inauguration a month earlier, looking forward to four years of conservative, pro-business government. The view wasn't quite so rosy in an office at Atlantic Richfield Co.'s headquarters here.

A group of Arco executives called issues managers saw trouble ahead. They predicted that Reagan budget cuts would prompt one state after another to try to compensate for lost federal money by taxing businesses. Arco, as a profitable oil and natural-resources company operating in twenty-eight states, would be a prime target.

A task force wrote a report on the likely state tax proposals, and by summer Arco lobbyists and top executives were ready. Sure enough, last winter and this past spring saw a deluge of state tax bills introduced, as many as ten a week. Well-prepared Arco operatives responded quickly, and, although four states did raise corporate taxes and four raised severance taxes, bills aimed specifically at oil companies in several states were defeated.

To Arco, the episode proved the usefulness of this new kind of executive that has arisen in recent years. The issues manager's job is to alert management to emerging political, social, and economic trends and controversies and to mobilize the company's resources to deal with them.

Tired of surprises

Archie Boe, the president of Sears, Roebuck & Co., who set up one of the first such departments when he headed Sears' Allstate Insurance unit, sees the system as "a pre-crisis approach." Arco established its issues-manager system partly because it felt its planning was "too numbers-oriented," says Breck Arrington, who heads Arco's twenty-eight-member governmental-issues team. He explains: "Single-line numbers forecasting, typically done by economic planners, didn't predict the Arab oil embargo or the environmental revolution. We needed a wider, more qualitative approach to supplement the other work."

In the late 1970s, Arco and a few other large oil, banking, and insurance concerns set up special trend-spotting departments, assigning them a task previously done somewhat haphazardly by top executives, government relations people, planners and public relations staffs. "They were fed up with unpleasant surprises," says Richard Drobnick of the University of Southern California business school. Today about seventy companies have issues managers.

An issues manager isn't the same as a futurist, who tries to tell management what will happen ten or twenty years from now. Rather, he or she considers the immediate future and the next one to five years, and is charged not only with identifying issues, but also with setting forth the specific ways the company might deal with them.

Box 4–3 (*continued*)

Corporations naturally take varying approaches to issues management. At some, like Monsanto Co., an issues manager organizes a committee of middle managers and other employes to do the work, with the results sent to top executives. Other companies, including Arco, have large staffs of full-time issues managers. At Arco, they include people trained as petroleum, chemical, and aeronautical engineers, lawyers, marketing managers, congressional consultants, and legislative analysts. There is a former journalist on the staff as well as a former English professor.

Some corporations emphasize legislative and governmental issues. Others, like Northwestern National Bank in Minneapolis, use issues managers to spot emerging concerns for their community and philanthropic programs.

Arco does both. Its system is organized around five clusters of issues: resources; environment; corporate and planning (including tax, antitrust, and labor matters); manufacturing processes; and Arco's participation in its many trade associations. Managers of the five clusters earn from $48,000 to $77,000 a year.

The Arco issues-management group monitors hundreds of publications, opinion polls and think-tank research reports. It provides 500 company middle managers and top executives with a daily publication called Scan, which summarizes governmental action—federal, state and local legislation, rules and regulations, court and agency decisions, hearing notices, investigations, meetings. It can provide copies of documents to Arco executives on one day's notice.

Right now, the group is tracking 140 issues in all. Among governmental matters, they include state taxes, the Clean Air Act review, natural gas decontrol and state legislation on hazardous wastes.

Eight-year curve

These are all mature issues, having reached the stage of governmental action. Many in the field believe issues tend to follow an eight-year curve. For the first five years or so, nascent issues are emerging in local newspapers, are being enunciated by public-interest organizations, and can be detected through public-opinion polling.

"At this stage an issue is low-keyed and flexible," says Margaret Stroup, the director of corporate responsibility at Monsanto. "If it affects their interests, companies can intervene to prevent the issue from ever reaching the legislative or active stage."

Issues managers have identified several "precursor" states where national issues frequently arise first. They are California, Oregon, Michigan, Connecticut, and Florida, Mrs. Stroup says.

In the fifth or sixth year of the eight-year cycle, national media get interested in an issue; then, governmental action typically results in the seventh or eighth year, according to professionals in the field. "If compa-

Box 4–3 (*continued*)

nies get into the game at this stage, all they can do is react," Mrs. Stroup says. "We like to get involved in the third to fifth year."

Identifying the issues leads to a more complicated task—analyzing them and determining what position the company ought to take. At Arco, issues managers may have to "broker" such positions among the various operating companies to come up with a final corporate stance.

For instance, if Congress required cuts in sulfur emissions in the East to combat "acid rain," low-sulfur Western coal might have a market advantage, and Arco's coal company would benefit. But compliance with the new regulations might cost Arco's aluminum company, based in Kentucky, about $4 million a month.

North to Alaska

Likewise, under natural-gas decontrol, the higher prices would aid Arco's oil and gas operations, but they would hurt its energy-thirsty refining and chemicals operation. Issues managers try to build a consensus among operating units before the issues get to top corporate management.

Such analysis and compromise finally move the company to action. As an example, not long ago a House bill on Alaska lands proposed to bar evaluation of the oil-and-gas potential of the William O. Douglas Arctic Wildlife Refuge. Arco's issues managers, who had been deeply involved in Alaskan affairs for years, marshaled a posse to head the bill off at the Senate.

It sent a barrage of maps, surveys and data to Arco's Washington lobbying office. Letters went to all members of Congress. Then Arco took a group of oil and environmental experts from Alaska and Los Angeles to Washington to discuss with key Senators and their aides what the company believed to be the high oil and gas potential of the wildlife range. Other experts were rounded up to testify that seismic testing wouldn't harm the refuge's caribou herd.

The final Alaska-lands bill let oil companies test for hydrocarbons in the wildlife refuge. Arco executives believe that the whole area would have been bottled up but for the efforts of their issues managers.

Issues managers can cite lots of other cases. With their advice, S. C. Johnson & Sons, a privately held maker of floor waxes and other chemicals, removed environmentally chancy fluorocarbons from its aerosol sprays three years before federal action forced others in the industry to do so.

Sears spotted the flammable-nightwear controversy early and got non-flammable goods into its stores before government action required this. A later issue arose over Tris, a flame retardant suspected of causing cancer; again Sears acted early, removing its Tris-treated garments from stores before the government required it to.

Bank of America, alerted early by issues managers about "redlining," moved to change its lending policies two years before Congress required banks to disclose whether they were barring all loans in certain parts of

---

Box 4–3 *(concluded)*

a city. The bank says the early action cut its eventual cost of compliance with anti-redlining laws and spared it "a lot of grief and antagonism" from cities and public-interest groups.

Some companies that don't have issues managers as such note that they have others whose broad assignment is to keep track of trends and controversies. "We wouldn't touch it," Forrest Shumway, the president of Signal Cos., says of issues management. "We already have enough high-paid help around who can detect new trends." Another executive terms the issue-spotters "just another bureaucracy."

Issues managers themselves have some concerns about how fast their field is developing. One fears that "bored public-relations people and speech writers are trying to hop onto the issues-manager bandwagon to enrich their jobs. Sadly, some of these people aren't all that good."

Rona Klingenberg, the issues director at Prudential Insurance, says the job actually is one of "aiding the company's response to change." She says the term "issues manager" may wrongly imply that the official can do more than he actually can, and she worries that the job may have "a short life cycle, like the consumer-affairs jobs at corporations a few years back."

Source: Earl C. Gottschalk, Jr., "Firms Hiring New Type of Manager to Study Issues," *The Wall Street Journal*, June 10, 1982.

EXPERTS—A FIFTH FORECASTING METHOD

Expert panels

Expert panels are one of the most widely used and least accurate forecasting methods. Nevertheless, the reason for their continued use in government forecasting is clear enough. In some areas of public policy, no alternative method is available. This is often the case, for example, in new areas, where adequate historical information—the life-blood of extrapolation—is unavailable; in areas that involve judgment about the effects of many converging factors; and in areas where events are dependent primarily on the decisions of public officials rather than environmental factors.

Forecasting with expert panels is generally considered preferable to forecasting with a single expert because groups can interact to compensate for the biases and ignorance of individual members. Studies of forecasts that have gone wrong show that one very common cause has been a failure to consider a sufficient number of factors external to the area of the forecast; in the long run, such overlooked external factors can prove more significant than internal factors. A well-balanced, interdisciplinary panel should have fewer blind spots than a single expert.

But committees or panels have several disadvantages:

1. A group can exert strong social pressure on its members—pressure, for instance, to agree with the majority even when the individual feels that the majority is wrong. This is especially true in the production of group forecasts, since these are not really matters of fact but only informed opinion.

2. Experiments with small groups have shown that frequently it is not the validity of a proposed position but the number of comments and arguments for or against the position that carries the day. Thus a strong vocal minority or even an individual may overwhelm the remainder of the group by pushing views vigorously, even though the arguments presented may have little merit.

3. Since the group takes on a life of its own, frequently reaching agreement comes to be considered of greater importance than producing a well-thought-out and useful forecast. The result of group discussion may only be a watered-down least common denominator which offends no one, even though no one really agrees with it.

4. Members of the group may come to have vested interests in certain points of view, especially if they have presented them strongly at the outset. Their objective becomes one of winning the remainder of the group over, rather than reaching what might be a better conclusion. They will be impervious to the facts and logic of the remainder of the group, and will concentrate only on winning the argument.

5. The whole group shares a common bias. This usually arises from a common subculture shared by the members—especially a subculture peculiar to the area of public policy in which the members are supposed to be experts.

Fortunately for the policymaker, methods have been developed within the last decade to mitigate these problems yet still capitalize on the obvious advantages of panels. The Delphi technique is certainly the most important of these newer methods. In this technique, participants do not meet and are not identified until the poll has been completed, so as to minimize the influence of "big names" and dominant personalities. The use of mail removes geographic limitations in selecting panelists. Expertise may be equated with special knowledge about a topic, informed opinions about the attitudes and intents of some population, or both. In Delphi polls, unlike surveys of intentions and attitudes, individual participants are given one or more opportunities to compare and (if they choose) revise their estimates. Typically, Delphi polls involve far fewer participants than do public surveys, partly because of the greater demands made on Delphi participants and partly because of the greater complexity and cost of Delphi studies. An example of a Delphi appears in the next chapter.

How expert are the experts?

Dozens of carefully constructed studies have demonstrated that expertise beyond a minimal level is of little value in forecasting change. Evidence comes from a variety of fields: economics, stock market, psychology, sociology, medicine, and sports. Almost all studies have shown that expertise above a minimal level—say, taking an introductory course in a subject—was not related to accuracy.

A few studies have shown expertise to be useful in some fields, but the differences between experts and nonexperts have always been small. In one study, sportswriters were a little more accurate than graduate students and faculty members in forecasting football scores. And bookmakers' forecasts, in turn, were slightly better than those of sportswriters.[18]

Forecasters fail partly because people, whether expert or not, tend to avoid information that refutes their preconceptions. In an experiment, P. C. Watson, a psychologist, presented people with a three-number sequence: two-four-six. He told them that this sequence had been generated by a rule that he had in his head. The subjects were then asked to figure out the rule by proposing additional three-number sequences (e.g., eight-ten-twelve). After each try, Watson would tell the subjects if the new sequence agreed with the rule, and when the subjects felt confident, they were to write the rule down.

The rule Watson had in mind was "three numbers in increasing order of magnitude." In other words, the rule was simply that the second number be larger than the first, and the third number be larger than the second.

Only 25 percent of the subjects discovered the correct rule. The majority selected other hypotheses—guessing, for example, that the rule was, "Add two to each successive number." Then they looked for evidence only to confirm their pet hypotheses. They would not attempt to *refute* their hypotheses by proposing sequences that didn't conform to them. In other words, most subjects refused to entertain the possibility that their hypotheses were wrong.

Toward better forecasts

There are four ways to get better forecasts. First, the experts should be asked explicitly to list the reasons why their forecasts may be wrong.

---

[18] This research is summarized in J. Scott Armstrong, "The Seer-Sucker Theory: The Value of Experts in Forecasting," *Technology Review*, July 1980, pp. 19–24.

This helps keep them in touch with reality. Second, they should be asked to list alternative possibilities that cover the range of potential outcomes. Third, averaging the predictions of several cheap experts is probably more reliable than accepting the forecasts of a single expensive expert. Robin Hogarth of the University of Chicago found that averaging the predictions of as many as ten people generally produced better forecasts than relying on the judgment of one well-qualified individual.

Finally, the experts should not have spent a lifetime providing advice and performing paper studies. They should have had, somewhere in their careers, hands-on experience. Lucius Aemilius Paulus, the Roman consul who was to lead the war against the Macedonians some twenty centuries ago, expressed the idea well:

> I am not one of those who think that commanders ought at no time to receive advice; on the contrary, I should deem that man more proud than wise who regulated every proceeding by the standard of his own single judgment. What then is my opinion?
>
> That commanders should be counseled, chiefly, by persons of known talent; by those who have made the art of war their particular study, and whose knowledge is derived from experience; from those who are present at the scene of action, who see the country, who see the enemy; who see the advantages that occasions offer, and who, like people embarked in the same ship, are sharers of the danger. If, therefore, anyone thinks himself qualified to give advice respecting the war which I am to conduct, which may prove advantageous to the public, let him not refuse his assistance to the state, *but let him come with me into Macedonia.*[19]

CONCLUDING OBSERVATIONS

Prognosis is commonly the weakest part of policy analysis. Good forecasts require either a theoretical understanding of the problem or phenomena sufficiently regular for extrapolation. Since most, if not all, forecasting in public affairs involves human beings neither condition obtains entirely.

For a variety of reasons, public affairs is inherently unpredictable. One reason derives from the nature of conceptual innovation. Suppose some time in the Stone Age I predict that, within the next ten years, someone will invent the wheel. "Wheel," you ask, "What is that?" I tell you all about rims, spokes, hubs, and axles. But now no one is going to invent the wheel in ten years, because I just did. In other words, the invention of the wheel cannot be predicted, because to do

---

[19] Quoted in Norman R. Augustine, *Augustine's Laws* (New York: Viking Press, 1983), p. 220.

so is to invent it. This example can be easily generalized to any area in which radical conceptual innovation takes place.[20]

Another reason why systematic prediction in public affairs is difficult derives from the fact that individuals cannot predict all of their own future actions. If *I* cannot predict myself which of two or more courses of action I will take, that would seem to make it even more difficult for a policy maker to predict it. And if I cannot predict all my future choices, then neither can the policymaker predict his. And his future choices, unknown to him, will affect my behavior in unforeseeable ways.

A third source of unpredictability, which was only touched on in this chapter but will be covered in the next, is the random element in human affairs. Trivial contingencies in history can powerfully influence the outcome of great events—for example, Napoleon's cold at Waterloo, which led him to delegate command to Marshall Ney, with disastrous consequences for the French. Trivial contingencies explain the breaks or discontinuities policymakers so often experience in trends—and most modeling assumes will not occur.

Does this unpredictability vitiate efforts to forecast? No, but it does demand some change in the character of forecasts. Policymakers need not know exactly when some calamity will occur; rather they need alternative scenarios of the future and the likelihood each will occur. Policymakers need not know the details of future events, but they do need enough to enable them *today* to set goals.

FOR FURTHER REFLECTION

1. What important trends do you think were omitted from the list of "trends worth tracking" given in Box 4–2?
2. The history of petroleum geology abounds with predictions that we were about to run out of crude oil. In 1914, the U.S. Bureau of Mines projected that future production would amount to only 5.7 billion barrels (we have since produced over 34 billion). In 1939, the Department of the Interior said that the U.S. oil supply would last only thirteen years (we have since discovered more than the total known supply at the time). In 1949, the Department of the Interior said that the end of the U.S. oil supply was in sight (oil production was increased by more than a million barrels a day in the next five years). The same kind of errors also appear in estimating the known reserves of other minerals.

   Some of the problem might be found in the way in which we conceptualize raw-material supplies. Accordingly, the U.S. Geologi-

---

[20] Compare Karl Popper, *The Poverty of Historicism* (New York: Harper & Row, 1966).

214

Figure 4–25
Conceptualizing raw material supplies

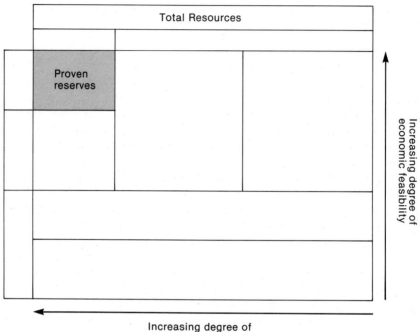

Increasing degree of
economic feasibility

Increasing degree of
geological assurance

cal Survey has adopted a box to show the place of known reserves
in the overall scheme of total resources. That box appears as Figure
4–25 with only proven reserves indicated. Can you complete it?
3. Using the data in Exercise 11, Chapter 3, determine for which pair—
(Y,X) or (Y,Z)—the slope of the predictive equation should be steepest. What is the value of b for each pair?
4. Study the table below, which shows the decline in union membership
as percentage of workforce since 1975. Extrapolating from these
data, predict the year in which membership will reach zero. How
much would you bet on this prediction? Explain.

1975	29%
1977	26
1979	25
1981	23
1983	21
1985	17

5. Read the following verbal description of a system and try to construct
a causal-loop diagram.

Prior to 1907, the deer herd on the Kaibab Plateau, which consists of some 727,000 acres and is on the north side of the Grand Canyon in Arizona, numbered about 4,000. In 1907, a bounty was placed on cougars, wolves, and coyotes—all natural predators of deer. Within fifteen to twenty years, there was a substantial extirpation of these predators (over 8,000) and a consequent and immediate irruption of the deer population. By 1918, the deer population had increased more than tenfold; the evident overbrowsing of the area brought the first of a series of warnings by competent investigators, none of which produced a much needed change in either the bounty policy or that dealing with deer removal. In the absence of predation by its natural predators (cougars, wolves, coyotes) or by man as a hunter, the herd reached 100,000 in 1924; in the absence of sufficient food, 60 percent of the herd died off in two successive winters. By then, the killing of so much vegetation through browsing precluded recovery of the food reserve to such an extent that subsequent die-off and reduced natality yielded a population about half that which could theoretically have been previously maintained. Perhaps the most pertinent statement relative to the manner of the interregulatory effect of predator and prey is the following: "We have found no record of a deer irruption in North America antedating the removal of deer predators. Those parts of the continent which still retain the native predators have reported no irruptions. This circumstantial evidence supports the surmise that removal of predators predisposes a deer herd to irruptive behavior."

Source: E. J. Kormondy, *Concepts of Ecology* (Englewood Cliffs, N.J.: Prentice-Hall, 1969).

6. In the figure below you will see seven different boxes that each contain a brief phrase. Each of these phrases describes some variable in an urban environment. Draw on this figure arrows to show how the variables are related. When you feel that some variable affects some other variable, represent this by an arrow connecting the two. In addition to drawing arrows among the variables you should also place either a plus or minus sign next to the head of *each* arrow that you draw. A plus sign means that the two connected events change in the *same* direction. Some events that you connect, however, will move in opposite directions. Whenever you have two events linked by an arrow and the two events move in opposite directions, then put a minus sign next to the arrow.

Work your way systematically around the diagram. In addition to drawing variables between the variables, you should also place either a plus or a minus sign next to each arrow that you draw. When you draw an arrow, that simply says that the event at the blunt end of the arrow has an effect on the event at the sharp end of the arrow. The plus and minus designation permits you to identify what kind of effect occurs. A plus sign means that the two connected events change in the same direction. But some events that you

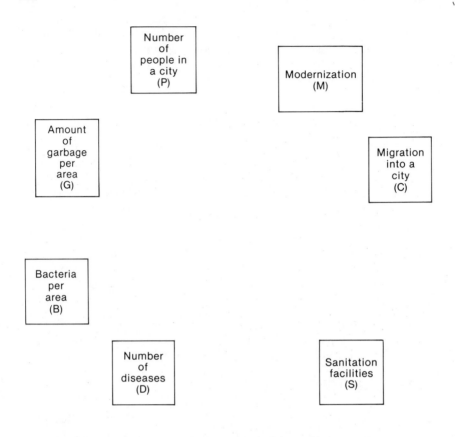

connect will move in opposite directions; in such cases, put a minus sign next to that arrow.

7. Can you reconstruct the supply and demand curves as a causal-loop diagram? That is, can you portray the dynamics of the market, the way price signals cause producers to produce or not, and consumers to buy or not?

8. Explain in your own words the following comments on computer simulation.

> . . . the future price of energy is not a key input for estimating the future price and quality of food; actions by governments concerning agricultural price controls and subsidies, and the amount of agricultural research done, among other forces, are likely to be far more important in the long run of twenty and more years. Population growth may even not be a central variable if viewed in the conventional fashion of more people implying a higher price of food; in the long run the effect may be the opposite, as greater population density leads to better farm-to-market transportation, and to a host of institutional and technological developments, as has been the history of humanity until now. Ignoring

most or all of the interdependencies among the sectors touched on by *Global 2000* may not be disastrous, as *Global 2000* suggests it is and necessarily will be. It may even be a prudent scientific strategy to ignore them. (This assertion may seem preposterous until you examine the track records of predictions about the resources and environment made without extensive consideration of such interdependencies, and compare them with predictions of the global modelers who insist—at least in principle—on including such interdependencies in models.)

Source: Julian Simon and Herman Kahn, *The Resourceful Earth* (New York: Blackwell, 1984).

9. One good method of forecasting is to watch bellwethers, that is, jurisdictions that more often than not are early adopters of new programs. Which countries, states, and cities would you consider bellwethers? Why?

10. Canada has one of the slowest population growth rates in the world. In 1983, with a population of about 25 million, it experienced a 1.0 percent annual growth rate. If this trend continues, when should Kenya surpass Canada in population?

Chapter 5

Strategic Thinking

Everyone knows Dirty Harry and Rambo. These characters do not waste time in philosophical musings; they see a problem and then *act*. This chapter suggests an alternative modus operandi. Before grabbing the Smith & Wesson or Uzzi, policymakers ought to ask themselves a few questions. What do I wish to achieve? What are my goals and objectives? Do my actions bring me closer to their realization? What are my priorities? How should I allocate my resources (time, energy, etc.) and that of my organization? These are high impact questions. They can increase the odds that problems like those in the previous two chapters are alleviated with minimum waste and few hitches.

But first we must clear our minds of caricature. While few people over the age of twelve would accept Dirty Harry and Rambo as decision-making models, a number of middle-aged bureaucrats and academicians may accept this view:

> Human beings make choices. Choices are properly made by evaluating alternatives in terms of goals and on the basis of information currently available. The alternative that is most attractive in terms of the goals is chosen. By using the technology of choice, we can improve the quality of the search for alternatives, the quality of information, and the quality of the analysis used to evaluate alternatives. Although actual choice may fall short of this ideal in various ways, it is an attractive model of how choices should be made by individuals, organizations, and social systems.[1]

This highly rational view of the decision process has not gone unchallenged. Choice situations contain more uncertainty, more politics, more

---

[1] According to Michael D. Cohen and James G. March virtually all theories of policymaking profess this faith in the rationality of choice. Although they concocted this statement, they do not subscribe to it. *Leadership and Ambiguity: The American College President* (Boston: Harvard Business School Press, 1986), p. 216.

blurring of means and ends, and less adequate information than the rational view allows. Charles E. Lindblom of Yale University has developed a concept of strategy as it applies to policymaking.[2] He considers strategy to be "adaptations" that policymakers fashion in order to make headway against problems—to muddle through. This particular strategy encompasses incremental change to the status quo, consideration of only a few alternatives (or maybe only one) and a limited number of consequences, and adaptation of goals to the means available to achieve them.

Lindblom's incremental approach is as modest as the rationalist's approach is grandiose. Rather than try to resolve these two polar views, as some scholars already have,[3] I propose that we quietly slip around this friendly feud and address this question: What do highly successful policymakers actually *do* once a problem has been identified?

PROLOGUE: REFLECTIONS ON THE THEORY AND PRACTICE OF GOAL SETTING

A rather large gap exists between the conventional wisdom on policymaking and the actual behavior of policymaking makers. The former is usually discussed in terms of rational choice (as suggested above); the latter is characterized by long hours, fragmented episodes, ambiguity, even a little anarchy, and oral communication. The policy planning that these people do does not seem very systematically done.

To understand why effective policymakers act as they do, it is essential first to recognize the fundamental challenge facing most of them: to figure out what to do despite uncertainty, great diversity, and an enormous amount of potentially relevant information. The severity of this challenge in government is much greater than the student of planning would suspect. The very nature of the policymaker's job requires a complex and subtle way of thinking. An examination of effective policymakers suggests that they have found just such a way of thinking.

The case of Joan Claybrook

During her first six months as administrator of the National Highway Traffic and Safety Administration (NHTSA) in the Carter administration,

---

[2] David Braybrooke and Charles E. Lindblom, *A Strategy of Decision* (New York: Free Press, 1970). See also by Lindblom, "The Science of 'Muddling Through,'" *Public Administration Review* 19 (Spring 1959), pp. 79–88; Lindblom, *The Intelligence of Democracy* (New York: Free Press, 1965); *The Policy-Making Process* (Englewood Cliffs, N.J.: Prentice-Hall, 1968); *Politics and Markets* (New York: Basic Books, 1977); and "Still Muddling, Not Yet Through," *Public Administration Review* 39 (November/December 1979), pp. 517–26.

[3] See, for example, Amitai Etzioni, "Mixed Scanning: A 'Third' Approach to Decision Making," *Public Administration Review* 27 (December 1967), pp. 385–92.

Joan Claybrook spent considerable time developing a list of loosely connected goals and objectives that addressed her long-, medium-, and short-term responsibilities. Prior to her confirmation, she had "no grand vision with a specific set of outcomes that were supposed to result after four years in office."[4] Once on the job, she quickly realized that she could not keep up with all the activities of the agency. That is why developing a grand strategy, a set of overarching goals, became crucial.[5]

Specifically, she adopted three goals to rely on in choosing particular courses of action:

1. Passenger cars should be designed similar to the designs of NHTSA research vehicles.
2. To build the agency's reputation for competence, standards called for by statutes should be issued in a timely manner and enforced.
3. The agency should recognize its obligation to attend to the needs and concerns of purchasers and operators of motor vehicles.

These three goals suited Claybrook's allocation of time and effort. Like other effective policymakers, her grand strategy helped her maintain a satisfactory balance among the competing demands she faced and an ability to defend her actions. But where did her goals come from?

Developing goals

Decision-making techniques tend to assume the *prior* existence of a set of consistent goals. Most theories of decision making accept the idea that goals exist and that policymakers act on those goals. So for policymakers, the message is: determine values, then act. The interesting question of where these goals come from is, however, seldom carefully examined.

Obviously, Claybrook's goals flowed in part from the legislation that NHTSA was established to implement. But this answer is not entirely satisfactory. In the first place, it merely exchanges one puzzle for another. How then did Congress arrive at *its* goals? Furthermore, the answer tells us nothing about how Claybrook came to develop her own particular agenda. Surely, there were many other goals she could have chosen to emphasize.

---

[4] David Whitman, "Joan Claybrook and NHTSA." Teaching Case C95-81-385. (Cambridge, Mass.: Kennedy School of Government, 1981).

[5] John P. Kotter reports that the same imperative faces top business executives. "What Effective Managers Really Do," *Harvard Business Review*, November/December 1982, pp. 156–67.

The great challenge facing policymakers is, in a nutshell, how to design a policy consistent with their (1) definition of the problem, (2) political environment, (3) resource constraints, and (4) values.

A problem definition does not tell the whole truth. For example, some important aspects of the problem may have been ignored. Borrowing a concept from statistics, we can refer to this inadequacy of problem definition as "Type I errors."[6] They are errors of omission. A second inadequacy results when we include in our problem definition irrelevant factors. This is an error of commission or "Type II error" in the language of statistics. Both errors will adversely affect the design of a policy. But a Type III error is perhaps the worst. This error occurs when the problem is correctly defined but it is the *wrong* problem. If the wrong problem is being tackled, then something less than the best policy will be recommended.

In developing goals, policymakers must consider politics and the availability of resources. Congressional intent reduced the degrees of freedom Claybrook had in forming her grand strategy, but constituency wishes reduced those of Congress in drafting the laws she will implement. And both executive head and legislator are constrained by the availability of funding and the capabilities, procedures, and traditions of the organization that will implement the policy.

To see how values enter the equation, consider the goals of primary and secondary education. Among them are:

- Increasing knowledge and skills.
- Fostering good citizenship and cooperation.
- Improving character.
- Freeing parents to work.
- Changing the social structure by providing for mobility.
- Fostering creativity and individualism.

How one prioritizes these goals invariably is a function of one's own values.

But must goals and values at all times precede action? To put it bluntly, could the Dirty Harry–Rambo approach ever make sense?

Michael D. Cohen and James G. March's study of college presidents suggests that policy-makers sometimes treat action as a way of creating goals; they seem to act before they think.[7] The idea is not as foolish as

---

[6] In statistics, the type I error is committed when a true null hypothesis is rejected; that is, the null hypothesis was true, but we decided against it. The type II error is committed when we decide in favor of a null hypothesis that is actually false. Generally, a null hypothesis is a statement that a population parameter (such as mean) has a specified value.

[7] Cohen and March, *Leadership and Ambiguity,*

it may seem. "Conventional theories of decision making allow us to entertain doubts about almost everything except the thing about which we frequently have the greatest doubt—objectives." Therefore, why not treat goals as hypotheses. "If we can experiment with alternative goals, we stand some chance of discovering complicated and interesting combinations of good values that none of us previously imagined."[8] According to Thomas J. Peters and Robert H. Waterman, many excellent corporations seem to take this approach. A common trait of such companies, they find, is a "bias for action"; rather than develop elaborate plans, these companies prefer to experiment—letting goals and objectives emerge out of this process.[9]

Whether this approach works equally well in the public sector I am not prepared to say. But it does seem that more policy is made on a let-us-try-something-and-then-see-what-happens basis than is generally recognized. Indicative of such policy is the immigration bill passed in 1986. No one really knew how many employees would go to jail or how many illegal aliens would get citizenship. Congressional supporters did not even pretend to understand what the bill said. Representative Charles Schumer called the policy "a gamble, a riverboat gamble. . . . we are headed into uncharted water."[10] After six years of arguing the need to get control of the border, Congress apparently decided that it was time to try something.

A variation of this let-us-try-something approach to developing goals occurs when policymakers imitate. For example, Edward I. Koch tells in his book *Politics* how Harry Truman and Fiorello LaGuardia have served as role models for him as mayor of New York.[11] Imitation is not necessarily foolishness. Rather, it is a prediction that, if policymakers duplicate the behavior or attitudes of someone else, they will fare well in terms of current goals and may increase their chances of discovering attractive new goals for themselves.

These are provocative ideas, to be sure, but the central point of the chapter remains this: Effective policymakers think strategically. The term conceptual skill is too general for our purposes. What we really need to talk about is conceptual skill as it manifests itself in policymakers. The preferred term for that is *strategic thinking*.

---

[8] Ibid., p. 223.
[9] Thomas J. Peters and Robert H. Waterman, Jr., *In Search of Excellence* (New York: Warner Books, 1982), Ch. 6.
[10] Quoted in *The Wall Street Journal*, November 10, 1986.
[11] Edward I. Koch, *Politics* (New York: Warner Books, 1985), pp. 7–8.

THE CONCEPT OF STRATEGIC THINKING

What it is

Some policymakers exhibit it, some do not. High intelligence does not guarantee it. Robert E. Lee, John F. Kennedy, and Jimmy Carter were highly intelligent men, but as we shall see, none exhibit much capacity for strategic thinking. What are the characteristics of strategic thinkers? Most importantly, they set goals in order of priority to ensure that available resources are better *concentrated* on the problems they face. Secondly, in any critical situation, they look for the few factors on which the success of their policy will rise or fall. How they discover these factors involves no mystery. It does involve, however, clearly defining the problem—just as we discussed in the two preceding chapters.

Thirdly, strategic thinkers recognize the interrelatedness of their environment. They recognize that if they do A, then B will occur—but B in turn will have consequences (C, D, and E) that will reverberate throughout society. A shorthand way of saying this is to say that strategic thinkers take a systems view of society.

Fourthly, strategic thinkers ensure that goals, plans, and programs are flexible—adaptable to changing circumstances. They foresee and provide for a next step in case of success or failure, or partial success— which is the most common case in public policy. Their policy formation allows this exploitation or adaptation in the shortest possible time.

Strategic thinkers know through experience that some goals are better than others. Clear and simple goals are better than vague and complex ones. Realistic and challenging goals are preferable to goals that are "mission impossible" or "a piece of cake." Finally, a policy should consist of goals that are internally consistent—not at cross purposes. Likewise, each goal should be consistent with the plan established to attain it—a point first made in Chapter 1.

Clear-cut nomenclature is essential to clear thought. Before discussing these characteristics in a public policy context, a military analogy or two might be useful in revealing more sharply the distinction between strategic thinkers and nonstrategic thinkers.

The grand strategy of Hannibal

The term *strategy* refers to the actual direction of military forces, as distinct from the policy governing their employment and combining that employment with other factors: economic, political, psychological. Since such policy is really an application of a higher-level strategy, the term *grand strategy* has been coined to describe it.[12] Grand strategy, then, is to strategy as public policy is to programs (or alternative courses of action). In either case, and this is the crucial point, the former should guide the latter. That is to say, specific military strategies should be decided on within the context of grand strategy; similarly, programs should be decided on within the context of an overarching public policy. If we press our military analogy a little farther, we can see in the starkest light why these directions are so vital.

The map in Figure 5–1 shows Hannibal's path of invasion into Italy during the Second Punic War (218–201 B.C.). Hannibal's grand strategy, as the map reveals, was not to march directly on Rome—given his lack of an adequate siege train and the strong fortification of the city, he knew that such a grand strategy could not have worked. Instead, he chose to swing south, achieve as many victories as possible against the Roman legions, and thus encourage the defection of Roman allies to his side. Month-to-month battles, despite their undisputed brilliance, were to Hannibal only means toward the end of breaking Rome's hold on its Italian allies.

After some stunning defeats, Rome appointed Quintas Fabius. Unfortunately for Hannibal, Fabius could also think in terms of grand strategy: recognizing that to try to defeat Hannibal on the battlefield was unlikely to work, he wisely chose to conduct a campaign of delays and small wars—the one thing Hannibal could not afford. B. H. Liddell Hart, the eminent British historian, elaborates:

> The strategy of Fabius was not merely an evasion of battle to gain time, but calculated for its effect on the morale of the enemy—and, still more, for its effect on their potential allies. It was thus primarily a matter of war-policy, or grand strategy. Fabius recognized Hannibal's military superiority too well to risk a military decision. While seeking to avoid this, he aimed by military pinpricks to wear down the invaders' endurance and, co-incidentally, prevent their strength being recruited from the Italian cities or their Carthaginian base. The key condition of the strategy by which this grand strategy was carried out was that the Roman army should keep always to the hills, so as to nullify Hannibal's decisive superiority in cavalry. Thus this phase became a duel between the Hannibalic and the Fabian forms of the indirect approach. . . .
>
> Hovering in the enemy's neighborhood, cutting off stragglers and foraging parties, preventing them from gaining any permanent base, Fabius remained an elusive shadow on the horizon, dimming the glamour of Hannibal's triumphal progress. Thus Fabius, by his immunity from defeat, thwarted the effect of Hannibal's previous victories upon the minds of Rome's Italian allies and checked them from changing sides. This guerilla type of campaign

---

[12] Liddell B. H. Hart, *Strategy* (New York: Praeger Publishers, 1954), p. 39.

Figure 5–1
Hannibal's theater of operations

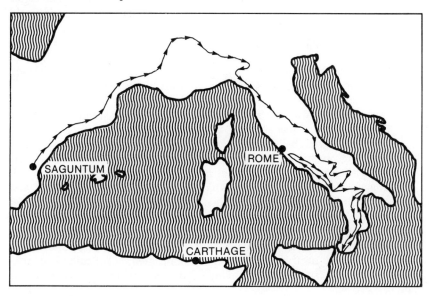

also revived the spirit of the Roman troops while depressing the Carthaginians who, having ventured so far from home, were the more conscious of the necessity of gaining an early decision.[13]

But this grand strategy was neither understood nor tolerated for long by the Romans. They had always won by offensive strategy. Fabius's policy earned him the name of "Cunctator," or delayer, and resulted in his replacement by two consuls, Paullus and Varro.

Hannibal, informed of the dissatisfaction of the Roman people with the policies of Fabius, and knowing that two thirds of the Roman troops were green, tried in every way to entice them into battle. Inaction angered his troops; supplies were hard to get; and he feared desertion. In an effort to force the issue, Hannibal made a night march to the vicinity of Cannae (CAN-ee) forcing the Roman army to follow. What happened the next morning was an example of strategy as opposed to grand strategy. Hart describes the action:

> Varro moved the Roman army out of camp to offer battle—and the kind of battle which Hannibal desired. As was customary, the infantry of both sides were posted in the centre, and the cavalry on the flanks—but Hannibal's detailed disposition was unconventional. For he pushed forward the Gauls

---

[13] Ibid., pp. 47–48.

and Spaniards, who formed the centre of the infantry line, while holding back his African foot, posted at each end of the line. In that way the Gauls and Spaniards formed a natural magnet for the Roman infantry, and were, as intended, forced back—so that what had been a line bulging outwards became a line sagging inwards. The Roman legionaries, flushed with their apparent success, crowded into the opening—where the press grew ever denser, until they could scarcely use their weapons. While they imagined that they were breaking the Carthaginian front, they were actually pushing themselves into a Carthaginian sack. For at this juncture Hannibal's African veterans wheeled inwards from both sides, thus automatically enveloping the thickly packed Romans. . . .

Meanwhile, Hannibal's heavy cavalry on the left wing had broken through the opposing cavalry on that flank and, sweeping round the Romans' rear, dispersed their cavalry on the other flank—who had been held in play by the elusive Numidian horse. Leaving the pursuit to the Numidians, the heavy cavalry now delivered the final stroke by bursting into the rear of the Roman infantry, who were already surrounded on three sides and too tightly jammed to offer effective resistance. Thenceforward the battle became a massacre. According to Polybius, out of the 76,000 men in the Roman army, 70,000 fell on the field of battle. Among them was Paullus, whereas Varro, ironically, succeeded in making his own escape from the crash which he had caused.[14]

Following his victory at Cannae, Hannibal was urged by his generals to move immediately on Rome. That he did not do so is a further tribute to his grand strategy. Rome could not be captured and Hannibal could not afford a war of attrition; his hope lay in the belief that by continued effort he could swing Rome's allies to his side. That he failed to do so is not so much a criticism of his policy as a tribute to Rome's policy toward its allies. Hannibal was realist enough to appreciate that no ultimate success could crown his efforts unless those allies were weaned away from Rome. But his efforts in this direction met with only partial success, owing to opposition from his home, Carthage, and his inability to carry on in the face of such opposition.

The essential feature in the grand strategy of both Hannibal and Fabius was that both men set goals. And it is largely this act—setting goals—that makes the formulation of grand strategy in the military analogous to the formulation of policy in civilian government. Below we will consider one more example intended to bring out an important aspect of goal setting.

The grand strategy of the North

On April 12, 1861, Fort Sumter was fired upon, initiating the bloody conflict between the states which was to last four years. Both sides

---

[14] Ibid., pp. 48–49.

hastily began preparations, neither fully appreciating the tremendous problems involved.

In 1861, neither side had an overall strategy. Jefferson Davis, the Confederate president, was a graduate of West Point; he had been in the regular army and had seen service in the Mexican War. Despite this military background, he never developed an overall strategy and never appreciated the significance of the Mississippi River. Abraham Lincoln, in contrast, was a great war president. He was an outstanding illustration of Clausewitz's dictum that an acquaintance with military affairs is not the principal qualification for a director of war but that "a remarkable, superior mind and strength of character" are better qualifications. In his *Lincoln and His Generals* (1952), T. Harry Williams writes:

> [Lincoln] saw the big picture of the war from the start. The policy of the government was to restore the Union by force; the strategy perforce had to be offensive. Lincoln knew the numbers, material resources, and sea power were on his side, so he called for 400,000 troops and proclaimed a naval blockade of the Confederacy. These were bold and imaginative moves for a man dealing with military questions for the first time. He grasped immediately the advantage that numbers gave the North and urged his generals to keep up a constant pressure on the whole strategic line of the Confederacy until a weak spot was found—and a breakthrough could be made. And he soon realized, if he did not know it at the beginning, that the proper objective of his armies was the destruction of the Confederate armies and not the occupation of Southern territory. His strategic thinking was sound and for a rank amateur astonishingly good.[15]

But it was not until the emergence of Ulysses S. Grant as commander in chief that a fully coordinated strategy was put into effect. Both sides, particularly the North, overrated the importance of the two capitals; hence the bloody campaigns around Richmond, which by themselves could not be decisive.

Figure 5–2 traces the evolution of the North's grand strategy: first, a naval blockade of the South; second, the east-west cleavage of the South by subjugating the Mississippi River area; third, William T. Sherman's drive across Georgia to split the already severed eastern portion of the Confederacy; and lastly, the closing of the pincers on Robert E. Lee and Joseph E. Johnston by Grant and Sherman.

Although Lee is usually ranked as the greatest Civil War general, he was not very interested in grand strategy. As a theater strategist, operating in a limited geographic area, and certainly as a battlefield tactician, Lee often demonstrated more brilliance than Grant. The staffs of the two men illustrate their outlook. Lee's staff was not, in the modern sense, a planning staff. Lee had to perform labors that should have

---

[15] T. Harry Williams, *Lincoln and His Generals* (New York: Vintage, 1952), pp. 7–8.

Figure 5–2
Grand strategy of the North

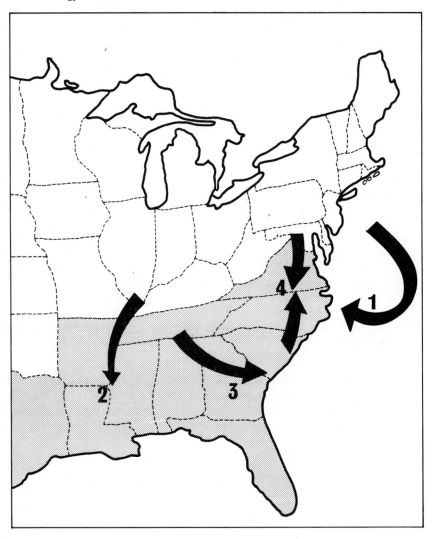

fallen to his staff; buried in trivia, he had little time left for the big picture. Most of Lee's staff officers were lieutenant colonels; some of the men on Grant's staff were major and brigadier generals, officers who themselves were capable of leading corps. "Grant's staff was an organization of experts in the various phases of strategic planning."[16]

---

[16] Ibid., p. 313.

Now I wish to leave the battlefield in order that we might take an extended look at how grand strategy, or strategic thinking, applies to some of the more pacific issues of public policy. Perhaps the best way to set the stage for this examination is to recall another great moment of strategic thinking in American history.

The Founding Fathers assumed that people inevitably tended toward conflict and struggle. This then was *the* problem they faced in 1787: How to control selfish factions or interest groups, oppressive local majorities, and popular follies and passions. James MacGregor Burns, one of America's most prominent scholars, writes:

> [James] Madison's answer went straight to the heart of the grand strategy of the men who would come to be known as the Federalists. The solution was not to try to remove the causes of faction, for a free society would always produce differences. The solution was to dilute the power and passion of local factions by enlarging the sphere of government into a nation of many regions, interests, and opinions. Like a careful cook, Madison would blend indigestible lumps and fiery spices in the blander waters of a large pot.
>
> It was this plan to "enlarge the sphere" that Madison brought to Philadelphia. . . .
>
> The delegates . . . conceived of themselves as engaged in a grand "experiment"—a word they often used—the outcome of which would shape their nation's destiny. . . . They saw themselves—in a word they would never have used—as pragmatists, as men thinking their way through a thicket of problems, in pursuit of that goal.
>
> That goal was liberty—liberty with order, liberty with safety and security, liberty of conscience, liberty of property, liberty with a measure of equality, but above all, liberty. They defined this term in many different ways, they had varying expectations of it, they differed over its relationship to other values, and later these differences would help spawn a series of tragedies. But conflict over this supreme goal did not deter the delegates at the time. Rather, liberty served as a unifying symbol and goal around which practical men could rally.[17]

TOWARD A THEORY OF POLICY DESIGN

Though Madison and Lincoln found themselves in radically different circumstances, both were able to attain their goals. Both had certain ideas in mind and were able to alter external circumstances so as to realize those ideas. A question of great moment to students of public policy is whether analytic, partly formalized, partly empirical proposi-

---

[17] James MacGregor Burns, *The Vineyard of Liberty* (New York: Knopf, 1982), pp. 30, 33.

230

tions about this process can be developed—propositions that are intellectually tough enough to apply in a variety of settings.

My research, described in the next chapter, suggests that any intelligent approach to policy design has to encompass and treat as interdependent at least six principles:

- *Concentration:* Are resources concentrated on the truly decisive aspects of the problem?
- *Clarity:* Are the goals clear and the steps to their attainment straightforward?
- *Changeability:* Does the policy have enough flexibility or cushion to ensure that it can be adjusted to changing conditions?
- *Challenge:* Do the goals challenge the organization yet remain realistic?
- *Coordination:* Does the policy allow for the exchange of information among implementing officials and the effects of feedback loops outside it?
- *Consistency:* Are the goals consistent with the objectives, the objectives with actions? Are the goal consistent internally (with one another) and externally (with other policies)?

This section gives special attention to these six Cs and elaborates a policy design framework. (See Figure 5–3.)

Concentration

After a meeting with Stalin in 1946, Secretary of State George Marshall decided that the United States must design a coherent foreign policy and act. He called George Kennan, the head of his policy planning staff, to his office. Marshall was brief, to the point: Europe was in a mess. Something would have to be done. He asked Kennan to form a committee to give him recommendations. He then added, characteristically, that he had only one bit of advice for the committee: "Avoid trivia."[18]

Here we have a fundamental principle whose understanding may prevent a fundamental error (the most common error in policymaking)—that of squandering scarce resources (time, money, influence, etc.) on lower priority items. The principle can be condensed into a single word, *concentration*. Actually, this needs to be amplified as the *concentration of strength against strategic factors*. For this principle to have any real value, strategic factors must be explained, and we will do that in a moment. For now we need only note that "strategic factors" serves as a kind of antonym for trivia.

---

[18] George Kennan, *Memoirs 1925–50* (Boston: Little, Brown, 1967), pp. 325–26.

Figure 5–3
Policy design framework

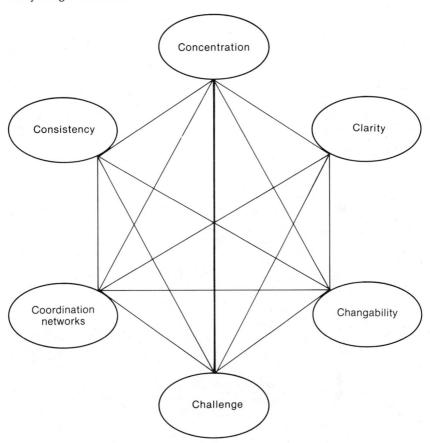

Examples in foreign, domestic, and economic policy. But to state the principle is not of much practical aid for execution; real-world examples are required.

- Working day and night for three weeks, Kennan's planning staff considered many alternatives, debated them, and made a series of decisions that were embodied in the recommended plan for the economic reconstruction of Europe. One of the staff's principle contributions was its *decisive emphasis* on the rehabilitation of the German economy and the introduction of the concept of German recovery as a vital component of the recovery of Europe as a whole. As Alfred Sloan, chairman of General Motors, pointed out at the time, Germany had always been, and was still, the "spark plug" of the European economy.

If Germany were allowed to collapse, Europe would follow, and if Europe collapsed, America would follow.[19]

- Many criminal justice experts believe that neither rehabilitation nor deterrence really works, and so it is useless to send people to prison with either purpose in mind. To be more precise, the evidence suggests that some people are "rehabilitated" by prison, in the sense that they find the whole experience so dreadful that they drop out of crime; however, these dropouts appear to be roughly offset by those who are made still more crime-prone by prison—those for whom it truly is a "school for crime." Peter W. Greenwood of the Rand Corporation argues that imprisonment can nevertheless be used to hold down crime rates. His proposal: *concentrate resources* on the relatively small fraction of criminals who account for high fractions of crime.

  It is no secret that criminal activity is very unevenly distributed among career criminals, most of whom commit only a few offenses per year. Greenwood cites data indicating that those who commit robberies average only around three per year; the figure is about the same for auto thefts; and for burglaries it is around six or seven. If, however, you differentiate between high-rate and low-rate offenders, you find that the former group is about five times as active as the latter. Greenwood has developed a model designed to predict the group in which any arrested criminal would fall; high-rate types are predicted by, for example, a record that includes juvenile convictions before age sixteen, heroin use during the two years before the arrest, and unemployment during most of that period. He suggests that more selective sentencing policies might get a lot more mileage out of the prison system. For example, we could get "a 20 percent reduction in the robbery rate with no increase in the overall number of offenders incarcerated."[20]

- Assuming a trade imbalance is a problem, and certainly many Americans do, what might be done to bring imports and exports into balance? Some policymakers argue that most of the *pressure for adjustment should be concentrated* on countries with surpluses in their balance of payments. If surplus countries adjust by raising imports, the volume of world trade expands and the world economy grows. Under this plan, countries running a trade surplus might be forced to expand their imports to avoid having to pay a 25 percent surtax in the U.S. market. The purpose is not to impose a 25 percent surtax, but to force countries

---

[19] See Charles L. Mee, Jr., *The Marshall Plan* (New York: Simon & Schuster, 1984), pp. 77, 90–92, 140–41, 165–66, and 230–31.

[20] Peter W. Greenwood, "Selective Incapacitation" in *Crime and Public Policy*, ed. James Q. Wilson (New York: ICS Press, 1983), p. 236.

to reduce their surpluses. The plan would also avoid an indiscriminate surtax on goods from economically depressed Third World countries.

How not to concentrate: A White House perspective. True concentration is the fruit of careful calculation and self-discipline, which is perhaps why the principle is so often violated.

- President-elect John Kennedy appointed a task force on depressed areas on December 5, 1960, and when he publicly received its report a month later, he declared that the depressed areas should be assigned "the most important domestic priority," a pledge which puzzled those who remembered that, both at the beginning of his campaign on August 21, 1960, and near the end of it in a letter to the Farm Bureau Federations of Arkansas-Tennessee-Mississippi dated October 11, he said that "the farm problem . . . the decline in agricultural income" is "the No. 1 domestic issue in this campaign . . . the No. 1 domestic problem in the United States"; or that at Atlantic City on September 19 he had assured the United Chemical Workers that he considered unemployment to be "the No. 1 domestic problem which the next President of the United States will have to face"; or that in the October 10 issue of *Missiles and Rockets* he had told its readers that "certainly national scientific goals will be our first objective."[21]

  As subsequent events proved, these remarks were not just campaign hyperbole but also indexes of a policy void that was to plague the Kennedy years. Instead of setting priorities in foreign policy, Kennedy found himself constantly reacting to Communist initiatives. His policy was pragmatic and operational, more in the nature of a firefighting exercise than a careful and long-range campaign for fire prevention. In much the same way, Kennedy handled the issue of civil rights. He did not aggressively push for new civil rights laws; rather as *Newsweek* observed in late 1963, Kennedy had been satisfied to use "the easy foil of rabble-rousing bigotry." He would put out a fire, not effect fundamental institutional change. The method did not change. He awaited the occasion to which he could react, which he could seize by a dramatic exhibition of his personal leadership. He was a pragmatic realist who sought to create and to manipulate a "consensus" in his support by waiting until an issue had become an emergency, or could be represented as one: until a fire had started, which he would put out.[22]

- President Johnson announced on July 28, 1965, that (contrary to his campaign promises) he would increase the number of American troops

---

[21] Henry Fairlie, *The Kennedy Promise* (Garden City, N.Y.: Doubleday Publishing, 1973), p. 125–56.

[22] Ibid., pp. 209–10.

in Vietnam from 75,000 to 125,000 with additional forces to be deployed as necessary. This move is generally regarded as the critical decision that led to open-ended escalation.

Recently declassified White House documents in the Johnson library in Austin, Texas, reveal that he did not have a plan for winning the war or for getting out of the war. Incredibly, Johnson's national security adviser, McGeorge Bundy, recently remarked: "You can argue that we should have gone in to win. . . . But my problem is that I don't know how to do that, *even now.*"[23]

- President Nixon's eventual strategy—Vietnamization—emerged on an improvised basis without a thorough policy review. His may have been a classic case of the chief executive appeasing various bureaucratic constituencies by giving them a bit of what they wanted: bombing for the military, speeded-up pull-out for the secretary of Defense (and to appease public opinion), and negotiations for the State Department. Because Nixon's plan did not provide enough force to compel North Vietnam to negotiate or sufficient concessions to entice Hanoi to the table, it offered only extended stalemate—like the improvised strategies of the Johnson era.

- President Jimmy Carter took up the issue of welfare in 1977. He appointed committees that eventually became so large they had to meet in auditoriums. Despite Carter's instructions that no additional funds should be committed, the committees recommended a program that would have cost the federal government an additional $174.4 billion. President Carter had devoted extraordinary effort to devising his welfare plan. Word was passed that this was a priority matter for his party and his administration. Carter's welfare economists used up almost a year of their president's time on a proposal that the full House Committee on Ways and Means never even considered. In the Senate, there was little disposition to act until the House had acted. In the end, however, this expensive and self-deluded policy formulation process failed. Moreover, in the process, it destroyed the prospects of any significant advances. The Carter administration, having expended such efforts on welfare reform would never again muster its resources or its nerve in the cause of other social policy innovations.[24] Thus, concentration requires not only that policymakers establish priorities among their goals but also that they allocate resources accordingly. As this example illustrates, concentration also means that policymakers allocate their time and spend their *political* resources wisely.

---

[23] Quoted in *The Wall Street Journal,* June 14, 1985. Emphasis added.
[24] Daniel Patrick Moynihan, *Family and Nation* (New York: Harcourt Brace, 1986).

• President Reagan rarely gave much attention to broad questions of strategy during the military build-up in the early 1980s. Consequently, more by default than design, he chose a maritime strategy that emphasizes naval forces and Third World contingencies, rather than a NATO-oriented coalition strategy that emphasizes the West's capacity to resist a conventional Soviet attack in Central Europe.

Robert W. Komer, a former senior defense official, asserts that a maritime strategy is wrong for the United States. His essential reason for rejecting it is simple—Eurasia is the great prize in the Soviet-American competition, and naval power, capable of operating only along the Eurasian periphery, cannot prevent the spread of Soviet power into key regions such as Western Europe or the Middle East. "We could obliterate every Soviet naval base, we could sink every Soviet warship, we could capture every Soviet merchant ship, we could drive them totally from the seas and we still could not prevent them from taking over Western Europe or Persian Gulf oil or anything else on Eurasia. You do need a powerful sea-control Navy, but you don't need the kind of Navy that they're building."[25]

The concept of strategic factors. Chester Barnard served for many years as chief executive officer of the New Jersey Bell Telephone Company. In his highly respected book, *The Functions of the Executive*, he develops a very important idea, the "limiting factor." As he explains it:

> If we take any set of conditions, or circumstances, we recognize that it consists of elements, or parts, of factors. Now, if we approach the system or set of circumstances with a view to the accomplishment of a purpose, the elements or parts become distinguished into two classes: those which if absent or changed would accomplish the desired purpose, and these others. The first kind are often called limiting factors, the second, complementary factors. *The limiting factor is the one whose control, in the right form, at the right place and time, will establish a new system or set of conditions which meets the purpose.*[26]

If a machine is not operating because a screw is missing, the screw is the strategic (limiting) factor. If an automobile is inoperative because it has no gasoline, then gasoline is the limiting factor. These are simple illustrations, but they embody a major concept. Instead of taking an automobile apart and analyzing each part to find out what is wrong, the more efficient approach is to search for the strategic factor.

---

[25] Robert W. Komer, *Maritime Strategy or Coalition Defense?* (Cambridge, Mass.: Abt/University Press of America, 1984).

[26] Condensed from Chester I. Barnard, *The Functions of the Executive* (Cambridge, Mass.: Harvard University Press, 1938), pp. 202–203. Emphasis added.

This concept has many applications in the development of policy. Every organization should ask itself just what major strategic factors must be recognized and perfected in order to make the organization successful. Barnard's concept of the strategic factor says to the policymaker, "Look for the critical, the major, the basic element." This counsel can be important in the examination of the strengths and weaknesses of the policy, but it can also be valuable in the identification of the most important elements in the environment that should be studied to find new opportunities and reveal new threats.

Unfortunately, today we have little, if any, agreement in political science on what these strategic factors are. For this reason, I have attempted to identify for the first time the major strategic or critical factors that have a significant effect on the services of different types of public agencies, as seen from the viewpoint of the top administrators now operating them. Participants in the study were given the following working definitions:

> Strategic factor refers to an action, element, or condition that for an organization may be of critical importance in its success or failure. It can refer both to a force outside the agency as well as one within.

> Success, as the word is used in this survey, refers to the designed achievement of major objectives and goals established for your organization.

Each participant received a list of forty-five strategic factors (see Table 5-1). How was this list developed? First, I prepared a list of those strategic factors that appeared to me to be of most importance in the success of public policy throughout government. The idea was suggested by a similar investigation by Steiner of the strategic factors for success in business and industry.[27] After discussing my short list with academic colleagues and friends in the government, I was able over time to expand the list until it reached the length included in the questionnaire.

What exactly did I hope to obtain through this survey? Since the strategic factors for success vary greatly from organization to organization, I thought that a listing of the major factors might help guide policymakers in identifying the factors that were most significant to them and their organizations. Further, I hoped that the list might stimulate public administrators to think more carefully about the strategic factors important to them. There does not seem to me to be enough self-examination by public administrators of the causes of the success of their organizations. When failure looms, the natural question is: What

---

[27] George A. Steiner, *Strategic Factors in Business Success* (New York: Financial Executives Research Foundation, 1969).

Table 5–1
Strategic factors for government success

	Rating scale					
	(Unimportant) ⟵⟶ (Most important)					
Strategic factor	0	1	2	3	4	5
Get high-quality top management						193
Leadership—ability to unify conflicting opinions, to generate enthusiasm and sense of common purpose						159
Knowledge about the needs of clients						129
Better judgment—top management						127
Service to clients						116
Acquire sufficient funding						113
Ability to influence legislative process						103
Improve productivity of employees					129	
Stimulate creativity in employees					124	
Utilization of employee skills					122	
Ability to react promptly to changes					118	
Sufficient delegation of authority from political leadership					117	
Effective use of top manager's time					117	
Ability to define the organization objectives					115	
Policy analysis (e.g., comparison of costs to benefits and the assessment of impacts)					114	
Ability to deal with the public and the media					108	
Sufficient manpower level					106	
Improve on existing programs					102	
Perceive new program opportunities					102	
Better judgment—lower management					101	
Train future managers					101	
Keep abreast of technological and social change					97	
More quantitative tools—top management					96	
Attract professional personnel such as lawyers and engineers					93	
Better long-range planning					93	
Take risks					84	
Better overall control of operations					81	
Ability to project risks and rewards in long-range fixed-price contracts					55	
Ability to work with and use resources of sister agencies				108		
More quantitative tools—lower management				99		
Employee retraining				99		
Cost reduction programs				99		
Ability to deal with regulatory agencies such as EPA, OSHA, and EEO				90		
Better employee relations				90		
Computers in problem solving				87		
Better organizational structure				84		
Proper relationship among programs				81		
Good contracts with private enterprise				77		
Good relations with unions				75		
Management of research expenditures				73		
Wider base of clients				63		
More outside contracts				62		
Computers in financial control				74		
Inventory control				69		
Geographic location				49		

did we do wrong? But a question even more important to an organization should be continuously asked: What did we do right?

The basic list of strategic factors went to 751 top administrators. Each respondent held a position of responsibility in the administration of government at one of three levels—federal (n = 390), state (n = 117), and local (n = 244). The initial response rate was relatively high (over 34 percent).[28]

Each recipient of the questionnaire was asked, first, to assess how much each of the factors contributed to the success of his or her organization. The value scale for assessing the importance of these strategic factors was:

> 0—completely unimportant
> 1—of very little importance
> 2—of somewhat more importance
> 3—of average importance
> 4—of more than average importance
> 5—of the greatest importance

Modes were selected for each strategic factor. These were, of course, the scales that received the majority of ratings for a particular strategic factor. If most of the respondents, for example, rated a factor by checking scale 4, that was the mode for the factor. Table 5–1 gives the mode rank of strategic factors reported by all respondents in declining order of importance. Table 5–2 compares the strategic factors rated in the "top ten" by level of government.

The principal conclusions that emerge from an examination of the data, despite some weaknesses, are two-fold. First, it is possible to identify major strategic factors that top administrators hold to be dominant in the success of their organizations' policies. Second, different levels of government hold surprisingly similar views about the importance of particular factors for success.

Still, the survey does not presume to show policymakers how to unerringly select the right "grand strategy." But it is my hope that by identifying the majority of strategic factors that administrators in policy-making positions themselves regard as most important, the basis will be laid for a more systematic assessment of these factors.

Applications. One issue drawn from the area of health policy illustrates how the concept of strategic factors applies in more specific situations. Strategic factors, as we will see, greatly facilitate the task facing

---

[28] Participants were randomly selected from the following three sources: *U.S. Government Manuals, 1976/1977* (Washington, D.C.: Government Printing Office); *State Administrative Officials Classified by Functions* (Lexington, Ky.: Council of State Government, 1973); and *The Municipal Year Book* (Washington, D.C.: ICMA, 1976).

Table 5–2
The "top ten" strategic factors by level of government[*]

Federal	State	Local
1. Leadership	1. Get high-quality top management	1. Get high-quality top management
2. Get high-quality top management	2. Better judgment—top management	2. Leadership
3. Knowledge about needs of clients	3. Leadership	3. Better judgment—top management
4. Service to clients	4. Knowledge about needs of clients	4. Acquire sufficient funding
5. Sufficient manpower level	5. Service to clients	5. Ability to deal with public and media
6. Effective use of top manager's time	6. Acquire sufficient funding	6. Knowledge about needs of clients
7. Better judgment—top management	7. Effective use of top manager's time	7. Stimulate creativity in employees
8. Ability to influence legislative process	8. Ability to deal with public and media	8. Effective use of top manager's time
9. Acquire sufficient funding	9. Improve productivity of employees	9. Service to clients
10. Stimulate creativity in employees	10. Stimulate creativity in employees	10. More quantitative tools—top management

[*]Ranking is based on number of times rated "most important." In cases of ties the factor that was also "of more than average importance" most frequently appears first.

every analyst: moving from diagnosis and prognosis (the subjects of the last two chapters) to a statement of goals (the subject of this one).

The issue I wish to focus on is catastrophic health insurance.[29] At first blush the idea seems an attractive alternative to a comprehensive national health insurance plan, which would be more costly. Catastrophic health insurance works this way. The federal government picks up all medical expenses above some threshold. Like all policy proposals, this one builds on a particular problem of definition—namely that some Americans are randomly struck by high-cost illness and that these costs constitute only a small share of total health costs.

Case-by-case review of medical records in selected hospitals gives, however, a quite different picture of the problem. In the first place, high-cost illness is seldom a single medical emergency. More likely, it comprises a series of treatments and hospital stays over a long period of time. Evidence suggests that high daily hospital charges reflect the

---

[29] The discussion which follows is based on Christopher J. Zook, Francis D. Moore, and Richard J. Zeckhauser, " 'Catastrophic' Health Insurance—A Misguided Prescription?" *Public Interest* 62 (Winter 1981), pp. 68–81.

240

use of a large total volume of standard resources rather than the application of complex, new technology. Further, unexpected complications often arise during the course of treatment that add to the already high cost.

Another fallacy in the conventional definition of the high-cost illness problem involves the high concentration of medical expenditures. A mere 13 percent of the patients in a typical hospital consume about one half of the medical resources, concentration of medical resources appears to be increasing over time. Thus, the most expensive patients are becoming both absolutely and relatively more expensive to treat.

The conventional view of the problem also posits that high-cost illness strikes randomly and that neither patient nor doctor can control costs. Not true. The costs involved in high-cost illness are due, in part, to persistent unhealthy personal habits: smoking, overeating, lack of exercise, risky sexual practices, and overconsumption of alcohol. Such persons are hospitalized substantially more than are others. For example, though 4 to 5 percent of the overall adult population is alcoholic, it has been estimated that 9 to 14 percent of the general hospital population is alcoholic. When hospitalized, patients with unhealthy habits like alcoholism are more expensive to treat and become high-cost patients.

From this analysis of the high-cost illness problem a couple of strategic factors emerge that should aid us in the design of health insurance programs. First, because the data suggest that catastrophic health insurance is likely to be more costly than some believe the high-cost 10 percent of patients account for 40 to 50 percent of hospital charges in one year, methods are still needed to instill cost efficiencies while insuring against genuine cases of financial hardship. Second, insurance schemes should reflect the differences in high-cost illnesses; identical insurance structures for the very different types of high-cost illnesses make no more sense than identical plans for fire and life insurance.

> There is no reason why insurance plans cannot address separately the different segments of high-cost users. . . . in more carefully tailored ways. The terminal cancer patient, the noncomplying diabetic, the repeatedly hospitalized alcoholic, the paraplegic, and the elderly widow with severe peripheral vascular disease are similar in their status as high-cost users of medical care, but dramatically different in their care requirements, their financial needs, and the lower-cost treatment alternatives that are available. Health insurance proposals should and can take these differences into account if they are to meet the patients' needs within reasonable costs. Since catastrophic health insurance, as embodied in present proposals, does not recognize differences, it is unlikely to be inexpensive or fully equitable, nor will it offer a "quick fix" to the most pressing health problems.[30]

---

[30] Ibid., p. 73.

From the foregoing analysis, the goals of a policy to deal with the problem of high-cost illness began to come into rough focus. I should emphasize that, at this point, we have only a tentative, first-cut solution. A more definitive goal statement will require much more testing and refinement. With that proviso in mind, several goals (along with options for attaining them) can be put on the table.

Cost-effectiveness: Provide different plans for different groups. Insurance plans should contain financial incentives to employ the most cost-effective modes of care for these illnesses. Does alcoholism need to be treated in a regular hospital? Why not have all the heart surgery in a region be done at one location, thereby making possible significant economies of scale.

Conservation: Make the provider or patient a primary decision maker and give him a stake in the conservation of scarce medical resources. Among other things, this strategy should lead to earlier intervention to lower the probability of future hospitalizations. Currently, reimbursement is after the fact.

Reduction in unhealthy behavior: Penalize individuals in some way for engaging in unhealthy behavior (greater taxation of tobacco and alcohol, insurance premium incentives to lose weight, community education programs, etc.).

This procedure—going from diagnosis and prognosis of the problem to distillation of strategic factors to a preliminary policy recommendation—can be applied to a wide variety, if not all, public issues. Table 5–3 offers a number of examples.

Because it is so important in policy design, concentration was discussed at some length. Now, we need to take a somewhat briefer look at the other five principles in our Six-C Policy Design Framework.

Clarity

Goals themselves need to be clear and simple. There should be little ambiguity regarding what the government wants to accomplish. Consider this paragraph from Winston Churchill's first speech before Parliament as prime minister: "You ask, what is our policy? I say it is to wage war by land, sea, and air. War with all our might and with all the strength God has given us, and to wage war against a monstrous tyranny never surpassed in the dark and lamentable catalogue of human crime. That is our policy." This is clarity on stilts. Its capacity to help a government concentrate efforts inside as well as outside the bureaucracy cannot be overemphasized. A further dividend of having a clear and simple policy is political. When an idea is too complex, it is just not reasonable to expect many people to rally around it. Ideas such as

242

Table 5–3
Using strategic factors to get from problem definition to policy recommendation

Problem diagnosis/prognosis	→	Strategic factor that policy design must address
Medical malpractice insurance premiums, are soaring, largely due to huge jury awards against physicians charged with malpractice. Access to affordable health-care services for the American public may be seriously jeopardized.	→	Concentrate on incompetent doctors, who generate a disproportionate high percentage of lawsuits—causing everyone's premiums to rise—but who do not have to pay any higher insurance premiums than highly competent doctors.
Sustained high unemployment is due to sluggish economy. In short, the problem is economic.	→	Lower interest rates in order to have a sustained expansion of the economy. The problem with manpower training programs is that, if you have very little growth in jobs, there is no point giving people training programs for non-existent jobs.
Sustained high unemployment is a structural problem, due to those sectors of labor surplus that surely are going to exist no matter what happens to the rate of growth of the economy as a whole. In short, the problem is sociological.	→	*Liberal analysis:* Place greater stress on basic educational skills—communications, computation, etc. These basic skills are necessary given the rapid structural changes in the U.S. economy; workers typically will have to be retrained every four or five years for different occupational careers. That means the premium will be on persons with high potential for training.

Conservative analysis: Administrators of inner-city schools could be less tolerant of disruptive influences, so that youngsters would face fewer distractions while they learn basic skills. Courts and law-enforcement agencies could get tougher with juvenile offenders, thus lowering the rewards of crime and increasing the relative value of legitimate employment. |
Social and economic problems in the Third World are due primarily to overpopulation.	→	Third World governments should educate citizens on birth control and establish a system of incentives and disincentives to see that these methods are followed.
Social and economic problems in the Third World are due to underinvestment in human capital.	→	For specific new programs to launch, leaders might look to Hong Kong and Singapore for they have grown rapidly and have achieved the highest standards of living in Southeastern Asia, without natural resources and with population densities far in excess of those in India.
Illicit drug use is a supply problem.	→	By neutralizing the money-laundering operations of international narcotics networks, the U.S. government could cripple the operations abroad that have thus far been immune to the process of bilateral negotiation. It should also continue its emphasis on prosecuting drug-related, organized-crime syndicates.

Table 5-3 *(concluded)*

Problem diagnosis/prognosis	→	*Strategic factor that policy design must address*
Illicit drug use is a demand problem.	→	From any study of drug control strategies, the most basic conclusion is that the *supply* of drugs can never be eliminated. The strategic factor therefore is demand. More resources for education are required to reduce drug abuse. Rather than preach or cajole, drug education programs should concentrate on the primary impetus for drug use among the young: peer pressure.
High U.S. trade deficit.	→	Concentrate on forcing surplus nations to expand their imports, rather than impose an across-the-board surtax on imports. The latter strategy would hurt nations that are very poor or that have a trade deficit with the United States. (See text.)
The war in Vietnam is a guerrilla war.*	→	Use search-and-destroy operations against the Vietcong.
The war in Vietnam is a conventional war. Hanoi is using the Vietcong as proxies to abfuscate the issue.*	→	Concentrate on North Vietnam. With an expanded naval blockade, drive the U.S. Army across the Demilitarized Zone between the two Vietnams and then cut through Laos to the Thai border, setting up defensive points. Vietnamese Army could then root out the guerrillas, and Americans could stay out of South Vietnamese villages.
The greatest threat to peace is the stockpile of nuclear arms the United States and the U.S.S.R. possess.	→	Find a satisfactory means to verify nuclear arm stockpiling to ensure compliance.
The greatest threat to peace is the proliferation of nuclear weapons to other nations. The world becomes much more unstable when Libya, South Africa, Argentina, Brazil, Pakistan, and South Korea all have nuclear weapons.	→	Follow Israel's example and destroy nuclear potential (even Israel's, if necessary) by using conventional force. The mere threat of using such force, if convincing, would almost surely be enough to make the most recalcitrant nation sign the non-nuclear pledge and open its facilities to inspection.
The greatest threat to peace is poor superpower relations. If you have arms control, you do not necessarily have peace; but if you have peace, then you can have arms control.	→	The strategic factor is psychological. Recognize that the Soviets are very tough bargainers but will deal if the president is reasonable. Start a dialogue.

*Note: This problem should be read from the perspective of an American policymaker in 1965.

the tax cut of 1981 or the nuclear freeze movement of 1983 may or may not have been good ideas, but this much is certain: They attracted support because they were easily understood. (There is, however, a downside to making goals too clear too soon—it may trigger early opposition to the policy. See Chapter 10.)

Yet another advantage of interjecting an element of clarity and simplicity into the design of process appears when the time comes—as it surely will—for the administrative apparatus to execute the policy. Nowhere in the dark and lamentable catalogue of recent U.S. foreign policy failures (as Sir Winston might have put it) can this be seen better than with American-Iranian relations. It was Iran, at least as much as anything else, that ruined the presidency of Jimmy Carter and deprived him of reelection. But what were the mistakes on his part that led to ruin? That Carter's decision in April 1980 in favor of a military expedition to rescue the hostages was a mistake does admit to much. Carter's parting word on that mission was: "It was a failure of military execution, not of political judgment or command."

This is a rash statement. Historically, U.S. military forces have not demonstrated a capacity to plan and conduct successful raids. This particular raid was an operation of such complexity, requiring the performance of so many strenuous and difficult tasks precisely timed and fitted together, that the president and high commanders should have realized that something could go wrong. They had a duty to see that the team committed to the operation would be as adaptable as possible to whatever unforeseen situation might arise. The various sections of the rescue team had trained hard, but no complete rehearsal, putting all the sections through it together, had been done. In his *All Fall Down: America's Tragic Encounter with Iran* (1986), Gary Sick reports that some of the participants met each other for the first time on the ground in the Iranian desert.[31]

The failure of two helicopters to press on through the dust storm to their rendezvous was, indeed, a fault of execution; the decision to rely solely on satellite reconnaissance, which could not show the dust storms that ruined the raid, was a failure of design. Once the rescue expedition had failed, Carter resisted any temptation to try it again, and the problem was turned back to the diplomats.

Six years later, the Reagan White House developed a plan for dealing with Iran that was so baroque it made Carter's plan look like the soul of simplicity. The basic idea was to sell arms to the Israelis who in turn would sell them to the "moderates" in Iran. The Iranians then would try to get the Shiites in Lebanon to release Americans whom they had kidnapped. Profits from the arms sale would be sent to a Swiss bank. Contras in Honduras would draw on these funds to aid the struggle against the Nicaragua government. Somewhere in this loop were retired U.S. Air Force generals, Anglican clergy, Danish shipping

---

[31] Gary Sick, *All Fall Down: America's Tragic Encounter with Iran* (New York: Random House, 1985).

companies, Saudi arms merchants, and sundry other folks. The plan required that all these transactions be done covertly. They weren't.

Changeability

Policies, plans, and programs should be designed so that they can be readily changed when new circumstances arise. This means that policymakers should try to foresee and provide for a next step in case of success, failure, or partial success. Plans should allow this exploitation or adaptation in the shortest possible time. Our limited ability to forecast far into the future, a theme presented in the last chapter, makes this principle particularly important.

Structuring flexibility. Logic dictates that policymakers purposely design the capacity to change into implementing organizations and have reserve resources ready to deploy as events demand. How does one do this? Three activities are essential in achieving flexibility: (1) establishing a *horizon-scanning activity* to identify the general nature and extent of the opportunities and threats the policy might encounter, (2) creating sufficient *resource buffers or slack* to respond effectively as events unfurl, and (3) developing and positioning *activists* with a psychological commitment to move opportunistically and flexibly at the proper moment.[32]

1. Policymakers are like race car drivers in at least one respect. If they fail to look ahead, they run the risk of not having enough time to change course when hazards emerge on their horizons. For this reason, change-oriented policymakers use the forecasting tools described in the last chapter to scan the future for potential economic, social, and technological threats. They force themselves to address the basic question of what adjustments, if any, should be taken now (or in the next year) in light of these forecasts. Some even develop contingency or "what if" plans. (For more about contingency plans, see Chapter 10.)

2. Change-oriented policymakers also ask themselves this question: What resource buffers do I need to deal with the uncertainties these events probably represent? They then consciously provide sufficient funding, more flexible organization structures, greater personnel redundancy, more active communications networks, and so on to allow rapid movement when necessary. "The essence of contingency planning," James Bryan Quinn says, "is not in estimating which events will occur and planning for those in detail, but in anticipating what type and scale of resource buffers and organizational flexibility are needed to exploit likely futures effectively."[33]

---

[32] Adapted from James Bryan Quinn, *Strategies for Change* (Homewood: Ill.: Richard D. Irwin, 1980), pp. 121–24.

[33] Ibid., p. 124.

3. Policies and the designated implementing agency should have, or at least develop, individuals whose role is to press proactively for movement as opportunities or threats develop around specific goals in a policy. Agency heads and political appointees generally serve this function, but (regardless of who they are) to be effective, they must have access to the top and perhaps to the legislature and not have to obtain approvals from multiple layers of organization. When these flexible response patterns are designed into the policy, the implementing organization is proactively able to move on to the new or modified goals that invariably evolve.

To the foregoing list of activities, we might add a fourth way of structuring flexibility. Procedures that purposely delay decisions and allow for feedback are particularly beneficial. Because of this, agencies like NASA have formalized the concept into *phased program planning* systems. Rather than just select a prime contractor for a project and then sit back and monitor progress towards completion, the agency established four phases in the life of a project: advanced studies (phase A), project definition (phase B), design (phase C), and development/ operations (phase D). Numerous firms would compete for contracts during each phase; sometimes, especially in the earlier phases, more than one contract would be let. As a major benefit, NASA would be able to keep its options open as long as possible. Phased program planning was not an end in itself; it was introduced only to ensure that research and development would be conducted in an appropriate number of sequential phases with maximum competition characterizing the "phase-by-phase increments of project execution" and each phase allowing for "the fundamental concept of agency top management participation at all major decision points."[34]

Paradox and tension in the design process. Policies are tentative adaptations to the world we live in, and they can exert their influence on the world they may help to change. The pattern of development may be characterized in the formula

$$P_1 \rightarrow TS \rightarrow EE \rightarrow P_2$$

where P is the initial problem, TS the trial solution or policy, EE the process of error elimination applied to the trial solution, and P_2 the resulting situation, with new problems. It is essentially a feedback process. It is not cyclic, for P_2 is always different from P_1. According to philosopher Karl Popper, virtually all processes of development and

[34] Arnold S. Levine, *Managing NASA in the Apollo Era* (Washington, D.C.: Scientific and Technical Information Branch, NASA, 1982), pp. 80–84 and 158–61. See also Grover Starling and Otis Baskin, "The Space Shuttle Program" in *Issues in Business and Society: Capitalism and Public Purpose* (Boston: Kent, 1985), pp. 263–98.

all learning processes can be looked at in this way—that is, in terms of an endless and gradual modification of existing policy under the pressure of novel demands.[35] Even complete failure of a poicy to solve a problem teaches us something new about where the difficulties lie, and perhaps what strategic factors any solution must allow for.

Thus we face a paradox: The function of goals is to guide activity that will generate new goals. In short, goals exist only to self-destruct. Herbert A. Simon explains:

> Making complex designs that are implemented over a long period of time and continually modified in the course of implementation has much in common with painting in oil. In oil painting every new spot of pigment laid on the canvas creates some kind of pattern that provides a continuing source of new ideas to the painter. The painting process is a process of cyclical interaction between painter and canvas in which current goals lead to new applications of paint, while the gradually changing pattern suggests new goals.[36]

It follows then that the idea of final goals is inconsistent with the nature of the development and learning process—not to mention our limited ability to foretell or determine the future. The real result of public policy is to establish initial conditions *(TS)* for the next succeeding stage of action. "What we call 'final goals' are in fact criteria for choosing the initial conditions that we will leave to our successors."[37]

We find tension as well as paradox in the design process. In most instances, as noted at the start, the six Cs for our design framework tend to be mutually reenforcing. But this is not always the case. Consider the tension that results when a new doctrine is announced.

A *doctrine* simplifies and makes accessible what was arcane and complex. "The American continents," President James Monroe told Congress in 1823, "are henceforth not to be considered as subjects for future colonization by any European powers." Three centuries of British foreign policy might be summed up in these few words: Whoever happens to be the strongest power in continental Europe will not be allowed to dominate the narrow seas around Britain. After World War II, the Truman Doctrine encapsulated American foreign policy. More recently, no president has seemed complete without one. The Reagan doctrine, for example, placed stress on aid to anti-communist guerilla movements. By relating a range of particular issues to general principles and values, it provides—or at least promises—coherence, consistency, and order where previously there was confusion. It has the dramatic impact that

---

[35] Karl Popper, *Objective Knowledge* (New York: Oxford University Press, 1972).
[36] Herbert A. Simon, *The Sciences of the Artificial* (Cambridge, Mass.: MIT Press, 1981), p. 187.
[37] Ibid.

goes with a firm declaration of purpose. It largely determines the terms in which issues are perceived and discussed. Once successfully launched, a doctrine can perform functions that are extremely useful to its adherents. It can be a powerful instrument for engaging attention and mobilizing popular support. It can make it more difficult for bureaucracies to procrastinate. It can be used to keep the administration honest, by making it difficult to renege on commitments that have been given a special authority and solemnity.

But doctrines, for all their clarity and simplicity, have serious drawbacks. By their nature they deal in broad categories and general principles, sacrificing selectiveness and circumstance. Doctrines tend to be fixated on goals not as trial solutions but as final ones. They pay more attention to the definition and justification of ends than to the appropriateness of means, the allocation of priorities, and the best use of scarce resources.

This tension between clarity and changeability should remind us why policy design must forever remain as much an art as a science. Are not similar tensions found in other professions? Do not aeronautical engineers make trade-offs in designing fighters; and physicians when designing treatments for patients?

Challenge

Another tension—and reminder of the artistic aspect of policy analysis—is the one between challenge and realism. Policies that present too much challenge to an organization fail to meet the standard of realism. Yet policymakers should not always be attacking sitting ducks. Goals should be as challenging as possible without becoming unrealistic. Why the emphasis on challenge? Simply because it maintains the vitality of an organization. Organizations are like bicycles: They fall over if they do not move forward.

Perhaps the point can be grasped better by considering real organizations rather than fanciful similes. Consider the plight of NASA as it approached its thirtieth birthday. Just before the Challenger explosion, Jack D. Kirwan, assistant editor of *Energy Journal*, suggested that the agency needed new goals, in harmony with its original ones, in order to gain "fresh sense of vigor and purpose." See accompanying box.

A more prevalent error in policy design is making goals too challenging rather than too mundane. Why do we so often see this lack of realism among policymakers who otherwise are intelligent, capable men and women? Perhaps it stems from unrealistic assumptions they have regarding the availability of resources, the controllability or predictability of human behavior, and the limitlessness of technical knowledge. I shall leave it to the reader to categorize these specimens of design hubris:

- Recently the mayor of San Antonio stated that there is only one way to stop the flood of illegal aliens from Mexico into the United States. The U.S. government should work with the Mexican government in order to fix its troubled economy and unemployment problem. The diplomatic skills this would require on the part of the American "advisers" would have to be, to say the least, extraordinary. But, even assuming some modern day Metternich could be located with such wisdom, how would he impart it to the Mexicans? Elsewhere in this book I have noted that after tens of billions of dollars and twenty years of effort, Washington still has not improved the relative economic conditions of Appalachia—which is in its own backyard.

- President Carter once seriously put forward the goal of making 20 percent of U.S. energy usage solar by the year 2000. That could only have been met by requiring buildings and industries to install solar technologies that would not be economical. The cost would have been astronomic, perhaps two or three times the cost of conventional energy and would probably have required subsidies far higher than all those thus far given for all conventional sources.

But what we are really talking about here is a question of balance. Goals must be workable, yes; but they must also be challenging. Fabius, of course, lost his job because the Romans grew impatient with a grand strategy so unlike the more "challenging" offensive one that they were accustomed to. But Hannibal had similar problems with his own grand strategy: though he was able to operate in Italy for many years, maintaining the morale of soldiers far from home proved a constant problem.

When we slide back into the arena of domestic policies, this question of balance—this task of finding both challenging and workable goals—does not vanish. And exacerbating the task is the tendency of some groups and political leaders to call for "fundamental change" rather than "cosmetic, partial solutions."

Nowhere is the tendency more prevalent than in the area of criminal justice. People who criticize an emphasis on the use of the police and the courts to cope with crime are fond of saying, "Such measures can't work so long as unemployment and poverty exist." While I must acknowledge that we have not done very well at introducing young people, especially blacks, into the workforce, I wonder how realistic a goal this might be for public policy in the criminal justice field. Moreover, as James Q. Wilson of Harvard argues, "It would be equally correct to say that so long as the criminal justice system does not impede crime, efforts to reduce unemployment will not work."[38] For if criminal opportu-

---

[38] James Q. Wilson, *Thinking about Crime* (New York: Basic Books, 1975), p. 227.

Box 5–1
NASA needs a new drawing board

Despite many candidates—the computer age, the atomic age, the information age—the name for our times that probably will stick will be the space age. In just a few short years, space changed from a spectator sport to a participatory one. And much of the glory of those times, the Mercury, Gemini, and Apollo programs, the first men on the moon, was summed up by four letters—NASA. But today that glory is tarnished and "remember when-ism" permeates the organization. What happened? How did Luke Skywalker get swivel-chair spread and, more important, what can be done about it?

John Lewis, a professor of planetary sciences at the University of Arizona, puts it neatly: "NASA is an institution that has reached bureaucratic old age. NASA has become extremely conservative since the 1960s. They have lost a sense of direction and have failed to develop anything new." Science writer G. Harry Stine says that NASA people "in the higher. . . . ratings have gotten fossilized." NASA's torpor is such that if the United States decided today to put a man back on the moon, it would take about sixteen years, according to a NASA engineer I interviewed. That's twice as long as it took (starting from scratch) back in the 1960s.

There are now two levels of space activity. One involves "paddleball" activities—sending something into space in order to transmit data back. These are, almost by definition, unmanned. The other (far more complicated and expensive) involves putting humans safely into space and keeping them there awhile.

As yet, money-making operations in space involve paddle-ball operations. Telecommunications is the prime example. This has been both successful and profitable. Remote sensing will soon join this category, and other operations will follow. However, the operational word here is unmanned. Sending an ELV (expendable launch vehicle) into space is in order of magnitude cheaper than putting a load of people up in a shuttle and bringing them down. Consequently, there is a real crap-shoot between the fledgling entrepreneurs with their private launch vehicles and NASA with the shuttle. And the dice are very loaded. As Patrick Cox wrote in *Reason* magazine earlier this year: "Against the highly subsidized shuttle, then, private ELV operators cannot compete on price. Without its huge subsidies, the shuttle would be a hands-down loser. But since taxpayers pick up somewhere between half and three quarters of the actual cost of a commercial shuttle launch, the shuttle beats ELVs in price by a wide margin."

Even with subsidies, shuttle costs are about $1,500 a pound. Like all government agencies, NASA's first object is to avoid budget cuts—particularly in today's era of tight budgets. Ironically, in NASA's case, marginal budget cutting tends to trim the muscle and keep the fat. In Mr. Lewis's words, "a reduced budget means that the big things get saved and the

---

Box 5–1 (*concluded*)

little get cut, 'the slaughter of the innocents.'" Thus innovative ideas are rendered stillborn.

NASA's original charter, back in the late 1950s, called for the agency to be basically a research and development organization. But it has left this noble and useful goal far behind. Rather than being a trellis to support private space activity, the trellis has become an end in itself—with very costly artificial flowers stenciled on.

The major problem, of course, is that the United States really has no long-term, overall grand strategy for space. (One day at a time may be great advice for alcoholics, but it's a lousy way to run a space program.) But thanks to the emphysematous effects of the budget deficit, massive, long-range funding is unlikely to be approved. But a policy should at least be spelled out. President Reagan should announce that the ultimate purpose of U.S. space policy is a permanently manned space presence. As Thomas Jefferson's Louisiana Purchase made the United States a continental power and the Panama Canal made the United States a world power, America's next goal should be to become a space power.

Among other things, this would be harmonious with NASA's original goals and might give it a fresh sense of vigor and purpose. As a former NASA employee, L. Jackson Gardner, puts it, "We were all Buck Rogers and we were going to the moon! Then it died." It might mean that NASA would stop worrying about private launch vehicles (and competition from the French Ariane rocket for that matter) and devote itself primarily to R&D—while the private guys look after P&L.

Source: Condensed from Jack D. Kirwan, *The Wall Street Journal*, December 6, 1985.

---

nities are profitable, many young persons will not take the legitimate jobs that are available.

And as a rejoinder to the "attack poverty" approach, Wilson writes:

The desire to reduce crime is the worst possible reason for reducing poverty. Most poor persons are not criminals; many are either retired or have regular jobs and lead conventional family lives. The elderly, the working poor, and the willing-to-work poor could benefit greatly from economic conditions and government programs that enhance their incomes without there being the slightest reduction in crime—indeed, if the experience of the 1960s is any guide, there might well be, through no fault of most beneficiaries, an increase in crime. Reducing poverty and breaking up the ghettoes are desirable policies in their own right, whatever their effects on crime.[39]

---

[39] Ibid., p. 228.

If such grandiose goals as the elimination of unemployment and poverty are not very realistic, then what goals might we have for our criminal justice system? In Wilson's view, the deterrent capacity of the criminal justice system depends in no small part on its ability to evoke sentiments of shame in the accused. Yet anyone familiar with the police stations, jails, and courts of our larger cities is keenly aware that accused persons caught up in the system are exposed to very little that involves either judgment or solemnity, that evokes any sentiment of shame. "They are instead processed through a bureaucratic maze in which a bargain is offered and a haggle ensues at every turn—over amount of bail, degree of the charged offense, and the nature of the plea. Much of what observers find objectionable about this process could be alleviated by devoting many more resources to it, so that an ample supply of prosecutors, defense attorneys, and judges were available."[40]

The purpose of the foregoing discussion is not to show how the crime problem can be solved but to show, in one specific area of public policy, how we tend to posit sweeping goals that are often unattainable (given limited resources) and have only limited efficiency. I have further tried to illustrate how rigorously thinking through the problem *can* lead to some goals (e.g., an ample supply of prosecutors, defense attorneys, and judges) that are workable and challenging.

Perhaps an additional, even more specific example would help us see the point more clearly. Goals for heroin addiction policies that differ in scope are sometimes loosely distinguished as those that attack "symptoms" of the problem and those that attack its "root causes." Presumably, goals attacking symptoms are those designed primarily to reduce heroin consumption among people currently using the drug (see column 4 of Table 5–4). Policies attacking causes have broader scopes: they seek to influence more aspects of behavior than simply heroin consumption and generalize their influence to a larger portion of the total population (column 1).

"The classification in terms of symptoms and causes," Mark H. Moore writes, "produces ardent judgments about the relative merits of specific programs; it strongly implies that policies attacking symptoms are cynical, impermanent, inefficient, or otherwise undesirable, and that policies attacking causes are self-evidently superior."[41] There is a cozy common sense in this. If you define the goals of heroin policy broadly, as is usually done, "you must intuitively judge that a policy restricted to reducing the heroin consumption of current users will not have a substantial impact on the problem. Too much of the user's adverse behavior

---

[40] Ibid., pp. 230–31.
[41] Mark H. Moore, "Anatomy of the Heroin Problem," p. 646.

Table 5–4
Scope of goals for heroin addict policies

Influence the behavior of the general society		Influence only the behavior of people already using heroin	
(1)	(2)	(3)	(4)
Influence a broad range of behavior	Influence heroin consumption only	Influence a broad range of behavior	Influence heroin consumption only
Macro employment policies	Prohibition of all sales and use of heroin	Therapeutic communities	Ambulatory detoxification
Welfare programs	Drug education programs	Individual psychotherapy	"Barebones" methadone maintenance
Public health programs	Early detection and quarantine programs	Methadone maintenance with ancillary services	
Antipoverty programs	Antagonist immunization programs	Probation and parole	
Job training programs			
Prohibiting discrimination in hiring		In-patient psychiatric hospitals	
Juvenile delinquency programs		Sheltered work programs	
Jails and prisons			

Source: Adapted from Mark H. Moore, "Anatomy of the Heroin Problem," *Policy Analysis* 2, no. 4 (Fall 1976), pp. 639–62.

and unhappy condition will persist despite the reduction in heroin consumption. Too many people whose behavior we would like to influence—siblings, parents, spouses, neighbors—will remain out of reach."

But if a sole reliance on narrow goals would be a mistake, so might a sole reliance on broader ones. According to Moore, there are two reasons to believe that the broader policies would fail.

First, such policies in general have had much weaker effects than expected on the overall behavior and condition of people: many of the great social programs of the sixties failed to improve the lives of those they were designed to serve. The time for great confidence in the magical effects of anti-discrimination laws, job training, and antipoverty agencies has passed. Second, because heroin users are separated from society by racial discrimination, by discrimination against people with criminal records, and by their own poor attitudes, health, and skills, they tend to be among the last aided by expansion in employment or extension of general social services. Even when broad policies are aggressively pursued, users require special attention and support to overcome the remaining barriers. Such attention and support can be provided only by policies with somewhat narrower scopes: in some cases, the very narrow policies will be sufficient for this; but in others, more comprehensive and intensive programs [column 3 of Table 5–4] will be required. Thus, there is an important complementary effect among programs with different scopes: combinations are likely to provide greater leverage than any one class of policy pressed alone.[42]

Again, my purpose here is not to resolve the issue of either crime or heroin addiction but to show the range of goals that exists and to raise the question of balance between the too broad and too narrow.

Coordination

Policymakers must concern themselves with two types of coordination, internal and external. Let us consider internal coordination first, because it is the simpler of the two.

Policy must establish some mechanism for ensuring that progress towards policy goals is monitored in order that adjustments can be made as required. All key participants within the network of individuals and institutions involved in program operation must be coordinated in this network. One of the keys to Joan Claybrook's success was not only that she had a set of goals on her own agenda but also that she created communications networks.

> We had a staff meeting every Monday morning that was attended by assistant administrators, the executive secretariat, and my personal secretary. That was when people could raise issues that needed attention. . . . we could generally draw up a list of where everything was at and that helped put pressure on top of projects, some of which I would pursue with special attention. For example, during my first six weeks, I held a five-hour meeting every Saturday morning to clear out the backlog of defects investigations, some of which had been open for six years.[43]

The other type of coordination is—more abstract than Monday morning staff meetings. External coordination involves the idea of a system—an idea that should be rather familiar by now. (It made its first appearance in Chapter 1 as a core idea: a set of elements in dynamic interaction organized for a goal. In Chapter 2, we encountered the policymaking system in which K Street, Capitol Hill, and the White House are important elements. In Chapter 4, we took intellectually another important

---

[42] Ibid.
[43] Whitman, "Claybrook and NHTSA."

step in using the systems idea when we modeled problems ranging from heroin addiction to corn production.) One of the principal structural characteristics of every system is a communication network that permits coordination among the elements of the system. Feedback loops play a particularly important part in the behavior of a system through integrating the effects of flows between variables. Numerous examples of feedback were given in the previous chapter (e.g., price equilibriums).

The idea of policy arises from the recognition that the social system is just that, a system. Once this fact is recognized, there is no alternative save to act in accord with it. That is to say, *the purpose of policy is to guide government activities in accordance with the properties of a system.*[44]

The first of a system's properties is the best known: everything relates to everything. If one part is changed, all other parts are affected. It thus becomes necessary to think of the total effect, not just the partial one.

This fact has an important corollary. Given the interconnections of things, it follows that there is no significant aspect of national life about which there is not likely to be a rather significant national policy. It may be a hidden or unintended policy—but it is a policy nevertheless. In the course of the 1960s, for example, the Selective Service System emerged as a national youth policy of enormous consequence. In effect, the draft meant that youth of higher social status would in considerable measure be excused from fighting in a difficult and dangerous war. Almost certainly, this contributed importantly to a sequence of events which led large numbers of this group into unprecedented opposition to society as a whole. Yet Selective Service was never seen as a youth policy. From the first, it had but one object, to maintain the armed forces at a lesser cost than would be required if the members thereof had to be induced to serve by the same kind of inducements that operate in the labor market generally. Not infrequently, the strongest proponents of the draft have been persons who wished to see the money "saved" so that it could be used for important social services to help the less advantaged. They certainly never considered that in the process they might be sending just such persons to war, while exempting more privileged youth.

A second property of systems can be seen at work in the Selective Service example: systems are frequently *counterintuitive* in their operation. That is to say, commonsense expectations as to what will follow from a given intervention are frequently wrong. Thus, by the end of the 1960s, it was not persons who were being drafted who appeared

---

[44] The following discussion is based on material from the National Goals Research Staff, *Towards Balanced Growth: Quantity and Quality* (Washington, D.C.: Government Printing Office, 1970), pp. 175–76.

256

to protest the draft most; rather, it was persons who for various reasons were exempted or deferred. On closer examination, it may be that there is a perfectly reasonable explanation for this, for the term counterintuitive is not intended to be mysterious. It is nothing unusual in personal experience for things not to work out as expected.

This is no less true of government activity. But it is within the power of government to detect such situations. How? By relying not on hunches but on systemic analysis. By moving away from a program orientation to a policy orientation.

Clearly, that is the best way for the United States to tackle its trade deficit. A policy built on one pillar is not a policy but a program. What then might a coordinated approach to the trade issue look like? Here is one suggestion, consisting of not one but four pillars:

> The first pillar relates to basic trade principles. When dealing with a problem as sensitive and emotion-packed as trade, one must work hard to rethink a proper sense of direction. In other words, it is important to resist the temptation of short-term political or economic benefits, which would in the long run be detrimental to the country. . . .
>
> A dose of reality leads us to the second fair trade pillar. The administration must demonstrate to the American people that we are doing our best to ensure that there is a "level playing field" on which American business can play. . . .
>
> Our third pillar has a long-run orientation. It relates to the need for a truly effective international organization to provide the "rules of the road" for international trade. . . .
>
> The fourth pillar of trade policy relates to the impact of an inordinately strong dollar on our U.S. trade balance. . . . it is imperative that we get a handle on this problem and reverse the trends. . . .[45]

The security chapter in the Kissinger Commission Report to the President on Central America might be cited as a rare example of how one traces the complex and involuted interconnections of foreign policy: "The ability of the United States to sustain a tolerable balance of power on the global scene at a manageable cost depends on the inherent security of its land borders. This advantage is of crucial importance. It offsets an otherwise serious liability: our distance from Europe, the Middle East, East Asia. . . ." This is certainly true. It gives pause to consider the full extent to which American foreign policy and American security policy are all premised on hemispheric peace. (It also gives pause to consider that the Soviet Union is lacking in precisely this strategic luxury.) In the event that the hemisphere becomes hot, the report notes, "we would either have to assume a permanently increased defense burden,

---

[45] Clayton Yeutter, "Follow the Four Trade Pillars." Speech given at the Center for the Study of American Business at Washington University in St. Louis, January 1986.

or see our capacity to defend distant trouble spots reduced. . . ." This is a legitimate and farsighted concern. Indeed, it may be the final goal of Soviet policy in the region to disrupt Mexico and deprive the United States of the peace here that has underwritten its security commitments elsewhere. And there is still time to act; the day that Mexico may fall is still distant enough to permit us a wide variety of means of prevention. The Kissinger Report is grave, but it is admirably unhysterical. It states that this strategic nightmare may be put off as much by the use of diplomacy as by the use of force.

In fact the security requirement put forward by the Kissinger Commission is worthy of respect. The United States would tolerate a variety of political and social systems in its hemisphere, but it would not tolerate an alliance between any of these systems and its enemies. Reform and revolution, yes; the Soviet Union and Cuba, no. As the report concludes:

> The general strategic objective that should animate U.S. diplomacy in dealing with the present threats in Central America can be simply stated: to reduce the civil wars, national conflicts, and military preparations there at least to the dimensions of the Central American region. As a nation we are certainly not opposed to indigenous reform in Central America. . . . Nor are we threatened by indigenous revolutions that use local resources and appeal to local circumstances. What gives the current situation its special urgency is the *external threat* posed by the Sandinista regime in Nicaragua. . . .[46]

Tracing the complex and involuted interconnections by which inputs produce outputs in a large social system is not work for amateurs. This task is seldom done in social policy, save in economics, and there, most economists would insist, it is done imperfectly. It is just that most persons who have considered the matter feel that it has to be done, and accordingly someone will have to learn how.

Consistency

Policymakers should be concerned with three kinds of consistency. First, goals should be consistent with objectives; objectives, in turn, should be linked to actions. (Table 5–5.) Since this logic was discussed in the opening chapter, I need say no more here.

Secondly, goals, which are the backbone of a policy, must be internally consistent—they must not work at cross purposes. For example, in writing the 1985 farm bill Congress had three goals in mind:

1. "Protect" farmer income. The bill called for nearly $40 billion in subsidies through 1988.

---

[46] Kissinger Commission Report to the President on Central America (Washington, D.C.: Government Printing Office, 1984), p. 30. Emphasis added.

Table 5-5
The U.S. future in space: Linking possible goals and objectives

Objectives:	Increase space activities' efficiency; reduce their net cost*	Involve the general public directly*	Derive economic benefits*	Derive scientific, political, and social benefits*	Increase international cooperation*	Study and explore the physical universe*	Bring life to the physical universe*
1. Establish a global information system/service re natural hazards	N	N	P	Y	Y	N	N
2. Establish lower-cost reusable transportation service to the moon and establish human presence there	Y	P	P	Y	Y	Y	Y
3. Use space probes to obtain information re Mars and some asteroids prior to early human exploration	N	N	N	Y	Y	Y	N
4. Conduct medical research of direct interest to the general public	N	N	P	Y	P	N	N
5. Bring at least hundreds of the general public per year into space for short visits	N	Y	Y	Y	Y	N	Y
6. Establish a global, direct, audio broadcasting, common-user system/service	N	P	P	Y	Y	N	N
7. Make essentially all data generated by civilian satellites and spacecraft directly available to the general public	N	Y	P	Y	Y	N	N
8. Exploit radio/optical free space electromagnetic propagation for long-distance energy distribution	N	N	Y	P	Y	N	N
9. Reduce the unit cost of space transportation and space activities†	Y	N	Y	Y	N	N	N
10. Increase space-related private sector sales†	Y	N	Y	N	N	N	N

*Y: Yes; N: No; P: Perhaps; depends on how carried out.
†This would advance the prospects of successfully addressing all other "goals."
Source: Office of Technology Assessment, *Civilian Space Stations and the U.S. Future in Space* (Washington, D.C.: Government Printing Office, November 1984), p. 16.

2. Increase farm commodity exports. Goal number one, which keeps price-support levels so high that American farmers are out of world markets, negates this goal.
3. Keep the farm bill's total cost below a $27.5 billion ceiling. Goals one and two negate this goal.

There are other interesting little contradictions in farm bills. For years, big land speculators in the West have been plowing up substandard range land and planting it in winter wheat. Environmentalists say this "sodbusting," threatens a new dust bowl. They are right. The U.S. government has been financing sodbusting through investment incentives in the tax law combined with agricultural subsidy programs. Yet it has also paid farmers millions of dollars to take land out of use.

Finally, policy should be *externally* consistent. For example, the farm bill should not conflict with national goals in other areas. As you might suspect, it does. By surpassing the $27.5 billion ceiling noted in point 3 above, it *increases* the budget deficit. Further, it offers no guarantee that it will help cure the trade deficit.

Contradiction plagued Carter's foreign policy perhaps more than any modern president. He told the nation that it had to overcome its "inordinate fear of Communism" and work with Moscow to reduce the nuclear threat, but the Soviet Union was "the epitome of evil" against which American virtue had to be "defined and preserved." Contradiction plagued the conception of the MX missile: Was the MX an insurance policy against the (theoretical) vulnerability of the Minuteman missiles or a first-strike weapon against Soviet missile silos? And how could it be reconciled with arms control? A still further contradiction weighed on Carter's policy toward Latin America: He sincerely wanted to put an end to paternalism (hence his admirable effort on the Panama Canal settlement), but he also wanted to prod delinquent states on human rights and nonproliferation. In Nicaragua and in El Salvador, his policy fell between two stools: his concern for, if not democracy, at least decency, and his fear of communism.[47]

An excellent example of an internally consistent policy was containment. To resist Soviet expansion following World War II, President Truman, Dean Acheson (Secretary of State), and George Kennan (veteran diplomat) articulated a containment policy. Kennan formally explained the policy in a famous article that appeared in the July 1947 issue of *Foreign Affairs:* "It is clear that the main element of any policy toward the Soviet Union must be that of long-term, patient but firm and vigilant containment of Russian expansive tendencies." Viewed in the wider

---

[47] These contradictions are well documented in Gaddis Smith, *Morality Reason & Power: American Diplomacy in the Carter Years* (London: Hill and Wang, 1986).

260

Figure 5–4
How four policies are connected

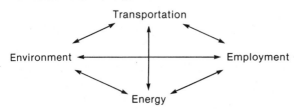

context of Soviet-American relations, we might say that containment was the strategic factor, or as Kennan himself puts it, "main element." But the point I wish to stress here is this: Kennan never believed in responding militarily to Russian threats at every point along the line or in shouldering the responsibility for holding the line all by ourselves. Kennan instead proposed collective, selective responses to Russian probings. The broad strategy of containment had three ends: to restore a balance of power and build up war-stricken allies, to exploit tensions in the then-monolithic Communist International and thereby to reduce Moscow's means of projecting power, and (in the long run) to moderate and negotiate Soviet global behavior. Political, economic, and military means all might have been called on in aid of such a strategy, but it must be considered as essentially political strategic doctrine—and certainly not a narrowly military one.[48] Each of the ends of this broad strategy were entirely consistent and mutually supportive.

External consistency, to repeat, refers to the notion that one government action does not thwart its other actions. How difficult the achievement of such consistency can be in practice may be seen by considering recent federal efforts in the areas of the environment, transportation, unemployment, and energy. It is no exaggeration to say that each of these four policies affects, and is affected by, the other three. The situation may be visualized as in Figure 5–4. Without trying to exhaust the possibilities, let us consider a few of the links and their implications for what we are calling the external consistency.

▪ *The transportation-employment connection.* In virtually every major city in the United States, unemployment rates are a function of the inadequacy of public transportation systems. Area workforce reviews repeatedly come to the same conclusion: many job openings listed by state

[48] See Barton Gellman, *Contending with Kennan: Toward a Philosophy of American Power* (New York: Praeger Publishing, 1984).

Figure 5–5
Conceptual environment/cost trade-off curve at a fixed level of
energy production

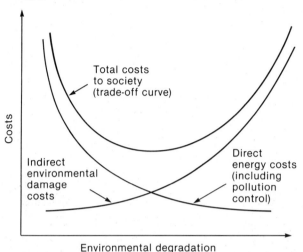

Note: Direct energy cost + Indirect environmental damage cost = Total costs to society.

employment commissions go unfilled because public transportation is inadequate.

- *The energy-transportation connection.* Among commuters in metropolitan areas, 53 percent drive to work alone in their automobiles; another 21 percent are automobile passengers. Only about 8 percent use buses, streetcars, or subways. Therefore, new federal taxes aimed at reducing energy consumption might be rebated to the public in the form of a more flexible subsidized public transit system.

- *The environment-energy connection.* In general, at a given level of energy production, the direct cost of supplying energy to the consumer decreases as such associated processes as land reclamation, waste disposal, and air and water pollution control are minimized or neglected. Thus, the direct cost of energy decreases as environmental restrictions are eased. At the same time, indirect social and environmental costs (e.g., pollutant-induced diseases, disabilities, shortened life spans, deterioration of buildings, reduced productivity) increase as environmental degradation increases. These trends are shown in Figure 5–5.

- *The unemployment-environment connection.* Although cleaning up the environment has led to a number of plant closings, environmental programs overall create employment. Two studies of jobs associated with the construction of municipal wastewater treatment plants indicate that the total number of jobs associated with $1 billion of expendi-

Box 5–2
Policy inconsistency: A paradigmatic case

It is hard to discuss inconsistencies in public policy without mentioning federal policy with respect to cigarette smoking. In 1964, the famous report on smoking and health by an advisory committee to the surgeon general of the United States declared that cigarette smoking was a leading cause of lung cancer in males, and that it presented "a health hazard of sufficient importance . . . to warrant appropriate remedial action." Accordingly, the government began taking measures to lessen cigarette smoking for the sake of public health. In 1970, cigarette advertising was taken off the air by act of Congress. Today, against the $400 million a year being spent on print advertising of cigarettes, the government is spending less than $2 million a year on educational programs concerning the hazards of cigarette smoking.

But the government continued to outweigh its own countermeasures with the estimated $97 million that it spent in 1977 in support of the tobacco-growing industry. These support measures included a loan program for tobacco sales abroad (under the Food for Peace Program!), expenditures to administer tobacco price-support programs in the United States, and a program for government inspection and grading of domestic tobacco crops.

tures for this purpose ranges from 53,000 to 82,000, even though only about 20,000 workers are directly employed to construct the facilities.[49]

Recapitulation

The six variables we have discussed in this section are relevant to policy design in any organization. To review, let us see how one university president used them.[50]

In the first decade of the century, the Massachusetts Institute of Technology was a poor, small (about 1,500 students), and struggling organization. Perhaps even its very survival was at stake. Like the archetypal small, growing business, the institute had been plagued from

[49] U.S. Council on Environmental Quality, *Environmental Quality 1976* (Washington, D.C.: 1976), pp. 153–54.

[50] This account is based on Roy McLennan, "The Chief Executive of M.I.T," *Journal of General Management* 3, no. 4 (Summer 1976), pp. 29–45.

the start by a shortage of capital. MIT's financial malaise was physically reflected in buildings and facilities as well as in academic salaries.

There was a need for organizational leadership to reinterpret MIT's mission in the light of current and future environmental conditions. A major attempt had been made in 1904 to solve the organization's problems. This had taken the form of a move inside MIT to make it Harvard University's engineering school and in this way to obtain access to the university's healthier funding. A voluntary takeover of MIT had been proposed within the institute.

About that time the organization's chief executive resigned. Given the circumstances outlined above, it was hardly any wonder that the two distinguished academics officially known to have been offered the presidency after the resignation had turned it down. For years many others would not touch it either: MIT had too many problems for its presidency to appeal to leading American scientists and technologists, and filling the post with a competent person was difficult. In the meantime, the organization soldiered on under a caretaker arrangement.

The presidential hiatus was finally broken in 1909 with the election of Richard C. Maclaurin to the presidency. Maclaurin, a thirty-nine-year-old New Zealand- and Cambridge-educated mathematician, had had an unusually broad education and professional experience. He began studying the institute intensively and talking to its faculty and alumni associations. In late 1908, he read and reread an authoritative two-volume work concerning MIT's founder, W. B. Rogers. With this book, he began what became a careful and systematic study of the origins, history, and development of the institute, including its goals, values, and mission. He "saturated himself with its spirit and tradition."

His inaugural address showed his close identification with the mission Rogers had proclaimed for MIT: the actual discipline a student took up was less important than the *process* of learning. Maclaurin's subsequent behavior and style in the role of president showed how deeply he had internalized this idea. At the subsequent alumni dinner, he announced the policy of his administration on two central issues which had hung fire for years, the location of MIT and relations with Harvard.

"He stressed that the thing to do first is to secure a new site, and on that new site raise a new [Massachusetts Institute of Technology] with all the characteristics of the old." To secure this objective, a million dollars would probably be needed. If the cost seemed high, people should consider the alternative of doing nothing—the decline of the organization—which was totally unacceptable. Maclaurin was stressing a longer-term objective, not the short-term crisis of balancing the books. He was equally definite on the second issue: "There will be no more talk of merger with Harvard. But in the domain of applied science there is much we can do for our mutual help. . . . [T]o make cooperation real and practical, we must be strong enough for independence."[51] Any kind of alliance with Harvard which was based on MIT's dependence was not to be considered. But joint ventures with the university, based on the two organizations' independence, were worthy of exploration.

Although goal-setting issues faced by political leaders, generals, and business executives are frequently studied and discussed, the need for goal setting is also encountered by management in other types of organizations. And here the same principles and conceptual schemes can be applied. Further, the case of Maclaurin illustrates how an organization can have, and usually does have, more than one goal. In such cases, good practice dictates that these goals be put in order of importance or priority.

THE USE (AND ABUSE) OF HISTORY IN POLICY ANALYSIS

Setting goals is perhaps the most crucial juncture in the policy process. After all, the identification of the problem (Chapter 3) and the forecasting of its probable course (Chapter 4) were tasks that pointed in only one direction—namely, the setting of goals. The follow-on tasks, generation of options (Chapter 6) and examination of their consequences (Chapters 7 and 8), will be carefully driven by what goals were set. Because historical materials can and should play an important role throughout this process, this is an appropriate place to consider the past's abiding influence on the present.

Such a consideration seems overdue, for in recent years history has been out of fashion among political leaders and their advisers. They are often people of masterful intelligence, trained in law, economics, or perhaps political science, but without a sense of history. To be sure, policymakers seize on certain crucial events in their lives—the Great Depression, Munich, Korea, Vietnam, the Civil Rights movement—but the rest of history remains for them a parade of forgotten memories. To put the matter plainly, to be ignorant of history is to be, in a very fundamental way, intellectually defenseless—unable to understand the workings either of our own society or other societies. We cannot hope that policymakers will know how the world got into its present situation—or even what the present situation is—if they know so little of the events that came before them.

I think the links between policy analysis and history are vital to the security of the nation and to a decent order at home. But I do not think these relationships are clear, nor do I think they are getting the

---

[51] Ibid., p. 32.

attention they deserve. Accordingly, let me state four general propositions at the outset and then follow up with an explanation of each.

Proposition 1: All current problems have historical contexts.

Proposition 2: Each generation learns certain lessons that influence how it views the present.

Proposition 3: While history teaches lots of little lessons, it teaches one big lesson about setting goals—nothing ever works out quite the way policymakers intended or expected.

Proposition 4: Historical analogies can suggest new options or fresh approaches to problems.

Putting problems in their historical context

A number of modern presidents exhibited a sense of history—Truman, Eisenhower, Kennedy, and Nixon come most readily to mind. More recent presidents have not had a record as good.

If President Reagan had viewed the Lebanon problem in historical context, he probably would not have sent a battalion of Marines there in 1983. When the first Marines began to die, he said he never dreamed that the Lebanon conflict would burgeon into a civil war. Yet, Lebanon had been the site of a bloody civil war since 1975, with 100,000 killed in 1981 alone. Viewed in that context, the U.S. involvement was like sending children into a massive typhoon.

In the spring of 1981, the Reagan administration made another error that could have been avoided. At the urging of Budget Director David A. Stockman, the president proposed sweeping changes in social security. The proposals would have meant considerable reductions in benefits for those already retired and especially for those about to retire. The reaction was swift and brutal. The plan was rejected out of hand, and the Democrats exploited the issue in the 1982 midterm elections.

It is clear that Reagan should have known better. What is less clear is that Reagan stumbled into a trap laid down by Franklin D. Roosevelt half a century earlier. A supporter complained to Roosevelt that the government was wasting a fortune having a large staff of clerks recording entries in individual social security "accounts" and answering inquiries about account balances when the system was nothing more than an income transfer from workers to retirees. Roosevelt replied that the trappings of a pension system created a public psychology that ensured that "those sons of bitches up on the Hill can't ever abandon this system when I'm gone."[52]

---

[52] Quoted in Richard E. Neustadt and Ernest R. May, *Thinking In Time* (New York: Free Press, 1986), p. 102.

Reagan's predecessor, Jimmy Carter, displayed an odd lack of a sense of history. Carter, an engineer by training, cared little for history; his instinct was to get things fixed and move on to the next problem.

It is not surprising that policymakers seldom bother to look deeply into the history of the issues that confront them every day. Politicians live for the present and the short-term future, that is, the period between now and the next election. The demands on a senior government official's time are overwhelming, and retrospection, therefore, almost always gets short shrift. Fortunately, bureaucracy does have a few people trying to analyze what happened yesterday. See accompanying box.

Generational learning and prognosis

Perception and misperception. To a remarkable degree, concepts formulated forty years, or two generations, ago continue to dominate American outlook on foreign and domestic policy. Probably the best way to explain the endurance of these concepts is by reference to some principles of cognitive psychology. The cognitive approach emphasizes the ways in which people distort decision making by gross simplifications in problem representation and information processing. Some psychologists suggest that human beings may be incapable of rational decision making. (Recall Core Idea 7.) In any event, considerable evidence suggests that people process and interpret information according to a set of mental rules that bear little relationship to those of formal logic.

According to cognitive psychologists, we cannot explain policy decisions without reference to policymakers' beliefs about the world. These beliefs, organized as images, shape the way in which policymakers respond to events. In the area of foreign affairs, for example, the primary source of images about world politics for policymakers is stereotyped interpretations of dramatic historical events. These events have a powerful effect on the thinking of younger people whose opinions about the world are still highly impressionable. Images formed by adolescents and young adults linger and someday shape the approach these people take when in positions of authority. This may explain why generals are prepared to fight in the last war and diplomats are prepared to avoid it.[53]

Now we come to a dilemma. On one hand, policymakers must relate new information to the conceptual framework they have developed; otherwise, they will confuse thought and inconsistent action. But the pursuit of consistency becomes irrational when it closes their minds to new information, different points of view, or alternative scenarios of

---

[53] Robert Jervis, "Hypotheses on Misperception," *World Politics* 20 (April 1968), pp. 454–79.

Box 5–3
Collecting the lessons of history

The nation's capital is filled with people trying to analyze today's events. Wayne Rasmussen, on the other hand, is trying to analyze what happened yesterday.

Mr. Rasmussen is a government historian, one of 450 scattered through the federal bureaucracy, looking backward, catching and preserving examples and instructive tidbits from years gone by.

He does not make policy. But by uncovering little remembered or forgotten facts, dusting them off and presenting them anew, he can influence those who do. And while the job may seem an ideal opportunity to highlight America's best features, Mr. Rasmussen and other official historians insist they are neither publicists nor government cheerleaders.

"We bring historical perspective to bear on current problems," said Mr. Rasmussen, chief historian of the Agriculture Department. "We don't tell anybody what they should do next year, but we can tell them what happened last year. They can take it from there."

Safeguarding the cautious

Duties vary within different agencies, but all historians, from the lone chronicler at the Federal Bureau of Investigation to the 234 historical researchers at the United States Air Force, share a meticulous and sometimes crucial role. They are, as Mr. Rasmussen says, "the institutional memory of Washington."

"It's amazing how details slide away, particularly when there is a turnover in administration," said Mr. Rasmussen, who challenges trivia mavens to name the Secretary of Agriculture from just eight years ago (Bob Bergland). "Many 'new' ideas have been tried in the past," he added, and his staff of seven historians seeks to put those ideas in context.

When angry farmers drove tractors into the capital a few years ago, for example, Mr. Rasmussen's history of the American agricultural movement was circulated in the White House. Its conclusions, that farm groups were not strong enough to make a significant impact on the market and were generally not violent, served as the basis for administration policy.

Old top-level parleys

Well-honed hindsight is useful abroad as well as at home, according to William Z. Slany, chief historian at the State Department. By preserving diplomatic details, from the Yalta Conference in 1945 to the latest news briefing from the Presidential spokesman Larry Speakes, Mr. Slany and his staff of twenty-one help to save administrators from being "lost at sea" when dealing with foreign leaders.

"History is just another part of the assortment of information that is necessary to conduct the nation's diplomatic business," he said.

Box 5–3 (*concluded*)

President Franklin D. Roosevelt first aimed the spotlight on federal history in 1942, soon after the United States entered World War II, when he learned that virtually no official records remained of World War I. Mr. Roosevelt resolved that the United States would never again fight a war without knowing the history of the one before it, and commissioned a federal history of World War II, setting the wheels in motion for other historical projects.

Objectivity seems no problem

Since then, according to Richard A. Baker, historian of the Senate and president of the Society for History in the Federal Government, a 500-member trade organization: "The military in particular has proved that federal employees can fairly and objectively write the histories of the agencies that employ them."

In recent budget-cutting times, official historians have begun to worry some about the future. They have sometimes been labeled an expendable service.

"Most history offices have proven the worth of learning from our past," Mr. Rasmussen said, "but we still have to sell ourselves."

"You would hate to conduct your own life without memory of what you were like ten years ago," Mr. Baker said.

Mr. Slany agreed. "Especially as we confront our rivals, I don't think anyone wants to be left without historical background," he said. "Besides, we know the Russians have a lot of historians too."

Source: *New York Times*, July 8, 1985.

---

the future. Policymakers must therefore strike a balance between consistency on the one hand and flexibility on the other. The tendency is to err in the direction of consistency and to cling to concepts long after they have lost their usefulness. The consequences are not good. Policymakers respond to information supporting existing beliefs and ignore or reshape contradictory information.[54]

Implications. From the foregoing analysis two practical conclusions might be drawn. First, policymakers should consider how generational learning might have affected other people relevant to the success of their policy.

For example, a careful consideration of the Russian historical experience might be in order. Why do Americans and Russians disagree so

---

[54] Ibid. Jervis marshals considerable evidence to support these views.

profoundly about arms control? The American arms-control community believes fundamentally in the principle of "mutual assured destruction" (MAD), that is, the deterrence of war by the certainty that whoever provoked it would suffer as terribly as his victim and that neither would "win." The Russians, still profoundly affected by their own wartime experience, are determined at all costs to survive, as they have survived before, and, if war comes, to fight it as best they can. They see the nuclear weapons of both sides as *weapons,* not as *deterrents.* The Russians' historical experience gives them a mortal dread of another war, whether nuclear or conventional; but if war came, that historical experience would move them to try to fight it through regardless of losses—and further, if they were convinced that it was coming, to strike a pre-emptive blow in order to cripple their adversary.

It is this Soviet will and capacity to pre-empt that seems to render invalid all American "war fighting" doctrines. Freeman Dyson, a Princeton physicist, writes:

> Our war fighters with their elaborate plans of limited war have never been able to face the fact that Soviet doctrine of massive pre-emption makes such plans meaningless. Our arms controllers with their fixation on assured destruction have never been able to understand that the driving force of Soviet policy is a determination to survive, and that this deeply rooted will to survive makes assured destruction impossible.[55]

It is this incompatibility of concepts, Dyson thinks, that has hampered arms-control negotiations in the past and might continue to do so in the future. Both doctrines grew naturally out of different historical experiences of the two sides. Both are firmly rooted and will not be easily changed.

Lest I leave the impression that only Americans have difficulty in appreciating the experiences of others, we might consider the following assessment of Helmut Schmidt, West Germany Chancellor during the Carter presidency and one of the most urbane of modern politicians.

> Schmidt seems to have taken no notice of events and details offering him possibly useful inferences about Carter. . . . With a little simple question-asking, Schmidt might have seen Carter's details against the special events of Southern, even Georgian, history. . . . Schmidt might then have assumed that he would be greeted with a sermon and that a great deal of courteous ritual would have to precede any getting down to business. One veteran of the Carter administration, also long acquainted with Schmidt, feels sure in retrospect that, with only a little imaginative effort, Schmidt could have made Carter a dogged friend and ally. We are inclined to agree. With a good deal less brainpower than Schmidt but, partly for that reason, more

---

[55] Freeman Dyson, *Weapons and Hope* (New York: Harper & Row, 1984).

experience in the exercise of personal charm, British Prime Minister James Callaghan managed to use Carter occasionally as the equivalent of an extra Labour Party whip.[56]

The second conclusion that we might draw from the theory of generational learning is as simple and useful as the first. Policymakers should rethink, from time to time, their own assumptions about the way the world works.

Examples of policymakers who failed to reassess their conceptual frameworks litter the history of twentieth-century diplomacy. In October 1938, nearly everyone in England cheered Prime Minister Neville Chamberlain when he conceded virtually everything to Hitler at Munich to bring "peace in our time." How could he have been so mistaken? Chamberlain and his generation had been brought up in the England of Queen Victoria and were middle aged when World War I began. Their world was that of the British Empire; global problems—not racial antagonisms of Central Europe—were what really mattered. Furthermore, appeasement payed. It payed off well enough when the British settled their differences with the French in Africa in 1904 and with Russia in Central Asia three years later. Because Churchill saw things quite differently at the time, we know that people can rethink those concepts they hold so dear. But it is no easy feat.

Munich was an event that deeply influenced the thinking of a generation of American policymakers. If democracies fail to act, then aggressors are encouraged to go ahead. This line of analysis appeared valid not only in Korea in 1950, when the communist North attacked the South; but also in Iran in 1947, when the United States put pressure on the Soviets to withdraw; in Greece and Turkey the same year, when the United States proposed a program of economic and military aid "to support free peoples who are resisting attempted subjugation by armed minorities and outside pressures"; in Berlin in 1948, when the United States responded to a Soviet blockade of the city with a massive airlift; and in Cuba in 1962, when the United States turned back Soviet ships carrying ballistic missiles to the country. But was the analysis equally valid in Southeast Asia in July 1964? Many would say no. Yet on the eve of American intervention in Vietnam, Lyndon Johnson described the challenge in Southeast Asia as fundamentally similar to the earlier challenges. "The great lesson of this generation," he told a sympathetic college audience, "is that wherever we have stood firm, aggression has ultimately been halted."[57]

---

[56] Neustadt and May, *Thinking in Time*, pp. 187–90.

[57] Quoted in Richard N. Lebow, "Generational Learning and Conflict Management," *International Journal* 11 (Autumn 1985), p. 565.

Later generations became wedded to their own conceptual frameworks. The heightening anxiety about nuclear war in the early 1980s is probably rooted in, among other things, generational changes. It takes only one generation of successful peacekeeping to engender the belief that peace is a natural condition; memory of the rigors of maintaining that peace around the world wanes. The view becomes this: Peace is threatened principally by those involved in preparations for war, that is, the military-industrial complex.[58]

And what might be said of younger generations? Much to the puzzlement of the Democratic party leadership, the youngest voters are the most likely of all age groups to vote Republican. But the concept of generational learning unlocks that puzzle rather quickly: most of these young men and women have known only two presidents in their lifetime—Democrat Carter and Republican Reagan.

The momentum of historical experience.   Policymakers are influenced not only by the events of their life but also by the historical experiences of their cultures. Policymakers in the United States, for instance, view events in South Africa through the lens of the Civil Rights movement of the 1960s. They recall that their forefathers won their initial liberty from the British with bayonets and that the end of slavery came for American blacks with wrath and carried a terrible swift sword.

Americans are sometimes puzzled by the suspicion, if not hostility, with which Latin Americans view them. But such suspicion is not without historical foundation. Consider the long record of the direct and indirect involvement of Washington into the affairs of those nations. There have been some fifteen major interventions in the Caribbean basin between 1903 (Panama) and 1984 (Granada). There have also been indirect interventions. For example, in 1973, President Salvador Allende of Chile was overthrown and killed in a military coup. The United States, as was later shown, had supported the opposition to Allende. In the 1980s, the United States provided aid to rebel forces in Nicaragua. The dim mists of time do not obscure as much of the past as we might think.

A final word of caution.   Old concepts are not necessarily wrong concepts. For nearly two generations a remarkable consensus dominated American thinking on foreign trade. Protectionism is bad. There was no debate; everyone agreed, but we have forgotten why. Today, with

---

[58] Richard Ned Lebow of Cornell University writes: "Whereas the Cold War image emphasized the aggressive nature of Soviet foreign policy and totally ignored legitimate defensive motivations, the competing image is extremely sensitive to these defensive needs but denies or seeks to explain away any offensive objectives on the part of Moscow. Both interpretations represent one-sided and simplistic views of both the Soviet Union and the nature of superpower conflict. For this reason, their policy prescriptions also tend to be unrealistic." Ibid., p. 582.

some 300 protectionist bills now before Congress, Congress is awash in protectionist schemes, and it takes a septuagenarian to recall that the lesson was painfully learned. "Some of us remember the 1930s, when the most destructive trade bill in history, the Smoot-Hawley Tariff Act, helped plunge this nation and the world into a decade of depression and despair," President Reagan told a radio audience on September 1, 1985. "If the ghost of Smoot-Hawley rears its ugly head in Congress, if Congress crafts a depression-making bill, I'll fight it."

The stockmarket crash of 1929 came in the midst of debate in Congress over the tariff; it had spent the year adding item after item to the protection list. In mid-1930 the Smoot-Hawley Bill became law, with the highest tariffs in the nation's history. What might have been an ordinary correction—early 1930 showed a recovery in share prices and stabilization in industrial production—turned into the Great Depression. The economy fell until 1933 and fully recovered only with World War II.

After the war, America led the world to a historic open economic order. Following the path set by the Roosevelt administration's reciprocal trade agreements, the international community created such institutions as the Bretton Woods monetary agreement and the General Agreement on Tariffs and Trade. The long postwar boom began. These experiences etched into national conscience, and in particular into the minds of President Reagan's generation, that free trade means prosperity and protectionism means depression.

Economists have of course made much of this argument. They find that the principal engine of economic progress is the law of comparative advantage; if each good is supplied by the lowest-cost producer, all will be richer. And the more widely comparative advantage works, the more wealth it creates. By blocking comparative advantage, protectionism hurts those on both sides of a barrier. Such arguments fell on deaf ears when 1,028 economists petitioned President Hoover to veto Smoot-Hawley; after the Depression they were readily accepted.

The validity of concepts does change, and therein lies the need for periodic review of those concepts. But not all old ideas are bad ideas.

What history teaches about goal setting

As the Smoot-Hawley example suggests, contemporary goal setters can gain valuable insights from a careful reading of history—even economic history.

Economic history. Table 5–6 summarizes two decades of American economic experience. What, if anything, can be learned from studying the events and disappointments of this grim past to set better goals for the future? Although economists and other analysts may differ in

Table 5–6
Lessons from the American economic experience, 1963–1983

November 1963	President Kennedy's assassination.
Early 1964	Kennedy-Johnson tax cut. Keynesians act to keep recovery going.
Mid-1960s	Spending buildup for Vietnam and Great Society adds more steam to economy.
Late 1960s	Inflation problem begins. Consumer price index up 5.4 percent in 1969, and 1 percent rises in early 1960s.
August 1971	President Nixon imposes wage-price controls and ends dollar convertibility into gold.
1972–73	Rapid money growth, Soviet wheat deal, anchovy shortage, and unwinding of price controls stir inflation again. Fixed exchange rates break down.
Late 1973	First oil shock: OPEC's fourfold price increase.
1974–75	Sharp recession with rapid inflation and weak dollar. Stock market plunges.
1979	Second oil shock, OPEC doubles prices.
November 1979	Chairman Paul Volcker changes Fed policy to emphasize control of money supply and to downplay control of interest rates.
1980	Interest rates soar to record highs. Carter recession.
July 1981	Start of Reagan's three-year cut in tax rates and of another severe recession. Inflation begins to drop.
1982	August bull market. World debt crisis erupts. Dollar begins major rise and recovery begins with 10.7 percent unemployment.
1983	Federal deficit hits $195 billion. Dollar still high. Debt crisis continues to spread.

degree about what there might be, there appears to be general agreement on a few key points:

1. *The United States must pay more heed to the international economy in setting its domestic economic policies.* In 1971, President Nixon, ignoring the lesson, stopped the outflow of U.S. gold and pursued a highly stimulative economic and monetary policy. That move set off waves in the world economy that accelerated inflation and eventually ended the Bretton Woods system of fixed exchange rates. The messy collapse of Bretton Woods and the resultant system of floating exchange rates were major causes of the breakdown of the golden age of growth and the unleashing of stagflation in the seventies.

2. *Presidents must make the tough decisions on how to use limited national resources while there is time and not subordinate those decisions to immediate political advantage.* Inflation began in the United States during the Vietnam War when President Johnson, with the economy approaching full employment, delayed, for political reasons, the difficult choice among three possible policies: raising taxes, cutting his Great Society programs, or

curbing military spending. And President Nixon gravely aggravated inflation a few years later with his New Economic Policy of August 15, 1971, simultaneously launching a highly stimulative fiscal and monetary policy, imposing wage and price controls, suspending the convertibility of the dollar into gold, and embargoing sales of certain American agricultural products. When the controls were lifted after his electoral victory in 1972, the suppressed inflation burst forth.

3. *Tight monetary policy must be used with great caution.* There is no doubt about the potency of monetary policy in checking inflation. But, in the process of squeezing inflation down over the past few years, tight money policy has taken an enormous toll in lost production, jobs, investment, and growth.

Since the fall of 1979, the Federal Reserve Board, has experimented with what some call "practical monetarism," paying greater attention to gradual growth of the money supply and less to the level of interest rates. But when tight money produced the recessions of 1980 and 1981– 82, the Fed swung to much more rapid rates of monetary expansion than sanctioned by the Fed's "target ranges" and paid more heed to interest rates. Thereby, discretionary monetary policy was used as a powerful tool for getting the economy out of deep recessions.

Other lessons. Whatever its value in improving judgment, history teaches no immutable lessons. The professional historian will be skeptical of those who claim that it does. The past is infinitely various, an inexhaustable storehouse of events.

Do arms-control treaties work? Do nations distrust each other because they are armed, or do they arm because they distrust each other? The record of arms-control negotiations in the twentieth century tends to support the latter judgment. The various arms-limitation agreements of the 1920s did not prevent the outbreak of World War II. By reinforcing a kind of optimism in Britain and France and thus inhibiting the possibility of military preparedness and diplomatic actions to deter war, these agreements may have actually helped bring that war about. Yet the Test Ban Treaty of 1963 has effectively prohibited testing in the atmosphere, in outer space, and under water by the United States, the Soviet Union, and Great Britain. (France did not sign it.)

Do arms-control agreements save money? Looking at the historical record, one would have to say rarely. Arms control appears to have had little effect on U.S. strategic weapons spending. During the tenure of Secretary of Defense Robert McNamara in the 1960s, U.S. spending on strategic weapons was cut almost in half. Then, throughout the 1970s, U.S. strategic weapons slowly climbed upward, despite a series of arms-control agreements with the Soviet Union. Moreover, limits on ICBM launchers probably accelerated the development of MIRVs (Multiple Independently Targetable Reentry Vehicles). Limits on ABMs (Anti Ballistic Missiles) accelerated the development of particle-beam and laser weapons. Limits on traditional strategic weapons such as ballistic missiles and bombers accelerated the development of cruise missiles. Limits on theater nuclear weapons such as those agreed to by Reagan and Gorbachev in 1987 triggered calls for increased spending on conventional weapons. Lesson: Limit the weapons currently being deployed, and nations will ingeniously find some other weapon on which to spend money.[59]

Do arms races always end in war? The longest and perhaps bitterest arms race in modern history was that between the French and the British navies between 1815 and 1904, yet peace was preserved throughout the period. Does overarming increase the risk of war? Even though the United States might deter the Soviet Union by adding more weapons, it might also increase their fear of attack and provoke them into a preemptive strike. In 1941, the United States cut off oil supplies to Japan in an effort to deter it from attacking Southeast Asia, but instead helped provoke the attack on Pearl Harbor.[60] Do sanctions work? Gary Clyde Hufbauer and Jeffrey Schott of the Institute for International Economics in Washington studied 103 episodes of trade sanctions since World War I. They conclude that sanctions are seldom successful, even by loosely defining success, except against small countries and only when the goals are modest. Moreover, the success rate is falling. Since 1973 the number of cases where sanctions have achieved any success has fallen to about one in four.[61] Yet, their research also tells us that sanctions do work as intended sometimes, and while no panaceas, sanctions are often effective at the margins.

Are negotiations and pressure complementary phases of foreign policy with communist states? History offers no example of successful negotiations with communists sustained exclusively by persuasiveness; for communist countries believe that settlements can only be based on the correct assessment of so-called correlation of forces between the contending forces. In both the Korean and Vietnamese negotiations, unilateral American restraint at the outset prolonged the wars and increased U.S. casualties.

One big lesson. Insofar as history teaches any lessons, it teaches that nothing ever works out quite the way policymakers intend or expect.

---

[59] Arms-control advocates like to point to the naval treaties of the 1920s and 1930s as example of how international agreements can prevent an arms race. They cite the fact that defense spending among the superpowers was relatively stable during those years. Yet the main decline in U.S. naval spending had already occurred by the time the great powers negotiated the Washington Naval Treaty of 1922. Naval spending was dropping until the treaty; arms control, in effect, froze naval expenditures at their 1922 levels.

[60] Joseph J. Nye, Graham T. Allison, and Albert Carnesale, *Hawks, Doves, and Owls: An Agenda for Avoiding Nuclear War* (New York: Norton, 1985).

[61] Gary Clyde Hufbauer and Jeffrey J. Schott, "Economic Sanctions and the United States' Foreign Policy," *PS* 18, no. 4 (1985), pp. 727–35.

Political science and sociology teach, in a sense, a can-do optimism, but history inculcates skepticism about people's ability to set firm goals or to manipulate and control purposefully their own destinies. History shows us repeatedly how the best-laid plans of the best minds usually go awry. Thus, history provides us with a perspective on what is possible and, more often, what is not.

Now, I will admit that too much of a historical sense, too much skepticism, is not very good for getting things done. Forgetfulness, Nietzsche once said, is a property of all action. But we need not worry: There seems little danger that our current crop of policymakers is too historically minded.

Let us see, then, if we can extract from our big lesson one or two concrete suggestions for today's policymakers. Perhaps policymakers of the older generation, so fond of citing the Munich lesson (don't appease!), and the young generation of policymakers, who prefer the Vietnam lesson (don't intervene!) should join to consider the lesson of 1914: *Events get out of control.* Most European leaders of the time expected a short war, a quick return to business-as-usual. Instead, four years of carnage destroyed 20 million people and three empires.

Accidents *can* happen. False alarms of nuclear attack *have* occurred. Recognizing the possibility of inadvertent nuclear war, what can policymakers do? Some steps would require Soviet cooperation—for example, regular bilateral talks on crisis prevention; establishment of additional hot lines among all five countries with nuclear arsenals; multinational measures against nuclear terrorists, and sanctions against nuclear proliferators; improvement of warning systems by placing unmanned tamperproof sensors in each other's missile fields. Other steps could be taken independently—for example, install electronic safety locks on nuclear weapons on naval ships similar to those on land-based weapons; pull back from the East German–West German border the short-range nuclear artillery that would be difficult to control from Washington in a crisis; improve procedures for maintaining civilian control over nuclear weapons; prepare top leaders far better than we do for dealing with nuclear crises.[62]

To summarize, history can help policymakers avoid past mistakes and manage better in similar circumstances next time. Not too long ago the idea that history can help policymakers would have been so obvious as not to merit the treatment given it here. Woodrow Wilson or Winston Churchill certainly assumed history to be a part of the intellectual furnishings of any educated person and a necessary foundation for any serious discussion of public policy. But educational philosophy

---

[62] Nye, et al. *Hawks, Doves, and Owls.*

has changed and these assumptions are, in some circles, no longer thought valid. If policy analysis must lower its sights—and some say it should—this may be because the demise of history in the curriculum has brought us a generation of analysts with no historical background.

Historical analogies and new options

As any careful reader of Sherlock Holmes knows, aside from his own unsurpassed experience in crime detection, Holmes was a systematic collector of historical case studies as well. He studied these famous cases of unusual cunning or ingenuity as paradigms or models to help him, by means of comparison and analogy, to solve the case at hand. He put it best: "I am generally able, by the help of my knowledge of the history of crime, to set them [i.e., the official police] straight. There is a strong family resemblance about misdeeds, and if you have all the details of a thousand at your finger-ends, it is odd if you can't unravel the thousand and first."[63]

Unfortunately, this is not the way policymakers tend to use analogies. Like all code words in ideological warfare, analogies are more than mere shorthand.

> They are used to prevent thought. They do so by instantly conjuring up a whole complex of circumstances and feelings to be drawn automatically from one situation and plugged into another. For "another Iran," read: hostages, helplessness, humiliation. For "another Cuba," read: adventurism, revolution, proxy mischief. For "another Afghanistan," read: imperialism, superpower bullying, disrespect for the rule of law. (For "another Nicaragua," see "another Cuba," above.)[64]

While analogies are usually deployed to thwart a policy, they are sometimes used to help make the case for one. The Reagan administration, for example, suggests that its Strategic Defense Initiative (SDI) is like the Manhattan Project, which was a success. Critics tried to rebut it by calling it "Star Wars," which seemed a clever analogy at first, something to link Ronald Reagan with another movie fantasy, but in retrospect it was probably a mistake. The public, after all, puts a lot of faith in Luke Skywalker and The Force. "Star Wars" just reinforces that successful, futuristic, high-tech image.

A better analogy, both politically and intellectually, would have been the nuclear plane. That project began in 1946 with a hope as simple and uncontroversial as Reagan's goal of eliminating nuclear weapons with SDI. Wouldn't it be nice if an airplane could stay aloft for weeks

---

[63] Arthur Conan Doyle, *A Study in Scarlet* (New York: Ballantine, 1975), p. 19.
[64] Charles Krauthammer, "Ghosts (Or: Does History Repeat)," *Time*, November 21, 1983, p. 95.

at a time? But actually building it proved difficult. In theory, it was possible to power an airplane indefinitely with a nuclear reactor. But a crew would have to be protected from the reactor's radiation, and it seemed that any shield would weigh so much that the plane could not get off the ground. Then, what if it crashed? Fifteen years and over one billion dollars later, Kennedy canceled the program.[65]

The real purpose of analogy in policy analysis. The main problem in the use of analogies in policy analysis results from erroneous notions about their purpose. To find that purpose I suggest we look to the area in which they have been used most fruitfully—science and technology.

Scientists often attribute their breakthrough to "method" or to a stroke of genius. Erased from their equations is the component called analogy. That neglect appears to be coming to an end. The role of analogy in science has come under increased scrutiny by scholars. Indeed, the search for hidden likenesses can be traced to the very roots of the scientific revolution. Early in this century, Ernest Rutherford and Niels Bohr found a model for the atom in the planetary model. That analogy— electrons orbiting the atom's nucleus like planets around the sun—still dominates the popular perceptions of atomic physics (though scientists now describe electron behavior in terms of statistical probabilities and jumps from one energy level to another).

Scientists use creative analogies and comparisons to extend theories and even to make new ones. Modern elementary particles are extensions and elaborations of the Greek atoms, and William Harvey found in the centralized Sun of Copernicus a model for the heart as the center of the circulation of blood. Issac Newton gave posterity the great machine, a clockwork universe in which everything moves according to inexorable law. One of the most striking examples of analogy comes from the work of Charles Darwin, who hit on "survival of the fittest" in his theory of evolution. Darwin's was the nineteenth-century world of *laissez-faire* economics, an age in which industrialists reigned supreme and young children were routinely put to work in mines and mills. Darwin immersed himself in the economic works of the period just prior to his discovery, imbibing the belief that society functions best when individuals are free to compete and struggle to their own advantage. Today, the very language of science—peppered with talk of black holes, the big bang, and gene splicing—hints at analogy continuing spurring scientific thought.

The crucial point about these examples is this: They show scientists using analogies not to refute colleagues or to justify their own beliefs

---

[65] See W. Henry Lambright, *Shooting Down the Nuclear Plane* (Indianapolis: Bobbs-Merrill, 1967).

but to *solve problems.* Policy analysts might proceed in a similar manner. *First:* Which other problem is this problem like? *Second:* How was that other problem solved? *Third:* How can the solution to that problem be adapted to this problem?

Let us take another look at the report of President Reagan's Commission on Central America issued on January 11, 1984, and quickly forgotten. In some ways, it was a remarkable document. For one thing, it put the military, economic, and social aspects of the problem in historical perspective. But its proposals were nibbled to death by opponents who objected to one part or the other rather than grappling with the report as a whole.

The following year the former chancellor of West Germany, Helmut Schmidt, suggested that the report be reconsidered.[66] It recognized the military threat from Cuba and the Soviet Union and the urgent need to deal with the region's economic and social problems, but this, he thought, could not be resolved by military means or even by a new Marshall Plan. The Marshall Plan idea was too narrow. It had the wrong name and smacked of U.S. domination. The hope lay, he said, in widening the economic restoration of the area using the other Central and South American nations—the Contadora group—to lead the way to a regional solution and bring European allies and Japan into a deal for peace and the economic reconstruction of Central America.

This was Schmidt's "new idea." He thought that the Central American problem was dividing the NATO allies. For that reason, they might be willing to contribute to an economic aid program for peace if the Reagan administration thought this might break the deadlock. The idea has drawbacks, but it is one of the few new ideas heard about the Central American problem in a long time. It calls on Europe and Japan to bring the Old World to the aid of the New for a change. And, it certainly demonstrates how analogies can be used creatively in problem solving by policymakers.

If this line of reasoning on the proper use of analogies is correct, then I think we can better see why the Vietnam analogy is not just overworked but useless. Because U.S. policy in Vietnam was manifestly unsuccessful, it held no promise for solving problems. By the same token, Bell Labs should not try to adopt a design for a perpetual motion machine to the solution of a problem in cryogenics. It is not because the fields of mechanics and cryogenics are incompatible, but because the perpetual motion machine is undoubtedly a failed notion.

Thus policymakers should look to the many relevant instances of *successful* wars against communist insurgencies: In Malaya in 1960, in

---

[66] James Reston, "A New Idea for Central America," *The New York Times,* January 25, 1985.

the Philippines in 1954, in Greece in 1949. Such an inspection should suggest the key components of a policy to stop a communist insurgency, for example, the strength of the local government. Of course, each element would have to be adapted to the problem at hand.

Ironically, even if Vietnam had been a successful policy, I am not sure it would make a good analogy for, say, El Salvador. Even cursory examination of the historical and political backgrounds of the two crises discloses major differences. El Salvador, for example, has a much smaller population than Vietnam (4.8 million compared to 41.5 million) and was never a part of a European colonial empire, as was Vietnam. It also is true that the United States today is far less deeply involved in El Salvador and in Central America than it was in Vietnam almost from the beginning. But the crux of the difference is geographical. Not only is El Salvador much closer to the U.S. border, its entire border consists of either ocean or U.S. allies.

The idea of analogy is a powerful one, and we will say more about it in the next chapter.

A PREVIEW OF THE NEXT THREE CHAPTERS

As emphasized in the first chapter, the purpose of policy analysis is to help policymakers choose specific alternatives, programs, or projects—that is, courses of action. It follows, therefore, that the heart of policy analysis consists of developing and assessing an adequate range of alternatives. But the connection between this effort and setting goals should be kept in mind: the quality of any alternative is largely determined by the definition of our goals. This section outlines how alternatives are selected; it also provides an overview of the subject matter of the three chapters that follow.

The assessment of program alternatives involves these fundamental concepts and methods: developing a range of alternatives, screening the preliminary alternatives, estimating the measurable consequences, assessing provisional orderings, determining the effect of constraints, reassessing the ordering of the alternatives, and checking the completeness of the assessment.[67]

Developing a range of alternatives

It is essential to search out a wide range of alternatives. The initial search for alternatives should not be constrained. Continuing, modify-

---

[67] The following discussion is based on U.S. General Accounting Office, *Evaluation and Analysis to Support Decision Making*, PAD 76–9 (Washington, D.C.: Government Printing Office, 1976), pp. 23–29.

ing, expanding, reducing, or abandoning an existing program should be included, as well as completely new alternatives. With regard to the existing program, consideration should be given to reexamining the validity of the existing objectives. The process of developing alternatives should include a thorough questioning of the need for any governmental intervention, which may have been justified on any of the following grounds:

The absence of suitable private alternatives or the absence of a private marketplace in which the needed service can be distributed.

The benefits to society resulting from universal use of the service or facility, such as sewage disposal.

Equal availability of a service, such as public education.

The distribution of benefits to disadvantaged people, such as the distribution of health benefits through medicare and medicaid.

The regulation of private activities, such as the certification of the effectiveness and purity of drugs.

The provision of incentives for desired private activities, such as the development of energy resources.

Broad classes of approaches that show potential for solving the problem being analyzed should be initially identified. One or more promising alternative approaches from each of the broad classes might be developed. If broad classes are *not* examined, then alternative approaches are usually unnecessarily limited to relatively small incremental changes in existing programs. For example, analysis of an incremental change in eligibility standards for the food stamp program is more narrowly defined than an analysis of overall income security or nutrition policy.

Reasonable alternatives from all sources, including those suggested by governmental agencies, legislative committees, and advocacy or interest groups, should be considered.

Screening the preliminary alternatives

A preliminary analysis of the likely consequences associated with the range of alternatives, including the status quo, should now be undertaken. This initial screening is intended to eliminate obviously inferior approaches and to reduce the original list of alternatives to a manageable size. It is helpful to make approximate calculations of cost and consequences, of break-even points, of technical and political feasibility, and so on.

Alternatives should not be ruled out too quickly based on implementation difficulties. Modification and combinations of alternatives usually become apparent and frequently provide the basis for new and superior alternatives. The search for alternatives is a continuing activity, and the analytical effort provides opportunities to invent or discover other alternatives.

Estimating the measurable consequences: Benefits, costs, and risks

Estimates must be made of anticipated measurable consequences as well as of all cost and resource inputs under various conditions and levels of available resources. Measurable consequences include effectiveness, side effects, and distribution considerations. In making such estimates, the data on actual costs and effectiveness found in prior appraisals of similar programs should be used together with actual operating data. It may also be necessary to use well-developed causal models to make such effectiveness estimates. Although these models must adequately simulate the real situation, an existing model may serve. Experience has shown that it is costly and time-consuming to develop a completely new model.

Some effort should be made to estimate side effects and their influence on resources. An estimate is needed, to the extent possible, of the differences of impact on the beneficiaries and the cost bearers (distribution considerations). Approximations may have to be used for side effects and distribution estimates, and various value judgments are involved in weighing both.

Assessing provisional orderings

Once the total and incremental consequences of the alternatives have been estimated, the alternatives should be arrayed in some order. In other words, do costs and benefits climb at a constant, increasing, or decreasing rate as the project approaches full funding? This ordering may be based on one of several available approaches.

One approach is *cost effectiveness*. This approach focuses on the resources expected to be consumed and how well the objectives are achieved. Using this framework, a preferred alternative is identified as one that produces the largest achievement for a given level of costs or that minimizes the resources expended for attaining a given level of effectiveness. While the cost-effectiveness approach provides a basis for ordering competing alternatives, it does not clearly allow for comparisons of alternatives associated with multiple, possibly conflicting, objectives. Other consequences of alternatives—side effects and distribution considerations—are not an integral part of the analysis and may require separate examination.

A second approach to ordering alternatives is *cost-benefit analysis*. Side effects and distribution considerations are incorporated into this approach. Major consequences, or benefits, are measured in dollars, and differences between monetary benefits and costs provide the basis for choice among alternatives. Theoretically, cost-benefit analysis is more useful than cost-effectiveness analysis in treating both differing and conflicting objectives. The streams of benefits and costs can be discounted to their equivalent present values, thus accounting for the effects of time. Conceptually, decision makers could select programs based on rankings of net present value benefits (or derivatives of these data) until the total available resources were exhausted. This approach requires that all measures be converted to dollars—a difficult task at best.

Each approach has both strengths and limitations, but all share certain limitations. One such limitation is uncertainty caused by such things as variations in assumption and in the quality of information on the alternatives. Because uncertainty is always present in anticipating future outcomes, undue emphasis should not be placed on small differences in the ordering of alternatives. The quantitative analysis which has been discussed should be supplemented with an analysis of nonmeasurable consequences. A serious attempt should be made to indicate the significance of nonmeasurable consequences and risks.

Determining the effect of constraints

Special efforts should be made to assess the impact of actual and potential legal, financial, and political constraints. Programs and policies must operate within the framework of law.

In addition to these sorts of constraints, there are constraints resulting from conflict with other objectives. An example of such constraints is the conflict between environmental, transportation, energy, and employment objectives.

But constraints are not inflexible. If decision makers were clearly aware of the potential opportunities forgone because of existing constraints, those constraints might change.

Decision makers must consider possible public reaction to alternative policy and program options, strategies that might increase the acceptability of these options, and the administrative or other operational barriers to implementation that may exist. The problems of implementation and acceptability may, to some degree, be dealt with in analysis. Usually, assistance can be provided to decision makers in identifying the "second or third best" alternatives that may have higher prospects for being adopted or implemented.

It has been argued that if acceptable considerations are avoided, the assessment of alternatives becomes more objective, less parochial, and less tailored to fit preconceived positions. True, but it may also be argued that if acceptable considerations are not included, the analysis may prove to be irrelevant.

Reassessing the ordering of the alternatives

Orderings of alternatives are always provisional. They are determined within the context of the factors and values considered to be important during the course of the analysis. The assumptions and values underlying the various orderings of the alternatives must be clearly presented to decision makers. Furthermore, even when the analyst thinks that the study is completed, decision makers may raise new issues, ask new questions, request further study, and ask for additional comparisons. As these requests are answered, the orderings of alternatives may shift.

Although attempts should be made to include as many factors as possible, other considerations affect policy and program choices. Some of these considerations may be completely beyond the analyst's knowledge or ability to estimate—even qualitatively. Nevertheless, the analyst should attempt to understand these considerations and to devise *sensitivity analyses that may help sharpen judgments.* Sensitivity analysis is a technique that consists of changing key parameters or assumptions and then calculating the sensitivity of the final estimates to those changes.

Analysts may even suggest new alternatives that balance the achievement of conflicting objectives in ways not perceived when the initial set of alternatives was developed with the decision makers. And, finally, they may identify alternatives that keep options open or avoid irreversible damage or risk. Experienced analysts will seldom attempt to use an optimizing technique for this sort of communication with decision makers because many of the important considerations are neither specific enough nor quantifiable. Both analysts and decision makers must be satisfied with what, in their judgment, is a good but not necessarily the theoretically best alternative. "The important thing," as Camus reminds us in the introduction to *The Rebel,* "is not, as yet, to go to the root of things, but, the world being what it is, to know how to live in it."

The purpose of the foregoing section was to outline in broadest strokes the concerns of the next three chapters. This trio of chapters attempts to provide a fairly rigorous introduction to how policy is formulated. In Chapter 6, the discussion will shift from the consideration of broad goals to the generation of alternatives to attain those goals. Chapter 7 will suggest ways in which the consequences of alternatives are measured. And Chapter 8 will suggest ways in which to compare and modify the consequences of different alternatives.

FOR FURTHER REFLECTION

1. Traditionally, when the West needed more water for its thirsty farmers, Washington provided it by building dams and diverting flows from areas of plentiful water to areas of scarcity. Although plenty of people in the West still cannot believe it, the era of huge water projects is over. Thus, if western states wish their farmers to be subsidized, they will have to do it themselves. That would mean tax increases for the growing proportion of westerners who live in towns.

   In 1980, Arizona's governor decided he needed a plan to get water to the farmers. What would you recommend? This question can be approached in one of two ways. You can outline the steps you would take or procedures you would follow in preparing your recommendation; substantive issue can be relegated to the background. Or you can focus on the substantive issues; this approach will require you to do a quick study of the water problem *and* Arizona politics and ecology. The first approach leads you to identify the key questions that need to be addressed; the second, to offer some answer.

2. Assume that you have been appointed to a task force established by a new mayor, city manager, or county executive in your area. Within six weeks you are to produce a document entitled *Setting Community Priorities: The Next Two Years*. The only guidelines you have been given are to address, at a minimum, these areas.

   Human resources (government employees)
   Services to children
   Education
   Health
   Services to elderly
   Criminal justice
   Housing
   Mass transit

   What *are* your priorities? Can you support them?

3. Discuss the implications of the following passage for policy analysts.

   > [S]uppose Woodrow Wilson had not been President of the United States in 1914 but instead Theodore Roosevelt, who had been his opponent in the election of 1912. Had that been the case, America might have entered the war much earlier, perhaps at the time of the *Lusitania* in 1915, with possible shortening of the war and incalculable effects on history. Well, it happens that among the Anarchists in my book *The Proud Tower* is an obscure Italian named Miguel Angiolillo, whom nobody remembers but who shot dead Premier Canovas of Spain in 1897. Canovas

was a strong man who was just about to succeed in quelling the rebels in Cuba when he was assassinated. Had he lived, there might have been no extended Cuban insurrection for Americans to get excited about, no Spanish-American War, no San Juan Hill, no Rough Riders, no Vice-Presidency for Theodore Roosevelt to enable him to succeed when another accident, another Anarchist, another unpredictable human being, killed McKinley. If Theodore had never been President, there would have been no third party in 1912 to split the Republicans, and Woodrow Wilson would not have been elected. The speculations from that point on are limitless. To me it is comforting rather than otherwise to feel that history is determined by the illogical human record and not by large immutable scientific laws beyond our power to deflect.

Source: Barbara Tuchman, *Practicing History: Selected Essays* (New York: Alfred A. Knopf, 1981).

4. Why don't policymakers simply arrive at goals and announce them in precise, integrated packages advocated by theoretical strategists and, indeed, expected by their organizational constituents? In fact, they may establish a few broad goals by decree, but more often (and for good reason) they avoid such pronouncements. Why?

5. Exacerbating the problem of policy coordination are the multiplicity of agencies that help administer each program. Column A lists eight functions. For each function, at least two agencies with responsibility can be found in column B. What are they? (Anyone who answers all correctly gets a Ph.D. in Bureaucracy.)

A	B
A. Aerosol products	1. National Oceanic and Atmospheric Administration
B. False advertising	2. National Highway Traffic Safety Commission
C. Energy information	3. U.S. Geological Survey
D. Mail fraud	4. Antitrust Division (Dept. of Justice)
E. Regulating securities industry	5. Environmental Protection Agency
F. Highway building	6. Federal Trade Commission
G. Control of fish products	7. Department of Housing and Urban Development
H. Mobile homes	8. Food and Drug Administration
	9. Consumer Product Safety Commission
	10. Postal Service
	11. Federal Power Commission

A	B
	12. National Marine Fisheries Service
	13. Department of Transportation
	14. Security and Exchange Commission
	15. Federal Energy Administration
	16. Bureau of Mines
	17. Federal Communication Commission

6. In theory, at least, plans and programs should be a function of changing conditions. (The classic illustration of this principle is the buggy whip factory.) Some military experts argue that technological change has passed the Marine Corps. What changes do you think they are referring to? If they are correct, then how do you account for the fact that the Corps is 196,000 strong—larger than the entire British army?

7. Chapter 1 discussed the relationship between goals and objectives (Figure 1–1). What objectives would you suggest for the following goals: (1) to place the management of the city on a sound financial basis; (2) to make streets and homes safe; (3) to improve the health of all citizens?

8. What would a program that had a real chance of eliminating the poor in our society look like?

9. What was the strategic factor in Kennan's analysis of the need for rapid recovery in Europe immediately after World War II?

10. Using the Six-C Policy Design Framework suggested in this chapter, assess the following six goals for a U.S. science policy suggested by Lewis M. Branscomb, vice president of Research and Development for IBM:

    (1) Government should assure a healthy environment for private innovation. But it should not substitute itself for the more effective private sector in the process of technology generation.

    (2) For some technologies, the potential payoff is so long delayed and so uncertain that private investors are unlikely to respond. In such cases, federal participation may be warranted.

    (3) Federal demonstration programs that test neither technology nor market acceptance should not be undertaken.

    (4) The United States' long-range, nonproprietary scientific and engineering research is a bountiful source of ideas for the technologies of the future. It must be sustained in its world leadership position by federal funds.

(5) The government should continue to bestow most of its basic research funding on U.S. university laboratories, thus sustaining both education and research through a single set of investments, and should expand the role (but not the size) of the national laboratories.

(6) Government policies should encourage companies to assist and collaborate with universities. Such partnerships leverage the federal research investment and pay important, if unquantifiable, economic dividends.

Chapter 6

Options

"The sun shown," Samuel Beckett writes in the opening passage of *Murphy*, "having no alternatives, on nothing new." Not so with public policy. One could argue that innovation is now becoming routine in American politics because of the two groups of mutually dependent professionals discussed in Chapter 2: *policy entrepreneurs*, who specialize in identifying problems and finding solutions; and *politicians*, who are constantly in the market for new ideas. Indeed, one political scientist has identified the U.S. Senate as "the incubator of policy innovation in the American system," where ambitious politicians looking for programs link up with energetic policy entrepreneurs who have programs for sale.[1]

But let us set aside the politics of policymaking for awhile and follow here a somewhat different line of inquiry:

- What are the major policy tools available to government? That is, once the goals of a policy have been established, what courses of action might be followed in order to attain those goals?

- What is a "new" policy? We hear a great deal these days about the need for new ideas, new policies. We hear practically nothing at all, however, about how new these new policies really are. The second section of this chapter therefore asks a purposely naive question: How does one judge the newness of a public policy?

- Finally, what effect does the mind of the policymaker have on the formulation of policy? In recent years, cognitive psychology has begun to offer some interesting answers to this question.

---

[1] Nelson W. Polsby, *Political Innovation in America: The Politics of Policy Initiation* (New Haven, Conn.: Yale, 1984).

RANGE OF GOVERNMENT ACTION

Policymakers have a variety of means available to attain their goals. Figure 6–1 arrays nine major ones in terms of their tendency to use force or authority without regard for individual desire.

Coercive actions

A crime is any act or omission prohibited by law in the interest of protecting the public and made punishable by the government in a judicial proceeding brought (prosecuted) by it. Crimes are prohibited and punished on the ground of public policy, which may include the protection and safeguarding of government, human life, or private property. Additional purposes of the criminal law include deterrence and rehabilitation. (Civil law, which does not appear in the figure, defines the duties which, if violated, would constitute a wrong against the injured party. In contrast, criminal law establishes the duties that, if violated, would be a wrong against the whole community. Thus, criminal law is a part of public law, while civil law is a part of private law.)

Public policies forbid certain practices. If A complains to an administrative agency that B is engaged in illegal practices, then the agency may order B to "cease and desist." Public policies also allow certain practices by certain persons—if they have the proper license or fee. Only those persons who have a specific privilege, say, to drive a cab or own a radio station may do so; everyone else is restrained from doing so.

The scope of government assistance programs, while not quite worth an entry in Ripley's, does go beyond what most people might imagine. According to the Census Bureau almost half of all households in the nation—47 percent, to be precise—were receiving some kind of check from the federal government during the first quarter of 1985.[2] But, if the bureau's survey was truly encompassing, so that it covered all kinds of federal subsidies for individuals, it would probably show that two thirds of American households benefit in some direct fashion from federal programs. In 16 million households, at least one person was benefiting from such programs as food stamps, medicaid, subsidized rental housing, free school lunches, and Aid to Families with Dependent Children. Many households benefited under several programs.

If the study had embraced all of us who benefit directly and personally from "tax expenditures," such as the deductions we take for home mortgages and charitable contributions, the survey would have taken in just about everybody.

The question arises, why place these assistance programs near the

---

[2] U.S. Bureau of Census, *Survey of Income and Program Participation*, 1986.

Figure 6–1
Range of government actions

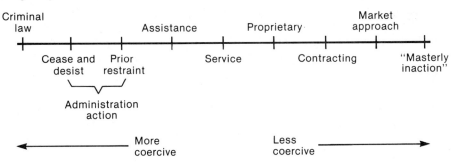

coercive end of Figure 6–1? The first point to be made is that these benefits are not manna; they flow to Paul's household not from heaven but from Peter's household via our tax system. Peter has no choice in the matter. To be sure, Peter can vote for or against assistance to Paul, and Peter himself probably receives assistance of one sort or another, but the crucial fact remains that Peter *must* pay.

Assistance programs are slightly coercive from Paul's perspective as well. In order to receive means-tested assistance Paul *must* fill in certain forms and make his case, so to speak. Failing to do so properly can result in the revocation of assistance.

Noncoercive actions

In contrast to assistance programs, services are generally available to all. No eligibility standards are applied, no special charges made. Services might also be contrasted with prior restraint and "cease and desist" orders. Service programs attempt to obtain results by direct government action rather than regulation. Government itself can clean up toxic waste dumps, or it can regulate how industry disposes of its toxic waste.

Proprietary activities like the Postal Service are conducted on a self-supporting basis. Peter can keep his money if he wishes, and Paul can use the service, if he wishes—but for a fee.

Since World War II, new policies have often involved contracting out governmental functions to private corporations and institutions for administration. The Atomic Energy Commission and the National Science Foundation relied heavily on this procedure, as did the medicare program and the Community Action Program. It is hard to imagine a political consensus to establish any of these programs without a previous understanding that the government, while supplying the money, was to leave the actual work to the likes of Cal Tech, Union Carbide, Prudential, Blue Cross, and others—and not to the federal bureaucracy. Since 1983, the state of Texas has paid private employment agencies to help public agencies place the unemployed. Examples could be multiplied.

Market approaches to public policy have been fashionable since the late 1970s. Shortly after taking office, President Jimmy Carter declared that one of his major goals was to free the American people from "the burdens of overregulation. We must look, industry by industry, at what effect regulation has. . . . Whenever it seems likely that the free market would better serve the public, we will eliminate governmental regulations." The biggest step involved the airlines. From 1978 on, airlines were allowed to select the routes they wished to fly and to alter their fares. Until then the Civil Aeronautics Board (CAB)—not the market—had allocated routes and set fares. The result of deregulation: cheaper fares, more competition, and a shift to smaller planes on fewer routes.

The Reagan administration hoped to carry deregulation even further. Reagan wished to see two criteria used to assess all regulations: (1) government action is justifiable only if it produces more benefits than costs, and (2) the regulation must be the least expensive way of achieving the objective. When he signed Executive Order 12291 on February 17, 1981, Reagan transformed with a stroke of his pen what had been a useful economic tool into an imperative of national policymaking—cost-benefit analysis. (See Chapter 8.)

As the 1984 election approached, the deregulation became less of a priority. At this point, it is unclear what the future of deregulation will be. Critics charge, for instance, that deregulation of banking has been pushed too far.

However, deregulation is not the only reform now seriously considered by advocates of market options. Also mentioned are these:

- Gradual privatization of social security system: Some think Congress will eventually be forced to phase-out social security and phase-in private programs to protect citizens in their retirement years.

- Education vouchers: Some advocate injecting competition and choice into the education monopoly of public schools. Total spending on education would remain the same, but the distribution of money would not: parents could decide where to spend their alloted sum.[3]

---

[3] The education establishment argues that consumer choice would be "unfair" to public schools, since these schools must accept anyone who shows up, including handicapped and foreign students who cost more to teach. Private schools by contrast can skim the "easiest" students. Yet this cavil, like that of hurting-the-poor, can be met by the credit system itself. Vouchers can be made redeemable at public schools. Bigger credits can be given to disabled children.

- Open up the entire health-care system to marketplace forces: The charge has often been made that government and insurance coverage insulates consumers and providers from the true cost of care; an open-ended reimbursement system rewards excessive admissions, excessive services, and the inefficient use of high technology; and a mass of regulations stifles the entrepreneurship and innovation the industry so badly needs to cut waste and create efficiency. To solve Medicare's crisis, then, policymakers might remove the excessive intrusion of government and provide positive incentives for consumers and providers to be cost-conscious.[4]

Masterly inaction

Sometimes the two most important words a policymaker can utter are: "Do nothing." Students of policymaking generally do not make much of this point. I suspect this reluctance to advise inaction stems in part from cultural and linguistic biases. John Wayne always knew what to do and did it; today Clint Eastwood and Sylvester Stallone know and do. Action, almost any action, is perceived to be good. Inaction suggests weakness, if not downright stupidity.

Not surprisingly, American historians generally rate as failures presidents who were perceived to be "inactive," that is, did not pass a lot of legislation or follow an aggressive (in the sense of busy) foreign policy. In the last few years, at least one inactive president, Eisenhower, has enjoyed a slight promotion to something more than a failure.[5] But I doubt that there will ever be much hope for Calvin Coolidge.

One British historian (need I emphasize British?) charges that "Coolidge's treatment" amounts to the systematic misrepresentation of public policy over a whole era.

> Coolidge was the most internally consistent and single minded of modern American presidents. . . . No public man carried into modern times more comprehensively the founding principles of Americanism: hard work, frugality, freedom of conscience, freedom from government, respect for serious culture. . . . But the notion . . . —"He slept more than any other president, whether by day or by night. Nero fiddled but Coolidge only snored"—was misleading. No president was ever better briefed on anything that mattered or less often caught unprepared by events or the doings of his term.
> It suited Coolidge, in fact, to mislead people into believing he was less sophisticated and active than he was (a ploy later imitated by Eisenhower).

---

[4] David B. Swoop, "Medical Crisis Is Only a Symptom," *The Wall Street Journal,* January 3, 1984.

[5] See, for example, Stephen E. Ambrose, *Eisenhower: The President* (New York: Simon & Schuster, 1984).

. . . In fact few men have been better prepared for the presidency, moving up every rung of the public ladder: parish councillor, assemblyman, major, State Representative, State Senator, President of the State Senate, Lieutenant-Governor, Governor, Vice-President. At every stage he insisted that government should do as little as was necessary. ("He didn't do anything," remarked the political comic Will Rogers, "but that's what the people wanted done.") But he also insisted that, when it did act, it should be absolutely decisive. . . .

Coolidge reflected America's Arcadian separateness during the 1920s by showing that, in deliberate contrast to the strident activism taking over so much of Europe and driven by the idea that political motion had replaced religious piety as the obvious form of moral worth, it was still possible to practice successfully the archaic virtue of stasis. Coolidge believed that all activity—above all of government—not dictated by pressing necessity was likely to produce undesirable results and certainly unforeseen ones. . . .

Political morality, he insisted, must always be judged not by intentions but by effects.[6]

Although the period of Coolidge's presidency (1923–29) was one of general prosperity and peace, writers and intellectuals tended to view it retrospectively as a time of gross materialism and no solid human accomplishment. Yet prosperity was very widespread. "What the Twenties demonstrates was the relative speed with which industrial productivity could transform luxuries into necessities and spread them down the class pyramid. Indeed to a growing extent it was a dissolvent of class and other barriers."[7] Perhaps the most important single development was the spread of education. Between 1910 and 1930, total educational spending rose fourfold.

I have dwelt on Coolidge and titled this subsection "Masterly Inaction" (a concept propounded by Lord Melbourne, the nineteenth-century prime minister of Britain) in an attempt to overcome the popular notion that leadership equals doing something and that patience equals indecision.

It is ironic that one of the first changes Reagan made when he entered the White House was to hang a portrait of Coolidge, for unlike Coolidge, Reagan did not seem to realize that American interests in the world cannot all be of equal importance; that presidents must have priorities and defend the national interest selectively and ad hoc; and that passivity, even retreat, are as important options as activity and attack.[8] Let us consider Reagan's actions in two trouble spots.

• Why did Reagan have to send a handful of Marines to Lebanon in 1983? He never identified a specific American interest that would justify

---

[6] Paul Johnson, *Modern Times* (New York: Harper & Row, 1983), pp. 219–21.

[7] Ibid., p. 224.

[8] Ernest van den Haag, "The Busyness of American Foreign Policy," *Foreign Affairs*, Fall 1985, pp. 113–29.

the risk and investment. Perhaps the troops were sent because he and his advisers had no idea of how, diplomatically or politically, to manipulate other countries in order to get what they wanted and deserved. Once the Israelis invaded, all the United States had to do was wait. Instead, by sending in the Marines, the president allowed the Israelis to withdraw to safer territory, leaving the United States as the focus of anger and as the inheritors of the fury against the Israeli invaders because the United States is their sponsor.

- Iran has been a virtual laboratory for American busyness. During Reagan's first term, it seemed unlikely that the United States would intervene diplomatically or militarily in the Iraq-Iran war. This was fortunate since it would serve American interest if neither party emerged totally victorious or totally defeated. The stalemate protected American interest without any cost. Then, in November 1986, it was revealed that the United States had arranged covert arms sales to Iran. Arms trade with Iran proved to be one of the great presidential follies of modern times.

As these two cases illustrate, one of the most effective options policymakers have is often to do nothing, to hold back power and influence at crucial moments, to isolate a situation, to wait until something really can be done—instead of jumping prematurely and with naive hope that everything can somehow be fixed.

The tendency for policymakers to lapse into busyness does not limit itself to diplomacy in faraway lands. Aaron Wildavsky of the University of California has aptly described the busyness of educational policy:

> For instance, no one can accuse local educators of inertia; they are always in motion, tinkering with the organization of their schools. Teachers teach alone, in twos, and in teams. They are supervised by specialists in subject matter, by specialists in presentation, by specialists in age groups, and by generalists whose virtue is that they are not specialists. Students are arranged by ability, by age, and by interest to secure homogeneity, and they are regrouped by ages, interests, or disabilities to secure homogeneity. School districts are centralized and decentralized; principals are given and denied hierarchical authority; teachers are assigned in almost every conceivable combination, as are the curricula and methods they use. No one can accuse schools of being unresponsive. In a manner of speaking everyone gets what they want. But innovation may turn into obfuscation when the assertion of multiple objectives—the whole child, the emotional child, the social child, even the educated child—creates a moving target, blurring the achievement of any one. Changing objectives and changing organizations becomes the object of change. And the more things change. . . .[9]

---

[9] Aaron Wildavsky, *Speaking Truth to Power* (Boston: Little, Brown, 1979), pp. 79–80.

Some students of public policy argue that the more options the better, but I would argue that the more options that are available, the more likely it is that they will include some that are mischievous. After all, in any situation, there are usually only a few wise courses of action. Faced by any new situation, former Secretary of State Dean Rusk advised policymakers to always ask before acting: What difference does it make?

CLASSIFYING ALTERNATIVES

A useful way of categorizing the alternatives that might emerge during the formulation of public policy is as follows:

1. *Incremental.* This popular decision-making process makes relatively small (i.e., incremental) changes in existing policy. When one hears such verbs as *update, strengthen, add, cutback, extend, retrench, tighten,* and *open up,* it is quite likely that the alternatives under consideration fall into this category.
2. *Branching.* This process develops alternatives in one area of public policy by adoption. For example, can techniques used to control monopoly be used to control industrial pollution? But this gives the impression that the search is an ad hoc, one-time affair. As we will see below, such is not the case: the adoptions, taken together, form a pattern. To describe this pattern, I use the word *branching*—a word with much more explanatory power than the adoption.
3. *Inventive.* A few alternatives are neither modifications of existing policy nor borrowings from other policy areas. When these alternatives represent a sharp break with the past and attempt to use inputs (money, human resources, etc.) more productively, we say that they are truly new, or inventive.

In the two subsections that follow, we will deal with incremental and branching alternatives. Because inventive alternatives are a little more difficult and, in certain respects, important, we will deal with them in a separate section.

Incremental

Charles E. Lindblom argues that the real world presents insurmountable problems to generating very many imaginative solutions to social problems.[10] Specifically, he notes the following constraints on the use of these efforts: the limited intellectual capacities of human beings, inade-

---

[10] Charles E. Lindblom, "The Science of 'Muddling Through,' " *Public Administration Review* 19 (Spring 1959), pp. 79–88.

quacy of information, the costliness of analysis, the impossibility of constructing a satisfactory set of criteria by which to judge the value of a decision, the closeness of fact and value (means and ends) in policy-making, and the diverse forms in which policy problems actually arise.

But for Lindblom the principal constraint is the limit on our ability to conceive all of the possibilities inherent in a complex social problem: People may intend to be rational, but rationality has its limits. Even the increased use of computers to help deal with masses of data cannot guarantee that we will consider adequately all of the possibilities that might impinge on a complex problem; inevitably we find that we must drastically simplify the problem to deal with it. This simplification could involve the development of formal models, as discussed in Chapter 3, but such formal models, according to Lindblom, would always be deficient. Adequate models of social problems would be extremely costly to develop and to keep supplied with information—assuming that people could design them to be flexible enough to cope with changing values. For example, a complete analysis of how much money to place in the federal budget for cancer research would have to include, among other things, consideration of all the other possible ways of using this money (e.g., for kidney research, educational research, salaries for military personnel, lower taxes) and all the possible implications of these alternatives (the future of the Papacy, the profitability of uranium mining, the prospects for interplanetary travel, the popularity of rock music, etc.).[11]

Because of the problems inherent in this rational-comprehensive approach to the development of alternatives, Lindblom rejects reliance on analysis and advocates a method of successive, limited comparisons—incremental decision making—for public policy problems. These limited, as opposed to comprehensive, policy reviews would be defined by the interplay of political forces. To Lindblom, the self-corrective feedback mechanism of the group political system is more reliable than abstract models supported by shaky social science theory.

The basic elements of the incremental approach, which seems to be a kind of mirror image of the rational-comprehensive approach, are summarized below:

---

[11] Lindblom's portrait of what he calls the "rational-comprehensive model" has something of the straw man in it. None of the model's advocates would press maximization to this absurd length. As two members in good standing of the rationalist school state: "We most emphatically do not believe that the objective of an optimizing analysis is to find the best of all possible courses of action; such a task is hopeless. . . . Only after a set of 'reasonable contenders' has thus been defined does it become possible to apply formal procedures for choices among them." Howard Raiffa and Robert Schlaifer, *Applied Statistical Decision Theory* (Boston: Harvard University Graduate School of Business Administration, 1961), p. 3.

1. Rather than attempting a comprehensive survey and evaluation of all alternatives, the decision maker focuses only on policies that differ marginally from existing policies.
2. Only a relatively small number of policy alternatives are considered.
3. Only a few "important" consequences for each policy alternative are evaluated.
4. There is no one "right" decision or solution, but a "never-ending series of attacks" on the issues.
5. Incremental decision making is remedial—geared more to the correction of present social imperfections than to the promotion of future social goals.
6. Group political interaction plays a leading role in each of the above areas.

At least two strengths of this method should be emphasized. First, since it is impossible to take into account all of the factors that may be relevant, simplification becomes essential. One must isolate the really important from the inconsequential. One must decide on the few factors which should be included in the "first-cut" analysis and on the additional factors which should be included in the "second-cut" analysis—if there is time for a second cut. The objective is to isolate the most critical factors and to describe their essential relationships. The ideas of the incremental method provide the framework for this task: only those alternatives that differ incrementally from current policy and from each other need be examined.

In addition to its logic of simplification, the incremental method carries distinct political advantages. To the extent that incremental alternatives are variations of the familiar—which does not necessarily mean the successful—it is likely that, all things being equal, they will be more acceptable, more salable than more trailblazing alternatives.

The best examples of incrementalism in operation are adjustments to budgets. Given a problem, decision makers simply respond by raising the level of funding in relevant existing programs. The premise on which this response rests is, roughly, that the level of service is a function of the level of expenditure. This premise is widely held among government officials, though its empirical basis is somewhat shaky: in some cases, the correlation between service and expenditure is actually negative.[12]

Branching

Though it is not widely recognized, the second method of developing alternatives appears almost as frequently in governmental policymaking

---

[12] Ira Sharkansky, *The Routines of Politics* (New York: Van Nostrand, 1970), Ch. 7.

as incrementalism. The principle on which it rests, however, lacks the simplicity of incrementalism. Indeed, we must approach it through the back door. And Gerald Holton's studies on the development of science provide that entrance.[13]

Holton argues persuasively that the process of building up an actual scientific theory requires explicit or implicit decisions, such as the adoption of certain hypotheses and criteria of preselections that are not at all scientifically "valid" in the sense usually accepted. Holton calls these styles of thought "themes" and finds them running throughout the history of science. To illustrate: for Descartes the theme of *conservation* in the laws of physics (e.g., the law of conservation of momentum) springs from the invariability of God. Because God wished the world to remain in motion, the variation must be as invariable as possible. Since Descarte's time, we have learned to change the basis of the conservation law, and we have extended its application from the colliding of billiard balls to many other events (for example, scattering of photons). But we have always clung to this law, even at times when laboratory observations seemed to make it very difficult to do so.

A second example of thematic analysis might be the notion of *discreteness* or *atomism*. This theme has been important in scientific thought from the first—indeed, from the atomism of Democritus (c. 460–370 B.C.)—and usually coexisted with and was arrayed against the equally ancient theme of the *continuum*. In the early part of the nineteenth century, with Dalton, atomism ceased to be regarded as a "mere" philosophical position and began to go to the forefront of the stage. Holton writes:

> The twentieth-century victory of discreteness was really the climax of a whole century of preparation for this new style of thinking in all branches of science. *We see here rather beautifully a family of related developments—the theme of discreteness expressing itself in physics, biology, and chemistry.* For between 1808 and 1905, physics, biology, and chemistry saw the introduction of remarkably similar conceptions. In each of these fields it was found fruitful to assume the existence of fundamental, discrete entities. Thus Dalton (1808) proposed that matter consists of atoms which maintain their integrity in all chemical reactions. In biology, Schleiden for plants (1838) and Schwann for animals (1839) proposed the theory of cells, by the various combinations of which living tissues were assumed to be built. Mendel's work (1865) led to the idea that the material governing heredity contains a structure of definite entities, or genes, which may be transmitted from one generation to the next without change. . . .
>
> Meanwhile, heat, electricity, and light, which were the parts of physics

---

[13] Gerald Holton, "The Thematic Imagination in Science," in *Science and Culture*, ed. Gerald Holton (Boston: Beacon Press, 1965), pp. 406–7.

300

that the eighteenth century had visualized largely in terms of actions of imponderable fluids, were being rephrased in a similar manner. In Joule's kinetic theory (1847), sensible heat was identified with the motions of discrete atoms and molecules. The electron, a particle carrying the smallest unit of negative charge, was discovered (1897). Finally, the energy of the sources of radiation and then of radiation itself was found to be quantized (1900 and 1905). It was as if these new views in the sciences stemmed from a similarly directed change in the mental models used to comprehend phenomena—a change in style where the guiding idea is no longer a continuum, but a particle, a discrete quantum.[14]

What has all of this to do with public policy? Simply this: When public policy is studied longitudinally, an interesting pattern emerges which I call "branching." Longitudinal study shows that the development of public policy is not unlike the growth of a tree: branching out from a few seminal ideas or themes are multifarious variations that lead to further variations. The upshot is that, for any given year, much of the ostensibly new policy under consideration can, on closer inspection, be traced back to a few seminal ideas. Consider the Social Security Act of 1935, which provided for unemployment insurance, retirement and death benefits, and a nationwide framework of incentives, supports, and standards for financial assistance to persons in three groups (the aged, the blind, and dependent children). A remarkable amount of subsequent legislation constituted, essentially, nothing more than variations on that basic theme. A more recent case is the Communications Satellite Act of 1962. The unprecedented financial arrangements under which the Communications Satellite Corporation was launched were, essentially, similar to those found in the Rail Passenger Act of 1970. And today some in government are pressing for the creation of a similar federal agency to operate the space shuttle.

Numerous illustrations of the branching phenomenon appear. Perhaps the best known was the Gramm-Rudman-Hollings "deficit reduction" plan, which appeared to many to be quite novel. The trunk to which this branch can be traced—self-imposed statutory mandates— lies in the early 1970s, when Congress elected to make inflation adjustments in social security automatic. Soon after the automated social security adjustments came the new "budget process" of 1974. It was designed to substitute yet another automatic and impersonal process for the political struggle over money among the congressional committees. (Those hopes, too, were disappointed.)

The 1980s witnessed little progress toward the problem of disposal of toxic wastes. The Superfund (the congressional grant of billions of

---
[14] Gerald Holton, "Science and New Styles of Thought," *Graduate Journal* 7, no. 2 (Spring 1967), pp. 399–423. Emphasis added.

dollars for removal of the many hundreds of dangerous-waste sites in the United States) is of course literally a device to clean up past mistakes. Its slow progress since its establishment in 1980 and its enormous expense show just how costly these mistakes can be. Public policy towards polluters can best be characterized as the gangbuster approach in which the bad guys who pollute are apprehended by federal agents. An alternative would be for the government to make it advantageous financially to dispose of wastes properly. William J. Baumol and Edwin S. Mills, two Princeton economists, therefore propose the application of an old idea: *subsidies* for proper and safe disposal of toxic wastes.[15] Inspection and coercion are useless, because we have no way of knowing who produces the wastes or who is currently holding them. Only a financial incentive that succeeds in inducing these persons to comply voluntarily has any chance of working, and may prove far less expensive than cleaning up the damage caused by indiscriminate dumping, as experience with the Superfund suggests. But the idea of offering financial in ducements to solve environmental problems is not original with Baumol and Mills. For over half a century, economists have advocated fees for discharges or the sale of marketable permits to polluting companies by the government to reduce the profitability of emissions.

Branching, apparently, is a cross-national phenomenon. Social security, a classic example, had its origins in Bismark's Germany. Where did the Reagan doctrine—support for freedom fighters or "assertive deterrence"—originate? Arguably, the Soviet Union had invented this doctrine by its extensive support of rebel movements in the 1970s. What we witnessed in the 1980s was a virtual role reversal with the United States supporting rebels in Afghanistan, Nicaragua, and Angola.

The branching model is an antidote for the persistent tendency to label too many public policies as "innovative" and to accept too readily the hyperbole of the media, interest group leaders, and politicians. More to the point, the branching model leads us to a critical observation: the number of truly seminal ideas in the polity (such as those embodied in the two examples cited above) is unexpectedly small.

INVENTION IN PUBLIC POLICY

Though one of the most important areas of political life, creativity in public policy remains one of the least understood. The objectives of this section, accordingly, must be and are modest. First, the section attempts to set forth a definition of invention in public policy that is

---

[15] William J. Baumol and Edwin S. Mills, "Paying Companies to Obey the Law," *The New York Times*, October 27, 1985.

reasonably serviceable for empirical investigation. Second, it presents a general framework within which research could be conducted. Third, employing the operationalized definition and the research framework, it offers some preliminary and highly tentative propositions about inventive public policy in the United States.

Problems of definition

In view of the relative infancy of work in political science on social inventions, it becomes necessary to reach into other disciplines for guidance on how to construct an operational definition. Because so much more work has been done on technical inventions than on social inventions, we might begin by looking at some of this research.

Simon Kuznets's essay "Inventive Activity: Problems of Definition and Measurement" provides a particularly fertile ground from which to launch our inquiry.[16] Kuznets notes three characteristics of technical inventions that, with certain modifications, can help us identify social inventions and, by extension, find those public policies that are truly inventive.

1. *An inventive alternative builds on a new combination of available knowledge concerning properties of the social system.* The requirement of *newness* serves, presumably, to eliminate the chance of counting branching alternatives (discussed above) as inventive ones. Clearly two alternatives identical in principle do not represent two new breakthroughs in public policy.

The Manpower Development and Training Act of 1962, which had been oriented toward experienced workers who had lost their jobs because of technological change, was amended in 1963 (Public Law 88–214). The amendments, however, simply extended the coverage to help illiterate jobless and out-of-school youth. In short, the amendments constituted not a break but an evolution. Similarly, the establishment of the Department of Health, Education and Welfare in 1953 was not a break with the past but a regrouping; more specifically the Federal Security Agency was replaced by a cabinet-level department.

The requirement that an invention be a combination of *available* knowledge further sharpens our definition. Specifically, the requirement makes a distinction between scientific discoveries, on the one hand, and practical policy proposals that embody new combinations of existing knowl-

---

[16] Simon Kuznets, "Inventive Activity: Problems of Definition and Measurement" in National Bureau of Research, *The Rate and Direction of Inventive Activity* (Princeton, N.J.: Princeton University Press, 1962).

edge, on the other. Thus, fundamental discoveries in the social sciences (new theories, new management techniques, etc.) are not included.[17]

The requirement is important for several reasons. Any scientific finding is *potentially* useful, but, most scientific discoveries are immediately useless—certainly so far as the scientists are concerned, for they are not attempting the application of the results to useful ends, even if they are aware of such ends. Moreover, since scientific discovery is usually general in character, each scientific discovery provides a basis for a wide variety of potential practical uses—inventive public policy among them.

2. *An inventive alternative must be the product of a mental effort above the average.* Although we do not insist on a flash of genius, we should distinguish between inventions and the host of routine improvements in technique that are made in the daily administration of a program and are the result of low-level and rather obvious attentiveness or know-how. Concrete examples would probably serve better than further generalization.

In April 1963, the Senate passed an administration-backed bill that would have set up a Youth Conservation Corps. Designed to provide jobs for unskilled and unemployed youths in a stable and healthy atmosphere while accomplishing needed conservation work, the bill offered considerable benefits. Yet it was so obviously adapted from the Civilian Conservation Corps idea of the 1930s that to refer to it as "an act of insight" would be manifestly inappropriate. On a similar basis, the Food and Agriculture Act of 1965, which applied to cotton the type of program that had already been successful in reducing surpluses of feed grains, though beneficial in many ways, could not be described as inventive.

In contrast, the National Science Foundation Act of 1950, the Public Works and Economic Development Act of 1965, and the Narcotic Addict Rehabilitation Act of 1966 evinced insight. The first stemmed from Vannevar Bush's 1945 report to the president (*Science: The Endless Frontier*), which persuaded the government, via an analogy with the western frontier of the 1800s, to support undirected research and to develop a national policy for science; the second, from the notion that some towns ("development centers"), though not necessarily in a depressed condition themselves, had a potential for economic growth that would benefit

---

[17] For a fascinating study of the major social science discoveries of this century, which ranges from the theory and measurement of social inequalities (1900) to conflict theory (1960) and stochastic models of social processes (1965), see Karl W. Deutsch, John Platt, and Dieter Senghaas, "Conditions Favoring Major Advances in Social Science," *Science,* February 5, 1971, pp. 450–59.

nearby depressed areas; and the third, from the clinical observation that narcotic addiction was more a medical than a criminal problem.

3. *An inventive alternative must be productive.* It must be a practicable course of action that, when employed, will either reduce the cost of delivering already authorized services or deliver new services for which the demand is sufficient to justify the costs to government. The reason for suggesting this characteristic is obvious enough: we are interested in inventive alternatives because they contribute to the output of government.

The point merits emphasis. Today a number of scholars and public officials have begun to view the improvement of public sector productivity (i.e., the ratio of output to input) as one of the top issues of the decade; and with 15–20 percent of working Americans in government and over one fifth of the gross national product absorbed by government purchases, this is hardly surprising. But the reasons for the importance of productivity in the public sector go deeper than these figures indicate. To the extent that resources are finite, we also need to consider ways to increase public sector productivity. Attention to innovative policy, as partially defined above, is certainly one way in which this can be done at the macrosystem level.

Yet one can easily think of alternatives that do very little to increase productivity. For example, some policies are designed to distribute rights and privileges universally and to ensure the equality of all citizens. These policies, however, are not necessarily compatible with economic efficiency, though they may help bring about a more just society. Other policies seek neither efficiency nor equality; they are really designed as placebos for various subgroups within the populace. According to Murray Edelman, the mass public responds more to *symbols* than to concrete facts or actions: "A dramatic, symbolic life among abstractions becomes a substitute gratification for the pleasure of remodeling the concrete environment."[18] As he points out, government has only a limited number of tangible rewards (jobs, programs, money, etc.) that it can dole out to various groups. Since highly organized groups tend to garner most of these rewards, governments must dispense symbolic rewards to the others. Finally, a number of policies and programs—especially in the regulatory area—appear to have an overall negative effect on productivity. Candidates for this category include the following:

- The Federal Communications Commission delayed for ten years the operations of the domestic communications satellite.
- The Federal Power Commission encouraged the overconsumption of

---

[18] Murray Edelman, *The Symbolic Use of Politics* (Urbana: University of Illinois Press, 1964), p. 6.

natural gas—our cleanest fuel—by setting the price at a level far below the likely market price.

- The Interstate Commerce Commission created great expenses for trucking firms by insisting on its authority to set every route and rate for every category of freight. Thus, in some instances, trucks are not permitted to take the most direct route to their destination and return empty even if cargoes are available.

- The Federal Drug Administration's regulations are so heavily biased to keep drugs off the market that Victor Fuchs of Stanford University observes that since "penicillin and fluorexene, two valuable drugs, are both lethal to some laboratory animals," if these drugs were just being developed today, clear evidence of their toxicity in animals would probably result in their rejection long before approval was sought to market them.

- A General Accounting Office report on the effects of environmental and land use regulations found that more than six billion board feet of mature timber in national forest dies every year because federal rules prohibit its harvest.

Thus, a wide variety of easily identifiable policies are not productive in the sense in which I employ this term. Less easily identified, however, are the policies that *are* productive. Stated more fully, the difficulty with this criterion is that it requires knowledge concerning the economic benefits of an alternative. Today, though not easy, the measurement of government productivity is possible. Output from public programs can, in other words, be measured; for example, third-grade reading levels, infant mortality rates, robberies per 100,000 population, and concentrations of suspended air particles are, to a degree, quantifiable.

But, when first launched, practically all programs are still far from such tests of productivity. To be sure, a program once authorized must "walk," that is, it must perform the task its supporters claim it can perform. But feasibility is a far cry from economic usefulness; and no airtight assurance of the latter can be given at the time the inventive alternative is proposed.

Faced with the same problem in his attempt to define and measure technical inventions, Kuznets simply shifted the formulation to *potential* usefulness. The question then arises as to whose judgment is to be accepted. The least demanding criterion would rely on the judgment of the advocates of the alternative. This standard does not provide a very firm base for identifying productivity, but at least it permits an inclusive definition of inventive programs based on the assumption that they would not be inaugurated unless each of their supporters believed that they were potentially useful.

This whole matter of productivity has, to my view, obvious bearing on a variety of questions concerned with measurement. In a number of instances, knowing the savings of a program *before* it goes into operation is fairly simple. Thus HEW knew in 1974 that it could save at least $89 million a year by adopting a proposed plan to limit government payment for prescription drugs under medicaid and medicare programs to the lowest price at which the drugs were generally available and to the least expensive of several competing brands in cases where the products were chemically identical.

But not every public policy needs to be subjected to such rigorous measurement simply to determine whether, by virtue of some new technique it incorporates, the ratio of output to input is increased. Consider the Health Maintenance Act of 1973 and the Water Resources Planning Act of 1965. The former provides not only a financial incentive to doctors to keep their subscribers healthy but also considerable savings to the subscribers; while the latter provides statutory authority to the Federal Water Resources Council to achieve maximum benefits from existing water resources.

Conversely, it is not too hard to tag some proposals as unproductive. Of the eighty-six reorganization plans transmitted to Congress from 1949 through 1969, only three—Reorganization Plan No. 3 of 1952, which would have ended Senate confirmation of postmasters; Reorganization Plan No. 1 of 1965, reorganizing the Bureau of Customs; and Reorganization Plan No. 5 of 1966, abolishing the National Capital Regional Planning Council—were supported by precise dollar estimates of savings. Plan No. 3 was disapproved by Congress. As Seidman writes: "Granted executive branch reluctance to offer savings estimates which can be taken down and later used in evidence by the Appropriations Committees, the failure to itemize expenditure reductions clearly reflects the reality that economies are produced by curtailing services and abolishing bureaus, not by reorganization."[19]

Applying the definition

Using this definition of invention, it might be instructive to review congressional legislative authorization to see how much of it used inventive alternatives. By focusing on five postwar presidents, we can travel through a variety of political milieus: postwar adjustments (Truman), middle-of-the-roadism (Eisenhower), storm and stress (Kennedy-Johnson), and program consolidation (Nixon). To make the survey manageable, however, we will consider only domestic policy.

The primary source of data for this study was the *Congressional Quar-*

---

[19] Harold Seidman, *Politics, Position, and Power* (New York: Oxford University Press, 1980).

terly Almanac, 1949–72 (vols. 5–28). The chief value of the *CQA* is that it provides a synoptic description and a legislative history of all major legislation introduced in each of the twenty-four years under investigation. A concentrated reading yielded a little over one hundred legislative actions that, based on the *CQA's* summaries of and excerpts from the hearings, appeared to meet the definition of inventive activity—new combinations of existing knowledge in proposals potentially useful and resulting from a mental performance above the average (no routine improvement in technique). The difficulties in measuring an activity so defined are perhaps obvious enough but still need underlining.

By examining primary and other secondary sources on this group of potentially inventive policies, it is sometimes (not usually) possible to find explicit statements and facts either coinciding or conflicting with the established criteria. This line of analysis resulted in a tentative list of forty-two legislative actions that appeared truly inventive (see Table 6–1).

Interpretation

Perhaps the surest inference to be drawn from these data is that innovative policies are rare. This has serious implications, and we will consider them shortly. For the moment, however, we will be concerned with suggesting some reasons for the low invention rate.

One possible reason is found in the Constitution, which was based squarely on the very Newtonian idea of balancing forces. In this schema—permeated by an elaborate system of checks and balances and epitomized by Calhoun's notion of concurrent majorities—inventive acts are easily defeated and become rare. Routine acts, which are less likely to upset this balance, become the rule.

Another possible reason for the low inventive rate is, as we saw earlier, the tendency of policymakers to rely on the incremental and branching methods. If the first reason is ingrained in the Constitution, then it is fair to say that the second appears linked to humankind's inveterate distaste for taking risks. No reformer is likely to change either of these conditions.

Where do seminal ideas—so few in number, so large in effect—originate? To be more precise, at what point in the American policymaking system are innovative ideas first seriously considered as the possible bases for new legislation?

Since many of these ideas are venerables, there is ample basis for caution here: otherwise one could face a historical inquiry of awesome proportions. Consider, for example, the idea of rehabilitation, which was the basis for the 1964 amendments to the U.S. Code (Title 18, Section 4082). Conceivably, this idea could be traced back to a ruling

308

Table 6–1
A tentative list of inventive public policies, 1949–1972

Housing Act of 1949
Federal Property and Administrative Services Act of 1949
National Science Foundation Act of 1950
Budget and Accounting Act of 1950
Agricultural Trade Development and Assistance Act of 1954
Government Accounting Act of 1956
National Defense Education Act of 1958
National Aeronautics and Space Act of 1958
TVA Revenue Bonds Act of 1959
Housing Act of 1961
Juvenile Delinquency Act of 1961
Area Redevelopment Act of 1961
Public Welfare Amendments of 1962
Trade Expansion Act of 1962
Communications Satellite Act of 1962
Manpower Development and Training Act of 1962
Independent Offices Appropriation Act of 1963
Revenue Act of 1964
Economic Opportunity Act of 1964
Land and Water Conservation Fund Act of 1964
Wilderness Act of 1964
Atomic Energy Amendments of 1964
Water Resources Research Act of 1964
Health Insurance for the Aged Act of 1965
Elementary and Secondary Education Act of 1965
Heart Disease, Cancer, and Stroke Amendments of 1965
Prisoner Rehabilitation Amendments of 1965
Water Quality Act of 1965
Solid Waste Disposal Act of 1965
Public Works and Economic Development Act of 1965
State Technical Services Act of 1965
Housing and Urban Development Act of 1965
Narcotic Addiction Rehabilitation Act of 1966
Model Cities Act of 1966
Intergovernment Cooperation Act of 1968
National Environmental Policy Act of 1969
Postal Reorganization Act of 1970
Defense Production Act of 1970
Resource Recovery Act of 1970
Office of Technology Assessment Amendments of 1970
Revenue Sharing Act of 1972

of King Athelstan of England (A.D. 940) which decreed that a fifteen-year-old boy liable to the death penalty should not be executed but placed under the supervision of the bishop.

Table 6–2 shows six major sources of inventive ideas in the American policymaking system. Perhaps the most important thing to note is that, notwithstanding academic cliché regarding the preeminence of the executive, congressional sources account for over 38 percent of these ideas.

Table 6–2
Sources of inventive policy, 1949–1972

	Number	Percent
Executive department or agency	17	40
Congressional committee	11	26
Presidential commission	5	12
Presidential task force	4	10
Congressional commission	3	7
Other (GAO and IRS)	2	5
Total	42	100

Traditionally, in building the case for the preeminence of the executive, political scientists were content to cite gross figures (about 80 percent) on the number of legislative proposals generated by the executive branch. One could argue that this figure should be tempered with a distinction between inventive policies and routine policies.

According to Robert A. Dahl, the politics of highly pluralistic, highly organized societies leads to a cycle of immobility and emergency.[20] It would seem to follow, therefore, that inventive legislation is most likely to occur during periods of national crises. Surprisingly, the data do not support this conclusion. For each of the forty-two policies, a determination was made of the specific cause that gave rise to the basic innovative idea. These causes were then placed into one of three broad categories: perceived benefits ($n = 23$), reaction to burdens or frustrations ($n = 15$), and national trauma ($n = 4$). It is in the third category that one expects to see the most entries, but only four innovative policies between 1949 and 1972 were found to be the result of anything like a crisis. These four were the Housing Act of 1949 (World War II), the National Defense Educational Act of 1958 (Sputnik), the National Aeronautics and Space Administration (Sputnik), and the Trade Expansion Act of 1962 (the Common Market). Conceivably, the fifteen policies caused by burdens of frustrations could be said to have been caused by crises, but even so a majority of twenty-four policies would still have been the result of expected benefits. Moreover, there is good reason for not including these fifteen, since many were chiefly the result of a president's desire to develop his own legislative program.

Daniel Bell's work on postindustrial society suggests another interesting line of inquiry concerning the causes of and preconditions to inventive policy.[21] According to Bell, the generation of public policies in mod-

---

[20] Robert A. Dahl, *Pluralist Democracy in the United States* (Chicago: Rand McNally, 1967).
[21] Daniel Bell, *The Coming of Post-Industrial Society* (New York: Basic Books, 1973).

ern society is increasingly determined by theoretical knowledge. If such knowledge is indeed important, then it would seem likely that its influence would be greatest on innovative—as opposed to routine—policy. The tentative findings, however, offer little to support this view.

Actually, only one clear-cut example of the shaping of innovative public policy by theoretical knowledge was observed: the influence of a mathematically formalized body of economic theory on the Revenue Act of 1964. Similarly, in his magisterial study of policy development under three recent presidents, James L. Sundquist is also hard pressed to find evidence that the academic community, perhaps the leading source of theoretical knowledge, originated any ideas that became the basis of major public policies.[22]

Two brief explanations for this contradiction are offered. The first is suggested by studies of technological innovation. "Invention," writes S. Colum Gilfillan, a pioneering sociologist in this area, "need not be based on prior science. It often precedes and evolves the opposite science."[23] The second explanation is suggested by Bell himself: the meager influence of theoretical knowledge is the inevitable result of the meager amounts spent on research in the area of domestic policy. "In 1968 . . . the total private and public outlays for urban facilities . . . were greater than the expenditures for national defense, $92 billion as compared with $81 billion. Yet while the Defense Department will have spent between $7 and $8 billion for research and development in 1970 and 1971, the Department of Housing and Urban Development will have spent a total of $22 *million*."[24]

To assess changes in the rate of policy development during the last few decades, the inventions were grouped into three periods based on when they were first conceived. The results are shown in Table 6–3. As the table indicates, the overall lapsed time for policy development has declined. Surprisingly, between period 1 and period 3, the primary reduction in total lapsed time is more the result of the decrease in the gestation period (4.22 years) than the decrease in the entrepreneurship period (2.72 years). This suggests that the acceleration in the rate of policy development may be attributable to the increasing sophistication of political leaders in identifying potential policy applications of new social techniques or seminal ideas. Politics becomes the acquisition of this property.

---

[22] James L. Sundquist, *Politics and Policy* (Washington, D.C.: Brookings Institution, 1968), p. 393.

[23] Colum Gilfillan, "The Social Principles of Invention," in *Research Development, and Technological Innovation*, ed. James R. Bright (Homewood, Ill.: Richard D. Irwin, 1964), p. 93.

[24] Bell, *Post Industrial Society*, p. 261.

Table 6–3
Summary of rates of policy invention

		Mean lapsed time (years)		
		Gestation*	Entrepreneurship†	Total
1.	1935–56	5.36	3.43	8.79
2.	1957–63	1.43	0.78	2.21
3.	1964–72	1.14	0.71	1.85

*The period of gestation was measured from the year in which the idea was first conceived to the year in which the idea was formally proposed either by the president (usually in one of his messages to Congress) or by a member of Congress (always in an introduced bill). Pinpointing the moment of conception is not easy. The negative income tax idea illustrates these difficulties. In 1943, while working in the Treasury Department on income tax matters, Milton Friedman became concerned about the problem of fluctuating earnings. Given graduated tax rates, persons whose incomes rose and fell from one year to the next paid more tax over a long period of time than did persons with equivalent gross earnings whose annual income was steady. Friedman conceived of a negative income tax to even things up. In a good year, such persons would pay taxes to the Treasury; in a bad one, the Treasury would pay taxes to them. By the late 1940s, it had further occurred to Friedman and his fellow economist George Stigler that a negative income tax could do more than smooth some of the bumps in the citizen's experience with Form 1040. It could become a permanent device for eliminating poverty: that is to say, it could be paid routinely to persons whose income never entered the positive brackets. But it is virtually impossible to say with any precision when during this period the negative income tax proposal was conceived.

† Following the proposal comes an indeterminate period of entrepreneurship that is terminated only when the bill becomes law, that is, has been adopted.

There are other reasons as well. In an age of space exploration, requiring an extraordinary integration of people and technology in the pursuit of specific goals, it is to be expected that an appreciation of societal problem solving (or, at least, the image of it) would spread. Politicians, accordingly, are more inclined to search for new social invention. And the gestation period might also be expected to decrease because of the growing tendency for groups within society to press actively and directly—often, as in the case of truck drivers during the energy squeeze of the early 1970s, quite forcefully—for immediate problem resolution.

Two recent examples of creativity: A proposal and a reality

The shared economy. Policymakers are inclined to accept 7 percent unemployment as an unavoidable cost of stable prices. They fear that a concerted effort to reduce joblessness would trigger another round of inflation and recession. Martin Weitzman, an MIT economist, suggests an elegant way to break the link between employment and the business cycle.[25] The core of his idea is something like profit sharing: to change our system of fixed wages to one in which workers' incomes are deter-

[25] Martin Weitzman, *The Shared Economy* (Cambridge, Mass.: Harvard University Press, 1984).

mined by company performance. Understanding why almost everyone would benefit takes a little effort.

Most workers are paid according to contract. From the employer's perspective, how much they are paid depends almost entirely on how many hours they work times the hourly rate. If the cost of extra hours is less than the extra revenues the work would yield, the employer hires more people. If workers insist on higher wages or sales fall, they get laid off.

Weitzman asks us to imagine a different pattern. Suppose that labor, instead of negotiating for so many dollars an hour, negotiated for a share of company revenues. Then, suppose the agreement leaves the employer free to hire as many more workers as he wants. Attitudes toward hiring would be transformed.

Imagine that General Motors, for instance, had agreed in such negotiations to pay its workers 70 percent of revenues. Since it would keep 30 percent, GM would want to keep hiring as long as the additional workers made any contribution to revenues. Those already employed would, in effect, pay part of any new workers' wages. If there were then a recession, GM would have a strong incentive to avoid layoffs. Revenues would fall, but pay would remain a fixed percentage of revenue, so the company would gain nothing by idling productive workers.

That sounds great for GM and the workers who would otherwise be unemployed. But what about the rest of GM's workers, whose income would now fluctuate according to company revenue and additional hiring? Why should they buy the Weitzman idea? There are two reasons. One is that the pay loss, averaged out among a whole workforce, would be small. The second is job security. Surely most people who work for a living should be willing to take a temporary pay cut to keep fellow workers on the job during recessions.

In good times, if GM hired so many people that wages dropped substantially, the union would be free to bargain for a larger share of the profits, just as it is free now to bargain for higher wages. And, if most companies switched to the Weitzman share agreement, the widespread competition for workers would ensure that no company could get away with sub-par compensation.

Government policymakers would no longer have to accept low growth as insurance against inflation. Since inflation could never become locked into higher wages, it would not feed on itself through workers' expectations of more inflation.

Sharing sovereignty in Northern Ireland. Strife in Northern Ireland between Protestants, who want to remain part of Britain, and Catholics, who would just as soon be part of Ireland, has claimed 2,500 lives since 1969 and turned a once-prosperous province into a slum. In 1985, the governments of Britain and Ireland agreed to share responsibility in Northern Ireland. The plan offered an ingenious way around the obstacle of sovereignty in the province—by passing around it.

The accord looks to the creation of a unique mechanism in Belfast, the capital of Northern Ireland. It is called an "intergovernmental conference" and is jointly headed by British and Irish ministers and served by a pooled secretariat. It is empowered to deal on a regular basis with all the political and security issues that are being disputed by the province's 1 million Protestants and 600,000 Catholics.

This amounts to giving predominantly Catholic Ireland a major consultative role in the affairs of hitherto British-run Northern Ireland. To compensate for the dilution of British influence in Northern Ireland, British Prime Minister Margaret Thatcher could point to the accord's explicit affirmation that the province will remain a part of Britain as long as a majority of its citizens desire. Moreover, that guarantee is now formally endorsed by the Irish Republic. And if the new arrangement takes hold, the North will benefit from greatly increased economic assistance, with the likelihood that the United States will be a generous contributor.

Protestants should come to understand that if they strangle the proposed experiment, the main beneficiaries will be the extremists of the Irish Republican Army and its political allies. Their cause breeds on despair, on the conviction that only violence can redress the grievances of the North's minority. To prove them wrong, London and Dublin tried imaginatively to transcend what cannot be reconciled by fashioning this ingenious experiment.

PSYCHOLOGICAL PERSPECTIVES ON CHOICE

Policy, like song, begins in the mind. While we need not know in what part, we are interested in knowing how. This section, which draws on research in cognitive science, is aimed at the elucidation of how individual policymakers fashion meaningful responses to problems. It is concerned not with structural or biological questions but with function and such activities as problem solving, creating, even whether "logical thinking" comes naturally to us or is always artificial and often useless.

Do policymakers exhibit the rational thought processes extolled by philosophers such as Francis Bacon and Rene Descartes or, for that matter, exhibited by fictional characters like Sherlock Holmes and Mr. Spock (who was only half-human)? If the truth be told boldly, logic frequently takes second place to emotional considerations. Chief Justice Charles Evans Hughes was speaking not as a philosopher when he said to William O. Douglas, "You must remember one thing. At the constitutional level where we work, 90 percent of any decision is emotional. The rational part of us supplies the reasons for supporting our predilections."[26]

But the contrast between logic and emotion, though a source of fascination, should not be drawn too sharply. We know officials who look to define the right course in terms of issues, for whom it is an intellectual process, a classic policy-planning exercise revolving around principles and ideas. But we also know officials who say, "What do I have to get done, who do I have to move, and who are their bosses?" These people see problems in terms of organization and human relationships. And sometimes we encounter officials who seem to mix the two approaches.

How psychological factors dictate choices

If human beings ever really believed in their supreme rationality, much of psychological thought has tended to disabuse them of that notion. A new assault on the idea of human rationality comes from research that examines some of the specific psychological factors that influence—and distort—decision making. The new studies focus on the subtle power of one's mental frame of reference in dictating what are often the simplest choices.[27]

Ordinary individuals are often surprised to find themselves reversing judgments of a situation when they are forced to shift from one mental frame of reference to another, and even experts can be fooled into making contradictory decisions by subtle manipulation of the way they are led to think about a problem. Research indicates that traditional, rationalistic notions of how policymakers decide almost certainly have to be revised to take account of subtle psychophysical factors that are often ignored.

The recent findings also suggest that citizens and political leaders could easily be subject to manipulation designed to play on the psychological factors that influence decision making. Among the more interesting conclusions of this research by cognitive scientists are these:

- People are more sensitive to negative consequences than to positive ones—more worried, for example, about losing a given amount of

---

[26] On the irrational processes in high-level decision making, see Robert Axelrod, *Structure of Decision* (Princeton, N.J.: Princeton University Press, 1976). The Hughes quote appears in Morton Hunt, *The Universe Within* (New York: Simon & Schuster, 1982), p. 129.

[27] This discussion is based chiefly on Amos Tversky and Daniel Kahneman, "The Framing of Decisions and the Psychology of Choice," *Science*, 211 (1981), pp. 453–58; and "Judgment Under Uncertainty: Heuristics and Biases," *Science* 185 (1974), pp. 1124–31.

money than eager to win the same amount. Thus most people are unwilling to bet $10 on a coin flip for equal stakes; in one laboratory experiment, most college students refused to stake $10 on a coin flip unless they stood to win $30. Amos Tversky, Stanford University, suggests that such concern over negative consequences may have had evolutionary advantages for human survival; species that worried less may have been happier, but they presumably died off.

- People have no sensible mental model for dealing with very improbable events, so they either ignore them entirely and assume they will not happen or, if forced to consider them, grossly overestimate their likelihood. That explains the popularity, for example, of one-in-a-million lottery tickets or the exaggerated fear of shark attacks in some people who saw the movie *Jaws*. It also helps explain the fear of nuclear power. (For more on decision making under uncertainty, see Chapter 8.)

- People overvalue the complete elimination of a lesser hazard and undervalue an equivalent reduction in a greater hazard. In one recent study, people favored a hypothetical vaccine that was described as fully effective against one of two viruses, each of which causes half the cases of the same disease. They were less impressed when the same vaccine was described as cutting the overall risk of contracting the disease in half.

- When people are called on to make assessments, they tend to anchor their judgments on some initial point of reference—whether or not it is relevant to the task. In another experiment, people were randomly placed in two groups and assigned a number that was determined by spinning a wheel of fortune in their presence. They were told to assume that this number was an initial estimate of the percentage of African nations in the UN. Their task was to adjust this figure to reflect their own estimate of the correct percentage. Although the two groups were homogeneous and therefore should have arrived at identical estimates, the roulette values turned out to have a marked effect. The group whose roulette value was 10 percent estimated the African nations at 25 percent; the other group, with a roulette value of 65 percent, estimated the African nations at 45 percent. Even a monetary reward for accuracy could not reduce this obvious anchoring effect.

Anchoring also occurs strongly in intuitive numerical estimation. For example, within five seconds try to estimate the products of

$$8 \times 7 \times 6 \times 5 \times 4 \times 3 \times 2 \times 1$$

Now, independently of the above answer, estimate the products of

$$1 \times 2 \times 3 \times 4 \times 5 \times 6 \times 7 \times 8$$

316

In experiments, the median estimate for the first sequence was 2,250, while the median estimate for the second sequence was 512. The correct answer to both is 40,320.

What seems to happen is that anchors influence judgments in such an important—and unconscious—manner that even when they are selected openly and trivially, as with a wheel of fortune, they can exert a profound influence.

- People make choices among alternative solutions, depending on how the problem is *framed*. In one experiment, students, physicians, and health economists were asked to choose between alternative programs to combat a hypothetical disease that was expected to kill 600 people. When the options were described in terms of the lives they would save, a large majority preferred a program that was guaranteed to save 200 lives rather than a program that had a possibility, but no certainty, of saving all 600. But when the very same programs were described in terms of the lives that would be lost, the results were reversed. An even larger majority rejected the program that was guaranteed to lose 400 lives and preferred to gamble, against the odds, on the program that might save everybody but more probably would lose all 600.

  The two sets of answers were clearly inconsistent. The participants were simply reacting differently to different formulations of the same question—giving opposite answers, depending on how the outcomes were described. The root of their dilemma was an apparently deep-seated psychological tendency to avoid risks when seeking gains but to accept risks in order to avoid losses. A large majority of people seem to prefer a sure gain over a decision that could lead to something better but has the element of a gamble, of uncertainty, to it. Yet they reject a sure loss in favor of a decision that could lead to something worse but has the element of a gamble.

Thus, policy analysts could influence decisions made by political authorities simply by how they choose to formulate a problem. They could do so without distorting or suppressing information, merely by the framing of outcomes and contingencies. This might happen accidentally or could be exploited deliberately. For example, lobbyists for the credit-card industry strove to ensure that any extra charges imposed on the consumers to cover the costs associated with credit-card purchases be labeled a "discount" for those who pay cash rather than what it really is—a "surcharge" on those who use credit cards. Because losses loom larger than gains, consumers would be less willing to accept a surcharge than forgo a discount.

One defense against inconsistent reasoning and outside manipulation is to practice framing problems and choices in more than one way to see if your preferences remain the same as the formulations change. Mere sophistication and expertise in the subject matter offers little protection.

Bounded rationality

Yet humans are not irrational either. In the policymaker's world, logic often fails because logic was designed not to deal with things and events but, rather, with the consistency or inconsistency of statements. The logic textbook says that it is false to say "All crows are black," since there are albino crows in the world. But the human mind often needs to, and does, distinguish degrees of truth. The human mind, in short, has common sense. Policymakers, like the rest of us, tend to focus on what can happen in the world under such-and-such conditions. The soundness, the speed, and the complexity of the reasoning they exhibit seems primarily a function of the degree of familiarity and organization of the information being processed rather than a function of any general intelligence of the policymaker. So a Nobel laureate in physics may not necessarily make a good undersecretary of state or chess player.

Marvin Minsky of MIT concludes that no cognitive system—whether a human being or a computer—can operate according to laws of formal logic.[28] Such programming would churn out any number of valid but useless inferences from every true statement, but it would not know which conclusion should *not* be drawn or which *ought* to be deduced under ordinary circumstance. For this reason, experienced chess players and computer chess programs do not explore every possible move, which would run into the millions, but zero in on only a few.

For instance, we may wish to consider various modes of personal transportation. We could isolate the major attributes or parameters; for example: power sources, types of passenger support, and the media within which the vehicle operates. Then, for each parameter, alternative possibilities are listed. See Table 6–4.

If one element is encircled in each column and all circles are connected, every resulting chain of circles represents one possible solution of the original problem. A possible solution is indicated in Table 6–4.

The main difficulty of this analysis lies in its excessive richness: the combinational process proliferates in geometric progression, and we quickly arrive at tens of thousands of solutions. As an example, if we use a table of eight parameters of four values each, we will have 4^8 or

---

[28] Marvin Minsky, "A Framework for Representing Knowledge," Artificial Intelligence Memo No. 306. (Cambridge, Mass.: MIT Artificial Intelligence Laboratory, 1974). See also his *The Society of Mind* (New York: Simon & Schuster, 1986) especially pp. 185–94.

Table 6–4
Morphological analysis for personal transportation

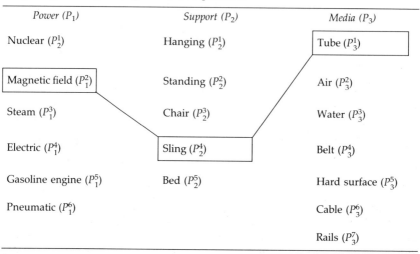

Power (P_1)	Support (P_2)	Media (P_3)
Nuclear (P_2^1)	Hanging (P_2^1)	Tube (P_3^1)
Magnetic field (P_1^2)	Standing (P_2^2)	Air (P_3^2)
Steam (P_1^3)	Chair (P_2^3)	Water (P_3^3)
Electric (P_1^4)	Sling (P_2^4)	Belt (P_3^4)
Gasoline engine (P_1^5)	Bed (P_2^5)	Hard surface (P_3^5)
Pneumatic (P_1^6)		Cable (P_3^6)
		Rails (P_3^7)

65,536 different solutions, assuming that there are no internal contradictions. If it only requires half an hour to study each of these 65,536 solutions, the required work represents roughly fifteen work years. This is out of practical possibilities.

Perhaps we need a new term to describe rationality in situations such as those that face policymakers—where the complexity of the environment is immensely greater than the computational powers of their brains and computers. Herbert A. Simon, one of the early leaders in cognitive science, has given us such a term, *bounded rationality*. The Apollo mission to the moon, for example, was a triumph of bounded rationality. Contrary to the popular view, going to the moon was a complex matter along only one dimension: It challenged organizational capabilities. Though it was no mean technological accomplishment, it required hardware not a great deal different from that found in the German rocket program in World War II and refined by the American rocket program during the 1950s. Although Apollo had several side benefits, in the final analysis it was a success simply because men walked on the moon.

In contrast, the development of the Space Shuttle was not an example of bounded rationality. NASA was not charged with a single, highly operational goal such as "develop and fly a semireusable space vehicle." Beyond that, it also had to push the state-of-the-art in four major areas of technology—and with scarce resources (Apollo's were enormous). It also had to satisfy the specific needs of a variety of other groups ranging from the military (who wanted the bay doors a certain size), to the scientific community (who wanted a space telescope placed in orbit), to industry (who sought profits from space industrialization). Finally, it had to carry on its flights not just tough, experienced test pilots but civilians—including members of Congress, school teachers, and scientists. The complexity of that environment probably exceeded what the human mind was capable of effectively handling.

Perhaps what made the U.S. Constitution so successful an invention was that its framers had limited objectives. Herbert A. Simon has examined their own views of their goals, as reflected in *The Federalist* and other documents. What is striking about these documents is their practical sense and the awareness they exude of the limits of foresight about large human affairs. Most of the framers of the Constitution accepted very restricted objectives for their artifact—principally the preservation of freedom in an orderly society. Moreover they did not postulate a new man to be produced by the new institutions but accepted as one of their design constraints the psychological characteristics of men and women as they knew them, their selfishness as well as common sense.[29]

Thus, it would seem that the success of policy planning on a large scale depends on modesty and restraint in setting goals and drastic simplification of the real-world situation. Yet, even with restraint and simplification, difficult obstacles remain. To help overcome them, policymakers may wish to use heuristic search techniques.

Heuristic search

Broadly defined, a heuristic search is employed when policymakers use knowledge to identify promising paths in looking for a solution, as opposed to using trial and error. There are, of course, a great many ways in which knowledge can be used to identify promising paths, and therefore many varieties of heuristic search. We will discuss these nine general varieties:

Selective search.

Satisficing.

Learning from experience.

Analogy.

Trying something.

Means-ends analysis.

Decomposition.

---

[29] Herbert A. Simon, *The Sciences of the Artificial* (Cambridge, Mass.: MIT Press, 1981), p. 163.

320

Synectics.

Thought experiments.

Selective search. Except when the number of possibilities is very small, the human problem solver avoids the kind of trial-and-error search that blindly looks at every alternative, one after another. It is a major characteristic of the human problem solver to do selective search, not exhaustive search.

Take for example this anagram:[30]

DRY OXTAIL IN REAR

How would you go about finding the one word that is made up of all these letters? To look at every possibility would be an exhausting, if not impossible, task. You would not want to waste your time looking for the anagram among possibilities that begin with RD or XY; you know better. You would more likely want to explore more promising avenues, or what we might call bands of interest, in which the prospects of finding a good specific solution are good. (The solution is printed at the bottom of p. 321.)

Selective search incorporates two main notions: first, the idea of moving from the level of very general solutions to determining specific solutions; and second, the idea of attaching values to solutions at the higher levels as a basis for deciding which plans to pursue at levels of greater specificity. Urban transportation, Central America, and health care provide good examples of the procedure.

But first a word of warning. Since this book is mainly about the philosophy and methodology of policy analysis, the examples that follow are intended not as recommendations but as illustrations. My aim is merely to show how a heuristic search might be used. Heuristic searches are not truth detectors—though sometimes they may sit by the well from which it springs.

Few areas of national policy are in greater flux than urban transportation. In addition to rather dramatic changes in the level of funding, important changes are also occurring in the content of federal policy. One need not look far to find the reason. Briefly put, it is the inevitable result of the increasing incompatibility between the car and the city. A complete recitation of all the problems that can be associated with the automobile is beyond the scope of this book. In place of such a recitation, the opening paragraph of Wilfred Owen's *The Accessible City,* which presents an excellent overview of the problem, will suffice:

---

[30] Example from George Polya, *How to Solve It* (Princeton, N.J.: Princeton University Press, 1973), p. 160.

In an age of urbanization and motorization, the way people live and the way they move have become increasingly incompatible. The results are congestion, pollution, and a growing sense of frustration. Where all-out efforts have been made to accommodate the car, the streets are still congested, commuting is increasingly difficult, urban aesthetics have suffered, and the quality of life has been eroded. In an automotive age, cities have become the negation of communities—a setting for machines instead of people. The automobile has taken over, motorist and nonmotorist alike are caught up in the congestion, and everyone is a victim of the damaging side effects of the conflict between the car and the community. The automobile is an irresistible force that may become an immovable object, and in the process destroy the city.[31]

Now, two principal alternative classes of solutions to this problem can be identified: (1) capital-intensive public transportation and (2) bus lines. The former refers to systems which require large fixed investments, such as rapid rail transit and rail commuter lines. Within each alternative, a number of specific programs are available. For example, funding for capital-intensive transportation might be directed toward research and development of technologically advanced systems, such as monorails, pneumatic propulsion tube systems, magnetic suspension systems, personal rapid transit, and conveyor belts. Funding for bus lines, on the other hand, might be directed toward completely subsidizing operation expenses or, in short, free-fare transit. An analysis might proceed by first analyzing capital-intensive transportation, as a class of solutions, and then zero in on one alternative in the other class, namely, a free-fare transit program.[32]

Taking a broad view of both classes, the first thing to strike the analyst is the relatively high costs of capital-intensive public transportation. Los Angeles' long-discussed subway project, Metro Rail, is estimated to cost $3.3 billion for the 18.5 miles, or over $178 million per mile. A light rail system in Houston, where no excavation would be required and property values are lower, is estimated to run about $40 million per mile. Where will this money come from?

Capital-intensive transportation also has certain political and technological drawbacks. Fixed rail systems favor middle-income commuters

---

[31] Wilfred Owen, *The Accessible City* (Washington, D.C.: Brookings Institution, 1972), p. 1.

[32] Discussion of free-fare transit is based largely on James I. Scheiner and Grover Starling, "The Political Economy of Free Fare Transit," *Urban Affairs Quarterly* 19, no. 2 (December 1974), pp. 170–84. Data on fixed rail systems is from "Mass Transit: The Expensive Dream," *Business Week*, August 27, 1984; and Judith Cummings, "Los Angeles Breaks Ground in Metro Rail Project," *New York Times*, September 30, 1986.

EXTRAORDINARILY.

from the suburbs over the poorer working residents of the central city. Developments in telecommunications—for example, CATV, Picture-phone, rapid facsimile, and new data networks—might lead to a decentralization of office employment now concentrated in the central business district. Radically improved communications may substitute for interoffice business trips; work could be done from closed-circuit TV consoles. In such a world of the not-too-distant future, rapid rail systems, no longer economically justifiable, might become objects of purely archaeological interest. And there are other problems. Advanced electronic gadgets and circuitry often entail uncertainty in operations. San Francisco's Bay Area Rapid Transit (BART) is a case in point: doors fail to open or close on schedule; automatic controls stop trains inexplicably; and brake signal lights come on for no apparent reason.

In contrast, the idea behind free-fare transit is simple: to reduce automobile ridership, and finance the city's bus lines as the city's police and fire departments are financed, that is, through general revenues rather than user fees. Significantly, a number of cities—including Atlanta, Seattle, Houston, Denver, San Diego, and Tulsa—have already tried free-fare on an experimental basis.

In analyzing this idea, the crucial question seems to be this: How do the costs compare with the benefits? The freeway bus lane can be built for an average of $10 million per mile, and some bus lanes, which simply absorb the median or outside shoulders of a freeway, can be built for as little as $2 million per mile. Full public financing of operating expenses nationwide, including increased ridership due to free-fare, would cost on the order of $2.3 billion. But this figure by itself tells only half the story. Although questions on the cost of free-fare transit have concerned government policymakers and the public for some time, approximations of the cost versus the benefits of such a strategy are rare indeed. This lack of data makes it impossible to justify free-fare on financial grounds: furthermore, until some measurement of the cost-benefit trade-offs is developed, policymaking in this area will tend to be more arbitrary than objective.

Basically, free-fare offers two kinds of benefits: those which are the result of a reduction in intercity auto travel and those which are not. A conservative figure on the cost of intercity auto travel is $49.1 billion. It is conservative because it includes only property damage, traffic fatalities, and delay (due to congestion), excluding such important considerations as noise pollution, opportunity costs, medical expenses, and, above all, operator expenses. How much of this $49.1 billion would be eliminated depends partially on how many automobile drivers are attracted. Best estimates, based on the several experiments referred to above, say that auto usage would drop 13.2 percent. Therefore, the benefits should be worth at least $6.6 billion ($49.1 billion × 0.132). This represents a cost-benefit ratio of almost three to one (6.6 ÷ 2.3).

A complete cost-benefit analysis would, however, go beyond these somewhat rough figures. For instance, in addition to the benefits derived solely from reduced automobile travel, the analysis might need to include the following:

Free-fare bus service, unlike capital-intensive transportation, does not require the public acquisition of any new land. Not only is land acquisition costly in the short run, but it also deprives the public coffers of property taxes in future years.

Operating a free-fare transit system will be 15 to 20 percent less on a per mile basis than current costs. There are a number of reasons for this paradox. First, to the extent that free-fare induces drivers onto public transit, the bus itself is able to move faster—and increased vehicle speed means lower operating costs. Second, free-fare reduces running time by reducing boarding time, which can consume as much as 18 percent of total running time. Under free-fare, box queues would be eliminated and passengers could board through both front and rear doors. Third, fare collection equipment maintenance and cash, token, and transfer handling require about one person for every ten buses—under free-fare, this expense would be eliminated. For a 100-bus operation, approximately $100,000 annually could be saved in personnel reduction alone.

Free-fare would contribute to urban renewal and full employment.

Lastly, free-fare would help compensate for the economic, physical, and legal restrictions that are placed on the mobility of millions of Americans who are unable to drive. In fact, an examination of the current population shows that in the United States more than half of the population is without immediate access to a car.

Although the foregoing procedure and the attendant analysis might seem lengthy, an analysis that had to explore all of the alternatives within both classes of solutions would have been much longer, more expensive, and quite impossible.

The bands-of-interest procedure can also be applied to policy issues as disparate as Central America and health care.

The debate over aid to the Nicaraguan contras simmered through much of the 1980s. By the mid-1980s, the fundamental facts had ceased to be contested. The Sandinista regime came to power in 1979 promising democratic renewal, but instead proceeded to turn itself into a Marxist-Leninist regime on the Cuban and Soviet model. It built up an army larger than that of all the other Central American countries combined.

It is sustained by a minimum of 8,000 Cuban advisers, of whom at least 3,000 are military; Bulgarians, East Germans, Libyans, and the largest Soviet embassy in the hemisphere, outside of Washington, provide the military, administrative, and intelligence sinews. It is this Soviet and Cuban presence, and the size of its armed forces, not just its internal arrangements, that make the regime a strategic threat.

This state of affairs gives the United States three broad policy choices:

1. It can let existing trends in Nicaragua continue and then seek to contain the resulting military, intelligence, and political machine. The National Bipartisan Commission on Central America rejected this approach unanimously in 1984 as being beyond the physical resources of the Central American countries and requiring a large, permanent, major U.S. military presence, which neither Central American nor U.S. public opinion would sustain.
2. It can seek to overthrow the Sandinista regime. This is impossible without direct U.S. military intervention. But the costs of such a policy would be substantial, and it would guarantee that the president's term would be marred by implacable congressional opposition and domestic and international upheavals.
3. The third option might be where the band of interest is found. The most promising course is—according to this analysis—a combination of negotiation and pressure designed to deprive the Sandinista regime of the capability to subvert or to undermine its neighbors. Now analysis can focus on the three components of such a policy: a balance of incentives and pressures, a forum, and a detailed negotiating position.

What are the general options for handling rising health-care costs?

1. The first one is triage: the denial of access to health care or at least to reimbursement to selected classes of patients or for selected complaints. There is already quite a bit of triage in medicare, which does not pay for dentistry, eye glasses, or hearing aids—the three most common health care needs of the elderly. Some have proposed denying medical care to old people who are terminally ill or beyond being restored to functional health. The British National Health Service severely restricts access to elective surgery.
2. The second option for handling health-care costs is through rules and regulations. In control by triage, there are impersonal general rules based in part on medical considerations of health needs but even more on economics. Rules and regulations handle health-care costs through administrative fiat: "Thou shalt do this" and "Thou shalt not do that."
3. The last option is to use the market mechanism as a regulator to the fullest extent possible. The individual family pays its own health-

care costs up to, say, 10 percent of its pretax income. The government would pay health-care costs above that amount—that is, "catastrophic-illness" costs—without any upper limit. The money would be provided for either through compulsory catastrophic-illness insurance or out of general tax revenues.

Where might a band of interest be found here?

Triage is undoubtedly an effective way to cut costs. But the price is very high. The benefits do not outweigh the costs saved. Of all modern medicine, elective surgery probably does the most good in relieving suffering and restoring health and function. To deny it to people because it costs so much is not good economics. But the greatest weakness of triage as the way to control health-care costs is that it brazenly favors the wealthy and penalizes the poor.

Rules and regulations never cut costs; they always raise them. The federal government recently decided that hospitals will be reimbursed a fixed amount dependent on the diagnosis at the medicare patient's admission. But for elderly people, the admissions diagnosis turns out to be wrong, or at least seriously deficient, in more than half of all cases. So hospitals will be forced, in order to survive, to demand of the medicare patient's physician the most comprehensive and most highly reimbursed diagnosis that can still be justified. Further, rules and regulations are in themselves exceedingly costly. The ones we already have add at least 10 percent to the costs of both the physician and the employer providing health insurance and probably more to the costs of the hospital.

A market system with income-related catastrophic-illness reimbursement has built-in cost control. Consumers do pay attention to health-care costs if they have to pay for them themselves. Moreover, a market-based health-care system favors advances in medicine more than any other way of paying for health care. And it is the fairest and most equitable system: The poor have the same health care available as the affluent, and the cost burden is fully proportional to ability to pay. Therefore, this option might be our band of interest.

Satisficing. In order to understand this procedure, we must first understand *optimizing.* Specialists in management science describe optimizing strategy as having the goal of selecting the alternative with the highest payoff. Such a strategy requires estimating the comparative value of every viable option in terms of expected costs and benefits (see next chapter). But, as pointed out earlier, human beings rarely adopt this approach; people simply do not have the time, money, or computational capacity to maximize.

As a result, policymakers *satisfice,* that is, they look for a course of action that is "good enough," that meets a minimum set of requirements.

Business executives know that the perfect product may cost them the market, whereas one 98 percent as good could save it.

> Product release is held up another three months. And then another two. And then forty-five days. "We've got to make sure that the software is *totally* compatible with *all* the rest of the product family," the logic goes. . . . But sometimes the last 2 percent takes twelve months. In the meantime ten competitors have approximated the solution, and gotten theirs into the marketplace faster and first. (At Data General, Tom West wrote these lines on the Magic Marker board in his office: "Not everything worth doing is worth doing well.")[33]

Simon argues convincingly that the satisficing approach fits the limited information-processing capabilities of human beings. Given their limited ability to foresee future consequences and to obtain information about the variety of available alternatives inclines them to settle for a barely "acceptable" course of action that is better than things are now. Rather than collect information about all the complex factors that might affect the outcome of their choice, estimate probabilities, and work out preference orderings for many different alternatives, policymakers are content to rely on "a drastically simplified model of the buzzing, blooming confusion that constitutes the real world."[34]

Therefore, whenever policymakers look for a choice that offers some degree of improvement over the present state of affairs, their analyses are usually limited to just two alternatives—a new course of action that has come to their attention and the old one they had been pursuing. If neither meets their minimal requirements, they continue to look *sequentially* until they find one that does. Thus they work their way through a problem space in a serial fashion, taking one thing at a time rather than simultaneously searching a wide variety of possible solutions.

Given the historical realities of the matter, I am inclined to think that the U.S. policymakers have satisficed on the problem of poverty. If there ever was a case for optimality over satisficing, surely we will find it here. Or will we? Let us see. Certainly the welfare system, as it exists now in the United States, is not optimal by either liberals' or conservatives' standards. The liberals' optimal solution would be to have welfare entitlements and their attendant fringe benefits increased to the federal government's statistical poverty level of around $12,000 for the dependent family of four. The purity of the idea is the source of most of its appeal. If poverty is a lack of money, then if people are given enough money, they will not be poor.

---

[33] Thomas J. Peters and Nancy K. Austin, *A Passion of Excellence* (New York: Warner Books, 1985), pp. 179–80.

[34] Herbert A. Simon, *Administrative Behavior* (New York: Macmillan, 1976), p. 40. See also Simon's *Models of Man* (New York: Wiley, 1957).

The conservatives' optimal solution is based on the belief that the welfare system has cruelly corrupted the people it was supposed to help and broken down the family structure among poor people. When the availability of assistance causes poor people to prefer dependency to strenuous efforts toward self-reliance and self-sufficiency, the poor will choose dependency, according to this belief. Their solution, therefore, consists of scrapping the entire federal welfare and income-support structure for working-aged persons. It would leave the working-aged person with no recourse whatsoever except the job market, friends, family members, and charity. This idea too has its purity: Cut the knot, for there is no way to untie it.[35]

But before we could adopt either solution a great deal more must be known. Would the near-doubling of entitlements urged by liberals be a bonanza for convenience stores, slum landlords, and used-car salesmen, but not raise welfare recipients out of poverty? Would the elimination of entitlements hurt the truly needy and cause all to give up hope? To be sure, many programs give too little weight to the preservation of incentives to work, to keeping families together, and to diligence in education. But this can be redressed. Satisficing does not suggest that policymakers can do no good at all but that they must pick their shots.

Learning from experience. Human beings are adaptive creatures; they learn from experience. Generally speaking, when a series of actions leads them toward a goal but comes to a dead end, they do not start anew; rather they keep the parts that have worked and discard those that have not.

It is useful to think about this recycling process, since it reminds us that remodeling old ideas may be as important in the policy process as creating a policy from scratch.

> The amount of recycling we have seen, where proposals are made, defeated, and reemerge later on, in the test ban treaty, in the creation of the Atomic Energy Commission, and in the establishment of a Council of Economic Advisors, suggests that at any point in history there is a limited stock of ideas which provide an agenda for policymakers. Keeping these ideas afloat is an activity in which political leaders interact with the specialists who invent the ideas in the first place. Over time, these ideas are frequently modified as they are adapted for political use.[36]

Moreover, in the course of trying to solve a complex societal problem, policymakers may see the shortcomings of their first plans and alter them to more effective ones. This helps explain why feedback is an essential component in our model of the policy process.

---

[35] See Charles Murray, *Losing Ground: American Social Policy, 1950–1980* (New York: Basic Books, 1984), pp. 227–33.

[36] Polsby, *Political Innovation*, p. 112.

Feedback can also occur across jurisdictions. Once a rail transit system looked attractive to Houston, but it quickly tarnished. In Atlanta, for example, the first phase of construction for the Metropolitan Atlanta Transit Authority (MARTA) was $24 million over budget and six months late. The experience helped sour sentiment in Houston.

Analogy. Another widely applicable heuristic method—especially when confronted by a problem that seems new—is to think of some analogous situation and use it as a guide. Analogical reasoning, I believe, underlies the branching process in public policy noted earlier. It is a natural tendency of the human mind to interpret new experiences, and new problems, in light of old ones, and to make inferences based on similarities. Logicians and Mr. Spock may look down on it, but humans could not survive without it.

> Analogy pervades our thinking, our everyday speech and our trivial conclusions as well as artistic ways of expression and the highest scientific achievements. Analogy is used on very different levels. People often are vague, ambiguous, incomplete, or incompletely clarified analogies, but analogies may reach the level of mathematical precision. All sorts of analogy may play a role in the discovery of the solution and so we should not neglect any part.[37]

The central idea of the Peace Corps—government-sponsored contributions by Americans of their technical skills to projects abroad—weaves together several analogies: missionary work, volunteer work abroad, technical assistance, and national service for youth. It is impossible to say where the idea first came from. Peace Corps semiofficial literature traces the idea to the nineteenth-century American philosopher William James, who called for "conscription of our youthful population . . . to coal and iron mines, to freight trains . . . to dish washing." James was not suggesting specifically foreign social service but more generally some moral equivalent to war.

> So long as antimilitarists propose no substitute for war's disciplinary function, no moral equivalent of war, analogous, as one might say, to the mechanical equivalent of heat . . . they fail to realize the full inwardness of the situation.[38]

More typically the expression "the moral equivalent of war" is used without understanding. Public officials tend to seize on this analogy because it is interesting and novel, failing to grasp James' illuminating analogy. Without much reflection, they fabricate out of it what *they* would make it mean. At the start of the oil embargo in the late 1970s,

---

[37] Ibid.

[38] William James, *The Moral Equivalent of War in Memories and Studies* (New York: Longman, 1911), p. 5.

President Carter used Moral Equivalent as a synonym for economizing fuel. The country should tighten its belt, he hoped to suggest, as it had in World War II. This meaning was the exact opposite of James' analogy, which suggests the release of aggression through the useful *expenditure of energy.*

Privately funded voluntary organizations also provide something of an analogy for the Peace Corps.

> One of the best known of these, and the one which attracted the attention of early Peace Corps supporter Hubert Humphrey, was the American Friends Service Committee, which as long ago as 1919 dispatched teams of young people to serve in underprivileged areas. This work-camp concept was extended to overseas nations by the A.F.S.C. in 1960, and teams of young people were working in India and Tanganyika in that crucial summer when the Peace Corps was becoming a campaign issue. . . .
>
> Operation Crossroads Africa, founded in 1957, was also aimed at "fostering communication"; its volunteers worked with their hosts on public improvement projects in African communities. President Kennedy later credited the small-scale Crossroads program with being the "progenitor of the Peace Corps."
>
> The first government-connected program of this type was the International Volunteer Service. I.V.S. was founded by an interdenominational religious group in 1953, in response to a plea by foreign aid officials for private support. I.V.S. coordinated private technical assistance programs under government contract or private donation, and sent teams of young Americans into Laos, Vietnam, Egypt, and elsewhere, to teach agriculture and home economics.
>
> The list of such private "progenitors" over the past half century could be greatly expanded. Most resembled the Peace Corps only in their concern for foreign development, for they were essentially financial assistance programs; those few which did feature volunteer teams of young people (e.g., Operation Crossroads Africa) did not have them actually "living in" a host community for any length of time, as part of its middle-level technicians.[39]

Policymakers may consider themselves lucky when, trying to solve a problem, they discover a *simpler* analogous problem. Take our frequently used example of rising health costs. The consideration of a simpler analogous problem—namely, shipping fees of railroads and trucks—led policymakers to start thinking about cost containment in the complex milieu of modern medicine.

One more point about analogical reasoning must be made. Analogy can sometimes provide the basis for those policies we termed inventive. The crucial criterion is this: Analogies used in branching are obvious and mundane—one need look no further than cost containment in health

---

[39] George Sullivan, *The Story of the Peace Corps* (New York: Fleet Publishing Corporation, 1964), p. 23.

care for an example—but analogies used in inventive policy require nonobvious connections. Inventive policies yoke together remote entities.

The ability to make such connections is not common and is indeed one of the hallmarks of creativity in any endeavor. But at least two other conditions are required: a knowledge base and a positive atmosphere. Having relevant knowledge does not guarantee creativity, but it is certainly important. It may provide the analogy that helps the policymakers form a solution. The chief requirement for a positive in the atmosphere is that alternative generation and criticism must be separate. Policymakers must turn off the inner voice of criticism during the phase of alternative generation.

Both conditions were clearly visible in what Winston Churchill once called "the most unsordid act in history," the Marshall Plan.[40] In 1947, the Truman administration faced the threat of economic collapse of war-devastated Europe. Secretary of State George C. Marshall asked the head of his policy planning staff, George Frost Kennan, to make some recommendations on what should be done.

Kennan's talent—which was considerable—was the ability to take hold of a notion and see all of its parts in relation to one another; he could grasp both broad generalities and specifics, and relate them all to one another. Kennan quickly assembled a group that included Charles Bohlen, aged forty-three, who had been in the Foreign Service for eighteen years and, like Kennan, was a specialist in Russian affairs; Carlton Savage, aged forty-nine, who had been in the department for twenty years and was chosen to become the executive secretary of the new planning staff; John Davies, aged thirty-nine, an old China hand who had more recently been assigned to Moscow; Joseph Johnson, former professor of history, more recently chief of the Division of International Security Affairs; Burton Berry, aged forty-six, a nineteen-year veteran in the Foreign Service, most recently on assignment in Eastern Europe; James Angell, aged forty-nine, a professor of economics from Columbia University; and George McGhee, aged thirty-five, a former Rhodes scholar, most recently serving as special assistant to Will Clayton.[41] The remarkable thing about this group was the wealth of knowledge and experience it contained. No young whiz-kids here.

As leader of the group, Kennan seems to have made it quite clear to the members that open-minded debate was to be encouraged. In his *Memoirs* he gives us an inkling of what went on by quoting a synthetic

[40] Quoted in J. M. Jones, *The Fifteen Weeks* (New York: Viking Press, 1955), p. 256.
[41] Charles L. Mee, Jr., *The Marshall Plan* (New York: Simon & Schuster, 1984), pp. 87–88.

example of the sort of debate that preceded the formulation of the plan:

> You say: "This shouldn't be so difficult. Why don't we tell these people to draw up a plan for the reconstruction of their economic life and submit it to us and we'll see whether we can support it or not?"
>
> That starts it off. Someone says: "That's no good. They are too tired to draw up a plan. We have to do it for them."
>
> Someone else says: "Even if they do draw up a plan, they wouldn't have the internal economic discipline to carry it out. The Communists would spike it."
>
> Someone else says: "Oh, it isn't the Communists who would spike it— it is the local business circles."
>
> Then someone says: "Maybe what we need isn't a plan at all. Maybe we just haven't given them enough in the past. If we just give them more, things will work out all right."
>
> Another then says: "That's probably true, but we've got to figure out how the money is going to be spent. Congress just won't pour money down any more ratholes."
>
> Then somebody says: "That's right; we need a program. We've got to figure out just what's to be done with the money and make sure that it does the whole job this time."
>
> To that someone else replies: "Ah, yes, but it would be a mistake for us to try to draw this program up all by ourselves. The Commies would just take potshots at it and the European governments would shrug off the responsibility."
>
> Then someone says: "That's absolutely right. The thing for us to do is to tell these Europeans to draw up a plan and submit it to us and we'll see whether we can support it or not."
>
> And then you ask: "Didn't somebody say that before?" And we're off again.[42]

The group would eventually present Secretary Marshall with a proposal for supplying American funds to aid European recovery. Not only did the plan prevent the crisis from worsening but it also enabled England, France, Italy, West Germany, and other allies to restore their economic vitality.

Try something. "But above all try something." These five words were spoken by Franklin Roosevelt, and they encapsulate another important heuristic method. In the face of complexity, try something. Suppose that we are running a school for hyperactive children. We want to run it so that the children learn as much as possible but finding out what is best for them is a complicated problem. Should we emphasize discipline or freedom, physical activity or sitting quietly, the carrot and the stick, warmth and affection, or what? Since our school is small,

---

[42] George F. Kennan, *Memoirs* (1925-1950). (New York: Bantam, 1969), pp. 345-46.

we cannot afford a massive research program, but we can "try something." We take a single step by varying a single factor at a time (e.g., physical activity) while keeping other aspects of the school program constant. If academic performance improves, we accept this step and try a new step. We continue to improve the school by taking the steps that help and rejecting those that do not until we run out of things to change.[43]

Thomas J. Peters and Robert H. Waterman, Jr., in their influential *In Search of Excellence: Lessons from America's Best-Run Companies,* maintain that excellent companies exhibit a willingness to try things out, to experiment. "Learning and progress accrue only when there is *something* to learn from, and the something, the stuff of learning and progress, is any completed action. . . . There is absolutely no magic in the experiment. It is simply a tiny completed action, a manageable test that helps you learn something, just as in high school chemistry."[44]

In March 1961, President Kennedy established the Peace Corps by Executive Order on a "temporary pilot basis"; this was six months prior to Congress passing legislation that would make the Peace Corps a permanent agency. Edwin Bayley, who had been hired to be the agency's director of public information, recalls this early period:

> The moment I showed up (in late February), they gave me a desk, a typewriter and several documents and told me to write the executive order declaring the formation of the Peace Corps. What's it going to do? I asked, foolishly. That's for you to figure out from those papers, they said. The documents were the Reuss bill, the Humphrey bill, a transcript of Kennedy's remarks at Michigan—just a sentence or two—the Albertson study (and) an ICA study by a team headed by Warren Wiggins.[45]

Unfortunately, government does not always remember how to test and learn; sometimes they seem to prefer analysis and debate to trying something out. When considering different transit plans, cities will hire consultants for several hundred thousand dollars to do computer simulations and other paper studies of their options. But they may have gotten better, faster, and cheaper results by actually running small pilot experiments.

Means-ends analysis. This technique suggests that we reach our goal by taking a sequence of steps, each of which reduces the distance to the goal (the end). Sherlock Holmes solved not a few cases by a process of reasoning backward or means-ends analysis. The most com-

---

[43] Example from John R. Hayes, *Cognitive Psychology: Thinking and Creating* (Chicago: Dorsey Press, 1978), pp. 186–87.

[44] Thomas J. Peters and Robert H. Waterman, Jr., *In Search of Excellence: Lessons from America's Best-Run Companies* (New York: Harper & Row, 1982), p. 134.

[45] Polsby, *Political Innovation.*

prehensive explication of this particular way of thinking is given in *A Study of Scarlet:*

> In solving a problem of this sort, the grand thing is to be able to reason backward. That is a very useful accomplishment, and a very easy one, but people do not practice it much. In the everyday affairs it is more useful to reason forward, and so the other comes to be neglected. There are fifty who can reason [forward] for one who can reason [backward]. . . . Let me see if I can make it clear. Most people, if you describe a train of events to them, will tell you what the result will be. They can put those events together in their mind, and argue from them that something will come to pass. There are few people, however, who, if you told them a result, would be able to evolve from their inner consciousness what the steps were which led up to that result. This power is what I mean when I talk of reasoning backward. . . .[46]

With apologies to Holmes, we will illustrate the workings of means-ends analysis through a crude experiment with an ape in a cage. Imagine a banana is tied high up off the ground in the center of the cage. Off to one side, stage right, rests a long stick; on the other side of the cage stands the ape. Besides eating bananas, the ape can do these three things: grasp, walk, and hit things with a stick.

The ape's first goal (end) is to obtain the banana, but he cannot grasp it because of the large horizontal distance (remember: he is on the opposite side of the cage) and vertical distance (remember: the banana is hanging from the roof of the cage). Therefore, he sets up a subgoal to reduce the horizontal distance between him and the banana. The *means* for this is ability to walk. Next he establishes another subgoal: to reduce the long vertical distance between him and the banana. The *means* for this is his ability to hit with the stick. Now, with the banana at his feet, he establishes a third and final goal: reduce short vertical distance between the banana and his mouth. His *means* for this is his ability to grasp. The most impressive thing about the ape's performance is its ability to establish sequences of subgoals in order to overcome difficulties encountered in a direct approach to solution.

Means-ends analysis, which our ape illustrates in a crude fashion, has been embodied in a computer program that has considerable problem-solving power and generality. The program, called General Problem Solver (GPS), has solved a variety of problems including logic proofs, trigonometric identities, formal integration, and series extrapolation.[47]

Let us now leave the ape in his cage, content with his banana and

---

[46] Arthur Conan Doyle, *A Study in Scarlet* (New York: Ballantine Books, 1975), p. 136.

[47] Allen Newell and Herbert A. Simon, *Human Problem Solving* (Englewood Cliffs, N.J.: Prentice-Hall, 1972).

proud of his performance, and carry the discussion of means-ends analysis back to the policy arena.

Today much of the focus of poverty debate is on budgeting matters. Means-ends analysis could change that focus to the extent that it forces policymakers to think about the final subgoals prior to the elimination of the dole. In those stages, the primary responsibility for extricating the able-bodied poor from poverty rests with the poor themselves, while the function of government will be to help them do so. This analysis does not preclude federal activism in ensuring opportunity but suggests that such activism should be directed at empowering the poor to make choices, such as deciding what school they want to send their children to and what neighborhood they want to live in. Externally imposed solutions, such as tucking the poor away in housing projects and providing schools of abominable quality, change nothing.

Means-ends analysis requires the analysts to face squarely such end game issues as lax law enforcement and educational standards. Above all it requires a desire to argue *backward* from a society in which the dole has in fact been eliminated instead of arguing forward from an already held position.

Decomposition. To solve a complex problem, one powerful heuristic method is to discover ways of decomposing it into semi-independent components. The solution of each component problem can then be carried out with some degree of independence of the solution of the others, since each will affect the others largely through its objectives and independently of the details of the actions that accomplish those objectives.

As World War II drew to a close, the U.S. government began to face a set of problems concerning its relationship to science that, in some respects, were unprecedented. To what extent would government continue to pay for the development of science? Who would set research priorities? To tackle these problems all at once would be indeed difficult.

In November 1944, President Roosevelt wrote his chief science adviser Vannevar Bush a letter that would set in motion an investigation that would lead to the establishment of a National Science Foundation. In the letter Roosevelt asked Bush four key questions:

- How could scientific knowledge developed during the war be released quickly?
- How could medical research be facilitated?
- How could the government assist research by other organizations?
- Could a program of scientific education or training be developed?

Bush immediately responded to the letter by forming four task forces of scientists, government officials, and educators to address each question and report back to him. From their reports—or, more accurately, a synthesis of these reports—evolved Bush's recommendation for a National Science Foundation.[48]

When and how much one uses decomposition are open questions. How far development of solutions to components will be carried before the overall policy is developed in detail—or how far the overall policy should be carried before various components are developed—will depend on the problem and the policymaker. These important questions are familiar to architects and composers.

Wolfgang Amadeus Mozart once described his manner of composing in a letter:

> All this fires my soul, and provided I am not disturbed, my subject enlarges itself, becomes methodized and defined, and the whole, though it be long, stands almost complete and finished in my mind, so that I can survey it, like a fine picture or a beautiful statue, at a glance. Nor do I hear in my imagination the parts successively, but I hear them, as it were, all at once. What a delight this is I cannot tell!

To hear in a single instant an entire original composition seems incredible. While Mozart's scores seldom contained erased passages, Beethoven's sketch books suggest a painful creative process. This is illustrated in Figure 6–2. American composer Walter Piston apparently had yet another approach to creation. He once told a friend that he had completed a new piece. "Can I hear it, then?" his friend asked. "Oh, no," Piston replied, "I haven't yet selected the notes." Apparently, Piston meant he had planned the structure of the piece in the abstract—the number of movements, shifts in tempo, and so on—but had still to decide on specific vehicles with which to carry out his conception.[49]

A cognitive scientist is likely to say that these creative individuals have a general schema—an abstract mental representation of what a composition should be. This schema is sufficiently general to apply to a variety of works. Some "slots" of the schema are relatively inflexible, while others are quite flexible and may be entirely different from one case to another. The process may be described as "top-down" (rather than "bottom-up"). That is, we do not assume that a composition begins afresh with the first element and then proceeds moment-to-moment until the finale.

These same variations in approach to creation are evident in public policy. The contribution of Kennan's group was not the comprehensive and detailed Marshall Plan but three design criteria:

---

[48] Polsby, *Political Innovation*, pp. 92–56.
[49] Howard Gardner, *Frames of Mind: The Theory of Multiple Intelligences* (New York: Basic Books, 1983), pp. 99–127.

Figure 6–2
The creative process: Mozart (top) and Beethoven (bottom) compared

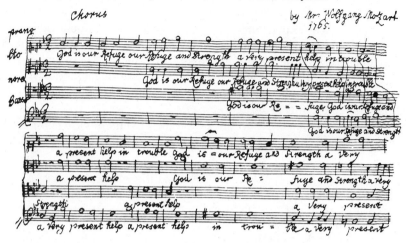

Source: The Bettmann Archive.

1. The principle that the Europeans should themselves take the initiative in drawing up a program and should assume central responsibility for its terms.
2. The offer should be made to all of Europe—that if anyone was to divide the European continent, it should be the Russians, with their response, not we with our offer.
3. The decisive emphasis on the rehabilitation of the German economy and introduction of the concept of German recovery as a vital component of the recovery of Europe as a whole.[50]

Others, in Europe and the U.S. government, would fill in the slots of Kennan's schema.

The Tax Reform Act of 1986 offers a more recent example of architectonics, or structural design, in policy formulation. One of the principles that tax reformers settled on early was "revenue neutrality," on the theory that a radical rewrite of the tax code would be difficult enough without getting it tangled up in the debate over whether the government should raise its total tax take in order to reduce deficits.

Synectics. It is appropriate that our discussion of decomposition and architectonics be followed by a consideration of synthesis or the joining together of apparently unrelated elements. This heuristic method is cross-cutting, that is, it can be used, and sometimes must be, in conjunction with other heuristics. For example, in William J. Gordon's book *Synectics*, the main goal is to teach people to make use of analogies in problem solving.

In 1965, two proposals for some kind of health program came before the House Ways and Means Committee. One of these was the King-Anderson bill which included a year of hospital care, nursing home care, or visiting nurse service, financed through the social security system for all those over sixty-five; it did not include surgery, physicians' fees, or drugs.

The ranking Republican on Ways and Means, John W. Byrnes, offered the other proposal. To prevent the Democrats from getting all the credit for a bill that was clearly going to pass, Byrnes called for subsidies to enable elderly persons to buy private insurance policies. The program would be federal both in financing and administration; the means test for participation was eliminated, but premium charges would be based on beneficiaries' incomes. Byrnes could rightly claim that his benefits were far broader than those of the King-Anderson bill, since they included drugs and doctors' and surgeons' fees.

Thus the committee, headed by Wilbur Mills, was presented with

---

[50] Kennan, *Memoirs*, p. 361.

338

two mutually exclusive alternatives. Then something surprising happened. Theodore R. Marmos tells the story:

> HEW officials were exhausted from weeks of questioning and redrafting, and viewed the discussion of the Byrnes bill as a time for restful listening. But Mills, instead of posing a choice between the two bills, unexpectedly suggested a combination which involved extracting Byrnes' benefit plan from his financing proposal. On March 2, Mills turned to HEW's Wilbur Cohen and calmly asked whether such a "combination" were possible. Cohen was "stunned," and initially suspicious that the suggestion was a plot to kill the entire administration proposal. No mention had even been made of such innovations. Cohen had earlier argued for what he called a "three-layer cake" reform by Ways and Means: H.R. 1's hospital program first, private health insurance for physicians' coverage, and an expanded Kerr-Mills program "underneath" for the indigent among the aged. Mills' announcement that the committee appeared to have "gotten to the point where it is possible to come up with a medi-elder-Byrnes bill" posed a surprise possibility for a different kind of combination. That night, in a memorandum to the president, Cohen reflected on Mills' "ingenious plan," explaining that a proposal which put "together in one bill features of all three of the major" alternatives before the committee would make Medicare "unassailable politically from any serious Republican attack." Convinced now that Mills' strategy was not destructive, Cohen was delighted that the Republican charges of inadequacy had been used by Mills to prompt the expansion of H.R. 1.[51]

Marmon explains the significance of this artful synthesis of two quite different bills:

> By changing from opponent to manager, Mills assured himself control of the content of H.R. 1 at a time when it could have been pushed through the Congress despite him. By encouraging innovation, and incorporating more generous benefits into the legislation, Mills undercut claims that his committee had produced an "inadequate" bill. . . . Mills's conception of himself as the active head of an autonomous, technically expert committee helps to explain his interest in shaping legislation he could no longer block, and his preoccupation with cautious financing of the social security system made him willing to combine benefit and financing arrangements that had been presented as mutually exclusive alternatives. The use of general revenues and beneficiary premiums in the financing of physicians' service insurance made certain the aged and the federal treasury, not the social security trust funds, would have to finance any benefit changes. In an interview during the summer of 1965, Mills explained that inclusion of medical insurance would "build a fence around the Medicare program" and forestall subsequent demands for liberalization that "might be a burden on the economy and the social security program."[52]

---

[51] Theodore R. Marmon, *The Politics of Medicare* (Chicago: Aldine, 1970), pp. 64–65.
[52] Ibid., p. 69.

Thought experiments. Many creative people use analogical thinking deliberately and consciously as a way of generating insights and discoveries. Einstein's *Gedanken* (thought) experiments are a case in point. In one of the most celebrated of these, he visualized himself as a passenger riding on a ray of light and holding a mirror in front of him. From this fanciful analogy of physical events, Einstein gained insight that led him to deduce his special theory of relativity.

It is easy to see how such an analogy can be valuable in generating insight into societal problems. William Raspberry is a syndicated columnist based in Washington, who specializes in black affairs. Recently he suggested this thought experiment: assume that, by devoting all our efforts and resources to its removal, we are finally able to lay racism to rest. What then?

> Obviously we'd have to do something else. Simply removing racism would put most of black America in exactly the same situation that low-income whites are in today. In other words, the end of racism wouldn't solve black problems; it would only make the solutions possible.
>
> So, assuming success in the elimination of racism, the immediate question would be: What is the next step in order to turn this new opportunity into practical gain? There are a thousand answers to that question, many of them worthy of serious national debate. But I have another question: Why don't we just move directly to the next step right now?
>
> And what might some of those next steps be?
>
> For some, the next step might consist of helping people to overcome the deleterious effects of past racism; cultural, attitudinal, educational and otherwise. For others, it might be to help the jobless find work, perhaps by fashioning tax programs and other incentives for the private sector to hire more of the hard-core unemployed; perhaps by rewarding employers who give enthusiastic youngsters a chance to show what they can do, even if potential doesn't reveal itself in written tests. For still others, it might be to prepare young blacks to take advantage of the post-racism opportunities: by encouraging them to take their education seriously, by remodeling their behavior, by postponing short-term pleasure in the interests of longer-term goals.
>
> For some, the logical next step might be to address the black economic situation.
>
> Blacks might, for instance, be encouraged to pool their resources to launch their entrepreneurially minded brothers and sisters into businesses that would make it possible to retain some of the considerable economic muscle of the black community *in* the black community, thereby creating both wealth and jobs.
>
> Or, they might, more conservatively, consider enhancing black economic leverage by concentrating their capital—including the Sunday morning collections of black churches—in specific institutions, perhaps black-owned institutions, which could then be the source of business and mortgage loans for blacks.

The possibilities of "next steps" are subject only to the limits of imagination. The point is: Why not take those steps now, without waiting for the problematical demise of racism?

The model I have in mind is that of West Coast Asian-Americans who, if they had waited for the end of anti-Oriental prejudice, might still be living in poverty, rather than outstripping white Americans in education and income, as they in fact are. They still suffer from race prejudice, but they suffer in relative comfort.

Unfortunately, the current model seems closer to that of the Indian reservation, with the emphasis on the level of funding of, and the degree of sympathy manifested by, the Bureau of Indian Affairs.

The truth—far easier to see on the reservations than in the ghettos—is that even if you could assure that every Indian on the reservation were given the most nutritional food, warm clothing freely supplied, and permanent, centrally heated and cooled housing, the result would be not salvation but cultural, spiritual, and economic genocide.[53]

Groupthink

"How could I have been so stupid?" President Kennedy asked after realizing how badly he had miscalculated when he approved the Bay of Pigs invasion of Cuba. Every policymaker has his or her own Bay of Pigs. Often the explanation for such mistakes lies in the personal errors discussed earlier. But policymakers usually operate in a group setting—task forces, committees, executive committees, cabinets, commissions, study groups, etc. And there the problem may lie.

Group cohesion sometimes results in a loss of willingness and ability among group members to evaluate one another's ideas and suggestions critically. Desire to retain cohesion, to hold the group together and avoid unpleasant disagreements, leads to an overemphasis on agreement and an underemphasis on the critical appraisal of alternatives. Irving Janis of Yale University calls this tendency *groupthink*. He identifies eight symptoms of groupthink:

1. Illusions of group invulnerability. Members of the group feel it is basically beyond criticism or attack.
2. Rationalizing unpleasant and disconfirming data. Refusal to accept contradictory data or to consider alternatives thoroughly.
3. Belief in inherent group morality. Members of the group feel it is "right" and above any reproach by outsiders.
4. Stereotyping competitors as weak, evil, and stupid. Refusal to look realistically at other groups.

---

[53] William Raspberry, "Forget Racism and Move onto the Next Step," *Houston Chronicle,* November 18, 1984.

5. Applying direct pressure to deviants to conform to group wishes. Refusal to tolerate a member who suggests the group may be wrong.
6. Self-censorship by members. Refusal by members to communicate personal concerns to the group as a whole.
7. Illusions of unanimity. Accepting consensus prematurely, without testing its completeness.
8. Mind guarding. Members of the group protect the group from hearing disturbing ideas or viewpoints from outsiders.[54]

When and if a group experiences groupthink, Janis recommends the following actions to avoid a potential fiasco:

- Encourage a sharing of viewpoints.
- Avoid, as leader, seeming partial to one particular alternative.
- Establish subgroups to work on the problem and then share their proposed solution.
- Have members discuss issues with outsiders and report back on the reaction they got.
- Invite knowledgeable outsiders to observe group activity. (During the Cuban missile crises, Kennedy had former Secretary of State Dean Acheson sit in on the deliberations of the Executive Committee of his National Security Council.)
- Assign one member to play "devil's advocate."[55]

CHECKING THE ASSESSMENT

We must now pause briefly to survey the ground we have been covering. In the preceding chapter, we introduced the important idea of goal setting and said that alternative courses of action (programs) ought to be selected with the goals set firmly in mind. Goals determine alternatives.

Alternatives, as we saw in this chapter, come roughly in three categories: incremental, branching, and inventive. At this juncture in the formulation of public policy, the analyst and policymaker will probably find themselves confronted with the problem of selection. Which alternatives should become elements in the policy? Though no computer program has yet been written that would answer that question, a number of guidelines have proven useful over time.

1. Are the objectives of the plan explicit? Were any special problems, either conceptual or practical, encountered in specifying an adequate set of quantifiable

---

[54] Irving Janis, *Groupthink* (Boston: Houghton Mifflin, 1982), pp. 174–75.
[55] Ibid., pp. 260–76.

measures of success for each objective? Are the objectives operational, that is, capable of becoming the basis for work and achievement?

Everyone—well, at least policy analysts—would like to believe in a fairytale world of consensus and cooperation. Unfortunately, the political realities of conflicts of interest, differences in personal ambitions, and scarcity of resources keep trampling through. For this reason, formal statements of objectives may have to be intentionally ambiguous to obtain a consensus on action. Value judgments underlying the objectives may not be shared by important groups: consequently, the end results intended may be perceived by some as implying ill effects for them. Explicit statements of objectives tend to imply a specific assignment of priorities and a commitment of resources.

Having registered that warning, we can now turn to what objectives should be. To the extent feasible, statements of objectives should: (1) capture a complete understanding of the intended benefits; (2) identify recipients of unavoidable adverse consequences or unintended benefits; (3) include important qualitative aspects, even though measuring degrees of attainment may be exceedingly difficult; and (4) take account of multiple objectives which may be complementary or conflicting.

Oversimplified statements of objectives may result if activity milestones are contained in them (e.g., to increase the number of emergency rooms by 20 percent by 1990). Objectives stated in this way may overly constrain an assessment of alternatives, the purpose of which is to determine efficient levels of attainment of an ultimate benefit (e.g., good health). But objectives must be specific with respect to the nature and direction of change so that progress can be measured. A statement such as "to reduce deaths, additional complications, disability, and suffering of persons with acute injuries by improving emergency care" would satisfy these criteria. Quantitative goals or targets are also needed, but these must reflect priorities among plans and programs. Accordingly, they can best be set as part of the budget and long-range financial planning process and should be reexamined regularly as budget priorities shift. Box 6–4 shows a number of measures used in transportation policy.

In appraising results of ongoing programs, if targets or activity milestones have been furnished to managers, the targets or milestones should not be accepted uncritically (e.g., a specified student/teacher ratio). An attempt should be made to find out whether deficiencies in attaining the milestones are caused by unrealistic expectations or by the way the program was implemented or operated.

Nor should objectives become straitjackets. Peter Drucker offers an illuminating analogy:

> The proper way to use objectives is the way an airline uses schedules and flight plans. The schedule provides for the 9 A.M. flight from Los Angeles

Box 6–4

Performance measures for transportation policy

The table below summarizes some of the more important performance measures of the nation's transportation system that have been identified by the U.S. Department of Transportation for measurement and reporting by state and local governments. These provide a basis for understanding how our nation's transportation facilities are currently performing, how they are expected to perform in the future, and how that performance might vary among the states and urban areas. When collected and examined over a period of time, this information permits the evaluation of particular investment programs and policies in terms of changes in system performance.

Highways

1. Freeway capacity measures.
2. Average travel speeds.
3. Congestion levels on freeways.
4. Amounts of total highway travel occurring on freeways.
5. Average trip lengths (time and distance).
6. Accident injuries and fatalities.
7. Population and job dislocation from highway construction.
8. Pollutant output levels.

Urban public transportation

1. Accessibility of residential population.
2. Average operating speed.
3. Average vehicle occupancy.
4. Fleet utilization.
5. Fares.

Marine terminals

1. Cargo (tons and number of containers) handled per day.
2. Cargo handled during peak day of the year (by type).
3. Average number of weeks per year port is closed by ice.
4. Number of ferry passengers served during peak day of year.

Airports: Air carrier (A/C) or reliever airports serving hubs

1. Annual and peak-hour passenger enplanements.
2. Peak-hour delay per operation.
3. Access time from central business district to airport.
4. Out-of-pocket cost to travel from central business district to airport.
5. Distance to nearest alternative A/C airport.
6. Population and jobs relocated as a result of future airport construction or modification.

Box 6–4 *(concluded)*

7. Population and jobs within thirty minutes driving time of each primary system airport.
8. Noise exposure within the thirty and forty NEF contours (number of residents and employees).

Source: U.S. Department of Transportation (1975: 51–52).

---

to get to Boston by 5 P.M. But if there is a blizzard in Boston that day, the plane will land in Pittsburgh instead and wait out the storm. The flight plan provides for flying at 30,000 feet and for flying over Denver and Chicago. But if the pilot encounters turbulence or strong headwinds he will ask flight control for permission to go up another 5,000 feet and to take the Minneapolis-Montreal route. Yet no flight is ever operated without schedule and flight plan. Any change is immediately fed back to produce a new schedule and flight plan. Unless 97 percent or so of its flights proceed on the original schedule and flight plan—or within a very limited range of deviation from either—a well-run airline gets another operations manager who knows his job.[56]

In sum, "Objectives are not fate; they are direction. They are not commands; they are commitments. They do not determine the future; they are means to mobilize the resources and energies of the business for the making of the future"[57] Determining valid objectives is a complex and frustrating task. A study may have to proceed without fully satisfying these requirements. If this is the case, objectives should be reexamined and clarified as the study progresses.

2. Were any potentially interesting alternatives eliminated early in the analysis? If so, why? Under what circumstances might they become attractive? To what assumptions or data is the ranking of the alternatives sensitive? Are there any actions which can make the leading alternatives significantly less affected by the uncertainties? Is it likely that additional information about the leading alternatives would change the ranking? How, when, and at what cost could this information be obtained? Can the policy or program decisions be held open while new studies, evaluation, or research efforts are completed?

One of the most important elements in any search for alternatives is to know when to stop. George Bernard Shaw summed it up well: "The open mind never acts: when we have done our utmost to arrive

---

[56] Peter Drucker, *Management: Tasks, Responsibilities, Practices* (New York: Harper & Row, 1974), pp. 101–102.
[57] Ibid., p. 102.

at a reasonable conclusion, we still, when we can reason and investigate no more, must close our minds for the moment with a snap, and act dogmatically on our conclusions. The man who waits to make an entirely reasonable will dies intestate." It was recognition of this element that led Herbert Simon to develop the concept of *satisficing*.

We need to peel away a few outer layers of the satisficing model to see its assumptions more clearly. The core is this: the benefits of analysis must be balanced against the costs of analysis to determine whether an analysis should be done in the first place and, if it is done, how complete it should be. John Rawls states the rule more directly: "we should deliberate up to the point where the likely benefits from improving our plan are just worth the time and effect of reflection."[58]

Because the rule is so important, I would like to develop it a bit more. The rule tells us that the analysis of public policy should begin or that the analysis of a decision problem should continue only as long as the expected benefits of analysis exceed the expected costs of analysis. The expected benefits of analysis depend on two factors: the probability that the analysis will yield a different decision (p) and the difference between the value, that is, "the expected utility," of this decision and the value of the decision that would otherwise have been made (d). The expected benefits of the analysis equal p times d. If the cost of the analysis is c, then the net benefits of the analysis will be p times d minus c. Therefore, a decision maker should begin or continue to analyze a decision problem as long as the decision maker thinks that $pd > c$ (i.e., that p times d exceeds c). In the $pd > c$ rule, we have the mathematical formulation of Simon's satisficing.

How can the $pd > c$ rule be used? For an analyst used to thinking in terms of this rule, it will probably become second nature. But conscious and deliberate use of the rule will sometimes be helpful in deciding whether to make some incomplete analysis a bit more complete. That is, a decision maker might use the rule to decide whether it is worthwhile to consider an additional course of action or gather some additional information. In any event, the decision maker will probably use the rule in a rough, verbal way. In particular, p might be estimated by phrases such as *fair chance, less than likely,* or *virtually certain; d* might be estimated by phrases such as *hardly any difference* or *substantially better;* and c might be estimated by phrases such as *little costs* or *very expensive.*

3. Do the alternatives have an appropriate time horizon?

A significant part of every analysis is the time horizon on which it is based. A well-formulated alternative not only reveals what objectives

---

[58] John Rawls, *A Theory of Justice* (Cambridge, Mass.: Harvard University Press, 1971).

are to be accomplished but also says something about *when* they are to be achieved. Offering a new service, opening a new office, or expanding an existing service becomes a significant strategic objective only if it is accomplished by a certain time: delay may drain it of all strategic significance.

Objectives must, however, be established far enough in advance to allow the organization to adjust to them. The larger the organization, the farther its strategic time horizon must extend, since its adjustment time is longer. The force of the rule also helps explain why new programs sometimes require new organizations or contracts.

The analysis should be careful not to examine the consequences of the alternative against a static environment. The efficacy of alternatives must be judged with respect to the environment *as it appears to be changing*. The forecasting methods introduced in Chapter 4 can be of help. The question of precisely how—that is, what the procedure is for examining alternatives in the context of tomorrow's society—will be addressed later. (See Chapter 8.)

An appropriate time horizon suggests that policymakers eschew a penny-wise, pound-foolish approach. For example, given a choice between rapid adjustment of the national economy to changes in the world market or protection of the national economy from the world market, liberals will be tempted to opt for the latter. Protection can be achieved through tariffs, quotas, marketing agreements, bailouts, business tax breaks, restrictions on factory closings, "enterprise zones" in which minimum wages are reduced, and wage concessions by labor unions. These measures will save some American jobs in the short run. But in the long run they will erode the real incomes of Americans. We will become a nation of assemblers, extractors, and retailers—poor by the standards of the rest of the world.

On the other hand, given a choice between tough spending cuts to reduce a massive deficit or tax increases to maintain programs that are cost-effective, conservatives will be tempted . . . well, you know.

Emphasis on the bottom line in domestic policy by the Reagan administration in the mid-1980s led to several potentially costly errors in long-run decisions. Rather than stockpile oil in the Strategic Petroleum Reserve when it was cheap, the administration called for a moratorium on purchases. Others worried about the long-term social costs of abolishing the Job Corps: Would it deprive disadvantaged youth of a much-needed way to get into the workforce?

4. Is the alternative workable? Are sufficient resources available? Is there a contingency plan?

A word that should be in every policy planner's lexicon is *hubris*. According to *Webster's New International Dictionary* (2d ed., unabridged), it means "wanton insolence or arrogance resulting from excessive pride or from passion." When studies are being worked out with paper and pencil, the difficulties in meeting the program objectives in a world of people holding conflicting values and charged with different signs of the zodiac can be forgotten.

Still, program objectives should be challenging. The problem then is one of knowing how high to set aspirations; but for this no calculus exists. At a minimum, however, analysts must try to determine the degree of consensus on objectives within the organization that must administer the program and whether the organization has the necessary competence to carry out the program.

The analysts must also examine the relevant legal constraints. Laws, property rights, international conventions, agency rulings, and so on can reduce any list of feasible solutions. It takes time and due process to build superhighways through people's living rooms; it often takes legislative, executive, and judicial action for rules to be made or broken.

Further, the analysts must ask unflinchingly whether the resources needed to make the program a success are available. Raising this question cuts against the grain of much policy planning in government, where the general tendency is to look only a year ahead.

But well-thought-out public policy requires procedures that force policymakers to look several years ahead. Significantly, the Congressional Budget and Impoundment Control Act of 1974 takes a first small step in this direction by requiring that the Congressional Budget Office estimate five-year costs of all bills reported out of congressional committees, that outlay projections accompany appropriation bills, and that reports on any tax expenditure legislation include five-year projections of revenue losses. Finally, at the start of each fiscal year the CBO is required to report on spending, taxing, surplus or deficit, and tax expenditures for each of the next five years. Unfortunately, all this information did not prevent huge budget deficits in the 1980s.

As a final check it is useful, if not imperative, to play the what-if-game or, to put it more formally, engage in contingency planning. In Chapter 10 we will consider specific methods for trying to disaster-proof a policy.

5. Were all of the costs and risks captured? How reliable are the estimates? What is the range of uncertainty? Were side effects and distribution considerations adequately considered? Are there significant differences among the alternatives?

The fundamental reason why analysis is needed to clarify objectives probably reveals itself more in this final group of questions than in any other. It is simply impossible to define appropriate alternatives and objectives without knowledge about the benefits, the costs, and the risks associated with all of the alternatives and objectives that are under consideration. Because the questions involved in the consideration of benefits, costs, and risks are so important, I have chosen to treat them separately, and at some length, in the next chapter.

To sum up quickly. Modern government must deploy expensive and complex resources in the solution of tough problems and in the pursuit of transitory opportunities. The time required to develop resources is so extended, and the time scale of opportunities so brief, that an agency which has not carefully delineated and assessed its strategy is adrift in white water. In short, though a set of goals and objectives that meets the criteria covered in this section does not guarantee success, it can, I think, be of considerable value in giving administrators time and room to maneuver.

FOR FURTHER REFLECTION

1. How have personal experiences shaped the worldview of recent presidents? How have such experiences shaped yours?
2. Government contracts with the private sector for an enormous amount of goods and services—from paper clips to policy studies to space stations. In recent years, some contractors have been charged with greatly inflating their prices. How can government ensure that it gets the most return for its dollars?
3. According to cognitive psychologists, the mind takes shortcuts in dealing with real-world problems too complicated for present day computers. But these shortcuts do not always serve us well. One shortcut is to judge the likelihood of something happening by how easy it is to call other examples of the same thing to mind. Does the letter K appear more often as the first letter in a word or the third letter? Because it is easier to recall words that begin with a letter than those that contain it somewhere in the middle, most people judge K commoner at the beginning. (Actually, K appears twice as often in the third position.) Based on the preceding discussion, explain why people overestimate the probability of airplane accidents, terrorist attacks in Europe, fires, murders, and meltdowns, and underestimate the risk of death from strokes and emphysema?
4. How might a market approach be used to:
   a. Improve the level of service in urban transportation.
   b. Allocate aircraft arrivals and departures at major airports.
   c. Protect domestic industry hurt by imports.
5. Using techniques suggested in this chapter, generate new alternatives for the three issues mentioned in the last question above.

Chapter 7

Costs, Benefits, and Risks

All government action involves cost, and most of it involves risks. The unfortunate thing is that, despite the costs and risks, no action guarantees policymakers benefits in return.

Thinking about costs, benefits, and risks is nothing new for policymakers. No doubt Joseph thought in these categories when he advised the Pharaoh on the storage of grain: take one fifth of the produce of Egypt during the seven years of plenty and put the corn under armed guard in the cities. This food would be a reserve for the country against the seven years of famine that followed.

Still, I doubt whether the Pharaoh's councillors ever dreamed of methods as sophisticated as those available to modern policy analysts. Just because sophisticated methods are available, however, it does not follow that they will be used. Consequently, present-day decision making is sometimes no better, and frequently even worse, than it was in Joseph's time.

Seeing the costs involved in a project does not require mathematical virtuosity, but it does demand a willingness to *think costs*. Considering the following examples will give you an idea of what I mean.

- The State Purchasing and General Services Commission of Texas decided to build a parking lot on property adjacent to the Capitol. The half-acre lot was purchased for $2.6 million. Demolition of a building already on it cost an additional $27,400, and the construction of the parking lot, which would provide fifty-four parking places, was $60,000. That means that the total cost per space was $51,618. Is this the modern equivalent of pyramid building?

- Here is another division problem. According to a 1985 report by the Office of Technology Assessment, disease and lost productivity due to smoking cost the United States $65 billion a year. The figure reflects medical costs, premature death, and time lost from work due to smoking-related disorders. That is more than $2 for every pack of cigarettes consumed, or $10 million dollars an hour.[1]

- Less than once a month, a handicapped person boards a bus in St. Louis using a wheelchair lift. With an annual lift-maintenance budget of around $532,000, that comes to about $44,000 a trip.[2] The justification for this enormous expense is equity for the handicapped.

It would be a disastrous mistake to interpret the prescription *think cost* to mean that we may safely ignore benefits. Nothing would get done by the government, and the public weal would suffer. Yet, by its very nature, many public undertakings such as building a canal or exploring space carry a large price tag; and in view of the cost and suffering, one can easily lose sight of the benefits. The decision whether to wage war is of course the quintessential example. It is not hard to agree with the words to the 1970 song by Barrett Strong and Norman Whitfield:

War
What is it good for
Absolutely nothing.

But easy agreement is not the way of the analyst—nor is mindless jingoism. Since crass appeals to economics (World War II ended the Depression, led to wide usage of penicillin, etc.) are inappropriate in this context, the analyst must frame the analytical question carefully. The crucial question seems to be this: Does "the destruction of innocent lives" and the "tears of thousands of mothers' eyes when their sons go out to fight to give their lives" somehow outweigh the lives of prisoners in Auschwitz or the cries of millions of blacks in the antebellum South?

Not so easy a question. Which brings us to what, for some, may be a disquieting revelation: Literature can at times give us a bigger piece of the answer than can facts and figures alone. In his Pulitzer Prize–winning novel about the Battle of Gettysburg, Michael Shaara puts one of his characters in a tough situation. Just before the battle, Colonel Chamberlain has assigned to his regiment a group of soldiers who have decided to fight no more.

> They were silent, watching him. Chamberlain began to relax. He had made many speeches and he had a gift for it. He did not know what it was, but when he spoke most men stopped to listen. Fanny said it was something in his voice. He hoped it was there now.

---

[1] U.S. Congress, Office of Technology Assessment, *Smoking-Related Deaths and Financial Costs*, staff memo (Washington, D.C.: Government Printing Office, September 1985).
[2] Jack Booth, "Accessible Transit: A Costly Issue," *Dallas Times Herald*, January 18, 1986.

"I've been ordered to take you men with me. I've been told that if you don't come I can shoot you. Well, you know I won't do that. Not Maine men. I won't shoot any man who doesn't want this fight. Maybe someone else will, but I won't. So that's that."

He paused again. There was nothing on their faces to lead him.

"Here's the situation. I've been ordered to take you along, and that's what I'm going to do. Under guard if necessary. But you can have your rifles if you want them. The whole Reb army is up the road a ways waiting for us and this is no time for an argument like this. I tell you this: we sure can use you. We're down below half strength and we need you, no doubt of that. But whether you fight or not is up to you. Whether you come along, well, you're coming."

Tom had come up with Chamberlain's horse. Over the heads of the prisoners Chamberlain could see the Regiment falling into line out in the flaming road. He took a deep breath.

"Well, I don't want to preach to you. You know who we are and what we're doing here. But if you're going to fight alongside us there's a few things I want you to know."

He bowed his head, not looking at eyes. He folded his hands together.

"This Regiment was formed last fall, back in Maine. There were a thousand of us then. There's not three hundred of us now." He glanced up briefly. "But what is left is choice."

He was embarrassed. He spoke very slowly, staring at the ground.

"Some of us volunteered to fight for Union. Some came in mainly because we were bored at home and this looked like it might be fun. Some came because we were ashamed not to. Many of us came . . . because it was the right thing to do. All of us have seen men die. Most of us never saw a black man back home. We think on that, too. But freedom . . . is not just a word."

He looked up in to the sky, over silent faces.

"This is a different kind of army. If you look at history you'll see men fight for pay, or women, or some other kind of loot. They fight for land, or because a king makes them, or just because they like killing. But we're here for something new. I don't . . . this hasn't happened much in the history of the world. We're an army going out to set other men free."

He bent down, scratched the black dirt into his fingers. He was beginning to warm to it; the words were beginning to flow. No one in front of him was moving. He said, "This is free ground. All the way from here to the Pacific Ocean. No man has to bow. No man born to royalty. Here we judge you by what *you* do, not by what your father was. Here you can be *something.* Here's a place to build a home. It isn't the land—there's always more land. It's the idea that we all have value, you and me, we're worth something more than the dirt. I never saw dirt I'd die for, but I'm not asking you to come join us and fight for dirt. What we're all fighting for, in the end, is each other."[3]

---

[3] Michael Shaara, *The Killer Angels* (New York: Ballantine Books, 1975), pp. 29–30.

CAPTURING ALL THE COSTS AND BENEFITS

Table 7–1 illustrates what might be called the first rule of selecting alternatives: try to consider *all* of the benefits and costs involved in a course of action. The rule, I must hasten to add, is far easier to state than to apply, for knowing which benefits and costs are relevant and how they should be valued can be quite difficult.

The matrix in Table 7–1 can be a powerful aid to the analyst who is trying to capture all the benefits and costs. To structure the discussion of this section, it is helpful to build around it. And to keep things as simple as possible, we will assume for now that all benefits and costs accrue at once—though in the next chapter we will see that the time dimension cannot be disregarded in actual practice.

Real benefits and pecuniary effects

The first distinction is between *(a)* benefits that increase consumer satisfactions (the community's welfare) or decrease the costs of the re-sources required to produce goods and services and *(b)* benefits that represent changes in some people's well-being at the expense of the well-being of other people (i.e., a redistribution of income).

An example should help clarify this most important distinction. If a new six-lane highway replaces a two-lane road that formerly connected cities A and B, then what are the *real* benefits of this project? Well, a number could be mentioned: reduced travel time and increased safety are perhaps the most apparent. But say that the new highway runs through C, whereas the two-lane road did not. Further assume that in C and adjacent to the highway is a five-year-old McDonald's. Very likely, the annual profits for this enterprise will go up. Question: Can these increased profits be counted as a real benefit of the project?

The answer is no, because no net welfare gain has occurred. If Herb, while traveling from his home in A to a park in B, stops at the McDonald's in C and spends $5 for food, the owners of the McDonald's in C would benefit by an increased profit, of course. But their gain would be a dollar-for-dollar loss to Herb.

To sum up, then, because no net welfare gains for the economy as a whole were present in our McDonald's example, we must consider the increased profits as *pecuniary effects*, not real benefits. And the general rule for the policy analyst is this: strictly pecuniary effects should be omitted in any estimates of the efficiency benefits of a proposed program or project.

I say "efficiency" benefits because, in certain cases, a major objective of a program could be to transfer a benefit from one group or area to another. In such cases, the pecuniary effects would be counted as a real benefit. So, once again, we see how very crucial a clear view of

Table 7–1
Cost-benefit matrix

		Benefits	*Costs*
Direct	Tangible		
	Intangible		
Indirect	Tangible		
	Intangible		
Pecuniary effects			

goals and objectives can be in the analysis of public policy. Indeed, an unambiguous statement of goals and objectives helps us not only to sort out real benefits from pecuniary effects but also to differentiate benefits and costs that are direct from benefits and costs that are indirect.

The direct and indirect categories

As one might guess, direct benefits and costs are those directly related to the main objective of the program; indirect (or secondary) benefits and costs are by-products.

The U.S. space program provides a mine of examples of indirect benefits (or "spin-offs" as they are called in the patois of NASA). The *direct* benefits of NASA research and development expenditures, as well as those of similar high-technology programs, are to increase the national well-being through direct applications of aerospace technology such as communications satellites and improved aircraft. But also significant are the indirect benefits that accrue along the way; these can be applied to many sectors of the economy.

Similarly, the Strategic Defense Initiative should have important consequences for national economic development, regardless of its national defense consequences. The technology used to create X-ray laser weapons could be applied to super-microscopes; the know-how garnered in designing particle accelerators could be applied to irradiating food products. Spinoffs and applications as yet unimaginable could create whole new generations of telecommunications and computer-related products that could underpin information-processing systems in the next century. Meanwhile, Japan is now aggressively pursuing commercial development of such technologies.[4]

---

[4] Malcolm W. Brown, "The Star Wars Spin-Offs," *New York Times Magazine*, August 24, 1986.

Unfortunately, in other areas of public policy, making the distinction between direct and indirect benefits becomes more difficult. But in all cases the first question must be, What does this activity seek to attain? To answer this, the analyst will probably need to carefully consider legislative intent.

To bring the issue into sharper focus, let us consider the case of legalized gambling. What the analyst counts as direct benefits depends on the objectives. The objective of maximizing tax revenues from gambling is by no means the same as the objective of eliminating illegal gambling in order to reduce corruption or the objective of minimizing government interference in the exercise of personal preferences. Therefore, given two programs legalizing gambling, effects counted as direct benefits for one of the programs might be indirect for the other.

Thus far we have been considering only benefits, but as was noted at the start, costs can also be dichotomized into direct and indirect categories. Indeed, when we fail to consider fully the right-hand column in our cost-benefit matrix, we are making public policy then become a kind of cargo cult—an assertion of faith that somehow government can see to it that everybody gets something for nothing.[5]

When analyzing costs, several types must be considered. The direct costs of an alternative include *capital costs,* that is, costs associated with the acquisition of equipment and facilities and *maintenance and operating costs* (often referred to as M&O), that is, resources consumed in operating an activity for a given period of time. Operating costs, or expenses, include labor costs, materials consumed, and services received.

A frequent tendency in policy debates is for the advocates of a particular program to underplay operating costs. For example, the Pentagon and Rockwell International, the prime contractor for the B-1 strategic bombers, were reluctant to give Congress or the public the detailed cost information that would allow intelligent assessment of the proposed program. The projected costs were not the cost of the full system, since they did not include the B-1's weapons or the cost of operating and maintaining the B-1 fleet. The Air Force, practicing its own version of a cargo cult, also asked for a new tanker whose primary task would have been to refuel the B-1; estimates for these items, however, were also kept separate.

Indirect costs also include those created for other government agencies and for society. Costs created for other agencies occur when agencies are given the free use of facilities no longer needed by the other agencies—for example, when it is proposed that a training school be estab-

---

[5] Cargo cults are religious movements that exhibit belief in the imminence of a new age of blessing, symbolized by the expected arrival of a special "cargo" of goods from supernatural sources.

lished on the site of an unused military base. Just because the training school is not required to rent the facility does not mean that the resource is free. Since alternative uses for the base probably exist (including its sale), an appropriate cost figure needs to be calculated. Similarly, a university might decide to launch a new degree program or establish a new center. The direct costs are probably obvious: additional facilities and staff. Less obvious would be the overload that the new program or center would create for, say, the university's fiscal office. A complete accounting of costs would not ignore these indirect costs.

It would be hard to think of a public program that involved no social costs. By social costs, we simply mean those that "spill over" onto groups in society other than the groups involved in the program. Additional expressways in urban areas are examples of how social costs arise. In addition to the direct costs of concrete and labor, a policy analyst must consider the social costs of additional air and noise pollution, increased congestion in downtown areas, increased urban sprawl, and continued difficulties for public transportation.

Environmental programs: A case study in measuring costs and benefits

How much does clean air cost? Some estimate that compliance with the Clean Air Act of 1970 alone may have reached as much as $400 billion (in 1980 dollars) by 1987. Studies by the EPA put the total cost at around $300 billion (in 1977 dollars).[6] Because the U.S. economy has experienced a variety of economic problems during this period (low productivity growth, unemployment, high inflation, trade budget deficits), figures like these attract attention.

In order to get better answers to questions about the impact of environmental programs in general, the Council of Environmental Quality has proposed a framework for carrying out environmental economic analysis.[7] By dividing environmental costs into four broad categories and explaining how each should be considered in formulating environmental policies, the framework is an excellent example of how the analytical method works. Following are the four categories of costs:

- *Damage costs* are those resulting from the damage that pollution causes, for example, blighted crops, ill health, and higher death rates.

- *Avoidance costs* are the financial costs and the other economic and social costs of attempts to avoid pollution-caused damage. Avoidance

---

[6] Lawrence Mosher, "The Clean Air You're Breathing May Cost Hundreds of Billions of Dollars," *National Journal*, October 10, 1981.

[7] U.S. Council on Environmental Quality, *Annual Report* (Washington, D.C.: Government Printing Office, 1975), pp. 494–543.

costs may vary from outlays for air conditioners to the many kinds of costs incurred by people when they move away from polluted central cities.

- *Abatement costs* are the value of the resources devoted to reducing the amount of pollution plus any indirect adverse effects of these expenditures on economic growth, employment, and production.
- *Transactions costs* include the value of the resources used in research, planning, administration, communication, and monitoring for pollution control.

Current pollution control policies attempt to reduce damage and avoidance costs substantially by increasing abatement and transactions costs. From the strict viewpoint of economic efficiency, the goal of our environmental policies should be to minimize the sum of the four types of costs—to continue to expend additional resources on abatement and transactions costs so long as the last increment of such expenditures buys at least an equivalent value in reduced damage and avoidance costs. This discussion, therefore, will attempt to rectify the imbalance by presenting similarly extensive analyses of damage, avoidance, and transactions costs.

Damage estimates. There are four stages in estimating the economic costs of pollution damages. As indicated in Figure 7–1, polluting emissions affect ambient environmental quality, which in turn causes damages, which have economic costs, some of which are quantifiable.

Uncertainty exists at the very outset. How much pollution is there and what types of pollutants are being emitted? EPA's estimates are still based on "typical" production processes with "typical" emissions. As with most such estimates, probably very few situations correspond to the typical.

Uncertainty increases at the next step—the determination of ambient conditions. The science of predicting ambient quality remains inexact despite efforts to describe mathematically the processes by which pollutants disperse, become assimilated, degrade, and combine with other chemicals. There is little sure knowledge about how pollutants interact with one another and with other chemicals in the environment.

How much damage occurs is perhaps the most difficult thing to ascertain. Pollution is known to affect health adversely, but there is little idea of the extent to which it does so. We know that lead can damage health, but we are unsure how much airborne lead enters the human bloodstream or the degree to which it impacts human health. Given the myriad genetic, socioeconomic, and environmental factors that affect health, it is usually impossible to prove beyond doubt that a particular pollutant—SO_x from a power plant, for example—causes health damage, much less how the damage may vary with exposure. And yet we know

Figure 7–1
Estimating environmental damage costs

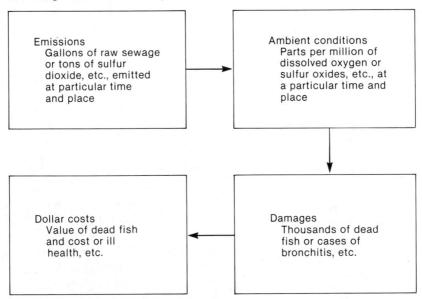

much more about such questions than we do about intangible and psychological damage, for instance, how noise affects people's well-being.

Materials damage is easier to measure, but even here it is difficult to deal with the interactions of pollutants with one another and with other environmental components to cause more, less, or other damage than they do alone. Sulfur dioxide alone causes little if any damage to many materials, but together with water it can form sulphuric acid, whose effects can be severe. The most controversial step is the last one, placing a value on the damage that occurs.

Estimating the dollar cost of painting a pollution-soiled building or of replacing ruined crops is a relatively straightforward process. But the value of a human life, or of a clear sky, or of a place for recreation, or of a species that contributes to the diversity, complexity, and stability of an ecosystem, cannot be fully translated into dollars. To the extent that we can quantitatively estimate damage costs with reasonable confidence, it will be easier to make efficient environmental decisions. We must keep in mind, however, that this procedure often understates the full magnitude of the damage and usually ignores important issues concerning its distribution.

Avoidance costs. The discussion thus far has dealt with efforts to estimate pollution damage *directly.* But to the extent that people are aware of such damage, its costs should also be reflected indirectly in the market prices of labor and land. Everything else being equal, people will demand higher wages to work where pollution levels are high. Conversely, they will be willing to pay more for unpolluted residential and industrial sites in order to avoid pollution damage.

Land prices are being used more and more in attempts to estimate the monetary value that people place on pollution damages. Among other advantages, property values can reflect many of the psychic costs that cannot be measured easily by other techniques. Environmental damage would be much worse if we did not act to avoid it. People install air filters in their homes to avoid respiratory disease; they cover unused clothing with plastic bags to prevent soiling; they travel long distances to find clean beaches; and some ultimately move their homes at great expense so that they can live in a clean environment. The list goes on, and we do not know all the items, let alone their dollar value.

Abatement and transactions costs. Now that our environmental programs are older, we are beginning to obtain empirical information on the magnitude of these costs. A major problem in comparing estimates of pollution abatement costs is to distinguish between what is a pollution control expenditure and what is not. The costs of installing, maintaining, and operating an "end-of-the-pipe" device that has no function other than abating pollution are easy to identify. But more and more often, pollution abatement is being integrated into the production process, where it may both reduce pollution and improve production efficiency.

Another definitional problem is whether to include all pollution abatement costs or just the additional expenditures required by law.

Solid waste management provides a clear example of the difference. Even if there were no environmental legislation, we would not allow trash and garbage to pile up in backyards and streets, but would pay to have it disposed of. It is unreasonable to attribute all of these disposal costs to environmental legislation.

Although most of the funds that governments spend for pollution control go directly to abatement of pollution, significant amounts are also spent on transactions costs, such as planning, monitoring, and enforcement. These expenditures, primarily those of the federal, state, and larger local governments, are often hard to identify because they are not separated from direct abatement expenditures or because they appear in budgets of departments other than the one responsible for pollution control. The private sector may also spend considerable amounts in planning pollution abatement strategies, in filling out government forms, and for other purposes that should be included as transactions costs. To the extent that these costs are reported, however, they are lumped with abatement costs, and no differentiation is possible.

Even if we cannot make rigorous quantitative estimates of costs, we should use all of the information that we have in formulating environmental policies. We have committed ourselves to a thoroughgoing program of reducing environmental damage. It is important to carry out this program as intelligently as we can.

Intangibles

Costs and benefits—whether direct or indirect—that are not easily measured in dollars we call intangibles. To use the expressway example again, we can say that construction costs are fairly tangible; market prices are easily obtained. Even the costs of the resulting air pollution, in terms of damaged health and property, can be measured—though the numbers here are "squishier." But what dollar value should be assigned to the destruction of a community to make room for the expressway or to the deleterious aesthetic effects of spreading more asphalt? Clearly, with considerations such as these, we enter the realm of intangibles.

Actually, there are probably fewer intangibles than might at first be supposed. In many instances, the market can be used to advantage to aid in the task of measurement. One example is a suggestion for dealing with the problem of airport noise and its deleterious effect on urban residential areas. Homeowners suffer losses from noise created by airplanes, and as the courts have been a poor resort for relief to homeowners, the market has been advanced as a mechanism for both quantification of the effect and redress for losses sustained. It has been suggested that losses in the value of homes as a result of their location under the flight paths of urban airports be borne not by the homeowners but by the airport and air passengers. This could be accomplished by a system of payments from the beneficiaries of air travel to those suffering such losses. Such a scheme would compensate those who suffer losses from airplane noise and would provide incentives for the better location of airports and for less noisy airline operations.

Generally speaking, the measurement of benefits is trickier than the measurement of costs. The situation is perhaps easiest when the benefits to the users of a government service can be calculated on the basis of the amounts they are willing to pay. Thus the value of electric power plants and city water systems can be calculated accurately in advance on the basis of experience elsewhere. But how does one measure the amount a person is willing to pay for spending a day at a city park if similar facilities are not actually sold to the users? Or the value of cultural enrichment (as opposed to professional training) from higher education?

A difficult but often fruitful approach in such cases is *shadow price* estimation. The objective is to impute benefits on the basis of what prices would have cleared the market for government outputs if the outputs had been made under the same conditions as private goods.

The most common way of estimating shadow prices is to use the market price of private sector goods that are similar to the public outputs. There are, after all, usually private educational, health, housing, and recreational markets.

Where private sector markets are not available to provide shadow prices, we must make our own estimates on the basis of assumptions about consumer behavior. Leisure is not traded in the market, but if individuals refuse to work an extra hour at $7.50 per hour, we may conclude that they value that hour of leisure at no less than $7.50 and can call $7.50 per hour the shadow price of their leisure. This information can frequently be used in the analysis of public transportation programs to value travel time saved.

The difficulty facing the analyst is that the comparable private commodities are sometimes very different. If the characteristics of the service of a private medical clinic are sufficiently similar to that of a public clinic, the data of the private clinic may be usable, but the differences between a public park and a private camp are huge and difficult to compare. Here a more indirect use of market data may be made; this application of market data relies on the responses of the private sector in gaining access to free public services. Public services are free, but access to them may be costly. How much I am willing to spend in time and money to see the Grand Canyon surely must say something about how much it is "worth" to me.

The above methods of estimating what individuals will pay for government outputs are still rudimentary and imperfect. However, they give far more information than do impressions or the weighing of mail from pressure groups. It is clear that these methods are not precise enough to eliminate judgment on the part of the decision maker, but the estimates will improve with practice and will provide a framework within which the decision maker can gain insight into the effects of public programs on the national welfare.

To conclude this discussion we might try cutting our teeth on one of the most difficult yet unavoidable issues in the whole area of intangibles, namely, the value of a human life.

Putting a value on life

What is the value of a human life? Pick a figure: $158 million, $4.5 million, $600,000, $28,000. An objection frequently raised to such a question is that "we can't put a price on a human life." But the fact remains that government policymakers must—implicitly at least—put a price on lives whenever they make decisions about the coverage of a health insurance policy, the installation of a traffic light, the extension of a food stamp program, the protection of steel workers from cancer-causing fumes of coke ovens, or innumerable other matters. Which is to say that policymakers are putting a price on life quite a bit nowadays.

Given limited resources, national policymakers cannot afford to say that they will spend "whatever it takes" to save lives. Once you cast yourself as a humanitarian willing to spend billions to save a few lives, you rapidly find yourself in an untenable position, because that billion might save many more lives if invested elsewhere, so the national policymakers spend on lifesaving only up to a point. That point expresses their judgment about the value of life in their society.

A number of methods have been suggested to deal with the problem, and the federal agencies still seem a long way off from settling on any one of them. A frequently used method is based on lifetime earnings, that is, the value of a life is the future earning power of an individual at the time of death. In the next chapter, we will examine how this method can be used in helping one decide among different cancer detection programs.

Thomas C. Schelling of Harvard proposed an alternative, generally referred to as the willingness to pay approach.[8] In essence, it says that the value of your life is reflected in the payments you would demand to accept a small risk of death or, alternatively, the payments you would willingly make to reduce the risk. Economists explaining the model have helpfully devised wonderful scenarios, some worthy of Hollywood. You are asked, for example, how much money you would insist on to join a group of 10,000 persons, one of whom will be selected at random for execution. An answer of $200 implies that you value your life at $2 million—that is, at 10,000 × $200. (That does not mean you would accept certain execution for $2 million, however.) Another much-discussed scenario asks you to envision a game of Russian roulette in which you are being forced to play but have the right to buy back various numbers of bullets for a price, with the price and the odds again dictating a life value.

Most analysts who have thought about life valuation seem skeptical of results based on survey data; they do not believe people filling out questionnaires think deeply or answer truthfully about how they would behave in a purely hypothetical situation. So an effort has been mounted to derive life values from people's actual behavior. Paul Portney at Resources for the Future derived values from people's willingness to pay extra for homes in areas with little pollution. Portney ended up with life values of around $600,000 to $900,000 in today's prices.[9]

---

[8] Thomas C. Schelling, "The Life You Save May Be Your Own," in *Problems in Public Expenditure Analysis*, ed. Samuel B. Chase, Jr. (Washington, D.C.: Brookings Institution, 1968).

[9] Paul Portney, "Urban Air Quality and Acute Respiratory Illness," *Journal of Urban Economics* 20, no. 1 (1986), pp. 21–38.

The life values that carry the most weight among policy analysts come from another direction, however. This method tries to calculate from a person's behavior what price he puts on his own life. In general, the more risk a person is willing to accept, the less value he places on his life. In the case of workers, for example, analysts have meshed statistics on occupational death and injury with statistics on pay to arrive at estimates of the money workers are willing to accept for putting their lives at greater jeopardy.

The average worker is considered to stand one chance in 10,000 of dying on the job. If a worker, for an extra $200 a year, is willing to accept a job where he has two chances in 10,000 of dying, then he is figured to value his life at $200 times 10,000 or $2 million. If the same worker gets only $20 extra for the added risk, then the economist says he has valued his life at $200,000.

Workers in such high-risk jobs as fire fighters, power plant operators, and bartenders, who often are not adequately compensated for the added danger, have priced themselves at about $500,000 according to W. Kip Viscusi of Duke University. A worker who seeks out an average-risk job, which would include most jobs in modern manufacturing plants,

Table 7–2
Cost-benefit matrix for the Satellite Solar Power System

		Benefits	Costs
Direct	Tangible	Increased electrical energy production Help in energy independence Improved balance of trade through foreign sales Makes fossil fuel available for other uses	Capital outlays Financing Satellite design Ground station design Large launch vehicle development Technology development Launch and assembly costs Maintenance costs Replacement expendables Crew transport On-orbit crew support Training Security system Management
	Intangible	Increased international prestige Better international relations through power-sharing potential	Use of some scarce natural resources Damaged relations with some countries due to military potential

Table 7–2 *(concluded)*

		Benefits	Costs
Indirect	Tangible	Technological spin-offs (cells for home heating and cooling, etc.), materials, and processes Reduction in pollution by reducing number of conventional power plants Reduction in power distribution grid costs because of flexibility in placing ground stations Can lead to further space exploitation large manufacturing stations, etc.	Launch vehicle pollution Reduction in jobs in fossil-fuel power plant industry Retraining for different types of jobs Land costs and international complications if launches are desired from equatorial site
	Intangible	Reduced excavation of land for oil shale or uranium ore Minimized risk of station failure as compared to ground-based (nuclear) plant failure More equitable energy distribution	Microwave beam effects Atmosphere Birds Airplanes Communications Noise pollution at launch site Complex corporate organizational problems Effect on humans and animals of sight of "other moons"
Pecuniary effects		Relative improvement in position of aerospace industry Increase in land values at sites of power conversion bases	

places a higher value on his life, about $3 million, by Viscusi's estimates. Most white-collar workers, who are considered to have the safest jobs, are said to value their lives as high as $10 million.[10]

Probably the best way to summarize this section is to apply the cost-benefit matrix to one specific program. I have selected a futuristic one: the Satellite Solar Power System. The SSPS is an extremely large structure

---

[10] W. Kip Viscusi, "Regulating Uncertain Health Hazards When There Is Changing Risk Information," *Journal of Health Economics*, 3, no. 3 (1984), pp. 259–73.

(several kilometers in length) that would be placed in orbit by NASA to capture solar energy and microwave it to earth. There the solar energy would be converted into electrical power. Table 7–2, pp. 362–363, gives a breakdown of the more significant costs and benefits involved.

DISTRIBUTIONAL CONSIDERATION

The distribution of benefits

Programs differ with regard to their distributional implications. Thus the benefits from one program may accrue primarily to people in high-income groups, whereas the benefits of another program may accrue to blind and handicapped persons and the benefits of still other programs may accrue to a particular geographic region of the country. Many of the pecuniary benefits discussed earlier in the chapter may have important distributional implications. Such distributional implications should not be ignored. Policy analysts, like judges, should not be reluctant to invoke the ancient query *"Cui bono?"*: To whose benefit do decisions redound? Burton A. Weisbrod suggests, therefore, a way of adding distributional considerations to the efficiency considerations that the cost-benefit matrix treats.[11] See Table 7–3.

The vigorous pursuit of distributional effects often leads to surprising results. Consider these three examples:

- Court decisions have held that expenditure per pupil in public schools must be roughly equal for all students in any given state. The legal argument has been that of "equal protection of the laws." Who will benefit from this? Senator Daniel P. Moynihan of New York has speculated that it will be the teachers, who already receive over two thirds of operating expenditures.

  That these are estimable and deserving persons none should doubt, but neither should there be any illusion that they are deprived. With exceptions, they are not. Where the teacher is a married woman, family income is likely to be in the top quintile of income distribution, even the top 5 percent. Without abusing probabilities (nor asserting the existence of detailed evidence), it may be said that increasing educational expenditures will have the short-run effect of increasing income inequality.

  Now is this what the courts intend? Possibly. The Establishment is said to do such things all the time. But the far greater likelihood. . . . is that courts simply don't know what they are doing. They

---

[11] Burton A. Weisbrod, "Income Redistributional Effects and Cost-Benefit Analysis," in *Problems in Public Expenditure Analysis,* ed. Samuel B. Chase, Jr. (Washington, D.C.: Brookings Institution, 1968).

Table 7–3
Program benefits by age, income, region, and color of beneficiary

Region and age	Income						Total
	Low		Middle		High		
	White	Nonwhite	White	Nonwhite	White	Nonwhite	
North							
0–18 years							
19–64 years							
65 years and over							
South							
0–18 years							
19–64 years							
65 years and over							
West							
0–18 years							
19–64 years							
65 years and over							
Total							

appear to have seized on undeniable instances in which "rich" districts contain "rich" kids and "poor" districts, "poor" kids, and where both expenditures and outcomes are so clearly unequal that any fair-minded person would feel that something ought to be done.[12]

- According to the director of the Small Business Administration's Security and Investigations Division, a special government program designed to help minority-owned businesses get contracts really benefits whites. While more than 50 percent of the stock in such businesses was owned by minority persons, whites, experienced in the businesses, controlled the management and took 90 percent of the profits. As one former SBA director put it before a Senate subcommittee, "They take a foreman, put 'president' on his hard hat, give him a station wagon and still make the same profits as they did before."[13]

- Politics in the United States has always been sensitive to regional differences. The Sunbelt states as a group received far more money from Washington in grants and federal spending than they sent to

---

[12] Daniel P. Moynihan, "Equalizing Education: In Whose Benefit?" *Public Interest*, 29 (Fall 1972), pp. 69–89.
[13] *Houston Post*, July 8, 1977.

Table 7–4
Annual expenditures per family on gasoline, by
fifths of families ranked by money income

Families ranked by money income	Average annual gasoline expenditures	
	Dollars	Percent of income
Lowest fifth	139	6.6
Second fifth	290	5.2
Third fifth	419	4.5
Fourth fifth	497	3.6
Highest fifth	605	2.5

Source: U.S. Congressional Budget Office, *President Carter's Energy Proposals: A Perspective*, Staff Working Paper (Washington, D.C.: Government Printing Office, June 1977), p. 118.

Washington in taxes. In this money exchange, according to one calculation, the Northeast lost about $11 billion annually, the Midwest $20 billion, whereas the South and West *gained* $12 billion and $11 billion. (The $8 billion balance went to Washington, D.C.)[14]

The distribution of costs

Thus far we have considered only the distribution of benefits. But equally important is how the burden of costs is shared.

In an effort to give American consumers a better idea of how their tax dollars are spent, we might use a "T-dollar," a simple computational device to "unit-price" government expenditures and translate large sums of money into terms more suitable for dinner table discussion. In 1984, for example, there were an estimated 85.4 million households in the United States. Divide that number into $1 billion, and you get $11.70— or the amount that each family contributes to each $1 billion of federal spending. Thus an aircraft carrier costs about $1 billion or about 12 T-dollars a family.

This may be a better way of doing things. I do not know. In any event, these T-dollars tell us very little about the incidence of particular

---

[14] *National Journal*, July 2, 1977. This line of reasoning is sound as far as it goes. But if you subtract defense contracts and salaries from those figures, the result is a more balanced distribution of federal largess among the regions: $579 in the Northeast, $523 in the Midwest, $560 in the South, and $580 in the West. So the argument that federal spending shortchanges the North turns out to hinge on how one allocates among the states the Pentagon's $42.8 billion of defense contracts and $28.2 billion of salaries. And, of course, most of the Pentagon's prime contractors subcontract to firms in other states.

Table 7–5
Tax hit list

Taxpayer group	Gross income	Percentage decrease or increase in taxes paid (from 1986 to 1988)
Single person with one child	$ 20,000	−26.8
Single retiree, over 65	25,000	−23.5
Married retiree, over 65	44,000	−11.0
Married couple with two children	30,100	− 7.1
Single person with no children	30,000	− 6.8
Single person with no children	64,000	− 2.7
Married couple with two children	61,050	+ 4.0
Married couple with no children	91,500	+16.5
Married couple with two children*	265,000	+79.2

*Tax shelter of $50,000 would be disallowed. This group's taxes would increase by $19,748 (from $24,950 to $44,698).
Source: Based on analysis by Arthur Andersen & Co. of the tax bill proposed by the tax conference committee in August 1986.

budget measures, that is, how the burden falls on different income levels. And, to that extent, they tell us very little about equity. But how does one analyze the distribution of costs?

Take the proposal for the imposition of a crude oil equalization tax and a standby gasoline tax. The initial burden imposed by these price increases will vary according to gasoline usage. On average, expenditures for gasoline increase with family income (see Table 7–4), but note how the expenditures *decline* as a percent of income. In this sense, the rich do pay less.

Table 7–5 shows how the costs and benefits of tax reform affect nine different groups in society.

The two preceding analyses, though fairly straightforward, can be extremely helpful to policymakers in understanding more fully the consequences of what they are proposing. We will conclude our brief discussion of the distribution of costs by considering two approaches that attempt to carry the analysis a step farther—the first by relating the distribution of the burden to the distribution of benefits, the second by relating the distribution of the burden to "willingness to pay."

In contrast to European universities, the state universities in the United States, and particularly the land-grant colleges, were founded on a radical concept: education for the people as a whole, not the privileged classes alone. These institutions were to provide education for the sons and daughters of the nation's workers, whose access to the elite private institutions was blocked by financial entry barriers. The institutions, in the words of Joseph R. Williams, the first president of

Michigan State University, were to be "good enough for the proudest and cheap enough for the poorest."

"Although the state universities, land grant colleges, and lately the community colleges have undoubtedly contributed to this goal," Walter Adams writes,

> it is nevertheless true that the recent escalation in tuition levels has detracted from their achievements. So has the regressive financing of public higher education. As Theodore W. Schultz points out, "the financing of higher education is in general quite regressive . . . because it adds to the value of the human capital of those who attend college relative to those who do not go to college, because it increases the lifetime earnings of college graduates in part at the expense of others, and closely related, because higher education provides educational services predominantly for students from middle and upper income families and a part of the cost of these educational services is paid for by taxes on poor families." In short, says Schultz, "the financing is such that substantial amounts of valuable assets are being transferred by society to a particular intellectually elite set of individuals."[15]

Robert Dorfman is concerned with the distribution among segments of the population of the benefits and costs of programs protecting the environment. The difficult part of this analysis is estimating the distribution of benefits. Dorfman writes,

> We do not have to review here the diversity of the benefits of those programs, the difficulties of estimating their magnitudes, or the obscurity of their values to different segments of the population. All available estimates are open to serious question. For our purposes the most appropriate and inclusive estimates appear to be ones derivable from some surveys made by the Gallup Organization on behalf of the National Wildlife Federation, which has provided the survey results to us. In 1969 the National Wildlife Federation survey of public opinion about environmental matters included the following question: "Would you be willing to accept a $X per year increase in your family's total expenses for the cleanup of the natural environment?" The question was asked for $X = \$20, \$50, \$100,$ and $\$200$. The tabulations available

---

[15] Walter Adams, "Economic Problems Confronting Higher Education," *American Economic Review* 67, no. 1 (February 1977), pp. 86–89. What, then, are the policy implications? Adams suggests several: "Assuming that it is our goal to promote vertical mobility through greater access to higher education, as well as to promote greater distributional equity in revenue/expenditure patterns, the following measures would constitute steps in the right direction: (a) correction of the significantly regressive state and local tax systems—a measure which can, of course, be justified on broader social welfare grounds; (b) the adoption at public colleges and universities of tuition schedules calibrated progressively to family income; (c) added inducements for qualified low-income students to attend college, including the offer of "full ride" privileges normally reserved to talented athletes; (d) creation of an educational bank, primarily to relieve financial pressures on the lower middle class, which would lend any qualified student the full cost of his/her education under conditions of lifetime repayment through, for example, a surcharge on the income tax.

show the percent willing at all four levels for the survey population as a whole, and the percent willing to pay $20 and $200 for three income ranges.[16]

The next step was to bring these estimates together with most estimates. Dorfman provides the following interpretation:

> The cost of the pollution control program to middle bracket families was just about what they would be willing to pay to obtain a clean environment. Lower bracket families, on the average, were required to pay some $60 more per family than they regarded environmental cleanup as worth, while the average burden on the upper income families was about $60 less than they said they would be willing to contribute to obtain a clean environment.[17]

Who would be the winners and losers of social security, state lotteries, tax cuts, control of acid rain, airline deregulation, bank deregulation, unisex pensions, unisex insurance, import quotas, and tax reform? You might want to jot down your guesses and then compare them with the author's in Table 7–6.

UNCERTAINTY AND RISK

The quest for certainty

"Uncertainty and expectations are the joys of life," William Congreve once wrote, but I doubt whether very many policy analysts would agree with him. For uncertainty and risks in public policy are difficult to handle, yet impossible to ignore.

An element of uncertainty can be found in virtually all policy decisions. It may range from a mere falling short of certitude to an almost complete lack of knowledge about the outcome of an action. Although instances of the former are few, one might cite peacetime wage and price controls as an action on which analysts are in general agreement as to outcome: such controls do not provide a long-term cure for inflation. Using historical records, analysts can predict fairly accurately the relative safety of different transportation modes (air, rail, bus, etc.). And, with their computer models, they can also predict the revenue generated by different tax proposals. Such projections often yield interesting results. See accompanying box.

But clouds of uncertainty billow around issues. Take energy. Analysts have been trying to get a fix on the energy problem for over a decade. What will happen next? One view is the spot crude oil market will last for several years with prices either stable or dropping. But not everyone agrees with that view. The twenty-one-nation International Energy Agency warns that a major new oil crisis might erupt in the

---

[16] Robert Dorfman, "Incidence of the Benefits and Costs of Environmental Programs," *American Economic Review* 67, no. 1 (February 1977), pp. 333–40.

[17] Ibid., p. 336.

Table 7–6
Distribution of some costs and benefits in eleven programs, actual and proposed

Program	Winners	Losers	Comment
Social security	One fourth of all payments go to people with incomes higher than the vast majority of contributors	Younger workers and children	A typical worker who retired in 1982 could expect to receive in social security payments three times what their investment would have earned in the economy. By contrast, today's thirty-year-olds will receive as little as 73 percent of the value of their contributions when they retire.[1]
State lottery	Rich	Poor	While middle-income people play lotteries in greater numbers than other classes, the poor spend much more for lottery tickets in proportion to their income than the rich.[2]
Reagan 1981–82 tax cut	People earning under $50,000	People earning over $50,000	Conventional wisdom said that this would push more of a tax load onto the poor. But cuts in the top rate draw the rich out of shelter and channel more of their income into taxable investments.[3] However, when these tax policy changes are combined with spending reductions in entitlement programs, low-income families lose the most money.[4]
Student tax credits	Families with incomes above the national median	Families with incomes below the national median	If the nation wants to give priority to encouraging youngsters from less-advantaged families to attend college, current and proposed tax breaks do not appear to meet that goal as well as conventional student aid based on need. Specifically, 75 percent of the tax savings from extending dependent status for college students goes to families with incomes above the median of $23,000.[5]
National program to control acid rain at its source	East, Southeast, and Canada	Middle West	The largest source of acid rain is widely believed to be the Middle West's coal-fired power plants. The most vulnerable areas are in the East, the Southeast, and Canada. Middle Westerners do not want to pay for the reduction of pollution that the government says may or may not harm lakes, forests, and buildings hundreds of miles

			away. Efforts to devise an acid-rain program, the cost of which would be shared by the whole country, are opposed by the Westerners, who believe they do not cause the problem and should not have to pay for its solution.[6]
Airline deregulation	Passengers and carriers	Some cities	Deregulation generally has had a positive impact, saving passengers $6 billion annually through lower fares, and (improving airline) earnings by $2.5 billion annually. The benefits have been greatest for business passengers notwithstanding increased delays. But service to some small communities did deteriorate in the early 1980s, as unregulated carriers quickly shifted operations to more profitable routes that were previously barred to them.
Banking deregulation	Affluent	Middle- and lower-income people	For most consumers, the average cost of maintaining a checking account has climbed more than 100 percent in the last few years. But while these consumer costs have risen, people who can keep $2,500 or more on deposit are finding that they can command much higher interest rates from banks. Deregulation has eradicated hidden subsidies by which depositors were paying for services that borrowers used. Deregulation in the industry's view has simply distributed the costs more equitably.[8]
Military draft	Taxpayers	Eighteen- to twenty-year-old males	
Unisex pensions	Women	Men	The insurance industry reasons that women live nearly eight years longer than men on the average, so they should get less each month because they will collect payments longer. Under unisex rates, women would receive more in pension payments.
Unisex insurance	Men	Women	The most obvious effect of the elimination of sex as a rating factor in insurance policies is increased rates for young female drivers (up 20 percent) and decreased rates for young male drivers

Table 7-6 (concluded)

Program	Winners	Losers	Comment
			(down 20 percent). Before the laws were changed in several states young men were charged higher rates because they had more accidents.[9]
Japanese car quota limit	Japan and American auto industry and its workers	American consumers and exporters	Japan's decision in 1986 to limit its exports to about one fifth of the U.S. market eased the pressure on Japan to open its own market to American exports, notably building products. The quota permitted Japanese automakers to raise their prices by about $2,500 a car. And their American competitors were able to charge about $1,000 more than would otherwise have been possible. The quota saved about 44,000 American jobs. That means consumers paid an astonishing $300,000 for every job defended—about ten times the pay of these workers.[10]
Tax Reform Act of 1986	Some six million people with incomes at or below poverty line.	People with tax shelters. States with a sales tax.	The investment tax credits are killed, and scores of special breaks eliminated. A strict 21 percent minimum tax on profits means no more cases of giant corporations paying no taxes. The act removes distortions created by a maze of incentives and exemptions. No longer will executives waste their ingenuity devising elaborate schemes to turn ordinary income into capital gains. Dollars will flow to the most productive uses rather than being diverted into half-empty office buildings and shopping malls that offer tax advantages.

[1] Congressional Research Service (1985)
[2] Daniel Suits, Department of Economics, Michigan State University (1983)
[3] Department of Treasury (1984)
[4] Congressional Budget Office (1984)
[5] Lawrence E. Gladieux, College Board (1984)
[6] New York Times (1985)
[7] Steven Morrison and Clifford Winston, Brookings Institution (1986)
[8] Consumer Federation of America (1983) and American Bankers Association (1983)
[9] U.S. News & World Report (1983)
[10] Robert Crandall, Brookings Institution (1985) and U.S. International Trade Commission (1985)

Box 7–1
Soak the rich?

As someone once pointed out, the only difference between the rich and other people is that the rich have more money. So, why doesn't Congress make them pay more in order to balance the budget?

What policymakers will discover is that, apart from fairness, sharply higher taxes on wealthy Americans—even total confiscation of all income—would make only a small dent in the budget deficits. Levying a flat 75 percent tax on persons with adjusted gross incomes of $1 million or more in 1984 would result in only $3.6 billion in additional money—enough to run the government for two days. The same flat tax on all incomes of $100,000 or more would yield $39.2 billion in new income-tax revenue. In fact, if all persons with income of $100,000 or more paid a 100 percent tax, the $68 billion in added revenue would be less than half of the projected budget deficit for 1985.

It is unlikely that any such proposal would advance very far in Congress. But, even if it did, these figures suggest that ending budget shortfalls will take far more than boosting taxes on the wealthy. •

Source: Data from U.S. Internal Revenue Service, *Statistics of Income, 1984.*

1990s, dealing a devastating blow to the major industrialized countries. By the end of the century, the IEA predicts the world might well be between nine and twenty-one million barrels a day short of the oil it will need.

So who's right? I am not certain. But it is crucial, as we march into the decade, not to think we understand when we lack comprehensive clues. We must remember that there is much about energy that we did not know in the past, so we ought to be reasonably prepared for widely different scenarios that may emerge in the future. For example, we do not know:

- The extent to which new non-OPEC reserves will be available when we want them. The industrialized countries need to keep discovering new reserves of their own, particularly in such major producing areas as Alaska, the North Sea, and Canada.
- The extent to which the Soviet bloc may become a net importer of oil, thus reducing the present surplus on world markets. Given Russia's technical inefficiency and especially the difficulties in producing and delivering Siberian oil, it could happen.
- The degree to which OPEC may choose to restrict production.
- The possibility that political events, such as an expanded Middle East war, could seriously affect worldwide crude oil availability.

• The degree to which consumers will again increase their use of oil as the current worldwide recession ends.

Risky business

In recent years, the mass media have given considerable attention to the risks in modern life and their public policy implications. Do fluorocarbons damage the atmosphere? Just how safe are dams? Does exposure to asbestos, vinyl chloride, carbon tetrachloride, and polychlorinated biphenyls (PCBs) cause metabolic disorders, birth defects, or even cancer? Are microwave ovens safe? Examples are virtually limitless. Rather than randomly sample them, let us focus on two: Strategic Defense Initiative and nuclear energy.

Star Wars. By the 1990s, the Soviets might be able to target the entire U.S. "triad" of missiles, bombers, and submarines. Yet alternative programs such as the MX, Midgetman, and others may not remedy this situation. One answer is to build a defense against Soviet nuclear weapons. The plan is called the Strategic Defense Initiative (SDI).

Since 1983, debate on strategic defense has centered on exotic systems able to catch missiles and other nuclear weapons so early in their flight as to shield U.S. cities. These Star Wars systems excite controversy, but there is little technical uncertainty over the Antiballistic Missile (ABM) systems, which fire hit-to-kill rockets from the ground. Even some Star Wars critics concede the feasibility of these relatively simple means for providing U.S. missiles a measure of defense. Given rapid increases in computer speed and missile accuracy, such ground-based ABMs can take two or more shots at a given warhead, at increasing distances. America tested this capability in 1984. This makes an attack on the defense itself far more difficult, and thus makes defense a solid proposition.

The advantages of limited defense can best be understood in contrast to present strategy, which rules out defense as contrary to the spirit of Mutual Assured Destruction (MAD) and the letter of the ABM treaty. Under MAD, each U.S. offensive weapon built can be countered with a linear expansion in Soviet warheads. If Americans build two missiles, the Soviets can knock them out with four warheads. The challenge for the Soviets is even smaller, since weapons carry multiple warheads.

SDI would totally change this equation. An attacker could not be sure how many of his missiles or bombers would penetrate any given layer of defense; for each layer, the attacker would have to multiply the number of warheads in his initial attack.[18]

---

[18] Consider a two-layer U.S. defense, with each layer stopping 80 percent of a given attack. To be reasonably sure of getting 8,000 warheads through to destroy up to 4,000

In the conventional view, U.S. defenses will only spur further Soviet buildups of offense. Yet, in the 1960s, the Soviets observed the United States making a great effort to upgrade air defenses against a potential bomber threat. The Soviets' response was to cancel their bomber program for many years. Thus, a likely Soviet response might be to slowly de-emphasize nuclear weapons—investing in areas likely to yield some return—or to speed up a large-scale Soviet effort to develop the same kinds of defenses. This would not eliminate competition, but it could channel it in a positive direction, a "good arms race" in which the faster each side goes, the better.

The transition period, in which the United States would have both offensive and defensive weapons, could last ten to thirty years. In the opinion of many, like Les Aspin, chairman of the House Armed Services Committee, this period "would be far more dangerous and unstable than anything we've lived through so far."[19] The nightmare some imagine is that, for the first time, nuclear war might be made thinkable, and military planners would be able to calculate nuclear victory as follows: a first strike that knocks out more than 90 percent of the victim's offensive nuclear forces, plus defenses good enough to blunt most of what remained for a retaliatory blow. It appears that policymakers have not yet thought through exactly what combinations of offensives and defenses would make the balance more or less stable. Besides, the transition from offenses to defenses probably could not be made safely without Russian cooperation, which is uncertain at best.

In sum, the nuclear age forces policymakers to face two hard questions. Has a president the right to expose his fellow citizens forever to the risks of an increasing number of volatile leaders in other countries? Has a president the right to expose his fellow citizens to the risks of a transition to a safer world?

Nuclear power. When the first detailed analysis of the risks of reactors was published in 1975—long before Chernobyl was a household word—nuclear power looked promising. According to the *Reactor Safety Study*, the probability of an accident serious enough to release large amounts of radioactivity into the plant, and possibly outside it, was about one in 20,000 years of operation.[20]

But complaints were heard soon after the study—known as the Rasmussen report for its chief author, Norman Rasmussen of the Massachu-

---

vital Western military targets, the Soviets would have to expend 264,000 warheads, many times their present force. Obviously, such figures become less certain the farther they are extended. That is the point: It makes Soviet military planning more difficult.

[19] Quoted in Leslie H. Gelb, "Star Wars Advances: The Plan versus the Reality," *The New York Times,* December 15, 1985.

[20] U.S. Nuclear Regulatory Commission, *Reactor Safety Study.* USNRC Rep. NVREG-75/014. (Washington, D.C.: Government Printing Office, 1975).

setts Institute of Technology—was released, and the Nuclear Regulatory Commission (NRC) sent its engineers back to do another analysis. In July 1982, they finished a revised assessment of the risks, and the new odds were not nearly as reassuring. The study, based on the experience of more than seventy commercial reactors over the decade ending in 1979, put the chance of a serious accident at one in 1,000 years of operation, twenty times greater than the earlier estimate. And researchers warned that this estimate may not be very accurate, either. Nuclear power is safe, federal regulators insist, but just how safe is hard to determine.

Predicting the absolute probability of accidents is impossible. The NRC study, which was based on more than 19,000 reports of malfunctions, helped determine accident trends and focus inspections and improvements. Nevertheless, probability estimates, like nuclear power plants, can fail. For one thing, the NRC report was based on the experience of relatively young reactors and their reliability may decline with time. The accident at Three Mile Island in 1979, the worst the American industry has suffered, was classified as an "incredible" event, meaning safety experts had not thought the chain of events that occurred at the plant near Harrisburg, Pennsylvania, was sufficiently likely to pose a threat.

Because nuclear technology is so complex, safety specialists have had to develop *fault trees* to trace how problems can spread through a plant when a given piece of equipment fails. Some risk analysts will draw the tree of faults with one more box labeled "other," and then they try to quantify "other." With hindsight, the Rasmussen report can be said to have missed several large "others." One was the risk of fire, like the blaze that damaged cables controlling vital equipment at the Browns Ferry complex in Decatur, Alabama. Another occurred at the Rancho Seco plant near Sacramento, California, when a worker dropped a light bulb into a control panel, causing a short-circuit that disabled some of the reactor's controls. Though regulators argue that modifications ordered as a result of these incidents make their repetition unlikely, critics say other accident sequences are waiting to happen.

Risk in perspective

We need a good book on the risks we all run just by virtue of living in a modern industrial society. We especially need a book that will help us think about government policy. When should we demand laws to bar risky products and behavior? When should we merely ask for more disclosure about the risk associated with those products? In what circumstances should we allow individuals to decide for themselves what risks to run? While many authors evidently find these questions interesting, few want to tackle them.

The story of the Three Mile Island reactor, which shut down for six and one-half years, is illustrative. No one died or was injured at Three Mile Island, and the Pennsylvania Health Department found no evidence that cancer death rates were higher near the plant as a result of the accident. But the Three Mile Island incident did fuel a chain reaction of opposition to nuclear power and effectively derailed the nuclear power industry in the United States. Utilities generally went back to building coal-burning plants instead of nuclear reactors, despite clear evidence of the hazards of using coal for power. So, in a sense, the accident did cost the nation hundreds of lives, as well as raise the costs of electricity.

According to Bernard L. Cohen of the University of Pittsburgh, every time another coal-burning plant is built—five to ten times a year—many hundreds of innocent Americans are condemned to early death. Ten thousand Americans die every year as a result of coal mining and coal-burning air pollution, according to some estimates. Even if all the electricity in the United States were produced by nuclear reactors, Cohen estimates, the risk to the average American would be equivalent to a regular cigarette smoker taking one extra cigarette every ten years or an overweight person gaining .03 ounces or increasing the speed limit from 55 to 55.02 miles per hour. Several other nations manage to produce substantial portions of their electricity in nuclear plants without problems.[21]

But people who fear nuclear power are not reassured by sober, scientific risk assessments. Nor are they not the only ones who have trouble keeping their risks in proper order. We ban cyclamates (which may have produced tumors in a few overdosed rats) but not cigarettes (which kill 350,000 Americans a year). We panic over EDB in muffin mix but ignore the cholesterol in steaks. We push an antinausea pregnancy drug off the market with little or no evidence it did harm but do almost nothing about alcohol, a known cause of serious birth defects.

Statistics that show how safe airplane travel is do not reassure millions of people who cannot shake their fear of flying. Data that proves that thousands of lives could be saved every year by using seat belts does not persuade nonusers to buckle up.

Some Americans, who blithely build on earthquake faults, jaywalk, and drive under the influence are the same ones who picket a school that has a child with AIDS in it, demand that trucks loaded with nuclear

---

[21] Bernard L. Cohen, "The Hazards of Nuclear Power," in *The Resourceful Earth*, ed. Julian L. Simon and Herman Kahn (New York: Basil Blackwell, 1984), pp. 545–65.

waste stay off our roads, and refuse to cook in aluminum pans. Perhaps it is easier to protest a nuclear reactor or demand a toxic waste cleanup than to stop smoking, diet, exercise, and fasten a seat belt. But it will not pay off as well in longevity.

Decision making under risk conditions

Faced with probability considerations like those in the nuclear power plant case above, how does the decision maker proceed? The Bayesian probability approach suggests a general procedure. The decision maker lists the set of possible outcomes that a particular decision might have, along with the value of each (X) and the probability of each (P). These subjectively weighted outcomes are then summed to obtain what is known as the *expected monetary value* (EMV) of each decision. The idea, which we will illustrate with two concrete examples, may be expressed by the formula

$$EMV = P_1X_1 + P_2X_2 + \ldots + P_nX_n$$

A frequently used example to see how the idea works is the case of the undecided wildcatter.[22] The decision that the wildcatter must make is whether to drill or not to drill at a particular location. Now he already finds himself in an uncertain environment, not knowing for sure how much the drilling will actually cost, how much raising the oil will cost, or how extensive the oil deposit is on the site. We will simplify the situation by just considering the last-named uncertainty.

Therefore, let us assume that if the wildcatter drills, three outcomes are likely: a dry hole, a wet hole, and a soaking hole. The value of each outcome to the wildcatter is the revenue obtained *minus* the cost of drilling. If the hole is dry, he is out $70,000, the cost of drilling. If it is wet, he will clear $50,000 ($120,000 revenue minus $70,000 in drilling costs). And if it is soaking, he will clear $200,000 ($270,000 − $70,000).

The probabilities of these outcomes vary. Let us assume that the wildcatter estimates them to be .5, .3, and .2. Now we are in a position to calculate the *EMV* of the decision *to drill*.

$$EMV \text{ (to drill)} = .4(-\$70,000) + .4(\$50,000) + .2(\$200,000)$$
$$= \$32,000$$

If our wildcatter were entirely rational, he would drill, although he *might* lose $70,000.

Of course, some individuals are more inclined to take risks than others. Which brings us to one of the most interesting and practical aspects of modern decision theory, namely, the work that has been

---

[22] Adapted from Howard Raiffa, *Decision Analysis: Introductory Lectures on Choices under Uncertainty* (Reading, Mass: Addison-Wesley Publishing, 1968).

done and the techniques that have been developed to supplement statistical probabilities with the analysis of individual preferences in the assumption or avoidance of risk. (Although referred to here as "preference theory," this is more classically denoted as "utility theory.") Purely statistical probabilities, as applied to decision making, rest on the questionable assumption that decision makers, such as our wildcatter, will follow them. It might seem reasonable that if a person had a 60 percent chance of a decision being the right one, he would take it. But this is not necessarily true, since the risk of being wrong is 40 percent and the decision maker might not wish to take this risk, particularly if the penalty for being wrong is severe, whether in terms of monetary losses (his last $70,000) or safety (the reactor melts down). In other words, not many of us would risk losing, say, $40,000 on a 60 percent chance that we might make $100,000, whereas we might readily risk $4 on a chance of making $10.

Therefore, in order to give probabilities practical meaning in decision making, we need a better understanding of the individual decision maker's aversion to or acceptance of risk. While we do not know much about attitudes toward risk, we do know that some people are risk averters in some situations and gamblers in others and that some people have a high aversion to risk and others a low one. The typical risk or preference curve may be drawn as in Figure 7–2. This set of curves shows both the risk averter's and the gambler's curves as well as what is referred to as a rational player's curve.

For any value on the curve (x, P), the risk averter is indifferent between getting X dollars for certain and getting in lottery. For example, at point A, the risk averter is indifferent to getting $50 for certain and getting in a lottery that would offer an .8 chance at $100 and a .2 chance at losing $50.

Our second example of decision analysis under risk conditions concerns not oil but hurricanes. Government decision makers have the option of either seeding a hurricane or not seeding it. Seeding can help reduce the maximum sustained wind of a hurricane and thus reduce property damage. But seeding costs $25,000 and is hardly a surefire method for damage reduction.

Our objective, of course, is to minimize damage. The procedure is essentially the same as that used in the wildcatter problem, except that this time we can structure the problem with a decision tree (see Figure 7–3). The expected losses if seeding is used will be the expected property damage plus the cost of seeding, calculated as follows:

$$\text{Expected loss (seeding)} = 0.038\,(335.8) + 0.143\,(191.1) + 0.392\,(100.0)$$
$$+ 0.255(46.7) + 0.172(16.3) + 0.25$$
$$= \$94.33 \text{ million}$$

Figure 7–2
Typical preference curves

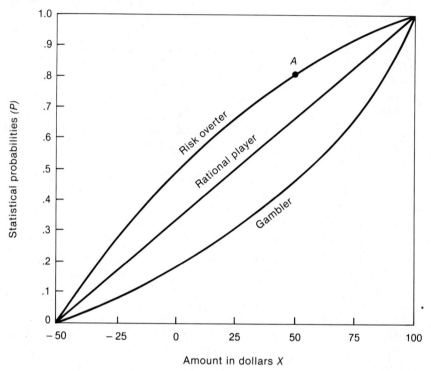

Amount in dollars *X*

Note: The rational player is indifferent between getting *X* dollars for certain and getting a *P* chance at $100 and a (1−*P*) chance at $−50. For example, such a player is indifferent between getting $25 outright and getting a .0 chance at $100 *and* a .5 chance at losing $50. Why? Because .5 ($100) + .5 ($−50) is the same as $25.

The expected loss if seeding is not used will be $116 million, calculated as follows:

$$
\begin{aligned}
\text{Expected loss (not seeding)} = {}& 0.054(335.8) + 0.206(191.1) \\
& + 0.480(100.0) + 0.206(46.7) \\
& + 0.054(16.3) = \$116 \text{ million}
\end{aligned}
$$

The analysis would, therefore, seem to suggest that seeding is the proper course of action.

But not necessarily. Both the wildcatter's decision and the hurricane-seeding decision were highly simplified. For example, the wildcatter might have wanted to first take a seismic reading, but the cost of the reading must be balanced against the reduced chance of drilling if the

Figure 7–3
Decision tree for hurricane seeding

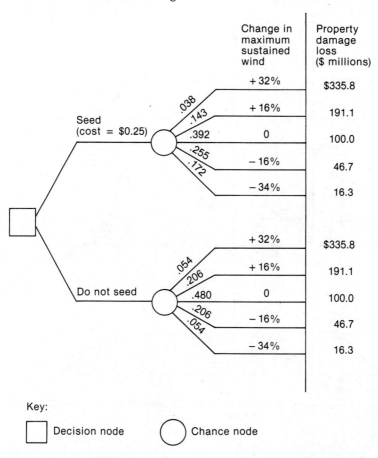

	Change in maximum sustained wind	Property damage loss ($ millions)

Key:

☐ Decision node   ◯ Chance node

hole is dry. Or the government decision maker might want to factor into the seeding problem the costs associated with disaster relief and flood insurance. These and other complications can also be handled with a decision tree, though one with many more branches than Figure 7–3.

Subjective probabilities

Thus far I have said very little about how we obtain probability estimates. Yet decision analysis can be no better than the quality of such estimates.

Figure 7–4
Typical probability distributions

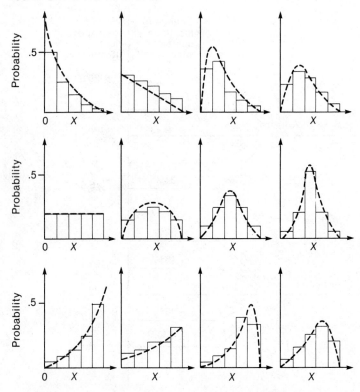

Source: Franz Edelman and Joel A. Greenberg, "Venture Analysis: The Assessment of Uncertainty and Risk," *Financial Executive* 37, no. 8 (August 1969), pp. 56–62.

Figure 7–5
Assessing the lower and upper quartiles

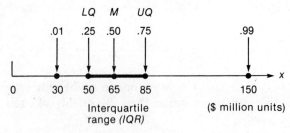

Since we are dealing with uncertainty, what we are after is not a single estimate (e.g., "The dollar value of crimes is $100 million") but a probability distribution. This means that we want to show how likely different values of X are between two extreme values. Recall that in the hurricane-seeding example we did not say "If seeding occurs, the chances of reduced wind velocity are .25." What we did say was that, if seeding occurred, several things could happen to wind velocity (e.g., +32 percent, +16 percent, no change, −16 percent, and −34 percent) and that a probability could be associated with each of these possibilities (e.g., .038, .143, .392, .255, and .172). These estimates could be plotted against their respective probabilities, and a smooth curve could be drawn that connected the five points; this curve would be the probability distribution. Of course, not all probability distributions look the same. Several are illustrated in Figure 7–4.

Let us consider an example of how an analyst might develop a probability distribution for use in decision analysis. Our analyst is interested in the dollar value of flood damage that would accompany a severe hurricane in a certain large city. We will denote this uncertain quantity by X.

After weighing carefully all the information available—data from the Weather Bureau, the Office of Civil Defense, insurance files, and so on, together with the views of experts in relevant areas—our analyst decides that the value X is just as likely to be below $65 million as above it. In other words, $65 million is the .5 fractile, or the median of the distribution.

The next step is to assess the lower and upper quartiles of the distribution. In the best judgment of our analyst, these are $50 million and $85 million, respectively. Let us be clear on what this means. In the analyst's opinion, the probability of X being less than $50 million is numerically equal to .25, while there is a .75 chance that X is less than $85 million.

Our analyst now begins to consider extreme points, the .01 and .99 fractiles. In the analyst's opinion, they are $30 million and $150 million, respectively. This means that the probabilities that X lies below $30 million and above $150 million are .01 and .99. This also means that the probability that X lies above $30 million and below $150 million is numerically equal to .98. These assessments are illustrated in Figure 7–5.

Before we can get from this point to a probability distribution similar to the ones in Figure 7–5, two preliminary steps are necessary. First, we must show the cumulative distribution; and second, based on the cumulative distribution, we must draw a histogram.

Figure 7–6 shows the cumulative distribution of the value of property

384

Figure 7–6
Cumulative distribution

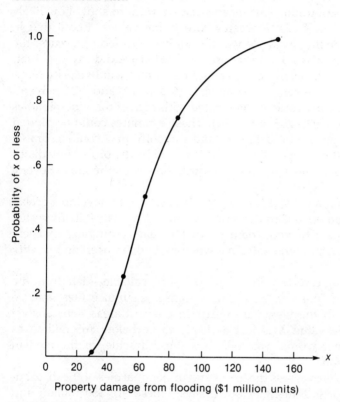

Property damage from flooding ($1 million units)

damage from flooding. Note how each of the five points on the graph correspond to the five points on the line. Using Figure 7–6, the analyst can develop a table like the one shown below.

Interval	Probability that X lies within this interval
Less than 30	.01
Between 30 and 50	.24
Between 50 and 70	.34
Between 70 and 90	.22
Between 90 and 110	.12
Between 110 and 130	.04
Between 130 and 150	.02
Greater than 150	.01

This table, in turn, enables the analyst to develop a histogram, as shown in Figure 7–7. Finally, by connecting the midpoints, it is fairly

Figure 7–7
Probability distribution of property damage

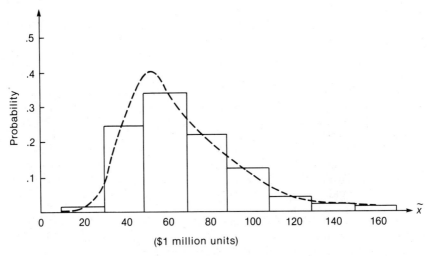

($1 million units)

easy to draw in the probability distribution (indicated by dashed curve).

Objectivist, or non-Bayesian, mathematicians, sometimes called "classicists" or "sampling theorists," object to the use of subjective (or "personal") probabilities such as these, arguing that only objective probabilities are meaningful. To paraphrase Raiffa, they refuse to make probability statements; as far as they are concerned, X is either greater than .25 or it is not. They choose not to get involved in any subjective betting games in which one tries to formalize psychological attitudes. But advocates of the Bayesian probability approach reply that the use of prior probabilities is logical and consistent.[23] Though this debate lies somewhat beyond the scope of this book, the basic idea cannot be swept under the rug. Few thinking adults do not raise their eyebrows slightly on first encountering Bayesian probabilities.

The future of risk management

The *estimation* of risk is a scientific question and therefore a legitimate activity of scientists and policy analysts. The *acceptability* of a given level of risk, however, is a political question, to be determined in the political arena. For example, lab tests show that immense quantities of saccharin cause bladder cancer in rats, and the FDA moves to ban it. There is a loud protest from diet-drink makers and consumers, and Congress votes to keep saccharin on sale. This two part process (estima-

---

[23] Ibid., p. 283.

tion—acceptability), which now shapes many regulatory decisions, seems likely to continue. Two men who have thought hard about risk management help us understand why.

Lester Lave of Carnegie-Mellon University asks "How safe is safe enough?"

> The answer depends on more than the risk of an activity. Safety goals also depend on the benefits and costs of enhancing safety. Try banning automobiles to end the carnage on the highways. Try banning pharmaceuticals because their side effects pose risks. The hard question is: How much safety do people want, considering the benefits and costs of making products and processes less risky?
>
> In searching for some alternative to zero risks, the courts have introduced the notion of *significant risk*. The Supreme Court found that the Occupational Safety and Health Administration had not shown there was a "significant risk" at the old benzene standard. Thus, OSHA had no basis for revising the standard.
>
> Recently, some agencies have grappled with "significant risk." The Nuclear Regulatory Commission set a risk goal for nuclear power. Risks to the surrounding population may not be increased more than 0.1 percent, one part in 1,000. The Food and Drug Administration now acts as if a food additive is not really a carcinogen if it would cause less than one cancer per million lifetimes of those exposed. . . .
>
> However arbitrary these numbers seem, they have helped these agencies to ignore minimal risks.[24]

Paul Slovic, a psychologist and past president of the Society of Risk Analysis, thinks that the key motivator for protective action by the public is the *perceived* probability of a loss. For this reason, it seems unlikely that risk management can ever become a purely scientific issue of estimation.

> It occurred to us that a person may not wear seat belts because his perceived probability of being in an accident is extremely low. A little calculation showed that the risks of being injured in an automobile trip were indeed minuscule— about one trip in four million ends in a fatal accident and one trip in 100,000 produces a disabling injury. The problem is that we take so many automobile trips, about 50,000 in an average lifetime. Over that many trips, the probabilities add up to a risk that is not trivial. One out of every 100 people dies in a car accident; one out of every three suffers an injury that is "disabling" for one day or more.
>
> We reasoned that if we could get motorists to look at the *cumulative risk* of driving, they would recognize the probability of a serious accident as high enough to justify making a "once-and-for-all" decision to always wear a seat belt. . . .
>
> People's attitudes and behaviors reflect their experiences. . . . But each safe trip rewards the nonuse of seat belts; the bother of buckling up has been avoided without injury. On the other hand, motorists who do use belts put forth that effort without any noticeable reward.

Moreover, the feedback we receive about our own driving skill is misleading. We can drive in an unsafe manner, yet still make trip after trip safely. People recognize that accidents do occur, but consider themselves personally invulnerable. All too often, in the course of 50,000 trips, this belief proves false.

The government generally should not intrude into the private lives of its citizens. But in those cases in which people do not and cannot appreciate the risk from a particular hazard, and thus fail to protect themselves, government has a duty to protect them. This seems to be such a case.[25]

APPLICATION: OFFSHORE OIL LEASING DECISION

In 1973, while on a fellowship in the Marine Policy Program at Woods Hole Oceanographic Institution on Cape Cod, Massachusetts, William R. Ahern was charged with the following policy research topic: Should Georges Bank, a rich international fishery on the continental shelf about 100 miles east of Cape Cod, be leased by the Department of the Interior for oil and gas development? In deciding this issue, Ahern applied a number of principles of policy analysis. By way of conclusion let us see how he applied those principles and consider the answers he found.[26]

The first principle

Exploration suggests that Georges Bank might contain commercially attractive deposits of oil and natural gas. Should the secretary of the interior lease these tracts to oil companies for development?

The first principle suggests that the analyst try to identify all possible major outcomes of the decision. The outcomes of the decision in favor of development can be listed by visualizing what happens physically if the lease sale is made. In approximate chronological order, these are the major outcomes:

- The federal government receives payments for the leases.

- The oil industry makes expenditures to explore for oil and gas and, if successful, to buy and place production structures and support facilities.

- Employees are hired by the oil industry.

- Oil and gas are produced and transported to shore.

- Royalty payments are made to the federal government; and the risk of oil spills is created, with possible attendant impacts on the fishery and on shore.

---

[24] Lester Lave, "The High Cost of Regulating Low Risks," *The Wall Street Journal,* August 19, 1983.

[25] Paul Slovic, "Informing and Educating the Public about Risk," *Risk Analysis* 6, no. 4 (1986), pp. 403–15.

[26] William R. Ahern, "Applying Principles of Policy Analysis to an Offshore Leasing Decision," *Policy Analysis* 1, no. 1 (Winter 1975), pp. 133–40.

Identifying the outcomes of the decision against development is much more difficult step in formulating the framework for the analysis. Policy analysts frequently take a decision and frame it as a "yes" or "no" choice, comparing the benefits and costs of the "yes" decision alone. Had Ahern done this, he would have taken the potential oil and gas production, the federal revenues, and the expenditures and employment resulting from a "develop" decision and compared them with the potential environmental damage to the fishery and the New England shore. "But the results would have been misleading, because if a 'no' decision were eventually made, the status quo would go marching off into the future, producing outcomes in all the possible areas of impact that would have existed under the 'yes' decision. The decision is actually a choice between two alternative packages of outcomes, with each package containing advantages and disadvantages."

The question, then, is What happens if Georges Bank is *not* leased and no oil and gas production occurs there? Answering this question requires placing all the major outcomes of a "yes" decision in context. If the oil and gas under Georges Bank are forgone, then the equivalent amount of oil will most likely be imported into the United States and carried to New England ports in tankers and barges. This is because the marginal source of additional oil for the United States is foreign nations, and for the East Coast it is primarily the Middle East. All of the oil used in New England is currently carried there by sea. And there is excess demand for gas, which is satisfied by the dirtier and more expensive substitute, oil. In sum, the package of outcomes resulting from a "no" decision consists of: imports of oil from foreign nations; taxes and royalties paid to foreign nations; duty payments made to the federal government; and payments made to owners of foreign oil tankers and barges. This is the package of outcomes that should be compared with the outcomes of developing Georges Bank. The Georges Bank decision, then, no longer stands in misleading isolation, with its advantages looking very large to proponents and its disadvantages looking very large to opponents. The choice is between producing oil and gas on Georges Bank and importing the equivalent amount of oil.

The second principle

The second principle suggests that the analyst should try to predict all major outcomes using explicitly stated assumptions and explicitly stated uncertainties. Outcomes should be described quantitatively whenever possible and appropriate, because the values of numbers are easily understood and compared. Some useful information is conveyed by the statement that offshore production results in fewer major oil spills than does the equivalent amount of international tanker traffic in oil, but clearly not as much information as is conveyed by stating that off-shore production results in 40 percent fewer spills. Numbers are best for describing outcomes simply because we can reach agreement on their values and because they enable us to convey how much more and how much less the values are. (See Box 7–2.)

This prediction of outcomes is a hazardous crystal-ball activity, but the honest predictor should deal explicitly with the uncertainties. Ahern estimated that the potential annual oil production from Georges Bank could be twenty-three million barrels. "But I would not make a bet on that. Because of all the geologic and economic uncertainties, I made a low estimate that no oil production at all could occur and a high estimate that as much as 152 barrels a year could be produced. Now I would give odds, maybe even twenty to one, that the production would be within that range. The analyst should provide his 'most likely' estimate, but he should also provide the range of possibilities so the decision maker realizes what is at stake."

In environmental and safety analysis, an estimate is frequently made of the "worst credible" damage possible. By itself, this estimate can be highly misleading. Using data on past oil spills from offshore production and predictions of possible oil production from Georges Bank, Ahern drew a probability distribution to estimate the number of major oil spills that might occur if the bank were developed. The result showed that if his high oil production estimate came true, and subjectively he gave this less than a 2.5 percent chance, then there would be a 5 percent chance of as many as thirty-five major oil spills occurring during a forty-year production period. This is a scary and impressive number. But it is the extreme tail of the possibilities, which have a joint probability of occurrence of 2.5 percent times 5 percent, or 0.125 percent. However, a very different picture emerges from the "most likely" estimated number of spills, which was derived by using the most likely oil production estimate and the fifty-fifty point on the probability distribution. This expected number of major oil spills over a forty-year period is 2.5. So now advocates of different positions can predict "only 2.5 spills" or "thirty-five major oil spills" over forty years—two very disparate conclusions. It is the analyst's job to give the decision maker the full range of possibilities rather than only a single-point estimate; the latter is often selected to illustrate a bias and generally turns out to be wrong.

The third principle

The third principle suggests that the analysts predict the net outcomes in context. "The estimated outcome rarely will occur in isolation. To publish only the impact of a punch in the nose on a man being hanged

---

Box 7–2
Specify!

Most students describe such probability assessments with words or phrases like "probably," "unlikely," "almost certainly," or "hardly any chance." But these terms are ambiguous: most people use the word "probably" to describe a fairly wide range of probabilities; furthermore, various studies have shown that some people use "probably" to mean something like a 50 or 60 percent chance, while others take it to mean at least a 90 percent chance.

Numerical probability assessments have the advantage over such words and phrases in that they are much more specific: 101 numbers are available to describe probabilities from 0 percent to 100 percent to the nearest percent. Furthermore, they are unambiguous (the meaning of a 70 percent chance can be clearly defined); and they permit a decision maker to perform certain arithmetic calculations that may help determine the preferred decision.

Two types of students tend to be particularly reluctant to accept the use of subjective probability assessments. The first type includes science and engineering students who have been rigorously trained in the use of objective statistical data. Such data, we must point out to them, are often unavailable or simply do not exist. In these cases, one must rely on subjective probability assessments. The only question is whether to make these assessments consciously and explicitly or to use some unconscious, intuitive process. The former tends to lead to better decisions.

The other students who tend to be uncomfortable with subjective, numerical probability assessments are those in literature, history, languages, and the fine arts who have had little exposure to mathematics. They are bothered not by the subjective nature of the assessments but by their being expressed as numbers. But "a 95 percent chance," we point out, is just as good an English phrase as "extremely likely." Indeed, it is better, at least in cases where precision of expression is important, because it is more specific. . . .

Significantly, words like "probably" or "unlikely" may reflect more than imprecise communication. They may reflect imprecise thought. The student who says "it will probably rain tomorrow" never really bothered to determine exactly how likely it was to rain. He used the word "probably" to mask his unwillingness to think carefully about this uncertainty. According to George Orwell, our language "becomes ugly and inaccurate because our thoughts are foolish, but the slovenliness of our language makes it easier for us to have foolish thoughts." One of the advantages of using precise probabilities—10 percent, 75 percent, etc.—is that before the student can use them he must think.

Source: Robert D. Behn and James W. Vaupel, "Teaching Analytical Thinking," *Policy Analysis* 2, no. 4 (Fall 1976), pp. 663–92.

is to give a misleading impression." Ahern calculated that the oil and gas production platforms could prevent fishing over possibly 150 square miles of the Georges Bank fishery. At first, this outcome appears undesirable. But the fishery is being rapidly overfished by large trawler fleets from Poland, West Germany, and the Soviet Union. In a few years, it will probably be destroyed. Thus, in an ironic twist, the platforms would help conserve the fishery resources. They would give the cod, flounder, and herring somewhere to hide.

Another example of dealing with net outcomes was Ahern's estimate that Georges Bank might provide New England with 150 billion cubic feet of gas a year. The importance of this estimate is difficult to comprehend unless the figure is placed in the context of total possible New England gas consumption. But that would require a forecast of energy use. To place all outcomes in their proper context can entail a vast amount of work. But a rough attempt must be made—otherwise the conclusions will be of limited use to the policymaker. The best situation, of course, is one in which the big picture has already been analyzed and forecast by someone else, preferably someone with no ax to grind. This was not entirely the case here, but the Department of the Interior had made a forecast of New England gas use. So Ahern reported that the gas obtainable from Georges Bank could be roughly equivalent to 30 percent of the department's estimate of 1985 New England gas consumption. Ideally, the analyst's sources for contexts and big pictures present ranges of possibilities, so that the impacts of the decision outcomes can be presented realistically as ranges too.

To his surprise, Ahern concluded

> that the leasing would be desirable, from both a national and a New England point of view, because it dominated the alternative, bringing in foreign oil by tanker, in all the categories of outcomes. Tanker traffic results in more oil spills of a more damaging character than does the equivalent amount of offshore oil and gas production. It seems more desirable to invest in domestic oil and gas production facilities than to have the investment in a foreign country, probably in Saudi Arabia. It seems better that the dollars from New Englanders' purchases of oil flow to the U.S. government, U.S. businesses, and U.S. workers than to Middle Eastern governments, foreign workers, and foreign oil-tanker owners. Thus, on both economic and environmental grounds, I concluded that Georges Bank should be leased as soon as possible.[27]

But, as Ahern was quick to note, the opposite conclusion can be reached if the development decision is framed as a comparison of the costs and benefits of a "yes" decision, if the actual alternative and its set of outcomes are not identified, and if outcomes are not placed in their

---

[27] Ibid.

proper perspective as net outcomes occurring in a broad context. Ahern concluded: "Policy analysis is still very much an art rather than a science. But I hold that the three principles discussed . . . can be used both to do and to evaluate any analysis that purports to be a basis for decision making."

FOR FURTHER REFLECTION

1. In 1985, the Secretary of Education proposed cuts in federal educational assistance to college students, drawing outrage from practically every quarter of academe. Specifically, the secretary called for a $32,500 family income eligibility cap for federally subsidized, guaranteed bank loans, and a $25,000 income cap for a range of other programs: Pell Grants, federally subsidized student jobs, direct federal loans, and certain other government grants that require no repayment by recipients. Various university administrators contended that the proposal would force colleges to turn away qualified students who are unable to afford steep tuition. Other critics insisted that some high school seniors would be unable to pay for any college, and that some students currently enrolled would be unable to complete their studies.

   Assume that you are an analyst for a senator who considers himself "a fiscal conservative but progressive on social issues" and have been asked to prepare a briefing paper about the proposal. The senator asks: Rhetoric aside, how draconian are the proposed cuts? Are there other alternatives? What factors should be considered in making a decision?

2. A true die is rolled twice. What is the probability of getting a total of six? Is this a subjective probability?

3. An agency must decide whether to go forward with a research and development project to develop a new process. If the project is successful, the social benefit will be $500 million; if it is not, it will lose $100 million. Experts say that the probability of failure is 0.8. Use a decision tree to set this problem up. What is the expected monetary value (EVM) of the project? What is the EMV of a no-go decision?

4. Choose between:
   a. A sure gain of $3,000, and
   b. An 80 percent chance of winning $4,000 and a 20 percent chance of winning nothing.

   What does your answer tell you about yourself as decision maker?

5. Choose between:

     a. A sure loss of $3,000, and

     b. An 80 percent chance of losing $4,000 and a 20 percent chance of losing nothing.

     What conclusions do you draw about your decision-making style now?

6. State lotteries have become a popular way of raising money. Critics see a host of hidden costs and pitfalls. Do you see any?

7. In trying to value a human life, how much weight should be placed on the person's own willingness to pay? If a worker places a low value on his life by certain actions (e.g., where he works), should society as a whole do the same?

8. When the government purchases an input for a program or project that is subject to a sales tax, should the producer's or the purchaser's price be used in the cost calculation?

9. Unlike most private firms, government is very large relative to the economy. Sometimes public projects induce changes in market prices. For example, a government irrigation project could bring so much land into production that the market price of food falls. If the market price changes, how should the additional amount of food be valued—at its original price, at its price after the project, or at some price in between?

10. Every year, more than 290 million tons of hazardous waste—more than a ton for each man, woman, and child—are produced in the United States, according to federal officials. The problem of what to do with toxic substances has spawned numerous debates. One solution is to have the material loaded aboard specially built and equipped ships and incinerated on the Atlantic Ocean many miles east of New Jersey. Sites off the Georgia-Florida coast and in the Gulf of Mexico have also been considered. Assume that, while doing an internship at the EPA, you have been asked to help in the analysis of this proposal. What points might you raise?

11. Imports account for more than 75 percent of the shoes Americans buy, compared with 48 percent in 1980. Congressional delegations from a dozen states argue that domestic producers have been injured and propose a 24 percent cutback in the import of shoes. Assume that, while doing an internship with the U.S. International Trade Commission, you have been asked to help in the analysis of this proposal. What points might you raise?

12. How do people formulate strategy? First, they decide what their opponents, say, the Russians, are likely to do. Then they plan how they will react, and so on. The more detailed these scenarios become, the more likely they will seem. But imagine the following scenario of a limited nuclear attack on the United States.

1. Soviet forces carry out limited attack. . . .
2. U.S. sensors correctly characterize nature of attack. . . .
3. U.S. leaders correctly interpret soviet intent. . . .
4. U.S. leaders send appropriate retaliatory orders to U.S. forces. . . .
5. U.S. forces carry out counterattack as ordered. . . .
6. Soviet sensors correctly characterize nature of U.S. counterattack. . . .
7. Soviet leaders correctly interpret U.S. intent. . . .
8. Soviet leaders successfully send "stand down" order to forces.[28]

According to prevailing strategic doctrine, an "appropriate" U.S. counterattack (Step 5) would induce the U.S.S.R to end the hostilities without triggering an all-out nuclear exchange (Step 8). In a real war, however, there would be a chain of individual events—for example, orders not received or not carried out properly—any one of which could divert this simple scenario into other outcomes.

Assume that there is a 90 percent chance of being right at each juncture of the above scenario and that things go reasonably close to plan. What would be the overall odds that the "predicted" outcome would occur?

13. What is an endangered species (e.g., elephant and cheetah) worth?

---

[28] Based on Ashton B. Carter, "The Command and Control of Nuclear War," *Scientific American* 252, no. 1 (January 1985), p. 39.

Chapter 8

Assessing Impacts

Thinking about costs may get us to first base, but it will not take us to home plate. Discovering hidden costs and measuring benefits gives us insight but not answers. So, what policymakers now need are methods to put the analysis of the preceding chapter into a format that provides a better basis for decision. Above all, they need methods that allow them to stand back from the proposed solution and see its overall impact.

Three analytical methods, while not panaceas, have proven useful in recent years: cost-benefit analysis, cost-effectiveness analysis, and technology assessment (or impact assessment). This trio, separately or together, can help the policymaker in addressing the most important question about a proposed course of action: What difference will it make in the morning?

PRELIMINARIES: THE PRINCIPLE OF MAXIMUM SOCIAL GAIN

The three methods to be examined build on a common assumption: Public goods are not exempt from the principle of efficiency. Yes, other principles, like equity, apply—and we will consider them in the last chapter—but the emphasis here is on efficiency.

It will be recalled from our earlier discussions that the public sector provides certain goods because spillovers or other market failures keep the private sector from producing the proper amounts of those goods. Because these public sector goods involve the production of an output by the government, the same model used to form a judgment of the "goodness" or "badness" of private sector production can be used here as well. Now, however, the question must be: Is the government producing the right things in the right quantities? To answer this question we focus on the costs and benefits of decisions. Since the goal is to

Figure 8–1
Representing social benefits

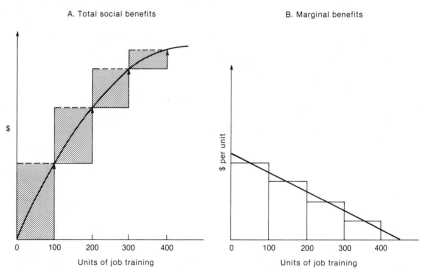

A. Total social benefits   B. Marginal benefits

$ / $ per unit

Units of job training   Units of job training

satisfy the preference and desires of the citizens, the familiar notions of willingness to pay (demand) and cost are again relevant.

Take, for example, the public sector's provision of job-training services. What is the willingness of people to pay for the "outputs" generated by job training? If job-training services are provided, the incomes of trained workers will tend to go up; that is a benefit for which the trained workers would be willing to pay something. The productivity of the trained workers will go up; that is a benefit for which business would be willing to pay something. The prices of the goods that these trained workers produce may fall because of their increased productivity; that is a benefit for which consumers would be prepared to pay something. Some retrained workers may be able to move out of poverty; that is a benefit for which society as a whole would be willing to pay something. All of these willingnesses to pay are incorporated into the total social benefits (TSB) curve shown in Figure 8–1A.

Note that although the total benefits rise with increased production, the shaded rectangles indicate that they rise at a decreasing rate. This means, in the language of economics, that the *marginal benefit*—the extra benefit added by each last extra unit of job training—will be decreasing. The fact that total benefits increase at a decreasing rate is shown in Figure 8–1B by the declining steps of marginal benefits. If we make our units smaller and smaller, the steps in the total benefits smooth out and the total benefits become the smooth curve in Figure 8–1A.

Figure 8–2
An optimal level of social benefits

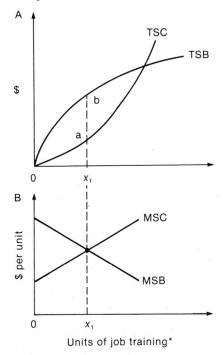

* E.g., the number of graduates.

Smoothed marginal benefits are shown in Figure 8–1B by the *downward-falling* line.

A further question must be asked before we can know whether public goods are being produced in the right amount. This question, not surprisingly, pertains to the costs to society of providing our training program. All of the social costs of providing the program (instructor salaries, buildings, etc.) are summarized in the total social costs curve (TSC) of Figure 8–2A. For reasons that will soon be apparent, Figure 8–2A also shows the total social benefits curve.

Figure 8–2B shows the marginal social costs (MSC) and the marginal social benefits (MSB) curves. As Figure 8–1B showed, these incremental curves are uniquely related to the "total" curves and can be located as soon as the "total" curves are known. The efficiency objective of the public sector should now be clear: *provide job-training services until the social gains of the next unit fail to exceed the social costs.* This optimum amount of job training is located at X_1 in Figure 8–2.

Figure 8–3
Life cycle costs and benefits

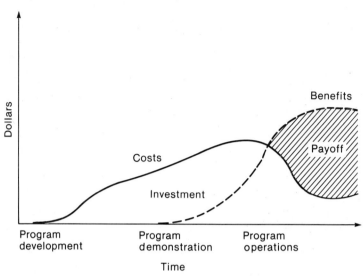

At output X_1, the difference between TSB and TSC (line *ab* in Figure 8–2A) is maximized. At X_1, the marginal social benefit (MSB) equals the marginal social cost (MSC). Hence, X_1 is the "right" amount of job training for the public sector to provide; it is consistent with the principle of maximum social gain.

COST-BENEFIT ANALYSIS

Cost-benefit analysis (CBA) is a leading method for helping us to follow the principle of maximum social gain. Essentially, CBA is a way of looking at the flow of costs and benefits from a program over time (see Figure 8–3). Programs for which costs exceed benefits are clearly in violation of the principle of maximum social gain—though they might still be justified on equity grounds.

To perform CBA, one must know three things. First, one must obviously know how to measure costs and benefits. This was discussed in the last chapter, but here we need to say a little about exactly how the cost-benefit matrix might be used in an actual CBA.

Obviously, the direct benefits to users must be included. But how about the indirect benefits? In the past, good practice dictated that all appropriate indirect benefits be considered at least by major category.

But which indirect benefits are relevant to CBA? John F. Due and Ann F. Friedlander make this observation:

> In general, only real or technological benefits, those increasing output potential of society other than through direct use of the activity, are relevant, whereas strictly pecuniary benefits are not. Included in real benefits are reductions in outlays and resources used for other governmental activities, such as those for highways when new rapid transit lines are built. [For example,] if the building of an irrigation dam reduces flooding or provides more pleasant scenery for tourists driving past the lake created by the dam, these are real externalities and should be included in the measured benefits. The building of a subway, by lessening the traffic on expressways, saves time for persons continuing to use their cars and reduces accidents, air and noise pollution, and investment in expressways and parking structures. These benefits alter the physical conditions of production or consumption for persons other than those directly using the activities.[1]

The second thing one needs to know about CBA is how to determine the present value of future benefits. A dollar in benefits now is worth more than a dollar in benefits ten years from now. Why is this so? Because interest can be earned on money. So in order to evaluate a particular program and to compare alternatives, a discount factor must be used to reduce the values of future benefits and costs to their present values. Below we will take a closer look at how this is done.

Thirdly, for CBA to be of any use, policymakers should know prior to the actual analysis what constitutes an acceptable relationship between the costs and the benefits of a program. For this, decision rules are necessary. This matter is also discussed below.

The discount factor

The mathematics of determining the present value of future costs and benefits is fairly elementary: just multiply by the appropriate discount factor. The formula for discount factors is

$$DF = \frac{1}{(1 + i)^t}$$

where t is the year under consideration and i is the discount rate. If, for example, one is interested in the present value (say, in 1988) of benefits in the year 1995, t would be 7. For convenience, Appendix B provides discount factors for up to 50 years at various rates.

---

[1] John F. Due and Ann F. Friedlaender, *Government Finance* (Homewood, Ill: Richard D. Irwin, 1973), p. 168.

The determination of i is not quite so easily explained. In fact, depending on the assumptions one makes, a number of discount rates are possible. Three approaches to selecting a discount rate might be noted[2] :

1. Rate of return in the private sector. The opportunity cost of a government program may be defined as the amount that funds would earn in private investment—the typical earnings rate of money capital in new private investment. This approach is favored by persons who seek to minimize government investment activity, since it produces the highest of alternative discount rates and therefore allows justification of a minimum of governmental activities.

Suppose that the last $1 million of private investment in the economy yields an annual rate of return of 20 percent. If the government takes $1 million from the private sector, then society loses the $200,000 that would have been generated by the private sector investment. Thus, the opportunity cost of the government program is the 20 percent rate of return of the private sector.

A couple of objections to this approach might be noted. First, risk is greater with private enterprise; if a project is unsuccessful, the owners of a firm may lose their entire investment. The government faces no similar risk, particularly in view of the wide range of projects being undertaken by the government. Second, the use of this discount rate is based on the assumption that the resources taken by government are diverted from private investment. But if the project is financed by taxes, the resources are in part diverted from consumption, not investment, and the opportunity cost of use in the investment sector is not relevant.

2. The social rate of time preference. Some experts think that the discount rate should measure the value that society (not capital markets) places upon consumption that is sacrificed in the present. Society as a whole should therefore give additional weight to the interests of future generations; accordingly, the social rate of time preference is less than the borrowing rate. If individuals would save more (provided that the other individuals were also saving more) in the interest of more rapid economic growth, the argument would have some validity. But there is no evidence that this happens. Since future generations will presumably have higher real incomes than the present generation, there seems to be little need for formal consideration of their interests relative to that of the present generation. Furthermore, if the government wishes

---

[2] Ibid., pp. 173–75. See also David F. Bradford, "The Choice of Discount Rate for Government Investments," *American Economic Review*, no. 65 (December 1975) pp. 887–99.

to increase the overall rate of real saving, it may do so by encouraging private investment as well as public investment.

In any event, how does one *measure* the social discount rate? The only feasible method is to ascertain the current government bond rate. If persons are, on the whole, willing to purchase the existing issues of bonds at 8 percent, presumably this figure reflects the time preference— the amount that persons must be paid in order to induce them to save rather than consume. But there are several problems. From all indications, most saving is done for reasons unrelated to compensation form time preference, and thus the figure is of no particular significance; it measures the compensation necessary to induce persons to buy bonds rather than to forgo present consumption. The actual bond rate is dependent in large measure on monetary policy, reflecting the current objectives of the Federal Reserve System to expand or contract the supply of money capital.

3. The government borrowing rate without reference to time preference. The complexities and inadequacies of these two approaches suggest the use of a simple rule: the rate of interest at which a particular government can borrow, without any effort to justify this figure on a time preference basis. In a sense this is the direct cost to the government of obtaining the funds. Admittedly it is an artificial figure because of the influence of monetary policy on the rate, and it is substantially lower than the figure of marginal productivity of capital in private enterprise. But given the fact that government investment is in large measure competitive with private consumption, not private investment, use of the figure is perhaps logical. Certainly it is the simplest approach. This approach would currently produce a discount rate of around 10 percent and thus would justify a much greater range of government projects than would the 20 percent or so rate of return on private equity investment.

The foregoing analysis focused on investment decisions by the federal government. Fortunately, the problem becomes much simpler when one turns to the determination of present values for state and local government programs. These governments have a given rate at which they can borrow; this is the rate that they should use.

How much difference does the discount rate selected make? Quite a bit, as Figure 8–4 shows for one program, the liquid metal fast breeder reactor. Discount rates can be decisive in determining the future of programs, and for that reason they can generate acrimonious political debates. It is equally useful to answer the question by considering the effect of proceeding with projects oblivious to discount rates.

Now, equipped with a little better appreciation of discount rates, let us see how the discount factor can be applied. Assume a ten-year program which will commit the government to the stream of expendi-

Figure 8–4
**Dollar benefits from the liquid metal fast breeder reactor with a
1993 introduction**

A. At a 7.5 percent discount rate   B. At a 10 percent discount rate

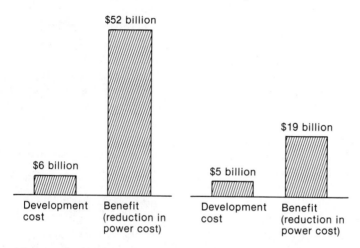

tures appearing in column 2 of Table 8–1 and will result in the series
of benefits appearing in column 3. The discount factor for a 10 percent
discount rate is presented in column 4. The present value cost for each
of the ten years is calculated by multiplying column 2 by column 4;
the present value benefit for each of the ten years is calculated by multiplying column 3 by column 4. (The figures in column 4 are from Appendix
B.) Present value costs and benefits are presented in columns 5 and 6,
respectively.

Decision rules: Ratios versus absolutes

The example in Table 8–1 looks at costs and benefits as a ratio and
as an absolute difference. Ultimately, the test of whether to go with a
project or not hinges on budgetary constraints. Consider the following
three projects (assume that the projects are alternative highway systems
that can be built across a given area):

Project	Benefits	Costs	Ratio	Net benefit
A	30	3	10	27
B	64	8	8	56
C	100	40	2.5	60

In the absence of a budgetary constraint, it would clearly be desirable
to build project C, which would yield a net benefit of 60. But assume

Table 8–1
A hypothetical cost-benefit analysis

(1)	(2)	(3)	(4)	(5)	(6)
				Present value cost	*Present value benefit*
Year of operation	*Expected yearly cost*	*Expected yearly benefit*	*Discount factor for 10 percent*[*]	*(column 2 × column 4)*	*(column 3 × column 4)*
1	$10	$ 0	0.909	$ 9.1	$ 0.0
2	20	0	0.826	16.5	0.0
3	30	5	0.751	22.5	3.8
4	30	10	0.683	20.5	6.8
5	20	30	0.621	12.4	18.6
6	10	40	0.564	5.6	22.6
7	5	40	0.513	2.6	20.5
8	5	40	0.467	2.3	18.7
9	5	40	0.424	2.1	17.0
10	5	25	0.386	1.9	9.7
				$95.5	$117.7

The sum of column 5 is the present value cost: $95.5.
The sum of column 6 is the present value benefit: $117.7.
The present value net benefit is the difference between the present value total benefit and the present value total cost: $117.7 − $95.5 = $22.2.
The benefit-cost ratio is 117.7/95.5 = 1.23.
[*] Though the formula for computing discount factors, given i and t, has been provided, in actual practice one would simply look the discount factors up in a table such as that found in Appendix B.

that the projects are no longer mutually exclusive and that numerous versions of the same project can be undertaken up to the limit of the budget. An example might be teacher-training programs (A, B, and C would be alternative forms of training). In such a case, we should follow the ratio criterion, and if our budget were 120, we would undertake 40 versions of project A. Finally, assume the budget to be relatively small in comparison with the costs of the projects. Now we might run into the problem of indivisibilities. If the constraint were exactly 8, we would find that project B should be our favored alternative.

In sum, ratios are applicable when we are dealing with a budget constraint, but no constraint with respect to the number of projects that can be undertaken. The net benefit approach is to be employed when the projects must be treated as mutually exclusive ventures.

Some illustrative examples

A few years back, the Department of the Interior published a massive document that identified four sites for power plants on the Snake River in the Pacific Northwest. Each site had a different power-generating capacity and different environmental effects. Table 8–2 summarizes the findings.

404

Table 8–2
Cost-benefit analysis of four power projects (in $1,000)

	Appaloosa	High mountain sheep with China gardens	High mountain sheep without China gardens	Pleasant valley
Benefits				
Power	$49,267	$60,748	$35,944	$44,165
Fish and wildlife enhancement	6,590	None*	None*	None
Recreation	406	336	336	305
Flood control	200	245	245	74
Total	$56,463	$61,329	$36,525	$44,544
Costs				
Federal investment	$16,083	$18,705	$10,377	$15,021
Annual operative	4,687	5,570	3,180	3,966
Total	$20,770	$24,275	$13,557	$18,987
C/B ratio[†]	2.72	2.53	2.69	2.35

All columns under heading *Project*.

* Very large adverse effects on spawning fish.
[†] Based on 3¼ percent discount rate over 100-year period.
Source: U.S. Department of the Interior, *Resource Study of Middle Snake* (Washington, D.C.: Government Printing Office, 1968).

As can be seen from the table, the Appaloosa project had the highest cost-benefit ratio of the four projects. But the precision of 2.72 is deceptive; it masks disagreements among experts. For example, John Krutilla, a senior research associate for Resources for the Future and a leading water resource economist, testified at Federal Power Commission hearings that, on the basis of a detailed analysis of the four plans in terms of 1967 prices, Appaloosa project was the least desirable economically. Employing a 9 percent rate of interest, which he considered a more realistic measure of the opportunity cost of capital, Krutilla found only project 2, High Mountain Sheep with China Gardens, to be economically feasible—that is, an investment in which the benefits exceeded the costs—and this only by totally disregarding the destruction of the river's natural character.[3]

One should not get the impression from the foregoing discussion of CBA that this method applies only to such matters as water resources and energy projects. As our next two examples should show, it is equally applicable to investments in human resources.

For the last two decades, the subject of investments in education has continued to receive attention from policymakers. Much of the re-

[3] Cited in Lawrence G. Hines, *Environmental Issues* (New York: W. W. Norton, 1973), p. 145.

search in this area, however, has been concerned with aggregate investments in job training. For good reason, then, Adger A. Carroll and Loren A. Ihnen decided to focus on a specific type of investment in education—two years of post-secondary technical school.[4] Their method was CBA.

The researchers compared the earnings of graduates from a technical school in North Carolina with those of demographically and educationally similar high school graduates in order to estimate the additional income attributable to the two years of technical education. These average earnings differentials increased from $555 per year in the first year after graduation to $1,038 per year in the fourth year. By projecting these differentials into the future and comparing the results with educational costs, including forgone earnings, a rate of return of 16.5 percent was calculated. The present value of these net benefits, discounts at 5 percent, was $33,713 per graduate; discounting at 10 percent, it was $11,494. The benefit-cost ratios were 4.5:1 at a 5 percent discount rate and 1.5:1 at a 10 percent discount rate.

Should Congress pass a law requiring that all cars be equipped with air bags? This option is much more expensive than seat belts, but vehicle occupants would be protected whether they chose to be or not. Such a "cost-benefit" analysis was done for five insurance companies in 1981 by William Nordhaus, a professor at Yale and an economic adviser to the Carter White House. Nordhaus assumes that full-front air bags would cost $425 in large quantities. From studies of what is spent to save lives with kidney dialysis and other health and safety programs, he imputes a social value to each life saved of $480,000. Then he plugs in conservative assumptions about air-bag effectiveness, nonfatal injury costs, vehicle life, voluntary use of seat belts, and so forth. The "present value" of benefits in reduced injury and death, Nordhaus finds, is double the cost of equipping all new cars with air bags. And the benefits minus the costs equal $47 billion.[5]

Caveat

To conclude: not only must analysts understand the basic skills of CBA (discounting, present values, decision rules, etc.) so that they can use it when appropriate, but they must also be clear on what CBA

---

[4] Adger A. Carroll and Loren A. Ihnen, "Costs and Returns for Two Years of Post-Secondary Technical Schooling," *Journal of Political Economy*, December 1967, pp. 862–73.

[5] M. J. Fisher, "Claybrook Complains: Reagan Team Deflates Air Bag Cause," *National Underwriters* 85 (January 9, 1981), p. 2. See also Kenneth E. Warner, "Bags, Buckles, and Belts: The Debate over Mandatory Passive Restraints in Automobiles," *Health Politics Policy and Law* 8 (Spring 1983), pp. 44–75. Peter Passell estimates that about one in five U.S. traffic deaths could be prevented by air bags in "Have They Let the Air Out of a Great Safety Idea?" *Medical Economics* 61 (March 19, 1984), pp. 166–74.

cannot do so that they can reject it when its use is inappropriate. Some analysts want to believe that the B/C ratio is the rule that solves all problems, but we have seen that that can depend on budgetary constraints. Other analysts want to believe that CBA is highly accurate, but we have seen, at least in the liquid metal fast breeder reactor and Middle Snake River projects, that discount rates, which contain not a little subjectivity, can make a decision difference.

Still other analysts want to ignore the very important relationship between equity and efficiency. On equity grounds, a technical school project having a 1.5:1 benefit-cost ratio might be preferable to a technical school project having a benefit-cost ratio of 5:1 if the former resulted in additional income to a particularly disadvantaged segment of the population. On the other hand, analysts too infatuated with the CBA technique can sometimes make quite inefficient decisions. For example:

- Suppose that there is a water shortage in a city. Assume that, given the current situation, consumers would be willing to pay enough to cover the cost of constructing the dam and aqueducts that would provide a new source of water. Does this not mean that the project is economically efficient? Answer: Not necessarily. It might be better to reallocate the existing supply. This could be done by letting the price of water rise until demand equals supply. The cost of reallocation is the value of the water forgone to those consumers who reduce their consumption of water. The benefit of the project cannot exceed this alternative cost of supply. *Thus the project is efficient only if its cost does not exceed the alternative cost of reallocation.*

- Suppose that it is claimed that a new power plant is justified because the cost of obtaining additional electricity from present capacity exceeds the cost of the new plant. Is this a valid argument for constructing the new plant? Answer: Not necessarily. The cost of obtaining more electricity from the new plant may be less than the cost of obtaining it from current capacity but exceed the benefits of the additional electricity to consumers. In this case, more electricity is not justified, whatever the source.[6]

As you might expect, assumptions play a big part in shaping the outcome of a cost-benefit analysis. The left-hand column in Table 8–3 presents an apparently straightforward analysis of the national highway speed limit. The comments on the right show you where another analyst might disagree. You might wish first to examine the analysis with the comments covered to see how many potentially false assumptions slide by and how many you catch.

---

[6] Larry Seidman, "A Course in the Economics of Policy Analysis," *Policy Analysis*, Winter 1975, pp. 197–214.

Table 8–3
Measuring the costs and benefits of the 55 mph speed limit: A critical appraisal

Steps	Comments

Costs

1. The major cost of the National Maximum Speed Law (NMSL) was the additional time spent driving as a result of slower speeds. To calculate the number of hours spent driving in 1973, divide the total number of vehicle miles by the average highway speed (65 mph) and then multiply by the average occupancy rate per vehicle.

   Next, find the number of hours spent driving in 1974 by dividing total vehicle miles by the average highway speed in 1974 (58 mph). The NMSL caused some people to cancel trips and others to find alternative modes of transportation, and as a result, time calculations based on 1974 mileage would be an underestimate. Therefore, we should use 1973 mileage.

   Using the following formula, where *VM* is vehicle miles, *S* is average speed, *R* is average occupancy rate, and *H* is the number of hours lost,

   $$H = \left(\frac{VM_{1973}}{S_{1974}} - \frac{VM_{1973}}{S_{1973}} \right) \times R$$

   The number of hours lost driving in 1974 based on this equation, is estimated to be 1.72 billion.

   Why use 1973 mileage without any adjustment? The average growth rate in travel before 1973 was 4 percent. Therefore, the formula should be

   $$H = \left(\frac{1.04VH_{1973}}{S_{1974}} - \frac{VM_{1973}}{S_{1973}} \right) \times R$$

   Using the above formula, the estimated number of hours lost should be 1.95 billion—not 1.72 billion.

2. To estimate the value of this time, begin with the average wage rate for all members of the labor force in 1974—$5.05. The value of one hour's travel is not $5.05 per hour because very few persons would pay this sum to avoid an hour of travel. We estimate that the people will pay up to 33 percent of their average hourly wage rate to avoid an hour of commuting. The value of time spent traveling is therefore about $1.68 per hour.

   Why take a percentage of the $5.05 figure based on what commuters would pay to avoid an hour of travel? We should avoid reducing the value of people's time for two reasons. First, the value of time in cost to society is equal to what society will pay for productive use of that time. Time's value is not what a commuter will pay to avoid commuting because commuting has other benefits, such as solitude for thinking, or the advantages of suburban living. Second, the value of time spent driving for a trucker is many times the industrial wage rate. Discounting would greatly underestimate the value of commercial drivers.

3. Application of the cost figure ($1.68) to the time lost figure (1.72 billion hours) results in an estimated travel cost of $2.89 billion.

   Applying the value of one hour's time to the hours lost as calculated above (1.95 billion) results in an estimated travel cost of $9.85 billion.

4. The NMSL also has some enforcement costs. Total enforcement costs for signs, advertising and patrolling are about $810,000.

   Total enforcement cost should be about $12 million—not $810,000.

Table 8–3 *(continued)*

Steps	*Comments*

Costs

a. New signs were posted. Cost estimates from twenty-five states for modification of speed limit signs totaled $707,000; for fifty states, this results in an estimated $1.23 million. Spread out over the three-year life of traffic signs, we get an estimate of $410,000.

OK

b. The federal government engaged in an advertising campaign encouraging compliance. The Federal Highway Administration's advertising budget for 1974 was $2 million. About 10 percent of this, or $200,000, was spent to encourage compliance with the NMSL. Assume that an additional amount of public service advertising time was donated, for a total of $400,000.

Not OK. The Federal Highway Administration does other advertising, not all $2 million should be counted part of NMSL. Public service advertising estimate also seems low.

c. Compliance costs are difficult to estimate. The cost of highway patrols cannot be used because these persons were patrolling highways before the NMSL. Assume that states did not hire additional personnel solely for enforcement of the NMSL. Therefore, we assume that enforcement of the NMSL will not entail any additional costs above enforcement of previous speed limits.

Compliance costs pose some problems, but they can be estimated. In 1973, some 5,711,617 traffic citations jumped by 1,713,636 to over 7.4 million. Each additional traffic citation includes an opportunity cost to society. If a law enforcement officer were not issuing traffic tickets, he could be solving other crimes. Assuming that it requires fifteen minutes for a law enforcement officer to issue a speeding ticket, the total cost of law enforcement is $2.9 million. This figure is based on the average cost of placing a law enforcement officer on the streets at $6.75 per hour. This figure is clearly an underestimate because it does not count time lost waiting to catch speeders.

Approximately 10 percent of all speeders will demand a court hearing. Estimating an average of thirty minutes for each hearing and an hourly court cost of $45 results in an additional cost to society of $3.8 million for 171,000 cases. Given the overloaded court dockets, this opportunity cost may be even higher.

Benefits

1. The most apparent benefit of the NMSL is the amount of gasoline saved. The average gasoline economy improves from 14.9 miles per gallon at 65 miles per hour to 16.1 at 58 miles per hour. Use this information to estimate the number of gallons of gasoline saved by traveling at lower speeds. Gallons saved will be calculated by the following formula

Why estimate gasoline saved by comparing 1973 and 1974 miles-per-gallon figures in relation to vehicle miles traveled? The federal figures for average miles per hour are estimates based on several assumptions. Given the conflict between industry estimates, Environmental Protection Agency estimates, and Energy Department estimates, any miles-per-hour estimate must be considered unreliable. The number of vehicle miles traveled is also based

Table 8–3 (continued)

Steps	Comments

Benefits

$$G = \frac{VM_{1973}}{MPG_{1973}} - \frac{VM_{1973}}{MPG_{1974}}$$

$$= \frac{697 \text{ b-gals.}}{14.9 \text{ mi/gal.}} - \frac{697 \text{ b-gals.}}{16.1 \text{ mi/gal.}}$$

$$= 3.487 \text{ billion gallons}$$

on gallons of fuel sold multiplied by average miles per hour. Hence, this figure is also subject to error.

Studies of the efficiency of gasoline engines show that the effect of reducing the average speed of free-flow interstate highways would save 2.57 percent of the normal gas used. In 1979, American motorists consumed 106.3 billion gallons of gasoline. Saving 2.57 percent would total 2.73 billion gallons.

In 1974, the average price of gasoline was 52.8 cents per gallon. This market price, however, does not reflect the social cost of gasoline, due to government price controls on domestic oil. The marginal (or replacement) cost of crude oil is the price of foreign oil. Therefore, the price of gasoline must reflect the higher cost of foreign oil. Use the market price of gasoline in the absence of price controls, which is about 71.8 cents per gallon. This figure yields an estimate of $2.50 billion in benefits through gasoline saved.

Why not use the market price? There is no way to determine whether a marginal gallon of gasoline will be imported or come from domestic reserves. In addition, the costs and benefits of the NMSL should not be distorted simply because the U.S. government does not have a market-oriented energy policy. In 1974, gasoline cost 52.8 cents per gallon, and therefore a gallon of gasoline saved was worth 52.8 cents.

2. A major second-order benefit of the 55-miles-per-hour limit was a large drop in traffic fatalities, from 55,087 in 1973 to 46,049 in 1974. Part of the gain must be attributable to reduction in traffic speeds. Studies by the National Safety Council estimate that up to 59 percent of the decline in fatalities was the result of the speed limit. Applying this proportion to the decline in fatalities provides an estimated 5,332 lives saved. The consensus of several studies is that a traffic fatality costs $240,000 in 1974 dollars. Using this figure, the value of lives saved in 1974 is estimated at $1,279.7 million.

OK.

3. The NMSL also resulted in a reduction of nonfatal injuries. Use the 59 percent figure found in the fatality studies. Between 1973 and 1974, nonfatal traffic injuries declined by 182,626. Applying the estimated percentages results in 107,749 injuries avoided. Generally, three levels of injuries are identified: (1) permanent total disability, (2) permanent partial disability and permanent disfigurement, and (3) nonpermanent injury. In 1971, the

OK.

410

Table 8–3 *(concluded)*

Steps	Comments

Benefits

proportion of traffic injuries that accounted for injuries in each category was .2 percent, 6.5 percent, and 93.3 percent, respectively. The National Highway Traffic Safety Administration estimated that in 1971 the average cost of each type of injury was $260,300, $67,100, and $2,465, respectively. The average injury, therefore, cost $8,745 in 1974 dollars. Applying this figure to our injury estimate results in $942.3 million as the social benefit of injury reduction.

4. The final benefit of the reduction in property damage fell from 25.8 million to 23.1 million. About 50 percent of this reduction was the result of lower speeds. The NMSL saved 1.3 million cases of property damage at an average cost of $363. Therefore, the total benefits from property damage prevented is $472 million.   *OK.*

Conclusion

Our estimates of the costs and benefits of the NMSL result in the following figures (in millions):

A better estimate would be as follows:

Costs

Time spent traveling	$2,890.0	
Enforcement	.8	
	$2,890.8	

Benefits

Gasoline saved	$2,500.0	
Lives saved	1,297.7	
Injuries prevented	942.3	
Property damage	472.0	
	$5,212.0	

Net benefits: $2,321.2 million
Benefits to costs ratio: 1.8

Costs

Time spent traveling	*$9,848.0*	
Enforcement	*12.0*	
	$9,860.0	

Benefits

Gasoline saved	*$1,442.0*	
Lives saved	*998.0*	
Injuries prevented	*722.0*	
Property damage	*236.0*	
	$3,398.0	

Net benefits: $−3.398
Benefits to costs ratio: .34

Source: The steps and data were suggested by Charles T. Clotfelter and John C. Hahn, "Assessing the National 55 m.p.h. Speed Limit," *Policy Sciences* 9 (1978), pp. 281–94. The critical comments are based on Charles A. Lave, "The Costs of Going 55," *Car and Driver*, May 1978, p. 12.

COST-EFFECTIVENESS ANALYSIS

Because of the relative ease of measuring benefits in dollars, the first real application of CBA was to water resource projects such as dams, river basin developments, and irrigation. As we have seen, CBA can be used with some success in the areas of recreation and education;

it can also be used in such areas as urban development, transportation, and pollution. Still, certain areas—for example, defense, regulation, criminal justice—remain less than accessible to CBA because the measurement of benefits in dollars is just too difficult.

But, to make rational choices among alternatives, is it absolutely essential that we be able to measure benefits in dollars? Cost-effectiveness analysis, a first cousin of CBA, seems to suggest that it is not. Cost-effectiveness analysis, like CBA, is based on the assumption that outputs of public programs are useful and valuable. Unlike CBA, it does not require that we actually measure the value of the benefits obtained. Thus, the choice among alternatives comes down to this: choose the program that gives the greatest return in some value per dollar. The question is: What value?

The Department of Transportation (Table 8–4) suggests that one possible value for analysts to focus on when selecting among automobile safety programs is lives saved or, as the Department of Transportation prefers to put it, "fatalities forestalled." Based on this value, mandatory safety belt use is an overwhelming favorite: for every $506 spent on the safety belt program, one life can be saved, whereas the government must pour $7,680,000 into roadway alignment and gradient countermeasures in order to obtain the same result, that is, one life saved.

An interesting application of cost-effectiveness analysis involves the use of beta carotene to prevent cancer deaths. (The body converts beta carotene into Vitamin A.) Faced with limited resources, the United States obviously must set priorities for research to identify preventable causes of cancer. A quantitative approach to priority setting, based on principles of cost-effectiveness analysis, can offer guidance in this process. An illustrative application of such a model suggests that the National Institutes of Health–supported clinical trial of dietary beta carotene offers a greater expected reduction in cancer mortality per research dollar than a program of determining the amount of carcinogens in high-volume industrial chemicals. Milton C. Weinstein calculates that a program costing $420,000 per year could prevent 384 cancer deaths, or about $91 per year of life saved.

Let us now take a closer look at cost-effectiveness analysis in the health field.[7]

One of the first analytical studies at the Department of Health, Education, and Welfare was a study of disease control programs. The basic concept was simple. HEW (now Health and Human Services) could support a number of categorical disease control programs whose objectives are to save lives or to prevent disability by controlling specific

---

[7] Milton C. Weinstein, "Cost-Effective Priorities for Cancer Prevention," *Science,* 221 (July 1983).

Table 8–4

Ranking of countermeasures by decreasing cost effectiveness in present value dollars per total fatalities forestalled—ten-year total

Countermeasure	Fatalities forestalled	Cost ($ millions)	Dollars per fatality forestalled
Mandatory safety belt usage	89,000	45.0	506
Highway construction and maintenance practices	459	9.2	20,000
Upgrade bicycle and pedestrian safety curriculum offerings	649	13.2	20,400
Nationwide 55-mph speed limit	31,900	676.0	21,200
Driver improvement schools	2,470	53.0	21,400
Regulatory and warning signs	3,670	125.0	34,000
Guardrail	3,160	108.0	34,100
Pedestrian safety information and education	490	18.0	36,800
Skid resistance	3,740	158.0	42,200
Bridge rails and parapets	1,520	69.8	46,000
Wrong-way entry avoidance techniques	779	38.5	49,400
Driver improvement schools for young offenders	692	36.3	52,500
Motorcycle rider safety helmets	1,150	61.2	53,300
Motorcycle lights-on practice	65	5.2	80,600
Impact-absorbing roadside safety devices	6,780	735.0	108,000
Breakaway sign and lighting supports	3,250	379.0	116,000
Selective traffic enforcement	7,560	1,010.0	133,000
Combined alcohol safety action countermeasures	13,000	2,130.0	164,000
Citizen assistance of crash victims	3,750	784.0	209,000
Median barriers	529	121.0	228,000
Pedestrian and bicycle visibility enhancement	1,440	332.0	230,000
Tire and braking system safety critical inspection—selective	4,591	1,150.0	251,000
Warning letters to problem drivers	192	50.5	263,000
Clear roadside recovery area	533	151.0	284,000
Upgrade education and training for beginning drivers	3,050	1,170.0	385,000
Intersection sight distance	468	196.0	420,000
Combined emergency medical countermeasures	8,000	4,300.0	538,000
Upgrade traffic signals and systems	3,400	2,080.0	610,000
Roadway lighting	759	710.0	936,000
Traffic channelization	645	1,080.0	1,680,000
Periodic motor vehicle inspection—current practice	1,840	3,890.0	2,120,000
Pavement markings and delineators	237	639.0	2,700,000
Selective access control for safety	1,300	3,780.0	2,910,000
Bridge widening	1,330	4,600.0	3,460,000
Railroad-highway grade crossing protection (automatic gates excluded)	276	974.0	3,530,000
Paved stabilized shoulders	928	5,380.0	5,800,000
Roadway alignment and gradient	590	4,530.0	7,680,000

Source: U.S. Department of Transportation, *National Transportation: Trends and Choices* (Washington, D.C.: Government Printing Office, 1977), p. 99.

Table 8–5
Cancer control program: 1968–1972 (estimated)

	Uterine-cervix	*Breast*	*Head and neck*	*Colon-rectum*
Grant costs (in thousands)	$ 97,750	$17,750	$13,250	$13,300
Number of examinations (in thousands)	9,363	2,280	609	662
Cost per examination	$ 10.44	$ 7.79	$ 21.76	$ 20.10
Examinations per case found	87.5	167.3	620.2	496.0
Cancer cases found	107,045	13,628	982	1,334
Cost per case found	$ 913·	$ 1,302	$13,493	$ 9,970
Cancer deaths averted	44,084	2,936	303	288
Cost per death averted	$ 2,217	$ 6,046	$43,729	$46,181

Source: Grosse, "Problems of Resource Allocation," p. 1210.

diseases. The study was an attempt to answer this question: If additional money were allocated to disease control programs, which programs would show the highest payoff in terms of lives saved and disability prevented per dollar spent? The study defined "disease" liberally; motor vehicle accidents were included along with tuberculosis, syphilis, cancer, and arthritis.

Table 8–5 illustrates the approach to one set of diseases—cancer. Robert N. Grosse and his colleagues at HEW looked at cancer of the uterine cervix, the breast, the head and neck, and the colon-rectum. They estimated cost per examination and the probable number of examinations that would be required for each case found. From this was derived the number of cases that would be found for an expenditure level, and estimates of the cost per case were found. An estimate was made of the number of deaths that could be averted by the treatment following the detection of the cancers, and then they calculated the cost per death averted, which ranged from about $2,200 in the case of cervical cancer up to $40,000 to $45,000 in the case of head and neck and colon-rectum cancer.[8]

The HEW then plotted the program costs; these included both the cost of the treatment and the cost of the federal detection program (see Figure 8–5). On the horizontal axis of Figure 8–5, estimates of deaths averted are ordered by the increase in the cost per death averted in each program. Segments of the curve identified to each disease cover the extent of the program that it was estimated could be mounted in

[8] Robert N. Grosse, "Problems of Resource Allocation in Health," in *The Analysis and Evaluation of Public Expenditures*, U.S. Congress, Joint Economic Committee (Washington, D.C.: Government Printing Office, 1969).

Figure 8–5
Cancer program costs (estimated)

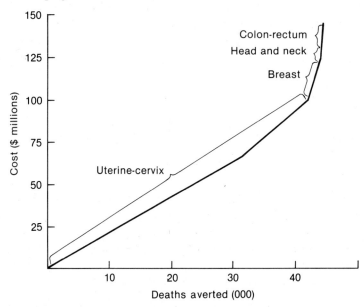

*Seat belt, restraint, pedestrian injury.

the years 1968–72 before running into sharply increasing costs. In concept, the cervical cancer curve is cut off where costs become higher than the costs for the breast cancer program, and so on. From this analysis one might say that if only $50 million were available, cervical cancer should get all the funds. If we have $115 million, the breast cancer control programs look quite competitive. Head and neck and colon-rectum cancer *detection* programs do not look attractive as major cancer control programs when viewed in this context. Thus the analysts recommended that HEW concentrate on research.

The same kind of analysis was performed for each of the five programs studied (Figure 8–6). There seemed to be a very high potential payoff for certain educational programs in motor vehicle injury prevention, such as trying to persuade people to use seat belts, not to walk in front of a car, and so on. And then, as we move up this curve, again ordered by the cost of averting death, we begin adding the others. But this criterion, deaths averted, was not completely satisfactory. The number of fatalities attributed to arthritis were negligible. Second, there is the question: Does it matter who dies? Does it matter whether the person who dies is a 30-year-old mother of a family, a 40-year-old father of a family, or a 75-year-old grandfather?

Figure 8–6
Deaths averted versus costs

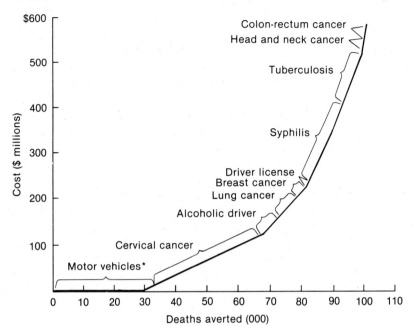

*Seat belt, restraint, pedestrian injury.

Source: Robert M. Grosse, "Problems of Resource Allocation in Health," U.S. Congress, Joint Economic Committee, The Analysis and Evaluation of Public Expenditures (Washington, D.C.: Government Printing Office, 1969).

Finally, let me illustrate with a hypothetical example how *marginal analysis* might be used to determine the preferred mix of disease control programs (hypothetical). Assume that we can determine, as in the following table, the number of lives saved by different expenditures on disease A and disease B:

Disease A

Expenditures	Lives saved
$ 500,000	360
1,000,000	465

Disease B

500,000	200
1,000,000	270

If we only knew the effect of spending $1 million, we might opt for a program in which all of our money was spent on controlling disease

A, as we could save 465 lives instead of 270 if we spent it all on disease B. Similarly, if we only knew the effects of programs of a half million dollars, we would probably prefer A, as we would save 360 lives rather than only 200 lives.

But if we knew the results for expenditures of both half a million dollars and $1 million in each program, we would quickly see that spending half of our money in each program was better than putting it all in one program, assuming that we had $1 million available:

Our calculations would be:

Expenditures	Lives saved
$1,000,000 on A	465
$1,000,000 on B	270
$1,000,000 $\left\{ \begin{array}{l} \$500,000 \text{ on A–360} \\ \$500,000 \text{ on B–200} \end{array} \right.$	560

But suppose that we had still more discrete data, as in the following tables, which give us the effect of each $100,000 spent on each control program:

Disease A

Expenditures	Lives saved
$ 100,000	100
200,000	180
300,000	250
400,000	310
500,000	360
600,000	400
700,000	430
800,000	450
900,000	460
1,000,000	465

Disease B

Expenditures	Lives saved
$ 100,000	50
200,000	95
300,000	135
400,000	170
500,000	200
600,000	225
700,000	240
800,000	255
900,000	265
1,000,000	270

We could then spend the $1 million even more effectively:

Expenditures	Lives saved
$1,000,000 $\left\{ \begin{array}{l} \$600,000 \text{ on A–400} \\ \$400,000 \text{ on B–170} \end{array} \right.$	570

Box 8–1

The cost-effectiveness of basic research in biologic science

When, as is bound to happen sooner or later, the analysts get around to the technology of medicine, they will have to face the problem of measuring the relative cost and effectiveness of all the things that are done in the management of disease. . . .

In fact, there are three quite different levels of technology in medicine, so unlike each other as to seem altogether different undertakings. The analysts will be in trouble if they are not kept separate.

1.   First of all, there is a large body of what might be termed "nontechnology," impossible to measure in terms of its capacity to alter either the natural course of disease or its eventual outcome. A great deal of money is spent on this. It is valued highly by the professionals as well as the patients. It consists of what is sometimes called "supportive therapy." It tides patients over through diseases that are not, by and large, understood. It is what is meant by the phrases "caring for" and "standing by.". . .

The cost of this nontechnology is very high, and getting higher all the time. . . .

2.   At the next level up is a kind of technology best termed "halfway technology." This represents the kinds of things that must be done after the fact, in efforts to compensate for the incapacitating effects of certain diseases whose course one is unable to do very much about. It is a technology designed to make up for disease, or to postpone death. The outstanding examples in recent years are transplanted hearts, kidneys, livers, and other organs, and the equally spectacular inventions of artificial organs. . . .

It is a characteristic of this kind of technology that it costs an enormous amount of money and requires a continuing expansion of hospital facilities.

3.   The third type of technology is the kind that is so effective that it seems to attract the least public notice; it has come to be taken for granted. This is the genuinely decisive technology of modern medicine, exemplified best by modern methods for immunization against diphtheria, pertussis, and the childhood virus diseases, and the contemporary use of antibiotics and chemotherapy for bacterial infections. The capacity to deal effectively with syphilis and tuberculosis represents a milestone in human endeavor, even though full use of this potential has not yet been made. . . .

The point to be made about this kind of technology—the real high technology of medicine—is that it comes as the result of a genuine understanding of disease mechanisms, and when it becomes available, it is relatively inexpensive, relatively simple, and relatively easy to deliver.

Offhand, I cannot think of any important human disease for which medicine possesses the outright capacity to prevent or cure where the cost of the technology is itself a major problem. The price is never as high as the cost of managing the same diseases during the earlier stages

---

Box 8–1 *(concluded)*

of no-technology or halfway technology. If a case of typhoid fever had to be managed today by the best methods of 1935, it would run to a staggering expense. At, say, around fifty days of hospitalization, requiring the most demanding kind of nursing care, with the obsessive concern for details of diet that characterized the therapy of that time, with daily laboratory monitoring, and, on occasion, surgical intervention for abdominal catastrophe, I should think $10,000 [in 1971 dollars] would be a conservative estimate for the illness, as contrasted with today's cost of a bottle of chloramphenicol and a day or two of fever. The halfway technology that was evolving for poliomyelitis in the early 1950s, just before the emergence of the basic research that made the vaccine possible, provides another illustration of the point. Do you remember Sister Kenny, and the cost of those institutes for rehabilitation, with all those ceremonially applied hot fomentations, and the debates about whether the affected limbs should be totally immobilized or kept in passive motion as frequently as possible, and the masses of statistically tormented data mobilized to support one view or the other? It is the cost of that kind of technology, and its relative effectiveness, that must be compared with the cost and effectiveness of the vaccine. . . .

It is when physicians are bogged down by their incomplete technologies, by the innumerable things they are obliged to do in medicine when they lack a clear understanding of disease mechanisms, that the deficiencies of the health-care system are most conspicuous. If I were a policymaker, interested in saving money for health care over the long haul, I would regard it as an act of high prudence to give high priority to a lot more basic research in biologic science. . . .

Source: Adapted from Lewis Thomas, "The Lives of a Cell." Reprinted by permission from *The New England Journal of Medicine* 284, no. 19 (May 13, 1971), p. 1082.

The lack of marginal data resulted from both a lack of such data for most programs and a lack of economic sophistication on the part of the Public Health Service analysts who performed the studies. Despite the theoretical shortcomings, the results were useful when applied with some common sense.

TECHNOLOGY ASSESSMENT

While the cost-benefit and cost-effectiveness calculuses are desirable methods in principle for making policy regarding many issues, sometimes exact numerical estimates of either benefits or costs are impossible, given the complexity of modern society and our knowledge about it. For these reasons, it is often an illusion to think that a single correct policy can be found by listing benefits and costs of all alternatives and choosing the one whose net sum or return per dollar is greatest. Policymakers must also exercise judgment where uncertainties, *unintended consequences*, and incomparabilities abound. To make that judgment more informed, policymakers can use a third method—technology assessment.

The problem defined: Unintended consequences

- Edward C. Banfield argues that, strange as it may seem, government programs to aid the cities are directed mainly toward the problems of comfort, convenience, amenity, and business advantage.[9] Insofar as these programs have any effect on serious urban problems, it is to aggravate them. Take housing and urban renewal programs:

  Since the creation in 1934 of the Federal Housing Authority (FHA), the government has subsidized home building on a vast scale by insuring mortgages that are written on easy terms and, in the case of the Veterans Administration (VA), by guaranteeing mortgages. Most of the mortgages have been for the purchase of new homes. (This was partly because FHA wanted gilt-edged collateral behind the mortgages that it insured, but it was also because it shared the American predilection for newness.) It was cheaper to build on vacant land, but there was little such land left in the central cities and in their larger, older suburbs. These were almost always zoned so as to exclude the relatively few Negroes and other "undesirables" who could afford to build new houses. In effect, then, the FHA and VA programs have subsidized the movement of the white middle class out of the central cities and older suburbs while at the same time penalizing investment in the rehabilitation of the run-down neighborhoods of these older cities. The poor—especially the Negro poor—have not received any direct benefit from these programs.

- Martin S. Feldstein argues that unemployment insurance creates two major distortions in the economy, both of which increase unemployment.[10] First, it encourages benefit recipients to remain jobless longer than they otherwise would. Second, it makes it easier for companies to lay off workers, especially in seasonal and cyclical industries.

---

[9] Edward C. Banfield, *The Unheavenly City Revisited* (Boston: Little, Brown, 1974).

[10] Martin S. Feldstein, "The Welfare Loss of Excessive Health Insurance," *Journal of Political Economy* 81, no. 2 (March–April 1973), pp. 251–73.

Feldstein argues that while unemployment insurance benefits seemingly replace only one third to one half of a jobless worker's previous gross wages, they actually replace much more—in some cases nearly 100 percent—because these benefits are exempt from taxes. As a result, the existence of unemployment insurance benefits causes workers to take more time searching for new jobs in the hope that a higher wage will quickly offset the relatively small amount of income lost during the search. "The unemployed make the rationally correct decision for themselves," Feldstein says. But since the time spent in job search represents lost production, "extended search is socially wasteful."

- Policy analysts are also debating the ultimate impact on society of the widespread use of day care.[11] They are investigating the long-range effects on a society in which ever-growing numbers of adults will have been raised in day-care settings. In the past, mothers took care of babies, but this is no longer the case. The effects of day care on family bonds are important because as families go, so goes society. Does day care reduce the stress on parents and make it possible for them to enjoy their children more? Or does day care for very small children deprive them of the bonding to a single person that psychologists believe produces an emotionally responsive person with a strong sense of identity? Are children in day care less compliant and more assertive—to the point of being aggressive? In particular, what are the long-term effects of low-quality day care—improper socialization, reading problems, behavior problems leading to societal problems?

  These are important public policy questions. Families are changing in all modern industrialized nations, and children do best in societies that adjust to that fact. Should the United States have nationally subsidized day care support systems like most other modern industrialized countries? Should the private sector be required to adopt policies that enable working mothers to stay home with newborns? Would the long-term social benefits outweigh the program's costs?

- Some lawyers and environmentalists have argued that research into methods of agricultural mechanization has had adverse social impacts. Mechanization critics often use the mechanical tomato harvester developed at the Davis campus of the University of California to illustrate the negative consequences of such mechanization. Twenty years ago, 44,000 Mexican men, called braceros, picked the tomatoes used to make catsup and tomato paste. Today, as a result of the work of UC plant scientists and engineers, fewer than 10,000 women sort twice as many tomatoes. Critics argue that 34,000 farm jobs were eliminated,

---

[11] For a summary of the research literature on day care see Allison Clarke-Stewart, *Day Care* (Cambridge, Mass.: Harvard University Press, 1982).

and that it is unlawful and irrational to put farm workers on welfare just to reduce harvesting costs. They also charge that the mechanization that results from ag research may eliminate small farmers because break-even production levels are too high. University administrators who support this research respond that without mechanization, rising wages would have forced much of the tomato-processing industry to follow its workforce to Mexico. This relocation would have displaced transportation and cannery workers in the United States, as occurred in the asparagus-processing industry. No one can say whether the tomato harvester, on balance, destroyed or created jobs in the United States, but it is clear that by making tomato work easier, American women were attracted into the tomato harvest.[12]

Biotechnology critics, meanwhile point to the potato-patch experiment. At the University of California at Berkeley, scientists developed a genetically engineered organism which, if sprayed on potato plants, could protect them from frost—which costs U.S. farmers ten of millions of dollars each year. But critics suggest that the microbe could possibly change weather patterns and disrupt delicate ecological balances.[13]

- The new automation technology, using computers, robots, and artificial intelligence, has reawakened fears that machines will replace human beings and create mass unemployment. Do those fears make any more sense today than they did at the dawn of the Industrial Revolution when textile workers smashed the machinery they thought would put them out of work? According to a study by the Office of Technology Assessment, the change in national employment induced by programmable automation (PA) will not be massive in the near term. Depending on macroeconomic conditions, use of automation can increase without significant growth in national unemployment. However, PA will exacerbate unemployment problems for individuals and regions. The potential long-term impact of PA on the number and kind of jobs available is enormous, and it is essential that the federal government, educational institutions, and industry begin to plan with these considerations in mind. The impact of programmable automation on the work environment is one of the most significant, yet largely neglected issues. Depending on how it is designed and used, PA can substantially change the nature and organization of the manufacturing workplace and consequently influence levels of job satisfaction, stress, skills, and productivity.[14]

---

[12] Marjorie Sun, "Weighing the Social Cost of Innovation," *Science* 223 (March 1984), pp. 1368–69.

[13] Patricia A. Bellow, "Agricultural Research, Once Little Noticed, Grows Controversial," *The Wall Street Journal,* November 21, 1984.

[14] Office of Technology Assessment, *Computerized Manufacturing Automation: Employment, Education, and Workplace* (Washington, D.C.: Government Printing Office, 1984).

The methodology of technology assessment

A relatively new class of policy studies is technology assessment. Joseph F. Coates of the Office of Technology Assessment of the U.S. Congress gives this authoritative definition: technology assessment comprises studies that systematically examine the effects on society that may occur when a technology is introduced, extended, or modified, with special emphasis on those consequences that are unintended, indirect, or delayed.[15]

A number of points ought to be kept in mind with regard to this class of impact studies. Perhaps the foremost is the broad sense in which we use the word *technology*. The methodology of technology assessment, in our sense, can be applied to new social programs, such as guaranteed annual income, deinstitutionalization, and national time management policy.

In addition to this broad usage of technology, Coates suggests six other points worth bearing in mind about technology assessment.

Technology assessment is a policy tool.

Technology assessment is likely to be iterative and part of an interlocking set of studies.

New technological knowledge creates new ignorance.

A major policy need is the organization of certainty and uncertainty to define effective strategies and tactics for managing any particular technology.

More information and analysis, rather than less, promotes better decisions.

In the long range, indirect and unanticipated effects of a technology are often more significant than the immediate or planned consequences.

TA should be tailor-made to fit each study, and this makes a flexible approach essential. Nevertheless, a number of basic preliminary steps have been found to be common to those TAs already completed and have proven useful. For example, there is almost unanimous agreement on the importance of clearly defining both the assessment task and the technology to be studied.

Below we will consider, in skeletal form, an approach to TA that might, if anything could, be considered classic. In May 1970, the Office of Science and Technology, Executive Office of the President, contracted with the MITRE Corporation for an exploratory technology assessment

---

[15] Joseph F. Coates, "Some Methods and Techniques for Comprehensive Impact Assessment," *Technology Forecasting and Social Change* 6 (1974), pp. 341–57.

project. The objective was to lay the foundations for a methodology that could be used to make assessments in many different fields of technology.

The generalized methodology that MITRE developed has seven steps, but there is nothing inviolate about these steps. Their order may be altered; some may be performed concurrently; and project ground rules may sometimes even dictate skipping one or two steps. The seven steps are: (1) define the assessment task; (2) describe relevant technologies; (3) develop state-of-society assumptions; (4) identify impact areas; (5) make a preliminary impact analysis; (6) identify possible action options; and (7) complete the impact analysis.

1. *Discuss the relevant issues and any major relevant problems; establish the scope (breadth and depth) of the inquiry; develop project ground rules.*

The definition of the task should be reviewed periodically during the course of the study, because new insights will be forthcoming as to what aspect of the technology or its consequences are most important and can be researched most effectively.

Many authorities feel that if technology assessment is to add a new dimension to the planning process, this should be in establishing a tradition, as well as a procedure, for making comprehensive or total assessments. Ideally a technology assessment should strive to make as broad an analysis of impacts as possible—the bad as well as the good, the indirect as well as the direct, the delayed as well as the immediate, the economic-social, environmental-political-legal, etc., effects on bystanders as well as on target groups or participants, and so on.[16]

Technology assessors should—must—take a much broader view of their responsibilities than that of a lawyer who has been hired simply to defend the interests of a litigant. In effect, they should say to the funding agency: "When you hire me, you inevitably get more than you bargain for. My professional obligations require me to consider not only your interests, not only the criteria you believe to be important and relevant, but also a great many other factors, including some that you may not have thought of and may not even care about. My clients are all the affected groups in society, including some who may not even know they're clients; and some of them may have interests that conflict with your own. My findings may lead to the conclusion that your innovation ought to be abandoned even though it would be beneficial to you. That risk is part of the price you must pay for getting any objective assessment of your innovation at all."[17]

---

[16] Martin V. Jones, "Technology Assessment Methodology," *The Futurist*, (February 1972),

[17] Robert Feldmesser, cited in Martin V. Jones, "Generating Social Impact Scenarios: A Key Step in Making Technology Assessment Studies," *Readings in Technology Assessment* (Washington, D.C.: George Washington University, 1972).

However compelling the logic of this position, it is likely that even the most socially enlightened and heavily funded organizations will probably have to limit the breadth of their assessments in one fashion or another. Frequently, there is likely to be a choice between covering many impacts in a superficial manner and covering fewer impacts in greater depth. Persons undertaking technology assessments should be aware of the different ways in which the scope of an assessment can be narrowed:

Assess only one facet of a broad, major field of technology.

Reduce the number of topics covered; for example, do not discuss action options, or discuss only a few opinions rather than many.

Limit the number of societal groups whose welfare is assessed in the impact analysis.

Reduce the time period covered by the assessment analysis.

Reduce the types of impacts studied; for example, confine the analysis to economic impacts.

Limit the number of levels of impacts studied; for instance, examine only initial impacts and ignore secondary and tertiary impacts.

Limit the precision of impact measurements; for example, seek qualitative rather than quantitative measurements.

2. *Describe the major technology being assessed; describe other technologies supporting the major technology; describe technologies competitive with the major and supporting technologies.*

In some cases, technology assessments are made with little attempt to analyze the technologies themselves. For instance, a government agency may want to know what the societal consequences would be if the cost of home computer service were reduced to that of monthly telephone charges. It is possible to proceed immediately to analyze societal responses without examining the technical aspects of home computer service, but there is a danger that such an assessment may overlook some of the most important consequences of the technology. For example, the air pollution hazards created by the automobile have resulted from the types of power plants and fuels used. If seventy years ago assessors had attempted to estimate the automobile's potential impact on our way of life, they would never have foreseen the air pollution problem unless they had gotten down to the power plant and fuel details.

3. *Identify and describe the major nontechnological factors influencing the application of the relevant technologies.*

Nontechnological factors accelerate, dampen, or otherwise affect the development and application of technology. The impacts of technological innovation in the construction industry have been considerably dampened by labor union constraints, contractor restrictions, and local building codes. Because of these institutional obstacles, new technology has not been applied as rapidly as would otherwise have been the case.

Automotive-generated air pollution has become a major problem largely because employment practices result in peak concentrations of urban traffic at certain hours of the day and on certain days of the week. However, if present trends toward a four-day week and a further staggering of work hours continue, these societal trends, which have little or nothing to do with automotive technology, could in ten to twenty years contribute substantially toward reducing the seriousness of automotive-generated air pollution.

In many cases, technological and nontechnological factors interact to such an extent that it is difficult to separate the effects of one from the other. A good example is the way that increased drinking of alcoholic beverages has interacted with automotive technology to cause appalling numbers of highway injuries and deaths.

4. *Identify impact areas—determine the societal characteristics that will be most influenced by the application of the assessed technology.*

A number of checklists have been developed that give an assessor some guidance as to the conditions or characteristics of society that may be affected when a technology is applied. Figure 8–7 is a case in point.

5. *Trace the processes by which the assessed technology makes its societal influences felt.*

According to Sara Kiester, a professor of social psychology and a member of the Robotics Institute at Carnegie-Mellon University, new technology has three orders of effects. The first is the intended technical effects—the planned improvements in efficiency that justify investments in new technology. The second is the transient effects—the very important organizational adjustments made when a technology is introduced but that will eventually disappear. The third is the unintended social effects—the permanent changes in the way social and work activities are organized.[18]

While the computer is today's most prominent new technology, it has much in common with earlier innovations in communications like the telephone and photocopier.

- When the telephone was introduced, it was supposed to improve business communication, and it did. In the end, though, the social effects have been even more striking; the telephone made it possible for people to sustain friendships and help each other quickly and

---

[18] Sara Kiesler, "The Hidden Messages in Computer Networks," *Harvard Business Review*, January–February 1986, pp. 46+.

Figure 8–7
Impact relevance tree for social impact analysis

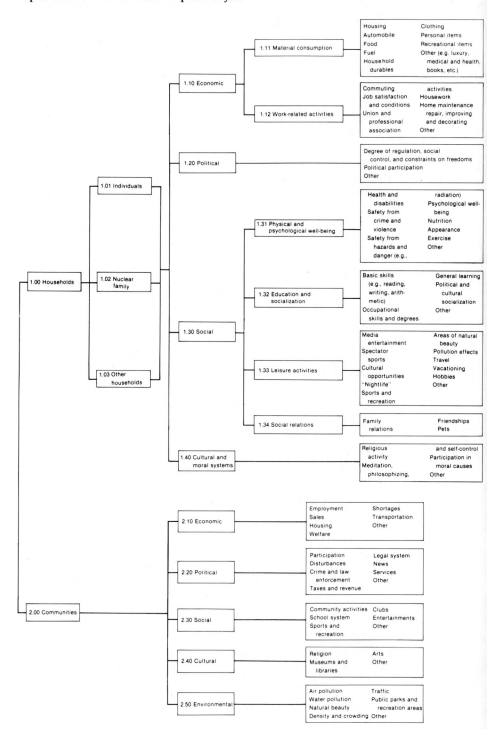

Figure 8–7 *(concluded)*

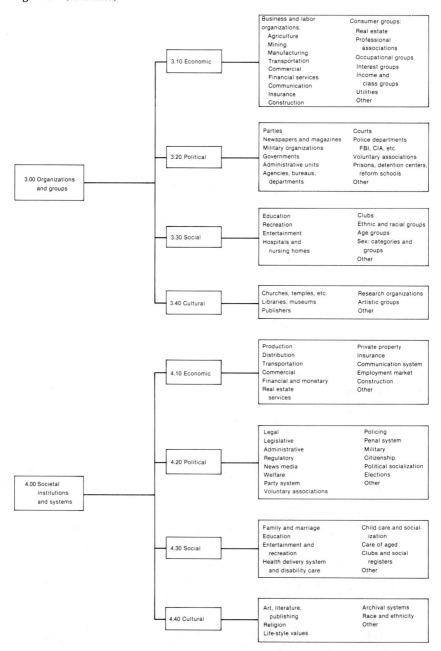

Source: Kurt Finsterbusch, "A Policy Analysis Methodology for Social Impacts," *Journal of the International Society for Technology Assessment* 1, no. 1 (March 1975), pp. 7–8.

easily. Among other things, because it encouraged sustained interaction outside the school, the telephone also made teenage peer groups socially important. The workplace has also felt the social impact of the instrument. Kiesler writes:

> When it was introduced, many managers imagined they would use the telephone to enhance their control; they thought that when they were physically absent, they could use the telephone as a broadcast device for transmitting orders and information to their employees. But the telephone performed even better as a conversation medium than as a broadcast medium. Thus it gave employees a chance to talk back to their supervisors, to exchange information, and to send it up the hierarchy as well as receive it. The telephone did not militarize the workplace but democratized it.[19]

- In discussing the process by which photocopying made its societal influence, D. M. Morrison offers these provocative thoughts:

> The photocopier has, its detractors say, fostered waste, encouraged sloth, stifled creativity and punched holes in the copyright laws. Bureaucrats complain that the machine now makes confidential exchanges all but impossible; foes of official secrecy complain that fear of Xerox-abetted leaks has made bureaucrats more secretive than ever. Whatever the complaint, in view of the social, economic and moral consequences of the office copying machine, the time has plainly come to ask: What hath Xerox wrought? . . . There are 2.3 million copying machines in the United States, and last year they emitted an estimated 78 billion copies—enough to paper Long Island from shore to shore and, if laid end to end, to girdle the globe 546 times at its widest point. Those numbers are double the figures of five years ago, and are expected to more than double again in five years. . . . The urge to reproduce is producing some alarming results. A new impersonality has crept into human discourse as Xerox copies are used more and more in place of personal communication. Americans seem to be losing the faculties of compression, digestion, and economy in their written communication. After all, why bother to summarize when you can simply attach a photocopy of the original? . . . The photocopier has made many Americans too lazy to copy documents by hand, to use carbon paper, to express something in their own words, to read—perhaps too lazy to think.[20]

---

[19] Ibid., p. 47.
[20] D. M. Morrison, "What Hath Xerox Wrought?" *Time*, March 1, 1976, pp. 69–70.

Based on these two examples we might hazard a couple of generalizations. First, the societal influences of new technologies are hard to foresee. Hence, we tend to exaggerate the technical changes and transient issues and underestimate the societal influences. "Second, the long-run social effects of a new technology are not the intended ones, but have more to do with the technology's indirect demands on our time and attention, and with the way it changes our work habits and our interpersonal relations."[21]

Returning to computers, most presume the first-order consequences to be more timely and convenient information. But the overlooked third-order consequence is that information sent via computer (computer mail) limits the information communicators get about the social context.

> Consider first the absence of dynamic personal information. Senders have no way to link the content or tone of messages to the receivers' responses so they can evaluate how their messages are being received. Similarly, without nonverbal tools, a sender cannot easily alter the mood of the message, communicate a sense of individuality, or exercise dominance or charisma.
>
> When communication lacks dynamic personal information, people focus their attention on the message rather than on each other. Communicators feel a greater sense of anonymity and detect less individuality in others than they do talking on the phone or face-to-face. They feel less empathy, less guilt, less concern over how they compare with others, and are less influenced by norms. . . .
>
> Why is this effect important? When social definitions are weak or nonexistent, communication becomes unregulated. People are less bound by convention, less influenced by status, and unconcerned with making a good appearance. Their behavior becomes more extreme, impulsive, and self-centered. They become, in a sense, freer people.[22]

6. *Develop and analyze various programs (that is, action options) for obtaining maximum public advantage from the assessed technologies.*

An action option is a public or private intervention into the process of technology development and application, in an effort to accelerate, dampen, or otherwise redirect the "normal" course of events. There are a wide variety of ways to intervene:

- Control over funds.
- Financial incentives (taxes, loans, off-peak pricing, depreciation allowances, college scholarships).
- Laws and regulations (licenses, fines, registration, mandatory standards).

---

[21] Kiesler, "Hidden Messages," p. 47.
[22] Ibid., p. 48.

- Exhortation and indoctrination.
- Construction and operation (drug treatment centers, traffic control systems).

Step 6 highlights one of the ways in which TA differs from CBA. More important, it suggests to the analyst that decisions about new technologies need not be received as simply "go–no go" decisions. In other words, with certain modifications a potentially valuable but, in its present form, dangerous technology can become acceptable. As Ralph Turvey puts it, "The question is not one of abolishing adverse unfavorable effects, but is one of reducing them in some cases where investigation shows that on balance such a reduction is worthwhile."[23]

Take the adverse effect of jet noise on households living around an airport. In this case, there is scope for both the creator of the adverse effect and the sufferer from it to adjust the scale and nature of the activities that produce the effect. Airlines can reduce the number of night jet takeoffs, modify engines to reduce noise, and alter the speed and angle of ascent, and the households around the airport can install soundproofing. (We must, I am afraid, rule out the option action suggested by Art Buchwald on the landing of the Concorde in New Jersey. The governments of France and Great Britain were naturally eager to have the landing approved; but the citizens of New Jersey were very much opposed. Buchwald therefore proposed this compromise: the Concorde could land but not take off. After landing in New Jersey, it would be disassembled and shipped by Amtrak to New York, where it would be allowed to take off.)

7. *Analyze the degree to which each action option would change the specific societal impacts of the technology being studied.*

In the case of enzymes, for example, we could consider establishing a laboratory to test their toxicity, and then spell out what the impact of using enzymes in consumer products would be if the laboratory were set up—and if it were not.

If these seven steps are followed in adequate fashion, policymakers have a basis for making a rational choice among the various action options at their disposal.

LIMITS TO ANALYSIS

This chapter and the preceding three dealt with the formulation of public policy. In these four chapters, we noted a wide variety of techniques and methods that could be used in the formulation process.

---

[23] Ralph Turvey, "Side Effects of Resource Use," *Environmental Quality in a Growing Economy* (Baltimore: Johns Hopkins University Press, 1966).

But what happens to the fruits of all this analytic effort? In the next two chapters, we will see how administrative and political realities constrain what an analyst may recommend. But administration and politics are not the only limitations. As numerous authorities have noted, analytical approaches to policy formulation have certain built-in shortcomings.[24] It is my belief that these shortcomings will attenuate as better techniques appear, as our experience with using them increases, and as larger cadres of trained practitioners become available. But it is also my belief that the inherent shortcomings of policy analysis can never be bred out; like death and taxes, they will be with us always.

Therefore, it becomes important for policy analysts, as well as decision makers, to recognize and keep constantly in mind these limitations. These can be summarized under four closely related points.

1. For most complex situations, it is unrealistic to assume that important factors (e.g., human and artistic qualities) can be expressed in numerical form.

2. As noted at the start of this book, the spirit of policy analysis is by definition to divide and conquer. By decomposing a complex problem into simpler problems, one is supposed to get his or her thinking straight; then, one need only paste these analyses together with a glue of logic and come out with a course of action. The trouble here is two-fold. In the first place, many problems are so fuzzy that breaking them down is impossible. In the second place, many problems cannot be solved very well in bits and pieces. Pollution is a case in point. To break the problem of pollution down into its components and then attempt to solve each (for example, SO_2 discharge from factories) is a strategy that blithely ignores how each source and type of pollution interrelates.

3. In theory, an economic analysis of any proposed public policy should identify all the significant costs and benefits, estimate their size, and weigh them impartially in order to determine whether the benefits exceed the costs. In reality, this is extremely difficult because of the complex interdependencies inherent in modern society. Consequently, no one knows—or can know—what all the likely impacts of any given program on, say, an urban area will really be. Further, it is impossible—or, at best, extremely difficult—to measure the magnitude of many impacts that are known. In some cases, they are inherently immeasurable. This is especially true of psychological impacts. In other cases, the effects of an intended program cannot be separated from those of other actions or forces occurring simultaneously. In still other cases, known impacts could be measured, but only at tremendous costs in complicated and

---

[24] See, for example, Ida Hoos, *Systems Analysis in Public Policy* (Berkeley, Calif.: University of California Press, 1972); and Alice M. Rivlin, *Systematic Thinking for Social Action* (Washington, D.C.: Brookings Institution, 1971).

432

lengthy studies. Finally, since many effects cannot be measured, it is impossible to know which ones are large enough to be significant and which ones can be ignored because they are relatively trivial. For these reasons, it is inescapable that both the identification of impacts and the selection of those regarded as important enough to analyze, are to a degree arbitrary acts of judgment which cannot be made on a "purely scientific" basis.[25]

4. Even assuming that the analyst can foresee these impacts, the question of how to weigh their distribution then arises. No policy affects every citizen identically. This being the case, what calculus is there to tell us how benefits are to be distributed among age groups, regions, races, and income levels? Is a twenty-year-old single black woman more deserving of benefits than a forty-year-old married white male? If so, how much more? What other factor might be relevant? Is preservation of the bowhead whale more important than preservation of the Eskimos' way of life?

I suspect that analysts would be wasting time and effort if they spent too much time trying to answer such questions, for politicians and decision makers are unlikely to pay attention to them. They and their constituents have strong, intuitive ideas about the relative importance of different benefits and their distribution. Indeed, what Shelley recognized even in the earliest days of the Industrial Revolution might be invoked here: There are "eternal regions where the owl-winged faculty of calculation dare not ever soar."

FOR FURTHER REFLECTION

1. When oil prices began to drop in the 1980s, many began to talk about the wisdom of an oil import fee as a convenient way of raising money to help reduce the federal deficit. A fee would offer several other advantages and disadvantages. Investigate arguments for and against. Which side do you find more persuasive? How would you rebut the objections of your opposition?
2. Using the discount factors in Appendix B, compute the net present value of the following three projects.

a.

Year	0	1	2	3	4	5
Benefit	0	200	300	400	500	600
Costs	1,000	100	100	100	100	100

Discount rate = 10 percent

[25] Anthony Downs, "Evaluating Efficiency and Equity in Federal Urban Programs," in *Economic Analysis and Efficiency of Government*, Part I, U.S. Congress, Joint Economic Committee (Washington, D.C.: Government Printing Office, 1969).

b.

Year	0	1	2	3	4	5
Benefits	0	20,000	25,000	30,000	40,000	10,000
Costs	60,000	0	0	0	0	20,000

Discount rate = 8 percent

c. Same project as *b*, but use 15 percent discount rate.

3. Suppose there is a water shortage in a city. Assume that, given the current situation, consumers would be willing to pay enough to cover the cost of constructing a dam and aqueducts to provide a new source of water. Is the project economically efficient?
4. The 1972 amendments to the Federal Water Pollution Control Act required industries to use "best available" technology by mid-1983. Do you think that this is proper public policy? Why or why not?
5. In response to growing transportation problems, the Houston Chamber of Commerce organized a study of the area's mobility needs. Given the chamber's influence, the proposal became the transportation plan for the area. The plan presented a variety of statistics to demonstrate the severity of Houston's congestion problems. Average highway speed had decreased from 36.6 mph in 1969 to 24.4 mph ten years later. The amount of land area accessible within a thirty-minute drive from downtown had decreased from 457 square miles to 282 square miles. Peak congestion now lasted a total of seven and a half hours per day, as opposed to a previous two-hour average. Finally, five out of six of the state's "most congested highways" were situated in Houston. To address this need, the plan recommended (among other things) 300 miles of new freeway and additional lanes on 170 miles of existing freeways. Shortly after the plan appeared, the Metropolitan Transit Authority proposed an 18.2-mile "rapid rail transit" system.

   Perform back-of-the-envelope calculations on these data and comment about the dimensions of the existing problem and the way it has been defined. Explore alternative problem definitions and solutions. What data would you need next to identify the magnitude of this problem for your locale?
6. Critics say that both Army Corps of Engineers and Bureau of Reclamation programs offer plenty of opportunity for putting pork-barrel items into spending plans. Conservation groups single out as questionable the Tennessee-Tombigbee Waterway in Mississippi and Alabama. The cost of the canal, designed to provide another navigable route to the Gulf of Mexico, rose, opponents say, from a projected $323 million to $3-4 billion, and they doubt that it can ever return the investment. Defenders contend the 234-mile waterway will provide a needed shortcut to the Gulf for midwestern shippers, saving them $140 million a year, and that the project will cost no more

than $1.8 billion. What factors might account for these widely differing cost-benefit assessments?

7. What principles stand behind the following statement?

> There is no question of reducing environmental damage to zero. As long as the human race survives, complete elimination of such damage is literally impossible. It is not even desirable to get as close as possible to zero damage. Some pollutants in small quantities are quickly dispersed and rendered harmless by natural processes, and it is not worth the opportunity cost to eliminate others whose damage is slight. Use of a large quantity of resources for this purpose may so limit their supply that there will not be materials available for the construction of hospitals, schools, and other things more important to society than the elimination of some pollutants.

8. List some objections to cost-benefit analysis.
9. Should cities require fire sprinklers in homes and apartments?

Chapter 9

The Political Factor

The discussion of the last four chapters has been, in one respect, unrealistic. It assumes that if one has developed goals and objectives appropriate to the problem and fully explored the economic consequences of the alternatives, then he has done his job. Who can deny the force of his analysis? The numbers speak for themselves.

Well, numbers do not speak for themselves. And, when vital interests are at stake, one need not look far to find public officials unmoved by the most cogent of arguments. Clearly, something has been left out of our discussion. Let us call it the political factor.

So we arrive at another critical juncture in the policy process. The proposal must be defended within the executive branch and then sold to the legislative body. Certain skills and knowledge are requisite to success in this phase of this process. They are the subject of this chapter.

THE NATURE OF POLITICS

Politics and power can give us a feeling of discomfort. They are rough, unsystematic, untidy—especially in comparison to the analytical techniques described in the preceding chapters.

"You can't use tact with a Congressman," Henry Adams wrote in *The Education of Henry Adams* (1918). "A Congressman is a hog. You must take a stick and hit him on the snout." President Reagan used both the carrot and the stick in his dealings with Congress, though he used the carrot more than the stick in gaining Congressional approval of his budget plans. In telephone conversations with members of Congress, he asked, "Is there anything you're really interested in that you'd like to talk about?" To gain votes on his tax package, Reagan used the query "What can I do to help you make up your mind?" It elicited such answers as "Don't lift the quota on imported peanuts"; "Keep some form of the minimum social security benefit"; "Promise to review the third year of your tax cut if the economy is going to pot." In each case, the president gave his word.

While Reagan was better at this political bargaining than presidents Nixon or Carter, the real master of the modern era was Johnson. "If Lyndon found out somebody really wanted something very badly, he would hold it up until he could trade it off for something he really wanted," Stewart L. Udall, Secretary of the Interior in both the Kennedy and Johnson administrations, once remarked.[1]

Watching a group of Senate staff aides maneuvering a bill through its hearings, we can also experience the discomforting sensation that politics is rough, unsystematic, and untidy. Eric Redman, who spent two years as an aide to Senator Warren G. Magnuson, provides a rare glimpse inside this world. Magnuson had an interest in a bill establishing a national health service corps (NHSC), but the Labor and Public Welfare Committee, headed by Senator Ralph Yarborough, had jurisdiction over the bill. Magnuson wrote Yarborough a letter asking him to cosponsor the bill and, most importantly, to hold hearings. Time dragged on before Redman, who had prompted the letter, got up enough nerve to press the issue with Lee Goldman, a staff member of Yarborough's committee. Redman and Goldman met for lunch at the Carroll Arms restaurant near the Senate Office Building, and Redman recalls what happened next:

> Before we had been seated [Goldman] came bluntly to the point: it was impossible, he said, for the Health Subcommittee to hold hearings on S. 4106. He outlined in detail Yarborough's travel plans and the hearings already scheduled on other legislation. . . . not a single day remained free for a hearing on the NHSC. "In fact," he said as we sat down, "the only available day would be this Friday, but that's practically the day after tomorrow, and three days isn't long enough to prepare for a hearing, is it?"
>
> Allowing his pronouncement to penetrate fully, Goldman preoccupied himself for some minutes in slicing up one of the Carroll Arms's garlic pickles. Then he reopened the conversation, as if on a wholly different topic. "How's Maggie (Senator Magnuson) coming with the HEW Appropriation?" he asked. "I know there are some specific things Yarborough would really like to see Maggie put in that bill."
>
> Numbly, I understood at last what Goodman was after. Did he think I would do anything in return for a hearing on our bill? He apparently did not understand that I couldn't play the game; only Dirks and Barer senior aides could influence Magnuson on matters concerning HEW's funds. . . . In short, Goldman should talk to Harley Dirks if he wanted a "deal," not

---

[1] Quoted in the *New York Times*, July 26, 1985.

to me, and there appeared to be no basis for a "deal" in any event. Although I said this somewhat angrily, Goldman accepted the statement with more equanimity than disappointment, as if he held no firm expectations in the first place. With the business portion of our lunch evidently concluded, he steered the conversation to small talk and Senate gossip.

In the course of our discussion, however, Goldman mentioned offhandedly that he planned to leave the Hill in October to become chief lobbyist for the Association of American Medical Colleges (AAMC). This remark intrigued me immediately. The focus of the AAMC's lobbying effort is to obtain more federal money for medical education—and Magnuson controlled that money through the HEW Appropriations Subcommittee.

"Well," I said casually, "if you're going to go lobby for the AAMC, I guess you'll be seeing a lot of Senator Magnuson next year."

For the first time during our luncheon, Goldman's composure seemed to change. We moved on to other topics, but before we parted outside the restaurant, we had more or less agreed that perhaps three days might be sufficient to prepare for a hearing.

Twenty minutes later, back in Magnuson's office, I received a call from Goldman.

"I just talked with Senator Yarborough," he informed me. "Hearings on S. 4106 will be held this Friday."[2]

Concealed in the shadow, political dealings at best strike us as contrary to the resolute calculations of analysts. At their worst, they might seem an effrontery to democratic ideals. When President Reagan signed a bill in 1983 to rescue the social security system from imminent bankruptcy, he hailed it as "a clear and dramatic demonstration that our system can still work when men and women of good will join together" in bipartisan cooperation. The commission was also portrayed by members of Congress and journalists as a great bipartisan success. But, according to a number of close observers, the commission succeeded mainly as a front for secret bargains.[3] The secret bargaining sessions were a way for the president and the speaker of the house, Representative Thomas P. O'Neill, Jr., to negotiate through proxies. After the commission agreed on the size of the problem, much of the hard bargaining was done by a group of nine—five commissioners and four White House aides. The National Commission on Social Security Reform did not succeed where all others had failed—this inner group of nine did. In the words of one participant, "a secret gang built a compromise, wrapped it in a bipartisan flag, and rammed it through Congress." The final legislation, if not a work of art, was at least artful work.

---

[2] Eric Redman, *Dance of Legislation* (New York: Simon & Schuster, 1973), pp. 110–13.
[3] Paul Light, *Artful Work: The Politics of Social Security Reform* (New York: Random House, 1985).

Outsiders are also baffled or frustrated by another kind of politics. It arises not from the need to get a policy adopted but from the need to obtain cooperation in the policy's implementation.

> Many institution leaders do not want to face up to the need for politicking. Not long ago, when the director of the New York Health Corporation resigned, he declared, "I already see indications of the corporation and its cause being made a political football in the current campaign. I'm not a politician. I do not wish to become involved in the political issues here." And yet, in a previous article, he had said that he found himself "at the center of a series of ferocious struggles for money, power, and jobs among the combatants, political leaders, labor leaders, minority groups, medical militants, medical-school deans, doctors and nurses, and many of his own administrative subordinates." The corporation he headed has an $800 million budget and is responsible for capital construction of more than $1 billion; it employs 40,000 people, including 7,500 doctors and almost 15,000 nurses and nurse's aides. It embraces nineteen hospitals with 15,000 beds and numerous outpatient clinics and emergency rooms that treat 2,000,000 New Yorkers a year. And he's surprised that he's into politics—and doesn't like it![4]

The basic premise of this chapter can be stated quite simply: Successful policymaking demands that analysts become more sophisticated with respect to issues of power and influence. With that increased sophistication, they can increase the chances that a new policy—despite dozens of legislative obstacles—will be adopted and that the resources and support needed to implement it will be obtained. Without political awareness and skill, they risk being overwhelmed by destructive adversarial relationships with people whose help and cooperation are essential.

Improved understanding of the political factor by the analyst depends on closer attention to what policymakers bring to the analysis. What each policymaker sees and judges to be politically important depends on the "conceptual lenses" through which he or she looks at the facts. The principal purpose of this chapter is to explore some of the fundamental assumptions and strategies available to policymakers in thinking about power dynamics in public affairs.

Five approaches will be suggested:

1. *Behavioral:* The belief systems of individual participants shape politics.
2. *Institutional:* The procedures and culture of organizations shape politics.
3. *Pluralist:* The interplay of different groups and individuals shapes politics.
4. *Structural:* Hidden codes, which underlie surface events, shape politics.

---

[4] Warren G. Bennis, *The Unconscious Conspiracy* (New York: AMACOM, 1976), p. 155.

5. *Public choice:* The logical decisions of individual rational actors shape politics.

BEHAVIORAL MODELS AND POLITICAL ACTIONS

The first approach suggests that policymakers consider the relationship between political knowledge and political action. Presumably, once we understand a person's belief system or ideology, we can make some reasonable inference about how he or she might behave. Yet, all too often, policymakers and implementing officials tend to gloss over contradictory interests, incompatible ideologies, and opposing cultures as potential sources of disagreement. This implicit assumption—that everyone-is-just-like-me—is more than antipolitical. It is dangerous. Those who hold a mirror to the world and see only themselves are apt to be shocked and panicked when the mirror is removed, as inevitably it must be. The behavioral approach forces the policymaker to take into account different motivations, beliefs, and roles.

Understanding motivations, beliefs, and roles

In analyzing the political feasibility of, say, a statewide property tax for financing California's schools, a good way to begin is by identifying the participants:[5]

Supporters: state superintendent of public instruction, poor school districts, California Teachers Association, Democratic legislators, educational professionals.

Indifferents (fence sitters): governor, average-wealth school districts, and the public.

Opposers: California Taxpayers' Association, wealthy school districts, California Real Estate Association, farm and oil interests, and Republican legislators.

Next, the analyst should refine the terms *supporters, indifferents,* and *opposers;* more to the point, the analyst needs to quantify these terms. But, before any numbers can be assigned, the analyst will need to probe as deeply as possible the motivations, beliefs, and role perceptions of the participants as each participant has a range of motives that encourages him to assert policy preference or respond to the policy initiatives of others. But a difficulty enters here. Participants in the political process frequently like to keep their motives concealed in order to maximize

---

[5] Arnold J. Meltsner, "Political Feasibility and Policy Analysis," *Public Administration Review* 32, no. 6 (November–December 1972), pp. 859–67.

their bargaining position. What could be more delightful than being wooed when one is already in a romantic mood?

Fortunately, research into political personalities can help the policy analyst to ferret out motives. To illustrate the possibilities, let us consider efforts by psychologists and political scientists to merge disciplines to form a new field, political psychology.

Political psychology. Proponents of this new discipline assert that it has the potential of bringing greater clarity and soundness to policy-making and perhaps may improve the manner in which participants perceive and deal with each other.

Richard Merelman of the University of Wisconsin has attempted to describe the various psychological elements that motivated David A. Stockman, Reagan's first director of the Office of Management and Budget. Merelman sees in Stockman a surface layer of Machiavellianism, and, under that, the kind of intense sense of conscience embodied in Puritan ideology. The latter strain of conscience, he thinks, must be at odds with Stockman's more pragmatic side. Beneath all of that, he sees a man who fears being abandoned, a man with a great need to be dependent on a strong mentor. Thus, Merelman hopes to explain how Stockman could seem to be so pragmatic and loyal and yet, in comments that invariably cause him trouble, admit to holding principles at odds with the policies he implements.[6]

A similar approach to the uncovering of motives is taken by Bruce Mazlish in his *In Search of Nixon: A Psychohistorical Inquiry.*[7] Mazlish argues that as president, Nixon tended to duplicate the ambivalence of democratic society. On the one hand, as Mazlish recounts, there was the competitive, fighting "Tricky Dick," enamored of strength, who contrasted weak, self-indulgent students with the brave soldiers who "stand tall" in Vietnam. On the other hand, there was the Nixon who had an "obsession" (his own word) for peace, who visualized the "major role" of his presidency as an "attempt to make a contribution toward building world peace, with freedom for all people." In Freudian fashion, Mazlish traces the roots of Nixon's ambivalence to the nature of his parents—to a mother who was a devout Quaker committed to peace and to a competitive father, dreaded for his irritability and temper.

James David Barber has developed a classification of presidential-style types.[8] By style is meant "a collection of habitual action patterns in meeting role demands. Viewed from outside, a man's style is the

---

[6] Richard M. Merelman, "The Development of Political Activists," *Social Science Quarterly* 67, no. 3 (1986), pp. 473–90.

[7] Bruce Mazlish, *In Search of Nixon: A Psychohistorical Inquiry* (New York: Basic Books, 1972).

[8] James David Barber, *The Presidential Character* (Englewood Cliffs, N.J.: Prentice-Hall, 1972).

Figure 9–1
Style orientations of political executives

		Attitude towards job	
		Positive	Negative
Behavior in job	Active	Tends to show confidence, flexibility, a focus on producing results through rational mastery Examples: Jefferson, Franklin Roosevelt, Truman, Kennedy, Ford, Carter	Tends to emphasize ambitious striving, aggressiveness, a focus on the struggle for power against a hostile environment Examples: John Adams, Wilson, Hoover, Lyndon Johnson, Nixon
	Passive	Tends to show receptiveness, compliance, other-directed-ness, plus a superficial hopefulness making inner doubt Examples: Madison, Taft, Harding, Reagan	Tends to withdraw from conflict and uncertainty and to think in terms of vague principles of duty and regular procedure Examples: Washington, Coolidge, Eisenhower

Source: Adapted from James David Barber, *The Presidential Character* (Englewood Cliffs, N.J.: Prentice-Hall, 1977).

observed quality and character of his performance. Viewed from inside, it is his bundle of strategies for adapting, for protecting, and enhancing self-esteem." Two criteria are used to formulate the typology: activity-passivity in performing the presidential role and positive-negative affect (or feeling) toward the activity. Though Barber focuses mainly on presidents, his findings are, I think, applicable to a wide range of political executives (see Figure 9–1).

Barber argues that presidential style can be classified by examining rhetorical patterns, types of presidential activity (business) focused on, and patterns of relations with others (in terms of the active-passive, negative-positive dimensions). Presidential styles are viewed as deriving from a person's first political success; the style that brought initial success tends to be used again. The initial situation in which the style is used is accompanied by the development of new confidence, different patterns of adaptation to groups, and increased public acclaim and attention. The condition surrounding this situation can be evaluated in terms of the future president's motives, the resources the person has, and the opportunities available to the person.

Another relevant typological analysis is Barber's typology of first-term legislators based on their level of legislative activity and their willingness to serve for at least three or more additional sessions of the legislature. In the course of his analysis, Barber makes use of psychological characteristics other than motivation to distinguish among legislators.

Among these characteristics are self-perception and strategies of adjustment to others and to the situation, for example, submission, aggression, displacement, and projection.

The last two terms merit brief explanation. In the process of *displacement*, an idea or image is substituted for another closely related one. The original object may be unattainable because of personal or external constraints. For example, an executive, reprimanded by his superior for poor performance, ventilates his anger on his wife. In *projection* the individual attributes to the external world an unacceptable wish that originates with himself. In a simplified way it appears that what is pleasurable is taken in and what is painful is externalized and attributed to the outside world. A statement such as "I hate him" is turned around and changed into "he hates me." This common defense mechanism is characterized in paranoia by delusions of persecution and grandeur. Political leaders seem especially susceptible to the paranoid style, perhaps because of the large stage on which they act, which allows them to easily transform fantasy into reality. Involvement in a cause—and defense against its opponents—is often nothing more than a projective disguise of a person's intrapsychic needs.

Anthony Downs suggests a classification system applicable to virtually any policymaker or implementing official:[9]

- *Climbers* see organizations as arenas in which they can achieve personal goals such as advancement and raises.

- *Conservers*, like climbers, are motivated by self-interest, but they care primarily about holding what they already have. Downs thinks that, in the long run, once further advancement seems unlikely, the majority of officials become conservers of the status quo.

- *Zealots* dedicate themselves to pursuit of a policy goal that they regard as in the national interest.

- *Advocates* dedicate themselves not to a cause but to an organization. Conveniently, they see the preservation of the agency tantamount to the pursuit of the public interest.

- *Statesmen* take a broad view of the public interest and recognize that there are many noble and worthy causes and agencies.

The works of Merelman, Mazlish, Barber, and (to a lesser extent) Downs result from the kind of analysis that has often fueled debate over the validity of psychological interpretation done at a distance. In contrast, Kristin Luker of the University of California at San Diego offers

---

[9] Anthony Downs, *Inside Bureaucracy* (Boston: Little, Brown, 1967).

an analysis of the contemporary debate about abortion based on extensive interviews with both prochoice and prolife activists.[10]

Luker does not deny the power or integrity of the moral arguments on either side of the debate. But, in the end, she insists, it is a battle between women with very different—and ultimately contradictory—stakes in the world. The prochoice activists do not come from those social groups that have the most immediate practical interest in abortion, namely, welfare recipients and unwed mothers. Rather, the most vocal advocates of legalized abortion are upper-middle class women who have entered careers indistinguishable from those traditionally reserved for men. Breaking with the long-standing sexual segregation of the American labor force and rejecting jobs that have been the familiar lot of women, these women have opted instead for fully competitive professional careers as doctors, lawyers, and scholars. Accordingly, they have felt compelled to establish control over their reproductive processes, whose vagaries have always been a major source of prejudice against women aspiring to such careers. Contrary to the suspicions of their opponents, Luker's survey data show these career-oriented women value children and put great stock in being good mothers, and they entirely reject the notion that abortion is an acceptable means of birth control. But the right to abortion on demand has become for them a highly charged and nonnegotiable issue precisely because it symbolizes their expectation—and to a considerable extent achievement—of social and economic equality with men.

The women involved in the prolife movement, on the other hand, are nearly all housewives. They are distinctly less well-educated than their adversaries, and their husbands are not professionals, but skilled workers and small-businessmen. Most of them married while still quite young, and they have relatively large families. Their opposition to abortion, Luker shows, is as heartfelt and uncompromising as is the advocacy of the prochoice activists, and for comparable reasons. Abortion represents an affront to the one responsibility—namely, motherhood—that lends dignity and worth to their lives; indeed, it is the only resource on which they can confidently trade in their relations with their husbands and the outside world. Thus, in an exact (although inverse) analogy to their opponents, prolife advocates are not merely offended but profoundly threatened by the legalization of abortion.

Political psychologists have also applied their skills to understanding the behavior of policymakers in the arena of international relations. Once you have a belief, Robert Jervis of Princeton says, it influences

---

[10] Kristin Luker, *Abortion and the Politics of Motherhood* (Berkeley, Calif.: University of California Press, 1985).

how you perceive all other relevant information.[11] Once you see a country as hostile, you are likely to interpret ambiguous actions on their part as signifying their hostility. A more neutral observer might see many other possible explanations.

The point, though obvious, is often forgotten. In the political arena, people do not realize how their opinions shape their conclusions. They see all information as independent confirmations of their view, not realizing—as cognitive psychologists have shown—that their bias preselects the information they notice and determines how they will construe it. Jervis cites as an example the tendency of those on different sides of the debate over a nuclear test ban to view very different facets of the issue all in the same way. People often believe that the policy they favor is better than the alternatives on several logically independent dimensions. For example, those who favored a ban on nuclear testing believed that the health hazards from testing were high, that continued testing would yield few military benefits, and that a treaty would open the door to further arms control agreements. Opponents disagreed on all three counts. This kind of consistency, Jervis notes, is suspect because there is no reason to expect the world to be so neatly arranged that a policy will be superior on *all* dimensions.

While Jervis and other political scientists have turned to cognitive psychology to analyze behavior of policymakers in international relations, a different approach is taken by those with a psychoanalytic bent. Typical of these efforts is the work of Steve R. Pieczenik, a psychiatrist who has been a deputy assistant secretary of state. Just as states of vulnerability in an individual lead to anxieties which are handled by ego-defense mechanisms, national anxieties arise from states of balance-of-power vulnerability. Pieczenik has argued that the perceptions of one country toward another are filtered by these defenses.[12] The more threatening one nation perceives another to be, the more extreme the psychological defenses it will rely on. The most extreme defenses include projection, where one perceives one's own hostility to be coming from one's enemy; distortion, in which one twists facts to make them more acceptable; and denial, where one ignores altogether discomforting facts. These extreme defenses, Pieczenik contends, were used toward China in the period when the United States refused to recognize its political existence.

Although political psychology is now seen as a legitimate topic in the study of public policy, it is still viewed as untested. And those

---

[11] Robert Jervis, *Perception and Misperception in International Relations* (Princeton, N.J.: Princeton, 1976).

[12] Steven R. Pieczenik, "Foreign Policy, Ego Defense Mechanisms, and Balance of Power Vulnerability," *American Journal of Psychotherapy* 30, no. 1 (1976), pp. 4–13.

with a psychoanalytic bent would do well to remember Kissinger's observation: Even paranoids have enemies.

Inside the congressional mind. In considering the motives that might impinge on participants—at least those participants who owe their jobs to voters—we cannot afford to ignore the "electoral connection." But specifying exactly how the drive to be reelected actually influences the positions of participants on any given issue is a murky business—even for the most distinguished practitioners of political science.

Writing in the early 1960s, V. O. Key, though convinced that public opinion directly affected public policy, was never able to demonstrate it.

> Discussion of public opinion often loses persuasiveness as it deals with the critical question of how public opinion and governmental action are linked. The democratic theorist founds his doctrines on the assumption that an interplay occurs between mass opinion and government. When he seeks to delineate that interaction and to demonstrate the precise bearing of the opinions of private citizens on official decision, he encounters almost insurmountable obstacles. In despair he may conclude that the supposition that public opinion enjoys weight in public decision is a myth and nothing more, albeit a myth that strengthens a regime so long as people believe it.[13]

More recently, Dye summarizes the state of the art thus:

> There is very little *direct* evidence in the existing research literature to support the notion that public opinion is an important influence over public policy. Many surveys reveal the absence of any knowledge or opinion about public policy on the part of masses of citizens. This suggests that mass opinion has little influence over the content of public policy. How can mass opinion be said to affect public policy when there is no mass opinion on a great many policy questions? Studies suggesting that the masses of people have little knowledge of, or interest in, or opinion about a great many policy questions, clearly imply that public opinion has little impact on the content of public policy. Likewise studies which indicate that public opinion is unstable and inconsistent also imply that public opinion has little policy impact.[14]

For this reason, in trying to determine the issue position and its relevance for each participant, the policy analyst needs to examine not only the influence of public opinion but also the effect of the policymakers' own beliefs and roles.

Every participant has a set of beliefs, attitudes, and values that shape the way in which he or she views the political world. For some, the set may take the shape of a relatively well formed political ideology.

---

[13] V. O. Key, *Public Opinion and American Democracy* (New York: Alfred A. Knopf, 1961).

[14] Thomas R. Dye, *Understanding Public Policy* (Englewood Cliffs, N.J.: Prentice-Hall, 1986), p. 267.

For others, the set may be an amalgam of operational codes, that is, particular ways of handling given problems. Examples might include these: "public power development is preferable to private development"; "monetary tools are preferable to fiscal measures to combat inflation"; "the less government interference in our lives the better." The appellations "hawk" and "dove" as orientation toward international relations probably fall somewhere between a full-fledged ideology and an operational code.

What we are saying, then, is this. Simply dividing participants in a policy decision into friends and enemies is insufficient for judging political feasibility; it therefore becomes essential that we consider the background and the intensity of a participant's beliefs. Two last examples should show why this is so. In the area of health policy, "the American Medical Association elevated fee-for-service not as a bookkeeping convenience but as a principle. Instead of adopting the wisdom of the ancient Chinese, the AMA encourages payment by the illness rather than prepayment for health. For some doctors, prepayment conjures visions of group health and of violating the standards of excellence maintained by the individual doctor-patient relationship. The belief in fee-for-service is thus an intense defense mechanism against socialism."[15]

The area of energy policy provides an even more striking example of why we need to consider beliefs and ideologies. Edward J. Mitchell considers the case of natural gas deregulation, a long-standing energy issue.[16] Mitchell maintains that Table 9-1 is all "you have to know about deregulation politics."

Table 9-1 groups the members of Congress into twenty-one classes, using the liberal-conservative ratings of the Americans for Democratic Action (ADA). Inspection of the table shows extraordinary correlations between the deregulation vote and these ratings. A simple prediction rule is: members whose ADA rating is over 45 percent will vote against deregulation, and members whose ADA rating is under 45 percent will vote for deregulation. Following that rule, the analyst would be correct in 361 out of 387 cases, or better than 93 percent of the time. "This close relationship," Mitchell says, "is due to the fact that even moderately liberal and moderately conservative Congressmen *vote overwhelmingly in accord with their ideological leanings* and that there are very few Congressmen in the middle classes where the vote is fairly even. What this indicates is that the deregulation vote is more ideologically polarizing

---

[15] Arnold J. Meltsner, "Political Feasibility and Policy Analysis," *Public Administration Review* 32, no. 6 (November–December 1972), pp. 859–67.

[16] Edward J. Mitchell, "Energy and Ideology," Speech to the Business Council in Hot Springs, Virginia. Reprinted in *Congressional Record*, June 27, 1977, pp. E4098–E4099.

Table 9–1
ADA ideological rating and congressional vote on natural gas deregulation, 1976

ADA rating	Votes against deregulation	Votes for deregulation	Not voting	No. of Congress-men[*]	Votes against deregulation as a percentage of all voting
100	7	0	0	7	100
95	19	0	0	19	100
90	18	0	1	19	100
85	13	0	0	13	100
80	18	2	0	20	90
75	23	2	0	25	92
70	17	0	1	18	100
65	16	2	0	18	89
60	18	1	1	20	95
55	12	2	3	17	86
50	13	4	2	19	77
45	6	6	1	13	50
40	6	10	1	17	38
35	2	8	1	11	20
30	3	7	2	12	30
25	4	13	0	17	24
20	1	15	0	16	6
15	0	22	3	25	0
10	2	29	4	35	7
5	1	40	5	46	2
0	0	37	1	38	0
Total	199	200	26	425	

[*] Congressmen were excluded due to a large number of absences on votes used to compute ratings.
Source: Edward J. Mitchell, "Energy and Ideology." Speech to the Business Council in Hot Springs, Virginia. Cited in *Congressional Record* (June 27, 1977), pp. E4098–4099.

than the average issue used to construct the ideological ratings" (emphasis added).

Mitchell continues:

Among the 176 liberal Congressmen (those ranked 55 percent or higher on the ADA scale) the vote was 161 against deregulation, 9 for deregulation, and 6 not voting. Thus for the 41 percent of the Congress in the more liberal camp the vote was about eighteen to one against deregulation. Starting at the other end of the spectrum, of the 200 relatively conservative Congressmen (those ranked 35 percent or less on the ADA scale), the vote was 171 for deregulation, 13 against deregulation and 16 not voting. Thus, for the 47 percent of the Congress in the more conservative camp the vote was about thirteen to one for deregulation. This means 88 percent of the Congress was in an ideological grouping voting at least thirteen to one in accord with its ideological propensity. Indeed, there were only thirty Congressmen (in the 40 and 45 percent classes) that were not in a group voting at least 70 percent in accord with their side of the spectrum. On natural gas deregulation the so-called vital center is almost nonexistent!

This ideological model of the deregulation vote seems to have more predictive power than does the "electoral connection." For example, suppose that you took only those congressmen from oil- or gas-producing states—Texas, Oklahoma, Louisiana, Kansas, and New Mexico—and used the ideological model to predict their votes without knowing where they were from. The actual vote was forty for deregulation, two against. The model would predict thirty-nine for, three against. It would identify precisely the two congressmen who voted against deregulation, and would err only in that one liberal member of Congress (Barbara Jordan of Texas) switched on this issue.

Based on a considerably more sophisticated econometric analysis of the deregulation vote, Mitchell enumerates "all the things that do not matter":

Whether the congressman is a Democrat or a Republican.

Whether the congressman is from a gas-producing or a gas-consuming state.

Whether the congressman's state has had large shortages of natural gas supplies or virtually no shortage.

Whether or not the citizens of the state heat with gas.

Whether the congressman's constituents are rich or poor, blue collar or white collar, urban or rural.

"Why do Congressmen vote their ideologies as opposed to their constituents' interests?" Mitchell asks.

> The simplest answer is that either they or their constituents do not know their interests. They are thus thrown back upon their beliefs, or philosophy, or whatever one cares to call it. Like capital punishment—where the facts are in dispute, or abortion—where the facts are irrelevant, there is no basis other than ideology upon which to choose. And so an inherently nuts-and-bolts pragmatic question like the price of natural gas becomes an issue of philosophy and at that a much more philosophical issue than the average vote used to compute ideologic ratings.

Finally, knowing the role concept that a participant holds can give the analyst additional insight on what that individual's issue position will be. We know, for example, that many budget officials see their role as one of "keeping the lid on spending" by "profligate" agencies.

The role conceptions of legislators have been studied even more thoroughly. An example of the development of a descriptive typology using role concepts was provided by a study of the state legislatures of California, New Jersey, Tennessee, and Ohio.[17] The authors argue that the role concept is particularly useful for political science because it ties

---

[17] John C. Walhke et al., *The Legislative System* (New York: John Wiley & Sons, 1962).

together the concerns of institutional, functional, and behavioral analysis. The focus of their study was on the norms of behavior perceived by occupants of the position of legislator. They distinguished several different legislative roles.

One type of role is that applying to a legislator in his or her relations with all other legislators; thus one can elaborate the norms or "rules of the game" to which legislators expect other legislators to adhere. Among the other roles is the purposive role, which refers to behavior which legislators perceive as appropriate to the accomplishment of legislative goals. Five purposive role types are identified: *ritualists,* who perceive the legislative process in terms of the technical aspects of committee work, rules, and the procedures for enacting legislation; *tribunes,* who view themselves as the voice of popular opinion; *inventors,* who perceive their role as that of creating and initiating public policy; *brokers,* whose role perceptions focus on achieving compromises between conflicting interests; and *opportunists,* who meet only the minimum requirements of their role and use their legislative office to maximize their nonlegislative interests, either personal or political.

Another set of legislative role orientations focuses on orientations toward interest group activity. The role alternatives include *facilitators* (knowledgeable about group activity and friendly to it); *resisters* (knowledgeable about group activity and hostile to it); and *neutrals* (having either little knowledge or no strong reaction to group activity).

A third set of role relationships is based on the way legislators believe that they should decide on an issue, regardless of the geographic focus of their role orientation; these are labeled representational role orientations. Legislators who consider themselves to be free agents, deciding on the basis of principles, are *trustees.* In contrast, legislators who believe that they should always vote their district's will are *delegates.* Legislators who express both trustee and delegate role orientations are *politicos.* The ways in which municipal council members attempt to represent their constituency also seem to depend on representational roles. The trustee role emphasizes the representative's obligation to vote according to conscience and best judgment, regardless of whether the vote happens to follow constituents' preferences. The delegate role obligates the representative to vote according to perceptions of constituents' sentiments. Studies of city council members suggest overwhelming support for the trustee orientation toward representation.

To summarize: Before the analyst tries to ascribe any minimal values to the issue position, it is important to think through the motives, beliefs, and roles of the participant. This kind of research should also help in determining how relevant an issue is to participants.

The distinction between issue position and issue relevancy is essential to a proper understanding of political feasibility. Two participants, A and B, may both strongly favor an issue (give them both +3). But A has many other commitments and priorities, whereas B does not. A says to B, "Gee, we would really like to hold hearings on your Gallipolis Lock and Dam bill but . . . the backlog of committee business precludes holding a hearing on a new bill, especially one with little chance of enactment . . . the resignations have decimated the committee staff . . . I now have to do most of the committee work myself . . . I already have a three-foot stack of bills to edit, reports to write, and hearing transcripts to correct." B realizes, alas, that A's priorities have an ineluctable logic: the legislation A was putting in order was all destined to become law this session; the Gallipolis Lock and Dam bill was not.

To "adjust" for these other priorities, which will surely drain the amount of political resources that can be directed toward the issue, we multiply A's issue position by, say, one; but we multiply B's by three.

Integrated political analysis technique (INPAT)

Eventually, we arrive at a point where we need a more holistic appraisal of a proposal's political survivability. One approach that I have found useful is the integrated political analysis technique (INPAT).[18]

The foundation of INPAT is shown in Table 9–2. Ideally the analyst will want to develop a similar chart for each site in the adoption process. By sites, I mean those points in the process at which critical decisions—that is, decisions that determine whether the proposal lives or dies—are made.

Selecting participants. As suggested earlier in this chapter, participants in the adoption of policy fall into several general categories—the chief executive, members of the legislature or board, party leaders, top-level managers, and interest group leaders. It is also the case that influential persons in a community may not hold formal positions of leadership. Ex-officeholders, distinguished citizens, the extremely wealthy, and informal opinion leaders may all possess a considerable degree of influence and should not be overlooked. To make analysis manageable, one should stay clear of the temptation to develop an exhaustive list. On close inspection, it will probably become apparent that many discrete participants can be aggregated by a common core interest. Thus, rather than list all influential black leaders in a community

[18] Cf. Arnold J. Meltsner, "Political Feasibility" and *Policy Analysis in the Bureaucracy* (Berkeley, Calif.: University of California Press, 1976); Joseph L. Bower, "Descriptive Decision Theory from the 'Administrative Viewpoint,'" in *The Study of Policy Formulation,* ed. Raymond A. Bauer and Kenneth J. Gergen (New York: Free Press, 1968); and Michael K. O'Leary and William D. Coplin, "Teaching Political Strategy Skills with 'The Price,'" *Policy Analysis* 2, no. 1 (Winter 1976), pp. 145–60.

Table 9–2
Political feasibility analysis

Participants*	Analysis of motivations, beliefs, and roles	Issue position (A)	Issue relevance (B)	Analysis of material, physical symbolic, informational, and skill resources	Political power (C)	Total support (A) × (B) × (C)
						Total _____

* Each actor is assigned an *issue position*, ranging from strong support (+3) to strong opposition (−3); an *issue relevance* factor, ranging from highly relevant (+3) to unimportant (0); and, finally, a *political power* factor, ranging from strong (+3) to none (0).

separately by name, the analyst simply puts down "black caucus." Or rather than maintain separate categories for physicians, scientists, engineers, and lawyers, the analyst may find "professionals" a suitable and much more convenient substitute.

Inventorying political resources. Let us now turn to the quantity called "political resources." Each participant has something that can help satisfy the motivations of other participants; to that extent, these resources are critical in striking bargains either for or against an issue. The term *resources*, however, is somewhat broad to be of much use for a determination of political feasibility. As with issue position and issue relevance, we must first do a little probing. As a first cut, it might be useful to inventory the resources of each participant, using the following system of classification.[19]

Material (job with increased wages or lucrative contract).

Symbolic (assignment to high-status committee or panel).

Physical (street violence).

Information (who will benefit, or how much will it cost).

Skill (sense of timing or verbal facility).

Another method for identifying the more powerful participants involved in a policy issue is the reputational approach. First used by Hunter, this method requires analysts to ask the participants themselves to nominate the persons whom they feel to be most influential.[20] Although the initial list of names may vary in size from one study to another, it generally includes a sizable proportion of formal or institutional leaders. An important feature of the reputational approach is that it allows the participants to add to the list powerful individuals not known to the analyst.

The approach, however, is not without its critics:[21]

It has been argued, for example, that the validity of the approach depends on the nominator's ability to identify the powerful or influential. Not only is there no guarantee that the nominators occupy a privileged vantage point in this respect, but the relationship between perceived and actual influence has received little close attention. Questions have also been raised about the way in which nominations have been obtained. In many instances the respondent is simply asked to identify persons in the community who are the most "powerful," "influential," or "important." Such questions are highly ambiguous and subject to individual interpretation. The answers to such questions may also be unduly influenced by recent issues or happenings in

---

[19] Meltsner, "Political Feasibility," p. 861.

[20] Floyd Hunter, *Community Power Structure* (Chapel Hill, N.C.: University of North Carolina Press, 1953).

[21] Kenneth J. Gergen in Bauer and Gergen, *Study of Policy Formulation*, p. 194.

Table 9–3
The political feasibility of a city's criminal justice plan

Participant	Issue position	Issue relevance	Political resources	Total
Mayor	+2	0	3	+6
Black leaders	−2	+3	3	−9
Chamber of commerce	+1	+3	1	+3
District attorney	+3	+2	1	+6
Federal judge	+1	+1	1	+1
University community	−1	+2	2	−4
Newspaper editor	+2	+1	1	+2
Grand total				+5

the community. Difficulties have also been pointed out in establishing a cutoff point for nominations. The decision as to how many votes it takes before a person can be included in the "power elite," is often arbitrary and proves little about the number of persons who may actually form the power nucleus. Finally, it has been pointed out that the method itself yields what appears to be a static power structure, without regard to the actual nature of the power complex.

In spite of these shortcomings, the reputational approach does have a number of valuable attributes relevant to operationalizing the concept of political resources.

First, it is relatively easy to administer. There are no complex scoring systems, and it can provide a set of likely candidates in a short period of time. Second, if used properly it can reveal the identity of influential persons not holding formal positions of leadership. In addition, the reputational approach allows for familiarity with the thoughts and opinions of persons actually engaged in the process of public policy formation. It is a relatively nonartificial and direct method of assessment.[22]

Making rough calculations. Having followed the preceding steps, the analyst develops a chart, or a series of charts (one for each site), similar to the one shown in Table 9–3. Now the interesting part begins.

In a nutshell, the analyst wants to use this chart as a point of departure for determining ways in which the political survivability of the plan can be raised to a more sanguine figure than +5. This objective may be attained in several ways. In the discussion that follows, I want to distinguish (a) those ways that involve modifying the proposed plan or generating new information about its consequences from (b) those ways that involve hard bargaining and coalition formation. Since (a) is a more legitimate concern of the policy analyst than is (b), the emphasis will be on (a).

---

[22] Ibid., p. 195.

454

A good place for the analyst to begin is by asking what changes in the plan would tend to *increase* the commitment of the participants— especially the fence sitters, that is, participants whose issue position is either zero or close to it. (Participants who are strongly against the issue are generally best written off as lost causes.)

From earlier analysis, we know that all of the participants have a range of motives and beliefs that cause them to assert their policy preferences or to respond to the policy preferences of others. Moreover, these motives and beliefs determine the price that other participants will have to pay for the political support of fence sitters. As Meltsner puts it: "The analyst has little choice in this matter. He has to find out what the actors will want or take. If a pivotal actor's price is so high that he cannot possibly be satisfied, then the question of political feasibility is, for the most part, resolved. Motivations are a rough guide to what will succeed or what the traffic will bear."[23]

A classic ploy in such situations is *cooptation*, that is, the "absorption of nucleuses of power into the administrative structure of an organization."[24] The purpose of cooptation is to make possible the elimination or the appeasement of potential sources of opposition. Cooptation could mean the actual sharing of power, or it could merely stand as a symbol of such sharing. Federal agencies, like all organizations, would prefer not to share power if they can help it, since sharing can have its cost in organizational goals.

W. Henry Lambright of Syracuse University notes a particularly effective means of coopting legislators: link their interests with those of the program through the selection of contractors. Contracting-out provides enormous flexibility for an agency: just select companies in the district of key legislative constituents.

> Locational politics can be used by the agency to enlarge the program's geographical, legislative clientele. Contracts and subcontracts combine the interests of regional economies, unions, industry, and legislators with those of the program. The award of contracts makes for political support through economic dependency. Government-by-contract is cooptation by another name. It purchases legislative loyalty without necessarily increasing congressional scrutiny into executive decision-making. Indeed, it usually leads to less oversight. Congressmen are anxious for the project to survive; they do not want to cause problems (at least so long as the project appears to be running smoothly).[25]

---

[23] Meltsner, "Political Feasibility," p. 860.

[24] Philip Selznick, *TVA and the Grass Roots* (Berkeley, Calif.: University of California Press, 1949).

[25] W. Henry Lambright, *Governing Science and Technology* (New York: Oxford University Press, 1976), pp. 48–49.

Another, less obtrusive, ploy is merely planting a seed in the mind of the right party—suggestion is a potent persuasive tactic. Sometimes an entire plan can be adopted by merely planting a seed of thought in the mind of the right individual. Research by Rufus Browning suggests that some participants might be more receptive than others.[26] In particular, individuals high in achievements and power needs and low in affiliation needs are more likely to become organizational activists. Browning also indicates that differences in patterns of needs may be related to differences in patterns of behavior in political office. For example, individuals high in affiliative needs tend to be recruited by others having no great desire to hold office. Additional support for this proposition is provided by Barber's study of the motivation, recruitment, and performance by first-term state legislators, noted earlier.[27] Browning finds that political activists ranking high in need for power and low in other needs have little interest in influencing policy and focus their efforts on control and maintenance of the organization. Individuals high in need for achievement and low in affiliation and power needs tend to focus on policy matters rather than organizational control, but are not likely to persist in efforts to influence policy. Individuals who were oriented toward influencing policy and persisted in this interest and activity were found to rank high in both need for power and need for achievement.

The language in which a policy is couched can be quite important. Some words are evocative to some participants, making the issue more salient to such than it would otherwise have been. The expression *guaranteed income* can set a conservative's teeth on edge, whereas the same conservative may find that the expression *family assistance plan* has a nice, warm ring to it.

One of the most direct ways in which an analyst can contribute to the survivability of a policy is to supply friendly participants with information ("hard data," if there is such a thing). For example, a powerful technique of persuasion is policy analysis that reveals how a given policy, desired by one participant, can also serve the values of another participant (perhaps a fence sitter). Charles E. Lindblom of Yale University writes:

> The President fears that Congress will cut aid to Latin America. His most effective means of inducing Congress not to cut may be to find a value that he believes stirs congressmen—like restraining the spread of communism in Latin America—and show them how aid achieves that value. His own interest in aid may be quite different. There might not even be one common

---

[26] Rufus Browning, "The Interaction of Personality and Political System in the Decision to Run for Office," *Journal of Social Issues* 24 (July 1968), pp. 93–103.

[27] Barber, *The Presidential Character,*

problem to which President and Congress think aid is a possible solution. It is enough that he can influence them by analysis designed to connect his desired policy with their fundamental dispositions or values.[28]

Persuasion by the participants can take other forms, of course: "outright deceit and irrational and nonrational appeals of many kinds, including at one extreme, organized propaganda, and at the other, exploited lies of kinship and friendship."[29] But, no matter what the form, the ultimate objective is always the same, namely, to build coalition at each site sufficient to ensure the ultimate adoption of the policy.

In this section I have drawn upon the work of many social scientists in order to show how the behavioral approach can help us understand the dynamics of power in policymaking. But recall that there are at least four other pathways to political understanding: institutionalism, pluralism, structuralism, and public choice. Let us see what these four might offer that the first does not.

INSTITUTIONALISM AND POLITICAL FEASIBILITY

During a debate over changing the layout of the British Parliament, Winston Churchill, who opposed the move, remarked that we shape institutions and they, in turn, shape us. There is a profound truth here that might elude the behavioralist who finds it difficult to consider organizations *apart from individuals.* But organizations are not merely the sum of the personalities, or belief systems, of the individuals who occupy or run them. The training, traditions, routines, and incentives of organizations can actually order individual behavior.

No one has demonstrated the usefulness of this perspective any better than Graham T. Allison in his study of the Cuban missile crisis. Among his conclusions are these:[30]

- Existing organizational routines constitute the range of effective choice open to policymakers confronted with any problem. Policies that demand that existing organizations depart from their established routines to perform new, unprogrammed tasks are rarely accomplished.

- The key political factor is not the individual or monolithic "government," but a constellation of loosely allied organizations on top of which policymakers sit. This constellation acts only when component organizations (such as the Navy, the Department of State, the CIA— or some subunit of these) perform routines.

---

[28] Charles E. Lindblom, *The Policy Making Process* (Englewood Cliffs, N.J.: Prentice-Hall, 1980), p. 83.
[29] Ibid.
[30] Graham T. Allison, *The Essence of Decision* (Boston: Little, Brown, 1971), pp. 94–95.

- Organizations perform their tasks through standard operating procedures (SOPs). For example: "Given this kind of situation, the correct
way to handle it is as follows. . . ."

> These rules of thumb permit concerted action by large numbers of
> individuals, each responding to basic cues. The rules are usually
> simple enough to facilitate easy learning and unambiguous applica-
> tion. Since procedures are "standard" they do not change quickly
> or easily. Without such standard procedures, it would not be possible
> to perform certain concerted tasks. But because of them, organiza-
> tional behavior in particular instances appears unduly formalized,
> sluggish, and often inappropriate. Some SOPs are simply conven-
> tions that make possible regular or coordinated activity. But most
> SOPs are grounded in the incentive structure of the organization
> or even in the norms of the organization or the basic attitudes
> and operating style of its members. The stronger the grounding,
> the more resistant SOPs are to change.[31]

> Existing organizational orientations and routines are not impervious
> to directed change. Careful targeting of major factors that support
> routines—such as personnel, rewards, information, and budgets—can
> effect major changes over time. But the terms and conditions of most
> political leadership jobs—short tenure and responsiveness to hot is-
> sues—make effective, directed change uncommon.

The only weakness in Allison's exposition of the institutional approach
is that he applies it to only one case, and a unique one at that—the
Cuban missile crisis. Despite efforts by Allison and other scholars, such
a unique event provides less than a satisfactory basis for generalizations.
Fortunately it is not the only case in which an institution's training,
tradition, routines, and incentives shed light on decisions.

During the Arab-Israeli war of 1967, the U.S.S. *Liberty* was attacked
by the Israelis. One hour and twenty minutes later the Israelis realized
that the ship they had attacked with efficient ruthlessness was an American vessel. Two hours before the attack the *Liberty* had been a sophisticated intelligence-gathering ship; now it was a burning hulk, with thirty-
four crewmen dead and scores injured. Was the *Liberty* attacked intentionally or by mistake?

Based on recently published material from Israeli naval and air force
archives and transcripts from two internal Israel Defense Forces investigations, it appears that several crucial factors led to the mistake. Among
these was a report that the *Liberty* was moving at thirty knots per hour.
The ship's speed was a crucial factor in determining whether it was a

---

[31] Ibid., p. 83.

ship of war. Standard operating procedure for the Israeli navy in 1967 decreed that any ship moving faster than twenty knots in a battle arena was to be presumed hostile. A second radar check was ordered. Now the target's speed was given as twenty-eight knots. Both radar readings were incorrect, but those speeds were sent back to naval headquarters, and both were registered in the logbook. Now they were "fact." Minutes later the Israeli chief of naval operations decided to order an attack on the ship.[32]

Defense is not the only sphere in which institutional imperatives shape outcomes. Almost every mistake in the swine flu scare of 1976 had an organizational source. The operating procedures of the Advisory Committee on Immunization Practices were too clubby to allow it to provide candid advice on whether the president should approve a nationwide immunization program. The Center for Disease Control (CDC) was ill-suited to handle public relations, a vital task in implementing such a program. Like many experts, CDC professionals could only view the media and public as laymen to be told only what would be good for them. Moreover, the CDC's information staff was, essentially, a publishing house for fellow physicians, not a source of expertise in media relations. Finally, the CDC lacked the kind of comprehensive relationships with the states that would be required to implement a national program.[33]

The institutional approach applies to the legislative branch as well as the executive. For example, there is an institutional bias in Congress towards large, new weapons systems—as opposed to munitions and maintenance. Members of Congress prefer big, juicy contracts for their districts—not the development of highly accurate, relatively cheap missiles with conventional warheads. But this bias may be the most dangerous of all because it could cause the United States to forgo technological advantages.

THE PROCESS OF PLURALISM

The third approach to political enlightenment for the policy analyst builds on both the behavioral and institutional approaches. Like behavioralism, pluralism emphasizes the active side of politics, the processes of politics. Like institutionalism, the pluralist approach emphasizes the role of organizations in politics—especially that of interest groups and representative government.

---

[32] Hirsh Goodman and Zeev Schiff, "The Attack on the Liberty," *Atlantic Monthly*, September 1984, pp. 78–84.

[33] Richard E. Neustadt, Harvey V. Fineberg, *The Swine Flu Affair: Decision Making on a Slippery Disease* (Washington, D.C.: Government Printing Office, 1978).

In the pluralist view, politics is, in essence, an interactive process involving the struggle for power among different groups. These groups may consist of large interest groups forming grand coalitions, or of small cliques within a government, or even a single agency. Through most of Ronald Reagan's first term, the executive branch appeared to be as much an arena for power struggles as a mechanism for the execution of policy.

- In economic policy, guerilla war raged between the Department of Treasury's true believers in supply-side economics (tax cuts to increase output) and White House staff. David Stockman at the Office of Management and Budget wanted to balance the budget before cutting taxes because he wanted to preserve for himself a leading role in economic policymaking through trimming government expenditures; Murray Weidenbaum at the Council of Economic Advisors feared that the tax cuts would spur inflation; White House advisers James Baker and Richard Darman worried about the political consequences of large deficits. Only Treasury Secretary Donald Regan and his loyal underlings held to the faith.[34]

- War also raged over arms control—not between the Americans and Soviets but between Richard Burt of the State Department and Richard Perle of the Pentagon. Burt preferred an appearance of responsiveness to Soviet offers, while Perle remained fearful that by some soft-headed blunder an agreement might actually be reached. When Burt said, "I really want to win this one," he was not talking about a victory over the Soviets or over nuclear danger; he was talking about winning the president's approval for the particular proposal he preferred. And when Perle said triumphantly, "We're going to zero-out [Soviet] heavies," he was not talking about a real reduction in Soviet forces but about his success in pushing a proposal he *knows* the Soviets will never accept.[35]

The great virtue of the behavioral approach is that it alerts policymakers to the importance of the belief systems of participants in the political process. The great virtue of the institutional approach is that it forces the policymakers to confront the fact that the goals and procedures of organizations—as much as the wit and will of participants—prescribe what is politically feasible. What, then, is the great virtue of pluralism? It reveals to policymakers the crucial importance of bargaining.

---

[34] See Paul Craig Roberts, *The Supply-Side Revolution: An Insider's Account of Policy Making in Washington* (Cambridge, Mass.: Harvard University Press, 1983); and Herbert Stein, *Presidential Economics: The Making of Economic Policy from Roosevelt to Reagan and Beyond* (New York: Simon & Schuster, 1983).

[35] Strobe Talbot, *Deadly Gambits: The Reagan Administration and the Stalemate in Nuclear Arms Control* (New York: Alfred A. Knopf, 1984).

Bargaining

Conditions. It is a demonstrable fact that a great deal of bargaining goes on among the leaders of the U.S. political system. Indeed, bargaining may be thought of as a means of "reciprocal control among leaders" as policy moves toward adoption. But why should this be? In 1953, Robert A. Dahl and Charles E. Lindblom set out to find an answer, and the one they formulated serves as well today as any.

Though bargaining in some form can exist in any society, three conditions make it especially prevalent in the United States:

1. *Social pluralism.* If leaders agreed to everything, they would have no need to bargain; if on nothing, they could not bargain. Leaders bargain because they disagree and expect that further agreement is possible and will be profitable—and the profit sought may accrue not merely to the individual self but to the group, an alliance of groups, a region, a nation, unborn generations, "the public interest." Hence bargaining takes place because it is necessary, possible, and thought to be profitable. . . .

Social pluralism makes some bargaining necessary. For if groups working through a common government retain some degree of autonomy with respect to one another—and this is what social pluralism means—they can arrive at governmental decisions only through bargaining. Moreover, groups engaged in national bargaining—political parties, government bureaucracies, pressure groups, legislative chambers—are themselves composed of groups, and these in turn break down still further. Hence bargaining is found at all levels, not merely among top leaders, but between top leaders and subordinates up and down a lengthy chain of reciprocal control. . . .

Social pluralism goes a long way, therefore, to explain the existence of bargaining. But it does not, by itself, explain the extent of bargaining. For if autonomous groups were not interdependent, or if they were fully in agreement at the outset, they would scarcely need to bargain.

2. *Interdependence.* The more the actions of one group are thought to be capable of adversely or beneficially affecting another, the more the second group is likely to protect itself by attempting to control the first. In the United States, as in other [democracies], social pluralism has been accompanied by increasing interdependence. Hence the interdependent groups must bargain with one another for protection and advantage.

3. *Constitutional factor.* In the United States, the structure of government prescribed by the Constitution, court decisions, and traditions vastly increases the amount of bargaining that must take place before policies can be made. Federalism; the composition and procedures of the Senate; the bicameral legislature; the separation of president and Congress, and the checks and balances between them; differences in their constituencies; fixed and overlapping terms of representatives, senators, and the president; constitutional restraints on legislative authority; judicial review; the amending process; a decentralized party system; and the devolution of power to committee chairmen in Congress whose position is automatically derived from seniority— all these provide a variety of narrow defiles where a skillful and aggressive

Figure 9–2
Bargaining: Causes and consequences

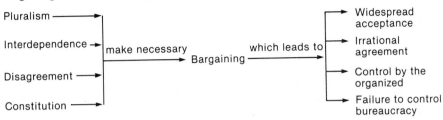

group may fatally mine the path of any group of threatening leaders. The necessity for constant bargaining is thus built into the very structure of American government.[36]

Consequences. To summarize, social pluralism, interdependence, disagreement, and the Constitution itself all come together in the adoption process to make bargaining essential. The bargaining process, in turn, has several profound consequences for public policy. The relationships may be shown schematically as in Figure 9–2.

Government policy requires *widespread acceptance* among the politically active. It seems highly probable that the extent of acceptance, if not agreement, among the politically active on any given issue that is required in the United States is notably higher than in, say, Great Britain. And, in so far as this is the case, it happens because there are many more positions in our political system from which political minorities can veto policy. Hence, the acquiescence of minorities must be obtained by bargaining. Many Americans regard this situation as highly desirable.

One alleged advantage of minority veto is that the need for widespread acceptance among the politically active turns the legislative process into a powerful instrument of civic education. "When a policy proposal has undergone two sets of committee hearings, debates in two houses, one or more formal statements from the president and a cabinet officer or two, a White House press conference, and numerous attacks, supporting speeches, and rebuttals by opinion leaders and pressure groups, it may be argued that the attentive public is almost certain to be as thoroughly educated about the bill as possible."[37] Another alleged advantage is that widespread agreement tends to muster stability in government policy once it is enacted.

But Dahl and Lindblom also see disadvantages: "To justify giving a minority a veto is to assert, in effect, that the majority either cannot

---

[36] Robert A. Dahl and Charles E. Lindblom, *Politics, Economics, and Welfare* (Chicago: University of Chicago Press, 1953), pp. 326–39.

[37] Ibid., pp. 338–39.

or should not control government policy. Either assertion is to deny the goal of political equality."[38] After all, John C. Calhoun in the first half of the nineteenth century used his rule of the concurrent majority—which basically said that every major interest in the country (whether regional, economic, or religious) is to possess a veto power on political decisions directly affecting it—to defend slavery. And I am certain Dahl and Lindblom would maintain today that it is difficult to show that the power of well-placed minorities to block government action in the area of energy policy is somehow less oppressive than the power of a majority to obtain an effective energy policy.

The need for widespread acceptance among the participants can sometimes produce *irrational agreement* through logrolling. Simply put, logrolling is a means of getting the acquiescence of every leader who has enough control to block or weaken your policy proposal, by trading your consent to the proposals of other leaders in exchange for their consent to your proposal. Because of logrolling, it is quite possible for all of the leaders to get their specific policies accepted, but the sum total of these specific policies may be quite unsuitable to a majority.

Dahl and Lindblom write: "The very process of logrolling obscures the general consequences of the final deal to the majority. For each party is so intent on his specific proposal that the final deal is analyzed almost exclusively in terms of its effects on one's specific proposal."[39] This is the case, for example, in the Congressional hearings for the annual pork barrel of river and harbor improvements. As Box 9–1 reveals, there is little interest in the general consequence of such programs for economic stability, government expenditures, and taxes.

One should have little difficulty understanding how bargaining can lead to irrational agreements. Bargaining along with the need for widespread agreement makes compromises almost inevitable; and for all its virtues, compromise does not always result in the optimal solution. This seems true regardless of time or place.

- *Washington, D.C., 1935:* The Social Security Act created three major kinds of programs: (1) a national system of old-age insurance financed through payroll taxes; (2) a national system of unemployment insurance, in which the federal government induced all states to establish programs as they saw fit; and (3) federal subsidies that set up programs of public assistance for the elderly poor, dependent children, and the blind. Social security was established in this cumbersome form because those who guided the Committee on Economic Security that drafted the legislation were cautious reformers. They were prepared

[38] Ibid., p. 338.
[39] Ibid.

Box 9–1
Power of Pork-Barrel Politics

The merging of new budget constraints with growing environmental pressures has changed—at least for now—the politics of pushing for the multimillion dollar projects. Nevertheless, the following excerpts from an article reporting on President Carter's 1977 battle with the water barons gives a good look at how the ties between Congress and executive branch agencies can lead to dubious projects.

For years, presidents have largely ignored the corps, leaving it free to respond directly to Congress. Working closely with lawmakers, the corps has adroitly spread the federal dam-building dollars (about $870 million this fiscal year) into as many congressional districts as possible, making a lot of friends on Capitol Hill. The arrangement guarantees a high level of dam construction far into the future; it takes an average of eighteen years to study, plan, and construct a dam—at a final cost that is generally double the original estimate.

"We view ourselves as doing what Congress says, and Congress views itself as following our advice," says Charles McIntyre, chief of planning at the corps' Huntington, W. Va., office, which is supervising the Paintsville work. "No one is responsible. It's all part of a great big system that works well."

But others disagree. "The corps is a bureaucratic monster," says Brent Blackwelder, a water-resources specialist at the Environmental Policy Center in Washington, D.C. "It long ago outlived its usefulness, and it now exists only to distribute federal pork for Congressmen."

Clearly, Congress loves water projects—dams, harbors, levees, and channels. Earlier this year, when the corps' generals appeared before the House Appropriations Subcommittee on Public Works to ask for a record $2.55 billion for fiscal 1978, the first question asked by Chairman Tom Bevill of Alabama was, "Why doesn't this budget contain money for any new projects?". . .

Lawmakers wax eloquent on the need for dams. "There's no silver behind our coins, no gold behind our dollars," says Rep. Jamie Whitten, a Mississippi Democrat and a senior member of the House Appropriations Committee. "The only chance we've got is to take care of our land. These projects are an investment in our country."

The prevailing system offers plenty of benefits to lawmakers. "A dam is concrete," says Rep. Carl Perkins, a Kentucky Democrat whose congressional district includes the Paintsville dam and six others already completed by the corps. "I think my constituents realize the protection and economic benefits of a dam, and a Congressman gets some appreciation for them."

Benefits to the Corps of Engineers are equally clear. Since Congress put the corps in charge of flood-control planning fifty years ago, the corps has grown from a military unit of 700 men with an annual budget of $63.4 million to a huge civilian bureaucracy of 28,000 employees with

Box 9–1 *(concluded)*

an annual budget of $2.5 billion. Currently the corps is designing or building 124 dams, whose total cost is estimated at more than $15 billion. . . .

When called before a House Appropriations subcommittee to defend President Carter's proposed deletion of funds for a revised list of eighteen projects, General Morris and Major General Ernest Graves, chief of civil works for the corps, simply read the president's objections from a White House statement. Then they smiled as one Congressman after another attacked the president's position. . . .

The corps is adept at stringing Congressmen along by stretching out corps studies of a project. The corps has been studying a $5 million flood-control project in Westchester County, N.Y., for twenty-two years. Says Rep. Richard Ottinger, a Democrat from the area: "The corps doesn't want to build a little project like mine, but they string me and others along for years because they think they will keep our vote on big projects if we think someday we'll get our little ones."

Another source of influence is the corps' control of information. Its economic, environmental, and engineering studies of a single project sometimes stack several feet high. . . .

In Paintsville, Kentucky, serious questions have been raised about the corps' analysis of costs and benefits of the Paint Creek Dam. The corps says the dam will lower flood waters and provide economic and recreational benefits. But some residents see the project as a threat to local economic resources.

But the dam seems likely to be built because Rep. Carl Perkins, chairman of the House Education and Labor Committee, wants it built. Presiding over $28.6 billion annually in federal education, labor, and welfare programs gives Mr. Perkins a lot of clout with his colleagues on the Public Works Committee, which authorizes dams, and in Congress, which ultimately appropriates money to build them.

Source: Condensed from Karen Elliot House, "Selling the Dam," *The Wall Street Journal*, June 17, 1977.

to compromise with congressional preferences on such issues as preserving state programs where they already existed or allowing state and local officials to make eligibility decisions (thus protecting the prerogatives of southerners to restrict public assistance for blacks). Moreover, plans for health insurance were left out of social security because Labor Secretary Frances Perkins and the others feared that intense opposition from doctors and insurance companies might scuttle the whole act.[40]

- *Austin, Texas, 1985:* Sponsors of a mandatory seat belt law introduced in the Texas legislature were also cautious compromisers. The belt requirement would not apply to occupants of pickup trucks or any other vehicle "constructed on a truck chassis or with special features for occasional off-road operation." The latter stipulation excludes four-wheel drive Broncos, Blazers, and similar vehicles. In other words, the proposed law would give pickup drivers the freedom to take risks that most of the driving public could not. Moreover, there are many more pickups on the streets of Houston, Dallas, and San Antonio than there are on the biggest western range. Yet pickups were excluded for political reasons. Sponsors of the bill realized that only by remaining all the potential opposition from the state's tremendous number of pickup owners would the bill would have a chance. We can recognize the pragmatism but not the logic of this play. Pickups may even be more likely to overturn on impact than a passenger car. Although the statistics are inconclusive, one automobile industry group estimates that one half of fatalities in light trucks could be saved with seat belt use.[41]

Figure 9–2 further suggests that the prevalence of bargaining results in public policies that are *controlled by the organized.* The adoption process—like the politics of issue development discussed in Chapter 2—tends to reflect the goals of the highly organized, because organizations provide leaders with the negotiable rewards and deprivations that make control over other leaders possible. "The highly organized, in turn, tend to be those individuals who identify themselves easily with one another; conversely, those who do not identify tend not to be organized."[42]

It follows, too, that there is *little unified control over government bureaucracies* by elected officials. "Each agency is a part of a special network of control relations consisting of its clients, who often can be stimulated to lobby in behalf of the agency when its control, status, or security is threatened; its bureaucratic allies; its bureaucratic rivals; its links with Congressional politicians, usually in the legislative committee with jurisdiction over its activities, or in the appropriations subcommittee handling

---

[40] Theda Skocpol and Kenneth Finegodl, "State Capacity and Economic Intervenion in the Early New Deal," *Political Science Quarterly* 97 (Summer 1982), pp. 255–78.

[41] Clay Robinson, "Seat Belts, Pickups and Politics," *Houston Chronicle,* March 3, 1985.

[42] Dahl and Lindblom, *Politics, Economics, and Welfare,* p. 339.

its budget; its links with Presidential politicians and their subordinates." Box 9–1 illustrates quite well how these networks operate.

From all of the foregoing, an important conclusion follows: *bargaining limits the degree to which rational analysis can be used in public policy in the United States.* For this reason, as I have argued throughout (perhaps at the risk of tendentiousness), analysis is incorporated into the play of power. And for *that* reason, policy analysts must give some thought to the question of political feasibility.

A closer look at how the organized control policy

Different policies mobilize different actors in different ways. James Q. Wilson of Harvard University suggests that public policies involving economic stakes can be classified in terms of the perceived distribution of their costs and benefits.[43] These costs and benefits may be widely distributed or narrowly concentrated. For example, income taxes and social security taxes are widely distributed; subsidies to a particular industry or regulations imposing costs on an industry that cannot be fully passed through to consumers are narrowly concentrated. Given this method of classification, Wilson describes four possible cases as indicated in Figure 9–3.

Majoritarian politics. In this case, all or most of society expects to gain, and all or most of society expects to pay. Interest groups have little interest in organizing around issues in this case because no small, definable segment of society (such as the textile industry, dentists, or farm states) can expect to capture a disproportionate share of the benefits or avoid a disproportionate share of the burdens. The passage of the Sherman Antitrust Act in 1890, the Federal Trade Commission Act in 1914, and the Social Security Act of 1935 arose out of circumstances that approximate those of majoritarian politics.

Client politics. In this case, the benefits of a prospective policy are concentrated in a relatively small group which thus has a powerful incentive to organize and lobby. The costs of the benefits are distributed at a low per capita rate over a large number of people who have little incentive to organize in opposition. For example, say that Congress holds hearings on a bill containing $93 million worth of subsidies to honey producers and there are about 10,000 beekeepers in the United States. That translates into an average subsidy of $9,300—surely enough to arouse interest in even the most apolitical beekeeper. On the other hand, 230 million Americans do not keep bees and, if they do not organize and protest the bill, they will be hit for about forty cents each.

---

[43] James Q. Wilson, *The Politics of Regulation* (New York: Basic Books, 1980), pp. 357–94.

Figure 9–3
How different policies tend to generate different politics

		Benefits	
		Widely distributed	Concentrated
Costs	Widely distributed	Majoritarian politics	Client politics
	Concentrated	Entrepreneurial politics	Interest-group politics

Source: Based on James Q. Wilson.

Who is going to fly to Washington to protest that? In fact, the vast majority of Americans will never even hear about the bill.

In recent years, however, an important organizational change has occurred that alters somewhat the normal advantage enjoyed by client groups in these circumstances—the emergence of watchdog or public interest associations like Common Cause that have devised ways of maintaining themselves without having to recruit and organize the people who will be affected by the policy.

Entrepreneurial politics. Antipollution and auto safety bills of the 1960s and 1970s were proposed to make air cleaner or cars safer for everyone at an expense that was imposed, at least initially, on particular segments of industry. Since the incentive to organize is strong for opponents of this type of policy—but weak for the beneficiaries—it may seem surprising that legislation of this sort ever passes. Nonetheless, it does, but it requires the efforts of a skilled entrepreneur like Ralph Nader who can mobilize latent public sentiment (by capitalizing on a crisis, revealing a scandal, or citing a "social injustice"). Such actions by the entrepreneur are intended to put the opponents of the plan publicly on the defensive (by accusing them of deforming babies, killing motorists, or depriving individuals of their rights), and associate the legislation with widely shared values (clean air, pure water, health, and safety). In recent years, presidents have shown an interest in this kind of legislation.

Interest group politics. In this case, a subsidy or regulation will benefit a relatively small group at the expense of another small group. The public does not believe that it will be affected in any way and though public sympathy may favor one side, its voice is likely to be heard in only weak or general terms.

Much labor legislation—the Wagner Act, the Taft-Hartley Act, the Landrum-Griffin Act, the proposed labor law reform act of 1978—is a product of interest-group politics. Wilson also cites the Commerce Act of 1886. The adoption of that policy resulted from interest-group politics as each affected party—long-haul and short-haul railroads, farm groups, oil companies, and businessmen representing various port cities—argued over how, if at all, railroad rates should be regulated.

Figure 9–4 shows the principal actors and relationships associated with each of these four policy types during their formulation and adaptation. These patterns, it should be stressed, are quite general ones.

THE FOUNDATIONS OF STRUCTURAL ANALYSIS

While pluralism is in the mainstream of the contemporary study of politics, particularly in the United States, it would be hard to find a subject less well-known than structuralism. Deriving from linguistics, anthropology, philosophy, and sociology, structuralism intimidates the most interdisciplinary minds. To make matters worse, structuralism comes in many variations. The subject almost fits Lord Palmerston's description of the Schleswig-Holstein question of the nineteenth century: Only three people had ever understood it, he said. One was dead. The second was in a lunatic asylum. He was the third and he had forgotten it.

Then why bother? The answer is that structural analysis deals with political issues obscured by pluralism. As noted in the previous section, pluralism regards politics in terms of action and process. But it ignores the limits within which action can occur. Structuralism tries to cut through the pasteboard masks, the surface manifestation of politics and lay base the underlying reality, the rules of the games that determine what is possible and impossible.

So, when we speak of "structures" here, we mean something quite different from what the pluralists and institutionalists do. We are not referring to the structure of organizations but to the structure of *relationships* that underlie and determine political events. In this view, politics is structured on a network of relationships of power.

An analogy may help. A person—let us call him Bob—who knows absolutely nothing about chess can observe and even report on a match that he sees. Bob can tell us how one player keeps moving white objects,

Figure 9–4
Four types of public policy: Relationships of principal actors

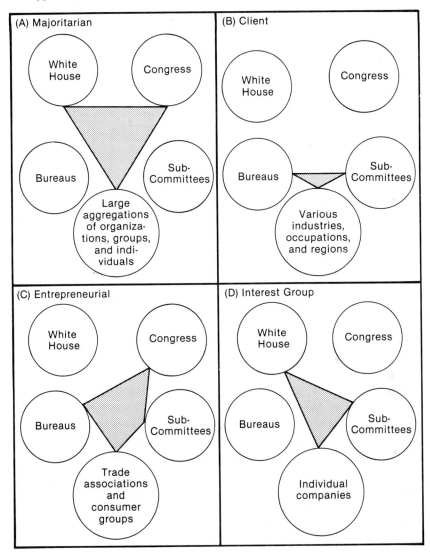

while the other moves black ones. He can begin to detect, in time, that certain pieces are able to move in certain ways. But an experienced player would see things quite differently from Bob. The experienced player would not just know the rules, he would know the nuances of the game. Well, a structuralist thinks of us as "Bobs" when we observe political processes—so mesmerized by surface events that we do not understand what is happening. We fail to detect the hidden rules and codes that govern political relationships.

We see, for instance, a member of Congress trying to get another water project for his state, and we assume that he is simply trying to bring home the bacon. But, to the structuralists, things are seldom as simple as they seem. The senator may also be trying to demonstrate his ability to get his way within the Senate, to show his colleagues that he is a figure of some consequence, a heavyweight who must be taken seriously. In other words, much legislative behavior that seems on the surface to be constituency-related may be involved with intra-Washington prestige and power.[44]

Similarly, we may see a member of Congress meeting with a lobbyist and assume that he is doing so because the lobbyist represents an interest group consisting of thousands of voters. But V. O. Key, Jr., argued persuasively that if interest groups try to threaten a public official with their claims to control votes, "they are usually pointing an unloaded gun at the legislators."[45] The reason is clear: interest group leaders are not very successful at inducing their members to vote one way or another as a reward or punishment to a legislator. The rank and file, in short, are too independent. Moreover, in the larger groups (e.g., the AFL–CIO) that contain enough votes to really count, there are crosscutting loyalties among the membership. In other words, although an individual member might understand the union's position, regional or racial or religious affiliations might override his or her desire to support it. As Key saw it, politics is a kind of closed game, played by interest group representatives, members of the House and Senate committees, and officials of administrative departments. The game takes the "form that it would take if there were no elections or no concern about the nature of public opinion; that is, those immediately concerned make themselves heard in the process of decision."[46] Interest group leaders are listened to with respect not because they wield power but because they are perceived to be representatives of interests entitled to be heard. (In a moment, I would like to restrict somewhat the applicability of this view of politics, but restrictions or no restrictions, the view is, I think, generally correct.)

---

[44] David R. Mayhew, *Congress: The Electoral Connection* (New Haven, Conn.: Yale, 1973); and Lawrence A. Dodd, "Congress and the Quest for Power," in *Congress Reconsidered,* ed. Dodd and Bruce Oppenheimer (New York: Praeger Publishers, 1977), chap. 14.

[45] V. O. Key, Jr., *The Responsible Electorate* (Cambridge, Mass. Belknap, 1966), p. 522.

[46] V. O. Key, Jr., *Public Opinion and American Democracy* (New York: Alfred A. Knopf, 1967) pp. 526–27.

Politics as symbolic action

Today political news is marked, motivated, and abundantly nourished by the symbolic. Understanding the mechanisms of the symbolic in which policymakers move means being political; not understanding them leads to mistakes. Of course, it is also a mistake to reduce political and economic events to mere symbolic mechanisms, but it is equally wrong to ignore this dimension in our analysis.

Edwin Meese III, Reagan's second attorney general, on several occasions tended to ignore this kind of analysis. Reporters expect a certain type of response to some questions. The reason is as Tom Wolfe points out in *The Right Stuff*, that "the public, the populace, the citizenry, must be provided with the *correct feelings.*"[47] About hunger, for instance, a policymaker cannot just step forward and declare, as Meese did while he was a White House aide, that proof of hunger in the United States is nonexistent or merely anecdotal and that some people taking advantage of soup kitchens might not belong to the ranks of the truly needy. That does not convey the proper feelings. Consequently, Meese was pilloried and pitied; the *Washington Post* ran back-to-back front-page stories about his cruel attitude (the first one stretching across eight columns at the top of the page).

Probably most reporters would be willing to admit privately that what Meese said was not scandalous and might, in part, be true. But publicly they were bound to maintain a different posture, and Meese, an experienced policymaker, should have known that. "But he stumbled into a trap," William Safire of the *New York Times* said.[48] "He tried to deal with a shibboleth question without properly pronouncing the shibboleth."

According to Safire, it is not safe to answer honestly certain questions. For instance, is a nuclear war winnable?

> The shibboleth questioner demands a "no." Certainly both sides in a nuclear war would suffer profoundly, but the purpose of our deterrent is to convince the other side that starting such a war would cause it to suffer more, even to "lose." The honest answerer is tempted to say, "If the Russians think we would win, they won't start a war, so why should I say we wouldn't win?" But that would be impolitic, opening the politician to the firestorm of charges of warmongering, and so he shuts up and repeats piously "all would be losers."

So Safire provides the required answer on hunger: call it political unfinished business. "Despite the great strides we have made in only three

---

[47] Tom Wolfe, *The Right Stuff* (New York: Bantam, 1984).
[48] William Safire, "On Language," *New York Times*, December 18, 1983.

years, I say to you that as long as one American is hungry, then we have unfinished business in this country!" (Ronald Reagan must have read Safire's column. At a press conference a few days later, he said "if there is one person in this country hungry, then it is one too many and we're going to do what we can.")

Symbols are more than pitfalls for policymakers like Meese to fall into and policymakers like Reagan to step around. Language and symbolism are important in the formulation and implementation of policy. They rationalize and justify policies that are largely the result of power and influence in order to make the results acceptable and legitimate.

Murray Edelman, a political scientist, sees language as a catalyst for focusing and developing interests and points of view. "Political argument, when it is effective, calls the attention of a group with shared interests to those aspects of their situation which make an argued-for line of action seem consistent with the furthering of their interests."[49]

Edelman makes two other points about language that are crucial for understanding the role of language in the policy process. First, language is an important substitute for the use of raw power or brute force. "Force signals weakness in politics, as rape does in sex. Talk, on the other hand, involves a competitive exchange of symbols, referential and evocative, through which values are shared and assigned and coexistence attained."[50] Language is used to provide meanings and justifications for desired choices so that the use of power is not as necessary and when it occurs, it is much more subtle and indirect. Secondly, Edelman thinks that political language, because it is symbolic, clouds analysis. Evocative political language makes difficult the accurate assessment of self-interest; it dulls the critical faculties rather than sharpens them. This theme emerges most clearly in Edelman's examination of poverty programs, which he says are primarily of symbolic value. Thus, the use of language in the political process can be viewed as a way of providing symbols rather than substance—especially to participants who are not closely involved in the political process and who have relatively little power.

Symbols can even cloud the judgment of those who have a clearly defined self-interest and are in dominant positions in the policy process. (Edelman does not appear to fully allow for this possibility.) Policymakers can become trapped in their own webs of symbols. For example, careful observers of criminal justice programs such as Lawrence T. Kurlander, director of Criminal Justice for the State of New York, and James Q.

---

[49] Murray Edelman, *The Symbolic Uses of Politics* (Urbana, Ill.: University of Illinois Press, 1964), p. 123.

[50] Ibid., p. 114.

Wilson of Harvard University have argued that these programs are largely symbolic. See Box 9–2. We might note three other areas of public policy where those in dominant positions might fall prey to an attractive symbol: administrative reorganization, economic sanctions, and bilingual education.

- James G. March of Stanford University and Johan P. Olson of the University of Bergen, Norway, have examined the political history of twelve twentieth-century efforts at comprehensive administrative reorganization in the United States and concluded that these efforts do not seem to have had much effect on costs, efficiency, or control. Why do presidents engage in such activities? The answer is that few presidents are comfortable with a role as overseer of the bureaucracy. In a society that emphasizes rationality, self-interest, and efficacy, politics honors administrative rhetoric. Reorganization "provides symbolic and ritual confirmation of the possibility of meaningful individual and collective action."[51]

- It would be hard to think of a more pristine example of symbolic policy than sanctions. Economic sanctions are a widely used, hotly debated tool of international diplomacy going back at least to ancient Greece. When the League of Nations moved to apply sanctions against Italy after its invasion of Abyssinia in 1935, a former British Prime Minister, David Lloyd-George, said jokingly that they "came too late to save Abyssinia, but they are just in the nick of time to save the Government," meaning the British government.

  President Carter's grain embargo against the Soviet Union and Reagan's restrictions against the Soviet-West European natural gas pipeline, against South Africa, and against Nicaragua are recent examples. The reality is that sanctions impose only marginal cost on an economy which is easily absorbed. For an embargo to have any bite, it needs broad international backing. Sanctions are especially popular devices when they do not hurt any domestic constituency.

- Richard Rodriguez, who wrote *Hunger of Memory*, the autobiographical account of a Mexican-American child's learning, suggests that bilingual education is more a symbolic than pedagogical issue.

  Bilingual education belongs to the 1960s, the years of the black civil rights movement. Bilingual education became the official Hispanic demand; as a symbol, the English-only classroom was in-

---

[51] James G. March and John P. Olson, "Organizing Political Life: What Administrative Reorganization Tells Us about Government," *American Political Science Review* 77 (June 1983), pp. 281–96.

Box 9–2
Criminal justice as symbolic action

Kurlander: It's a cruel joke to call criminal justice in this state a system. Among the practitioners and among the politicians, there's very little consensus on what we ought to be doing to combat the issues of crime. Indeed, in the political sphere, things tend to be enormously symbolic and we tend to focus on a variety of issues, none of which really contain the solution to the problem. For example, in this session of the legislature, the big issue was *voir dire*, the method in which we have lawyers select juries. It came to pass—and certainly Governor Cuomo supported the reform, but not to the point of trying to convince people that this was a cure-all for the system—that somehow if we changed the method of selecting juries our problems would vanish.

I have noticed in these past six months an enormous resistance to change. Try and think back to when prosecutors last had an innovative idea. I trace that to about 1972, when someone came up with the idea that we ought to focus on career criminals. In the Bronx, they instituted such a program. When we look at it a decade later, we found that the average age of those prosecuted was 24.6—essentially at the end of their criminal lives, when they were no longer going to be career criminals, they were labeled career criminals and sent to jail with draconian sentences.

Wilson: I sometimes think that we are waging largely a symbolic crusade against crime. When I go to a large metropolitan area and ask to see the data that would show what happens to offenders when they move through the system—from juvenile court to family court to adult criminal court and into the correctional system—most cannot supply that information. If we tracked the state of the American economy or the money supply the way we track offenders in the criminal justice system, the people responsible for it would be impeached.

The press covers crime by covering individual crimes—the more gory, the better the coverage; the higher the status of the criminal, the better the coverage. And when the case is settled by the jury, the coverage ends. We ought to cover crime the way the sports pages cover the American League. There ought to be box scores tracking burglars or robbers through the system, measuring the time it takes to get from one stage to the other, trying to find out why appeals occur, which are justified and which are not. We don't do those things because we think of crime as composed of individual events that have no systemic relationship one to the other.

Source: *Reforming the Criminal Justice System,* a symposium sponsored by the Manhattan Institute for Policy Research, July 14–15, 1983.

tended to be analogous to the segregated lunch counter; the locked school door. Bilingual education was endorsed by judges and, of course, by politicians well before anyone knew the answer to the question: Does bilingual education work? . . .

Because bilingual education was never simply a matter of pedagogy, it is too much to expect educators to resolve the matter. Proclamations concerning bilingual education are weighted at bottom with Hispanic political grievances and too, with middle-class romanticism . . .

It is no coincidence that, although all of America's ethnic groups are implicated in the policy of bilingual education, Hispanics, particularly Mexican-Americans, have been its chief advocates. The English words used by Hispanics in support of bilingual education are words such as "dignity," "heritage," "culture." Bilingualism becomes a way of exacting from gringos a grudging admission of contribution—for the nineteenth-century theft of the Southwest, the relegation of Spanish to a foreign tongue, the injustice of history.[52]

Methods of symbolic action

Because definitions and perceptions of events are socially anchored, public officials should ensure that policies are received as legitimate and just. For example, Congress passed the Windfall Profits Tax in 1980. Ostensibly, the oil tax was designed to return to the government some of the money the oil companies would have received through decontrol of oil prices on domestically produced oil; in reality, the tax had nothing to do with profits. Since it was based on the price of oil it was a form of excise tax, and excise taxes almost inevitably fall on the consumer. How was Congress able to get support for such a massive tax increase? Jeffrey Pfeffer of Stanford University offers this explanation:

> Suppose the tax had been called an Excise Tax on Gasoline, or the Oil Products Sales Tax, or the Oil Price Increase Tax, any of which might have been of equal accuracy. How can anyone object to taxing the profits of the big oil companies, particularly if the profits are "windfall" profits, as contrasted with "hard-earned" or "deserved" profits. The labeling of the tax as a tax on windfall profits, even when most of the people involved knew it was no such thing, had a powerful effect. It helped to create an atmosphere in which the tax could be passed, in spite of substantial industry opposition.[53]

---

[52] Richard Rodriguez, "Bilingualism Con: Outdated and Unrealistic," *New York Times*, November 10, 1985.

[53] Jeffrey Pfeffer, *Power in Organizations* (Boston: Pitman Publishing, 1981), pp. 179–80.

In other areas of public policy, the challenge is greater than erasing the words "Excise Tax" and penciling in "Windfall Profits." All nations love "glorious little wars." In foreign policy, Americans have historically embraced two, and only two, kinds of wars. One is the glorious little war. While intellectuals will no doubt have misgivings, since public enthusiasm sweeps away serious legal and moral questions, such quibbles hardly weaken popular support for events like the U.S. invasion of the islands of Grenada in 1983, in response to a request from the Organization of Eastern Caribbean States. From a broad public policy perspective, however, such easy victories may resolve little. If a conflict is sufficiently easy to be a glorious little war, it may be marginal to national interest.

Americans have also embraced "crusades," such as World War II. The difficulty, as one former defense secretary points out, is that

> the most likely conflicts of the future fall between crusades and such brief encounters as Grenada. Yet these in-between conflicts have weak public support. Even in the best of times—with national unity and at the height of our power—public enthusiasm for Korea and Vietnam evaporated in just a year or two. Indeed, any war that is not a clear-cut winner will not long enjoy public enthusiasm.
>
> The problem is that virtually no opportunity exists for future crusades and those glorious wars are likely to occur infrequently. The role of the United States in the world is such that it must be prepared for, be prepared to threaten, and even be prepared to fight those intermediate conflicts that are likely to fare poorly on television. Whether this nation, the leader of the free world, can measure up to such challenges will to a large extent define the future shape of international politics.[54]

Policymakers face many such conundrums. The challenge remains, basically, the same: to generate external support and develop external allies for a given perspective by making it appear consonant with the prevailing social values or goals of those potential allies. Admittedly, the challenge is much easier stated than met.

In an analysis of university presidents, Michael D. Cohen and James G. March derive some rules of action for operating in a political environment in which rules and procedures are unclear and power is shared.[55] We can build from these rules to develop a perspective on the adoption and implementation of public policy.

1. *Spend time.* Policymakers who are willing to spend time on a particular issue find themselves in a strong position for at least three reasons.

---

[54] James R. Schlesinger, Statement before U.S. Congress, Senate Foreign Relations Committee, February 6, 1985.

[55] Michael D. Cohen and James G. March, *Leadership and Ambiguity*, 2nd ed. (Boston: Harvard Business School Press, 1986), pp. 207–16.

First, time spent conveys (symbolizes) to others the importance of the issue. Seattle Seahawk coach Chuck Knox reversed that team's performance between 1982 and 1984 by improving its turnover ratio (i.e., the number of times they took the ball away from their opponents through fumble, recovery, or pass interception compared to the number of times they give it to their opponents). Knox gives what was, in his view, a prime reason for this shift: "I began starting every practice with a five-minute drill on some aspect of turnovers. I just wanted them [the team] to focus, each and every day . . . on the importance of the turnover."[56] Second, if policymakers are willing to spend time, they can expect more tolerant consideration of the problems they consider important. Third, by spending time on the homework for a policy, they become a major information source in an information-poor world. Finally, by investing more of their time in policy concerns, they increase their chance of being present when something important to the development of the policy is considered.

2. *Exchange status (or symbols) for substance.* As was indicated earlier, some areas of public policy—poverty, criminal justice, reorganization, sanctions, bilingual education—may have sufficient symbolic outcome to ensure support of some group for the proposed action or for some other action the policymaker wants.

3. *Facilitate opposition participation (cooptation).* The high inertia of government institutions and the heavy dependence of policymakers on groups and events outside their control make governmental power ambiguous. Top policymakers sense their lack of control despite their position of authority, status, and concern. Most people who participate in the policy process sense a disappointment with the limited control their position provides. Outsiders tend to see things differently. Not only do they think change relatively simple to achieve but they also would expect more of it. One obvious solution is to let them participate more in the policy process to give them a dose of reality. By extending the range of legitimate participation, the aspirations of occasional actors remain in bounds. On the whole, the direct involvement of dissident groups in the policy process is a more effective curb on exaggerated aspirations than a lecture on the burdens of high office by policymakers.

4. *Interpret history.* In a society in which most issues have low salience and in a government in which institutional memory is low, definitions of what is happening and what has happened become important tactical instruments. Events have meaning only through interpretations; interpreting events as consistent with the definition of the problem or the solution can help develop a social consensus around the chosen policy.

---

[56] Quoted in Tom Peters and Nancy Austin, *A Passion for Excellence: The Leadership Difference* (New York: Warner Books, 1985), p. 314.

If people had more of a sense of history, this tactic would be of limited use, for histories would be challenged and carefully monitored. The actual situation is this: On the one hand, people have limited interest in what happened; on the other hand, they believe that history can add legitimacy to current action. "The model of consistency is maintained by a creative resolution of uncertainty about the past."[57]

Thomas J. Peters provides an excellent discussion of the symbolic and other mundane tools that policymakers can use to communicate their expectations credibly to other participants.[58] Two of these are summarized below.

1. *Change or enhance the settings for interaction.* A new setting conveys that something new is going on; an enhanced setting will convey the meaning that the activity now occurring is more consequential and important. More specifically, Peters suggests the following tactics:

- Role modeling: by your actions shall your intentions be judged.
- Location of groups: moving the location of a group or a meeting to a new place to communicate what is important.
- Attendance: who is invited and excluded from meetings.
- Presentation format: what comes first versus last; what is emphasized.
- Questioning approaches: what items, issues, and aspects are probed; what is deemphasized in the questioning of subordinates.

2. *Provide a dominant value or vision expressed in a simple phrase.* Language can evoke support or opposition, can serve to organize social consensus, and can provide an explanation and rationalization for activity. Most will agree that Ronald Reagan did relatively well in this respect during his first term. Like other effective presidents, Reagan embodied certain values which he deeply held. As the *New York Times* (October 14, 1984) put it: "He is a true believer. He repeats [his simple dream] again and again because he believes every word of it." Most observers also agree that Reagan was much less effective during his second term. That experience raises a point often overlooked: The absence of an overriding vision does not just reduce effectiveness but can lead to a series of policy failures and loss of control. Proverbs 29:18 expresses the notion much more forcefully: "Where there is no vision, the people perish."

PUBLIC CHOICE APPROACH

The principal purpose of this chapter, it will be recalled, is to explore some of the fundamental assumptions and strategies available to policy-

---

[57] Cohen and March, *Leadership and Ambiguity*, p. 215.

[58] Thomas J. Peters, "Symbols, Patterns, and Settings: An Optimistic Case for Getting Things Done," *Organizational Dynamics*, Autumn 1978, pp. 3–23.

makers in thinking about power dynamics in public affairs. At first encounter, much about our fifth and final approach appears obvious. It is. But, like many obvious things in the world, we tend to overlook it. (Try describing the face of a "familiar" watch or clock or a telephone without looking at it.) Furthermore, if we can state the obvious with greater precision, so much the better.

In recent years, political science has witnessed the development of this approach. The names used to describe it vary (*collective choice, rational choice models, formal political theory*, etc.), but here we will call it *public choice*.[59] Like the behavioral approach, this approach asserts that the individual choice maker in the public arena is the main unit of analysis. But it further asserts that all decisions are rational in the sense that decision makers can discern their true self-interest and then select among alternative actions in terms of realizing that interest. This second assertion distinguishes the public choice approach from the behavioral approach, which views choice making as an often irrational, affective, or confused affair; it also distinguishes public choice from structural analysis, which assumes true self-interest to be sometimes obscured by symbols.

Public choice might be thought of as the theory of the "invisible foot," a perverse government analogue to Adam Smith's wealth-creating invisible hand. Under Smith's theory, individuals seeking their own good also produce benefits for society at large; the "invisible foot" notion suggests that the same self-interest is likely to produce harmful governmental interference in the private economy.[60]

One of their key propositions of the public choice approach is that politicians are like business executives and the rest of society in that they generally act in their own self interest: Not the least of the politicians' intentions being getting re-elected. The result is a system biased in favor of spending and against taxes, a combination which results in deficits. Public choice advocates further argue that, because government programs often produce bad results, the real choice a society faces is

---

[59] Unlike structuralism, public choice has been systematically examined in a number of works. See, for example, Michael Laver, *The Politics of Private Desires: A Guide to the Politics of Rational Choice* (New York: Penguin Books, 1981); Robert Abrams, *Foundations of Political Analysis* (New York: Columbia University Press, 1980); Dennis C. Mueller, *Public Choice* (New York: Cambridge University Press, 1979); and Clifford S. Russell, ed., *Collective Decision Making* (Baltimore, Md.: Johns Hopkins University Press, 1979).

[60] Adam Smith, *Wealth of Nations*, Bk. IV, ch. 2. In 1776, the great explicator of capitalism Adam Smith put forward his idea of the Invisible Hand. While individuals may not intend to promote the public interest but rather seek their own gain, the net result of their multifarious, selfish activities is to promote the public interest. Thus, the market place operates like an invisible hand to promote an end for which few individuals directly or consciously strive. "By pursuing his own interest he frequently promotes that of the society more effectually than when he really intends to promote it. I have never known much good done by those who affected to trade for the public good."

not between an imperfect situation created by the private sector and a situation to be made perfect by government intervention. Rather the choice is really between two imperfects: what we called market failures in Chapter 4 and what we might call *governmental failures* here. Both tend to be the inevitable side-effects of individuals acting rationally in their own self-interest.

The problem of private goals

Lacking the direct performance indicators available to business (from consumer behavior and the profit-and-loss statement), government agencies must develop their own standards by which to operate. These standards Charles Wolf, Jr., of the Rand Corporation, calls "private goals," that is, the goals that apply within governmental organizations to guide, regulate, and evaluate agency performance and performance of agency personnel.[61] These goals are private in the sense that they provide the motivations for individual and collective behavior in the agency—at least as much as the agency's public goals. This structure of rewards and penalties constitutes what Kenneth Arrow, a Nobel laureate in economics, refers to as "an internal version of the price system."

These private goals, Wolf thinks, "affect the results of nonmarket activities as predictably and appreciably as externalities affect the results of market activities, in both cases causing divergences between actual outcomes and socially preferable ones."[62] The existence of external private goals means that some social costs and benefits are not included in the calculus of private decision makers. The existence of private goals means that "private" or organizational costs and benefits are included in the calculus of social decision makers. Whereas externalities are central to the theory of market failure, what goes on *within* public bureaucracies—the private goals that motivate their action and performance—are central to any theory about public policy or *non*market failures.

Of the specific types of private goals that often accompany government activities, Wolf notes three:[63]

1. Budget growth. Lacking profit as a measure of performance, a government agency may view its budget as the proxy goal to be maximized. Performance of the agency's personnel and sub-units are evaluated in terms of their contribution to expanding its budget, or protecting it from cuts.

---

[61] Charles Wolf, Jr., "A Theory of Non-market Failures," *Public Interest* 55 (Spring 1979), pp. 114–33.
[62] Ibid.
[63] Ibid.

2. Technological advance. Compatible with the budget goal is the one favoring "advanced," "modern", "sophisticated," or "high techology" government agencies, whose activities might be justified in the first instance by one or more of the acknowledged sources of market failure, and may establish advanced technology or technical "quality" as an agency goal. In medicine, a bias toward "Cadillac" quality health care may result; and in the military a sometimes compulsive tendency toward development and procurement of the "next generation" of sophisticated equipment. Needless to say, the next generation is not always better.

3. Information acquisition and control. Frequently in government, information translates readily into power and influence. Consequently, information becomes valued in its own right. Acquisition and control of information may be particularly important as a goal for agencies involved in foreign policy—even if this internal goal of hoarding information ill serves the national interest.

Voting

The unwillingness to assign either politician or bureaucrat an exalted moral status or to consider them part of a noble process that produces better results than the market is largely a reflection of the public view of human nature. Gordon Tullock figures that people act from selfish motivations about 95 percent of the time. And they are no more high-minded as voters than as consumers, selecting the candidate they think represents the best bargain for them just the way they select cars or detergent.[64]

Voters and customers are essentially the same people, Tullock argues. Although it seems very modest, this indeed is a very radical—even if obvious—assumption. For decades, the bulk of political science has been based on the assumption that government aims at higher goals than individuals aim at in the market. The voter is sometimes assumed to be aiming at achieving the public interest, the man in the shop his private interest. To Tullock, this assumption seems illogical.

According to public choice researchers, politician, bureaucrat, and voter are all in the trough together. The statistics provide a quiet but eloquent explanation for the pressures that were manifest in Congress' debate on the budget. When 30 million persons are getting social security checks, it is hard to put a limit on cost-of-living adjustment in benefits. Checks for military retirement come into 1.2 million homes every month—and 351,000 of those homes have incomes in excess of $24,000

---

[64] See Gordon Tullock, *Private Wants, Public Means: An Economic Analysis of the Desirable Scope of Government* (New York: Basic Books, 1970).

a year. Voters dwell in such homes—lots of voters. So long as voters insist that these programs be maintained at current levels—so long as they are unwilling to give up anything—deficits will persist.

But not all the news from public choice researchers is bad. Among other things, they argue that logrolling—vote trading—is, on balance, a beneficial, not morally questionable, practice. It allows people to register their views and the intensity with which they hold them. The drawback, they say, is that logrolling gives members of Congress the means to press local interests at the expense of broader, national ones.

Although the mechanics of majority votes are familiar, it might be useful at this point to review these.[65] Consider a community with three voters, I, II, and III, who have to decide how to use a vacant building. Choice A is an abortion clinic, choice B is an adult book store, and C is counseling center for juvenile offenders. The voters ranked their preferences as shown in the table:

I	II	III
A	C	B
B	B	C
C	A	A

Thus, voter II most prefers C, but given a choice between B and A, would prefer B.

Suppose a referendum were held on whether to adopt A or B. Individual I would vote for A, while II and III would vote for B. Hence, B would win two to one. Similarly, if an election were held between B and C, B would win two to one. Choice B wins any election against its opposition and thus is the option selected by majority rule.

Majority decision are not always so clear cut, however. Suppose the preferences for the three options are as shown in the following table:

I	II	III
A	C	B
B	A	C
C	B	A

Now, if a referendum were held between A and B, A would win two to one. If it were held between B and C, B would win two to one. Finally, if it were between A and C, C would win two to one. These results are disconcerting. The first referendum suggests that A is preferred to B; the second the B is preferred to C. Conventional notions of consistency suggest that A should therefore be preferred to C—but in the third election, just the opposite occurs. Although each voter's

---

[65] Mueller, *Public Choice.*

preferences are consistent, the community's are not. This phenomenon is referred to as the *voting paradox.*

Note that the ultimate outcome depends crucially on the order in which votes are taken. If the first election is between A and B and the winner (A) runs against C, then C is the ultimate choice. But let us try a little *agenda manipulation* and make sure that the first election is B versus C. Now the winner is B. If B then runs against A, then A is chosen. This ability to control the order of voting confers power; in our example, it ensures that the community will get a counseling center rather than an abortion clinic.

Why did the first table of preferences give us a smooth election, while the second table gave a disconcerting one? The explanation turns on the structure of individual preferences. Consider again the people in the second table. Because voter I prefers A to B to C, it follows that A is more worthwhile to voter I than B, and B more than C. The schedule denoted I in Figure 9–5 depicts this relationship. The schedules labeled II and III do the same for the other voters.

Voter II is the guilty party. His preferences lead to the voting paradox. Note that voter I has a single point (A) at which all the neighboring points are lower. So too does III. But voter II has two peaks. If II had *any* set of single-peaked preferences, majority voting would lead to a consistent decision. This is why no voting paradox emerged from the first table. There, each voter had single peaked preferences.

To summarize, when all preferences are single peaked, majority voting yields a stable result. But when all voters' preferences are not single peaked, then a voting paradox may emerge. Because miltipeaked prefer-ences may be important in many situations during the policy process, majority voting cannot be depended on to yield consistent public choices.

Does this mean that democratic processes are not viable? Not accord-ing to James M. Buchanan (winner of the 1986 Nobel Prize in economics) and Gordon Tullock. As noted earlier, he views these inconsistencies of majority voting as having beneficial aspects:

> Majority rule is acceptable in a free society precisely because it allows a sort of jockeying back and forth among alternatives, on none of which relative unanimity can be obtained. . . . It serves to ensure that completing alterna-tives may be experimentally and provisionally adopted, tested, and replaced by new compromise alternatives approved by a majority group of ever-chang-ing composition. This is democratic choice process, whatever may be the consequences for welfare economics and social welfare functions.[66]

---

[66] James M. Buchanan and Gordon Tullock, *The Calculus of Consent* (Ann Arbor, Mich.: University of Michigan Press, 1962), p. 83.

484

Figure 9–5
The voting paradox: A graphic representation

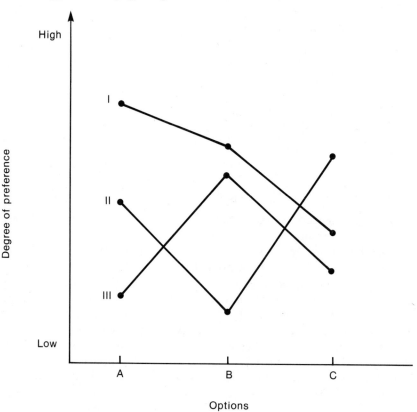

Coalition building: A laboratory experiment

Lawrence Fouraker reports on a set of laboratory experiments that tend to support the idea of Buchanan, Tullock, and other public choice researchers.[67] Fouraker noted that the results from conflict experiments with two persons of equal strength in an experimental bargaining situation could be explained very well by the level of aspiration of the bargainers.

The problem that the group faces is to divide a set of benefits earned by working together as a coalition; indeed, this is an aspect of almost all group-decision problems, even if it is seldom the whole problem.

---

[67] The following discussion is based on Joseph Bower, "Descriptive Decision Theory," pp. 138–41.

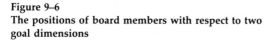

Figure 9–6
The positions of board members with respect to two goal dimensions

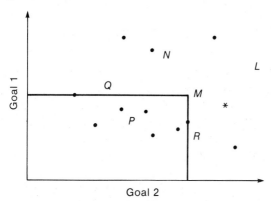

Source: Adapted from Bower (1968:140).

Assume that the majority rule enables the coalition to make its decision. Then, two possible states characterize all permutations of such "games of division": either the reward to the coalition is large enough to satisfy the aspirations of a winning subcoalition, or it is not. In the latter case, Fouraker would expect to find either a revision of aspiration by some individuals, after some frustration had been experienced in trying to reach a decision, or a complete failure to reach an agreement. Fouraker hypothesizes (1) that the winning coalition will be the smallest winning coalition, and (2) that the members of the winning subcoalition will be those individuals in the group with the minimum aspiration.

Consider this simple example. Suppose that the members of a three-person group dividing $10 have aspirations of $3, $3 and $5. Fouraker hypothesizes that the group will divide the money $5, $5, $0. The third person cannot make a counteroffer to either of the first two persons that will both satisfy his aspiration and improve the position of the person to whom he is making the counteroffer. The same is true even if there is slack, and the reward to be divided is $15.

Despite the obvious oversimplicity of the experimental situation, there are intuitive, appealing implications of the results for the real organizations. Suppose that the decision-making coalition with which we are concerned is a board that sets policy for a large organization and faces a choice among several alternatives. Obviously, in such a situation there will be more than one "goal dimension" along which aspirations are relevant.

Fouraker has suggested that the board can be represented by points on a coordinate system. Figure 9–6 is an example in two-goal dimensions.

Each point represents the interaction of the level of aspirations of a participant along the goal dimensions. He will not vote for an alternative below or to the left of the point. The capital letters denote alternatives. Assuming that majority rule decides, point M is the alternative that will be chosen by the minimum winning coalition. If the group leader (*) believes it important for the organization to adopt an alternative with higher goals along a given dimension, his job is to work at raising the aspirations of those members of the winning minimal subcoalition with the highest aspirations along the dimension with which he is concerned.

The graph also enables us to see the value of disparate points of view in an organization. To change the course of the group fairly radically, the leader needs to move only one or two participants, and moreover, he can count on the help of one or two strong partisans. A committee without diversity is one in which the points representing individuals all fall fairly close to a straight line from the origin. In such an instance, should change be desirable, it may be impossible to bring it about. Many individuals must be moved, and there are no dissidents to whom power can be shifted.

Fouraker further assumes that concessions by one coalition have the effect of raising the level of aspiration of the other coalition and thereby increase its demands. According to their model, concessions will not be reciprocated, so that if one wishes to maximize gain, one should make small concessions, if any.

Winner take less

One of the outstanding intellectual achievements of this century is game theory, developed by the mathematician John von Neumann in 1928 and extended to economics by von Neumann and the economist Oskar Morgenstern in their classic, *The Theory of Games and Economic Behavior* (1944). Game theory, a mathematical system for analyzing contests where opponents seek to outwit each other and design the best course of action under all circumstances, has had a steadily growing influence in fields as diverse as warfare, arms control, politics, business, and the humanities.

We can use game theory to understand a contest between members of a city council who support the mayor's economic development program and those who oppose it. The opposition has two basic strategies: (I) mainly support the mayor's program, or (II) attack the mayor's program and present an economic development program of their own. The mayor's supporters on the council can choose between two strategies: (A) fully defend the mayor's program, or (B) compromise with

Figure 9–7
Using game theory to predict and explain political strategy

		Supporter's Strategies	
		Completely defend the mayor (A)	Compromise with opposition (B)
Opposition's Strategies	Mainly support mayor (I)	Mayor triumphs; opposition avoids blame (2, 4)	Supporters win but upset mayor; opposition shares credit (3, 3)
	Attack mayor (II)	Mayor's program blocked, opposition incurs blame (1, 2)	Mayor loses much of programs; opposition looks effective (4, 1)

Key:

4 = best
3 = next best
2 = next worst
1 = worst

First number in pair is outcome for Democrats, second is outcome for Republicans.

the opposition, who have a majority on the council (if they hang together).

Each combination of strategies produces different pairs of payoffs, as Figure 9–7 shows. The best result, as judged by each group, is represented by the number 4, the worst result by 1, the next-best outcome by 3 and the next to worst by 2. In each pair, the opposition's payoff is listed first. For example, if the opposition plays a "mainly support" strategy (I) and the mayor's backers play the "completely defend" strategy (A), the payoff is to the backer's advantage (2, 4). The opposition succeeds only in avoiding the worst possible outcome of incurring public scorn for pure negativism in the face of the mayor's bold new program, but they still incur insults for criticizing parts of the program and then voting for all of it. The council members who support the mayor score a complete victory.

But suppose that the opposition switches to a strategy of strong attack (II) and offer their own economic development program. The mayor's supporters can respond to this attack by sticking to their "completely defend" strategy (A). With the influence of the mayor to back them up, his supporters can block the opposition's plan. But if the opposition sticks to its strategy (II), with its majority on the council, the supporters can not get the mayor's program either; the result will be a stalemate. Both parties suffer (1, 2), with the opposition losing more. Voters will be angrier with the opposition and punish it in the next election. But the mayor and his supporters will have nothing to show by way of an economic program.

However, if his supporters respond to the attack by switching to the compromise strategy (B), they will hand a political victory to the opposition, while surrendering most of the mayor's program. Outcome: (4, 1).

The mixture of an opposition strategy (I) and a supporter strategy (B) gives the second-best outcome for each coalition (3, 3), which is actually the best outcome for both coalitions under the circumstances. The mayor will get most of his program. The opposition, meanwhile, can claim that it has given the mayor most of his program but modified the outcome in a responsible manner.

MANAGING THE PROCESS: A SYNTHESIS

As we come to the end of our examination of politics, we find ourselves in the proverbial position of the six blind men who examined an elephant. "It's like a wall," the first said, touching the animal's side. "Like a snake," the second said, touching its trunk, "A spear!" a third said, touching a tusk. "A tree!" "A fan!" "A rope!" the others said, as they touched the elephant's leg, its ear, its tail. What, then, is the essence of politics? Is it beliefs systems, organizational procedures, group interactions, symbolic actions, or rational decisions? Can these five approaches be combined to form a coherent, composite picture of this beast called the political factor? Because the five views are mutually reinforcing— not contradictory—I think the answer is yes.

Generally speaking, a strong political action plan—whether to get a policy adopted or to secure its implementation—must contain three principal thrusts:

1. To seize the initiative.
2. To move forward gradually and logically.
3. To build coalitions.

While many experienced policymakers and implementing officials may argue that developing a detailed political action plan is impractical or unnecessary, it forces the student of public policy to think carefully through the political factor and take a stand on how they would attack this difficult problem. Frankly, most experienced policymakers do this planning almost unconsciously, by instinct as it were. From time to time, however, some do try to make their political thinking explicit. See Box 9–3.

Initiative

Successful policymakers are proactive. Franklin Roosevelt and his Secretary of Labor, Frances Perkins amply demonstrated this when they proposed social security. In 1934–35, the United States was in the midst of the Great Depression. There were popular movements demanding that government help people cope with unemployment, and the Townsend Movement for old-age pensions spread like wildfire across congressional districts. Francis Townsend and his followers demanded that the federal government pay each elderly man or woman $200 a month, provided that he or she retire and promise to spend the check in full each month, thus helping others to get jobs. Roosevelt, Perkins, and other key advisers were willing to take advantage of such popular pressures to help get new legislation through Congress. But they found the actual demands of the Townsendites absolutely abhorrent and were determined to establish fiscally sound programs of old-age and unemployment insurance, built on taxes from potential beneficiaries who were regularly employed. Roosevelt knew, however, he could not delay proposing legislation and acted.

But in seizing the initiative, policymakers must insure that their actions are supported by thorough analysis. To do otherwise is not merely bad economics—it is bad politics. To present a proposal backed up with faulty analysis and erroneous data can not only undercut your legislative supporters but also destroy one's credibility on future proposals. And the loss of credibility, in Washington at least, is the kiss of death.

As most long-term Washington bureaucrats know, a favorite tactic of high-ranking officials on launching a new policy proposal is to make some opening statement that clearly establishes them as highly knowledgeable in the area. (Staff analysts furnish this information.) Armed with a headful of cogent data, the official starts with an enormous political advantage. At the moment of his or her choosing, the official can say something like this, "What bothers me is the long-range effect of all this on the coal industry. It's all very well to talk about domestic fuel oil, but if you look at the probable effect of reducing the quotas on imported residual fuel oil as a function of price, you can see that by the middle 1990s thirty-eight cents per 1,000 BTUs will not even be competitive with nuclear power, let alone oil. It's obvious what that will mean to the coal industry."

Box 9–3
How to get your way in a state legislature: Guidelines for governors, agency heads, and staff

1. *Have one or two members who are willing to be a cutting edge for your cause.*

For instance, you need a couple of legislators who really care enough to go to bat for your postcard registration proposal. Thus, it is crucial to get the bill referred to the elections committee, on which your "angel" serves.

Be sure your legislation is drafted with a title and appropriate language for the jurisdiction of that committee. And draft it yourself because young, overworked generalists make up most of the legislature's small legal staff. Don't get stuck with a technical, but noncorrectable scrivener's error in something like your legislative-reapportionment proposal, which, as a constitutional amendment, could go into the fundamental governing document of your state.

2. *Get the leadership of both houses on your side.*

Try to meet separately with the leaders of both parties early in the session before the less noble causes of others completely distract them. The appropriations committee is far more likely to fund your financially and technically complex program to computerize your corporation's division if you brief the chairman "from soup to nuts" while you can still get more than a minute of his uninterrupted time. If you can get the governor to make a favorable reference to your proposal in his, or her, annual address at the beginning of the session, party members down the line will get the message on how to make points with the front office.

3. *Persuade the chairman of the relevant committee, and canvass all committee members before any important votes.*

Show committee members that there is something in it for them, with specific reference to their re-election campaigns. Don't expect a young ambitious Democratic state senator to be enthusiastic about your liberal lobbying reform proposal if, originally because of Watergate, he has been narrowly elected from a conservative, Republican-leaning district.

4. *Line up the special interests.*

You are foolish to spend so much time polishing up a stirring speech to deliver at the committee's public hearing on your bill. When the Democrats control the legislature, it is far more important that your organized-labor friends at the A.F.L.–C.I.O and U.A.W. put in a good word to any doubters for that visionary postcard registration statute.

5. *At least neutralize the proper state agencies.*

Woe to you if you are opposed by the state government agency with responsibilities in the areas affected by your bill. You must show the attorney general, or at least his deputy, that your measure to simplify the collection of penalty fees for late-filing corporations will not adversely affect his agency's bureaucratic size and power. You are in for tough

---

Box 9–3 *(concluded)*

sledding if your proposal would reduce the attorney general's budget or eliminate job positions in his department.

   6. *Know the legislature's schedule and deadlines.*

Beware of having your lobbying reform bill sit on the back burner until the day when a "friendly" legislator confides that it is really too late to treat such sophisticated, path-breaking legislation in the short time remaining.

   7. *Watch your bill's every move like a hawk.*

You never know who will, perhaps even unintentionally, act to gut your long-overdue reform. For this reason, as lobbyists well understand, physical proximity to the legislature is vital. Closely reasoned memoranda addressed from afar will not work any remote control. Be especially on guard against eleventh-hour amendments from the floor of the House or Senate, particularly if they are labeled "technical." A "technical" campaign financing bill may have, tucked away at the very end, an important policy provision allowing corporations to finance political action committees in your state.

   Source: Clifton Leonhardt, "How to Get Your Way with a State Legislature," *New York Times*, June 11, 1977.

Well, few things are less obvious than long-range forecasts of the economic consequences of specific government actions on specific industries. Still, if officials have acquainted themselves with the intricacies of an issue, their statements will surely carry more weight. While all this may sound very clever, it can be a very dangerous tactic if one is not really knowledgeable. For if someone is present who knows that the official is talking nonsense and decides to expose that fact, an entire career can be ruined (which would be, perhaps, a rough kind of justice).

Some kinds of information about the economic effects of a policy are, from a political standpoint, more important than others. For instance, Allan Altshuler ranks policy options in *decreasing* order of political acceptability as follows:[68]

- Options that consumers will buy voluntarily in the marketplace at a price high enough to cover their cost. If such options require public implementation, it greatly helps to be able to show that the decisions on their use are voluntary.

---

[68] Allan Altschuler, "The Politics of Urban Transportation Innovation," *Technology Review* 79, no. 6 (May 1977), pp. 50–59.

- Options that, though entailing some measure of perceived compulsion, do alleviate problems and reduce (or at least do not significantly increase) the cost of service. Ideally, such innovations involve direct compulsion of corporate enterprises rather than the public at large (government regulations which set performance standards for new automobiles). Alternatively, such innovations entail the exercise of traditional governmental powers in relatively unobtrusive ways (the use of improved traffic signal systems).
- Measures that do not entail significant public or private cost for the benefits they confer, but diffuse or defer the blame for whatever cost there might be.
- Options that entail substantial cost or interference with established patterns of behavior, imposed in such a manner that the blame will fall clearly and inescapably on the public officials who adopt the options.

Clearly, our high-ranking official in the hypothetical case about future energy policy described above would want to stress, and to support with as much quantitative data as possible, those features found toward the top of Altschuler's list.

While seizing the initiative is important, action should not be premature. Sometimes it is wise for top officials to test the temperature of the organizational and environmental waters before introducing a program. If the reaction to the test is adverse, then a revision is probably called for. Little is lost and—potentially—much is gained by taking this approach. For example, a new dean of an engineering school has developed a new organizational plan. Among other things, it entailed bringing an outsider to head all academic programs. He first tried his plan on his executive council. They did not like it, so he changed his plans. Or consider the case of a manager who truly wants to disguise the source of an idea while testing the water. This manager might "attribute the idea to someone else, or to an unidentified party, thereby removing his own personal status from the idea should it be soundly defeated."[69]

Good timing means more than knowing when to strike. Occasionally, it behooves top officials to let a bad situation get worse, for acting too early can bring criticism of "unwarranted action." This approach is essentially the one taken by Franklin D. Roosevelt in instituting rationing during World War II: he let the situation deteriorate until the public would accept rationing; had he acted earlier, he would no doubt have

---

[69] Richard H. Buskirk, *Handbook of Management Tactis* (Boston: Cahners Books, 1976), p. 95.

encountered sharp resistance. In more recent times, the attempts of the nation's leadership to develop an adequate energy policy have faced a similar dilemma: it is hard to take strong measures until a situation is palpable to all.

Finally we must not underestimate the dangers that this tactic—letting a bad situation get worse—entails. Some situations may worsen to such an extent that an action is really too late or, at best, too expensive. It takes consummate political skill and, I might add, courage to let a situation worsen to the point at which action can be taken.

Gradualism

Military strategy does not always apply to public policy. In combat, a sudden, vigorous onslaught *(coup de main)* often proves the most effective and, indeed, least costly course of action. Many experts think that the United States should have adopted such a strategy when it invaded Grenada in 1983. Because it did not, the Cuban forces had time to organize a stiff resistance, and the United States found itself committing more and more units piecemeal.

In the arena of domestic policymaking a *coup de main* is almost always ill-advised. In the first place, such a strategy probably would be exceedingly difficult because the American political system provides so many checks and balances that such a bold stroke could be easily vetoed. Moreover, even if the opposition was bowled over, today's success could cause resentment in the opposition, making cooperation in the future more difficult than ever. Remember, policymaking is a continuing process.

Political considerations aside, the sheer complexity of any social intervention makes a gradual approach advisable. Careful study of poliymaking leads to the realization that complex structures are best created and changed by stages, through a critical feedback process of successive adjustments. The notion that they can be created, or made over, at a stroke, as if from a blueprint, is an illusion that can seldom be realized.

Successful policymakers carefully assess and deal with the most important centers of potential opposition—and support. They take the time to get key people behind their policy to neutralize the opposition if necessary. They try to craft the policy so that, if people do not support it actively, they at least do not feel threatened by it. Following a gradual strategy allows time for committees to be formed so that people can better understand the proposal and perhaps become champions of it. Following a gradual strategy allows time to float trial balloons or, to use another metaphor, to test the waters, and following such a strategy allows time for new symbols to be developed and understood.

Coalitions

The third trust in our action plan concerns some of the processes through which additional power and support is mustered. In a pluralistic interdependent society, coalitions have to be developed within as well as outside of government.

Despite two landslide elections, President Reagan was never able to overcome the divisions within the United States regarding foreign policy and extend the base of national consensus. His failure in this regard proved once again that diplomacy cannot be sustained when the policy pendulum swings too far to either extreme. For example, a policy that seeks agreement with the Soviet Union for its own sake will run up against the national mood of self-assertion. A confrontational course evokes elementary fears of nuclear war and forfeits domestic and allied support. The Great Communicator never became the Great Educator who could take bipartisanship beyond the least common denominator. Without an unambiguous vision of the world for which to strive and the dangers to be overcome, bureaucracy and Congress, left to their own devices, segment what should be a national strategy into a series of ad hoc decisions.

Although political science has developed an extensive theory of coalition formation and coalition size, transferring that literature directly to the issue of coalition formation in an action plan is difficult.[70] Unfortunately, most of that literature was developed from studying experimental groups or studying voting blocs and coalitions in legislatures. Neither contest is representative of the situation that confronted Reagan on foreign policy.

Furthermore, some of the theory is inconsistent with observed events. For example, one of the theoretical ideas emerging from coalition research is that participants in the political struggle seek to form coalitions that are of the minimum winning size. Although actors want to win in order to share in the rewards acquired by the winning coalition, they want to share these rewards with as few others as possible; hence, a coalition of the smallest size necessary to win is the most desirable. Importing these ideas into a policymaking context, one would predict that a decision would be made whenever enough support was mustered behind one position or the other to ensure that a decision could be made. Then why do we so often find that, after the preponderance of support has come down on one side of an issue, the debate continues in an attempt to build a broader base of support for the policy? Jeffrey Pfeffer of Stanford University explains:

---

[70] See William H. Riker, *The Theory of Political Coalitions* (New Haven, Conn.: Yale, 1962).

The desire for widely shared consensus at times means that making the decision rapidly or as soon as it is politically possible to do so is sacrificed in the interests of getting as many organizational interests as possible behind the decision. One difference from the theory of the minimal winning coalition is that the situation addressed by the traditional, political science theories of coalitions is one in which the decision making ends the action, and a policy is decided and the rewards are divided. In ongoing organizations, implementation of and commitment to the decision may be as important, if not more so, than the decision itself. Making a decision in a context in which there is enough opposition . . . is probably an almost useless activity. Many excellent decisions have been doomed by implementation problems. Thus . . . instead of the observation of the principle of the minimum winning coalition size, what is observed more often is the maximum possible coalition size principle. In this case, the making of a decision is delayed until all the interests that can possibly be lined up in support of the decision have been approached and courted. It is only when it becomes clear that almost no additional concessions or political action can produce additional support for the decision, that the decision will be finally made.[71]

Perhaps the key principle that a policymaker must follow in building a coalition is to *invent options for mutual gains*. That would activate all important players positively in their own self-interest.

In a pluralistic society, policymakers and implementing officials can seldom with ease get people whom they do not control to march in some needed direction. Yet this is precisely the skill that they must have—because American society is so interdependent. When few possess this skill, good ideas go unrecognized or simply never get carried out.

This holds true at all levels of government and in all sizes of organizations. People who have been taught the basics of policy analysis often sing a predictable tune when thrown into a job demanding political leadership: "If I just had more formal authority, I could do the job fine. Because I do not, the policy is unlikely to be adopted—and if it somehow is, it will be impossible to implement." Too bad. They have not yet learned that power is where power goes.

FOR FURTHER REFLECTION

1. "The picture that one gets from many books on policy analysis is one in which people use sophisticated analytical tools to make decisions about program structure, resource allocation, risk, and other

---

[71] Jeffrey Pfeffer, *Power in Organizations* (Boston: Pitman Publishing, 1981), p. 156.

technical matters. Getting the information needed to use these tools does not seem to be a problem. Nor does implementing the decisions. It is a picture almost devoid of conflict, struggle, manipulation, antagonism, fighting, and the like. It is a very naive picture." Discuss.

2. The United States may be the first society in history of which it can be said that children are worse off than their parents. Consider these facts:

   a. Through social security alone, the federal government in 1986 transfered $200 billion in wealth from young to old.

   b. The year a thirty-seven-year-old was born, his father was paying a maximum of $60 a year in social security tax. Today that thirty-seven-year-old will pay about $3,000 annually in FICA taxes. The year that same thirty-seven-year-old was born, social security benefits accounted for 1 percent of the annual federal budget. Today the payments account for 21 percent of the federal budget.

   c. The major forms of federal aid to children (education, aid to families with dependent children, health programs, food stamps, child nutrition programs) have been cut in real terms over the past five years, while at the same time poverty among the young has more than doubled.

   Looking at numbers like these, one member of Congress said, "Things are way out of whack. We're not sorting out on the basis of need any more but on the basis of who can visit political retribution." Do you agree or disagree? How did this situation come to be? Recommend a political strategy for this member of Congress.

3. The price of a pound of sugar in the United States is more than five times the world price; the price of a quart of milk is probably more than twice as high as it would be without the government programs. With one hand, the government provides subsidies to indigent mothers to enable them to buy milk for their children; with the other, it doubles the prices of the milk. Explain.

4. Dahl and Lindblom (quoted in the chapter) seem to suggest that endless bargaining, a basic component of the American political process, is an anomaly. Do you agree or disagree? Does bargaining have any positive features?

5. C. N. Parkinson presents the following data concerning the British Admiralty in 1914 and 1928:

	1914	1928
Capital ships in commission	62	20
Officers and men in Royal Navy	146,000	100,000
Dockyard workers	57,000	62,439
Dockyard officials and clerks	3,249	4,558
Admiralty officials	2,000	3,569

Did the number of civil servants in the Admiralty vary in proportion to the size of the Royal Navy? What factors might have accounted for these results?

6. Conduct a political feasibility study using INPAT to affect some change at a local college (beer in the cafeteria, elimination of reserved parking for faculty, a new program of study, etc.) or to understand better some issue on the front page of today's newspaper.

7. The chapter suggested that effective policymakers do and probably should make use of symbols. But some symbols are worthier than others. Few would defend scapegoating, for example. What other misuses of symbols can you think of?

8. The power one needs in the policy process comes, of necessity, in many forms. Several were mentioned in the chapter. What others might be cited?

9. Some students of policymaking recommend that leaders build comfort levels, amplify understanding, build awareness, legitimize new viewpoints, control the agenda, use outside experts, selectively use objective criteria, coopt the opposition, look for zones of indifferences, create pockets of commitment, conduct "shootouts," empower champions, and engage in systematic waiting. What do you think these terms refer to? Can you think of examples?

Chapter 10

Levers for Implementation

Let us assume that the policy advocates had enough political skill, wisdom, and luck to successfully shepherd their proposal past the opposition. The story does not end here with everyone walking into the sunset. Another critical juncture looms ahead. Will the policy be implemented as its designers had hoped, or will it be asphyxiated in the bureaucracy, or will it simply prove unworkable in practice? Many things can go wrong. Some of these can be avoided by policymakers who consider the implementation phase *during* the formulation phase, and design accordingly. Other problems can be avoided by implementing officials if they do the right things during operations phase. This chapter is concerned with approaches to more effective implementation.

THE CONCEPT OF ACTION LEVERS

Saying is one thing; doing is another. Thus far, we have mostly concentrated on the saying part of the policy process—defining the problem, stating the goals, listing the alternatives, estimating the costs, and articulating possible impacts. But eventually all these worthy activities must translate into action. In Detroit, this would mean bending metal, getting rubber to pavement; but in Washington, state capitols, and city halls, it means writing and enforcing regulations, providing public goods and services, making inspections, issuing permits, letting contracts, acquiring funds, ironing out differences, and sustaining and protecting political support. Policy, in short, must be *implemented*.

Types

This chapter considers carefully the *action levers* that policymakers and administrators have available to them to influence the implementation process. Four kinds of levers exist. *Design levers* are certain features of a policy that can be added during its formulation to make implementation less difficult. *Operating system levers* are guidelines that can be institutionalized like start-up plans, public relations, incentive structures, pricing decisions, and contingency plans.

Organizational levers are a particularly effective means of controlling the outcome of a policy. Indeed, creating a new government agency, or altering an existing one, often can be more important to goal attainment in the long run than legislating general principles. The means and ends of policy cannot be separated.

When there is no active supportive constituency either inside or outside government, then *political levers* become vital to the sustainability of a policy. But even when implementing officials enjoy this kind of support, they still must use this lever to ensure that objectives are met. In the mid-1980s, some of the biggest challenges facing President Reagan's Star Wars ideas were not, as one would expect, scientific ones. Building political support for the controversial program was nearly as difficult as overcoming the scientific complexities. James Abrahamson, who headed the project, found himself spending about 40 percent of his time managing the program's political aspects: soothing the Europeans, fending off congressional budget cuts, and making speaking appearances before scientific and defense industry groups.[1]

Clearly, one of the elements in a successful policy is good management. But we must not let our concern with implementation lead us into rehashing the traditional concerns of public administration under a new term. In speaking of levers, I have sought to indicate a level of actions more strategic, more general, than what we traditionally refer to as public administration or management. Though inevitably there will be some overlap, these distinctions are worth keeping in mind.

Exogenous elements

Unlike the quality of management and the skillful manipulation of levers, some elements in a successful policy fall largely outside the control of policymakers and implementing officials. The most important of these exogenous elements are economic conditions, change of administrations, and the emergence of new issues. When the country enjoys relative prosperity, such as in the late 1960s or when military spending declines sharply in real terms as it did in the 1970s, or when inflation stealthily pushes citizens into higher and higher tax brackets, then a huge "fiscal dividend" is freed and policymakers proceed to spend

---

[1] Estimate made by Abrahamson's staff. Tim Carrington, "High-Tech Star Wars Program Is Challenged by Law-Tech Woes—Bureaucracy and Politics," *The Wall Street Journal,* August 27, 1985.

more on their pet programs. In times of severe budget constraint, such as was the case through much of the 1980s, many programs will suffer through lack of funding. The point can be made with only four numbers. In 1986, total federal government revenue was $769 billion, defense spending was $273 billion, social security and medicare $269 billion, and interest on the debt $136 billion. This leaves about 91 billion to fund everything else: conduct foreign policy; take care of the unemployed, farmers, and veterans; provide health care services for the 209 million Americans who are not 65 and older; provide for education and training; protect the environment; preserve natural resources; administer justice; support research and development; and help operate the nation's transportation system.

Changes in presidents—or even department heads—can also cause cataclysmic changes in programs. Under Reagan, the Strategic Defense Initiative was a well-funded program with plenty of momentum. Under a different president, the picture might change as quickly as did the status of the synthetic fuels program when Reagan replaced Carter in 1981. Carter had supported it; Reagan was against it. Until early 1983, the Reagan administration's drive to roll back auto-safety regulations had momentum. Reagan's first Secretary of Transportation, Drew Lewis, once said that he would like to see a four-year moratorium on auto safety rules. The future of the department's National Highway Traffic Safety Administration (NITSTA, also known as NIT-suh) was not bright. But the pendulum swung back the other way when Lewis' successor, Elizabeth Dole, arrived. She pushed so hard for highway and safety rules that employees began calling her the "Secretary of Safety."[2]

In this chapter, we will be concerned chiefly with the first three action levers: design, operating system, and organizational. The political lever, you will recall, was the focus of the last chapter.

DESIGN LEVERS

Policy design and policy formulation are quite similar processes; therefore many of the points made in earlier chapters about the formulation of public policy, if taken seriously, can ease the task of implementing officials. Among the key points were these:

- Has the problem been correctly defined? By correctly modeling the problem, causal relationships become apparent, allowing the policymaker to identify the linkage between a particular action and the goals of the policy.

---

[2] Albert R. Karr, "Auto-Safety Agency Stalls in Deregulation after Setting Fast Pace," *The Wall Street Journal*, December 9, 1983.

- Are the goals and objectives of the policy clear and consistent? Although I have in general extolled the virtues of clarity, we will see a little later in this chapter that there are circumstances in which obfuscation becomes a virtue.
- Have sufficient funds been allocated—or do policymakers hope that implementation can be done "on the cheap," or "on a shoestring"? The development and operation of the Space Shuttle program is a classic, tragic example of such hope.

The framers of social security provide a particularly good example of how being "implementation oriented" can work wonders. These framers believed that employed Americans should pay taxes before achieving eligibility for retirement benefits. That meant, of course, that only a few Americans would receive help soon, even though the need was desperate during the Depression. But to the social security framers the establishment of contributory social insurance was crucial, even if many years would pass before most Americans were covered by it. Building up a trust fund in advance of payments of benefits would, they reasoned, protect the federal Treasury from popular pressures and short-term political meddling. At the same time Americans would gain a sense of individual rights to the benefits they had earned through their contributions over the years. In effect, the federal government would form a contract with each working individual. The framers believed that this would be the best way to make the program politically secure for the long run.[3]

Where the formulators of policy are implementation oriented, the following kinds of questions are more likely to be heard. How many veto points are there within and among implementing institutions? Have sufficient sanctions and inducements been provided to enable implementing officials to overcome resistance? Has responsibility for implementation been assigned to sympathetic agencies? Jeffrey L. Pressman and Aaron Wildavsky sum things up nicely: "Implementation must not be conceived as a process that takes place after, and independent of, the design of policy."[4] It follows then that policymakers ought not to operate in ivory towers, safely sealed off from the grubby realities of the street below.

Deinstitutionalization: A cautionary tale

When the temperature drops below freezing in New York, city police are instructed to round up "street people" and transport them to warm

---

[3] See Alan Pifer, "The Public Policy Response to Population Aging," *Daedalus*, 115(1986), pp. 373–95.

[4] Jeffrey Pressman and Aaron Wildavsky, *Implementation* (Berkeley, Calif.: University of California Press, 1973).

shelters or hospitals. The city deems the measure necessary because many are deinstitutionalized mental patients who do not appreciate the dangers of sleeping outdoors in subfreezing temperatures.

The policy that led to the release of most of the nation's mentally ill patients from the hospital to the community is now widely regarded as a major failure. But who, specifically, formulated this ill-fated policy? What motivated these influential people, and what lessons are to be learned?

The result of deinstitutionalization has been a thirty-year decline in the number of patients in county and state psychiatric hospitals from 559,000 to about 125,000 patients. Impetus for turning these patients out into the community was the advent of such psychotropic drugs as Thorazine, which greatly ameliorated psychotic symptoms. Patient advocates saw no reason why mental patients who had these symptoms checked by regular medication could not be given their liberty.

The flaw of this reasoning is that it was predicated on the expectation that community mental-health centers (CMHCs) would ease patients into the world outside the asylum. Even if outpatient treatment had been feasible in principle, bureaucratic inertia would have to be overcome and public spending would have to follow. Today only 7 percent of the two million chronically mentally ill people nationwide live in state hospitals, yet 70 percent of the $6 billion spent by states on mental health goes to those hospitals. How can this be? Legislators and unions fought efforts to have hospital facilities shut down and jobs cut back. So, while the hospital staff-to-patient ratio has risen (to 150 per 100 patients in 1981 from 30 per 100 in 1960), the mental-health system's support of liberated patients in the community has been minimal. The federal government has financed more than 750 CMHCs, but mental-health experts say three times as many are needed.[5]

A vicious cycle has emerged that mental-health professionals refer to as the "revolving-door syndrome." Patients are stabilized in the hospital with antipsychotic drugs and then turned loose into the community, where they quickly deteriorate, necessitating reinstitutionalization. This high recidivism rate is due in part to deinstitutionalized mental patients living in isolation once they leave the hospital.

Other flaws in the design of the policy that had a profound effect on implementation were blithe assumptions about how local communities would behave. Patients were precipitously released regardless of whether local facilities could provide adequate follow-up care—regardless of whether those facilities even existed. Communities fought the establishment of halfway houses and clinics in residential neighbor-

---

[5] Figures from U.S. Health Care Financing Administration, *Health Care Financing Review*, Summer 1985.

hoods, and local governments were reluctant to fund them. The mental health centers that were established were designed more for treatment of people with occasional problems than for chronic patients. Families often found themselves unable to cope with the strains of caring for a disturbed sibling or parent or child.

In retrospect it does seem clear that questions were not asked that might have been asked. In the thousands of pages of testimony before Congressional committees in the late 1950s and early 1960s, little doubt was expressed about the wisdom of deinstitutionalization—only optimism about saving money. The point is borne out repeatedly by references in Congressional testimony, such as the following exchange at a House subcommittee hearing between Representative Leo W. O'Brien, Democrat of upstate New York, and Henry N. Pratt, director of New York Hospital in Manhattan:

> MR. O'BRIEN: Do you know offhand how much New York appropriates annually for its mental hospitals?
>
> DR. PRATT: It is the vast sum of $400 million to $500 million.
>
> MR. O'BRIEN: So you see that, through a real attempt to handle this problem at the community level, the possibility that this dead weight of $400 million to $500 million a year around the necks of the New York State taxpayers might be reduced considerably in the next fifteen or twenty years?
>
> DR. PRATT: I do, indeed. Yes, sir.[6]

Deinstitutionalization may have been a good idea, or it may have been a technological quick fix. But, if it was a sound idea, then policymakers should have thought through how the idea would be carried out. As the story indicates, formulation was clearly divorced from execution. Perhaps policymakers considered the later steps of implementation to be administrative matters or technical details that would resolve themselves. Experience shows, however, that details often make or break a program.

Ronald Reagan's election in 1980 was, in part, a reaction to the management style of Jimmy Carter, who made it his business to know all the details. Reagan, by contrast, was not a detail man. His philosophy seemed to be the less he worried and prepared, the more popular and effective he would be. He would concentrate on the big picture and leave details for smaller minds. Actually, this approach to policymaking can be very effective. But it can work only if he is supported by a competent and active staff. During Reagan's second term, this condition

---

[6] U.S. House of Representatives, Committee on Labor and Public Welfare. Subcommittee on health. *Mental Illness and Retardation: Hearings* (March 5–7, 1963).

504

did not always obtain. The result was missed opportunities (no arms control breakthrough with Gorbachev in Iceland when they first met in 1986) and fiasco (the transfer of money from an Iranian arms sale to the contras in Nicaragua).

Additional comments on designing for implementation

Why goals may sometimes need to be obscure. In Chapter 5, we spoke of the need for goals to be clear. The reasons are obvious.

My favorite example of just how unclear and indecisive a plan can be comes from General George B. McClellan, who commanded the army of the Potomac in the early stages of the Civil War. This was his plan at the Battle of Antietam: "to make the main attack upon the enemy's left—at least to create a diversion in favor of the main attack, with the hope of something more by assailing the enemy's right—and, as soon as one or both of the flank movements were fully successful, to attack their center with any reserve I might then have in hand." Nebulous as this conception was, McClellan's numerical superiority ensured he would not be defeated, but he missed a chance to end the war early with a decisive victory.

Still, there are situations in which clarity is no virtue, Chapter 5 and Antietam notwithstanding. James Brian Quinn of Dartmouth College gives three reasons *not* to announce goals.[7] First, goal announcement can centralize organizations. Such statements tell subordinates that certain issues are closed and their thoughts about alternatives are irrelevant. (Oddly enough, when lower levels of government demand clearer goals, they are often unwittingly working against their own desires for increased freedom and personal growth.) Second, explicitly stated goals—especially on complex issues—can provide focal points around which otherwise fragmented opposition will organize. For example, President Carter's first publicly stated energy plan in 1978 immediately drew the adverse comments from many parochial interest groups who only opposed a specific part of the plan; soon these highly fragmented forces appeared unified in their opposition to the total plan. Similarly, a land-use plan can quickly become a coalescing element for many disparate local interests.

A third reason for not announcing is this: Once a policymaker announces a goal, that goal can become difficult to change. Both the policymakers's ego and those of people in supporting programs become indentified with the goal. Changing the goal broadcasts that the policymaker was wrong; consequently, people often doggedly prolong outmoded—

---

[7] James Brian Quinn, *Strategies for Change: Logical Incrementalism* (Homewood, Ill.: Richard D. Irwin, 1980), pp. 65–96.

but publically committed—goals, rather than cut their losses and move on. Governments constantly continue obsolete military, energy, and social programs for just such reasons.

Why less is better. As a general proposition, policies should be designed to minimize the amount of human behavior that needs to be changed. Thus, the Occupational Safety and Health Administration might be inclined to prefer that manufacturers use machines with high noise levels eliminated rather than trust workers to follow safety rules and wear earplugs. Or the National Highway Traffic Safety Administration might be inclined to support mandatory installation of air bags in automobiles rather than trust drivers to remember to buckle-up. In both cases however, government will have to factor in cost considerations, since the first options tend to be many times more costly.

Policies should also be designed to affect the behavior of as small a percentage of the population as possible. Those who advocate better coordination of U.S. policies toward industry, trade, and technology— that is, an industrial policy—may be wise and even correct, but no one can accuse them of believing that small is beautiful. Even before the details of such a policy are revealed, it is clear that an effective industrial policy could require a reshaping of Congress, the federal bureaucracy, and some of America's most basic legal values. Industrial policy demands highly centralized coordination and planning. But American politics, relentlessly parochial, could reduce industrial policy to endless compromise and incoherence. Steel towns in Ohio, sugar-producing areas in Louisiana, shoe producers in New England, and other desperate communities have long attempted to stop the flow of jobs, talent, subsidies, and tax bases to other localities. By politicizing the process of economic change, industrial policy would transform thousands of such situations into explicit governmental choices that would benefit certain regions or firms over others. As we saw in the last chapter, the American political system is admirably designed and decentralized to confound just such choices.

Further, an industrial policy would also demand a different kind of federal establishment. The civil service would have to be completely renovated, equipped with the resources, political detachment, social status, and technical competence to engage in the awesome task of long-term planning. Federal officials would have to not only identify winners and losers (in the new argot, "sunrise" and "sunset" industries) but also administer a social and economic (hence political and moral) transformation for which neither American nor Japanese experience provides a relevant model.

Finally an effective industrial policy would require a different legal order and public philosophy. In recent decades, Congress and the courts have given individuals and groups extensive rights to challenge and delay government actions.[8] These rights could enable citizen's groups to raise innumerable obstacles to the government's industrial policies, diminishing their effectiveness. For industrial policy to succeed, Washington would have to deploy powerful incentives or apply coercion to influence where and how individuals live, work, invest, and borrow. New public values, then, would somehow have to be created favoring the political manipulation of private choices that industrial policy would surely entail. For all these reasons, the implementation of industrial policy could daunt the most competent administrators. It requires changing too much behavior of too many people.

Nevertheless, the fact remains that the implementation of public policy usually requires the cooperation of many independent or semi-independent participants and organizations. Federal officials trying to cajole state and local government officials into cooperating on some environmental issue may serve as a prime example of this phenomenon. As the number of such outsiders increases, the probability of successful implementation declines precipitously. To see why, just consider the probability of successful implementation of a project that must be agreed on by forty different participants, each of whom has almost a 95 percent likelihood of reaching an affirmative decision. As shown in Figure 10–1, the chances are less than one in five.

Participation by outside groups is a two-edged sword, however, when considered abstractly and mathematically as in Figure 10–1, it appears to lower the success rate of implementing officials. But wide participation can provide those same officials with a strong political base and, by providing differing perspective, reduce error rates and help avoid catastrophes and fiascoes.

In any event, this much is certain: for many government policies, and especially those in the regulatory area, public participation is mandatory. Box 10–1 provides a mini-case study of how this process has been institutionalized and what role the *Federal Register* plays in it. Figure 10–2 shows you how the many rules and regulations produced each year by the federal government are brought together with existing ones and presented in reasonably coherent fashion in the Code of Federal Regulations.

OPERATING SYSTEM LEVERS

What can implementing officials as well as policymakers do to help smooth the road to implementation? Well, some things—such as keeping red tape to a minimum—are obvious enough, though often ignored.

---

[8] See Peter H. Schuck, *Suing Government: Citizen Remedies for Official Wrongs* (New Haven, Conn.: Yale University Press, 1983).

Figure 10–1
The probability of successful implementation as a function of participants

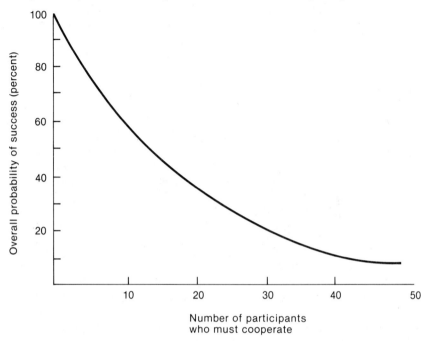

Other actions are not so obvious, and it is these that I want to concentrate on. Specifically, we will consider these topics:

1. Start-up decisions.
2. Public relations decisions.
3. Incentive decisions.
4. Contingency decisions.

In developing this short list, I have made a distinction between those decisions that concern both the policymaker and the implementing official and decisions that are almost exclusively the province of the line manager, or public administrator. In other words, there are a number of things that the public administrator can and should do to increase the probability of successful implementation that really go beyond what the staff analyst and policymakers can do. Perhaps the most obvious area of concern falls under the heading of leadership. But one could cite other concerns and techniques that the administrator who is serious about implementation must be serious about. To name a few: queuing theory, linear programming, theories of worker motivation, management by objectives, layout analysis, and so forth. Since this is a book about

Box 10–1
Making regulations: A four-step participatory process

"This could triple [the used car dealers'] paper work and I'm afraid in some cases absolutely cripple the Used Car Dealers' effort to maintain his place under the American free enterprise system." This was part of the comment W. H. Wilcox filed March 19, 1976, with the Federal Trade Commission in response to the FTC's proposed "window sticker rule" for used vehicles.

On Nov. 19, 1984—eight years after the FTC's initial proposed rule (and a year after Mr. Wilcox's death)—the FTC finally promulgated its controversial "Used Motor Vehicle Trade Regulation Rule," which took effect this May 9. A matter Mr. Wilcox complained about in the original proposal was the requirement that used car dealers keep the window sticker and sales contracts for three years after the sale. The May 9 promulgated rule deleted this requirement. (The rule has already been challenged in court by a consumer group. The reviewing court refuses to stay the rule pending the case's outcome.)

The FTC rule and Mr. Wilcox's reaction to it are an example of how an obscure federal publication—the Federal Register—can be used by businesses (or anyone) to practice preventive law.

Federal regulations are made in what is basically a four-step process. First, Congress passes an enabling act. By so doing, Congress gives an agency the authority to make regulations (also called "rules") and provides a policy or guideline for the agency to follow in making the rules.

Once the agency has the enabling act's authority, it takes step two: gathering evidence to propose a regulation fulfilling the enabling act's directive. Ideally, an agency will conduct or commission one or more studies. Agencies must have enough evidence, because agency rules and regulations are subject to court review.

Assuming the agency completes a study and comes up with its proposed regulation, it publishes it in the Federal Register, a newspaperlike federal publication appearing every business day. The Federal Register is the public's official notice of what rules federal agencies want to make, plus other tidbits such as federal meeting announcements, presidential proclamations and promulgated ("final") regulations. Generally a rule cannot become law unless the proposing agency first publishes it in proposed form in the Register.

Next comes the third and crucial step in the rule-making process—where preventive law can occur—the public comment period. Except where the agency for "good cause" finds it necessary to waive the period, the proposing agency must give the public at least thirty days to file comments on the proposed rule. This is the opportunity to speak out and educate the regulator about the ins and outs of the business to be regulated.

Point out refinements in the regulation that could take account of some facet of your business unknown to the regulator. Or show the regulator

Box 10–1 (*continued*)

how industry or trade-association activities already provide public protection from the evil the agency perceives. Or indicate a misconception implicit in the regulation itself.

For example, part of Mr. Wilcox's comment letter to the FTC noted that the original proposal appeared to be based on journalists' allegations of shenanigans in the used car industry. In so doing, he questioned the FTC's evidentiary basis for the rule, alleging that it lacked "hard data" to support its proposal. Had, for example, the FTC conducted a study of consumer satisfaction in used car purchases? If so, what was "n," the number of observations in the study? It may well be true that unethical conduct occurs, but what is its frequency and magnitude? This is the sort of articulateness that catches regulators' (and reviewing courts') attention.

While an agency has no legal obligation to do more than "consider" commenters' suggestions, they can serve as a barometer of public sentiment. Also, agencies . . . can learn. It is particularly crucial to comment on proposed regulations, because at this point in the regulation's life, the regulator's position is relatively fluid.

The final step in the regulation's development is when the agency promulgates it—again by publishing it in the Federal Register. Generally, promulgation refers to the time the regulation takes effect, although when highly technical regulations (for example, banking rules) are involved, their effective date is often delayed.

Preventive law through the filing of comments is fine, you might say. But how am I supposed to pay $300 a year for a Federal Register subscription and then read the Federal Register? Actually, one need not even subscribe. Trade associations ride herd on the agencies by following regulatory developments in the Register and filing comments on their members' behalf. Trade association representatives also roam the agency halls to see what is in the works even *before* a proposed regulation reaches the Federal Register. Also, the Regulatory Flexibility Act of 1980 encourages regulators to send copies of proposed regulations to trade publications.

After a regulation goes into effect, the general rule is that a person or organization may challenge it in court even though he or it did not comment on the proposed regulation or raise the objection later made in the lawsuit challenging the rule. In the case of a very few federal agencies' rule-makings, the Hobbs Act requires that a person file comments on proposed rules to later challenge the promulgated rule.

Is the example of Mr. Wilcox's comment on the early version of the used car rule and the later deletion of the record-retention requirements really a reflection of the power of public comments to proposed regulations, or is it something else?

A recent issue of Consumer Reports notes that the used-car trade contributed over $1 million to members of Congress. Also, there was a change

---

Box 10–1 *(concluded)*

of administration and regulatory personnel between the rule's first proposal in 1976 and its last promulgation in 1984. Thus, it could be argued that broader forces in the political and economic environment were as much responsible for the FTC's change of position as was Mr. Wilcox's comment.

But such thinking misses the point: Campaign contributions, voting and commenting on proposed regulations are all *legal* and *ethical* means the business community can use to make its case with the public and nation's lawmakers. If it makes it convincingly and the regulators subscribe to its views, it is the *Zeitgeist*.

Source: Bruce D. Fisher, "The Federal Register: Capitalist Tool," *The Wall Street Journal*, June 3, 1985.

---

policy analysis—not public administration or management science—we will limit ourselves to the four areas of decisions noted above.

Start-up decisions

The start-up period. The period of transition between program authorization and its steady state or full-fledged operation is commonly referred to as the start-up period. This period is often a traumatic time in the life cycle of a program, since it is at this time that the separate elements considered in formulation must be brought together and begin to function as a system. Indeed, not only must such technological components as equipment be integrated into an operational whole, but the establishment of working relationships with other groups and organizations must be solidified. Figure 10–3 illustrates the relationship between the start-up period and formulation and steady state operations in terms of the service output of a hypothetical program.

As a rule, the objective in managing the installation phase is to minimize the transition time, that is, to reach full-scale service delivery as soon as possible. Political realities and the budgetary cycle sometimes make this rule a life-and-death matter for the program. But in certain instances it is desirable to go slowly—so as to permit more careful study of the performance of the system over different output ranges or to allow management and the work force to learn to cope with operating problems when errors are less costly.

Learning curves. Determining when steady state and specific transient output levels will be achieved is of great importance in breaking in a program or project. Clearly, the ability to meet client demands,

Figure 10–2
Sample pages of the code of federal regulations

SUBCHAPTER C—MARINE MAMMALS [1]

PART 215—ADMINISTRATION OF THE PRIBILOF ISLANDS

Sec.

215.1   Visits to seal rookeries.
215.2   Dogs prohibited.
215.3   Importation of birds and mammals.
215.4   Reindeer and foxes.
215.5   Walrus and Otter Islands.
215 6   Local regulations.
215.7   Penalties.

AUTHORITY: The provisions of this Part 215 issued under secs. 101, 201, 207, 403, 80 Stat. 1091; 16 U.S.C. 1151.

SOURCE: The provisions of the Part 215 appear at 34 F.R. 13371, Aug. 19, 1969, unless otherwise noted.

§ 215.1   Visits to seal rookeries.

From June 1 to October 15 of each year no person, except those authorized by the Bureau of Commerical Fisheries, or accompanied by an authorized employee of the Bureau of Commercial Fisheries, shall approach any fur seal rookery or hauling grounds nor pass beyond any posted sign forbidding passage.

§ 215.2   Dogs prohibited.

In order to prevent molestation of the fur seal herds, the landing of any dogs at the Pribilof Islands is prohibited.

§ 215.3   Importation of birds and mammals.

No mammals or birds, except household cats, canaries and parakeets, shall be imported to the Pribilof Islands without the permission of the Bureau of Commercial Fisheries.

§ 215.4   Reindeer and foxes.

The reindeer herd on St. Paul Island is Government-owned. When it is determined that a surplus exists, hunting will be allowed to the extent of the surplus. A drawing will be held under local rules. Foxes may be hunted or trapped when prime during the months of December and January by holders of State trapping licenses.

§ 215.5   Walrus and Otter Islands.

By Executive Order 1044, dated February 27, 1909, Walrus and Otter Islands were set aside as bird reservations. All persons are forbidden to land on these Islands except those authorized by the Bureau of Commercial Fisheries.

§ 215.6   Local regulations.

Local regulations will be published from time to time and will be brought to the attention of local residents and persons assigned to duty on the Islands by posting in public places and brought to the attention of tourists by personal notice.

§ 215.7   Penalties.

Any person who violates or fails to comply with the regulations relating to the use and management of the Pribilof Islands or to the conservation and protection of the fur seals or wildlife or other natural resources located thereon shall be fined not more than $500 or be imprisoned not more than 6 months, or both. Any person who violates the provisions of Title I of the Fur Seal Act of 1966, which relate to the protection of fur seals, shall be fined not more than $2,000 or be imprisoned not more than 1 year, or both.

PART 216—REGULATIONS GOVERNING THE TAKING AND IMPORTING OF MARINE MAMMALS

Subpart A—Introductions

216.1   Purpose of regulations.   (2)
216.2   Scope of regulations.
216.3   Definitions
216.4   Other laws and regulations.

Subpart B—Prohibitions   (3)

216.11   Prohibited taking.
216.12   Prohibited importation.
216.13   Prohibited uses, possession, transportation, and sales.
216.14   Marine mammals taken before the Act.
216.15   Depleted species.

Subpart C—General Exceptions

216.21   Actions permitted by international treaty, convention, or agreement.
216.22   Taking by State or local government officials.
216.23   Native exceptions.
216.24   Same-taking and related acts incidental to commercial fishing operations.
216.25   Exempted marine mammals and marine mammal products.
216.26   Collection of certain marine mammals parts.

[1] 37 FR 28177, Dec. 21, 1972.

1. Chapter II of Title 50, Wildlife and Fisheries.
2. Part number.
3. Analysis of section headings.

Figure 10–2 (*concluded*)

§ 216.1   Title 50—Wildlife and Fisheries

Subpart D—Special Exceptions

Sec.
- 216.31 Scientific research permits and public display permits.
- 216.32 Waivers of the moratorium.
- 216.33 Procedures for issuance of permits and modification, suspension or revocation thereof.
- 216.34 Possession of permits.

Subpart E—Designated Ports

- 216.40 Importation at designated ports.

Subpart F—Penalties and Procedures for Their Assessment

- 216.51 Penalties.
- 216.52 Notice of proposed assessment; opportunity for hearing.
- 216.53 Waivers of hearing; assessment of penalty.
- 216.54 Assignment of presiding officer and agency representative; notice of hearing.
- 216.55 Failure to appear; official transcript; record for decision.
- 216.56 Duties and powers of the presiding officer.
- 216.57 Appearance of the respondent and the agency representative.
- 216.58 Evidence.
- 216.59 Filing of briefs.
- 216.60 Decisions.
- 216.61 Remission or mitigation.
- 216.62 Payment of penalty.
- 216.63 Forfeiture and return of seized property.
- 216.64 Holding and bonding.
- 216.65 Enforcement officers.

Subpart G—Notice and Hearing on Section 103 Regulations

- 216.70 Basis and Purpose
- 216.71 Definitions
- 216.72 Scope of Regulations
- 216.73 Notice of Hearing
- 216.74 Notification by Interested Persons
- 216.75 Presiding Officer
- 216.76 Direct Testimony Submitted as Written Documents
- 216.77 Mailing Address
- 216.78 Inspection and Copying of Documents
- 216.79 Ex parte Communications
- 216.80 Prehearing Conference
- 216.81 Final Agenda of the Hearing
- 216.82 Determination to Cancel the Hearing
- 216.83 Rebuttal Testimony and New Issues of Fact in Final Agenda
- 216.84 Waiver of Right to Participate
- 216.85 Conduct of the Hearing
- 216.86 Direct Testimony
- 216.87 Cross-Examination
- 216.88 Oral and Written Arguments
- 216.89 Recommended Decision, Certification of the transcript and submission of comments on the recommended decision
- 216.90 Director's Decision

Subpart H—Approval and Review of State Laws and Regulations

- 216.101 Purpose of regulations.
- 216.102 Scope.
- 216.103 Review of state laws and regulations—General.
- 216.104 Review of state laws and regulations implementing waiver.
- 216.105 Approval of state laws and regulations—Criteria.
- 216.106 Review of approved state laws and regulations.
- 216.107 Notification.
- 216.108 Enforcement.
- 216.109 [Reserved]

APPENDIX

AUTHORITY: Title I of the Marine Mammal Protection Act of 1972, 86 Stat. 1027 (16 U.S.C. 1361-1407), Pub. L. No. 92-522.

SOURCE: 39 FR 1852, Jan. 15, 1974, unless otherwise noted.

Subpart A—Introduction

§ 216.1   Purpose of regulations.

The regulations in this part implement the Marine Mammal Protection Act of 1972, 86 Stat. 1027, 16 U.S.C. 1361-1407, Public Law 92-522, which, among other things, restricts the taking, possession, transportation, selling, offering for sale, and importing of marine mammals.

§ 216.2   Scope of Regulations.

This Part 216 applies solely to marine mammals and marine mammal products as defined in § 216.3. For regulations under the Act, with respect to other marine mammals and marine mammal products, see 50 CFR Part 18.

§ 216.3   Definitions.

In addition to definitions contained in the Act, and unless the context otherwise requires, in this Part 216:

"Act" means the Marine Mammal Protection Act of 1972, 86 Stat. 1027, 16 U.S.C. 1361-1407, Public Law 92-522.

"Alaskan Native" means a person defined in the Alaska Native Claims Settlement Act (43 U.S.C. sec. 1602(b)) (85 Stat. 588) as a citizen of the United States who is of one-fourth degree or more Alaska Indian (including Tsimishian Indians enrolled or not enrolled in the Metlaktla Indian Community), Eskimo, or Aleut blood, or combination thereof. The term includes any Native, as so defined, either or both of whose adoptive parents are not Natives. It also includes, in the absence of proof of a minimum blood quantum, any citizen of the United States who is

---

4. The text of the regulations.

5. The authority under which the regulations are issued, namely, the Marine Mammal Protection Act of 1972.

Figure 10–3
Relationship among design, start-up, and steady state for four prototype programs—or why no one hits the ground running

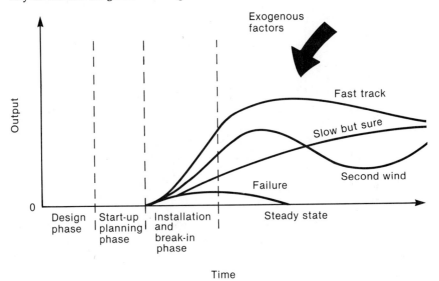

coordinate transportation services, and perform a number of other vital production functions depends on a realistic appraisal of progress over time. A common approach to making this appraisal is the development and analysis of learning curves. In its basic form, a learning curve is simply a line displaying the relationship between cost or time per unit and the number of conservative units of output.

Learning curve theory is based on three assumptions:

1. The amount of time required to complete a given task will be less each time the task is undertaken.
2. The unit time will decrease at a decreasing rate.
3. The reduction in time will follow a specific and predictable pattern, such as an exponential function.

Each of these assumptions was found to hold true in the airplane industry, where learning curves were first applied. Specifically, it was observed that, as output doubled, there was a 20 percent reduction in direct production worker-hours per unit between doubled units. Thus, if it took 100,000 hours for plane 1, it would take 80,000 hours for plane 2, 64,000 hours for plane 4, and so on. Since the 20 percent reduction meant that, say, unit 4 took only 80 percent of the production time required for unit 2, the line connecting the coordinates of output and

514

Figure 10–4
An 80 percent learning curve

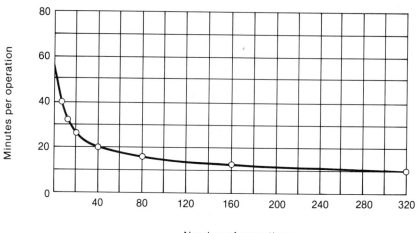

time was referred to as an "80 percent learning curve." By convention, the percentage learning rate is used to denote any given learning curve.

Figure 10–4 shows a learning curve. It could be drawn for a wide range of human activities besides building a plane, for example, how long it takes to process juvenile offenders in a new custodial unit (jail). One could even draw a learning curve for the time spent in mastering languages. Assuming similar levels of difficulty, the second foreign language should be acquired in a shorter period of time than the first was, the third less than the second, and so on.

Closely related to the concept of the learning curve are cost curves like the one in Figure 10–5. As time goes down with each performance of an act, so too should the cost.

Scheduling. Although it is perhaps easy to broadly define the activities that must be undertaken, the actual scheduling of a start-up is often a complex task. This is particularly true in the public sector where so many programs and projects are unique. To deal with this complexity, some formal mechanism of planning and control must be employed. The most common types of planning charts are Gantt and PERT.

A Gantt chart is simply a series of horizontal bars representing the time and sequence requirements of the various component tasks of a project. (See Figure 10–6.) A PERT chart takes the form of a tree similar to a bureaucratic organizational chart. A series of boxes defining the tasks are linked by lines that represent their dependencies. (PERT is an acronym for Program Evaluation and Review Technique)

Figure 10–5
Cost curve for shuttle operations

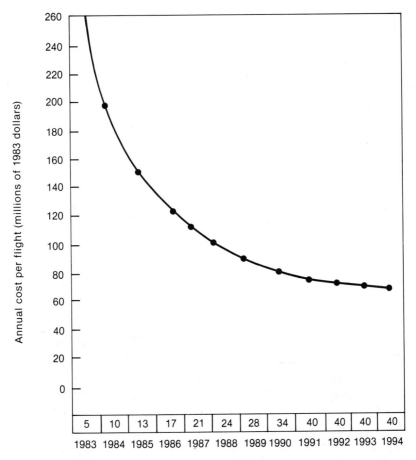

Fiscal Year

Source: "Economic Comparison: Shuttle-Only Fleet vs. Shuttle/Commercial ELV Mixed Fleet," Rockwell International Space Transportation and Systems Group, May 17, 1983.

Personal computers can help coordinate people and resources in the implementation of projects. These computerized planners, based on either the Gantt or PERT concept, take time and apply it visually to organizational problems. The appendix to this chapter gives a fuller treatment of both PERT and the use of computers in policy analysis.

The prediction of schedule involves uncertainties and risks. When the time actually required to complete a task is compared with the time that had originally been projected, a quite consistent correction

Figure 10–6
Scheduling research and development of wind energy with PERT

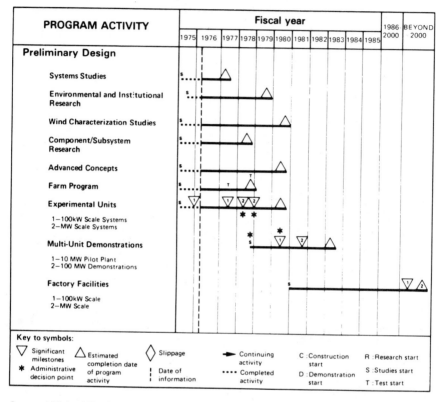

Source: *A National Plan for Energy Research, Development, and Demonstration,* Vol. 2 (Washington, D.C.: Government Printing Office, 1976), p. 107.

factor can be empirically derived. Since the late 1970s, a number of new systems were delivered to the U.S. armed forces by major industrial firms. On the average, according to reports submitted to Congress, these systems were delivered in one third more time than had been projected. The fraction one third seems to have enduring significance in determining the scheduling error associated with predicting major events in government undertakings. Data on how promptly various schedule milestones were met in a large sample of major development projects form the basis for Norman A. Augustine's Law of Unmitigated Optimism, which, in turn, defines the concept of the Universal Fantasy Factor: "Any task can be completed in only one third more time than is currently estimated." Augustine wryly observes that it is a "fundamental property of human character to be able to believe in all earnestness, after having missed twenty-two consecutive monthly schedules, that there is no reason whatsoever to question that the next month's schedule can be met."[9]

Why this pattern of program slippages? "It would seem to be," Augustine writes, "that plans are too often made on the basis that nothing in the future will ever go wrong—a 'success-oriented' plan—in the venacular. And if nothing will ever go wrong, there is no need to provide resources such as time, funds, manpower, or facilities for contingencies. The problem is, of course, that something always does go wrong." We will say more about contingencies presently.

As we said, the fraction one third seems to have enduring significance in determining the scheduling error. In 1798, Eli Whitney contracted to deliver 10,000 muskets to the Continental Army within twenty-eight months. As things worked out, they delivered them in thirty-seven months, or in about one third more time than had been anticipated. A number of new systems were delivered to the U.S. military forces 180 years later by major industrial firms. On the average, according to the reports submitted to the Congress, these systems were delivered in one third more time than had been projected.[10]

Policy planners also tend to underestimate the costs associated with a project. Obviously, when projects are stretched out, their costs will increase substantially. Less obvious, perhaps, is what happens when the implementation or development effort is accelerated. An examination of Figure 10–7 reveals that accelerating a program can be very costly indeed. Perhaps Figure 10–7 can also serve as a reminder of the importance of prognosis. To be constantly surprised by events means not only that policymakers will be continually engaged in crises management, but also that they will be enmeshed in costly crash programs.

In addition to giving attention to such basic techniques as learning curves and scheduling models during the start-up process, the policy analyst should also give attention to other pertinent considerations, such as information systems and personnel training. Since operating problems and questions are bound to arise during start-up, it is essential to set up an information system that can permit rapid adjustments. An information center, which may range from a simple filing system to a sophisticated computer-based information retrieval operation, should be established at the beginning of the project and be readily accessible to all responsible personnel (see chapter appendix). Such an information center should have a wide range of source material. In practice, the value of the information retrieval system increases tremendously with the maturation of the overall program. Similarly, a training

---

[9] Norman R. Augustine, *Augustine's Laws* (New York: Viking, 1986), pp. 158–59.
[10] Ibid.

518

Figure 10–7
The high cost of schedule changes

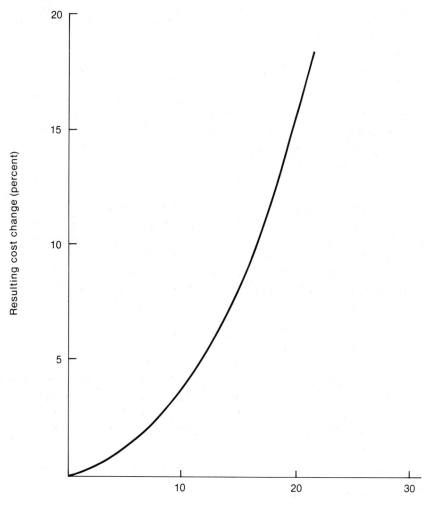

program might also be provided for administrators and other key person-nel.

Public relations

Information centers and other PR-related tasks are not—repeat not—the sole responsibility of staff assigned to those areas; they are also the responsibility of all policymakers and implementing officials. Fortunately, most recognize that today they have little choice in the matter—they and their organization must communicate with various relevant publics. It is a serious mistake not to appreciate how much public relations contributes to the functioning of society. Over 90 percent of all news is public relations assisted.

Officials who communicate with any of the agency's publics, or whose subordinates do, know what successful public relations requires and how to communicate effectively in the forms they use. Above all, this means that they know how to deal with the media and cooperate with those who do. Media relations remains the cornerstone of public relations because the media influences so many other audiences.

The media are, by nature, adversarial. Even if an individual reporter is not intellectually or ideologically opposed to an agency program, a sense of what makes a good story tends to make the reporter act anti-agency from time to time. Exposé titillates readers more than praise. In an agency with sound public relations, this bias is countered with cooperation, thoughtfulness, and professionalism. Officials answer questions from the media promptly. When executives cannot answer directly, they make every effort to be helpful, supplying the reporter with story material whenever possible. Every official and every communication avoids repeating negative information about the agency as much as possible, yet every effort is made not to mislead reporters, even by what is left unsaid. News releases and other communications measure up to the highest professional standards. Whenever time, the budget, and other conditions allow, news releases and other communications are tailored to meet the needs and desires of each recipient.

These actions avoid unfavorably affecting the attitudes of the media and therefore the *quality* of what is said. But often an agency implementing a new or easily misunderstood program needs to increase the *quantity* of its publicity. What can be done to gain additional publicity depends on at least five factors:

1. The interest inherent in the subject.
2. The media habits of the ultimate audience.
3. The cooperation of the source.
4. The budget.
5. The ingenuity of the public relations professionals.

Quantity and quality are, however, interrelated. Reporters tend to be friendlier toward publicity-seeking agencies and officials simply because those agencies and officials often help them do their jobs better. Interestingly, some officials who have always aggressively sought publicity and some public relations professionals who concentrate on program publicity scoff at the notion that the media are antigovernment. The media have never been so in their experience.

While the media are crucial to an agency's public relations effort, deliberately influencing other audiences often proves more effective and necessary during program implementation. Among these other audiences, implementing officials worry most about higher government officials (chief executives) and legislators. They gain and maintain access to appropriate lawmakers by cooperating wholeheartedly, even taking the initiative from time to time in helping lawmakers and their staffs. People who present the agency's position have done their analysis well and respond promptly and accurately to questions. The arguments made to chief executives and lawmakers on the agency's behalf are related to what is good for the nation, state, or community.

Agency officials minimize ill feelings by treating even the most outrageous and illogical opponents courteously and reasonably.

Also crucial to an agency's public relations effort is the support of public opinion. With that support, it can expect to be in a stronger position with chief executives and legislators. After all, in a democracy, public opinion is the ultimate sovereign. "Power gives power," Francis E. Rourke of Johns Hopkins University writes, "and once an agency has established a secure base with the public, it cannot easily be trifled with by political officials in either the legislative or the executive branch."[11] Rourke sees agency officials as cultivating public support essentially in two ways:

> The first is by creating a favorable attitude toward the agency in the public at large. The second is by building strength with "attentive" publics—groups that have a salient interest in the agency—usually because it has either the capacity to provide them with some significant benefit, or the power to exercise regulatory authority in ways that may have effect on the groups.
>
> These methods are not mutually exclusive. An agency can seek to create general public support while assiduously building alliances with interest groups that have a special stake in its work. This is in fact the strategy most agencies follow, to the extent that is available to them. Actually, comparatively few agencies carry on functions that have high visibility for the general public. An agency like the FBI, which has been performing a dramatic role in American life for several decades, does command a broad pattern of public support that stretches through all strata of society. Part of this public standing may be said to spring from skillful use of publicity—agencies like the FBI exploit every opportunity to catch the public eye with their achievements.[12]

Sometimes an agency may find itself suddenly thrust into the national spotlight. In such situations, how it handles public relations will shape

---

[11] Francis E. Rourke, *Bureaucracy, Politics, and Public Policy* (Boston: Little, Brown, 1984), p. 50.
[12] Ibid.

its future relations with lawmakers. This happened to the Nuclear Regulatory Commission in the wake of the nuclear accident at Three Mile Island in Pennsylvania in 1979 and to NASA after the explosion of the *Challenger* Shuttle in early 1986.

Fundamental to successively influencing all these audiences—the media itself, the chief executive, legislators, public opinion in general, and more special publics—is proper planning and communication. Public relations should not be confused with paid advertising. The media must be persuaded—not forced or deceived. Because mass communications differs from one-to-one communications, a carefully prepared plan based on a knowledge of the realities of public relations becomes essential. In particular, the communication ought to be tailored to the specific interest of its audience. (Agencies do not want the audience to think "Why are they telling me all this?") If the communication is designed to get action, then the agency ought to say precisely what action is required. (To restate Murphy's Law: If a message *can* be misunderstood, it *will* be misunderstood.) Finally, a communication plan should address the issues of source and form. Coming from one source, certain ideas may be believable; coming from another, they may not. Some facts and ideas may be communicated easily by certain forms, but with difficulty by others.

The conflicts between the media and government will continue, but those agencies with better public relations will be reported on more favorably by the media, besides gaining more support and encountering less opposition from other publics. These agencies will tend to get more of their ideas adopted as public policy. And agencies that raise their public relations standards to the level required by today's world will be more likely to see their programs survive.

Contingency decisions

Early in the nineteenth century, Clausewitz wrote (not jokingly) about the "friction" inherent in the environment of war. That friction, according to Clausewitz, arose from a combination of ignorance, fatigue, and danger which meant that, though most of the problems confronting a soldier might appear to be very easy in theory, their solution was terribly difficult in practice. Clausewitz believed that the real talent of the commander displayed itself as much in overcoming friction as in overcoming the enemy. He identified friction as the impeding element that prevented so many wars from being decisive.

The analogies between the friction of war and the problems of policy implementation are too patent to require drawing out. Moreover, examples and variations of Murphy's Law are legion. (Box 10–2) Laurence E. Lynn, Jr., even speaks of Murphy's First Law of Policy Implementa-

522

Box 10–2
Six unnatural laws

1. MURPHY'S LAW
   If anything can go wrong, it will.
2. O'TOOLE'S COMMENTARY ON MURPHY'S LAW
   Murphy was an optimist.
3. THE UNSPEAKABLE LAW
   As soon as you mention something . . .
   . . . if it's good, it goes away.
   . . . if it's bad, it happens.
4. NONRECIPROCAL LAWS OF EXPECTATIONS
   Negative expectations yield negative results.
   Positive expectations yield negative results.
5. HOWE'S LAW
   Every man has a scheme that will not work.
6. ZYMURGY'S FIRST LAW OF EVOLVING SYSTEMS DYNAMICS
   Once you open a can of worms, the only way to recan them is to
   use a larger can.

Source: Arthur Bloch, *Why Things Go Wrong* (Los Angeles: Price Stern, 1981).

tion: If anything can go wrong, it is probably happening at this very minute. He notes four corollaries:

Regulations designed to clarify organizational responsibilities will compound the confusion.

Policies that direct funds to a specific target group will miss the target.

Measures designed to streamline procedures will double the time required to complete a task.

No matter what you do, costs will increase.[13]

What can the policy analysts do?   "The ancient Goths of Germany," Laurence Sterne tells us, "had all of them a wise custom of debating everything of importance to their state twice; that is—once drunk, and once sober; drunk—that their councils might not want vigor; and sober— that they might not want discretion." The passage is not quoted to suggest that policy analysts be drunk when helping to formulate policy; rather, it is quoted to suggest that, once a bold policy has been developed, it should be debated once again. During the second debate, an attempt

---

[13] Laurence E. Lynn, Jr., "Implementation." Communication to the editor. *Policy Analysis* 3, no. 2 (Spring 1977), pp. 277–80.

should be made to assess the adverse consequences of the first decision. The analysts should take the best alternatives and consider them independently, visualizing each as though it were already in operation. They should, soberly, weigh the effect that each alternative will have on other things, and the effect that other things will have on it. They are not reconsidering the attainment of objectives, but estimating the possible future effects of the actions necessary to attain them. For example, if cost were an objective, they would not consider the costs of attaining each alternative as a consequence—they should have already done that—but would weigh the possible effects and trends of those costs over a period of time. They should ask: "If we were to do this, what would happen? What could go wrong?" As this point, they are looking for trouble, trying to find the potential breakdowns and shortcomings that have escaped their notice so far. These may be hidden and obscure.

Kepner and Tregoe suggest some promising places to which an analyst might look for "friction."[14]

People
  Motivation and attitudes
  Skills and abilities
  Performance and productivity
  Development and growth
  Health and safety
Organization
  Relationships among units, functions, persons
  Communications
  Responsibility and delegation
  Formal and informal organization
  Coordination
External influences
  Economic trends
  Competition
  Company image
  Legal and government
Facilities and equipment
  Space
  Flexibility and adaptability

Location
  Compatibility
Ideas and processes
  Security, proprietary position
  Adaptability
Material
  Sources and availability
  Quality
  Handling and storage
Money
  Capital or fixed
  Costs and expenses
  Return
Output
  Quality
  Quantity
  Pace and timing
Personal
  Goals and plans
  Family
  Strength and weaknesses
  Interests

---

[14] Charles H. Kepner and Benjamin B. Tregoe, *The Rational Manager* (New York: McGraw-Hill, 1965), pp. 191–92.

Alternative scenario planning.[15]   If the analytical staff has the time, it might be better to approach contingency planning more systematically than is suggested by the checklist above. In order to minimize the risk inherent in planning against a single, unforeseeable future and to be in a position to profit from different possible trends and events, many governmental agencies and private companies are finding it desirable to plan against, not one future, but rather a range of possible futures. For the techniques to be used effectively, alternative scenarios which are relevant, reasonable, and logically interrelated need to be developed.

Scenarios can be generated in a number of ways, with the method chosen depending on the intended use of the scenarios, the nature of the organization, and the personal preference of the planning group involved. Regardless of the method of generation, however, each scenario should have the following general characteristics.

Plausibility.

Self-consistency.

Inclusion of all critical, relevant factors.

Similarity to other scenarios in form and scope.

The main reason for taking the time to develop scenarios is that scenarios force us to compare our policies and plans against futures that we normally would not have. Actually, most policies and plans are based on the assumption of fairly optimistic futures (indicated by the shaded area in Figure 10–8).

Ideally, we would want to prepare about four scenarios. Two might represent rather bleak futures, one an average future, and one a bright future. The bleak futures, however, need not be all bad, that is, composed only of unfavorable events. The policy or plan should then be tested against each scenario, or four separate plans, one based on each scenario, might be formulated, and from these four plans one consolidated, master plan could be developed. Schematically,

$$
\begin{array}{l}
S_1 \longrightarrow P_1 \longrightarrow \\
S_2 \longrightarrow P_2 \longrightarrow \\
S_3 \longrightarrow P_3 \longrightarrow \\
S_4 \longrightarrow P_4 \longrightarrow
\end{array} \right\} \longrightarrow P_m
$$

Developing scenarios of material value to planning projects is, at best, an uncertain art. The scenarios must be relevant, thought-provoking, and comprehensive. Hence, it is essential that appropriate time and care be devoted to employment of the technique. The steps listed

---

[15] This section is based on NASA's Portable Energy Technology Assessment Workshop Contract No. NAS 2–8444 and on several valuable conversations that I have had over the years with James R. Bright.

Figure 10–8
Pollyanna policy planning

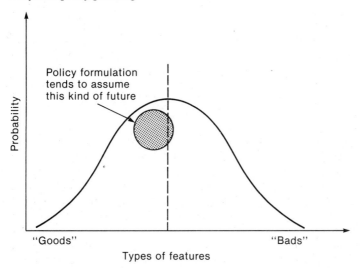

in Box 10–3 have proven useful in previous alternative scenario planning (ASP) applications.

Incentive decisions

The problems defined. Most public policy assumes some change in the behavior of public and private decision makers. Policymakers and implementing officials, therefore, need to ask themselves why it is reasonable to think that this change will occur. While they would hardly need to draw a box like the one in Figure 10–9, they do need somehow

Figure 10–9
The incentive problem

	Pre-intervention behavior	Post-intervention behavior (expected)
Public decision makers	A ⟶	B
Private decision makers	C ⟶	D

526

Box 10–3
Steps in alternative scenario planning

1. *Define the purpose and organize a development team.*
2. *Gather relevant data.*
3. *List all of the relevant factors in the social, political, technical, and ecological environments relevant for the project.*
4. *Determine the most pertinent factors.*
5. *Choose themes for the alternative scenarios.* Although the exact number of scenarios to be developed will vary, experience has shown that from three to six are usually appropriate.
6. *Arrange the most pertinent factors (step 4) into related groups.* This grouping will not only assist readers in understanding the thrust of the scenarios but will also aid the writers in maintaining consistency within the individual scenarios as they are developed. However, it is stressed that all of the factors considered in one scenario should be considered in all other scenarios.
7. *Define the present situation in terms of the chosen factors.*
8. *Develop the most probable scenario.* Once projections for each of the factors have been determined, the projections must be compared for consistency, and a narrative, correlated description of the postulated "most probable" future must be prepared. Since this scenario will probably be used to describe one or more points in time, transitional material explaining the development of given situations during relevant time intervals will increase clarity and acceptability.
9. *Prepare alternative scenarios.*
10. *Check all scenarios for consistency, clarity, and completeness.*

Source: Adapted from John H. Vanston et al., "Alternative Scenario Planning," *Technology Forecasting and Social Change* 10 (1977), pp. 59–80.

---

to address the fundamental issues it raises—namely, what incentives does the policy provide for getting from A to B and from C to D?

Getting from A to B—that is, inducing other government agencies to cooperate—is the bigger challenge. Consider these four examples:

- The Veterans Administration (VA) operates a vast program of free medical services. Private hospitals are frequently, and correctly, criticized for certain gross inefficiencies—for investment in costly, prestige-conferring, but rarely used treatment technologies; for allowing services, and thus costs, to rise to match whatever level of income is available; and for building elaborate new units in areas (such as those near medical schools) that are already well served, while neglecting rural and poor areas that are underserved. Yet VA hospitals are guilty of exactly the same inefficiencies, despite determined efforts by the Office of Management and Budget (OMB) to curtail them. Recognizing that the number of veterans requiring medical care will inevitably tend to decline in peacetime, OMB has tried to cut back VA medical expenses, but to little avail. The VA has powerful friends in Congress, and these friends saw to it that the agency would get hundreds of millions of dollars for "specialized medical programs," a fancy name for open-heart surgery facilities and intensive-care units. In contrast, with the advent of medicare and medicaid the federal government acquired powerful tools that it could use to control the behavior of private hospitals. For example, many hospitals are developing plans by which physicians would share in the benefits when costs are kept under the fixed amount to treat a specific ailment. See Box 10–4.

- Since 1972, the federal government has been attempting to reduce "noise pollution" by lowering environmental noise levels to seventy decibels or less. The Occupational Safety and Health Administration has imposed rigorous standards on foundries, and the Federal Aviation Administration is pressing the airlines to modify aircrafts to reduce noisy takeoffs. But as Paul H. Weaver has found, "for noise problems in the public sector, a rather less exacting standard seems to prevail." No standards have been set for perhaps the most pervasive big-city noisemaker, the subway trains, and the Noise Control Act gives special exemptions to the military and to the National Aeronautics and Space Administration, as well as to seminationalized industries such as the railroads.

- In Boston, the Housing Inspection Department (HID) is charged with responding to tenant complaints about unsafe housing conditions. It does so by sending out an inspector, writing up a report, and, if necessary, taking the landlord to court. When the HID must deal with the Boston Housing Authority (BHA), which manages the low-income public housing projects in the city, it is a different story than when it deals with private landlords. Whereas almost half of the complaints from tenants living in private housing were "cause for action" (required landlord compliance), nearly two thirds of the complaints from public housing tenants were of this sort. Though public housing complaints were more frequently well founded, they were much less frequently corrected. Only about 14 percent of a year's public housing cases, compared to at least 75 percent of the private housing cases, were reported as corrected at the time of the survey. This difference did not arise because public housing managers were callous but because the BHA as a public agency was required to serve goals that, as it turned out, were inconsistent with good maintenance. It had to

Box 10–4
Changing medicare's payment system

Should a physician get a financial bonus from a hospital for making patient-care decisions that help the hospital make money?

New rules effective last October 1 are designed to lower medicare expenditures in hospitals but may also cause fundamental changes in physician-patient relations. Under the old medicare rules, the federal government reimbursed hospitals for the costs of services they provided—so the more services, the more money from medicare.

Medicare will now pay hospitals a flat amount, set in advance, for the care of each hospitalized patient. The amount paid will depend not on the costs actually incurred in caring for any particular patient, but on the "diagnosis-related group" into which the patient fits. If a hospital's costs in caring for a patient are lower than the fixed DRG payment rate, the hospital will make money on that patient; if not, the hospital will lose money. With hospitals' own balance sheets at stake, Congress hoped hospitals would find ways to economize and slow the growth of medicare costs.

Economic rewards

Efficiency-minded hospital administrators will no doubt find ways to reduce costs, but they face one major obstacle: Most hospital costs—estimates run as high as 75 percent to 80 percent—result from the decisions of physicians, who typically bill for their own services and are paid separately from the hospital. Although not usually hospital employees, physicians are the ones responsible for deciding whether a patient should be admitted, what tests should be run, what procedures are needed and when the patient is ready for discharge. Physicians benefit economically from having patients in the hospital and have incentives to order more services, more tests and more days in the hospital. Extra treatments and tests can easily be rationalized in terms of patient benefit and quality of care. Furthermore, rightly or wrongly, physicians believe that a malpractice suit is more likely to result from a test not done than from doing a test that may not be strictly necessary or from discharging a patient a bit sooner from the hospital.

Can hospitals be expected to cut costs—by reducing the number of tests run and shortening patients' lengths of stay—without also changing the incentives for physicians who make the decisions? Not surprisingly, consultants who advise hospitals are devising ways by which hospitals can encourage more economical behavior by physicians. The most common approach is to educate physicians about the financial consequences of their patient-care decisions and to provide them with information about how their "practice patterns" compare with other physicians' (for example, in the average lengths of hospital stays for patients with particular diagnoses).

Box 10–4 (*continued*)

But education and persuasion may not suffice to change physicians' behavior, particularly in situations in which they use several different hospitals and have only limited loyalty to any particular one. Thus, increasing attention is being paid to arrangements by which hospitals would offer economic rewards to physicians whose patient-care decisions help restrain the hospitals' expenses. Many hospitals are now developing plans by which physicians would share in the economic benefits when costs are kept under the DRG payment level. In addition to the "for-profit" hospitals that are playing an increasingly prominent role in American health care, nonprofit hospitals are also exploring how to develop incentive plans for physicians without jeopardizing their tax-exempt status.

The details of physician-incentive arrangements are still being worked out. Some plans may tie the incentives very closely to patient-care decisions (e.g., by offering rewards for holding lengths of stay below some statistical norm), while in other plans the link between the reward and any particular patient-care decision may be more remote.

Surprisingly, the possibility that hospitals might offer economic incentives to physicians got virtually no attention when Congress was enacting the DRG law. It is not yet clear how many hospitals will establish physician-incentive arrangements. But once it begins, the practice could spread quickly. We must ask, will it have undue negative effects on patients and the health-care system as a whole?

First, in communities where physicians have a choice of hospitals, they may be inclined to admit their patients with good prognoses to the hospital that offers to share the savings, while sending their patients with more complications and potentially longer lengths of stay—often those from poor socioeconomic circumstances—to the hospital without a profit-sharing arrangement. This would result in further socioeconomic segregation in hospital care and put some institutions at an undeserved economic disadvantage.

Second, giving physicians a new financial interest in the economic health of a hospital may weaken the position of the physician as, first and foremost, the agent of the patient. Traditional ethical norms dictate that a physician's primary obligation is to patients, not to others—whether they be relatives, institutions or even the physician's own welfare. Physicians' adherence to this norm has undoubtedly been a large factor in the public's esteem for the profession, and it is important for the success of the therapeutic relationship as well. Since lay people have only limited knowledge about what treatments are beneficial or necessary, they must rely heavily on physicians' recommendations. Moreover, during treatment they often place not merely the most intimate aspects of their lives but life itself into their physicians' hands. For any of this to be possible, patients have to be able to trust their physicians as people acting on their behalf.

Box 10–4 (*continued*)

Neither patients nor physicians seem prepared by experience for the particular conflict-of-interest problems that may be created by hospitals offering physicians profit-sharing to reduce services to patients, even if we could be confident that the services that are eliminated weren't really needed.

The law generally requires people who operate in a fiduciary capacity—presumably including physicians—to disclose any interests adverse to their clients. (Some conflicts of interest are simply prohibited in a fiduciary relationship.) Alerting patients to the new financial incentives may be one way to reduce the potential problems. With this knowledge, a patient would be in a better position to evaluate the physician's recommendations, just as a patient now does in light of the opposite incentives. Some patients already operate in such an environment—indeed, some have sought out settings where physicians have fewer incentives to overtreat, by joining health maintenance organizations or other prepaid plans where the physicians get a fixed amount per patient, regardless of the procedures they employ in treatment.

Individual patients probably care less about the new system's potential for controlling medicare costs than about its possible impact on the quality of care they receive. Reductions in care—in the sense of fewer tests or shorter hospital stays—are not necessarily contrary to patients' interest in quality. Most students of the American health-care system believe that many unnecessary services are now provided. Fewer procedures and shorter hospital stays could decrease not only costs but also the incidence of iatrogenic, or treatment-induced, occurrences, such as a patient acquiring an infection in the hospital or being injured while undergoing an unnecessary procedure or during follow-up on an "abnormal" (though actually insignificant) lab result. Moreover, with a little luck, other, inherent safeguards—physicians' loyalty to their patients, the high standard of medical training, the risk of malpractice liability, and so forth—may prevent any real harm from occurring.

But the system being set up to evaluate care under the new rules does not appear to be adequate to monitor whether patients fare less well than they should because a physician—or a whole hospital—is skimping on necessary services for economic reasons. Although physicians involved in "peer review" programs have touted their potential for monitoring quality, the success of these programs was really measured by whether they held down services and, thus, saved more money than they cost. Even though it is hoped that the new reimbursement system will control certain types of unnecessary services, policymakers recognize that some incentives for unnecessary services remain in place (for example, the incentive to hospitalize patients in the first place). It is clear that the new "professional review organization" program that is to monitor services will be heavily focused on trying to prevent institutions from taking actions

---

Box 10–4 (*concluded*)

to inflate the amount of money they receive from the medicare program, for example, by manipulating patients' diagnoses to put them into "higher" DRG categories or by discharging and then readmitting patients under a new DRG.

Quality of care

The Health Care Financing Administration has requested suggestions on how professional review organizations could monitor the quality of patient care at the same time. Chances are it will deteriorate due to these changes in the economic relationships between doctors and hosptials. No one now knows how much changed incentives will reduce the number of services provided to patients and, if so, whether this will occur selectively so that only "unnecessary" services are affected. And neither the desire to hold down medicare costs nor the cynical view that profit-making is not exactly new to the practice of medicine should blind us to the risks that arise when physicians are offered bonuses by hospitals for holding back on things they would otherwise be doing for patients.

Source: Alexander Morgan Capron and Bradford H. Gray, "Between You and Your Doctor," *The Wall Street Journal*, February 6, 1984.

---

keep rents low and it could not pass on to tenants increases in operating costs that would be entailed by complying with housing inspections. In addition, one government agency is reluctant to take another government agency to court.

- Perhaps the clearest example of the weakness of intragovernmental controls can be found in the area of affirmative action employment policies. The Office of Federal Contracts Compliance (OFCC), located in the U.S. Department of Labor, supervises the efforts of federal agencies to ensure that contractors doing business with them have affirmative action hiring programs. Seventeen major agencies are required to comply with the rules and directives of OFCC that specify how each of them is to regulate the hiring practices of private institutions. In the opinion of almost everyone in and out of the agency, OFCC has failed to control effectively the compliance activities of other federal agencies: it lacks the power to control those agencies.

Although there is no perfect solution to this problem of one government agency trying to solicit cooperation from another, the existence of the problem does, I think, reinforce the need for having policymakers give more thought to building incentives into policy. How might this be done?

What to do. Charles L. Schultze, a respected economist and former
OMB director, suggests two general means for providing incentives:
(1) use private competition to stimulate the performance of public officials, and (2) develop better measures of performance so that the success
or failure of federal agencies and public officials can be at least judged
on relevant criteria.[16] Before reading further you might ask yourself
how these ploys apply to the four examples given above.

1. First, we can sometimes provide the spur of private competition
to stimulate the performance of public officials. In providing public
support to higher education, for example, we must choose between
giving direct aid to institutions of higher learning and giving aid directly
to students. The choice between the two will depend on many considerations. But one of these considerations should surely be the impact of
the form of support on incentives for performance. If assistance is given
to students, then colleges and universities must, in effect, "earn" the
subsidy to higher education by attracting students. Surely this provides
greater incentives for performance than does having the bulk of the
assistance directly provided to the colleges and universities by the government.

In a similar vein, we should experiment with providing Head Start
vouchers to the parents of children eligible for Head Start programs
and letting the parents choose the particular Head Start programs to
which they wish to send their children. This would require the operators
of the various Head Start programs to compete for customers, rather
than being given a monopoly position as a chosen instrument in each
locality.

2. To see how we can improve performance by developing better
measures, Schultze cites the case of government loan programs.[17] Many
of these programs rightly or wrongly, have the supposed objective of
providing loan capital to small enterprises which are too risky for investment by commercial lenders. The Small Business Administration is a
case in point. Measures have not been developed, however, that can
be used to judge the performance of various regional loan offices in
terms of overall program objectives. Defaulted loans, on the other hand,
are easily identified, and a significant default rate is sure to invite congressional questions. Loan officials, therefore, tend to avoid risky loans.
As a consequence, far from meeting their original objectives, the pro-

---

[16] Charles L. Schultze, "The Role of Incentives, Penalties, and Rewards in Attaining
Effective Policy," in U.S. Congress, Joint Economic Committee, *The Analysis and Evaluation
of Public Expenditures*, vol. 1 (Washington, D.C.: Government Printing Office, 1969), pp.
201–5.
[17] Ibid.

grams end up, in many cases, simply in making loans of commercial quality at less than commercial rates. It is difficult to expect public officials to pursue the basic objectives of a program unless they are judged on the basis of performance measures that have some relevance to those objectives.

Another means of promoting efficiency in public enterprises is to make sure that the budgets of those enterprises are charged with all the costs which they incur. Until recently, for example, military installation commanders were not charged in their budgets for the use of military personnel. They were charged for other items of cost or at least many other items of cost. Quite naturally, they tended to use as much as possible of the "free" resource—that is, military personnel—while economizing on civilian personnel, equipment, and the like.

A very particular kind of incentive problem arises in the case of federal grant-in-aid programs, which constitute a very large part of recent federal social legislation. Presumably the purpose of the grant is to increase the resources devoted to a particular objective (If the purpose of the program were to ease state and local overall financial burdens, revenue sharing or some form of tax credit would be much more appropriate.) But, as a matter of fact, little attention is paid to the problem of whether federal grant funds, designed to achieve a particular purpose, add to the resources currently being spent for that purpose by state and local governments or simply substitute for funds that otherwise would have been spent by those governments.

In addition to providing inventives for public officials who are not directly responsible for a program, in many cases policymakers need to think about modifying, in quality or quantity, the outcome of private production and investment decisions. In terms of Figure 10–9, they need to think about getting from C to D. Yet too often, by concentrating solely on the public sector side of a joint public-private problem, policymakers fail to provide adequate incentives for private decision makers. The result: public programs produce distinctively inefficient results.

Flood protection is a case in point. Between 1936 and 1969 the federal government spent some $7 billion on flood protection projects. Expenditures on such projects currently run about $500 million per year, with another $100 to $150 million per year spent on disaster relief to flood victims. Flood losses, nevertheless, are high and rising, and recently have averaged in excess of $1 billion per year. Schultze writes:

> National policy toward flood protection is straightforward: build flood protection works primarily at public expense and assist states, localities, and private citizens to recoup against flood losses. Where it can be shown that potential projects would prevent losses whose value exceeds the cost of the project, then these projects become eligible for public financing. . . .

534

Once the flood plain is developed, the standard benefit-cost calculation will often show that the construction of flood prevention works is worthwhile in terms of expected damage avoided. But in many instances, the optimum policy would have been not to have invested so heavily in the flood plain to begin with. Since states, local communities, and individual beneficiaries typically contribute only a fraction of the cost of federal flood protection works (ranging from 5 to 60 percent and averaging 25 percent), there has developed a set of incentives for uneconomic use of flood plain lands. Development occurs in flood plains. Either in response to or in anticipation of floods, strong and often successful pressure is brought to bear for federal flood protection. In many cases, floodproofing of individual buildings would be much cheaper than building flood control public works. But the costs of floodproofing are borne by the individual owner; the cost of public works is not. . . . The present policy, which concerns itself almost solely with public projects, not only fails to consider the establishment of incentives for economic private investment in flood plain lands, it sets up a series of monetary and political incentives which induce distinctly uneconomic investment decisions.

If, on the other hand, the government adapted a policy of requiring that flood plain investments be covered by mandatory flood insurance, whose premiums were actuarially scaled to the danger of flood damage, such rational location would be encouraged. Investors would have to weigh the potential advantages of the site against the insurance costs.

Another example of perverse incentives can be found in the Clean Water Act. Though the public is unaware of it, the Environmental Protection Agency spends considerably more money to subsidize the construction of local sewage-treatment facilities than it does to enforce all major federal antipollution laws. In fact, at $2.4 billion a year, the construction grants make up over half of the EPA's annual budget.

Congress expanded financial aid to the states in 1972 to help localities meet the tough new water-quality requirements passed that year. Congress hoped that a generous fiscal "carrot"—grants that paid up to 75 percent of all projected costs—would speed up construction of municipal treatment plants and reduce water pollution. But the generous grants actually hindered progress. Federal money was supposed to supplement local funding but instead has often replaced it. Many local governments simply put off building treatment plants on their own in the hopes of securing a federally funded project.

Even worse, because grants focus solely on construction, many cities were given incentives to build the most elaborate system available, whether needed or not, and whether or not they could afford to operate and maintain it. As a result, a good deal of money has been squandered. Moreover, the grant program has consistently promoted the decentralization of treatment facilities while studies of local treatment facilities have demonstrated the existence of *economies of scale.* (Economies of scale exist when expansion of the scale of production capacity of an organization causes total production costs to increase less than proportionately with output, and as a result, long-run average costs of operation fall.) As the volume of wastewater treated increases from 2 million to 8 million gallons a day, the unit cost of removing certain pollutants declines 50 percent. The consolidation of many small plants could have resulted in substantial savings. What has happened to the Clean Water Act is fairly typical with major capital investments in public works. Congress attempts to spread the money around to as many members' districts as possible. Accordingly, the largest systems, which treat about 70 percent of the wastewater in the United States, receive only about 40 percent of the funds.[18]

Using CBA in incentive decisions. Cost-benefit analysis was discussed in Chapter 8 as a technique to assist the public decision maker in choosing from among various alternative programs or projects. Harold Luft makes the argument that a relatively simple conceptual extension of CBA can be usefully applied to the implementation stage of the policy process.[19] The general idea is to carry out a CBA from the perspective of each decision maker or group that can influence the potential success of the project. This tells us the likelihood that it will be done. Below we will consider the procedure in greater detail and then see how it might be applied to evaluate the introduction of new testing and screening procedures in medical care.

The first step in this expansion of benefit-cost analysis, which Luft calls interest group analysis, is the explicit consideration of all the benefits and costs of the proposed project or policy change relevant to each identifiable group that is affected. It is desirable to evaluate the outcomes from the viewpoint of the groups involved and in a time frame that is most likely to affect the decision-making and implementation processes.

But the benefits and costs should not be described solely in monetary terms. It is also necessary to try to consider nonmonetary factors that may be important in the decision and its implementation. Examples include anxiety, disruption of social role, and the basic human resistance to change. Although it is generally not possible to measure the price that people attach to such intangibles, the recognition of these factors is important.

The next step is to develop some implicit estimates of the relative

---

[18] Paul Tramontozii, "Federal Projects Are the Biggest Pork Barrel of All," *Houston Chronicle,* August 25, 1985.

[19] Harold Luft, "Benefit-Cost Analysis and Public Policy Implementation," *Public Policy* 24, no. 4 (Fall 1976), pp. 450–51.

power of the various interest groups in the interest group analysis. This step is important for a number of reasons. Luft writes:

> If some groups benefit while others lose, and the [losing] groups have the power to block the project, then implementation will require specific additional action. Such action may be indicated by a careful examination of the interest-group analysis. It may become apparent that some of the interest groups are too broadly defined and that a closer look will identify subgroups who can be approached for support. For instance, even though physicians as a group have certain common interests, surgeons and internists may evaluate a specific proposal very differently. Another policy alternative may be to establish mechanisms whereby a winning group can compensate (or pay off) a losing group and thereby gain their support. Explicit payoffs are sometimes illegal or unethical, but there may be other methods to internalize pecuniary externalities. For instance, a new procedure may alleviate a disabling condition but also increase medical care costs. One would predict that an insurer providing disability or workmen's compensation coverage would favor such a procedure, whereas one providing health services coverage would be less than enthusiastic about the additional costs. A transfer payment from the first company to the second could lead to a mutually beneficial result, with both having something to gain from the new procedure. A single company providing both types of coverage would internalize the transfer.[20]

Of course, what Luft calls "transfers" are, essentially, a form of what we earlier termed "incentives."

Thus far we have discussed, in a general sort of way, some of the major aspects of interest group analysis and how it might be useful in the implementation of a program. Using an empirical example, Luft shows how this kind of analysis can be used in a prospective manner to help the chances of successful implementation. See Box 10–5.

Pricing decisions

Public policies usually raise questions about price. How much should NASA charge users of the space shuttle? How much should the National Park Service charge a family to spend a week in Yosemite National Park? Can a university raise its tuition 20 percent without reducing student enrollments?

Of course, when prices must be set in public policy, the objective is not simple profit maximization, as it is with business policy. Now I am tempted to say that the objective for public policy pricing is "fairness."

---

[20] Ibid., pp. 450–51.

Box 10–5
Interest group analysis: An example

The particular project in question is the use of a work evaluation unit for the objective testing of functional work capacity to supplement the usual information concerning the health status of patients who have recently had a heart attack. At present, the physician makes an appraisal of the patient's ability to work using clinical judgment that is based on very little evidence bearing directly on the patient's functional capacity. In such cases, the standard practice is to keep the patient at home for eight to twelve weeks, depending on relatively crude estimates of the amount of effort required on his job. There is no evidence, however, that patients who are sent back to work earlier, say in four to six weeks, have any greater risk of death. In fact, there are some expert opinions that early resumption of satisfying, productive activity will favorably influence the ultimate outcome of the episode.

Of course, one may question why there has not already developed a standard practice of shorter convalescent periods if there is no greater risk of death associated with earlier return to work. The root of the problem lies in the fact that a substantial fraction (about 4 percent) of population will die within a six-month period after discharge. Few physicians are willing to take the chance that any particular patient who is sent back to work sooner than usual will die. Although statistically the patient may have been at no higher risk, it is unlikely that the jury in a malpractice trial would be convinced of that.

Thus the work evaluation unit, by providing more information to further stratify patients into those with relatively higher and lower risk, can allow physicians to change their practice for a sub-group and expect to find a lower death rate in that group. If somehow the standard practice could be changed, there would be a gain in productive work: from society's viewpoint, this innovation should be undertaken.

This first-cut analysis, however, does not indicate whether the work evaluation unit will be successfully implemented. There are a number of key interested parties whose backing, or at least nonopposition, is necessary. These parties include the patient and his family, who must agree to the new procedure and the earlier return to work; the physician; the patient's employer; and the insurers. The relevant benefits and costs that are likely to result from the use of the work evaluation unit and earlier return to work are (1) more productive activity in the marketplace, (2) an increase in medical care costs, (3) a decrease in anxiety concerning a future cardiac event for most patients, (4) a decrease in the disruption of the usual social role in the family and the community, (5) a decrease in disability insurance payments, and (6) a change in standard medical practice.

The likely effects of using the work evaluation unit relative to current practice are also shown in the table, which displays the net impact that

538

Box 10–5 (*continued*)

Marginal effects of the use of the work evaluation unit as evaluated by each interest group

Interest groups	Effect 1	2	3	4	5	6
Society	+	−	+	+	+	0
Patient and family	+	−	+/−	+	−	0
Physician	0	0	+	+	0	−
Employer	+	−	+	+	+	−
Health insurer	0	−	0	0	0	−
Disability insurer	+	0	0	0	+	−

Key: + = Positive impact.
  − = Negative impact.
  0 = Negligible impact.
Box represents factors usually examined in traditional benefit-cost analyses.

each type of effect has on each of the groups. Traditional analyses normally look only at the boxed region of the matrix. As can be seen, there exist a variety of other important considerations for the decision maker. For example, reading across the first row, the social decision maker is likely to attach some positive value to the reduction in anxiety, the decrease in social role disruption, and the decrease in disability payments. We would not expect the social decision maker to feel strongly, either positively or negatively, about a change per se in medical practice.

The other interested parties are likely to have differing evaluations of the potential outcomes. As can be seen in the second row, although the patient and his family will receive increased income from his early return to work, they will at the same time lose supplemental income such as workmen's compensation or disability payments. Depending on the amount of such income in relation to his potential increase in earned income, an individual may or may not desire to return to work early. This tendency is strengthened when the tax implications of the various types of income are considered. (Most transfers are not taxed, whereas earned income is subject to payroll and income taxes.) A tradeoff must also be made between reducing the anxiety of the low risk patients and possibly increasing the anxiety of those in the high risk class. (Some of the patients identified as being at high risk may receive special medical or surgical treatment to reduce their risk of death.) However, the patient may not want to be told that he is in the high risk group.

The physician probably views with favor the reduction in the patient's anxiety and social role disruption, and is relatively indifferent to the patient's net financial state. It is very likely that the physician is uneasy about the change in standard practice. The employer stands to gain from the increased productive activity of having his worker return sooner than

Box 10–5 (*continued*)

expected, a factor that will also reduce experience-rated disability payments. On the other hand, the increase in medical expenditures may be passed on in higher company health-insurance premiums. Reduced anxiety and role disruption of the employee is likely to have positive benefits for the company. The change in medical practice may raise the perceived risk of accepting employees back at work sooner because of the fear of an increased risk of workmen's compensation claims. It is important to note that this does not have to be an actual increase in risk, but only a perceived increase. Those who return to work on the basis of the findings of the work evaluation unit are expected to have a lower death rate because of the identification and exclusion of high risk patients. It may take a while both for this lower death rate to become known and for the use of the work evaluation unit to become accepted practice and thus lower the perceived risk of a successful claim.

The health insurer is primarily concerned with the increase in medical expenditures, and therefore, until premiums can be adjusted, reduced reserves. The newness of the work evaluation unit precludes the availability of actuarial data and thus may add to the insurer's anxiety. The disability insurer may also be somewhat concerned by the lack of actuarial data, but the expected financial changes are to its advantage.

Although these costs and weights are hard to quantify, and may not be included in the traditional analysis, they are important considerations for the social decision maker who may adopt and subsequently attempt to implement the program. The matrix also points out the futility of expending a great deal of the analysts's time in working out exact values for earnings and disability payments to the patient when anxiety and social role disruption are likely to dominate the patient's decision.

The analysis can be carried a step further by realizing that not all interest groups have equal power and ability to organize around the issue in question. Clearly, the physician dominates the situation because only he or she can order the use of the work-evaluation unit and then make a recommendation based on its findings. The insurer may choose not to cover the medical expenses associated with the work evaluation unit and thus increase its effective price to the patient by fourfold or fivefold. The employer has substantial influence in two ways. If the firm believes that the test is really worthwhile, it can subsidize it or offer it through company physicians. Alternatively, it may choose to ignore the patient's physician and refuse to accept the worker back on the job until the "standard" amount of time has elapsed. Although the patient is free to choose not to comply with his physician's recommendations, the inequality of information in such a situation and the authority of the physician are so great that there is likely to be little conflict.

Using this discussion of relative power in conjunction with the information portrayed on the matrices, the decision maker can readily predict

---

Box 10–5 (*concluded*)

potential sources of implementation problems. Once a problem area (cell of a matrix) has been identified, it may be further broken down. For instance, the hypothesized outcomes and weights suggest that a key implementation problem with this proposal is the physician's fear of malpractice suits. The physician "group" can be broken down into general practitioners, internists, cardiologists, and board-certified cardiologists serving on the staff of a university hospital. The threat of malpractice can be significantly reduced if only board-certified, university staff cardiologists are permitted to perform the testing. This group can be assumed less likely to be challenged in court; i.e., when in doubt, first convince the experts. Until the effectiveness of the work evaluation unit is generally accepted, it may be somewhat risky for a general practitioner or internist to initiate its use and act on its findings without the consultation of one of these experts.

Source: Condensed from Harold A. Luft, "Benefit-Cost Analysis and Public Policy Implementation," *Public Policy* 24, no. 4 (Fall 1976), pp. 437–62.

And it is. But this one word hardly provides much guidance in setting prices.

Let me therefore suggest three principles that the policy analyst might keep in mind when thinking about prices: (1) with certain exceptions, public services should be sold rather than given away; (2) prices should equal marginal costs; and (3) prices should affect consumer behavior.

Selling public services. Selling public services offers several advantages. First, it provides the agency with an output measurement. If public services are sold at prices that approximate full cost, the revenue figure that is thereby generated is a measure of the quantity of services that the organization supplies. It is difficult to measure either efficiency or effectiveness without such an output measure. Second, it provides a way to motivate the client.

> Charging clients for services rendered makes them more aware of the value of the service and encourages them to consider whether the services are actually worth as much to them as their cost. If revenues generated by full-cost prices are not sufficient to cover total expenses, there is an indication that the service is not valuable enough to society to warrant the cost of providing it. It may be that the organization's costs are higher than necessary, or that a lower-cost service would satisfy the clients' needs.[21]

---

[21] Robert N. Anthony and Regina E. Herzlinger, *Managerial Control in Nonprofit Organizations* (Homewood, Ill.: Richard D. Irwin, 1975), p. 158.

Third, it provides a way to motivate managers. If services are sold, the responsibility center that sells them can become a "revenue center," that is, a unit whose output and input are both measured in monetary terms. The manager of a revenue center becomes responsible for operating the unit in such a way that revenue equals expenses. For example, if a university furnishes telephone services and university vehicles to the members of each department without charge, the users will have no inhibition about making long-distance phone calls and taking numerous jaunts. But when these expenses are charged against departmental accounts, then the faculty begins to weigh such needs against other possible uses of the available funds.

But certainly the most basic reason for user charges, the reason that lies at the heart of the three advantages stated above, is that it is in the interest of better allocations of resources. Despite these advantages, a number of important exceptions must be entered. In particular, the class of services that we defined earlier in the book as public goods should normally be furnished without charge to the client. Let us say that I would like to hear on radio a new release by Tangerine Dream or a new performance of Beethoven's *Missa Solemnis* before I buy the record. The market will probably not provide that service—only Top Forty records and Muzak. But a public radio station might. This, then, is one reason for public goods: to provide those goods and services that just do not get produced in the market. In addition, such public goods as national defense and clean air inevitably have to be supplied to a group of people rather than on an individual basis; these goods cannot be withheld from individuals who refuse to pay.

Moreover, in certain situations the selling of services is undesirable. Sometimes clients cannot afford a service that it is the goal of public policy to provide them (for example, legal aid). At other times, the collection of the revenue exceeds the benefits. This is the argument against levying toll charges on automobiles.[22]

Marginal cost pricing. It is an axiom of microeconomics that efficient resource allocation is achieved by setting the prices of various goods equal to their marginal cost.

Although "marginal cost pricing" is often made to sound academically arcane, it is easily understood as a matter of common sense. The demand for public services follows a pattern different from the demand for private goods in a perfectly competitive industry. In the latter case, sellers can sell all that they wish to sell at the market price. But in the case of a public service, sellers are able to sell more only if they reduce the price. If sellers of public service want a higher price, then they will

---

[22] Ibid., p. 161.

Figure 10–10
Marginal cost pricing

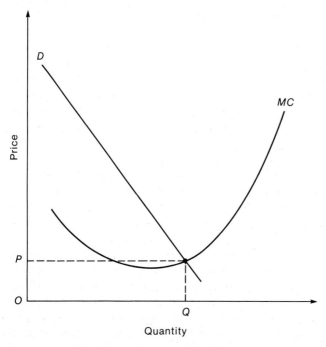

Ideally managers of public enterprises behave like perfect competitors: they continue to produce extra units up to the point (*Q*) where the last unit costs the government just its selling price (*P*).

have to accept a smaller quantity of sales. This can be shown graphically by drawing a typical demand curve that might face sellers of public services. (See Figure 10–10.)

Public agencies that provide these goods and services will, of course, have cost conditions similar to those of any business enterprise—*except that they may not feel the same pressure toward highly efficient operations that the competitive firms feel*. And this is the fundamental reason why our second principle is so important.

In the short run, as agencies begin to produce more and more of a particular service, the marginal cost for each additional unit of output tends to fall. Marginal or incremental cost at any output level is the extra cost of producing one unit more. For example, let us say that the state of Texas decided to make and sell armadillo traps. We now have the data shown in Table 10–1. We would find the marginal cost of producing the fifth trap by subtracting $160 from $210 to get $50. Recall the concept of marginal utility discussed in Chapter 8: marginal

Table 10–1
Hypothetical marginal costs from the sale of armadillo traps by the state of Texas

Output	Total costs	Marginal costs
0	$ 55	
		$30
1	85	
		25
2	110	
		20
3	130	
		30
4	160	
		50
5	210	

utility is to total utility exactly as marginal cost is to total cost. (See Figures 8–1 and 8–2).

But let us not be worrying too much about how marginal cost is derived; the main point is that in the short run marginal costs decline, reach a low point, and then rise. This U-shaped pattern appears in Figure 10–10 as the curve marginal costs *(MC)*. Note that marginal costs will cross the demand curve. Our second principle, to repeat, tells us that the price charged should equal marginal cost. Why? "Because marginal cost measures the resource cost to society of producing an additional unit while price measures the value of an additional unit to the consumer. The gain from increased output continues up to the point where the two are equal. Beyond this point, additional output involves a net loss to the economy since marginal cost will then lie above price or the value of the marginal utility.[23] Simply put, if the agency sets its prices above its costs, it is taking unjustifiable advantage of its monopoly status. Furthermore, the agency would be generating a profit. Who would benefit from such a profit?

Box 10–6 provides an application of this concept. It also provides a delightfully straightforward explanation of the concept—one that you might even prefer to Figure 10–10.

Prices and behavior. Prices almost always affect the behavior of consumers; to that extent, they should be a matter of no small concern in the design of a public policy. Indeed, in certain situations, an agency may need to depart from principle 2 (prices should equal marginal costs) in order to facilitate the achievement of a program's objectives. It may

---

[23] Richard A. Musgrave and Peggy B. Musgrave, *Public Finance in Theory and Practice* (New York: McGraw-Hill, 1973), p. 678.

544

Box 10–6

Marginal cost pricing and the guy next door

Imagine yourself in a supermarket when the manager announces that for the next five minutes bottles of your favorite soft drink will be sold two for one dollar rather than the regular price of one dollar each. "Buy one, get one free."

Back at home a half hour later, a neighbor with unexpected company calls to ask if you would sell him a bottle of the same soda. You agree, but before he gets there you must decide how much to charge him. Three possibilities come to mind—one dollar, fifty cents or nothing—but there doesn't seem to be any way of knowing which is appropriate.

It doesn't take long to narrow your choices to two. Only the most altruistic would figure that the neighbor was getting the free bottle anyway, and shouldn't have to pay for it.

If you concentrate on the average price per bottle, then fifty cents will seem correct. After all, it is impossible to say which bottle was purchased and which one was "free," so it may appear reasonable to split the difference and charge your neighbor fifty cents.

But before the neighbor arrives, you have two bottles of soda. Once he leaves you will have one bottle and fifty cents, if you charge according to average cost. Since the two-for-one sale was a one-time thing only, it will be necessary to spend an additional fifty cents of your own money to replace the bottle once it is gone.

So averaging costs to set a price reduces your wealth by the difference between replacement cost of the soda and its average cost to you.

Now, you may charge the neighbor fifty cents just to prevent hard feelings in case he later learns about the two-for-one special. But that is the consequence of placing friendship above economic considerations. If the deal is purely an economic one, then it is proper to charge the neighbor one dollar. This represents the soda's replacement cost, or the marginal cost incurred by you when selling the soda.

Sound simple? That's because it is. Unfortunately, however, government officials often have difficulty translating such ideas into policy.

Our nation's energy policies and the regulation of financial institutions have usually been based on the naive view that firms set prices according to their average costs of doing business. Instead, profit-seeking firms use marginal-cost pricing. Thus policies can (and often do) have consequences opposite to those intended.

Recall the experience with oil price controls in the 1970s. The price of domestic crude oil was held down to artificially low levels to try to lower the costs of producing gasoline. As everyone knows, though, gasoline prices have declined (rather than increased) since President Reagan abolished controls in early 1981. This is contrary to what price controllers had expected, so they generally explain the (three-year) decline as temporary.

Box 10–6 (*continued*)

But a different explanation emerges from the marginal-cost pricing perspective. Oil refiners produce gasoline (and other products) from crude oil purchased from both domestic and foreign sources. Controls held the price of U.S. oil to $2 or $3 a barrel while foreign suppliers charged $36 or more in 1979. Refiners rationally bought all of the U.S. crude available, and turned to OPEC members only as a last resort.

Like a person selling soda to his neighbor, however, refiners charge customers a price based on their marginal costs of selling oil. That is, because Exxon or Texaco had only a limited amount of $2 oil available, a sale of that oil meant they had to rely on OPEC sources to replenish their inventories. Since that meant an additional (marginal) outlay of $36 a barrel, then the price of gasoline had to be high enough to reflect this cost rather than the lower controlled price.

So price controls on oil allowed refiners to pay less than a market price on some of their inputs, while they charged a market price on all of their output. Thanks to Congress, refiners' profits were at an all-time high during the price-control years. Of course, U.S. landowners and others who sold crude to refiners were harmed in proportion to the latter's gain.

The 1981 removal of price controls gave domestic owners of oil reserves more incentive to find and sell crude, and they responded in kind. As new domestic supplies came into competition with foreign oil, OPEC and others were forced to lower their prices to the current range of $28 to $29. This lowered refiners' marginal costs of doing business, and allowed them to lower the price of gasoline.

In the financial-services industry much the same pattern has emerged. Banks (and savings and loans, etc.) receive funds from several sources, then lend those funds to borrowers at a rate high enough to cover their costs of doing business. The Fed's Regulation Q, which will be around until 1986, limits the maximum rates banks pay on small accounts (demand, NOW and passbook deposit), while rates on other funds fluctuate with market conditions.

To earn maximum profits, bankers charge borrowers an interest rate that covers their marginal costs. Since the total volume of small (low-interest) deposits is limited, lending those funds out means that banks must turn to more expensive sources for funding their operations—say, selling CDs or purchasing Fed funds. (Conversely, a reduction in loans allows a bank to eliminate its most expensive liabilities.)

Removal of Regulation Q ceilings will allow millions to earn more on their deposits and stimulate them to maintain larger balances than they have now. Banks will have less need for funds from money markets, so rates in those markets should trend downward. Banks and other lenders can be expected to charge borrowers lower interest rates, since their marginal funding costs decline with rates in the market.

546

Box 10–6 (concluded)

Meanwhile, because of the average cost—marginal cost confusion, Congress remains unwilling to remove price controls from certain categories of natural gas. Doing so, it is thought, would result in price increases for consumers—perhaps by 50 percent or more within a few months.

In reality, however, controls cause owners of artificially low-priced gas to hold down production, so pipeline companies must turn to more expensive (uncontrolled) sources to satisfy customer demands. That drives up the latter's price, increases marginal costs for pipelines and utility companies, and pushes up prices to consumers.

Decontrol would allow all natural gas to sell for the same price. The owners of decontrolled gas would increase production to profit from higher prices, and the now-familiar dynamic would be seen again. Lessened demand for higher-priced gas on the margin would bring down the market price of gas. And lower marginal costs for pipelines would ultimately help reduce the heating bills of consumers.

The lesson to be learned is that market participants respond to marginal costs, not average costs. If a firm's cost rise by X dollars when it produces and sells one more unit of output, then price will tend toward X dollars regardless of the firm's costs averaged over all units of output.

Policy makers intent on helping consumers, borrowers and others would do well to stop trying to control the various components of production costs. Such efforts usually end up reducing the total supply of the good or service in question, and customers pay higher retail prices as a result. Public officials should spend more effort understanding how the private economy works; then they wouldn't waste so much energy trying to fix it.

Source: Thomas L. Wyrick, Department of Economics, Southwest Missouri State University, from *The Wall Street Journal*, April 12, 1984.

deliberately price below full cost in order to encourage the use of certain services, or it may deliberately price above full cost in order to discourage the use of other services. The former is called a "subsidy" price; the latter, a penalty price.

A subsidy price encourages the use of services by certain clients who are unable or unwilling to pay a price based on full cost, or when as a matter of policy the organization wishes to allocate its service on a basis other than ability to pay (e.g., new drugs, low-cost housing, and socialized medicine). Unless the service is a public good, a price that is less than cost is preferable to providing the services free—for a low, even a nominal, price motivates clients at least to give some thought to the value of the service they received. But an organization may want to use a penalty price in order to discourage clients. For example:[24]

- A nonprofit regional stock exchange and clearing corporation charged proportionately more for small transactions than it did for large ones because it wanted to encourage another type of business indirectly and because the small transactions were a nuisance to its members.
- A hospital charged appreciably more for providing outpatient services to nonemergency patients than did other hospitals in the area because its staff and facilities were fully utilized in providing for its inpatients' requirements.
- The civil aviation department of the government of India charged one rupee for every person not making a flight but coming to the major airports in Bombay, Calcutta, and other cities to see friends and relatives off, even though zero cost was incurred for these persons. The reason given was to discourage the crowds of people around the airport.

Penalty prices may also be used in order to discourage certain socially undesirable activities, for example, user fees levied against polluters of rivers. "When it is public policy to include, in effect, a tax in the price, the price may be regarded as being higher than full cost (for example, prices in state liquor stores). Alternatively, this practice may be regarded as full-cost pricing, with the 'tax' as an element of cost."[25]

A pricing decision becomes especially challenging when an agency is thinking about initiating a price change. The traditional analysis of consumers' reactions to price changes is based on the assumption that all buyers learn about the price and accept it at face value. The magnitude of their response to the price change is described by the concept of *elasticity of demand*.

The concept refers to the ratio of the percentage change in demand (the quantity sold per period) caused by a percentage change in price. In symbols:

$$E_{qp} = \frac{\dfrac{Q_1 - Q_0}{Q_0}}{\dfrac{P_1 - P_0}{P_0}} = \frac{\text{Relative change in quantity}}{\text{Relative change in price}}$$

where:

---

[24] Anthony and Herzlinger, *Managerial Control*, p. 171.
[25] Ibid., pp. 170–71.

E_{qp} = Elasticity of quantity sold with respect to a change in price
Q_1 = Quantity sold per period after price change
Q_0 = Quantity sold per period before change
P_1 = New price
P_0 = Old price

And this is the way it works. Assume that the Pennsylvania Turnpike has a $6 toll and 45,000 users per week. The decision is made to cut the toll to $5. As might be expected the number of users increases— let us say to 65,000 per week. E_{qp} would be computed as follows:

$$E_{qp} = \frac{\dfrac{65,000-45,000}{45,000}}{\dfrac{5-6}{6}} = \frac{20}{45} \div \frac{-1}{6} = -2.65$$

A price elasticity of -1 means that sales rise by the same percentage as price falls; therefore, total revenue is unaffected. But a price elasticity *greater* than -1, as in the example above, means that sales rise by more than price falls in percentage terms; therefore, total revenue rises (in the turnpike example, from $270,000 per week to $325,000 per week). In short, price elasticity of demand gives more precision to the question of whether an organization's price is too high or too low. For example, suppose that we had found the price elasticity for the Pennsylvania Turnpike was $-.5$. This means that, by raising the toll, total revenue would increase. But, if the price elasticity is over -1 (as in our case), then it could increase its total revenue by *lowering prices*. This is why it is critical to measure price elasticity.

One does not have to be an economist or even calculate elasticities (see pp. 180–82) to see the problems of *underpricing*. Common sense tells us that people waste commodities that they do not value highly, or commodities that, though valued highly, are supplied cheap. In the Southwestern United States where water shortages are permanent and likely to worsen if present consumption rates continue, water prices are extremely low. People in Frankfurt, Germany, pay $2.82 per thousand gallons, whereas in Los Angeles, which is significantly more arid, people pay only sixty cents. Not surprisingly, U.S. consumption is much higher than it is in other developed nations: 180 gallons per capita per day versus 37 in Germany, 30 in France, and 53 in the United Kingdom.

However low the price of water might be for the average American, farmers get it almost free. The price of agricultural irrigation water in United States ranges between about one penny and a dime per thousand gallons. Consequently, highly subsidized farmers simply flood entire fields with water, rather than use a much more efficient sprinkler. Unless the consumers of water are made aware of its cost, it is difficult to see how any public policy to encourage conservation can succeed.[26]

ORGANIZATIONAL LEVERS

At the start of this chapter, we noted the various choices that confront policymakers in deciding where to house a policy, that is, in deciding who should be given responsiblity for the policy's implementation. As with policy decisions, there is no calculus by which we can derive clear-cut answers. Again we will seek to distill a few principles based on experience.

Simple versus complex organizations

"The fox knows many things, but the hedgehog knows only one big thing." This line by the Greek poet Archilochus might be applied to organizations. Some organizations relate all of these actions to a single central aim; they form, as it were, one coherent system. Other organizations pursue many ends, often unrelated and sometimes even contradictory. These latter organizations, to borrow from Isaiah Berlin, lead lives, perform acts, and entertain ideas that are centrifugal rather then centripetal; they move on many levels and seize on a vast variety of tasks. The first kind of organization belongs to the hedgehogs, the second to the foxes.

But which is better? In both the private and the public sector, Peter F. Drucker, a well-known management consultant and author, opts for the first type of organization:

> The experience of the fifties and sixties indicates that complexity is a competitive disadvantage. Complex businesses, despite their size and large resources, have again and again shown themselves exceedingly vulnerable to competition by a small but highly concentrated single-market or single-technology business. Among the "long-pull" performers the "stars" are also the highly concentrated, single-market or single-technology businesses, e.g., Eastman Kodak, GM, and the Swiss pharmaceutical companies.
>
> The outstanding public-service institutions similarly tend to be single-mission institutions rather than diversified. In the United States in the last thirty or forty years the examples of public-service achievement are the Port of New York Authority, the Tennessee Valley Authority (TVA), Rural Electrification, or the Social Security Administration in its earlier and relatively uncluttered days. Each of these agencies tried to do one thing at a time. But the "diversification craze" hit public-service agencies as hard in the fifties and

---

[26] Peter Rogers, "The Choice of the Appropriate Model of Water Resources Planning" *Water Resources Research*, 14, no. 6 (1978), pp. 1003–10.

sixties as it hit businesses. It led to the emergence of the "multiversity," willing, indeed eager, to tackle any job anyone was willing to give a professor a contract for; to the "conglomerate agencies" of the War on Poverty, tackling simultaneously all social ills known to mankind; or to the agencies of the environmental crusade, concerned with every problem of environment, pollution, and technology. These newer agencies dispose of vastly bigger budgets. They engage in scintillating intellectual debates—whereas the earlier ones tended to be rather dull and concerned with such boring matters as getting things done. But the new diversified or conglomerate public-service institutions have not accomplished much.[27]

The same contention applies to service staffs within businesses. The performers are single-purpose staffs, trying to do one thing and one thing only. Few of the highly diversified research labs which try to "cover all the basic sciences" achieve research results; such results seem to emerge mostly from labs that focus on one area, whether antibiotics or power metallurgy.

Between Archilochus and Drucker lies, I think, a principle that the policy analyst should heed. Stated formally: The best performance in implementing a program will probably occur if responsibility is given to a single-purpose organization. Few highly diversified agencies that try to cover a number of major policy areas have outstanding results in attaining their objectives. Results seem to emerge most readily from agencies that focus on one area.

Contracting

An equally important, and not unrelated, organizational issue centers on the question of whether to contract out some or all activities to the private sector. Presumably, the spur of competition results in lower costs. For this reason, some organizations explore such possibilities systematically as a part of their "zero-based" reviews. The opportunities are limitless, ranging from such specialized activities as building cleaning and maintenance to activities that are usually thought of as belonging exclusively to the public sector, such as fire protection and garbage collection.

E. S. Savas, for instance, has studied public and private residential refuse collection and has identified the prevalence and the comparative efficiency (the cost to the household) of the different organizational arrangements used to provide the service in metropolitan areas of the

---

[27] Peter F. Drucker, *Management: Tasks, Responsibilities, Practices* (New York: Harper & Row, 1974), pp. 680–81. More recently, Thomas J. Peters and Robert H. Waterman, Jr., in their best-seller *In Search of Excellence* (New York: Harper & Row, 1982) have made the same point. For their philosophy of "stick to the knitting" see especially pp. 292–305.

Box 10–7
To contract or not to contract

Cities of less than 20,000 in population are likely to lower their per-household cost of (garbage) collection if they form larger markets, of up to 50,000 in size, to be serviced by a single organization—public or private. . . .

The average city of over 50,000 can expect to achieve significantly lower costs by contracting with a private firm for service, provided that its procedures for awarding contracts or franchises are at least of average effectiveness, and provided that the local refuse-collection industry is at least as competitive as it is in the average community.

For cities larger than 100,000 in population, pragmatic considerations suggest that the best approach may be to divide the city into two or more districts, each with at least 50,000 in population (this procedure results in no appreciable loss of economies of scale) and to have a municipal agency service one or more of the districts while the city contracts with one or more private firms to service the remaining districts. By doing this, a large city might best assure a continued competitive environment and protect itself against possible collusion by its contractors or coercion by its employees. Such an arrangement might also be expected to reduce the city's risk of service disruptions due to strikes or business failures.

The important strategic point is that a city should, if at all possible, retain some options in service delivery and some standard for measuring and comparing performance.

Source: E. S. Savas, "Policy Analysis for Local Government," *Policy Analysis* 3, no. 1 (Winter 1977), pp. 49–74.

United States. Private firms play a major role, collecting residential refuse in almost twice as many cities as municipal agencies do; and in cities with over 500,000 in population, refuse collection by private firms under contract to the city is significantly more efficient than collection by municipal agencies. Savas has also advanced policy recommendations to improve the productivity of local government with regard to this and other municipal services. See Box 10–7.[28]

I have cited Savas's recommendation to show that it should not be assumed in every case that a profit-oriented company will perform a function more efficiently than a nonprofit organization, although there are those who act as if this were the case. The proper approach, of

---

[28] E. S. Savas, "Policy Analysis for Local Government: Public vs. Private Refuse Collection." *Policy Analysis* 3, no. 1 (Winter 1977), pp. 49–74.

course, is to make a careful analysis of the cost of the alternative ways of performing the function. Even if such an analysis leads to the conclusion that the function should continue to be performed by government, the fact that such comparisons are being made tend to keep the government organization on its toes.

On being the right size

Finally, policy analysts need to think through the question of whether the implementing structure is the right size. A more concise way of stating this principle is captured in the concept of *economies of scale.* Generally speaking, bigger enterprises can produce things more cheaply than smaller ones thanks to less overhead, bulk purchasing, and other such factors. But this does not necessarily mean that average total costs will continue to fall and fall as production or output rises higher and higher. In fact, Table 10–1 showed that marginal costs fall at first and then rise. Why? Because after a certain point there are diseconomies of getting bigger. I hope that I will be forgiven if I use a rather trite and less than precise saying to shed further light on why, after organizations reach a certain size, costs begin to mount and diseconomies set in: too many cooks spoil the broth. (Or in Spanish: *Tres al saco y el saco en tierra.*)

While it might be simple enough to talk about economies of scale with reference to big companies such as General Motors, how does the concept apply to the public sector? Education and medical care provide two excellent examples. The policy of public school consolidation, which has largely eliminated the one-room schoolhouse in rural America, has apparently failed to produce expected financial savings and educational quality, according to a study for the National Institute of Education.[29] The study found that the newer, larger regional schools cost as much or more to run than did the old, decentralized rural school systems. And the evidence indicates that the children receive no better education. Ironically, the study called the consolidation of rural schools and school districts "the most successfully implemented educational policy of the past fifty years."

As the report pointed out, consolidation proved popular because it promised rural people economies of scale, among other things. The authors devised a hypothetical case based on a study of Iowa high schools. In the case, three rural high schools of 140 pupils each were replaced by one new 420-pupil school. In the old, small schools, the

---

[29] Jonathon P. Sher and Rachel B. Tompkins, *Economy, Efficiency, and Equality: The Myths of Rural School and District Consolidation,* U.S. Department of Education, (Washington, D.C.: Government Printing Office, July 1976).

costs for professional personnel totaled $198,000. But in the new, consolidated school, they amounted to $157,000, a saving of $41,000.

This figure, however, was arrived at by ignoring several critical economic factors, the study said. First of all, higher transportation costs are involved in busing students to the centrally located schools. Furthermore, the larger schools attract more specialized teachers and administrators who demand higher salaries.

As for quality of education, the authors cite a recent study of high schools in Vermont, the most rural state in the nation, as evidence that bigger is not necessarily better. "The small high schools (in Vermont) appear to be performing every bit as well as their larger counterparts on the one available output measure—percentage of graduates entering college." And none of the recent studies that measure student achievement independent of IQ and social class "records a consistent, positive correlation between size and achievement."

In the field of health care, one of the most interesting studies of the effect of size on costs found that this relationship varied with the number of services and facilities offered by the hospital.[30] The authors concluded that "small hospitals with high service capability should not generally be built because they are likely to be of uneconomic size. Large hospitals having low service capability are also likely to be uneconomic, since there are few or no additional economies associated with increased size." In other words, if hospitals are not going to provide a large number of complex services, it is very inefficient for them to be small. A hospital of 200 beds can efficiently provide most of the basic services needed for routine short-term care—radiology, laboratory, nursing, and the like. Should that hospital grow to 600 beds and still provide only the same basic services, some inefficiencies are likely to develop because of increasing difficulties of administrative control. What is likely to happen, however, is that more specialized services will emerge in the 600-bed unit, services which could not possibly have been provided at a reasonable cost when the hospital had only 200 beds.

As Victor Fuchs of Stanford University observes, "Persons with direct experience in running hospitals tend to confirm the results of such econometric studies. The president of one major corporation that owns and operates a large chain of for-profit hospitals personally told me that his company would rather not build or operate one that had fewer than 200 beds, but they would be equally apprehensive about a hospital with more than 500 beds."[31]

---

[30] John W. Carr and Paul J. Feldstein, "The Relationship of Cost to Hospital Size" *Inquiry* 4, no. 2 (June 1967).

[31] Victor R. Fuch. *Who Shall Live?* (New York: Basic Books, 1974), p. 83.

New and restructural institutions: A macroapproach to implementation

In the middle of our journey, we come to a dark woods where the path is lost. When does a policy innovation require a new institution? When does the policy apparatus itself require revamping? These are difficult questions, indeed. And we have no sure compass to guide us through them.

Policy innovations usually require new or restructured institutions in order to succeed. The Employment Act of 1946 established the *Council of Economic Advisers;* the National Aeronautics and Space Act of 1958 established *NASA;* the Peace Corps Act of 1961, the *Peace Corps.* The Secretary's Reorganization plan of 1977 restructured the way in which the medicare program was administered in the Department of Health and Human Services; specifically, it gave to one operating component in the Department, the *Health Care Financing Administration,* the task of overseeing medicare, medicaid, and related programs. Similarly, the omnibus Budget Reconciliation Act of 1981 restructured the administration of block grants through the *Office of Community Services.*

Some of the problems of the Strategic Defense Initiative Organization stem from the way it was set up in 1984. The office was not given the authority to award contracts directly to the defense contractors and research laboratories that were to explore the prospects of missile defenses. Thus, the SDI office must depend on at least seven separate arms of the Defense Department, as well as offices in the Energy Department and the National Aeronautics and Space Administration, to carry out the projects.[32] Consequently, implementation of the program gets bogged down.

As these examples show, the design of new institutions should be an integral part of policy analysis. It would be, I think, instructive to briefly touch on a few of the many options that have been floating around policymaking circles in recent years. For each, we want to ask, What are the implications? Institutional design is not an aesthetic operation; the criteria by which we judge it must be, in the main, the political and economic consequences that flow from it.

The Constitution: Is it broke? The bicentennial of the U.S. Constitution took place in 1987. Most constitutional debate continues to be between partisans of activism and restraint in interpretation of the document. But a growing number of politicans and analysts believe that there is such a lack of coherence and consensus on public policy that structural reform of the Constitution, written and unwritten, is in order. Some observers are convinced that the weaknesses now apparent in

---

[32] Tim Carrington, "High-Tech Star Wars,"

American institutions—with the Republicans able to control the presidency much more often than the Democrats, who, in turn manage to control the Congress—result in a wearying and costly policy stalemate.[33] They point to the huge budget deficit and the indecisiveness in foreign policy as symptoms of a weak and inadequate policy apparatus—one that demands treatment before the entire system breaks down.

Is this assessment accurate? I am not sure, but it is difficult to deny or to ignore serious flaws in the structure. Let us consider four suggestions on how to minimize some of the chaos wrought by the separation of powers and other features of the Constitution.

1. One of the most significant suggestions is to allow the president to choose cabinet members from among sitting legislators in the Congress and to create a *team ticket* whereby voters would cast a single party ballot for president, senator, and representative. This team ticket proposal would make one political party the clear winner in every election and give representatives, senators, and presidents of the same party a strong incentive to align their respective agendas.

2. Somewhat less constructive, in my opinion, is the proposal for *a six-year presidency* with no chance of reelection. It would be detrimental to accountability. The principle of elections as a means of hiring and firing leaders would be compromised.

3. A number of members of the Washington establishment, including President Reagan, have proposed a constitutional amendment to empower the president to make *partial or line-item vetoes* of spending bills. Line-item vetoes, like whole bill vetoes, would be contingent negatives because Congress could overide them. Presumably a president would use the veto to eliminate various pork-barrel projects of which Congress is so fond.

The main problem with this proposal is that it is simply a nonstarter. It will not pass Congress because it would entail a major shift of power from the legislative to the executive branch.

4. Should the Federal Reserve System, which is relatively independent from both the president and the Congress, be rebuilt? The Federal Reserve Act was passed in 1913, and the Federal Reserve System ("the Fed") was inaugurated in 1914. The preamble to the act indicates the functions the Fed is to perform: "to furnish an elastic currency, to afford means of rediscounting commercial paper, to establish a more effective supervision of banking in the United States and for other purposes." More generally, the Fed was created to correct the then-existing defects in the banking system, defects which periodically created significant problems for the economy.

---

[33] See, for example, James L. Sundquist, *Constitutional Reform and Effective Government* (Washington: Brookings Institution 1986); and James MacGregory Burn, *The Power to Lead: The Crisis in the American Presidency* (New York: Simon & Schuster, 1984).

Some conservative critics of the Fed argue that the major source of instability in the economy is the instability in the money supply. Economists like Milton Friedman, who are known as monetarists, argue that the Fed controls the money supply; therefore, because the Fed causes the money supply to behave erratically, it causes the macroeconomy to behave erratically. In their efforts to achieve a stable macroeconomy, the monetarists face two tasks. Their first task is to shift the Fed's attention from interest rates to the money supply. The monetarists' second task is to compel the Fed to allow for slow and steady growth in the money supply. Liberals also criticize the Fed. Liberals begin their attacks by declaring that the Fed has an unwarranted preoccupation with inflation—that is, the Fed pays too much attention to the fight for price stability and too little attention to the fight for full employment. Liberals also believe the monetarists' view of the overriding importance of stable money growth for a stable macroeconomy is a gross oversimplification. Consequently, they contend that the Fed should have continued to pay attention to interest rates.

Reshuffling and restructuring the executive branch. Experience in the federal government over the past two decades shows that massive aggregation of departments has not been beneficial. Furthermore, the present disaggregated but highly successful arrangements of the federal conduct of research and development have contributed to a very rich harvest of science and technology.

Nevertheless, the proposal for a Department of Science and Technology has gained particular force in recent years. Faced with increasing foreign competition, many in government and industry see a need to strengthen and update the American science and technology base. Today, with science and technology distributed through the majority of mission agencies, it is difficult to keep, maintain, and direct a coherent policy. In short, the proposed department (Figure 10–11) might manage federal research dollars better. Moreover, if the reorganization is done properly, some overhead should be reduced—though that is not the principal benefit.

Critics of the proposal make these points.

1. Science and technology are integral to most of the existing federal departments and, as such, cannot easily be extracted.
2. While the department might be a good idea for large scientific projects, little projects require multiple doors to knock on for funding.
3. Inevitably, the department would be dependent on a single personality, the secretary. If it is not managed properly, it could be a disaster.

Arguably, the central strategic problem in defense is not budgetary levels, or the pros and cons of various weapons systems, but structure. More specifically, the current organization of the Department of Defense

Figure 10–11
Cabinet structure with the addition of a department of science and technology

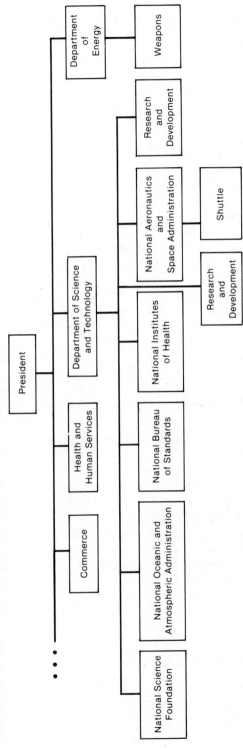

Note: According to the Commission, the department would not include the research activities of the Department of Defense or of such major regulatory agencies as the Food and Drug Administration and the Environmental Protection Agency.

Source: U.S. House of Representatives, Committee on Science and Technology, Subcommittee on Science, Research, and Technology, *Federal Organization for Technological Innovation: Hearings* (Washington, D.C.: Government Printing Office, June 7–14, 1984).

558

is a principal obstacle to either controlling the budget or choosing weapons wisely. The National Security Act of 1947 established a Joint Chiefs of Staff representing the heads of the military services. The chairman is first among equals, the chiefs operate on the basis of consensus—a practice that tends to produce a large staff, masses of memoranda, and the least common denominator.

This procedure would be only time-consuming had not modern technology destroyed the traditional distinctions between the missions of the services. Significant conflicts inevitably involve all of the services acting in concert with overlapping weapons systems.[34]

The consequences for overall policy are even more worrisome. Strategic planning occurs, if at all, in the Joint Commands, where the relevant services are brought together for specific missions. But the heads of the Joint Commands neither serve on the Joint Chiefs nor control their constituent elements in peacetime. By contrast, the inevitable and natural concern of the service chiefs—with their competitive and often mutually exclusive mandates—is the future of their services, which depends on their share of the total budget. Their incentive is more to enhance the weapons they have under their exclusive control than to plan overall defense policy.

Interservice rivalry, thus institutionalized, is magnified by the extraordinary swings of congressional mood with respect to the defense budget. The sharp increase of the 1960s was followed by a relentless assault on defense expenditures in the 1970s. The buildup of the Reagan administration had strong support in the beginning, but by the mid-1980s confronted growing opposition.

Faced with such a pendulum effect the service chiefs seek to protect their own by turning strategy into procurement. In periods of budgetary plenty they spread the increase over as many weapons categories as possible. In periods of budgetary stringency they tend to cut not the infamous $10,000 wrench but something visible and painful to evoke the greatest degree of public backlash.

The starting point of the most significant debate over defense organization since the establishment of a secretary of defense was a study presented to the Senate by senators Sam Nunn of Georgia and Barry Goldwater of Arizona. The study's most important recommendation was the abolition of the Joint Chiefs and a reorganization of almost all the other offices under the secretary of defense.[35]

---

[34] In his seminal book *The Pentagon and the Art of War* (New York: Simon & Schuster, 1984) Edward Luttwak has demonstrated the paralyzing impact of this state of affairs on operational planning and procurement.

[35] U.S. Congress, U.S. Senate, Committee on Armed Services, *Defense Organization: The Need for Change* (Washington, D.C.: Government Printing Office, October 16, 1985).

As in all public debates there are issues that no one wishes to admit are there and other, somewhat unreal issues that get far too much attention:

- As the defense establishment is now organized, the Navy has strong reason for fighting change. The Navy with its carriers has its own air force. The Marine Corps supplies the Navy with tanks and infantry. The surface fleet provides the long-range artillery. The Navy, in fact, is an all-arms military force. It may even be as good as it thinks it is.

- The non-issue in the debate is the furor aroused by consideration of the organization of a true general staff, composed of officers who join as captains or majors and remain on the general staff for the remainder of their military careers. Goldwater and Nunn considered this option but steered away, possibly because they anticipated congressional and public uproar. Nevertheless, there was during the course of the debate dark talk about creating a "Prussian or German general staff." (Even if this option had been suggested, critics might recall that the last one was good enough to create forces whose downfall required the combined might of the United States, the British Empire, and the Soviet Union.)

Reform in Congress. There is no shortage of suggestions for changing the way Congress operates. Some might seem marginal: reducing the number of standing and select committees and subcommittees (which seem to multiply like so many amoebae), or prohibiting proxy voting in committees. These changes may seem small and technical, but so was the American League's designated-hitters rule that some baseball aficionados felt was a "desecration" of baseball.

In recent years, however, budget reform has been high on the list of congressional reforms. The reasons are not hard to find. In 1985, for example, Congress failed to pass any individual appropriation bill and finally sent to the White House a single omnibus bill funding every federal agency—just past the deadline when the government ran out of money. More important, the deficit remains stuck in the $100 billion plus range. (Government spending is about 23 percent of GNP, while revenues are at 19 percent.)

The crucial question is whether trying to revise the process will alter the fact that the American body politic appears to want more government than it is willing to pay for. The beneficiaries of many federal programs—and their elected representatives—tend to regard the benefits as sacrosanct, like the Grand Canyon or the Lincoln Memorial.

Another proposal would create a *capital budget* for the federal government. This would enable the government to spread the recorded outlays for a long-lived investment (such as a building) over a period of years, just as corporations do. But a capital budget could expose the budget to new levels of accounting gimmickry. As happened in New York City, programs favored by politicians—education, for example—could be categorized as long-term investments in the nation's future, rather than current operating expenses to be counted in the deficit. That in turn would give Congress a green light to spend in those areas.

Other proposals, such as expanding the budget cycle from one year to two and enhancing the president's power to rescind outlays, may make good sense. But nobody claims they would solve the deficit. So budget "reform" may spark a lot of discussion in the coming years, but miraculous solutions are not likely to emerge.

Crisis and reform in the federal court. It hardly requires a Tocqueville to recognize that the federal courts and constitutional law are subjects too important to be left to lawyers and judges. Before turning to reforms let us sketch briefly a portrait of the problem.

From 1960 to 1983, Federal District Court cases increased by 250 percent and appeals to the Courts of Appeals rose by 789 percent. (The figures for the prior 25 years were 30 percent and 15 percent respectively.) Meanwhile, the number of district judges doubled, but the number of appeals judges did not change despite a caseload seven or eight times as heavy as it had been. The size of the Supreme Court has not changed at all. The principal method of accommodating the increase in caseloads has been a large expansion of supporting personnel, ranging from bankruptcy judges and magistrates to law clerks, staff attorneys, and law students.[36]

Why not simply multiply the number of federal judges? The inelastic capacity of the Supreme Court (at least as long as it sits as one panel) would nullify the increase. Why not rely more on supporting staff? It might threaten the unique character of the judiciary as the institution of government in which those with the power of decision do the actual work of deciding and explaining their reasons. A substantial volume of cases is in federal court only because the opposing parties live in different states. A searching examination finds possible justification for at most a small fraction of this diversity jurisdiction. Yet how this would be curtailed is not clear. Nor is it clear how—or even whether—more economic analysis could be factored into judicial decision making.

Considering the lengthy process historically required for any jurisdictional revisions, the effort to secure lesser ones, particularly if they were successful, could be an obstacle to achieving the needed, more fundamental reforms.

---

[36] Richard A. Posner, *The Federal Courts: Crisis and Reform* (Cambridge, Mass.: Harvard University Press, 1985).

If you feel slightly undernourished on finishing this discussion of institutional reform, it is probably because most proposals to grease the machinery of policymaking leave us wondering precisely what we want to use it *for*. Tens of millions of poor and lower-income Americans are not represented in the system very well. How can it best serve them—and how can the nation maintain prosperity for the majority of American without making the poor suffer? Questions of building a fairer and a more prosperous society make our hearts beat faster and inspire us to make the wheels of the policy process hum. Let us think on these things in the remaining two chapters of this book.

FOR FURTHER REFLECTION

1. At what level of initiation (federal, state, or local) is a policy most likely to be successfully implemented?
2. What examples of public policies can you give for each of the four implementation patterns shown in Figure 10–3?
3. Select a public program with which you are familiar. What were the action levers? What went wrong during implementation? What went right? Why?
4. Incorporate the following information into Figure 10–A2. While hiring the cast and getting the screenplay written, the agency will also have to hire a director.
5. How would you answer the three points raised by the critics of the science department?
6. "The United States possesses one of the worst top-leadership recruitment systems in the world." Discuss.
7. Assume that a high NASA official recently said that a 50 percent increase in launch fees for the shuttle would result in a two-thirds reduction in traffic. Represent this statement with a graph. What principle is involved?
8. The mayor wishes to do something about the growing number of badly deteriorating houses in the city. Develop an action plan that will work on this situation. Show how you could use a PERT chart.
9. Select one of the trends in Box 4–2 and develop a scenario for it. Which government agencies or jurisdictions would be most concerned by your scenario?

Appendix 10–1

A Brief Note on a Vast Subject: Computers and Policy Analysis

The purpose of this chapter appendix is not to introduce you to the fundamental concepts and key features of computers but to outline how they can contribute to the analysis of public policy. Familiarity with these applications should encourage you to embark (if you have not done so already) on a program of study so that you will be able to exploit the vast capabilities of the computer.

The use of computers has expanded enormously since their commercial introduction in the early 1950s, and new applications continue to emerge. Microcomputers in particular are becoming cheaper and more powerful and, as more software becomes available, easier to use. What follows is a partial list of applications relevant to policy analysis.

INFORMATION RETRIEVAL AND DATA MANIPULATION

Early applications of computers concentrated on file maintenance, data sorting, accounting, inventory status information, and other information and data summaries. Master files in government can be kept current with changes, deletions, and additions made by a computer. Such up-to-date data is valuable to the analyst attempting to define and forecast problems like those discussed in Chapters 3 and 4. Data also can be sorted, classified, and printed in a variety of desired forms: tables, graphs, matrix arrays, and the like.

Thus computers allow the analyst to manipulate data. There is nothing like a spreadsheet for financial analysis of almost any kind. Spreadsheets are those flexible grids of cells that allow the inspection and manipulation of complex relationships. Built-in functions such as Present Value (Chapter 8) allows one to concentrate on the results of the analysis instead of the job of building formulas to perform the analysis.

Project management is another fast growing application. One of the givens in program implementation (the subject of this chapter) is that jobs seldom proceed as planned. A large project may well require repeated recalculation to compensate for changes due to delays in the delivery of materials, employee absenteeism, or any of the myriad variables that can affect the venture. Assembling and tracking materials and people needed for a constantly changing government program is simply not the same thing as monitoring the production of handcrafted buggy whips. In this respect, the manipulations of project management resemble those of spreadsheeting, except that in the case of project management one is not asking the now familiar "what if?" questions, but rather "what now?"

One of the most crucial functions of project management software is resource leveling. Resource leveling is simply the resolution of conflicts in scheduling involving personnel, machinery, or other active components of a project—the old "you can't be in two places at once" predicament. If a certain engineer is working on the design of a monorail project in Albany on Tuesday, obviously he cannot be in Washington to oversee design work on a new bus that same day. Clearly, then, in a computerized project management plan, the two projects must be linked if such a scheduling conflict is to be highlighted, much less resolved.

Some project management software stresses the Critical Path Method (CPM) and the Program Evaluation and Review Technique (PERT) as well as the simpler Gantt chart discussed earlier in this chapter. Both CPM and PERT list all the activities required to complete a project or program and arrange them visually in the sequence in which they must occur. For example, in building a new prison, a state must first acquire the land on which to build. Before it can acquire the land, it must locate the site. Before it locates the site, it must decide what characteristics a new site must have. These activities must occur in sequence—the company cannot build before acquiring land, and it cannot acquire land before locating it.

A PERT representation of these activities would look like Figure 10–A1. By estimating how long each of the four activities will take, the state's department of corrections can decide when each step should begin, given a desired date for the prison's completion.

To see how PERT would apply, consider the production of a film by the Public Health Service (PHS). Tight schedules lower costs and ensure earlier release, but such scheduling requires an efficient plan

564

Figure 10–A1
A simple PERT network

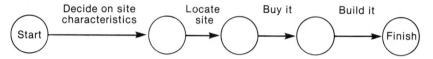

for the sequence of events. To produce this film, PHS must do five things: (1) acquire a script; (2) write the screenplay and hire a director, cast, crew, and technical consultants; (3) shoot the film; (4) prepare publicity and edit film; and (5) publicize the film. Some of these activities cannot occur before others have been completed, but others can. A simple PERT network indicates these relationships (Figure 10–A2).

Let us assume that the target release date is in early September, in time for the new school year. The estimated times in our PERT chart suggest that the latest to begin writing the screenplay and hiring for the movie would be 20 + 10 + 8 + 4 weeks, or forty-two weeks before early September, or about mid-November of the previous year.

An essential feature of PERT is that several activities can be carried out at the same time rather than in sequence. Identifying these activities saves time and thus money. PERT also permits the project managers to shift resources from noncritical activities and avoid delays. The key is to find the critical path through the network, that is, the path that takes the longest time. If any task on this path takes longer than expected, then the entire project may be delayed. In Figure 10–A2, the critical path is indicated by cross hatching; it represents the total time required

Figure 10–A2
A simple PERT network continued

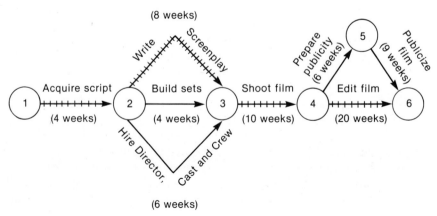

to produce the film. To repeat: Any delay of activities along this path will delay the entire project and should be avoided if possible.

Computer planning programs also control the way on which data are displaced in time-line charts (e.g., "day at a glance" and "work at a glance"). They also tie the time-line to other variables such as filter, scale, and slack. These three terms are briefly described below:

- *Filter* is used to spotlight certain tasks that are not to be matched with others. Among other uses, this option permits one to "hide" tasks that do not match. In other words, the display can be simplified to show only those undertakings that are connected. For instance, in the building of a dam, all activities related to the steel work and all those related to the concrete work may be filtered separately.

- *Scale* permits the specification of how much time is to be represented by each segment of the time frame. Certain jobs may need to be broken down into hourly segments, while others may require a span of days, weeks, or even months.

- *Slack* determines how unscheduled time is to be represented. For instance, the total allowable slippage that can occur without fouling up a project may be allocated among various subsidiary tasks.

The various tasks of a project can also be categorized as fixed dated, ASAP, and Aslap. The nature of fixed-date and ASAP tasks should be familiar to most people, the former being of the "Get it done by Friday or don't come in on Monday" variety, while the latter falls into the "It's needed yesterday" category. Aslap may be less familiar. It is the acronym for "as late as possible," and tasks subsumed under this heading depend on the prior completion of numerous other tasks. This kind of scheduling also comes in handy when the due date of a project is known but the best time to start it is not. Working backward from the end to the beginning, the computer will calculate when each project segment should begun.

Some software allows for a change in plans when tasks are not completed on time. In fact, this provision may be its most important function. One cannot deny the advantages of being able to ask, for instance, "What if the steel bars for the dam are delivered three days late?" and then have the computer automatically recalculate the whole project schedule to indicate how bad the snafu would really be.

CALCULATIONS

The computer can perform calculations from the elementary to the most sophisticated. There are many computer programs for performing analysis of variance and other operations discussed in Chapter 3. Among the best is the Statistical Package for Social Sciences (SPSS) and the

Statistical Analysis System (SAS) programs. If complex problems are being analyzed, the wisest course of action is to learn how to use these packages. Sometimes, however, a simple eight-function hand-held calculator with memory suffices.

In Chapter 4, we explained how things like population and GNP growth rates change over time. Difference equations are a tool for forecasting such change; essentially, they relate the value of a variable in a given time period to its values in periods past. Recall the compound interest model we used in Chapter 4:

$$A_n = P (1 + i)^n$$

Here A, the sum of money in a saving bank account at the end of the year, is related to the initial sum P; i is the rate of interest.

Given this general equation, finding how much money we have in, say, year thirteen, is easy. Unfortunately, general formulas like this one, which we can plug into, are not always available. In such cases, the best course might be to find the equation for the nth period in terms of the immediately preceding period or periods and then run the equation on a computer, starting at period 0. To do this number crunching on a hand-held calculator could be quite tedious.

Another calculation that computers perform well is solving linear programming (LP) problems. I have not discussed LP in this book because it is a technique more associated with management science than policy analysis. Generally speaking, it falls more in the category of nuts and bolts than strategy. Still, LP is powerful tool for allocating resources when supplies are limited or other constraints imposed.

Standardized computer programs for solivng LP programs greatly facilitate sensitivity analysis, allowing the analyst to see in an instant the effects of adding new variables and new contraints. For example, a linear programming model of an entire river system takes into account flood control, power production, irrigation, navigation, and salinity control. The analyst can ask what will happen to any one of these variables if another is changed by X amount. Because political considerations outside the LP problem could prohibit implementation of the optimal solution, the analyst should conduct extensive sensitivity analysis. The second-best or even the third-best solution might be more palatable politically.

Another nuts and bolts technique that computers handle superbly are queuing models. These models help the analyst make decisions about expanding service. By randomly generating the arrival of clients (who sometimes must stand in a line or a queue), the analyst can discover average waiting time and whether an expansion of service is economically justifiable. Again, these models can be constructed without the aid of computers, but to do so is time consuming.

STATISTICAL FORECASTING

Prognosis has been part of our culture in one form or another ever since the idea of a future was first conceived. As civilization evolves, the means employed in divination have become less crude (no more casting entrails), and the methodology more scientific. Thus the development of various electronic forecasting techniques should not come as a surprise. Among the latest of these are statistical forecasting systems that can run on personal computers. The programs are designed to be used for a wide variety of forecasting application, from general data analysis, model building, econometrics, and service demand evaluation to specialized niches such as predicting electricity demand. The analyst's primary task is simply to supply the historical data on the basis of which projections are to be made.

The data supplied can come from the spreadsheets or other computerized data bases noted above. All data files, however, must be in the form of a simple time series, twelve monthly figures, for instance. One cannot have two figures from June and one from each of the other months.

Suppose the analyst wants to forecast the monthly consumption of gasoline on the basis of past consumption as it relates to price. The consumption of gasoline, the variable being predicted, is the dependent variable, and the price of the gasoline the independent variable. This data must be drawn from a time span long enough for a valid statistical relationship to be established between the variables. Those variables, numbering two in the simplified example I have used, may total as many as fifteen in the case of a complex model.

Curve fitting, in less than the proper mathematical terminology, means fudging around with various curves until you find one that more or less fits the data with which you are working. Chapter 4 described how a regressional line can be fitted to a plot of data on a graph. Now, of course, computers can do that fitting. You merely select one of, say, eight available curves: a straight line (something I could never envision as a curve, but who am I to argue?), a quadratic, an exponential, the power of t, and a logarithmic curve, along with three hyperbolic curves, the simplest being y equals $a + b/t$. By pressing the return key, you may opt for automatic fitting, whereby the program tries out all the various curves for you and chooses the smoothest fit.

SIMULATION

Effective control to attain the desired goals of a policy depends on understanding the dynamic system that is to be controlled. Because of the complex interaction in such systems, neither analytical technique nor common sense provides us with a very sure guide as to what might happen after a particular action is taken. Computer simulation provides the tool to gain such knowledge and understanding.

When implementing a policy, we must question the goals and change them when appropriate. Let us briefly consider a dynamic model in which a change in goals has been suggested. In his pioneering work *Urban Dynamics*, Jay W. Forrester applied simulation to study the well-being of a city. His model included the city population aggregated in three groups: professional workers and management, labor or skilled workers, and unskilled worked or underemployed. It also included industry, housing, and real estate taxes on housing and industry. The flow of people into and out of the city was taken to be a function of the economic opportunities and the housing situation. Forrester's simulation model showed deterioration with time to a 45 percent rate of unemployment among the unskilled, a shortage of skilled workers, and high real estate taxes. (The high taxes were necessary to support the unemployed.) To upgrade the well-being of the city, Forrester studied the effect of alternative controls introduced through policies adopted by the city government. Two such alternative policies were slum clearance and job training to increase mobility from unskilled to skilled labor ranks. The simulation model was applied to each of the alternative policies.

THE SHAPE OF THINGS TO COME: EXPERT SYSTEMS

In the future, some computers will still process data, crunch numbers, and perform all the applications described above. New software and new computers will also be available.

Since World War II, computer scientists have tried to develop techniques that would allow computers to act more like humans. The entire research effort, including decision-making systems and robotic devices, is usually called artificial intelligence (AI). Most AI efforts remain in the research labs. A collection of AI techniques that enables computers to assist people in analyzing problems and making decisions, called knowledge-based expert systems, has recently proved its value, and numerous applications are now underway. Expert systems can assist with complex planning tasks, diagnose diseases, locate mineral deposits, configure complex computer hardware, and aid in troubleshooting locomotive problems.

Expert systems will change the way governments operate by altering the way people think about solving problems. This new technology will make it possible to develop quick, pragmatic answers for a wide range of problems that currently defy effective solutions. It will help policy analysts define problems and determine what knowledge is available to solve problems in ways they have never considered before. They will free experts to focus on the more difficult aspects of their specialty.

Professor Edward Feigenbaum of Stanford University, one of the leading researchers in expert systems, has defined an expert system as:

> An intelligent computer program that uses knowledge and inference proce-dures to solve problems that are difficult enough to require significant human expertise for their solution. Knowledge necessary to perform at such a level, plus the inference procedures used, can be thought of as a model of the expertise of the best practitioners of the field.
>
> The knowledge of an expert system consists of facts and heuristics. The "facts" constitute a body of information that is widely shared, publicly avail-able, and generally agreed upon by experts in a field. The "heuristics" are mostly private, little-discussed rules of good judgment (rules of plausible reasoning, rules of good guessing) that characterize expert-level decision making in the field. The performance level of an expert system is primarily a function of the size and the quality of a knowledge base it possesses.[37]

Feigenbaum calls those who build knowledge-based expert systems "knowledge engineers" and refers to their technology as "knowledge engineering." Early systems were usually called "expert systems," but most knowledge engineers now refer to their system as "knowledge systems."

The first systems were built by interviewing a recognized human expert and attempting to capture the expert's knowledge—hence the term expert system. Recently, however, several systems have been built that contain knowledge of a difficult decision-making situation that is quite useful, but hardly the equivalent of a human expert. "Knowledge systems" is rapidly becoming the preferred name since it avoids suggest-ing that all systems built by means of knowledge engineering techniques capture the knowledge of a human expert.

Knowledge engineers are concerned with identifying the specific knowledge that an expert uses in solving a problem. Initially, the knowl-edge engineer studies a human expert and determines what facts and rules-of-thumb the expert employs. Then the knowledge engineer deter-mines the inference strategy that the expert uses in an actual problem-solving situation. Finally, the knowledge engineer develops a system that uses similar knowledge and inference strategies to simulate the expert's behavior.

This does not suggest that most of today's expert systems are as good as human experts. The technology is new and just beginning to

---

[37] Edward A. Feigenbaum and Pamela McCorduck, *The Fifth Generation* (Reading, Mass.: Addison-Wesley, 1983).

be applied to tough policy problems. Today's knowledge systems are confined to well-circumscribed tasks. They are not able to reason from axioms or general theories. They do not learn and, thus, they are limited to using the specific facts and heuristics that they were "taught" by human experts. They lack common sense, they cannot reason by analogy, and their performance deteriorates rapidly when problems extend beyond the narrow task they were designed to perform.

But it is not unreasonable to consider developing a small expert system to assist a policy analyst in the study of a specific type of cost-benefit problem or to help policymakers decide how to respond to a particular type of crisis. In most agencies, these problems are probably sufficiently well-defined and adequately constrained so as to result in useful small systems. One would not want, however, to try to develop a system to help a policymaker analyze a social problem or to design a program to fix it. Most social problems tend to be poorly defined and broad-ranging. Moreover, they typically involve large amounts of common sense and reasoning by analogy, as we saw repeatedly in Chapter 6. These are things that existing expert systems cannot do. On the other hand, knowledge systems do not display biased judgments or jump to conclusions, and then try to maintain those conclusions in the face of contrary evidence. These are, alas, things that human beings can and probably will do.

Chapter 11

What Is Good Policy?

In the utopia of every rationalist can be found policymakers and administrators who evaluate their work, correct errors as they go along, and acknowledge mistakes as a way of improving performance. In practice, things are quite different. Who likes to admit mistakes, much less *look* for them? Because self-evaluation goes against human nature, external evaluative studies must reenforce in-house efforts.

In the rationalist's utopia, determining what is good policy would be a straightforward affair: Policies that achieve their goals are good, those that fail are bad. Period. But again reality intrudes. Because people are not clones, they have different political perspectives, and this variety results in a plethora of goals and priorities. Some people may, in fact, reject the very notion that goal attainment should be *the* criterion by which to judge public policy. This chapter will suggest seven.

SEVEN CRITERIA

Output (*not* input)

Because the products of government programs are usually difficult to measure independently of the inputs that produce them (Core Idea 14), measuring outputs involves more difficulties than might be at first imagined. It is important to understand why.

Government programs generally result in intermediate products or inputs that are at best only remote proxies for the intended outputs. For example, environmental-impact statements enforced by the Environmental Protection Agency have a final intended output that includes aesthetics and public health; forces and equipment developed and deployed by the military services are ultimately intended to produce national security. In the same way, the education of students at different levels in the public school system, research projects funded by the National Institutes of Health, and cases processed and payments disbursed by the social-welfare agencies, are all only intermediate products like impact statements and tanks. Units for measuring the final products of such activities are usually nonexistent, and it is often hard even to distinguish "more" from "less." Consider, for example, the difficulty of measuring or specifying "quantities" of national defense, or education, or even regulatory services, in terms that are *separate* from the inputs used in producing them.[1]

Because measuring outputs is so difficult, analysts tend to focus on the more visible inputs. After all, they have to measure *something*. But are outputs really that elusive? I think not.

Measuring outputs: Appalachian Regional Development Act. The first major Great Society program President Johnson signed into law was the Appalachian Regional Development Act of 1965, which was designed to bring industry, jobs, and government services to an impoverished, neglected region of the country. Since then more than $15 billion was attracted to the region over a twenty-year period. So *inputs* are not hard to find.

But neither are the outputs. One need only travel along Appalachian Corridor G in West Virginia. The highway curves smoothly through wide, newly blasted granite canyons and soars over resculpted green mountains—until barricades begin to appear and, suddenly, the concrete ends. Long, tortuous stretches over the steepest mountains are still traversed by the twisting, pot-holed two-lane blacktop of old U.S. Route 119. The disconnected sections of the four-lane highway are visual evidence that, despite all the inputs—billions of dollars invested, the establishment of the Appalachian Regional Commission, and so on—the goals of the act remain unfulfilled.

Numbers tell the real story. In nearly half of the 397 counties across the thirteen states that make up official Appalachia—from western New York to northeastern Mississippi—1980 per capita income was still about three-quarters the non-Appalachian national average. This has changed very little in the past twenty years. While unemployment in the region has always been among the highest in the nation, the gap is getting wider. Both the population and workforce of the central Appalachian region are declining. Contrary to Johnson's 1965 expectations, "the dole" in Appalachia is far from dead. From 1970 to 1980, while the cost of welfare payments nearly quadrupled for the nation as a whole, it increased four and a half times in the Appalachian region.[2]

---

[1] Charles Wolf, Jr., "A Theory of Non-Market Failures," *Journal of Law and Economics*, (1979), pp. 107–39.

[2] Data from Appalachian Regional Commission, *Annual Report* (Washington, D.C.: Government Printing Office, 1984); and Ben A. Franklin, "Despite 20 Years of Federal Aid, Poverty Still Reigns in Appalachia," *New York Times*, August 11, 1985.

Measuring outputs: Military equipment readiness. Between 1980 and 1984, the average annual real growth in spending on military equipment readiness was more than 14 percent. While the debate raged over this input, a few wondered about the output (that is, the actual state of combat readiness), for the statistics traditionally used to measure readiness showed little or no improvement. For example, if we look at the numerical readiness ratings, or C-ratings, for combat units, we find that the percentage of units in the top two readiness categories increased by only a single percentage point from 1980 to 1984. If we look at "mission capable" rates—the proportion of equipment that is in sufficient repair to carry out its assigned mission—we find a dramatic increase in the readiness of naval aircraft, but nothing else.[3]

The C-rating and mission capable rates are considered by the military to be the key numerical measures of readiness. But there are good reasons for claiming that these measures are defective, since military commanders can tinker with these numbers. Les Aspin, chairman of House Armed Services Committee notes an even more fundamental problem with these numbers:

> [T]hey really aren't measuring output. Budget dollars measure input; the Pentagon readiness statistics measure the level of effort, which is only a slightly less crude form of input. A squadron that flies more also wears out its aircraft faster; a squadron that gains more time in the air by flying in circles simply consumes more fuel. Flying hours and training days tell us the amount of time consumed, but not how that time has been spent.
>
> Many important elements of readiness simply can't be measured statistically. Take the Grenada invasion. For the relatively modest level of fighting there, our troops were ready by all the traditional measures of readiness. Yet they did not have anything better than Xeroxed oil company maps to work with. Considering that Grenada was in our own backyard and had been a sore spot for five years, it is curious that an up-to-date map did not exist and that thousands had not been printed. That's one of the things we pay the Defense Mapping Agency to do. That was a readiness lapse that won't show up in any statistics.[4]

Besides paying particular attention to how the military performs in actual operations (like Grenada or the Libyan air strike) and in practice exercises, the analyst can focus on output by asking for some real measures of readiness. "It is not how many combat hours a pilot put in behind the joystick, but what he has learned. That requires a test of pilot skills—the 'output' we hope we are getting for all those flying hours."[5]

---

[3] Organization of the Joint Chiefs of Staff, *U.S. Military Posture for FY 1987* (Washington, D.C.: Government Printing Office, 1986).

[4] Les Aspin, "Ready or Not," *New Republic*, October 29, 1984, p. 22.

[5] Ibid., p. 23.

An obvious parallel with trends in public education should not go unmentioned. Many states have followed the lead of Florida in requiring that all students be given the same standardized test of academic skills prior to promotion. Whatever the drawbacks to this form of evaluation, and no matter how fierce the resistance to it by some education professionals, it clearly measures output.

Measuring outputs: The effect of Reaganomics. Perhaps the most important single question about domestic policy in 1984 was whether Americans were better off economically than they had been four years earlier. By increasing the incentives to work, Reagan said in 1981, his tax and spending cuts would create three million new jobs and expand the economy.

In *The Reagan Record* (1984), John L. Palmer and Isabel V. Sawhill evaluate these economic policies.[6] The great strength of their assessment is that it focuses squarely on output. The curious thing about it is that the numbers refute their conclusions.

To determine the effect of Reaganomics on jobs, the authors cite an Urban Institute study by Robert Haveman, which concludes that these policies permanently increased the labor force by 800,000 to 2.7 million full-time workers. But assumptions matter. Haveman assumes that if Carter had been reelected he too would have proposed a tax cut. If one does not assume a Carter tax cut, then Reagan's policies can be credited with 1.4 million to 4.1 million full-time workers. Shortly after *The Reagan Record* appeared, the case for his taxes and spending was further strengthened, as two million more jobs were added.

To determine whether Americans were, on the balance, better off in 1984 than if Carter had been elected, *The Reagan Record* uses an econometric model to project that real disposable family income will rise 3.5 percent under Reagan but would have risen 4.0 percent under an alternative policy (presumably Carter's). But their projection missed the strength of the 1984 recovery. Real disposable family income was more than 7.2 percent higher in 1984 than it was in 1980. Therefore, by the author's own test, Americans as a whole were better off under Reagan.

It might seem (to paraphrase a famous American general) that there is no substitute for output, for goal attainment; it is, afterall, the public sector's bottomline. Or is it? If we could speak with the authors of *The Reagan Record* at the end of 1984, I doubt that they would still place quite so much faith in a single dimension evaluation. Is the fact that the Reagan administration disproportionately reduced benefits of low-income families irrelevant? In fairness, Moon and Sawhill do mention

---

[6] John L. Palmer and Isabel V. Sawhill, *The Reagan Record* (Cambridge, Mass.: Ballinger, 1984).

this. But the point is that they make output their pivotal criterion. Against this standard, Reagan wins in a walk.

So, let me open things up by proposing for starters six more criteria:

1. Side-effects (externalities).
2. Efficiency.
3. Strategy.
4. Compliance.
5. Justice.
6. Intervention effect.

Side-effects

Evaluators should consider negative side-effects or externalities (Core Idea 7). If goals are attained but the indirect costs extraordinary, can we call the policy "good"? Like the authors of *The Reagan Record*, the American officer firing on Ben Tre, Vietnam (February 8, 1968), had a one-dimensional conception of success. "It became necessary," he said, "to destroy the town in order to save it."

Throughout this book we have noted instances in which public policies designed to alleviate a societal problem generate unanticipated or very large side-effects, often far in the future or in areas remote from the one in which the problem occurred. Famine relief saves lives in the short-run, but this achievement carries a long-term threat: Free food undermines a country's farming sector.

The Elementary and Secondary Education Act (ESEA), the largest educational experiment ever undertaken in the United States, may have unwittingly created a program that segregates the lowest achieving children. Whereas schools mainstream handicapped children in order that they may benefit from being in a regular classroom, ESEA pulls out poor children and teaches them separately. The literacy gap between poor teenagers and other teenagers, not surprisingly, has increased dramatically since the program was begun.

In 1943 New York City began to regulate the rents that landlords could charge. The aim was to protect the tenants; the result has been a dearth of new housing construction, poor maintenance of existing buildings, and a severe housing shortage, which affects the poorest residents the most.

A couple of factors make externalities likely. Government tends to operate through large organizations using blunt policy instruments. Secondly, the buildup of strong political pressures for policymakers "to do something," the "there-ought-to-be-a-law" attitude on the part of many citizens may create an effective demand for action before there has been adequate time to consider potential side-effects. Moreover, the short time-horizon of elected officials predisposes them to overlook potential externalities.

To be sure, cost-benefit analysis and technology assessment (discussed in Chapter 8) try to take account of externalities and unintended consequences, but we have also seen the limitations of such analysis. Externalities are hard to see because the consequences of public policies may be far removed from the immediate problem. For example, a city wants to cleanse a section of its downtown that contains mostly panhandlers, prostitutes, drug pushers, derelicts, and adult moviehouses. All this would be replaced, say, with office towers, a merchandise mart, a hotel, and a center for the performing arts. The interesting objection to this urban renewal plan is simply that it is a big plan and, as such, is apt to result in unanticipated side-effects. *The unintended effects of an ambitious act of social engineering are apt to be more important than the intended effects.* Will the renewal project drive up land values causing the owners of businesses to sell to developers and *destroy downtown* thus destroy the economic vitality of downtown? Where will the area's street crowd go? Experience shows that when the seamy side of life is suppressed in one place, it tends to pop up in another.

Urban renewal at first envisioned "spot removal" of the worst slums, but soon people were talking about the redevelopment of entire city centers. As a consequence, cohesive communities were often atomized, the stock of low-income housing was reduced, and high-rise instant slums were erected. It would be hard to cite a better example of government operating through large organization using blunt policy instruments.

In his study of welfare programs, Charles Murray shows incisively how three undesired consequences seem to be inherent in social policies.[7] Specifically:

1. Any program, however generously designed, will necessarily leave many more worthy claimants uncovered and thus exert pressure for expansion.
2. Any program will also necessarily provide benefits to unworthy or unintended free riders.
3. Most programs hurt more people than they help.

These three principles of social policy emerge in part from Murray's fascinating parable of the $1 billion anticigarette campaign. In it, he poses the problem of designing a set of financial rewards that will stop people from smoking. After convincingly detailing many of the problems—of eligibility for the program, the preconditions for receiving its

---

[7] Charles Murray, *Losing Ground* (New York: Basic Books, 1984), pp. 211–18.

benefits, and the size of the reward—he arrives at an apparently optimal scheme. It would grant prizes of $10,000 to all five-year smokers of a pack or more a day who give up smoking for at least a year.

Murray shows that this scheme, or any like it, would not only fail to reduce smoking, it would reliably *increase* the number of smokers and number of cigarettes consumed. Among the 5 percent of the population already eligible for the program, the reward would indeed reduce smoking (though it would also reward some who would have stopped anyway). The problem is that the prize would increase the appeal of smoking for the 95 percent of the population that has not yet qualified by smoking a pack a day for five years. All the four-year smokers, the fifteen-cigarette-a-day smokers, the young beginning smokers, and the tentative nonsmokers would receive an additional incentive to increase their cigarette consumption.

Murray's problem cannot be circumvented by changing the rules of the program. Unless it is a one-shot prize—hardly a permanent or politically acceptable solution—it will dependably increase smoking. Any reward sufficient to induce a significant number of people to change their behavior for the good will also be sufficient to induce a larger number to change their behavior for the worse to qualify for the benefits. In every case, moreover, the target population will tend to be much smaller than the unintentionally affected group.

A similar puzzle appears in all programs to relieve any condition that most of the population can easily choose to adopt. Unfortunately, such conditions include—to varying degrees—most of the current targets of social policy. For example, unemployment, poverty, illegitimacy, and marital breakdown are obvious cases of voluntarily achievable afflictions; disability and even disease are less obvious but nonetheless relevant problems, in that they may be made more prevalent by the vast governmental attempts to relieve their effects. (Murray does not conclude that all social programs do more harm than good. He endorses social security benefits and unemployment insurance, for example, despite their effect in promoting early retirement and causing or extending unemployment.)

Efficiency

Assume a policy attains its goals and has little or no side-effects. Before evaluators may call it good, they must look at direct cost. Goals might have been attained but at too great a cost. This can occur either through inefficient administration (waste, fraud, and abuse) or through poor design (the program is inherently inefficient or profligate).

"Waste," Rhett Butler says in *Gone With the Wind*, "always makes me angry." One therefore can easily imagine what his reaction might be after a visit to the Pentagon. But defense has no monopoly on waste.

In recent years, environmental lobbies seem to have acquired many of the worst traits of the defense lobby. In the same way that being pro-defense is often an excuse to neglect cost overruns and badly built weapons, being pro-environmental appears sometimes as a license to disregard the failure of antipollution programs. By 1985, the Environmental Protection Agency had cleaned up only six out of thousands of hazardous waste sites, and the $1.6 billion superfund established in 1982 to finance this cleanup of abandoned dumpsites has primarily spawned planning, administering, and litigating.

To be sure, cleanup is not easy—there is no one technology that can be applied at each site. Moreover, EPA has had to spend much of its time identifying sites. But the only solution to the fund's failings that environmentalists seem to offer is to throw more money at the problem. Almost all the debate has been over the level and method of superfund financing—as if the program's efficiency was irrelevant.

Further, environmentalists have neglected the fund's weaknesses. For instance, a company that placed a single barrel of waste at a dump can be held legally responsible for the cleanup cost of the entire site. This is not only inefficient but also unfair, since companies fight vigorously to avoid admitting responsibility, and nothing gets done while lawyers get rich.

Environmentalists have not provided leadership in focusing the super-fund's resources. The gravest threat from hazardous waste dumps is that seepage will contaminate ground water and taint much of the nation's water supply. But, as a result of the superfund's "act now, understand later" mandate, policymakers know little more about groundwater pollution today than in 1980. The General Accounting Office reports that little has been done to determine how dump sites contaminate the water supply and to measure the dangers that various pollutants pose.[8] Yet, environmentalists have hardly protested the lack of research that would eventually enable policymakers to know what they are doing.

The environmentalists' great cause of the 1970s—the Clean Water Act of 1972—was also inefficient in certain important respects. Government and private corporations spent $120 billion complying with it. How much was achieved? No one really knows, but the Council on Environmental Quality estimates that only 11 percent of surface water streams are cleaner now than in 1972.[9] The act was characterized by a pork-barrel approach, infatuation with "best-available technology," and

---

[8] U.S. Geological Survey, *Hydrologic Events and Surface Water Resources*, Water-Supply Paper 2300 (Washington, D.C.: Government Printing Office, 1985).

[9] U.S. Council on Environmental Quality, *Environmental Quality, 1986* (Washington, D.C.: Government Printing Office, 1986).

utopian standards (zero discharge of pollutants). The superfund program repeats many of these same mistakes.

Strategy

Strategic evaluations concentrate on the definition of the social problem and on the implicit theories that lie behind ameliorative program.[10] A strategic evaluation, for example, might test the contention that a policy like the Appalachian Regional Development Act can, through a massive infusion of funds, spark an economic revival, as the Marshall Plan did for Western Europe. Jane Jacobs thinks this theory wanting and proposes an alternative one. See Box 11–1.

Theories have consequences. Assume that we think that every human predicament that is not a bodily disease is a mental disease. Thus drinking is "alcoholism"; smoking, "tobacco dependence"; gambling, "pathological gambling"; ingesting, inhaling, or injecting illegal chemical substances, "drug abuse"; and assaulting one's child or spouse, "child abuse" and "wife abuse." It follows then that the thousands of mentally ill people, previously housed in mental hospitals, who were deinstitutionalized and hence made homeless, should be re-rehoused—either in mental hospitals or public shelters. Theories, as I said, have consequences.

But is the theory that the homeless are mentally ill correct? Thomas Szasa, an iconoclastic professor of psychiatry, State University of New York Upstate Medical Center, has a radically different theory.[11] If life is a game or a contest, then it follows that not everyone can be a winner or a runner-up. He argues that the homeless are *not* (mentally) sick. Policymakers call them sick only because they want to treat them as if they were; they seek a technical solution to a moral problem—namely, what to do with the "have nots" of society. Szasz writes:

> As recently as in the last century, people concerned with helping the destitute distinguished between the deserving and undeserving poor. Although making such a distinction is next to impossible, it is a useful reminder of the fact that the problem of the homeless is moral rather than technical. But today, by treating those who are poor, helpless, victimized, desocialized, undisciplined, over-ambitious, greedy, destructive and self-destructive as essentially alike—that is, mentally ill—we foreclose the very possibility of any viable, piecemeal reform of our policies aimed at helping our modern *miserables*.[12]

---

[10] Dennis N. T. Perkins, "Evaluating Social Interventions: A Conceptual Schema," *Evaluation Quarterly* 1, no. 4 (November 1977), pp. 639–56.

[11] Thomas S. Szasz, *Law, Liberty and Psychiatry* (New York: Macmillan, 1963).

[12] Thomas S. Szasz, "New Ideas, Not Old Institutions, for the Homeless," *The Wall Street Journal*, June 7, 1985.

Box 11–1

Questioning the theory behind industrial development

The conventional prescription for poor and backward nations or regions is "industrial development." This seems a logical remedy for their plight since any economy that lacks industry must either go without manufactured goods or else, to an absurd degree, import almost everything its people require, paying with one or a few kinds of cash crops or resource exports. Such colonial-type economies, by definition, are not economically well rounded, cannot produce amply and diversely for their own people and producers as well as for others the way rich and more advanced economies do. They lack much range of opportunity, have no practical foundation for economic self-development, and are disastrously at the mercy of distant and often capricious markets for the few things they do produce. To wriggle out of their fix, it is true that they need industry.

In practice, however, the conventional prescription is reduced to two conventional strategies, used singly or in combination: attempts are made to attract transplanted factories from elsewhere; and ambitious programs are launched to build up major industrial facilities usually, except in the case of rich oil producers, financed by credits or grants. At first thought both strategies seem admirably to the point. What could be more straightforward? Unfortunately, in practice, they work miserably. Just such industrial programs and projects, for example, are largely responsible for the vast, unpayable debts with which Brazil and Mexico (and their foreign bankers) now struggle. They have helped to produce outright economic debacles in Uruguay, Turkey, Iran, Cuba, Ghana, and Tanzania, to mention a few varied examples. Countries or regions that have enjoyed far better than average success at attracting branch plants or other industrial transplants, like Ireland, Puerto Rico, the Canadian Maritime Provinces, or southern Italy, have been disappointed nevertheless. They expected the acquisitions to catalyze continued development, growth, and prosperity, and these haven't materialized. We live in a distraught time of failed and failing industrial development schemes.

I am going to argue here that the cause of these failures goes deeper than poor planning, recessions, the price of oil, political miscalculations, corruption, greed, and so on. At their root is a terrible intellectual failure, for the prescribed strategies themselves are foredoomed to produce disappointment, futility, and debacles. The germane prescription is more roundabout. What backward, stunted economies lack is productive cities that can replace their imports—and enough such cities. This is the lack that makes such economies stunted in the first place. Overcoming it is the only effective cure for what ails them. This is so because productive cities, containing proliferations of diverse, symbiotic producers, are the only types of settlements capable of replacing wide ranges of their imports with local production in a practical, economical fashion. Hence cities are the only kinds of settlements that can generate the industry resulting

---

Box 11–1 (*concluded*)

from this vital economic process, and the further industry built upon it. The world abounds in evidence, both positive and negative, of these realities; if we only look, it tells us why the conventional strategies, their superficial logic notwithstanding, don't work out as they are supposed to and never have.

Source: Jane Jacobs, "Why TVA Failed," *New York Review*, May 10, 1984, p. 41.

Jacobs and Szasz may or may not be correct in their alternative theories. But their evaluations of current policy are certainly strategic in that they question the theoretical basis of major public policies and suggest to policymakers new legislative initiatives. Not all strategic evaluations result in an alternative theory; in many instances, they simply cast doubt on an existing theory.

- By far the most troublesome atmospheric alteration has been the steady increase in carbon dioxide (CO_2). This and a few other minor gases have been lumped together under the term *greenhouse gases*. Their action is supposed to increase surface temperature, somewhat analogous to the glass panes of a greenhouse. Undeniably CO_2 has steadily increased on a global basis, probably since the 1860s, and at an accelerated rate since the end of World War II. These facts have prompted a staggering amount of literature pertaining to the climatic consequences of a continuing increase in atmospheric CO_2. There is a general agreement that the infrared-absorbing qualities of this gas will reduce the outgoing radiation from earth to space and thus raise the surface temperature.[13]

- Less skepticism surrounds the theory that sulfur emissions from coal-fired power plants in the Midwest are killing lakes and trees in the Northeast.[14] Still, drawing sound and scientific defensible quantitative links between acid disposition and environmental damage remains difficult. Many Florida lakes are highly acidic, suggesting that many lakes have always been acidic due to natural causes. Many factors—

---

[13] The greenhouse effect still has its skeptics. A major embarrassment for the theory is that the carbon dioxide content of the atmosphere has been steadily rising for the last 30 years, yet the predicted warming has not definitely appeared. Explanations can be provided, but are inevitably ad hoc.

[14] U.S. Office of Technology Assessment, *Acid Rain and Transportation of Air Pollution: Implication for Public Policy* (Washington, D.C.: Government Printing Office, 1984).

vegetation, soil, hydrology, geology, water, climate, and atmosphere—determine the acid status of a lake. Moreover, the sulfur dioxide emissions themselves actually declined by 28 percent in the decade ending in 1983.[15] Given the theoretical basis of the sulfate-acid rain link, the critical question for policymakers is how much to invest in a cleanup program.

Compliance

For better or worse, the founding fathers made the American government one of laws, not of men. Until a second Constitutional Convention changes that arrangement, it seems that a fourth test of good policy must be consonance with congressional intent and Constitutional standards.

Waiving all four preceding criteria, can it be said that the following policies are successes?

- Few people like to criticize federal education programs designed to aid poor and disadvantaged children. But the sad truth is that few such programs fulfill their promises. Consider the Education Department's largest single program, the previously mentioned Chapter 1 of the Elementary and Secondary Education Act. Under it, about $40 billion has been spent since 1965 to improve the schooling of "educationally deprived" children. But it turns out that more of this money has been spent on nonpoor than on poor children, *contrary to the program's principal rationale.*

- The dispute over the Interstate Commerce Commission (created by the Interstate Commerce Act of 1887) mirrors arguments about regulation and deregulation generally. Created to help farmers combat the growing power of the railroads, the commission was directed to promote "safe, adequate, economical and efficient service" in surface transportation. But it long has been criticized as a captive of the industries it was intended to regulate. To many observers, the ICC was not a protector of the people it was meant to protect. In the end, the railroads loved it, and the truckers loved it. The commission has strayed so far from congressional intent that it is hard to imagine that things would have been that much worse if the market had been allowed to work by itself.

- The Department of Defense has a long record in frustrating congressional intent. In 1983, Congress passed a law requiring defense contractors to give the Pentagon warranties that weapons will perform as

---

[15] From *Nonferrous Amelteors Have Been Reduced*, RCED-86–91 (Washington, D.C.: Government Printing Office, 1986).

intended. The Pentagon tried unsuccessfully to eliminate funding for the program, then pushed through what members of Congress called "loopholes so large an MX missile could be put through one." Another program pushed through Congress provided for an independent weapons-testing office within the Defense Department to evaluate weapons and detect any glitches before accepting delivery. The Pentagon took over one year to name a permanent head for the office.[16]

Justice and other normative standards

Who would say that every law that Congress passes and that the Supreme Court refuses to overturn meets the standard of justice? Surely not many Americans. For them, the fairness of a public policy is an intensely personal matter.

Some health officials have proposed that, in order to help control the spread of AIDS, drug addicts should be provided with free sterilized needles. Is this good public policy? Given the tremendous social costs associated with this disease and what we know about its spread, the proposal is not without merit, judged by our first five criteria. But it might run into trouble when evaluated in terms of morality, at least by some citizens.

The application of this criterion, interestingly enough, varies not only from citizen to citizen but also across time. Today no fewer than 96 percent of unmarried mothers choose to keep and raise their babies, whereas a generation ago only 20 percent did. Most of these young mothers join the public-assistance rolls, which means society pays the bills arising from the choices teenagers are allowed to make. How did the "right" to keep one's child come about? Conservatives could support the tradition that says a baby should remain with its natural mother. Reinforcing that right, however, was a new generation of social workers, who had been taught not to dominate their clients but to treat them as equals. It seems unlikely that we can return to earlier practices when an illegitimate birth was widely viewed as evidence of unfitness for motherhood. So the public policy question now becomes what can be done to ensure that these mothers and their offspring have a chance at decent lives.

While standards of justice may change over time, the criterion itself remains ever relevant to evaluative studies. For example, by the late 1980s, many conservatives seemed to accept the notion of government welfare payments to unwed mothers but suggested that teenage mothers

---

[16] Tim Carrington, "Pentagon Frustrates Reform Effects," *The Wall Street Journal*, December 26, 1984.

who live independently of their parents be denied benefits.[17] This subtle shift in position might be significant. Traditionally, the philosophical debate between conservatives and liberals has been framed in these terms: The conservatives said social programs do too much for the poor, while the liberals said too little. Their dispute was over the size of government. The new view is that the nature of government may be more important. The problem with the welfare state is not its size but its permissiveness.

Christopher Jencks, a distinguished liberal sociologist, recently suggested what he believed to be the correct terms in which debate over social policy should be cast.

> First, it does not simply ask how much our social policies cost, or appear to cost, but whether they work. Second, it makes clear that a successful program must not only help those it seeks to help but must do so in such a way as not to reward folly or vice. Third, it reminds us that social policy is about punishment as well as rewards, and that a policy that is never willing to countenance suffering, however deserved, will not long endure.[18]

According to Jencks, the liberal coalition that dominated Washington from 1964 to 1980 did quite well by the first of these criteria; they *did* help the poor. But, he adds, it did not do as well by the other two criteria. "It often rewarded folly and vice and it never had enough confidence in its own norms of behavior to assert that those who violated these norms deserved whatever sorrows followed." [19]

My point, then, is this. Normative considerations are an integral facet of any thorough evaluation of a public policy. In the chapter which follows, we will consider how the questions only raised here might be addressed.

Intervention effect

The criteria for good policy offered thus far can be readily appreciated by most citizens. But, in taking up the seventh and final criteria, we must return to the domain of the expert.

To understand the necessity of intervention effect, one need only accept the possibility that policy goals can be attained irrespective of its implementation. That is to say, what happened after the policy would have happened anyway, policy or no policy. Thus, the evaluator must

---

[17] Gary Bauer, Executive Director of Task Force to Study Federal Welfare and Family Policies, *The Family: Preserving America's Future* (Washington, D.C.: Government Printing Office, November, 1986).

[18] Christopher Jencks, "How Poor Are the Poor," *New York Review,* May 9, 1985, p. 49.

[19] Ibid.

be sure that the output can be clearly attributed to the intervention and not some other variable. To illustrate, let us begin with an old friend, the fifty-five-mile-per-hour speed limit.

Does the fifty-five-mile-per-hour speed limit really save lives?[20] These are the facts. The highway fatality rate has been trending downward since the horseless carriage began appearing on roads. In 1922 about eighteen people died in accidents for every 100 million miles traveled. By the end of World War II that rate had dropped to nearly half. And, although highway speeds were increasing, fatality rates continued to fall an average of 3.1 percent a year since then. That is because of safer highways, safer cars, more experienced drivers, and better emergency care.

But a peculiar thing happened in 1974. The fatality rate dropped 15.3 percent to 3.6 fatalities per 100 million miles, the sharpest drop ever. The most obvious explanation was the lower speed limit adopted nationwide in March of that year. Federal Department of Transportation (DOT) statisticians estimated that more than 9,000 lives were saved that year, and they assumed that the speed limit had an effect.

Then another peculiar thing happened. Drivers started ignoring the "double nickel," and average highway speeds crept up again—but the fatality rate dropped more than 25 percent in the next decade. The fatality rate dropped 12.7 percent in 1982 alone, even though the speed limit did not change from the year before.

Although it may sound strange at first, the sharp drop in the fatality rate may actually be more closely related to economics than to speed limits. The oil embargo of 1973–74 kept recreational drivers off the roads. Statistically, they tend to have more accidents if only because they tend to be tired, travel unfamiliar roads, and go much slower than the general traffic flow. Another possible explanation is that more people survive car crashes not because there are fewer crashes, but because there are better emergency medical services, more wearers of seatbelts, and safer cars. There is substantial historical evidence to support this. For instance, in 1946, as speeds went up after wartime gasoline conservation ended, the fatality rate dropped 12.7 percent, and then fell 10 percent more in 1947. A recession also began at the same time. The economic boom of the early 1960s also saw the highway fatality rate rise, but it dropped during the recession in 1982. In fact, a 1983 DOT study demonstrated that 98 percent of the variation in annual highway fatalities could be accounted for by an equation incorporating such economic factors as unemployment.

---

[20] This discussion is based on Damon Darlin, "Does 55-MPH Speed Limit Save Lives?" *The Wall Street Journal*, April 28, 1986.

Control groups provide the surest way of determining whether the intervention itself and not some external force caused the desired effect. Focusing now on accidents rather than fatalities, let us consider whether driver education courses reduce the number of traffic accidents involving young motorists. Since about 75 percent of public high school students take driver education, the question is not trivial. In a study funded by the National Highway Traffic Safety Administration and the state of Georgia, 18,000 high school students were divided into two groups.[21] One group took an extensive driver ed course, and the other group— the control group—took no driver education. The frequency of accidents among students who had the extension course was almost exactly the same as those in the control group. Conclusion: the driver education courses do not cut accidents.

Does hiring more police cut crime? Because many other variables might affect the crime rate—the onset of winter, changing demographics, new state and federal programs, rise in unemployment—a control group again should be established. In a study funded by the Department of Justice, cities that had increased their police forces were compared to those that had not to see whether the average citizen's chances of becoming a victim of street assaults or any other crime was reduced from the added manpower.[22] The study disclosed that even tripling the number of police in a neighborhood had no effect. Nor do foot patrols decrease crime. How can the conventional wisdom be so wrong? Many crimes occur indoors, but even where offenses occur in public and can be seen from the street, police strength may not be important. The criminal, after all, merely has to wait a moment until the patrol car has passed before committing his offense.

To accurately assess the intervention effect, evaluators must also consider the time frame of the study. Trends in poverty are a case in point. If we contrast 1950, 1965, and 1980, we find that economic conditions improved more between 1950 and 1965 than between 1965 and 1980, but that poverty nonetheless fell almost as much in the second period as in the first. Based on these data, it seems reasonable to conclude that the material condition of the poor improved more than it "should have" because of the poverty programs between 1964 and 1967.

To discredit this obvious conclusion, Charles Murray divides the years from 1965 to 1980 into two subperiods: 1965–1973 and 1973–1980. He then correctly notes that while poverty dropped dramatically from 1965 to 1973, it stopped dropping after 1973. Indeed, it even rose slightly if you use the official measure.

---

[21] *Houston Chronicle*, August 18, 1982.

[22] David Greenburg, "Age, Crime and Social Explanation," *American Journal of Sociology* 91, no. 1 (1985) pp. 1–20.

But changing the period under discussion completely changes the meaning of the intervention effect Murray is studying. Remember he is trying to evaluate the effect of reforms began in the mid-1960s. Remember, too, that the two most obvious explanations for a change in the poverty rate in any period are (1) changes in current economic conditions and (2) changes in current government benefits for the poor.

Let us look closer at what happened from 1965 to 1980. From 1965 to 1973 *both* economic trends and changes in government benefits made it easier to escape from poverty. From 1973 to 1980, in contrast, escape became harder: unemployment rose, real wages fell, benefits lagged far behind inflation, and eligibility requirements tightened. Under these circumstances it is hardly surprising that poverty fell dramatically from 1965 to 1973 and increased after 1973.

Murray cannot have it both ways. If the accounting period is to run from 1965 to 1980 (as it usually does in his influential *Losing Ground*), he cannot argue that social policy made the poor worse off in material terms, because the material condition of the poor improved dramatically over this interval. If the accounting period is to run from 1973 to 1980, as Murray wants it to for this particular set of statistics, he must face the fact that, at least according to the census statistics on which the official poverty count is based, everyone (even the richest 5 percent) lost ground after 1973. Why, then, should we expect the poor to have done better, especially when cash transfers to the poor were lagging behind both wages and inflation?

EVALUATION METHODOLOGIES

Associated with the preceding criteria are a variety of research methods. Some of these evaluation methods are very similar to analytical techniques discussed in earlier chapters. What is the difference between evaluation and analysis? A rough and ready rule of thumb might be that policy analysis is *prospective;* it looks ahead at the consequences of various proposals in order to help policymakers decide what to do today. In contrast, evaluation is *retrospective;* it looks backward to see how well a program has actually worked.

A diverse number of research strategies for evaluation have been described in the literature.[23] Among the more prevalent of these methods are the following:

---

[23] See P. J. Runkel and J. E. McGrath, *Research on Human Behavior: A Systematic Guide to Method* (New York: Holt, Rinehart & Winston, 1972); Edward A. Suchman, *Evaluative Research* (New York: Russell Sage Foundation, 1967); T. P. Tripodi et al., *Social Program Evaluation* (Itasca, Ill.: F. E. Peacock, 1971); Leonard Rutman, ed., *Evaluative Research Methods: A Basic Guide* (Beverly Hills, Calif.: Sage, 1977); and Donald T. Campbell and J. C. Stanley, *Experimental and Quasi-Experimental Designs for Research* (Skokie, Ill.: Rand McNally, 1963).

- *Laboratory study or experimental design* exercises full control over scheduling of experimental stimuli (the when and to whom of exposures and the ability to randomize exposures). Typically, a laboratory study would involve two randomly constituted groups. The experimental treatment would be introduced to one group and then the pretest and post-test scores of both groups would be compared. This method is extremely good in determining intervention effect.

- *Field experiment* exercises only partial control over experimental stimuli (the when and to whom of measurement). Typically, a field experiment would involve the periodic measurement of some variable, the introduction of an experimental event, and the identification of a discontinuity in the measurement pattern.

- *Case study* examines only a single group (towns, families, corporations) that have been affected by a program. Typically, the one-shot case study draws inferences based on expectations of what might have happened without experimental intervention.

- *Sample survey* uses static correlation studies, typically employing multivariate techniques to analyze data collected from large samples. (Discussed in Chapter 3.)

- *Administrative audit* examines program policies and practices in terms of compliance with internal and external standards.

- *Cost-benefit analysis* examines the relative effectiveness of alternative programs (expressed in dollars) judged in relation to economic costs. (Discussed in Chapter 8.)

Many researchers see the methodological issue in black and white terms: evaluations must be "hard" (based on quantitative data) or "soft" (based on qualitative information), experimental or anecdotal, and so forth. Advocates typically conclude with prescriptive statements about the "right" design—that is, a model that is to be always applied. But this chapter might be characterized as calling for a contingency approach to evaluation. An appropriate choice of research strategy can only be made in light of a particular set of research objectives. Is the evaluator chiefly interested in output, side-effects, efficiency, strategy, compliance, justice, intervention effect, or something else? Only when *that* question has been answered, should the question of methodology be broached. Other theorists support this view. Runkel and McGrath write:

> Too often in behavioral science the choice of strategy is made first, based on the investigator's previous experience, preferences, and resources, and then the problem is chosen and formulated to fit the selected strategy, rather

than the other way around. . . . The trick is not to search for the right strategy but to pick the strategy that is best *for your purposes and circumstances.*[24]

Rather than defend a single, ideal evaluation strategy, *a contingency approach* suggests that we look at all the methodologies in order to achieve an optimal fit between evaluation criteria and assessment method. With this in mind, let us explore one or two examples of each of the six types cited above.

The Minneapolis domestic violence experiment

Generally, experimental designs are laboratory studies, but sometimes they can be done in the field. Under a grant from the National Institute of Justice, the Minneapolis Police Department and the Police Foundation conducted such an experiment to test police responses to domestic violence.[25]

Purpose. The purpose of the experiment was to address an intense debate about how police should respond to misdemeanors, such as cases of domestic violence. At least three viewpoints can be identified in this debate:

1. The traditional police approach of doing as little as possible, on the premise that offenders will not be punished by the courts even if they are arrested, and that the problems are basically not solvable.
2. The clinical psychologists' recommendations that police actively mediate or arbitrate disputes underlying the violence, restoring peace but not making any arrests.
3. The approach recommended by many women's groups of treating the violence as a criminal offense subject to arrest. This approach merits brief amplification.

Just when psychologists succeeded in having many police agencies respond to domestic violence as half social work and half police work, feminists began to argue that police put too much emphasis on the social work aspect and not enough on the criminal. Widely publicized lawsuits in New York and Oakland sought to compel police to make arrests in every case of domestic assault, and state legislatures were lobbied successfully to reduce the evidentiary requirements needed for police to make arrests for misdemeanor domestic assaults. The feminist critique was bolstered by a study showing that in 85 percent of a sample of spouse killings, police had intervened at least once in the preceding

[24] Runkel and McGrath, *Research on Human Behavior*, pp. 116–17.
[25] Lawrence W. Sherman and Richard D. Berk, "The Specific Deterrent Effects of Arrest for Domestic Assault" *American Sociological Review*, vol. 49 (April 1984), 261–72.

Table 11–1
Expected versus observed repeat violence
over six months

Police action	Expected*	Observed
Arrest	17	9
Advise	19	20
Send suspect away	20	27
	56	56

* Among the 311 suspects, police arrested 91 (29.3 percent), advised 107 (34.4 percent), and sent away 113 (36.3 percent). Within six months, 56 of this group were again involved in an incident. If intervention had no effect, then we would expect to see about 29 percent of that 56, or 17 suspects, to have been previously arrested. The observed number, 9, was considerably lower.

Source: Data calculated from Minneapolis Domestic Violence Experiment.

two years. For 54 percent of those homicides, police had intervened five or more times. It was impossible to determine from the data whether making more or fewer arrests would have reduced homicide rate.

If the purpose of police responses to domestic violence calls is to reduce the likelihood of that violence recurring, the question is which of these three approaches is more effective than the others?

Experiment design. In order to find which police approach was most effective in deterring future domestic violence, the Police Foundation and the Minneapolis Police Department agreed to conduct a *classic experiment*. A classic experiment is a research design that allows scientists to discover the effects of one thing on another by holding constant all other possible causes of those effects. The design of the experiment called for random selection by a lottery, which ensured that there would be no difference among the three groups of suspects receiving the different police responses. The lottery determined which of the three responses police officers would use on each suspect in a domestic assault case. According to the lottery, a suspect would be arrested, or sent from the scene of the assault for eight hours, or given some form of advice, which could include mediation at an officer's discretion. In the language of the experiment, these responses were called the arrest, send, and advice treatments. The design called for a six-month follow-up period to measure the frequency and seriousness of any future domestic violence in all cases in which the police intervened.

Findings and policy implications. The Minneapolis domestic violence experiment was the first scientifically controlled test of the effects of arrest for any crime. See Table 11–1. It found that arrest was the most effective of three standard methods police use to reduce domestic violence. (These were not life-threatening cases, but rather the minor assaults that make up the bulk of police calls on domestic violence.) The other police methods—attempting to counsel both parties or sending assailants away from home for several hours, were found to be considerably less effective in deterring future violence in the cases examined.

It may be too premature to conclude that arrest is always the best way for police to handle domestic violence, or that all suspects in such situations should be arrested. A number of factors suggest a cautious interpretation of the findings. In the first place, because of the relatively small numbers of suspects in each subcategory (age, race, employment status, criminal history, etc.), it is possible that this experiment failed to discover that for some kinds of people, arrest may only make matters worse. Until subsequent research addresses that issue more thoroughly, it would be premature for state legislatures to pass laws requiring arrests in all misdemeanor domestic assaults. Further, Minneapolis may be unique in keeping most suspects arrested for domestic assault in jail overnight. It is possible that arrest would not have as great a deterrent effect in other cities where suspects may be able to return home within an hour or so of arrest.

Minneapolis is unusual in other respects: a large Native American population, a very low rate of violence, severe winters, and a low unemployment rate. The cultural context of other cities may produce different effects of police actions in domestic violence cases. Until these issues are resolved, one might question the *external validity* of the study.

But police officers cannot wait for further research to decide how to handle the domestic violence they face each day. They must use the best information available. This experiment provides the only scientifically controlled comparison of different methods of reducing repeat violence. And on the basis of this study alone, police should probably employ arrest in most cases of minor domestic violence.

The findings clearly support the legislation in Minnesota that made the experiment possible. In many states the police are not able to make an arrest in domestic violence cases without the signed complaint of a victim. In at least one state (Maryland), police cannot make an arrest without a warrant issued by a magistrate. This experiment shows the vital importance of state policymakers' empowering police to make probable cause arrests in cases of domestic violence. As a result of the experiment's findings, the Minneapolis Police Department changed its policy on domestic assault.

Field experiment: Workfare and project concern

Programs linking welfare to work. When modern national welfare programs began in the 1930s, welfare was largely uncontroversial because aid went to people who were not expected to work, such as widows, wives of disabled workers, the blind, and the aged. But in recent decades rising welfare enrollment and costs and falling expectations that mothers would remain at home with young children have brought a reexamination of the relationships between work and welfare.

In the 1970s, when Ronald Reagan was governor of California, he won enactment of a limited form of work programs. In 1981, as president, Reagan proposed national mandatory work requirements. Congress rejected this idea but authorized similar state programs. Since then, at least twenty-three states, including New York, New Jersey, and Connecticut, have required some welfare recipients to work.

Workfare requires people receiving assistance to work a certain number of hours (usually twenty) a week in return for the money they get, almost always in public service and for charities: carting away rubbish, sweeping leaves or snow by the few men on the rolls, cleaning offices and such for the many more women. The programs vary widely and many exempt some recipients, but the work plans are probably the largest social experiment going on in the country.

Massachusetts, for example, has established an education and training (ET) scheme for women on welfare. Many thousands applied, far more than could be accommodated, undermining the frequently heard charge that people on welfare do not want to work, and Governor Michael Dukakis was delighted to announce that 23,000 women had been placed in jobs, saving the state and federal governments a total of $70 million in one year. Alas, experts in the field unkindly pointed out that there was no *control group* and that in the booming economy of Massachusetts in the 1980s many of those women might have obtained jobs without the benefit of ET. Unemployment in the state was below 4 percent and, even the unemployment rate for black men was down to 5 percent. Still, it is hard to believe that the continuation of medicaid, the provision of daycare, and the training and help with finding jobs failed to make a difference.

Then came a report from the Manpower Demonstration Research Corporation of New York, a respected social policy research group, on four state and county programs in which a control group was conscientiously employed.[26] The women did not select themselves; they were simply the intake, over a given period, of women applying for AFDC. The amount of training varied. To generalize, while the programs rarely made dramatic improvements in individual lives or in welfare rolls, over time they did appear to result in higher real income for individuals and a smaller burden on the public treasury.

---

[26] Manpower Demonstration Research Corporation, *Summary and Finding of the National Supported Work Demonstration* (Cambridge, Mass.: Ballinger, 1980).

However, the concept has strong critics. They charge, in particular, that workfare fails to meet at least two criteria: efficiency and fairness. Mandatory programs, they think, could be costly to administer. Further, recipients are forced to work for far less than regular employees and get few or no benefits.

Evaluating desegregation. Project Concern was a fifteen-year study of black students educated in predominantly white suburban schools. Financed by the National Institute of Education, the study was conducted by the Center for Social Organization of Schools at Johns Hopkins University and the Rand Corporation.[27]

Most of the students in the program began it as first and second graders who lived in northern Hartford, a predominantly lower-income black community with a high crime rate and numerous abandoned dwellings. Black students ($n = 318$) from four inner-city elementary schools were randomly selected to attend sixty predominantly white schools in thirteen suburbs of Hartford. The other group ($n = 343$), preserved as a control group, remained at segregated schools.

For their study the researchers traced Project Concern members from the time they entered the program to 1981, when most had completed high school and were working or attending college. The analysis drew six conclusions about those who attended racially mixed schools as contrasted with those who did not:

- They were more likely to graduate from high school.
- They were more likely to attend predominantly white colleges and complete more years of college.
- They perceived less discrimination in college and in other areas of adult life in Hartford.
- They were involved in fewer incidents with the police and got into fewer fights as adults.
- They have closer and more frequent social contacts with whites as adults, are more likely to live in desegregated neighborhoods, and have more white friends in college.
- Women in the group were less likely to have a child before they were eighteen years old.

Critics of desegregation programs have argued that simply putting a black child beside a white child in a classroom does not lead to eventual social equality or acceptance, which, they say, should be among the primary purposes of such desegregation efforts. The evidence cited by

---

[27] Robert L. Crain and Rita E. Maynard, "Desegregation and Black Achievement," *Law and Contemporary Problems* 42 (Summer 1978), pp. 17–35.

594

Project Concern, however, shows that a desegregation project can lead to such changes.

The study found that those who had attended one of the schools in the integration plan overwhelmingly gravitated toward racially mixed settings as adults. Blacks who had remained at segregated schools, the study reported, generally projected a less receptive and sometimes hostile attitude toward living and working in racially mixed settings.

Project Concern illustrates that the side-effects of a policy do not necessarily have to be all negative. Just as we might find that the negative side-effects of a policy might overshadow output in importance, so too might positive side-effects. As the researchers wrote: "Evidence suggests that the test scores of minority students rise after desegregation. But this outcome is not the real test of the value of desegregation in the schools. The real test is whether desegregation enables minorities to join other Americans in becoming well-educated, economically successful, and socially well-adjusted adults." [28] The daily coexistence with whites showed the black students they could both compete and socialize with their white schoolmates. Thus, Project Concern strongly suggests that there is more to desegregation than just higher test scores for minorities; it suggests that the effect of integrating races in the school trickles into the community and into adulthood.

Case study versus sample survey: The causes and persistence of poverty

Probably no evaluation methodology has greater strengths than the case study. Eloquent descriptions of the lives of the poor have a capacity to attract public attention missing from more quantitative studies. Case studies give a fine-grained picture of a probem, capturing details and subtleties that slip easily through the net of the statistician.

But the strengths of the case study are, paradoxically, its weaknesses. Eloquence is not truth; indeed, great eloquence combined with emotionalism will suffocate the truth. Fine-grained pictures must be perforce limited in time and place. Many of participant-observation studies of poverty focus on small and extreme groups are a case in point. In *The Other America* (1962), Michael Harrington describes his two years of experience with skid row alcoholics in the Bowery in New York. In *La Vida* (1968), Oscar Lewis studies poor Puerto Rican families living in slums. In his study of gang delinquency in the *Journal of Social Issues*, Walter B. Miller studies adolescent groups in a slum district of a large eastern city. In *The Underclass* (1982), Kenneth Auletta describes the

---

[28] Ibid.

experiences of participants in two somewhat atypical projects run by the previously mentioned Manpower Demonstration Research Corporation (MDRC) in New York City.[29] Regarding the last-named study, critics have recently made this point:

> Auletta's generalizations about the underclass are too closely linked to his observations of participants in the MDRC-supported work demonstration. His four categories of the underclass directly parallel the four eligibility criteria for the MDRC Supported Work demonstration. In as much as MDRC program participants were selected on the basis of criminal records, drug addiction, and long-term welfare dependency, it is not surprising that Auletta strongly emphasizes the deviancy and violence of the underclass.[30]

It is useful to contrast these case studies of poverty with a major large-scale data collection project, the Panel Study of Income Dynamics (PSID). Actually, the project was conceived to test many of the key assumptions of the previously mentioned case studies about poverty and welfare dependency—especially the notions that the economic status of the poor is caused by psychological dispositions and that poor families are trapped in a "culture poverty," making it difficult for their children (or their children's children) to break the cycle.

The data for the PSID study were collected from a representative sample of the U.S. populations. Furthermore, the evidence of the intergenerational aspects of poverty and welfare dependency was reported *directly* by both parents and children, thus minimizing the reporting errors that pervade studies in which people are asked to recall conditions when they were growing up.

In summary, this is what the PSID study found:

> The culture of poverty and underclass arguments are generally inappropriate models for viewing the poor. Many poor people do have low levels of motivation, but this low motivation appears to have been caused by the events they have experienced. Resocialization strategies are unnecessary and inappropriate for the majority of people who come into contact with poverty. Poverty spells should be viewed, for most people, as temporary and unlikely to leave lifelong scars. Income maintenance programs can be designed without inordinate fear of fostering dependency among those in temporary need. Such programs should focus on the events that produce poverty spells and

---

[29] Michael Harrington, *The Other America* (New York: Macmillan, 1962); Oscar Lewis, *La Vida, A Puerto Rican Family in the Culture of Poverty: San Juan and New York* (London: Panther Books, 1968); Oscar Lewis, *A Study of Slum Culture: Backgrounds for La Vida* (New York: Basic Books, 1968); Walter B. Miller, "Lower Class Society as a Generating Milieu of Gang Delinquency," *Journal of Social Issues* 14 no. 3 (1958), pp. 5–19; Kenneth Auletta, "The Underclass," in *The New Yorker*, November 16, 1981, November 23, 1981, and November 30, 1981; and Kenneth Auletta, *The Underclass*, (New York: Random House, 1982).

[30] Mary Corcoran, et al., "Myth and Reality: The Causes and Persistence of Poverty," *Journal of Policy Analysis and Management* 4 no. 4 (1985) p. 522.

their consequences rather than on the presumed psychological characteristics of the poor.

At the same time, however, it should be recognized that there is an identifiable subset of the poor whose spells are not likely to be temporary, and it is on them that many programs' resources should be focused. An examination of this subset of long-term poor suggests that the conception of an underclass made up of youths or welfare mothers living in large cities may target attention to groups that have difficult, long-term problems, but it does not characterize most of the individuals in the United States who find themselves in persistent need.[31]

Auditing: How well OSHA saves lives in the workplace

Using only sample survey data to evaluate the Occupational Safety and Health Administration, I can arrive at a disturbing conclusion: OSHA seems to have had no effect on workplace safety whatsoever. In 1948, the workplace death rate was twenty-nine per 100,000 workers, according to the National Safety Council. The rate drifted downward unevenly to seventeen in 1971—this being the year Congress established OSHA. Using the data for the years 1948–1971 and the linear repression technique described in Chapter 4, I projected the trend to 1983 and found that, if the trend continued as it had been going prior to OSHA, the death rate in 1983 would be eleven. Of course, the actual rate for 1983 is now available, and guess what? It is eleven.

But, before we conclude that OSHA is redundant, we might want to consider an administrative audit of that agency by the Office of Technology Assessment.[32] In the study, OTA asserts that OSHA's inspections were infrequent and its penalties were so low that companies had limited incentives for complying with federal safety and health regulations. The average penalty for a serious violation, which is defined as one that creates a "substantial probability of death or serious physical harm," was about $172 in the fiscal year 1983.

OTA officials said that it was not within the study's scope to predict whether changes in enforcement efforts, such as more inspections and tougher penalties, would improve worker safety. But their general conclusion is that, given the low probability of inspections and the relatively low penalty rates, the incentive for complying with OSHA standards before an OSHA inspection occurs is actually quite low.

More typically, when Congress wants to know how efficiently a program operates, it will turn not to OTA but to the General Accounting Office. Recently the GAO has performed administrative audits to ad-

---

[31] Ibid., p. 518.

[32] U.S. Congress, Office of Technology Assessment, *Preventing Illness and Injury in the Workplace* (Washington, D.C.: Government Printing Office, April 1985).

Box 11–2
Using sample surveys to evaluate motorcycle helmet laws

The following is an excerpt from an interview with Gene Wirwahn, legislative director, American Motorcyclist Association. Ben Kelley, senior vice president, Insurance Institute for Highway Safety, has just asserted that helmet laws "reduce the death rate by about 30 percent."

Q: Don't statistics indicate that helmet laws do save a large number of lives?
A: The only correct statistic with which to assess the effectiveness of motorcycle-helmet laws is the number of fatally injured motorcyclists per 100 accidents. These data actually address whether helmet laws reduce the number of fatalities per accident.
Q: Do you have such figures?
A: Yes, we do.
   We have taken 18 states that have had the helmet law for at least three years and that properly report fatalities as the number of motorcyclists fatally injured. Using the number of fatalities per 100 motorcycle accidents for these 18 states, we compared the ratio for the years after implementation of the helmet law to the years before and found there was no statistically significant difference.
   The over-all average fatality ratio for those 18 states before helmet laws was 2.688 per 100 accidents, and the over-all average was 2.562.
Q: That's a reduction, isn't it?
A: Yes, but not a statistically significant one, and not large enough that it could not be said to have occurred by chance alone.
   The more correct phrasing of the conclusion would be that the proper statistics show that motorcycle-helmet laws have not had the effect that their proponents say they have.

Source: *U.S. News & World Report*, July 18, 1977, pp. 40–41

---

dress questions like these. How efficiently is American aid to the Philippines being spent? Does the EPA overpay for emergency cleanups of toxic waste? What are the kinds and causes of welfare payment errors, and how can the federal government's quality control systems be improved? [33]

---

[33] AFD, medicaid, and food stamps cost over $43 billion in 1985, and even a 1 percent payment error rate produces significant excess costs. See U.S. General Accounting Office, Briefing Report to the Chairman, Committee on Government Affairs, U.S. Senate, *Managing Welfare: Issues and Alternatives for Reforming Quality Control Systems* (Washington, D.C.: Government Printing Office, August 1986).

Are the benefits of Head Start worth the costs?

Chapter 8 discussed in detail cost-benefit analysis from the standpoint of a policymaker who was trying to decide whether to launch a new project. But CBA is equally useful in evaluating a program that has been in existence for sometime.[34]

In 1968, 123 black children from poor families and with below average IQs were selected and then randomly divided into an experimental group, which was offered high-quality preschool education at the age of three, and a control group without that advantage. Fewer than one in five of the parents had completed high school. Forty-seven percent of the children lived in single-parent homes.

Previous studies of the Head Start program had shown some educational gains for children who had been in early programs. But this research differed significantly in that it involved children one year younger than those in Head Start, and it followed them all the way to young adulthood.[35] By age nineteen the shift from school to "real-world" had already taken place and for the first time, the cost-benefit analysis could be based on actual data from complete school records, police reports, and state records of welfare payments. Employment histories were verified, and the retesting of the participants' functional competence focused on information and skills in the real world rather than on school achievement or intelligence tests.

Now, at age nineteen, their record showed that the rates of employment and participation in college or vocational training after high school for the preschool group were nearly double those of youths without preschool education; teenage pregnancies in the group were slightly more than half those among the non-preschool girls; preschool graduates were involved in 20 percent fewer arrests and detentions; nearly 20 percent fewer had dropped out of high school. The benefits to society as a result of the reduced crime rate were estimated at about $3,100 per preschool child. Economists who studied the subjects' records estimate that, over their lifetimes, the economic benefits to them and to society may be more than seven times the cost of operating the program for one year.

The crucial aspect of preschool education, the study stressed, is that it makes it easier for children to function in school. This better perfor-

---

[34] See Burton A. Weisbrod, "Benefit-Cost Analysis of a Controlled Experiment: Treating the Mentally Ill," *Journal of Human Resources* 16 (Fall 1981), pp. 523–48. Peter Kemper, et. al., "Benefit-Cost Analysis of a Supported Work Experiment," in Robert H. Haveman and Julius Morgolis, *Public Expenditure and Policy Analysis* (Boston: Houghton Mifflin, 1983), pp. 260–300.

[35] David P. Weikart, *Changed Lives* (Ypsilanti, Mich.: Scope Educational Research Foundation, 1984).

mance is visible to everyone, the child, the teacher, the parents, and other children. As a result, children develop confidence in themselves. Teachers react with higher expectations. Early scholastic achievement becomes the foundation for success in school and community, whereas scholastic failure paves the way for all-round failure and delinquency, according to the final report.

TERMINATION OF PUBLIC POLICY

Machiavelli got it wrong when he said, "There is nothing more difficult to take in hand, or more perilous to conduct, or more uncertain of success, than to take the lead in the introduction of a new order of things." What he should have said was that nothing is more difficult than to *end* an order of things.

Policies develop constituencies and constituencies vote. President Reagan's experience was typical. When he took office in 1981, Reagan vowed to halt "runaway government" by terminating superfluous federal agencies. His administration tried manfully to close many but only two were actually closed: the Civil Aeronatuics Board and the Community Service Administration. The latter was the first major federal agency to be abolished since World War II. The story of how members of Congress, prodded by special interests, succeed in keeping agencies' programs alive is too well-known to need repeating here.

Psychological factors also make policy termination difficult. Laboratory experiments show that individuals tend to make increasing commitments to a failing course of action, rather than cut their losses. Such entrapping dilemmas (known as the "Knee Deep in the Big Muddy" phenomenon) occur frequently, both within and outside of government.[36] Having already made an initial financial allocation to some high-risk borrowers, the bank loan officer must decide whether to approve an additional loan when the borrowers later claim that the initial loan will not be sufficient; having already spent hundreds of dollars to repair a car's transmission, buy new tires, and replace the shocks, the car owner must decide whether to spend additional money— now that the brakes require immediate replacement; having already lost thousands of lives, the U.S. government must decide whether to continue its involvement in a military conflict (such as Vietnam).

---

[36] B. M. Straw, "Knee-Deep in the Big Muddy: A Study of Escalating Commitment to a Chosen Course of Action," *Organizational Behavior and Human Performance* 16 (1976), pp. 27–44; and Joel Brockner, "The Role of Modeling Processes in the 'Knee Deep in the Big Muddy' Phenomenon," *Organizational Behavior and Human Performance* 33 (1984), pp. 77–99.

Perhaps because of these difficulties few authors hazard to summarize or suggest how to terminate a policy.[37] This is too bad. To ignore termination is to discount the value of evaluation, for these studies do more than provide policymakers with feedback on how to fine-tune programs. Evaluative studies can also send the message that a program is so fundamentally flawed or that environmental conditions (including the problem itself) have so radically altered that the only course of action now is termination. In a larger sense, to ignore termination is to deny society the application of its precious resources to more productive uses. Therefore, a few points about termination planning, distilled from experience, merit attention.

Documentation and evaluation. Surely a prerequisite for any termination plan must be a well-prepared case for it—one that is easy to understand and hard to refute. Better yet if the explanation can pass the "Otto test," named for the late Harvard economist and founder of Data Resources, Inc., a leading economic forecasting concern. That means that it can be understandable in thirty to forty seconds. Otto Eckstein learned in Washington that no one has time to waste and that you have to make your main points quickly.

Timing. Although policies have constituencies and special interest groups prod Congress, political climates can change. When constituencies shrink and interest groups weaken, policies are more susceptible to change. Policies are especially vulnerable at the start of a new administration, during the end of session rush to pass an appropriations bill, or after a blue ribbon panel recommends termination.

Rate. "If it were done when 'tis done, then 'twere well/It were done quickly." Macbeth's advice on how to terminate Duncan might apply to policy as well. To proceed gradually allows the opposition time to marshal its forces and map its strategy. Moving quickly might also help to reduce the opposition's misery. On the other hand, it could prove a wrenching experience. When jobs are at stake, as they often are in termination cases, time should be allowed for the displaced personnel to relocate. (Private firms sometimes use a consulting arrangement with former employees to cushion the blow of outplacement.)

Terminators and referees. First of all, there must be a terminator, that is, some one authority to curtail a program. Next, it is a good idea to appoint an expert in policy and institutional restructuring, though such individuals are scarce. Flex Rohatyn had some experience in rescuing distressed corporations, but he had to learn by doing when he and his Municipal Assistance Corporation helped extract New York

---

[37] For a couple of exceptions, see Gary D. Brewer and Peter de Leon, *The Foundations of Policy Analysis* (Chicago, Ill.: Dorsey Press, 1983), pp. 383–459, and Robert D. Behn, "How to Terminate a Public Policy," *Policy Analysis*, Summer 1978, pp. 393–413.

City from its financial crisis in the 1970s. Referrees can also protect legally the rights of multiple claimants when a public agency founders. A group of referees can make certain that a program's assets are equitably redistributed.

Survival tactics. The terminator should know survival tactics like those used by the organization targeted for termination and the interest groups that support them in order to prepare for them.

Weak points. Although the lion is the king of the beasts, it generally attacks the weakest animals in a herd. By the same token, "a frontal assault on an entire organization is less politic than selecting more vulnerable, discrete targets of opportunity (within an organization's policy and program array) and concentrating extraordinary attention and resources on them." Similarly, "if public education is oversupplied with teachers, reductions in force might be more easily attained by curtailing teacher training programs . . . than firing an entrenched, highly visible, and vocal cadre of teachers."[38]

POLICIES AS HYPOTHESES

Writers who pose questions in chapter titles have an obligation to offer answers, sooner or later. I maintain that a good policy is one that attains its goals with minimum waste and side-effects. A good policy attacks the right problem the right way—which means that it builds on a correct theoretical understanding of the problem and its solution. A good policy complies with legislative intent and constitutional law. Further, it is fair (more about that four letter word in the next chapter). And, finally, a good policy itself—not luck or circumstance—causes the desired change in the societal problem.

Ultimately, the best evidence that a policy is good is pragmatic: it works when it is tried. As Aaron Wildavsky explains:

> We value what works and we learn what works from experience, particularly experience that magnifies error and failure. The impetus for analysis flows from the clash between expectations formed from prevailing theory and our interpretation of experience. When predictions do not pan out we attempt to reimpose order on the confusion by suggesting new hypotheses about the world or by reexamining the claims to "facts." Inventing these hypotheses and discarding current theory for better theory are the learning analogues to establishing new government programs when faced with failures of current ones. We hope that new hypotheses expand into theories that better explain the world, just as we hope that new programs form better matches between resources and objectives.[39]

---

[38] Brewer and de Leon, "Foundations of Policy Analysis," p. 436.
[39] Aaron Wildavsky, *Speaking Truth to Power* (Boston: Little, Brown, 1979), p. 393.

But people do not ordinarily learn well from experience. For this reason, formal methods of evaluation, which seek to order that experience so that knowledge will be gained from it, are required. Those methods do not guarantee progress in public policy, for error recognition and error correction are not always compatible.

> The trouble is that what facilitates recognition often inhibits correction. To be readily recognized, error should be conspicuous and clear. The larger the error and the more it contrasts with its background, the easier it is to identify. Easy correction of error, however, depends on mistakes that are small in size (and hence in cost) and are necessarily close to what has gone on before. But small errors are likely to lack sharp resolution, merging imperceptibly into their backgrounds. Because they are cheap and reversible, these errors would be correctable if only they were detectable. Alternatively, big policies generate giant mistakes, which make them simple to spot but difficult to reverse, because the cost of changing past practice soars. If only big mistakes can be recognized, we would be able to detect only the errors we cannot easily correct.[40]

Taking evaluation seriously does not mean that we discard a policy as soon as we detect error; not only would that be politically naive, it would also be bad practice. Certainly, scientists and mathematicians do not discard their theories at the first sign of a contradiction. For example, policies directed at alleviating poverty rest on a set of theories regarding the demographic composition of the poor and the psychological dispositions of poor individuals. As we saw in this chapter, case study writers seem to think that a culture of poverty exists, but researchers on the Panel Study of Income Dynamics disagree.

Starting from a problem, there is a conjecture as to what might be done to alleviate it. Then follows a search for explanations, justifications, elaborations that will make the conjecture more plausible, more convincing. This "proof" is immediately followed by a barrage of counterexamples. Under the pressure of these counterexamples, the policy proposal is corrected and elaborated. New counterexamples are presented, new modifications of the proposals are made.

Following Imre Lakatos, we might call a counterexample that challenges one part of the proof a "local counterexample."[41] For example, the finding that lakes in Florida are highly acidic challenges popular theories about acid rain. Where could Florida's acid rain come from—Cuba, the Gulf of Mexico? A counterexample that challenges the conjecture itself Lakatos calls a "global counterexample." Certainly, Charles Murray's argument that the poverty rate went up *after* the War on

---

[40] Ibid., p. 340.
[41] Imre Laktos, *Proofs and Refutations* (Cambridge: Cambridge University Press, 1976).

Figure 11–1
A simplified model of the dynamics of policy assessment

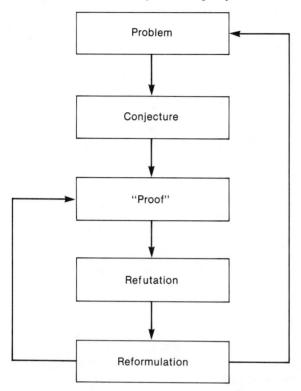

Poverty challenges our theories about programs to help the poor at a very fundamental level.

The Lakatos model, in a simplified form, appears in Figure 11–1. Perhaps the greatest value of the model is that it helps us understand what the role of evaluation in the policy is *not*. A single evaluative study is unlikely to provide policymakers with a yes or no answer; rather, each study plays its part in the larger process of conjecture-proof-refutation-reformation we have just been describing. Evaluation is not some system built up with inexorably inductive logic from first principles. Instead it should be seen as a clash of views, arguments, and counterarguments.

This view better explains the incredible number of evaluative studies that programs like Headstart generate. But this is by no means bad. Evaluation makes policymaking what it is: a slow and careful process of growth. To the extent that evaluation helps policymakers discover errors, it is an engine of change.

FOR FURTHER REFLECTION

1. Are there ever any good reasons *not* to evaluate?
2. How would you evaluate the quality of service in your state's social service agencies? How would you determine whether the police in your community are doing an adequate job?
3. Because of a recent rollback in property taxes and reduction in federal funds, the city manager for a city of 300,000 has decided that operating expenses must be cut 12 percent. Rather than cut across the board, he wants to do it selectively. He asks you to develop a set of "objective criteria" by which to make the cuts. What do you recommend?
4. The local police department has decided to adopt, on an experimental basis, a program that allows officers to take departmental vehicles home. The assumption is that the more police vehicles that are visible the better. Develop an appropriate evaluation design strategy.
5. How would you evaluate a state's workfare program (pp. 591–93)?
6. A county decides to contract with a private firm to house its prisoners. Design an approach to monitoring and evaluating the impact of the policy. Include in this design at least a specification of the variables to be observed, an identification of the ways in which changes will be measured, and a statement of the decision rules that will be used to draw a conclusion.
7. "There is nothing in a formal theory of evaluation that requires that criteria be specified in advance. In particular, the evaluation of social experiments need not be in terms of the degree to which they have fulfilled our prior expectations. Rather, we can examine what they did in terms of what we now believe to be important. That prior specification of criteria and the prior specification of evaluational procedures depend on such criteria are common presumptions in contemporary social policymaking. They are presumptions that inhibit the serendipitous discovery of new criteria. Experience should be used explicitly as an occasion for evaluating our values as well as our actions." Discuss. [Source: Michael D. Cohen and James G. March, *Leadership and Ambiguity* (Boston: Harvard Business School Press, 1974)]
8. Discuss the political uses of evaluative studies.
9. The new medicare payment system groups medical procedures into 468 diagnosis-related groups. After diagnosis, each patient is assigned a group number. Based on this category, the hospital is reimbursed a predetermined fee regardless of the total cost of treatment. In most cases, if costs exceed the reimbursement fee, the hospital takes a loss. Assess this approach to cost containment in terms of the program logic criteria.

10. The budget for the county hospital has been slashed. Preliminary analysis indicates that the best way to administer the cut is to close two underutilized clinics or to reduce some services. You are to head the team that will analyze these options and make recommendations on which to choose. First, develop some broad concepts that can be used to evaluate the performance of the hospital as a whole, the clinics, and the services. Next, develop very specific statistical indicators that can be used to evaluate clinic against clinic, service against service. These indicators must employ readily available data.

11. A major domestic concern facing mayors, governors, and presidents is unemployment. Evaluate efforts over the years to attack this problem through the creation of public service jobs and aiding the transition of laid-off workers into new jobs and skills.

12. There are two studies that proponents of mandatory helmet laws use to support their position. The first one is a study done by the National Highway Traffic Safety Administration Michigan-Illinois study. This project attempted to compare a helmet-law state—Michigan—with a nonhelmet-law state—Illinois—and concluded that states with compulsory motorcycle safety-helmet laws should have a 40 to 60 percent lower fatal or serious head-injury rate. The second one was done by the Insurance Institute for Highway Safety. It says that states with helmet-use laws have experienced, on an average, decreases in motorcycle-involved fatalities compared to those without laws. The statistics used show the number of fatal accidents in which a motorcycle was involved per 10,000 registered motorcycles. Assume that you are legislative director of the American Motorcyclist Association, a lobby group that opposes helmet laws. What questions or objections if any, would you raise about this evaluative research?

Chapter 12

Two Concepts of Ethics

Surely the task of policy analysis is more difficult today than ever before. In the face of a growing complexity in the substance of public policies, improvements in strategy may seem meager indeed. The distance between what analysts know and what they need to know appears to be greater than ever. Washington and Jefferson thought in terms of four million homogeneous people, most of whom were farmers; today's policymakers have to think in terms of nearly one-quarter billion people of all races and traditions, crossbred and inbred, plunked down on a continent between two great oceans.

Today's policymakers have to take into account not the simple opposition of two classes or two parties but the conflict of many—farmers and consumers, blue-collar workers and high technology workers, small businesses and transnationals, young and old, black and white, male and female. Contemporary policymakers cannot keep to problems within their borders. They are involved in the world's problems; all the economic winds and thermonuclear dangers blow through their land. Overlaying all these challenges is another, less visible perhaps, but no less worthy of our attention: The people with whom policymakers must deal differ in their sense of what the facts really are, in their ideals, and in the very groundwork of their morals. It is this challenge that I wish to address now.

Few policy decisions are purely technical. Ethical questions, questions about what we *ought* to do—as individuals and in organizations—appear throughout the policy process. Because analysts do not always appreciate this fact and because the methodology of policy analysis tends to emphasize the quantitative over the qualitative, we need to understand how and when ethical concerns emerge. The first section of this chapter addresses that question.

The remainder of the chapter deals with the more difficult question of how to handle ethical issues. Contemporary philosophers divided the ethics into many branches, but the argument here is that there are really only two approaches to the field. More specifically, ultimate ethical principles are either arbitrary choices or they are not. Section Two introduces you to one of these approaches by focusing on social welfare economics, a subject well discussed in the literature of policy analysis. Section three gives you a look at an older concept of ethics and then compares the two.

THE UBIQUITY OF ETHICS IN POLICY STUDIES

The role of ideology in diagnosing the problem

At a news conference in Washington on June 7, 1985, Patrick J. Buchanan, the White House director of communications, referred to the "philosophy" of the Reagan administration. Asked by a reporter whether he did not mean "ideology," Buchanan, "No, philosophy. We don't use ideology any more."

Why the reluctance to use the word ideology? What could be wrong about having a system of ideas that supplies a sense of intellectual cohesion and perhaps a plan of political action? Nothing, except that the word carries another connotation as well—the most disturbing thing about an ideology is its immunity to the voice of experience and concrete reality. Beliefs harden and chill into dogma. Neither policy analysts nor communications directors can afford to ignore this possibility. Nuclear war, nuclear weapons, abortion (pro-choice), opposition to abortion (pro-life), trade deficits, economic growth, free markets, immigration, population growth—a hundred pages could not exhaust the range and diversity of ideology in the United States today. But this passion to convert opinion into dogma and ignore the other side and other values is anathema to good analysis. *It makes a clear understanding of the problem virtually impossible.*

Helen Caldicott is a prime mover in the worldwide organization of doctors against nuclear war, Physicians for Social Responsibility. Speaking from a solid basis of medical experience, she is articulate and witty. Yet she lives in a completely different world than that of a general. If she tried to talk to a general, or the general to her, it would be a dialogue of the deaf.

> Why is it so easy for the warriors to ignore Helen? The warriors do not feel inclined to take her seriously, because she does not play her game according to their rules. Both the style and the substance of her argument violate the taboos of their profession. Her style is personal rather than objective. The substance of her argument is anecdotal rather than analytical. She

is careless about technical details. She does not think naturally in quantitative terms. The qualities that make Helen convincing to an audience of concerned citizens in Princeton, her sincerity and seriousness and down-to-earth goodness, are outweighed in the world of the warriors by her weakness in arithmetic.

If it is difficult to translate Helen's message effectively into the language of the generals, it is even more difficult to translate the legitimate concerns of the generals into a language which pays some respect to ordinary human values and feelings. The deliberately impersonal style of the warriors' world gives outsiders the impression that the warriors are even more inhuman than they actually are. There is prejudice and antipathy on both sides. The military establishment looks on the peace movement as a collection of ignorant people meddling in a business they do not understand, while the peace movement looks on the military establishment as a collection of misguided people protected by bureaucratic formality from all contact with human realities. Both these preconceptions create barriers to understanding. Both preconceptions are to some extent true.[1]

The debate over abortion, which once provoked such hopes and fears of a constitutional amendment and a government more concerned with and involved in the morality of its citizens, has settled into trench warfare. One of the reasons for the stalemate is that most Americans do not see abortion in the clear, black-and-white terms discerned by activists on the issue. A recent poll indicated deeply felt conflicts in the public that make unlikely solid support for either side. While 55 percent of the public said that abortion "is the same thing as murdering a child," 66 percent said that it is "sometimes the best thing in a bad situation" and 40 percent said that it "should be legal as it is now."[2]

Meanwhile, the activists continue a controversy marked on both sides by extreme vehemence and a denial of any merit to opposing points of view. One side asserts that a woman has an innate right of "control of her own body," which encompasses, it is said, arranging for the death of a fetus on a variety of grounds including psychological disinclination and economic inability to raise a child. At the other extreme is the existence of a "right to life," the assertion that the killing of even a zygote (a fertilized egg before the first embryonic division) is murder because the zygote has the "potential" to become a human being. If one earnestly believes that the fetus is human, then any rejoinder about not imposing one individuals' morality on another is nonsensical.

Similar problems appear in debates about economic policy. In the new competitive world economy, how does the United States become a winner? The essence of the choice can be seen in a dialogue that

---

[1] Freeman Dyson, *Weapons and Hope* (New York: Harper & Row, 1984), pp. 6–7.
[2] Poll based on 1,354 telephone interviews conducted December 14–18, 1985 by the *New York Times*, February 23, 1986.

Lester Thurow of M.I.T. had with Herbert Stein, Chairman of the council of Economic Advisers under President Nixon. Note how Stein's belief in the superiority of current market arrangements seems to shut his mind to concrete reality and experience.

> DR. THUROW: What makes you sure that the United States at the moment isn't Great Britain circa 1900? The rest of the world is breathing at our heels and they aren't going to slow down when they catch up. They're going to zoom right by and the United States fifty years from now will have half their per capita GNP.
>
> DR. STEIN: I'm not sure of that at all. But I'm not willing to make a major change in the system on the bet that that is the case.
>
> DR. THUROW: Let me ask you a question. Suppose you knew that it were true. Would you then be willing to change the system?
>
> DR. STEIN: No.
>
> DR. THUROW: You are saying that the system is more important than the result no matter how bad the result?
>
> DR. STEIN: Well, you have to give me a little room about how bad the result is, but I mean—
>
> DR. THUROW: I'll give you the result. Fifty years from now the American per capita GNP will be half that of the leading industrial country. Assume that were a fact. Would that then lead you to believe that we ought to change the system now?
>
> DR. STEIN: No.[3]

Finally, consider the following passage about India from Paul Ehrlich's *The Population Bomb:*

> I came to understand the population explosion emotionally one stinking hot night in Delhi. . . . The streets seemed alive with people. People eating, people washing, people sleeping, people visiting, arguing, and screaming. People thrusting their hands through the taxi window, begging. People defecating and urinating. People clinging to buses. People herding animals. People, people, people.[4]

What is remarkable about this passage is not that Ehrlich sees misery—after all, there *is* misery in India—but what he apparently does not see. He writes nothing about those people laughing, loving, or being tender to their children—all of which one also sees among poor Indians.

Ehrlich and other scientists have convinced a number of policymakers that rational population policies with respect to fertility, mortality, and

---

[3] Lester C. Thurow, *The Zero-Sum Solution: Building a World-Class American Economy* (New York: Simon & Schuster, 1985), p. 383.

[4] Paul R. Ehrlich. *The Population Bomb* (New York: Ballantine, 1968), p. 15.

immigration can be deduced directly from facts about population growth. While science can reveal the likely effects of various population levels and policies, it cannot show that population in a particular locale is too large. Such judgments depend on one's values. There are some values relevant to population policy:

- *Time discount rate.* The effect of children on the standard of living is clearly negative in short run. But if we give weight to the more distant future, then the overall effect of the additional child may be positive. (In Chapter 8, we discussed how the importance of the nearer versus the further future affects every investment decision.)

- *Altruism.* Should additional children or immigrants be welcomed into a community if these will be an immediate tax burden on you? Our willingness to share our wordly goods affects a variety of population-related policies.

- *Privacy.* How much of your isolation in the forest are you willing to give up so that others may enjoy the experience? (We can guess how Daniel Boone would have answered.)

- *Inherent value of human life.* Are some people's lives so poor that they would have been better off had they never been born? Is there no life so poor that it does not have value? (We do not have to guess how Mother Teresa would answer, nor do we have to guess Paul Ehrlich's response.)

- *A value for numbers of people.* The Bible says, "Be fertile and increase, fill the earth and master it." The "Greenpeace Philosophy" of the whole-protecting group says: "Ecology teaches us that mankind is not the center of the planet."[5]

As these examples suggest, it is impossible to define a value-neutral list of alternatives for assessment. People will consider different alternatives depending on what they have at stake and their perception of what constitutes a good outcome.[6]

---

[5] Julian L. Simon, *The Ultimate Resource* (Princeton, N.J.: Princeton University Press, 1981), pp. 332–35.

[6] Even when a project's objectives are clear, there is no way to make a value-neutral determination that enough alternatives have been considered. Consider the decision to site a toxic-chemical storage facility. Site evaluation is expensive: The area must be surveyed, the soil tested, and the underlying geologic structure evaluated. This process precludes analysis of all possible sites. An economist would tell us that an additional site should be considered if the expected marginal benefit from evaluating a site exceeds the cost of evaluation. But this calculation cannot be made mechanically. It requires a subjective assessment of the likelihood of different outcomes, the value to be ascribed to each outcome, and the rate at which we are willing to exchange certain costs for uncertain benefits. How large and how likely do the benefits have to be before we are willing to incur a three-month delay and $100,000 in additional site evaluation costs? Lawrence S. Bacow, "Exploring Environmental Impacts: Beyond Quantity," *Technology Review*, January 1982, p. 34.

Foreseeing consequences: A necessary condition for moral conduct

Only if we are aware of the consequences of our actions can we be moral. Policymakers, in particular, have an *obligation* to think through the possible impacts of their policy recommendations. In Chapters 7 and 8, I suggested that such an assessment was merely good operating procedure; here I wish to suggest that there exists a kind of moral imperative to do so. That being the case, let us see how one might proceed.

Governments frequently undertake activities that yield zero, or even negative, benefits but are worthwhile because of their distributional effects. Programs for the disadvantaged (through progressive taxation, transfer payments, job programs broadening equality of opportunity, the elimination of racial and sexual discrimination, and a lowering of barriers to access to capital) are clear-cut examples. Obviously, in addition to measuring the net benefits and costs of public programs, we need methods for considering the benefits that result from a more equitable distribution of benefits among members of the community.

Measuring redistributional benefits, however, is not easy. What makes such measurement especially difficult is that, when policymakers attempt to reduce certain inequities, economic efficiency is sometimes impaired. And yet, if the social system is to remain viable and democratic, some compromise between market efficiency and equity is essential—dollars should not always be allowed to transgress on right.

Clearly, some compromise is in order. But on what terms is a country such as the United States willing to trade equality for efficiency? Economics provides the following rule: promote equality up to the point where the added benefits of more equality are just matched by the added costs of greater efficiency. Although this rule may provide insight, it is hard to apply. As Arthur M. Okun has observed, "The consequences of most redistributive measures on both equality and efficiency are uncertain and debatable. Confronted with a proposed tax or welfare equalization, no legislator or voter can assess how much the program would add to equality or subtract from efficiency. Thus decision-makers do not get opportunities in the real world to test neatly their priorities between the two competing objectives."[7] Okun therefore proposes an experiment by which each of us can test our own attitudes about how we might make this trade-off between equity and efficiency.

Okun asks us to consider the American families who make up the bottom 20 percent of the income distribution (their aftertax incomes in 1984 were under $12,489), then to consider the top 5 percent of families

---

[7] Arthur M. Okun, *Equality and Efficiency* (Washington, D.C.: Brookings Institution, 1975), p. 99.

Figure 12–1
Okun's leaky-bucket experiment

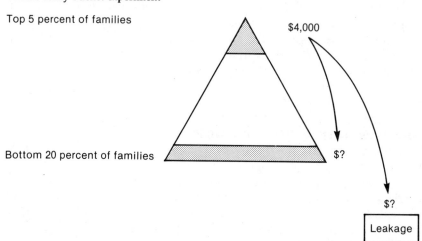

Top 5 percent of families

$4,000

Bottom 20 percent of families $?

$?

Leakage

in the income pyramid, whose aftertax incomes ranged upward from about $45,300 (see Figure 12–1). Assume that a proposal is made to levy an added tax averaging $4,000 on the income of the affluent families in an effort to aid the low-income families. Since the low-income group has four times as many families as the affluent group, that should, in principle, finance a $1,000 grant for the average low-income family. But the program has an unsolved technological problem: the money must be carried from the rich to the poor in a leaky bucket.

> Some of it will simply disappear in transit, so the poor will not receive all the money that is taken from the rich. The average poor family will get less than $1,000, while the average rich family gives up $4,000. How much leakage would you accept? Suppose 10 percent leaks out; that would leave $900 for the average poor family instead of the potential $1,000. Should society still make the switch? If 50 percent leaks out? If 75 percent? Even if 99 percent leaks out, the poor get a little benefit; the $4,000 taken from the rich family will yield $10 for each poor family. Where would you draw the line?

According to Okun, "Your answer cannot be right or wrong—any more than your favorite flavor of ice cream is right or wrong."

Okun continues:

> Of course, the leak represents an inefficiency. The inefficiencies of real-world redistribution include the adverse effects on the economic incentives of the rich and the poor, and the administrative costs of tax-collection and transfer programs. The opponent of redistribution might argue that my experiment obscures the dynamics of the incentive effects. He might contend that any

success in equalization today is likely to be transitory, as the adverse impact on work and investment incentives mounts over time and ultimately harms even the poor. What leaks out, he might insist, is the water needed to irrigate the next crop. In addition, anyone who views market-determined incomes as ethically ideal rewards for contribution would oppose the switch, regardless of the size of the leak.

On the other hand, some would keep switching from rich to poor as long as anything at all remains in the bucket. The philosopher John Rawls insists that "all social values . . . are to be distributed equally unless an unequal distribution of any . . . is to everyone's advantage."[8] In short, give priority to equality.

Okun's answer is not that neat:

> I cannot accept Rawls's egalitarian principle. It is supposed to emerge as a consensus of people in the "original position," when they develop social rules without knowing where their own future incomes will lie on the pyramid. But . . . that . . . principle would appeal only to people who hate to take any risk whatsoever. That is the implication of the view that no inequality is tolerable unless it raises the lowest income of the society. . . . Put the American people in an "original position," and I certainly would not expect them to act that way.
>
> If I were in Rawls's original position, I would argue that the social constitution should not seek to settle forever the precise weighting of inequality. It should instruct the society to weight equality heavily, but it should rely on the democratic political process it establishes to select reasonable weights on specific issues as they arise.

But unlike the opponent of income redistribution, Okun says that he would make the switch in the leaky-bucket experiment with enthusiasm if the leakage were 10 or 20 percent—though, unlike Rawls, he would stop short of the 99 percent leak. Since Okun feels obliged to play the farfetched games he makes up, he reports that he would stop at a leakage of 60 percent in this particular example. If the analyst's answer, like Okun's, lay somewhere between 1 and 99 percent, presumably the exact figure reflects some judgment of how much the poor needed the extra income and how much the rich would be pinched by the extra taxes.

Lester Thurow has addressed the equity issue with about as much specificity as one can. His solution to the nettlesome issue is ingenious and simple (as most elegant solutions are). He suggests that our general equity goal should be to establish a distribution of earnings for everyone that is no more unequal than that which exists for fully employed white males (see Table 12–1). "Since this distribution of earnings is

---

[8] John Rawls, *A Theory of Justice* (Cambridge, Mass.: Harvard University Press, 1971), p. 62.

614

Table 12–1
Distribution of earnings

| | Full-time, full-year | |
| | White males | All other workers |
Quintiles	(percent)	(percent)
1	7.7	1.8
2	13.9	7.2
3	18.2	15.8
4	23.5	27.0
5	36.7	48.2
Mean earnings	$16,568	$5,843

Source: U.S. Bureau of the Census, *Current Population Reports, Consumer Income 1977*, Series P–60, no. 118 (March 1979), p. 228.

the . . . incentive structure for white males, there are no problems with work incentives. With more than half of the labor force now participating in this natural lottery [for economic prizes], it is hardly a distribution of economic resources that anyone could consider un-American."[9]

Playing fast and loose with the evidence

Much earlier in our inquiry, I tried to establish the proposition that analysis is used in, and is subordinate to, the play of political power. That being the case, analysts must face pressures to manipulate the data, to bend the truth. Sometimes these pressures come from clients, other times they are self-generated.

Soft theories paraded as hard facts. Scientists have a special relationship with nuclear weapons. They invented them, which gives some of them a guilty conscience. They understand how they can be delivered or countered, which turns some into the partners of policymakers in enterprises such as the Strategic Defense Initiative or Star Wars. They command great public respect, which tempts some to present scientific theory as scientific fact in advocating this or that version of arms control. People respect science because when honest scientists disagree they at least try to obey important rules: to make plain the distinction between theory and evidence; to separate scientific issues from political ones; to listen with open minds to the criticisms of colleagues. In disagreements that touch on nuclear war, these rules are now being routinely breached. Many scientists are fighting their battles in newspapers and on television instead of in the sober columns of learned journals.

[9] Lester C. Thurow, *The Zero-Sum Society* (New York: Basic Books, 1980), pp. 200–201.

The theory that nuclear war will be followed by a life-extinguishing "nuclear winter" provides a cautionary tale. When it emerged in 1983 the idea was genuinely new. It was also important: people deserve to know that nuclear war could kill all life on earth, not just hundreds of millions of people in the countries involved. It is, none the less, just a theory. Eventually the detailed predictions began to unravel under closer scrutiny.[10] A nuclear winter is indeed possible, but, because of gaps in knowledge about the behaviour of the atmosphere and the oceans, nobody can be sure. Originally, proponents of the theory did say that their predictions were approximate. But this faint note of caution was lost in mass media reports. The false impression of certainty was reinforced when the spokesman for the hypothesis, Carl Sagan, an astronomer, used the (scientific) evidence to buttress his (political) opinion that there should be an immediate freeze on nuclear weapons.

Ignore or "select" the data. The federal government released to the press in 1978 a paper entitled *Estimates of the Fractions of Cancer in the United States Related to Occupational Factors.* Its authors were the National Cancer Institute, the National Institute of Environmental Health Sciences, and the National Institute of Occupational Safety.

The study was significant in several ways. First, it had never been published in a scientific journal or reviewed by other scientists; it had simply rolled off a government mimeograph machine. Second, it announced that six occupational carcinogens were going to cause as much as 40 percent or more of the cancers in the United States. This estimate clashed with estimates commonly made of the proportion of cancer associated with other factors. Tobacco had been said to account for 30 to 40 percent of all cancers in males, and tobacco interacting with alcohol had been said to account for 50 percent of male cancers. Nutritional factors had been said to account for 30 percent of all cancers in men and possibly more in women. In addition, sexual practices and reproductive habits had accounted for yet another proportion of the cancer rate. Clearly, if the new estimate that 40 percent or more of all cancer was linked to exposure in a factory was accepted, the other factors would have to shrink in significance. The implications of the study were stunning to many epidemiologists.[11]

Finally, the report predicted that past exposure to asbestos is expected to result in over two million premature cancer deaths in the next three decades. The asbestos death rates previously projected had been shock-

---

[10] U.S. General Accounting Office, *Nuclear Winter: Uncertainties Surround Long-Term Effects of Nuclear War*, NSIAD-86-62 (Washington, D.C.: Government Printing Office, March 1986).

[11] These studies are fully documented in Edith Efron, *The Apocalyptics: Politics, Science, and the Big Cancer Lie* (New York: Simon & Schuster, 1984).

ing enough—approximately 2,000 lung cancer deaths were being recorded among asbestos insulators (most of whom had also been heavy smokers). Never before had estimates of two million asbestos deaths been made.

Thomas Maugh of *Science* analyzed the study and explained its central error:

> In each case, the investigators have taken the highest risk ratio available— ratios obtained for workers exposed to massive concentrations of carcinogens—and multiplied that by the total number of workers who might have been exposed to the carcinogen, even though most or all of the workers have never been exposed to the concentrations upon which the risk ratios are based. . . . [The] investigators have also rather sloppily equated deaths with incidence, even though the number of deaths resulting from a tumor is clearly only some fraction of the incidence, depending on the tumor. In short, the HEW projections are clearly exaggerated.[12]

Richard Peto of Oxford mocked the study's asbestos estimates. Observing that they were "possibly 1,000" times higher than the 2,000 deaths indicated in previous studies, he said that the four million men said to be employed in the asbestos industry were "all being treated as though they had been asbestos insulators for years. It's comical."[13]

Partisanship in use of data appears in other areas of public policy, and one need not be a scientist or statistician to detect it. Lester Thurow has repeated over the past decade his considered conclusion that, despite all the spending programs of the welfare state, the distribution of incomes among American families has remained approximately fixed since the end of World War II.[14] How can he draw this conclusion, when most people think income distribution has changed? Thurow simply ignores relevant data. He chooses to use Census Bureau statistics that show money income received by families *before* payment of income taxes and that excludes nonmoney income provided by the government such as outlays for medicaid, food stamps, housing, and other in-kind benefits for the poor.

Ethical issues during implementation

Ethical policymakers will exercise restraint on the means chosen to attain the goals and objectives of a policy. More specifically, this means:

---

[12] Thomas, Maugh, "Justice, EPA Begin Hazardous Waste Drive," *Science*, 207 (1980), p. 162.

[13] Cited in Efron, *The Apocalyptics*, p. 212.

[14] Thurow, *The Zero-Sum Society*, pp. 156–157, and (with Robert L. Heilbroner), *The Economic Problem* (Englewood Cliffs, N.J.: Prentice-Hall, 1975), p. 215.

1. They will not violate the law or the civil liberties of individuals.
2. They will apply laws and regulations fairly.
3. They will knowingly do no harm.
4. They will not undermine citizen trust in government.

Though deceptively simple (cynics might say platitudinous), these four guidelines involve a profound "tension between restraint carried to the point of inertia and a blind commitment to results."[15]

Presidents at least as far back as Franklin Roosevelt have used extralegal means to protect their policies—and themselves. Roosevelt created his own intelligence unit, responsible only to himself and used the FBI to tap phones of staff aides, political opponents, and journalists.[16] Attorney General Robert Kennedy had FBI agents carry out raids on the homes of executives of U.S. Steel who had defied the economic policies of President John Kennedy. To carry out his civil rights policies, President Kennedy used the federal contract system and executive order rather than legislation. Under Johnson, phone-tapping increased markedly.[17]

But Nixon went further than any of his predecessors. His secretary of state, Henry Kissinger, describes the tension he faced:

> That wiretapping is distasteful is unquestionable. But so is the willful and unauthorized disclosure of military and diplomatic secrets in the middle of a war. . . . [A] dangerous practice was growing in the bureaucracy: Some who disagreed with national policy felt free to try to sabotage it by leaking classified information in clear violation of the law. . . . The media took the position that . . . it was up to the administration to keep its own secrets.[18]

By the spring of 1969, Nixon and Kissinger had become convinced that the leaks of military operations and sensitive negotiations with Hanoi were jeopardizing American lives. Attorney General John Mitchell and FBI Director J. Edgar Hoover recommended a program; Nixon ordered it; Kissinger assisted in identifying those persons to the FBI who had access to the leaked information. In reflecting about the subject, Kissinger writes:

---

[15] Donald P. Warwick, "The Ethics of Administrative Discretion" in *Public Duties: The Moral Obligations of Government Officials* ed. Joel L. Fleishman, Lance Liebman, and Mark Moore (Cambridge, Mass.: Harvard University Press, 1981), p. 123.

[16] Richard W. Steele, "Franklin D. Roosevelt and his Foreign Policy Critics," *Political Science Quarterly*, Spring 1979, p. 22. See also Robert Dallek, *Franklin D. Roosevelt and American Foreign Policy, 1932–45* (New York: Oxford University Press, 1979), pp. 224–26, 289–90, 313, 334–36.

[17] U.S. Congress, Select Committee to Study Government Operations with Respect to Intelligence Activities, *Final Report, Book III: Supplementary Detailed Staff Reports on Intelligence Activities and Rights of Americans* (Washington, D.C.: Government Printing Office, April 23, 1976), pp. 271–351.

[18] Henry Kissinger, *Years of Upheaval* (Boston: Little, Brown, 1982), pp. 119–20.

I believe now that the more stringent safeguards applied to national security wiretapping since that time reflect an even more fundamental national interest—but this in no way alters my view of the immorality of those who, in their contempt for their trust, attempted to sabotage national policies and risked American lives.

In retrospect it is also clear to me that while electronic surveillance is a widely used method of investigation in democracies, the wiretapping of one's associates presents an especially painful human problem. I was never at ease about it; it is the part of my public service about which I am most ambivalent. At the time, I simply preferred it to the alternative, which was to separate from their posts those who were suspected of unauthorized disclosures of information.[19]

Another of the ethical tensions that can arise during implementation concerns public participation. The case for public participation and openness has been made so effectively, and in so much a part of the contemporary American consensus, that it needs no elaboration from me. But participation has its costs, and the policy implementor must somehow balance these against the moral imperatives of openness. Harlan Cleveland of the University of Minnesota sums up the costs of participation this way:

> An open meeting is likely to be large. The larger it is, the higher the ratio of emotion to reason, nonsense to common sense. An open meeting favors simple formulations over complicated ones, certainty over ambiguity, the loudmouth over the reflective private person. An open meeting is more apt to generate confrontation than compromise, it will probably result in inaction rather than action, and it will likely be prone to caution and delay rather than innovation and impetus.[20]

I will be brief with regard to the second and third points. The second point raises the question of what is "fair." I will return to that question later in the chapter. The third point is actually the motto of the medical profession: *primum non nocere* ("above all, not knowingly to do harm"). I can think of no reason why policymakers should not follow it.

An example of why point four (not to undermine citizen trust) matters can be found in the rumor campaign that Reagan's national security adviser, John Poindexter, developed to destabilize Muammar Qaddafi in Libya. The idea was to combine real and illusionary events—through a disinformation program—to make Qaddafi think that there was a high degree of internal opposition to him in Libya and that the United States was about to move against him militarily. Misleading Qaddafi was one thing, but what troubled the American media was that it had

---

[19] Ibid., p. 121.

[20] Harlan Cleveland, *The Knowledge Executive: Leadership in an Information Society* (New York: E. P. Dutton, 1985), p. 61.

been misinformed as well. A *New York Times* editorial summarized the reasons for the journalistic outrage: "All media, all Americans, are vulnerable because they must trust their government to some degree. The deliberate abuse of that trust is a scandal of the first magnitude."[21]

Moreover, shortly after this episode occurred an American supplying arms to the contras was shot down in Nicaragua. He and his Sandinista captors claimed to be working for the CIA; the administration denied it. Whereas most Americans would be inclined to believe their government rather than a man under duress and a Marxist government, the Qaddafi episode had reduced the administration's credibility.

Tensions in evaluating policy

Ethical tensions arise during policy evaluation. One of the most controversial issues concerns how experiments are conducted on human subjects. Before putting a few contemporary examples on the table, let us consider one nearly two hundred years old. By telling the story, I hope to dramatize the tension between our attempt to shake off our subjectivity, to be "scientific," and our affective attachments to other human beings.

The forbidden experiment. Nearly two centuries have passed since the wild boy known as Victor was captured in Aveyron, France, and trotted around Paris on a leash as a specimen of natural man.[22] Although he was the talk of the town for a few months in 1800, he had been forgotten by the time he died, half-tame and mute, in 1828. Why does he still haunt our consciousness? The wild boy personified the "forbidden experiment" that has hovered over all speculation about human nature. If a child could be cut off from family, language, and all exchange with other human beings, what sort of creature would he be? Does a bedrock humanity exist beyond culture?

Eventually, a committee of experts decided that Victor was an idiot who had been abandoned in the forest by his parents. At this point, Jean-Marc Gaspard Itard, a young doctor, took over the case. For five years, Itard worked with Victor, slowly awakening his senses and developing his mental faculties. By 1806, the child who had wandered about naked in subfreezing temperatures had developed a fondness for warm baths and clean sheets. He ate fully cooked food with a fork and spoon.

Thus Itard boldly confronted the giants of his profession by curing the incurable and penetrating the inner recesses of human nature. His experiments with Victor looked promising, went wrong, were rede-

---

[21] Editorial, *New York Times*, October 9, 1986.
[22] The account of Victor is based on Roger Shattuck, *The Forbidden Experiment: The Story of the Wild Boy of Aveyron* (New York: Farrar, Strauss & Giroux, 1980).

signed, seemed to work, ran into impasses, were abandoned—and through it all the scientist slides imperceptibly into an emotional rapport with the creature that he had placed somewhere between plant and animal life. For instance, Itard tried to teach the young savage to recognize the sounds of vowels. Victor seemed to enjoy the game. Blindfolded and laughing, he held up different fingers as Itard made different vowel sounds. But he could not keep them straight. To stop the giggling and correct the errors, Itard rapped him over the knucles with a stick.

> Tears trickled down from under the blindfold, and I hastened to take it off. But, out of embarrassment or fear or absorption in his own feelings, he kept his eyes closed even though the blindfold was off. I cannot describe the pained expression on his face with his eyes closed and every so often a tear coming out between the lids. Oh! at that moment as at many others when I was ready to give up the task I had imposed on myself and when I looked on all my time as wasted, how deeply I regretted ever having known this child, and how I condemned the barren and inhuman curiosity of those men who first uprooted him from an innocent and happy life!

Itard decided to experiment with injustice. After an especially successful session of puzzle solving when Victor was beaming with pride and primed for a reward, Itard slammed the props to the floor and dragged the boy toward a closet in which he had been shut up on earlier occasions as a form of punishment. Victor resisted, flailed about in Itard's arms, and finally in a paroxysm of rage bit him on the hand. "How wonderful it would have been at that moment to be able to make myself understood to my pupil, to tell him how that pain filled my soul with satisfaction and repaid me for all my trials! . . . I had raised a savage to the full stature of moral man."

Itard wanted to understand Victor yet clearly did not want to harm him, and there lies the tension that haunts all experimenters: They want to know the effects of a proposed policy yet do not want to harm anyone who would not have otherwise been harmed.

Contemporary tensions. As we saw in the last chapter, in national policy experiments, people are randomly assigned to experiment groups and control groups. Welfare recipients are given different amounts of aid to see how differences affect their incentive to seek work. Ex-convicts are given different amounts of unemployment compensation to see how differences affect their commission of crimes. Suspects in domestic violence cases are either arrested for eight hours or given advice only to see how different police actions affect repeat violence. AIDS patients are either given a possible cure or a placebo to test the efficacy of the new drug. In these four examples, one group receives what appears at the outset to be potentially much better treatment than another. In the last example, one group receives, in effect, a death sentence.

Tensions also abound between program administrators, who believe in what they are doing, and evaluators, who may be skeptical. Some question whether the former should ever be involved in evaluation.

But evaluators often have their own ideological biases. Sarnoff A. Mednick at the University of Southern California was sharply criticized for reporting that, even when placed in healthy environments, the children of criminals are more likely than children of noncriminals to engage in criminal behavior.[23] The environmental school of psychology maintains that misbehavior is almost entirely caused by environmental deficiencies—slum conditions, poor education, lack of ready cash—all of which could be cured by outlays of government money. Anyone challenging the environmental position becomes a threat to a great number of persons who have a stake in maintaining the dogma (that is, persons maintaining the social agencies and politicians dispensing benefits), and it is not surprising that denunciations are swift and sweeping.

Had Mednick merely observed children of criminals brought up by their parents it could well have been argued that any apparent leanings toward criminal behavior were caused by their surroundings. Instead, he examined the records of 14,427 Danish children adopted shortly after birth by nonrelatives between 1924 and 1947. He compared the criminal records of real and adoptive parents, and similar records of the children. Among the natural children of parents having three or more convictions, he found 20 percent of the sons had at least one conviction, while only 13.5 percent of the sons of those real parents who have never been in serious trouble with the law had conviction records. There was no clear difference in violent crimes. The difference lay in crimes against property.

Given the ubiquity of ethics, what should the policymaker do? The next two sections review some important attempts to answer that basic question.

ECONOMIC ETHICS

Economics is probably the social science discipline that contains the most systematic ethical discourse. As advisers, economists are called on to read and evaluate a constant flow of policy proposals. Given the enormous diversity of public policies, they have tried to develop some kind of general framework to organize their thoughts about whether a government action is right or wrong. The framework used by most economists with a public policy orientation is *welfare economics*.

---

[23] Sarnoff A. Mednick, "Genetic Influences in Criminal Conviction: Evidence from an Adoption Cohort," *Science* 224 (1984), pp. 891–94.

In this section, we will approach economic ethics by examining its history. We will consider the "old" welfare economics, associated with the work of Jeremy Bentham, an English writer whose career spanned over sixty years from the early 1770s to 1832. Next, we will consider the "new" welfare economics that supplanted the old in the 1930s. Last, we will consider a more recent suggestion that cost-benefit analysis can incorporate ethical considerations.

In "old" welfare economics: Utilitarianism

Jeremy Bentham. In 1780, Jeremy Bentham gave an elaborate statement of the utilitarian viewpoint which was to have enormous influence on economic thinking during the last several decades of the nineteenth century. He began by asserting that all human motivation, in all times and all places, can be reduced to a single principle: the desire to maximize one's utility. By utility, he meant the satisfaction or pleasure derived from consuming some quantity of a good. "Nature," he wrote

> has placed mankind under the governance of two sovereign masters, *pain* and *pleasure*. It is for them alone to point out what we ought to do, as well as to determine what we shall do. . . . They govern us in all we do, in all we say, in all we think. . . . The *principle of utility* recognizes this subjection, and assumes it for the foundation of [its social theory].[24]

By reducing all motivations to a simple principle, Bentham thought that he had found the key to the construction of a science of human welfare. Pleasure and the avoidance of pain were ends, and because they could be quantified, we can understand this value.

In Benthamite welfare economics, the welfare of a society is defined by how well off its individual members are. Because each individual's utility can be calculated (or so Bentham believed), we can say algebraically that social welfare, W, is equal to the sum of all individual's utilities:

$$W = U_1 + U_2 + U_3 + U_4 + \ldots + U_n$$

An increase in any U *increases* W. A change that makes someone better off without making anyone worse off increases the social welfare.

Now suppose that public policy aims to maximize W. Assume further that as an individual's income increases, he become better off, but at a decreasing rate. In the jargon of economics, we say that his utility function exhibits diminishing marginal utility of income. But the idea is quite simple: The pleasure derived from the second million is not as great as from the first. Now assume that the utility functions of every

---

[24] Jeremy Bentham, *An Introduction to the Principles of Morals & Legislation* (New York: Pegasus, 1969), p. 85.

Figure 12–2
Optimal distribution of income in a very simple society

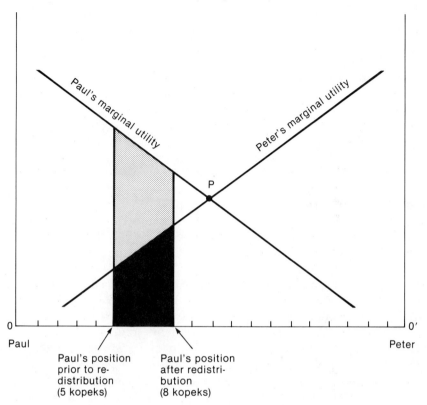

man and woman are identical. Finally, assume that the total amount of available income is fixed.

Under this set of assumptions and the equation stated above, what would the optimal income distribution be? The answer is *complete equality.* Although this answer might come to you in an intuitive flash, we can prove it by considering a society consisting of only two people, Peter and Paul.

In Figure 12–2, the horizontal distance 00′ measures the total amount of income available in this society, 20 kopeks. Paul's income is measured by the distance to the right of point 0; Peter's income, by the distance to the left of point 0′. Thus any point along 00′ represents some distribution of income between Paul and Peter.

The vertical distance above point 0 measures Paul's marginal utility of income. It slopes downward because, as we assumed above, each extra kopek is not quite as wonderful as the previous kopek. Because

Peter and Paul have identical utility functions, Peter's marginal utility of income is the mirror image of Paul's.

Assume that Paul's income is a meager five kopeks, and Paul's is fifteen. Suppose we take three kopeks from Peter and give them to Paul. What happens to the *sum* of their utilities? (Ignore Peter's complaints.) Because Peter is richer, his loss in utility is smaller than Paul's gain, so the sum of their utilities goes up. Taking three kopeks from Peter decreases his utility by the darkly shaded area. Giving three kopeks to Paul increases his utility by the darkly shaded area *plus* the lightly shaded area. Therefore the sum of their utilities increases under this transfer arrangement.

Similar reasoning suggests that as long as incomes are unequal, the sum of utilities can be increased by distributing income to the poorer individual. Only at point P, where incomes and marginal utilities are equal, is social welfare maximized or "optimal."

But wait. Can we really know that Peter and Paul derive the same satisfaction from the consumption of goods? Perhaps Paul read Henry David Thoreau's *Walden,* as he observed Peter rising to what he then saw as wealth. Perhaps he heeded the book's message, and simplified his life, resisted the attractiveness of the dominant cultural objective of pursuing goods, resisted a narrow definition of fortune. Perhaps it gave him the courage to do other things and to accept the consequences.

These objections to the model are not new. John Stuart Mill, a professed disciple and contemporary of Bentham, insisted that some pleasure could be judged as morally superior to other pleasures. If this is true, then there must be some higher principle than the pleasure principle of utilitarianism whereby moral judgments among different pleasures become possible. Mill asserted that some kinds of pleasure are more desirable and more valuable than others. For example, regardless of the quantity of pleasure involved, poetry may be judged to be more desirable and valuable than poker. Mill had no doubt that it was better to be Socrates dissatisfied than a fool satisfied. This utterly destroys the basis on which Bentham had constructed his economic theory.[25]

One other aspect of the argument for income equity merits scrutiny: the assumption that the total income in the society, distance 00', is fixed, that the size of the pie does not change as government redistributes its pieces from Peter to Paul.

Public policies to redistribute income will generally change people's work decisions and diminish total real income. Thus, a society whose goal is to maximize the sum of utilities faces the inescapable dilemma noted earlier in the chapter: the trade-off between equality and efficiency.

---

[25] John Stuart Mill, *Utilitarianism, Liberty, and Representative Government* (New York: Dutton, 1951).

Figure 12–3
Trade-off between equality and efficiency

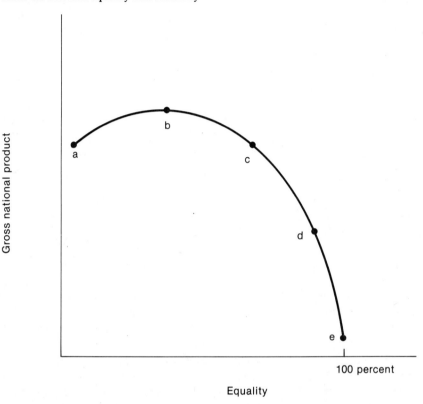

A society that rigorously pursues the goal of equality will, in the process, reduce the total income available. Figure 12–3 illustrates this lesson. The curve *abcde* represents possible combinations of GNP and income equality that are obtainable under the present system of taxes and transfers. If, for example, point *c* is the current position of the economy, raising taxes on the rich to finance more transfers to the poor might move as downward to the right, toward point *d*. The GNP falls as the rich react to the higher taxes by producing less. Achieving more equality, like most things in life, has its price. Some studies suggest that the price may be substantial. Edgar K. Browning and William R. Johnson estimate that each dollar increase in the disposable income of the lowest 40 percent of the income distribution requires a reduction of more than *nine* dollars of the disposable incomes of the highest 60 percent.[26]

---

[26] Edgar K. Browning and William R. Johnson, "The Trade-Off between Equality and Efficiency," *Journal of Political Economy*, April 1984, pp. 175–203.

John Rawls's theory of justice. In the equation above for the social welfare, we made no distinction about who received utilities (or "utils"). But some might wish to weight utils and give certain individuals more than others. Then the equation would need to be rewritten:

$$W = a_1U_1 + a_2U_2 + a_3U_3 + \ldots + a_nU_n$$

The higher an individual's *a*, the greater the weight that society attaches to a change in his utility.

"A decent provision for the poor," Samuel Johnson said, "is the true test of civilization." Suppose a society took Dr. Johnson seriously and attached a great value to increasing the utilities of its poor. This society would assign high *a*'s to individuals with low utilities and vice versa. Thus, the strength of this society's preferences for equality can be measured by the relative magnitudes of the social weights for high- and low-utility individuals. At the extreme, a society could give weight only to the individual with the lowest utility. Because the objective is to maximize the utility of the person with the minimum utility, this social objective is often called *maximin criterion*. Income distribution, the criterion suggests, should be perfectly equal *except* to the extent that departure from equality increases the welfare of the worst-off person. For example, Peter employs Paul, a poor person. Government taxes Peter and distributes the money to Paul. But Peter's taxes are so onerous that he must fire Paul. Moreover, Paul's paycheck had been greater than his government benefits. In this hypothetical example, the maximin criterion would still allow some income disparity.

John Rawls, an influential philosopher at Harvard, argues that the maximin criterion is *morally* correct.[27] He asks us to imagine a situation in which we have no knowledge of what our places in society will be—we do not know who our parents will be, our race, our physical handicaps, or our intelligence. In this position, Rawls believes that our opinions concerning distributional goals will be fair and impartial. What would you choose? Rawls thinks people will adopt the maximin criterion because of the insurance it provides against disastrous outcomes. You will find it harder perhaps to make your first million, but you have lessened your chances of freezing to death under a bridge.

At least four objections to Rawls's theory may be entered at this point. The first is empirical: Are people really that risk adverse?

> If you can make one heap of all your winning;
>> And risk it on one turn of pitch-and-toss,
> And lose, and start again at your beginnings
>> And never breathe a word about your loss;[28]

[27] John Rawls, *A Theory of Justice* (Cambridge, Mass.: Harvard University Press, 1971).
[28] Rudyard Kipling, "If" in M. E. Speare, ed., *The Pocket Book of Verse* (New York: Pocket Books, 1940), p. 346.

Was Kipling engaging in poetic excess or unmasking the human psyche? The second objection is ethical. Rawls seems to take for granted that individuals' incomes are common property which can be redistributed as government sees fit. He gives no attention to the fairness of either the processes that determine the initial income distribution or the procedures used to redistribute it. Some would argue that the process by which income is distributed is crucial.

One of the more cogent presentations of this libertarian position has come from Robert Nozick.[29] He claims that, if the world were wholly just, the only people entitled to hold anything—that is, to appropriate it for use as they wish—would be those who had justly acquired what they held by some just act of acquisition. For example, if equal opportunity had been available to all, then any resulting distribution of income would be just. Nozick's position has merit. Incomes, including those of the relatively prosperous or the owners of property, are not taken from other people. Normally they are produced by their recipients and the resources they own; they are not misappropriated from others; they do not deprive other people of what they have had or might have had.

Nozick is particularly effective at revealing the underlying contradiction in Rawls' egalitarianism—at least in free societies. Political action that deliberately aimed to minimize, or even remove, economic differences (i.e., differences in income and wealth) would entail such extensive coercion that the society might cease to be open and free. The successful pursuit of economic equality might exchange the promised reduction of differences in income and wealth for greater inequality of power between rulers and subjects.

The third objection is both empirical and ethical. Given sufficient social mobility in a society (an empirical question), the distribution of income is of no particular interest (an ethical conclusion). In other words, even if people at the bottom are poor, it is not a problem if the people there are constantly changing. But how much churning within the income distribution is enough? One government study found that one fifth of the people classified as being poor in the first of the study remained poor for the duration of the study (six years).[30]

The fourth objection, which strikes at the heart of utilitarianism, is a practical one. We do not know how to make people happy. Karl Popper, a prominent philosopher of science, writes:

> I believe that there is, from an ethical point of view, no symmetry between suffering and happiness, or between pain and pleasure. . . . human suffering

---

[29] Robert Nozick, *Anarchy, State and Utopia* (Oxford: Basil Blackwell, 1974).
[30] U.S. Department of Health, Education and Welfare, *The Changing Economic Status of 5,000 American Families* (Washington, D.C.: Government Printing Office, 1974).

628

makes direct moral appeal, namely, the appeal for help, while there is no similar call to increase the happiness of a man who is doing well anyway. . . . Instead of the greatest happiness for the greatest number, one should demand, more modestly, the least amount of avoidable suffering for all. . . .[31]

As a guiding principle of public policy, "minimize avoidable suffering" has the immediate effect of drawing attention to *problems*. If, say, a state education department set itself the goal of maximizing opportunity for school children, it might not be sure how to proceed. But it sets itself the goal of *minimizing disadvantage,* its attention would focus immediately on those schools with the worst staffing problems, most over-crowding, most decrepit buildings, and least instructional equipment. Doing something about them would be the first priority. Popper's approach encourages policymakers to think about removing specific social evils rather than building Utopias.

The new welfare economics: Pareto optimality

The subsequent evolution of economics took it far from the simple concept of utility as a measure of usefulness and motivation. To trace this evolution would take us well beyond the scope of this work. The important point is, however, this. The old welfare economics assumed that utility could be ascertained objectively (Bentham) or that aspects of experience were known to constitute the good (Mill and Rawls). In the new welfare economics such assertions were considered nothing more than personal preferences.[32]

To examine the new welfare economics, let us return to an example introduced in the first chapter: There are only two people, Adam and Eve, who consume two commodities with fixed supply. The only problem in this simple economy is to allocate fig leaves and apples between them.

Figure 12–4 will help us see the problem better. The length of the box, *Os*, represents the total number of apples in the economy or nineteen apples; the height, *Or*, is the number of fig leaves or thirteen. Every point within the box represents a specific allocation of apples and figs. For example, at point *p*, Adam consumes seven fig leaves and six apples, while Eve consumes six fig leaves and thirteen apples.

An *indifference curve* is a line connecting all combinations of the commodities in question that are equally desirable to a person. Suppose

---

[31] Karl Popper, *The Open Society and Its Enemies,* vol. 2 (Princeton, N.J.: Princeton University Press, 1964), pp. 284–85.
[32] Duncan MacRae, Jr., *The Social Function of Social Science* (New Haven, Conn., Yale, 1976), pp. 107–57.

Figure 12–4
Adam's indifference curve

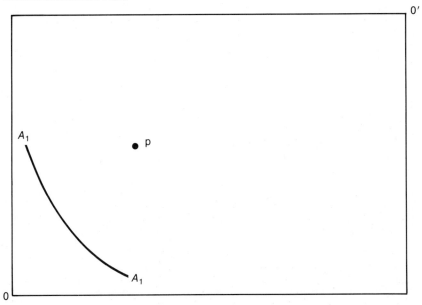

for instance that Adam is offered a choice between two bundles: bundle 1, which contains four fig leaves and two apples; and bundle 2, which contains one fig leaf and five apples. Will he prefer one to two, or two to one, or is he indifferent about which one he gets? Indifference curves like those shown in Figure 12–4 provide this preference information. Since both bundles are on Adam's indifference curve, A_1A_1, he would be equally pleased with either bundle.

Figure 12–5 shows several indifference curves for both Adam and Eve. The numbering of indifference curves corresponds to higher levels of happiness ("utility"). Adam is higher on indifference curve A_3 than A_2 or A_1. Eve is happier on E_3 than on E_2 or E_1.

Let us say that the distribution of apples and fig leaves is point g in Figure 12–6. Note that Adam's indifference curve A_gA_g runs through this point, as does Eve's E_gE_g. Could we reallocate apples and fig leaves in such a way that Adam is better off but Eve no worse? Point h is such a point. Adam is better off, and A_hA_h represents a higher utility level for him. Eve is no worse for the reallocation because she is still on her original indifference curve. This process of putting Adam on ever higher indifference curves can be continued until Adam's indifference curve just touches E_gE_g; that occurs at point p. At this point, the only way we can put Adam on a higher curve is to put Eve on a lower one. An allocation such as point p, at which the only way to make

630

Figure 12–5
Adam and Eve's indifference curves

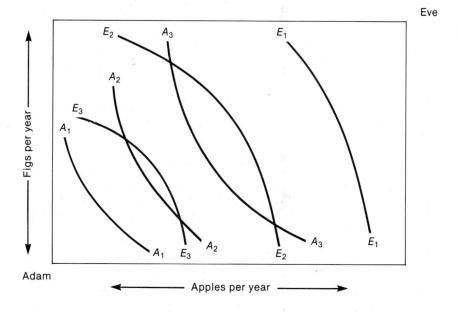

Figure 12–6
An optimal distribution in Eden

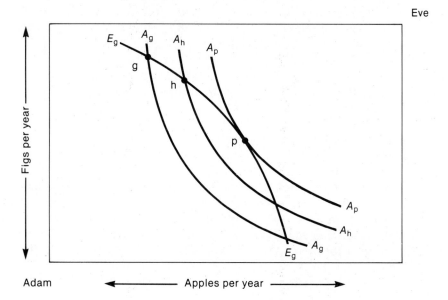

one person better off is to make another person worse off is called *Pareto efficient*.

A major contribution of the new welfare economics is the *fundamental theorem of welfare economics*. The theorem states that a *properly* working competitive market generates a Pareto efficient allocation of resources without any government intervention. (Conditions for a properly working competitive market were discussed in Chapter 4.) But it is not obvious that efficiency is everything; some argue that equity must also be considered, even traded off with efficiency. Furthermore, markets do not conform perfectly to the definition of competitive used in the theorem, though some approach it. Therefore, in the real world we do not achieve a competitive market determination of the allocation of resources.

In sum, the new welfare economics suggest that there is an opportunity for government to intervene in the economy to modify the distribution of income and enhance economic efficiency. But opportunities are not mandates. The Theory of Nonmarket Failures (Core Idea 13) should alert us to the fact that public policy does not always work better than an imperfect market. Therefore, once a situation has been identified in which government intervention *may* lead to higher social welfare, policymakers must ask hard questions. Will the costs of setting up a government agency to deal with an externality cost more than the externality itself? What unintended consequences might lurk behind the policy proposal?

Applied welfare economics: Cost-benefit analysis revisited

The preceding discussion focused on the preferences of individuals. Recall government robbing Peter to pay Paul and Adam and Eve swapping their apples and fig leaves. The realities of policymaking in Washington, in the statehouse, in the courthouse differ from those in economic lectures and Eden. If we wish to compare the effects of two public policies on an individual, there is something to be said for using *prices* instead of preferences. We could estimate the amount of goods each policy would produce for the individual and then estimate his preferences for the policies in terms of benefits (dollars) received. If the individual experienced costs as well, we could subtract them and estimate his preference for the two policies in terms of net benefits. The resulting analysis of benefits and costs could be considered an applied form of welfare economics.[33]

A poet might charge that using economic analysis to calculate the precise costs and benefits associated with a public policy borders on the immoral. At the very least, the exercise ignores higher human values.

---

[33] Ibid., p. 129.

It is not a surprise that many economists think otherwise. In their view, *any* value can be included in cost-benefit analysis provided we have the ingenuity to specify the relative importance of any value in comparison with other values. Indeed, modern economics is designed for considering relationships among values.

Actually, microeconomic theory in general and cost-benefit analysis in particular are well designed for considering relationships among values. The classical economists of the nineteenth century constantly spoke about the "theory of value." By value they meant price; they wanted to know how prices are determined, what forces and factors determine the value of any good or service in terms of another good or service. The use of one good, money, in price theory permits a ready comparison to be made between any two particular goods or services. This does not mean that money is the only value but simply that it frequently proves to be a useful way to measure the *relative* value among competing aims or goods.

To repeat a point made earlier, policy analysts should give recognition to values such as individualism, freedom, truth, justice, love, beauty, generosity, tolerance, community, environment, and so forth. Sometimes these values conflict with one another. We have already seen this in the case of equality of efficiency, and Box 12–1 provides several additional instances of this conflict. In such cases, when trade-offs have to be made, Charles Wolf thinks that economics can help:

> These trade-offs can alternatively be expressed as "opportunity costs": the cost of one social or ethical value is the foregone opportunity to realize more of a conflicting ethical or moral value. The opportunity cost of achieving more of one ethical "value" is the "price" of that increment. More equal distribution of income and wealth may be achieved at a cost of less rapid growth. . . . Insistence on cleaner air standards may be at the expense of greater vulnerability to an oil embargo, and so on.
>
> Hence, I suggest that the tools and concepts of economic price theory (for example, demand functions, supply and production functions, possibility frontiers, substitution possibilities, and elasticities), are potentially useful and applicable to the analysis of ethical issues in connection with public policy. Opportunity costs are no less a characteristic of social and ethical values, or of morals, than they are of food, clothing, shelter, education, recreation, medical care, and other "economic" values.
>
> . . . if ethical and moral values are to be better understood, and be more useful and more influential in public policy analysis and public management, then the opportunity costs associated with any single ethical value or group of values should be identified and evaluated in formulating and choosing among alternative courses of action.[34]

---

[34] Charles Wolf, Jr., "Ethics and Policy Analysis," in Fleishman, Liebman, and Moore, *Public Duties*, pp. 139–40.

Box 12–1
Health and competing values

But surely health is more important than anything else! Is it? Those who take this position are fond of contrasting our unmet health needs with the money that is "wasted" on cosmetics, cigarettes, pet foods, and the like. "Surely," it is argued, "we can afford better health if we can afford colored telephones." But putting the question in this form is misleading. For one thing, there are other goals, such as justice, beauty, and knowledge, which also clearly remain unfulfilled because of resource limitations. In theory, our society is committed to providing a speedy and fair trial to all persons accused of crimes. "Justice delayed is justice denied." In practice, we know that our judicial system is rife with delays. . . . We also know that part of the answer to getting a fairer and more effective judicial system is to devote more resources to it.

What about beauty. . . ? How often do we read that a beautiful stand of trees could be saved if a proposed road were rerouted or some other (expensive) change made? . . . Knowledge also suffers. Anyone who has ever had to meet a budget for an educational or research enterprise knows how resource limitations constrain the pursuit of knowledge.

. . . We may give lip service to the idea that health comes first, but a casual inspection of our everyday behavior with respect to diet, drink, and exercise belies this claim. Most of us could be healthier than we are, but at some cost.

Source: Victor R. Fuch, *Who Shall Live? Health, Economics, and Social Choice* (New York: Basic Books, 1974), pp. 18–19.

The application of economics to ethical issues will require more ingenious efforts to translate a wide range of values into practical terms. For example, if alternative flood control projects are being evaluated, outcomes should be assessed according to a wide range of norms, including reduced risk of flood, impacts on flora and fauna, losses and gains in recreational activities, and effects on oceangoing shipping. Obviously, each of these norms reflects a different view of social values, of what is important to differing groups and interests in the community. The policy options should be evaluated according to these several norms, as well as the attendant costs and direct economic effects. The policy analyst's aim should be to highlight the trade-off associated with each option, making the choice dependent on the relative weights assigned policymakers to the conflicting norms.

Still, economic reasoning cannot make a moral dilemma in public policy vanish. Suppose gas prices rise, inflicting an undue burden on poor consumers. Instead of permitting the increase, fairness to the poor might suggest rationing. But, in fact, rationing hurts both rich and poor, because the rich would be willing to pay the poor the market price to buy their ration coupons. The reason the poor would be willing to sell their coupons is that they are constrained to do so by their smaller incomes, a fact that suggests to many a moral problem in the first place. Therefore, instead of rationing, suppose we place a tax on gas and use its revenues to subsidize poor gas consumers. But this action does not get rid of the moral question. Why should the tax revenues go to poor gas consumers but not to even poorer nongas consumers? The more effectively economics resolves the smaller moral dilemmas of public policy, the closer it may nudge the political agenda to major questions of redistribution that lie outside its purview. Perhaps it is time to leave the realm of welfare economics and try to think about ethics in some other way.

POLITICAL ETHICS

Politics and ethics cannot be easily separated. Ethical questions are always in part political questions, because the human being is part of a historical people, a culture, an ethos, a political system, and an economic system. Moreover, political issues about civil rights, criminal justice, nuclear war, guerrilla war, illegal aliens, health care, and the like require that the policymaker be able to fashion and understand moral reasoning. American history does not teem with examples of policymakers who excelled at this sort of thing, but the few it does offer up are worthy of our careful consideration.

The Lincoln-Douglas debate reconsidered

A memorable series of debates occurred in 1858 in Illinois between Abraham Lincoln and Senator Stephen A. Douglas. No arguments in the English language have more shrewdness, luminosity, or moral force, than those used by Lincoln to demolish Douglas' proposal to allow the extension of slavery into free territory.

When a politician appeals to morals the public expects intolerance and overstatement, and perhaps a harsh demand for some unrealistic reform. But Lincoln could use moral arguments humbly and simply, and the people listened when he replied to Douglas's well-polished defense of slavery in the territories (the Kansas-Nebraska Act):

> I think I have no prejudice against the southern people They are just what we would be in their situation. If slavery did not now exist among them, they would not introduce it. If it did now exist among us, we should not instantly give it up. . . . If all earthly power were given me, I should not know what to do, as to the existing institution. . . . But all this, to my

judgment, furnishes no more excuse for permitting slavery to go into our free territory, than it would for reviving the African slave trade by law. The law which forbids the bringing of slaves *from* Africa; and that which has so long forbid the taking of them *to* Nebraska, could hardly be distinguished on any moral principle; and the repeal of the former could find as plausible excuses as that of the latter. . . .

But Nebraska is urged as a great Union-saving measure. Well, I too, go for saving the Union. Much as I hate slavery, I would consent to the extension of it rather than see the Union dissolved, just as I would consent to any *great* evil, to avoid a *greater* one. But when I go to Union saving I must believe, at least, that the means I employ have some adaptation to the end. To my mind, Nebraska has no such adaptation.

"It hath no relish of salvation in it." It is an aggravation, rather, of the only one thing which ever endangers the Union. When it came upon us, all was peace and quiet. . . . In the whole range of possibility, there scarcely appears to me to have been any thing, out of which the slavery agitation could have been revived, except the very project of repealing the Missouri Compromise. . . . Repeal the Missouri Compromise—repeal all compromises—repeal the Declaration of Independence—repeal all past history, you still can not repeal human nature. It still will be the abundance of man's heart, that slavery extension is wrong; and out of the abundance of his heart, his mouth will continue to speak. . . .

In our greedy chase to make profit of the Negro, let us beware lest we "cancel and tear to pieces" even the white man's charter of freedom. . . . Let us turn slavery from its claim of "moral right" back upon its existing legal rights, and its arguments of necessity. Let us return it to the position our fathers gave it, and there let it rest in peace. . . . In his [Senator Douglas's] view, the question of whether a new country shall be slave or free is a matter of as utter indifference as it is whether his neighbor shall plant his farm with tobacco or stock it with horned cattle. Now, whether this view is right or wrong, it is certain that the great mass of mankind take a totally different view. They consider slavery a great moral wrong; and their feeling against it is not evanescent, but eternal. It lies at the very foundation of their sense of justice; and it cannot be trifled with.

Lincoln spoke to "the great mass of mankind." He seemed to muse aloud, arguing with himself, seeking firm ground in a slippery world. Yet, he was a deadly opponent, for he tested Douglas' arguments by the principles of the American Revolution. More than six years later, on his way to his first inauguration, after the South had seceded, Lincoln spoke at Independence Hall in Philadelphia.

All the political sentiments I entertain have been drawn, so far as I have been able to draw them, from the sentiments which originated and were given to the world from this hall. I have never had a feeling politically that did not spring from . . . the Declaration of Independence. . . . It was that which gave promise that in due time the weight would be lifted from the shoulders of all men. . . . I would rather be assassinated on the spot than surrender it.[35]

This combination of moral fervor and respect for tradition was a relief from the logic-chopping about states' rights and property rights. Slavery was wrong because the Declaration of Independence was right. Nothing therefore could justify a permission for slavery to extend. Yet slavery existed, and no one knew how to end it wisely, so nothing could justify the hateful, loud, and extravagant talk of the abolitionists. Some voters who opposed the spread of slavery nevertheless hesitated to act on those sentiments lest they be thrown in company with ranting abolitionists. In the Peoria speech, Lincoln told them good humoredly that he thought this very silly.

> Stand with anybody that stands RIGHT. Stand WITH him while he is right and part with him when he goes wrong. Stand WITH the abolitionist in restoring the Missouri Compromise; and stand AGAINST him when he attempts the repeal of the fugitive slave law. . . . In both cases you are right. . . . In both you stand on middle ground and hold the ship level and steady. In both you are national and nothing less than national.

If the presidents had taken this stand strongly and consistently from 1853 onwards, the federal system might not have collapsed. But instead of morals and realism, the presidents tried expediency combined with sudden deeds of rashness. The bitter fruit of this policy would be the Civil War.

Political debates today

It is instructive to contrast the Lincoln-Douglas debates with contemporary debates over public policy. In the first place, ethical ideas today are employed with less precision. Take the idea of fairness. Like the metal shark in the film *Jaws*, the idea of fairness is a kind of prop, contrived by people who have a very particular vision of fairness— namely, redistribution—and who, far from viewing it as an issue, have made up their minds. Debate over lower tax rates on upper-bracket earners should be based, it seems to me, on what the real consequences of the policy are. If, after having discovered that lower tax rates on upper-bracket earners induce them to pay more taxes (because they earn more), there are still people who want to give them higher rates, let them say so. But they will have to admit that, in the name of fairness, they might have to settle for less revenue from the rich.

---

[35] Both the speech in Independence Hall and the Peoria speech are preserved in varying versions. The quotations used are from *Complete Works of Abraham Lincoln*, edited by John G. Nicolay and John Hay (New York, 1905).

Difficulties also exist with the priority of values. As pointed out earlier, we have seen rights often conflict, and it is seldom obvious which should take precedence in a given situation. Consequently, more and more moral judgments today are seen as *nothing but* expressions of preference. Questions about what constitutes the good life or the ends of human life are regarded from the public standpoint as systematically unsettlable; on these matters, individuals are free to agree or disagree.[36] These views form a great deal of contemporary moral utterance and, more specifically, policymaking.

Thus we are surrounded by interminable moral arguments that we have no rational way of settling. All has been reduced to choice, to the irrational, to various emotional tactics: you choose X and I choose Y. The public expression of this radical abandonment of reason is political protest. Placards denounce Y and cheer X. We seem unable to reason with each other.

Where does this notion that values may be *chosen* come from? At first sight, it seems strange to say that whether or not truth or courage is to count as a virtue depends on choice. Can a person actually *choose* lying or racism to be a virtue? Nevertheless, many educated people, including philosophers, hold that moral principles are, and can only be, matters of choice. They hold that moral judgments are either expressions of feelings or derivative from general principles ("do to others as you would have them do to you") for which no higher reasons can be given. It follows that important moral differences can be neither clarified nor settled through debate, for there is no matter of fact involved in the discussion. It is like a debate over whether Pepsi tastes better than Coke.

In *After Virtue: A Study in Moral Theory*, Alasdair MacIntyre argues that this belief about the nature of morality is fundamentally the same as that found in the thought of moral philosophers like Bentham and Rawls.[37] What these philosophers have in common is the belief that no account of "good" or "right" can be based on hard facts about the real world. We can say that a pair of running shoes is good if they help one run faster and avoid injury, but we can say this because we know the function of running shoes. Many philosophers believe that no functional account can be given of man.

It is not surprising that students of public policy who have been exposed to ethics leave their study feeling as if they have been digging and filling the same hole all day. It is hard—sometimes even exhilarat-

---

[36] Cf. Ronald Dworkin, *Taking Rights Seriously* (Cambridge, Mass.: Harvard University Press, 1977).

[37] Alasdair MacIntyre, *After Virtue: A Study in Moral Theory* (Notre Dame, Ind.: University of Notre Dame, 1981).

ing—working through the framework festooned with terms like axiologi-
cal intuitionism, naturalistic cognitivism, welfare economics, material
deontological ethics, teleological theories, and, of course, utilitarianism.
But in the end the student learns in the final analysis, it comes down
to individual *choice*.

MacIntyre attacks this ruling orthodoxy in moral philosophy. In so
doing, he attacks a popular way of discussing public policy. His argument
is, in the first place, that philosophers have been mistaken: the ultimate
premises of moral argument need not be arbitrary. MacIntyre believes
that our moral debates contain fragments of concepts that make sense
only within a different, largely forgotten scheme of thought. Because
we traffic in fragments, many problems in modern ethical debates are
inconclusive.

Roughly speaking, one concept of ethics in Western civilization pre-
vailed prior to the eighteenth century, another after that time. In a
fundamental sense, they represent the only two ways there are to think
about moral questions. Let us now consider this great moral transformation in the meaning of moral concepts and their place in political life.
Let us see how the fragments with which we now work were originally
at home in larger totalities of theory and practice, which they now
lack.

Concept I

Ancient Greece and medieval Europe differ from modern democratic
societies in three important ways. First, they considered value judgments
as judgments of fact. They believed that human beings could actually
know what was good. Second, both the Greek city-state and the medieval
kingdom were conceived as communities in which men and women
in company pursue the good. Thus roles or relationships contributed
to the achievement of the good. These communities were not what
modern democratic states take themselves to be: arenas in which each
individual seeks his or her own private good. Third, in these earlier
societies, the practice of certain virtues was essential to the realization
of the good life.

Because he summed up much that had gone before and stimulated
in turn much that came later, Aristotle (384–322 B.C.) provides an ideal
focal point to better understand these differences. The good for Aristotle
is whatever is aimed at. So the good for man is what men by nature
seek and say they seek. Their seeking is not identical with what they
wish, since their seeking is rooted in their nature in a way in which
their wishing need not be. What men seek may be given the formal
name eudaemonia (U-de-MO-nia), which we misleadingly translate as
"happiness." If we have to be more explicit as to what eudaemonia

means we should say "the good life" or "living well." This is elucidated in many ways; but it will evidently include the free activity of reason, for it is reason that distinguishes man from other animals. Thus, eudaemonia involves the fulfillment of man's function.

> To call something good therefore is also to make a factual statement. To call a particular action just or right is to say that it is what a good man would do in such a situation; hence this type of statement too is factual. Within this tradition moral and evaluative statements can be called true or false in precisely the way in which all other factual statements can be so called. But once the notion of essential human purposes or functions disappears from morality, it begins to appear implausible to treat moral judgments as factual statements.[38]

The virtues are acquired as habits that enable us to lead lives of free, rational activity. They are therefore a crucial component in what good men seek. Aristotle derives a partial account of a core concept of virtues—incorporating truthfulness, justice, and courage—that he considers basic to any common pursuit of the good.

Aristotle strikes us as deficient in at least one respect: He talks not about human ends, but about the ends of free Greek males, an end they do not share with women, slaves, and barbarians (those who are not Greek and make ugly noises when they speak). One of Christianity's historical achievements is to have rescued Aristotle from some of these narrow views.

The virtues are not just means to an end (happiness); they are, in their exercise, a part of the end. Similarly, what is wrong with vices—the disposition to take innocent life, to steal, to lie, to betray—is not just that their exercise produces unhappiness. A life filled with these vices is the worst life conceivable. Such a life, even if spiced with a number of pleasures, is utterly hateful, whereas the life of virtue, even if accompanied by pain and public disgrace, is intrinsically desirable.

The crucial point for us then is this. Concept I of moral theory and practice embodies objective and impersonal standards that provide rational justification for particular policies and actions.

Concept II

The virtue-centered moralities of Concept I were repudiated with the rise of science, between the fifteenth and seventeenth centuries. This repudiation paved the way for efforts in the eighteenth century to discover new foundations for morality. Both the proper ends of man and the laws of God disappear from the scene. The new view of man as an individual prior to and apart from all roles (recall Rawls's original

---

[38] Ibid., p. 59.

position) replaces the idea of man finding his fulfillment in his social role. The eighteenth century brought fully into existence for the first time a society of free individuals. This society is thought to be the "natural" society. The importance of the social environment and past history in nurturing private values is dismissed. Now what are called statements of fact cannot entail what are taken to be moral conclusions.

With the air cleared, philosophers set to work to put morality on a rational basis. But MacIntyre argues that this intellectual enterprise—in which Bentham played a conspicuous part—failed. Once the modern world repudiated the moral traditions of which Aristotle's thought was the core, all subsequent attempts by moral philosophers to provide some alternative rational secular account of the nature and status of morality *had* to fail.

Perhaps we are now in a better position to see why public debates cannot be settled and why contending parties appear so arbitrary. Our moral language and practice deploys ill-assorted fragments from the past, but not in their original context. Suppose a tribe of people lost their original moral and intellectual culture, except that fragments remained to them, rules ripped from their context, words whose original meanings had been lost and for which loose guesses had been supplied. Someone who undertook to weave these fragments into a rational whole would probably create a caricature. This has been our predicament. We do not understand our original moral culture.

The modern moral culture of individualism offers no solution to this disorder. It relies on what MacIntyre calls pseudo-concepts and moral fictions such as utility and human rights. Utilitarianism *by itself* solves nothing because it fails to give a cogent reason why anyone should listen to the utterances of newly autonomous individuals. Certainly in evaluating the consequences of given policies, policymakers should adopt elements of welfare economics and try to foresee the consequences of policies for individuals. When it is convenient, they should gather information about the values that individuals place on the diverse effects of a policy. This is all fairly obvious, but it does not help us distinguish right from wrong.

The idea of human rights *seems* simple enough, but it means different things—not all of them obvious—to different people. That was seldom better demonstrated than at a 1983 Conference on Human Rights held at the University of North Carolina.

> To Dennis Brutus, the South African poet and activist now in exile in the United States, "human rights" self-evidently includes the political rights denied by "the minority regime in Pretoria" to the 22 million blacks who are 80 percent of the population of South Africa.
>
> To Ernest Lefever of the Ethics and Public Policy Center, President Reagan's rejected nominee to head the State Department's Bureau of Human Rights,

the Sandinista regime in Nicaragua is a greater violator of human rights than was the Somoza dictatorship because the Sandinistas "insulted the Pope."

To Otis Graham of the University of North Carolina history department, the "underclass," that minority of Americans who remain in deepest poverty (most of them women and children who are not legally discriminated against), are human rights victims because "practically speaking, many of them will never have a chance."

To the Reagan administration, said Lars Schoultz of the University of North Carolina political science department—basing his judgment on a year's research in Washington—"human rights" is mostly a device to undermine "friendly, stable anti-Communist regimes"; thus, the administration believes that for the United States to promote human rights only "leads to a threat to our national security."

And to Charles Lyons, once a victim of segregation laws and racial discrimination, now the chancellor of Fayetteville State University, human rights means "the preservation of the dignity of the human being"—a definition that emphasizes the complexities of the term, and the problem.[39]

From this divergence of opinion it does not of course follow that there are no human rights; it only follows that no one knows what they are. But belief in them, MacIntyre says, is one with belief in witches and unicorns.

> The best reason for asserting so bluntly that there are no such rights is indeed of precisely the same type as the best reason which we possess for asserting that there are no witches and the best reason which we possess for asserting that there are no unicorns: every attempt to give good reasons for believing that there *are* such rights has failed. . . . Twentieth-century moral philosophers have sometimes appealed to their and our intuitions; but one of the things that we ought to have learned from the history of moral philosophers is that the introduction of the word *intuition* by a moral philosopher is always a signal that something has gone badly wrong with an argument. In the United Nations declaration on human rights of 1949 what has since become the normal UN practice of not giving good reasons for *any* assertions whatsoever is followed with great rigor. And the latest defender of such rights, Ronald Dworkin (*Taking Rights Seriously*, 1976) concedes that the existence of such rights cannot be demonstrated, but remarks on this point simply that it does not follow from the fact that a statement cannot be demonstrated that it is not true (p. 81). Which is true, but could equally be used to defend claims about unicorns and witches.[40]

In summary, Concept II rejects the notion of society as a community united in a shared vision of the good for human beings. It offers no agreement on which values are of fundamental importance. Society

[39] Tom Wicker, "A Disputed Idea," *New York Times*, October 10, 1983.
[40] MacIntyre, *After Virtue*, p. 69.

becomes only as a collection of citizens who have banded together for mutual protection.

Criteria of choice

How can there be an argument to show that there is a human end and that virtue consists in its fulfillment? Granted that such an argument has some plausibility, how can the argument be morally relevant to public policy in today's society, bureaucratic and individualist as it is? Below, in a very schematic form, is how I think MacIntyre might respond.

Any political order that requires us to pursue certain ends must derive those ends from what human beings characteristically seek. This seeking can only show itself in the concrete, in the behavior and proclamation of particular communities as they persist through time. Any serious thinking about morality must therefore begin with what people say, spontaneously or reflectively, about what things are worth aiming at. In this context, ethics becomes a branch of politics. Ethical questions are always in part social questions because human beings are part of a historical people, a culture, an ethos, a political economy.

It follows then that the policymaker will heed the narratives and stories that their cultures and its participants make exemplary. Rules about what to do make sense only within stories. These stories are both cultural and inherited by individuals. They are given original and distinctive shape by each individual and yet belong to all.

Learning from Lincoln. For precisely that reason, I chose to begin this section with the story of the Lincoln-Douglas debates. The debates— or, more to the point, the character of Lincoln—instructs at a variety of levels. Lincoln crystallizes most virtues fundamental in American society. The nickname Honest Abe suggests only the most obvious. (If one wishes to quibble that honesty is not really a shared virtue in an aggressively capitalist society like the United States, then one need only recall the zeal with which Richard Nixon was run out of office. Throughout the ordeal, Europeans remained baffled by the animosity Nixon kindled in the American people.)

There are far more subtle virtues in the Lincoln character. In his own distinctively American way, he possessed what John Keats called the quality that "went to form the Man of Achievement," that quality which Shakespeare possessed so enormously—"*Negative Capability,* that is, when a person is capable of being in uncertainties, Mysteries, doubts, without any irritable reaching after fact and reason."[41] Lincoln knew

---

[41] Quoted in David Donald, *Lincoln Reconsidered* (New York: Vintage Books, 1961), p. 143.

that there were limits to rational human activity, and there was no virtue in irritably seeking to perform the impossible.

Above all, he knew that the successful leader must have a patient confidence in the ultimate justice of the people. He knew that the popular will was slow, blundering, and often mistaken. But, in a free society, one had to believe in the soundness of their final judgment as it expressed itself over time.

King and Kennan as exemplars. Did Lincoln represent the last gasp of Concept I morality in American politics? Not quite. From time to time, even today, examples of Concept I appear. One of the best known of these was Martin Luther King, Jr.'s, "Letter from Birmingham Jail."[42] In the grand manner of Lincoln, King refused to cobble together an argument based on legal fine points, economic analysis, and sociological research. Segregation laws were *morally* wrong: "A just law is a manmade code that squares with the moral law. . . . An unjust law is a code that is out of harmony with the moral law." Then, to buttress the point, he reaches back to the great medieval philosopher, Thomas Aquinas, who had attempted to reconcile Aristotle with Christianity. The next lines suggest that segregation laws are inconsistent with the concept of a community in which men and women in company pursue eudaemonia or happiness:

> Any law that uplifts human personality is just. Any law that degrades human personality is unjust. All segregation statutes are unjust because segregation distorts the soul and damages the personality. It gives the segregator a false sense of superiority and the segregated a false sense of inferiority. Segregation, to use the terminology of the Jewish philosopher Martin Buber, substitutes an "I-it" relationship for the "I-thou" relationship and ends up relegating persons to the status of things.

George Kennan resigned from the state department in 1953 and began a new career as a historian in Princeton. Ever since his retirement from public service he has argued, to all who would listen, that the Soviet-American balance of power is to be valued as a foundation for a durable international order and inveighed against the moral disease of the crusading spirit in politics. Recently, Kennan has updated the argument.[43]

"Government is an agent, not a principal," he writes. "Its primary obligation is to the *interests* of the national society it represents, not to the moral impulses that individual elements of the society may experience." Note the rejection of any utilitarian summing of individual preferences. Does it then follow that there is no morality in the conduct of

---

[42] Martin Luther King, Jr., Letter appeared in *The Christian Century* (1963).

[43] George F. Kennan, "Morality and Foreign Policy," *Foreign Affairs*, vol. 64, Winter 1985–86, pp. 205–18.

foreign policy? Is it all cynicism? No, Kennan says. We should observe certain moral rules. First, avoid "the histrionics of moralism." This means act correctly "without self-consciousness or self-admiration, as a matter of duty or common decency." These are not matters of style, as some of Kennan's critics have charged. Kennan has not confused etiquette with morality; rather he recognizes, as Aristotle did, that virtues must become habits.

Kennan also recognizes that morality derives neither from intellectual constructs nor from eternal principles (as some say human rights does); rather, it must be discerned from particular peoples in particular times and places:

> When we talk about the application of moral standards to foreign policy . . . we are not talking about compliance with some clear and generally accepted international code of behavior. If the policies and actions of the U.S. government are to be made to conform to moral standards, those standards are going to have to be America's own, founded on traditional American principles of justice and propriety. When others fail to conform to those principles, and when their failure to conform has an adverse effect on American interests, as distinct from political tastes, we have every right to complain and, if necessary, to take retaliatory action. What we cannot do is to assume that our moral standards are theirs as well, and to appeal to those standards as the source of our grievances.[44]

The link between virtue and policy. To properly apply the law requires justice. To be just is to give each person what he or she deserves. (Contemporary moral philosophers say little or nothing about deserts, but people do.) In our society, much of the assignment of goods and penalties in accordance with desert is governed by elaborate rules and procedures. Still cases will arise in which it is unclear how the law should be applied and what justice requires. In such cases, Aristotle says we have to act *according to right reason*. What he seems to mean here can be usefully illustrated by a few contemporary examples.

- In the late 1970s, American Indian tribes in New England filed a series of land claims under the terms of almost forgotten legislation Congress had enacted in 1789 and 1790. Homeowners in general and retired people in particular were hard hit, since they faced the loss of lifelong savings invested in homes. In this situation, what does justice require?

  Rules of justice advanced by contemporary moral philosophers offer little help. Rawls argues that social and economic inequalities are to be arranged so that they are of greatest benefit to the least advantaged. Nozick asserts that the holdings of a person are just if he is entitled to them by the principles of justice in their acquisition. But we cannot

---

[44] Ibid.

know who is least advantaged until after the courts have decided the case.

Nor can we know who has just title in a case involving legal issues so complex, some of which go back to ancient English common law.

Indians in one town devised, however, this rough-and-ready solution: all properties of one acre or less on which a dwelling house stands will be exempt from the suit. The reasoning involved such considerations as the proportion of the land claimed which consists of such properties and the numbers of people affected. To judge by right reason is indeed to judge more or less, to find the mean between two extremes in a given circumstance. As Aristotle contends, vices and virtues depend on circumstances: the very same action which would in one situation be courageous could in another be rash or timid. Hence virtue requires not merely being law-abiding but also using judgment.[45]

- Let us consider a less parochial issue: low-income housing. Most of us imagine that we do the poor a favor by giving them neighborhoods whose sole criterion for residency is economic failure. Prove your poverty, and you become instantly eligible. Stop being an economic failure, and you have to move. But I doubt this is how we would devise a system for ourselves. What we would want, I suspect, is the establishment of criteria that would reward our virtues, not just our shortcomings. Certainly if we were poor we would want low-cost housing made available. But we might find it reasonable to reserve the best of the low-cost housing for those among us who exhibited the best behavior, those who took the best care of the property, who planted flowers or undertook minor repairs, those who at least saw to it that their children did not leave the place a shambles. If we were needy, we would want the chance to earn our way to better, more prestigious quarters through decent behavior—both because we *deserve* it and because it would strike us as a *reasonable way* to design public policy.

- Even public policies involving such controversial issues as affirmative action and abortion might be usefully modified if we applied to them right reason. I will briefly address the former and let Carl Sagan speak to the latter (Box 12–2).

Few people who support affirmative action would want their own employment, promotion, or school attendance based primarily on their sex or ethnicity. What they do want is some assurance that their

---

[45] MacIntyre, *After Virtue*, pp. 152–54. See also Paul Brodeur, *Restitution: The Land Claims of the Mashpee, Passamaquoddy, and Penobscot Indians of New England* (Boston: Northeastern University Press, 1985).

Box 12–2
Carl Sagan on abortion

There is no question that legalized abortions avoid the tragedy and butchery of illegal and incompetent "back-alley" abortions, and that in a civilization whose very continuance is threatened by the specter of uncontrolled population growth, widely available medical abortions can serve an important social need. But infanticide would solve both problems and has been employed widely, by many human communities including segments of the classical Greek civilization, which is so generally considered the cultural antecedent of our own. And it is widely practiced today: there are many parts of the world where one out of every four newborn babies does not survive the first year of life. Yet by our laws and mores, infanticide is murder beyond any question. Since a baby born prematurely in the seventh month of pregnancy is in no significant respect different from a fetus *in utero* in the seventh month, it must, it seems to me, follow that abortion, at least in the last trimester, is very close to murder. Objections that the fetus in the third trimester is still not breathing seem specious: Is it permissible to commit infanticide after birth if the umbilicus has not yet been severed, or if the baby has not yet taken its first breath? Likewise, if I am psychologically unprepared to live with a stranger—in army boot camp or college dormitory, for example—I do not thereby have a right to kill him and my annoyance at some of the uses of my tax money does not extend to exterminating the recipients of those taxes. The civil liberties point of view is often muddled in such debates. Why, it is sometimes asked, should the beliefs of others on this issue have to extend to me? But those who do not personally support the conventional prohibition against murder are nevertheless required by our society to abide by the criminal code.

On the opposite side of the discussion, the phrase "right to life" is an excellent example of a "buzz word," designed to inflame rather than illuminate. There is no right to life in any society on Earth today, nor has there been at any former time, beasts and vegetables are as alive as we. What is protected in many human societies is not life, but human life. And even with this protection, we wage "modern" wars on civilian populations with a toll so terrible we are, most of us, afraid to consider it very deeply. Often such mass murders are justified by racial or nationalistic redefinitions of our opponents as less than human.

In the same way, the argument about the "potential" to be human seems to me particularly weak. Any human egg or sperm under appropriate circumstances has the potential to become a human being. Yet male masturbation and nocturnal emissions are generally considered natural acts and not the cause for murder indictments.

The issues are clearly complex. The solution, equally clearly, must involve a compromise among a number of cherished but conflicting values. The key practical question is to determine when a fetus becomes human.

Box 12–2 (*concluded*)

This in turn rests on what we mean by human. Surely not having a human shape, because an artifact of organic materials that resembled a human being but was constructed for the purpose would certainly not be considered human. The reason we prohibit the killing of human beings must be because of some quality human beings possess, a quality we especially prize, that few or no other organisms on Earth enjoy. It cannot be the ability to feel pain or deep emotions, because that surely extends to many of the animals we gratuitously slaughter.

This essential human quality, I believe, can only be our intelligence. If so, the particular sanctity of human life can be identified with the development and functioning of the neocortex. We cannot require its full development, because that does not occur until many years after birth. But perhaps we might set the transition to humanity at the time when neocortical activity begins, as determined by electroencephalography of the fetus.

Source: Carl Sagan, *Dragons of Eden* (New York: Random House, 1977), pp. 195–97.

---

qualifications, their skills, and their potential will not be undervalued because of their sex or race. Justice requires that we not assume that a person cannot be a competent police officer or engineer or student just because he or she had insufficient opportunity or does not speak like a network anchorperson or look like our idea of a competent professional. Judge fairly, even if that means taking an unusually careful look at what a person has to offer. Yet some people persist in prescribing for others things that they would not want for themselves or their children—social promotions, lowered qualifications, etc. But this is pity, not justice.

This chapter has presented two opposing concepts of ethics: liberal individualism in some version or other and the Aristotelian tradition in some version or other. Whether the latter can be restated in a way that restores intelligibility and rationality to policymaking remains an open question. Meanwhile, I think we ought to face squarely the limits of the alternative in providing coherent, rationally defensible statements about the morality of public policy.

To put it plainly, by opposing Concept I to Concept II, I have sought to suggest that the common sense of ordinary, decent people makes sense—the sense often lost in the writings of ethical philosophers. In the real world, action and thought are so closely related that one cannot wait on the other. Policymakers cannot wait in the political arena for any completed theoretical discussion of ethics; it is a monstrous demand. There is no pausing until ethical philosophy is more certain. Policymakers have to act on what they believe, on half-knowledge, illusion, and error. Experience itself will reveal their mistakes; research and criticism may convert them into wisdom. But act they must, and act as if they knew the nature of human beings and could satisfy the needs of their fellow citizens.

FOR FURTHER REFLECTION

1. Identify a problem that seems to be confronting your local government or one that confronts national leaders, and then analyze it following the general format suggested in Figure 1–3 and elaborated in subsequent chapters.
2. Welfare economics is concerned largely with the determination of ways to satisfy human wants as best we can. But is this really a sensible goal? For example, suppose that people want the wrong things. Is it still sensible to try to satisfy these wants as completely as possible? Should not welfare economics be concerned, too, with how wants are created?
3. In judging various social mechanisms and policies, welfare economics tends to emphasize the outcomes of these mechanics and policies, as measured by the extent to which various human wants are satisfied. But should not welfare be concerned with means as well as ends? For example, suppose that a particular policy resulted in an ideal allocation of resources, but that it was achieved by trickery or coercion. Doesn't this matter?
4. To induce manufacturing firms to move within its city's limits, the city council has passed a bill which permits the city to provide free sewer and water and to abate property taxes for the first five years of operation of the firm. Discuss the normative issues posed by this proposal.
5. Carl Sagan is no Aristotelian, but what connections can you make between his analysis of the abortion issue and Aristotle's views of ethical reasoning.
6. Some American scientists have despaired of any possibility of improving the sophistication of the American public about science. Among them is Bowen R. Leonard, Jr., a senior scientist in the fusion technology program at Battelle Pacific Northwestern Laboratory. "I would judge that it is hopeless to educate the public on atomic energy, considering that the public is so uneducated in other subjects." Does this mean, he was asked in an interview, that future national decisions will have to be made increasingly by a relatively small group of experts? "I think it's going to have to come to that.

There are pressure groups insisting that judgments about technical matters be made by what they call unbiased people, that is, people with no knowledge of the subject. But is an uninformed decision really the kind of decision our nation needs to survive?" Discuss.[46]

7. Thomas Howell, an economist, makes this observation: "Environmentalists try to give the impression that they are trying to save the last few remaining patches of wilderness before it disappears under a cover of asphalt and concrete. The fact is that the land owned by the National Park Service is larger than Great Britain and that owned by the U.S. Forest Service exceeds the size of France. The environmentalists' real aim is to give preferential access to those with their kind of lifestyle and to keep out ordinary city people with limited vacation time and kids who cannot be turned loose in the wild. If you don't have the leisure, the money, the physique, or the 'commitment' to a special lifestyle, then the wilderness recreation lobby doesn't want you allowed in anymore. All their talk about 'the people' is political rhetoric." Discuss.

8. A large city is divided into the socioeconomic pattern indicated in Figure 12–7. How should services be distributed? At least three general patterns are possible:

   - *The more, the more:* New library funds go to those who already read; roads to where cars already travel; experienced teachers go to well-to-do schools.
   - *The less, the more:* This is the opposite of the first pattern. The Mexican-American neighborhood gets funds for its own library; streets in the poorest neighborhoods are paved as part of an urban-renewal project; the poorest schools get extra resources.
   - *Whatever will be, will be:* This pattern no one intends; it is simply the result of many influences and players pushing for their own views to prevail.

9. In a major policy study of alternative flood control projects along the Mississippi River, outcomes could be evaluated according to a wide range of norms. For example:

   - Reduced risk of flood.
   - Environmental changes and their effects on existing and new flora and fauna through the creation of new lakes.
   - Losses and gains in recreational activities.
   - Effects on river shipping.

---

[46] From Malcolm Browne, "The Untutored Public," *New York Times*, April 22, 1979.

650

Figure 12–7
The social economic pattern of a hypothetical city

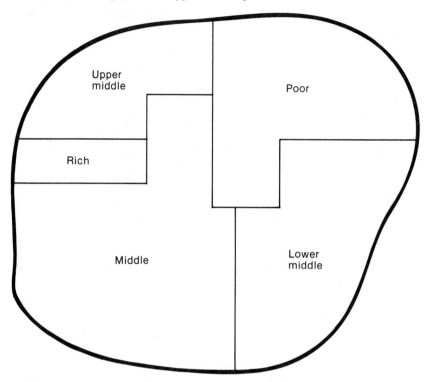

Each of these norms reflects a different view of social values, of what is important to different groups and interests in the region. What are these views, groups, and interests?

10. In 1966 Congress established rules for federal judges. Unless it could be shown that a defendant was likely to skip town and not show up for trial, minimum bail under minimum conditions had to be granted. Was the defendant likely to commit new crimes? Was he a danger to the community? Those questions could not be examined, and the result was the revolving door. A hypothetical auto thief stole one car. Then he got arrested, made bail, and so on, ad infinitum. In one recent study of release practices in eight jurisdictions, one out of every six defendants in the sample was rearrested during the pretrial period. Some were arrested as many as four times. Among defendants arrested on surety bonds, the rate of pretrial arrest reached 25 percent. The thinking behind the 1966 law was both reasoned and compassionate. To deny bail to an accused person is a serious matter. The defendant, if he has a job, loses his job;

his family suffers accordingly; he cannot consult effectively with his lawyer in building his defense. The wealthy defendant can make a high cash bond; the poor man cannot. For all these reasons, the 1966 law commanded wide support. In practice it has not worked. Some judges, forbidden to speculate on a defendant's potential for new crimes, have evaded the law by fixing astronomical bonds. Most federal judges have gone along—and career criminals have thumbed their noses as they went out the revolving doors. What should public policy be?

11. Competition in health-insurance markets, and the efforts of each individual and company to obtain the best possible value, will hasten the demise of community rating of health-insurance premiums. In the past, heavy users of care were, in effect, subsidized by those who used less health care. The ethical dilemma is clear. On the one hand, it is socially desirable to reward healthy behavior and efficiency and to punish excessive use of care. On the other hand, the fragmentation of insurance markets will mean very high premiums for some groups and the abandonment of collective responsibility for health care. What should be done?

12. The housing authority in Charlottesville, Virginia, needs your advice. How should they go about achieving safe, decent, and affordable housing for the city's low-income residents? Your preference would be to accept tenants on a first-come, first-served basis, letting the racial ratio work itself out. Blacks make up about 18 percent of the Charlottesville population, and some 30 percent of those whose income is below federal poverty levels. But you know from experience that first-come, first-served would result in segregated housing. To begin with, there is the long-standing tendency of Charlottesville residents to think of public housing as black housing. Second, black families on the waiting list outnumber white families by some two-and-a-half to one. Colorblind acceptance of applicants as their names reach the top of the list would leave the project so heavily black that whites would stop applying. Theoretically, that would be no problem. In practical terms, it would turn the housing development into exactly the sort of ghetto that you hope to avoid. What's the right thing to do?

Appendix A

Compound Sum of $1

Year	1%	2%	3%	4%	5%	6%	7%
1	1.010	1.020	1.030	1.040	1.050	1.060	1.070
2	1.020	1.040	1.061	1.082	1.102	1.124	1.145
3	1.030	1.061	1.093	1.125	1.158	1.191	1.225
4	1.041	1.082	1.126	1.170	1.216	1.262	1.311
5	1.051	1.104	1.159	1.217	1.276	1.338	1.403
6	1.062	1.126	1.194	1.265	1.340	1.419	1.501
7	1.072	1.149	1.230	1.316	1.407	1.504	1.606
8	1.083	1.172	1.267	1.369	1.477	1.594	1.718
9	1.094	1.195	1.305	1.423	1.551	1.689	1.838
10	1.105	1.219	1.344	1.480	1.629	1.791	1.967
11	1.116	1.243	1.384	1.539	1.710	1.898	2.105
12	1.127	1.268	1.426	1.601	1.796	2.012	2.252
13	1.138	1.294	1.469	1.665	1.886	2.133	2.410
14	1.149	1.319	1.513	1.732	1.980	2.261	2.579
15	1.161	1.346	1.558	1.801	2.079	2.397	2.759
16	1.173	1.373	1.605	1.873	2.183	2.540	2.952
17	1.184	1.400	1.653	1.948	2.292	2.693	3.159
18	1.196	1.428	1.702	2.026	2.407	2.854	3.380
19	1.208	1.457	1.754	2.107	2.527	3.026	3.617
20	1.220	1.486	1.806	2.191	2.653	3.207	3.870
25	1.282	1.641	2.094	2.666	3.386	4.292	5.427
30	1.348	1.811	2.427	3.243	4.322	5.743	7.612

Year	8%	9%	10%	12%	14%	15%	16%
1	1.080	1.090	1.100	1.120	1.140	1.150	1.160
2	1.166	1.188	1.210	1.254	1.300	1.322	1.346
3	1.260	1.295	1.331	1.405	1.482	1.521	1.561
4	1.360	1.412	1.464	1.574	1.689	1.749	1.811
5	1.469	1.539	1.611	1.762	1.925	2.011	2.100
6	1.587	1.677	1.772	1.974	2.195	2.313	2.436
7	1.714	1.828	1.949	2.211	2.502	2.660	2.826
8	1.851	1.993	2.144	2.476	2.853	3.059	3.278
9	1.999	2.172	2.358	2.773	3.252	3.518	3.803
10	2.159	2.367	2.594	3.106	3.707	4.046	4.411
11	2.332	2.580	2.853	3.479	4.226	4.652	5.117
12	2.518	2.813	3.138	3.896	4.818	5.350	5.936
13	2.720	3.066	3.452	4.363	5.492	6.153	6.886
14	2.937	3.342	3.797	4.887	6.261	7.076	7.988
15	3.172	3.642	4.177	5.474	7.138	8.137	9.266
16	3.426	3.970	4.595	6.130	8.137	9.358	10.748
17	3.700	4.328	5.054	6.866	9.276	10.761	12.468
18	3.996	4.717	5.560	7.690	10.575	12.375	14.463
19	4.316	5.142	6.116	8.613	12.056	14.232	16.777
20	4.661	5.604	6.728	9.646	13.743	16.367	19.461
25	6.848	8.623	10.835	17.000	26.462	32.919	40.874
30	10.063	13.268	17.449	29.960	50.950	66.212	85.850

654

Appendix A *(concluded)*

Year	18%	20%	24%	28%	32%	36%
1	1.180	1.200	1.240	1.280	1.320	1.360
2	1.392	1.440	1.538	1.638	1.742	1.850
3	1.643	1.728	1.907	2.067	2.300	2.515
4	1.939	2.074	2.364	2.684	3.036	3.421
5	2.288	2.488	2.932	3.436	4.007	4.653
6	2.700	2.986	3.635	4.398	5.290	6.328
7	3.185	3,583	4.508	5.629	6.983	8.605
8	3.759	4.300	5.590	7.206	9.217	11.703
9	4.435	5.160	6.931	9.223	12.166	15.917
10	5.234	6.192	8.594	11.806	16.060	21.647
11	6.176	7.430	10.657	15.112	21.199	29.439
12	7.288	8.916	13.215	19.343	27.983	40.037
13	8.599	10.699	16.386	24.759	36.937	54.451
14	10.147	12.839	20.319	31.691	48.757	74.053
15	11.974	15.407	25.196	40.565	64.359	100.712
16	14.129	18.488	31.243	51.923	84.954	136.97
17	16.672	22.186	38.741	66.461	112.14	186.28
18	19.673	26.623	48.039	85.071	148.02	253.34
19	23.214	31.948	59.568	108.89	195.39	344.54
20	27.393	38.338	73.864	139.38	257.92	468.57
25	62.669	95.396	216.542	478.90	1033.6	2180.1
30	143.371	237.376	634.820	1645.5	4142.1	10143.

Year	40%	50%	60%	70%	80%	90%
1	1.400	1.500	1.600	1.700	1.800	1.900
2	1.960	2.250	2.560	2.890	3.240	3.610
3	2.744	3.375	4.096	4.913	5.832	6.859
4	3.842	5.062	6.544	8.352	10.498	13.032
5	5.378	7.594	10.486	14.199	18.896	24.761
6	7.530	11.391	16.777	24.138	34.012	47.046
7	10.541	17.086	26.844	41.034	61.222	89.387
8	14.758	25.629	42.950	69.758	110.200	169.836
9	20.661	38.443	68.720	118.588	198.359	322.688
10	28.925	57.665	109.951	201.599	357.047	613.107
11	40.496	86.498	175.922	342.719	642.684	1164.902
12	56.694	129.746	281.475	582.622	1156.831	2213.314
13	79.372	194.619	450.360	990.457	2082.295	4205.297
14	111.120	291.929	720.576	1683.777	3748.131	7990.065
15	155.568	437.894	1152.921	2862.421	6746.636	15181.122
16	217.795	656.84	1844.7	4866.1	12144.	28844.0
17	304.914	985.26	2951.5	8272.4	21859.	54804.0
18	426.879	1477.9	4722.4	14063.0	39346.	104130.0
19	597.630	2216.8	7555.8	23907.0	70824.	197840.0
20	836.683	3325.3	12089.0	40642.0	127480.	375900.0
25	4499.880	25251.	126760.0	577060.0	2408900.	9307600.0
30	24201.432	191750.	1329200.	8193500.0	45517000.	230470000.0

Appendix B

Present Value of $1

Periods until Payment	1%	2%	2½%	3%	4%	5%	6%	8%	10%	12%	14%	15%	16%	18%	20%	22%	24%	25%	26%	30%	40%	50%
1	0.990	0.980	0.976	0.971	0.962	0.952	0.943	0.926	0.909	0.893	0.877	0.870	0.862	0.847	0.833	0.820	0.806	0.800	0.794	0.769	0.714	0.667
2	0.980	0.961	0.952	0.943	0.925	0.907	0.890	0.857	0.826	0.797	0.769	0.756	0.743	0.718	0.694	0.672	0.650	0.640	0.630	0.592	0.510	0.444
3	0.971	0.942	0.929	0.915	0.889	0.864	0.840	0.794	0.751	0.712	0.675	0.658	0.641	0.609	0.579	0.551	0.524	0.512	0.500	0.455	0.364	0.296
4	0.961	0.924	0.906	0.888	0.855	0.823	0.792	0.735	0.683	0.636	0.592	0.572	0.552	0.516	0.482	0.451	0.423	0.410	0.397	0.350	0.260	0.198
5	0.951	0.906	0.884	0.863	0.822	0.784	0.747	0.681	0.621	0.567	0.519	0.497	0.476	0.437	0.402	0.370	0.341	0.328	0.315	0.269	0.186	0.132
6	0.942	0.888	0.862	0.837	0.790	0.746	0.705	0.630	0.564	0.507	0.456	0.432	0.410	0.370	0.335	0.303	0.275	0.262	0.250	0.207	0.133	0.088
7	0.933	0.871	0.841	0.813	0.760	0.711	0.665	0.583	0.513	0.452	0.400	0.376	0.354	0.314	0.279	0.249	0.222	0.210	0.198	0.159	0.095	0.059
8	0.923	0.853	0.821	0.789	0.731	0.677	0.627	0.540	0.467	0.404	0.351	0.327	0.305	0.266	0.233	0.204	0.179	0.168	0.157	0.123	0.068	0.039
9	0.914	0.837	0.801	0.766	0.703	0.645	0.592	0.500	0.424	0.361	0.308	0.284	0.263	0.225	0.194	0.167	0.144	0.134	0.125	0.094	0.048	0.026
10	0.905	0.820	0.781	0.744	0.676	0.614	0.558	0.463	0.386	0.322	0.270	0.247	0.227	0.191	0.162	0.137	0.116	0.107	0.099	0.073	0.035	0.017
11	0.896	0.804	0.762	0.722	0.650	0.585	0.527	0.429	0.350	0.287	0.237	0.215	0.195	0.162	0.135	0.112	0.094	0.086	0.079	0.056	0.025	0.012
12	0.887	0.788	0.744	0.701	0.625	0.557	0.497	0.397	0.319	0.257	0.208	0.187	0.168	0.137	0.112	0.092	0.076	0.069	0.062	0.043	0.018	0.008
13	0.879	0.773	0.725	0.681	0.601	0.530	0.469	0.368	0.290	0.229	0.182	0.163	0.145	0.116	0.093	0.075	0.061	0.055	0.050	0.033	0.013	0.005
14	0.870	0.758	0.708	0.661	0.577	0.505	0.442	0.340	0.263	0.205	0.160	0.141	0.125	0.099	0.078	0.062	0.049	0.044	0.039	0.025	0.009	0.003
15	0.861	0.743	0.690	0.642	0.555	0.481	0.417	0.315	0.239	0.183	0.140	0.123	0.108	0.084	0.065	0.051	0.040	0.035	0.031	0.020	0.006	0.002
16	0.853	0.728	0.674	0.623	0.534	0.458	0.394	0.292	0.218	0.163	0.123	0.107	0.093	0.071	0.054	0.042	0.032	0.028	0.025	0.015	0.005	0.002
17	0.844	0.714	0.657	0.605	0.513	0.436	0.371	0.270	0.198	0.146	0.108	0.093	0.080	0.060	0.045	0.034	0.026	0.023	0.020	0.012	0.003	0.001
18	0.836	0.700	0.641	0.587	0.494	0.416	0.350	0.250	0.180	0.130	0.095	0.081	0.069	0.051	0.038	0.028	0.021	0.018	0.016	0.009	0.002	0.001
19	0.828	0.686	0.626	0.570	0.475	0.396	0.331	0.232	0.164	0.116	0.083	0.070	0.060	0.043	0.031	0.023	0.017	0.014	0.012	0.007	0.002	
20	0.820	0.673	0.610	0.554	0.456	0.377	0.312	0.215	0.149	0.104	0.073	0.061	0.051	0.037	0.026	0.019	0.014	0.012	0.010	0.005	0.001	
21	0.811	0.660	0.595	0.538	0.439	0.359	0.294	0.199	0.135	0.093	0.064	0.053	0.044	0.031	0.022	0.015	0.011	0.009	0.008	0.004	0.001	
22	0.803	0.647	0.581	0.522	0.422	0.342	0.278	0.184	0.123	0.083	0.056	0.046	0.038	0.026	0.018	0.013	0.009	0.007	0.006	0.003	0.001	
23	0.795	0.634	0.567	0.507	0.406	0.326	0.262	0.170	0.112	0.074	0.049	0.040	0.033	0.022	0.015	0.010	0.007	0.006	0.005	0.002		
24	0.788	0.622	0.553	0.492	0.390	0.310	0.247	0.158	0.102	0.066	0.043	0.035	0.028	0.019	0.013	0.008	0.006	0.005	0.004	0.002		
25	0.780	0.610	0.539	0.478	0.375	0.295	0.233	0.146	0.092	0.059	0.038	0.030	0.024	0.016	0.010	0.007	0.005	0.004	0.003	0.001		
26	0.772	0.598	0.526	0.464	0.361	0.281	0.220	0.135	0.084	0.053	0.033	0.026	0.021	0.014	0.009	0.006	0.004	0.003	0.002	0.001		
27	0.764	0.586	0.513	0.450	0.347	0.268	0.207	0.125	0.076	0.047	0.029	0.023	0.018	0.011	0.007	0.005	0.003	0.002	0.002	0.001		
28	0.757	0.574	0.501	0.437	0.333	0.255	0.196	0.116	0.069	0.042	0.026	0.020	0.016	0.010	0.006	0.004	0.002	0.002	0.002	0.001		
29	0.749	0.563	0.489	0.424	0.321	0.243	0.185	0.107	0.063	0.037	0.022	0.017	0.014	0.008	0.005	0.003	0.002	0.002	0.001			
30	0.742	0.552	0.477	0.412	0.308	0.231	0.174	0.099	0.057	0.033	0.020	0.015	0.012	0.007	0.004	0.003	0.002	0.001	0.001			
40	0.672	0.453	0.372	0.307	0.208	0.142	0.097	0.046	0.022	0.011	0.005	0.004	0.003	0.001	0.001							
50	0.608	0.372	0.291	0.228	0.141	0.087	0.054	0.021	0.009	0.003	0.001	0.001	0.001									

Source: Jerome Bracken and Charles J. Christenson, Tables for Use in Analyzing Business Decisions (Homewood, Ill.: Richard D. Irwin, Inc., 1965), except for the data on 2½ percent, the source for which is Mathematical Tables from Handbook of Chemistry and Physics, 6th ed.; (Cleveland: Chemical Rubber Publishing Co. 1938).
Note: These values are obtained by compounding at the end of each period. Other tables use different schemes of compounding, without changing the magnitudes greatly.

Appendix C

Practical Aspects of Managing and Performing Policy Studies

The chief aim of this book has been to discuss the conceptual aspects of policy analysis. In deciding which problems to study and in carrying out actual analyses, however, certain practical questions arise that need to be addressed. This Appendix discusses some of these practical aspects and offers suggestions for coping with them.[1] The list is not exhaustive, but it is indicative of the very real problems faced in this type of work.·

FORMULATING AN AGENDA OF STUDIES

One of the most important responsibilities facing any manager of an evaluation, analysis, audit, or other program review staff is developing the overall work for the organization. Planning a program of studies which will be of maximum benefit to decision makers should involve two principal tasks:

Identifying problems or issues which are evolving as major areas of concern.

Deciding which of the many candidate problems the organization should commit itself to studying.

Identifying emerging problems

A contribution can be made to resource allocation decisions by raising problems and exploring their ramifications in "issue papers." These

---

[1] Based chiefly on U.S. General Accounting Office, *Evaluation and Analysis to Support Decision Making*, PAD 76–9 (Washington, D.C.: Government Printing Office, 1976).

focus on problems which, there is reason to believe, will become the subject of a full-scale evaluation or analysis.

The ability to recognize emerging problems for issue papers depends on experience and good judgment. Developing an issue paper also requires an understanding of the problem area and its environment.

An issue paper may follow the format and style appropriate to a full-scale evaluation or analysis but is limited to an assessment of what is known about the problem. An issue paper could be as short as a few paragraphs or long enough to cover all or almost all of the points required in a full evaluation or analysis, but without the scope or definitiveness of a finished study. An issue paper should emphasize recommendations on the nature of further study efforts—for example, whether the problem should receive high-priority attention (and why), whether it should be pursued but on a long-term basis (and why), or whether it should be abandoned (and why).

Deciding which problems to study

Many problems, programs, and policy issues are in need of systematic study. However, scarce staff resources should be allocated to the most productive projects.

Issue papers can identify policy and program problems worth evaluating or analyzing. However, a complex series of judgments is still needed to select the particular group of problems whose solution would maximize the anticipated payoff. Although it is relatively easy to list the factors influencing these choices, it is seldom feasible to appraise all of them in a formal quantitative fashion. In some cases there can be little more than an informed guess about the potential utility of a study.

A systematic weighing of the following factors will be helpful.

1. *The anticipated payoff of a successful evaluation or analysis.* This payoff can take several forms: an ineffective program can be canceled and costs saved; a mismanaged program can be reshaped, with consequent improvements in effectiveness, reductions in costs, or both; or better alternatives can be substituted for current programs and policies, with gains in effectiveness, reductions in cost, or both.

2. *The chances for the successful performance of an evaluation or analysis.* This judgment depends on a basic understanding of the fundamental causal relationships; the requirements for additional information; the adequacy of current analytical methods; the quality of staff, consultants, or contractors; and the time and money available.

3. *The chances that a preferred course of action can actually be implemented.* This judgment depends on such things as the newness, simplicity, visibility, coverage, and timeliness of the preferred course of action.

4. *The need for resolving the problem or issue.* This need depends on the nature and the relative importance of the problem and the time remaining before a meaningful decision has to be made.

5. *The estimated cost of the evaluation or analysis.*

BEGINNING A STUDY

Certain tasks should precede major commitments of staff and other resources. These tasks include preparing a study plan, obtaining necessary agreements, selecting the study team, establishing lines of communication, and selecting appropriate methods.

Preparing a detailed study plan

Substantial effort should be devoted to drawing up a comprehensive and thorough study plan which will serve as a guide for all subsequent work. A study plan that is too broad in scope or too loosely stated is almost certain to create false expectations for some interested groups. Clearly, trade-offs have to be made between the time devoted to planning versus the time spent in doing a study and, within the planning period, between the time spent in preparing a general study plan and the time spent in preparing a detailed study plan.

As the study progresses, it is likely to deviate from original expectations. Perhaps the issue turns out to be different from the one which was postulated originally; the objectives may not have been stated precisely enough; a working assumption may not prove viable; other alternatives to the program may emerge; new facts may come to light; hoped-for data may be unobtainable; and so on. All of these developments call for some modification of the study plan. Changes in the study plan should be made, as appropriate.

Essential elements of the study plan would appear to be:

A clear statement of the problem to be studied, the questions to be answered, and decisions to be affected.

A careful listing of constraints and assumptions.

A statement of the methods to be used.

A specification of the resources to be committed (including identification of the key staff members and of any contracted tasks required).

The frequency, the format, and the recipients of reports.

Procedures for amending the study plan.

The time frame for the major components of the study and the final deadline.

When a study or a major part of it is to be performed by contract, there should be discussion and understanding by the parties concerning the essential elements of the study plan. This is likely to require lengthy dialogue with the decision makers. Persons with official responsibility for the policy of program and for the study should assess the feasibility and validity of the study plan. Any differences should be resolved before the study begins. Substantial time and effort may be necessary to arrive at a workable understanding. In the case of contract studies, the agency staff must be technically competent to oversee the study and must also be familiar with the various rules on contract management.

Selecting the study team

Most analyses or evaluations require contributions from several key persons. For large studies, subteams may be required for particular aspects. As in any group effort, someone must be in charge to (1) provide guidance, (2) manage the work on a day-to-day basis, (3) report to higher authority and (4) be generally responsible for meeting the terms of the study plan.

The coordinator or director should be experienced, with a technically sound but broad background, an instinct for the principal issues, and leadership abilities that elicit the best efforts of team members. It usually turns out that the team coordinator or director will have to be the principal editor of the final report—so writing skill is necessary.

A team studying any complex policy or program should be composed of experienced persons from various disciplines, with the stature required to obtain the information needed and to assure the credibility of the study. Regardless of their origins, however, all team members should be made to feel that they are coequals in an exciting intellectual experience and a useful endeavor.

One way to create such an environment—and at the same time to avoid duplication of effort—is to have an initial briefing on the terms of the study plan with all team members. Important aspects of the study plan, such as concepts, assignments, schedules, basic assumptions, the need for personal and agency coordination, and the reporting requirements, should be fully understood and agreed on in advance. Provision should be made for periodic briefings by each specialist to the team as a whole so that everyone has both a grasp of the study's overall progress and a chance to offer facts or insights on any aspect of the study.

It is often helpful to obtain reviews by competent and widely recognized independent professional analysts and evaluators and experienced program administrators. This advice adds a seasoned viewpoint which may improve the technical aspects of the study and may assist the

Figure A–1
Sample work plan

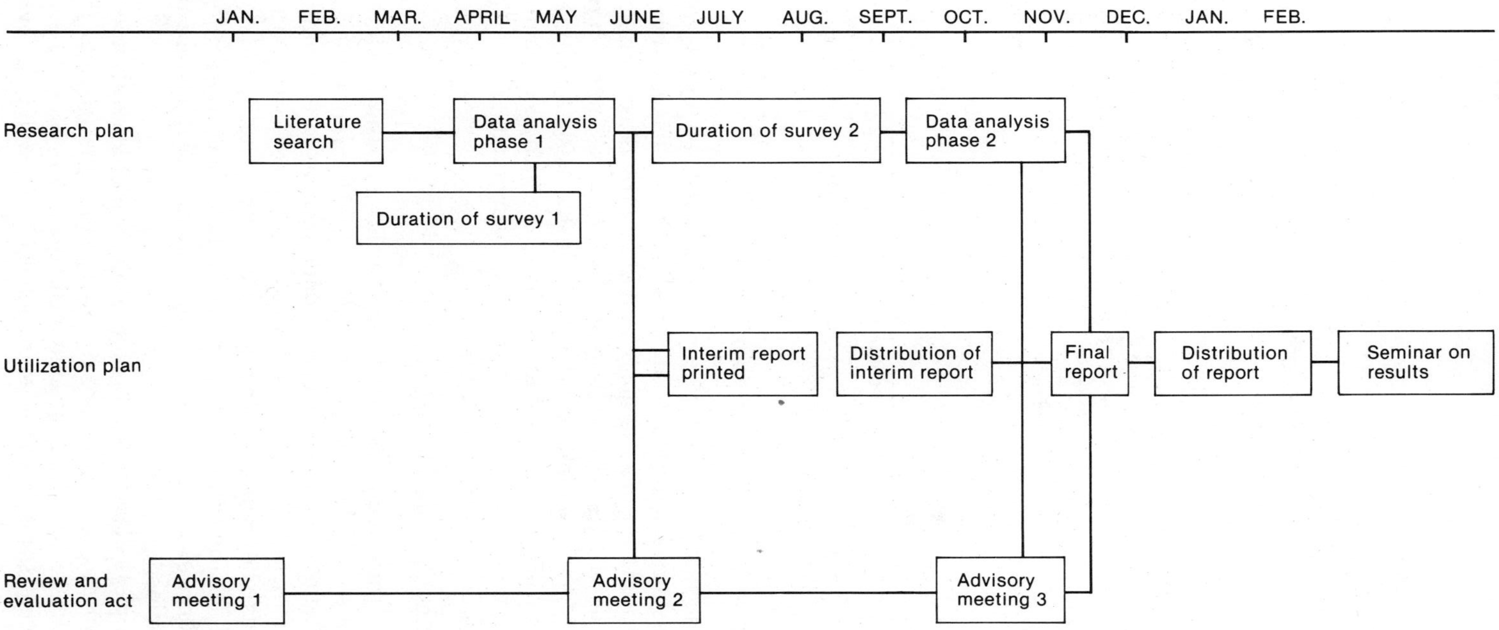

supervisor in assessing the technical adequacy of the work of staff members trained in different disciplines.

Work plan costs by task

Research activity		$230,300
Literature search and evaluation	$11,300	
Survey 1	65,200	
Survey 2	80,300	
Data analysis–Phase 1	33,500	
Data analysis–Phase 2	40,000	
Review and evaluation activity		$ 22,800
Advisory meeting 1	$ 7,600	
Advisory meeting 2	7,600	
Advisory meeting 3	7,600	
Utilization activity		$ 29,000
Printing of reports	$ 5,000	
Distribution of reports	2,000	
Seminar on results	22,000	
Total costs		$282,100[*]

[*] Includes administrative and management costs.
Source: National Science Foundation, *Technology Assessment in Selected Areas: Program Announcement* (Washington, D.C.: Government Printing Office, May 1977).

Establishing lines of communication

If the study effort is sufficiently large, official points of contact among various interested groups and users of the study should be designated. This should ensure the quick and clear flow of communications of all kinds among the groups having a major interest in the progress of the study. Open communications provide the basis for a more complete assessment or appraisal and a climate in which recommended changes are more likely to be accepted and implemented.

Selecting appropriate methods

Analytical methods which yield valid and (hopefully) unequivocal results should be used. However, the methods must also satisfy the constraints of time, money, and data peculiar to the study. If the constraints imposed are so rigid as to compel the study to use methods judged to be analytically inappropriate, the study should be undertaken only after the responsible authorities have been fully informed of the risk that reliable conclusions and recommendations are not likely to be obtained.

No particular approach or technique is inherently the appropriate one. In practice, there are too many attempts to mold the policy or program issue to fit a specific technique. This should be avoided. For a specific study, various approaches, each having its own particular logic, should be considered. Usually, a blend of methods and techniques will be required to provide insights into the full consequences of the various alternatives. The reasons for selecting a particular approach or blend of approaches should be clearly stated so that others can understand the rationale for the particular choice.

Whatever approaches and methods are selected, they should satisfy the following criteria:

1. *Validity:* How much confidence is there that the results can actually be used?
2. *Relevance:* Are the results useful to decision makers?
3. *Significance:* Will the results go beyond what is apparent from direct observation? Will the results tell the decision maker something new and important?
4. *Efficiency:* Does the value of the insights obtained exceed the cost of using the approach?
5. *Timeliness:* Will the analytical information be available in time to meet a management or legislative decision point, such as the renewal of expiring legislation?

Modeling and statistical inference are two particularly useful methods which are frequently used by evaluators and analysts.

A model is an abstraction from or a representation of the key elements in some real system. If the key elements and their relationships are adequately specified, relevant, and valid, a model can predict the consequences of untried alternatives and variations in data and assumptions.

Statistical inference techniques are widely used to analyze data obtained from the various collection instruments and analytical models. However, the conditions and assumptions underlying these methods must be satisfied if statistical inference techniques are to be used. Mistakes can occur, for example, if prepackaged computer programs are used without understanding the assumptions and conditions.

CONDUCTING A STUDY

In the performance of any evaluation or analysis, practical decisions of many types must be made, and practical problems are frequently encountered. Some of the most common ones are discussed here.

Collecting relevant data

In performing studies, there is often a temptation to collect all of the information which might be of use. Although every piece of information may have some value in the right place, is it relevant and worth what it costs to acquire it? Questions which should be continually applied to any data collection effort are:

Exactly what question is this piece of data intended to answer?
What analytical model demands it?
What calculation cannot be done without it?

Testing the reliability of data

An attempt should be made to estimate whether data are reasonable at the time they are first generated; that is, how does this new piece of information square with everything else that is known or can be deduced relating to it? This is especially important when complex calculations are involved. How does the answer compare with the rough calculations? The exercise of making rough calculations frequently gives the staff member new insights into the data.

There are numbers of one kind or another which are widely published. Everyone seems to use these numbers unquestioningly. However, careful analysis has often demonstrated that some data have a different interpretation than what is commonly supposed.

Occasionally, attempts may be made to withhold information. It is not uncommon to hear that data:

Are too hard to assemble.
Do not exist in the form wanted.
Are only a working paper.
Are privileged.

When faced with situations of this type, the analyst should (1) consider the value of the information to the study, (2) attempt to obtain a release of the appropriate information if it is needed, and (3) propose to the study coordinator that a formal request be sent for the needed information. In some cases, essential data will have to be "constructed" or "extracted" from secondary sources.

Frequently, data collected from different sources about the same subject matter will be in apparent conflict. The first practical step in getting the right data is to reconcile the conflicting interpretations of the data. An appropriate question might be: Are the data truly two different sets of values describing exactly the same event or situation? A second step would be to examine how the data were derived. The apparent conflict may be a simple function of the data collection methodology. After these procedures have been employed, it may be appropriate to use an analytical technique to determine the significance of the differences. Additional assurances may be obtained by having the data reviewed by experts in the field.

Protecting the confidentiality of information about individuals

It is often necessary in evaluation and analysis to collect data about individuals. In most research involving human subjects there has been a firm commitment to protect the confidentiality of personal data. It is important to make certain that data on individuals are not personally identifiable in the study or in unsecured files. If it is necessary to obtain information from the same individuals in subsequent time periods, special controls and procedures should be required to assure that systems of records do not disclose individually identifiable data.

Federal agencies and some federal contractors are required to comply, where applicable, with all provisions of the Privacy Act of 1974 to protect the confidentiality of individually identifiable data. These provisions include:

Public disclosure of the fact that an agency maintains a system of records about individuals.

Strictly enforceable procedures for assuring that individuals have access to their records and the opportunity to correct them.

Controls on the disclosure of individuals' identifiable data.

Administrative, technical, and physical safeguards to prevent unauthorized access to such data.

In planning a study, care should be taken to require individually identifiable information to be collected only when no other approach can enable the issue to be validly studied. When such data are collected, they must be properly protected.

Documenting and referencing

Documenting appraisals of the results and assessments of alternatives is important. The documentation should be sufficient to enable other individuals or teams involved in reviewing the policy or program to follow the analysis and, as needed, to reconstruct parts of it or to use it in another study. Basic assumptions should be clearly identified and recorded. The rationale for using direct or surrogate measures should be stated explicitly. Oral interviews should be summarized in writing, dated, and filed. Original documents should be retained. Complete files of relevant raw data and work papers should be kept and filed so that they can be retrieved easily for review. Information which cannot be readily filed should be adequately described and referenced in the files.

The study team should design, use, and save work papers. Well-designed, clearly labeled, and fully legible work papers offer an important insurance policy to the study team. The work papers constitute the evidence gathered. A review of the work papers will show whether the study team has been thorough or whether it has overlooked an important fact or an important element of a problem and whether all similar elements of the analysis or evaluation have been treated consistently. The work papers should be checked against the study plan to assure that the plan has been carried out or that changes have been fully explained. Developing the total costs of each of a series of alternatives is an outstanding example of the need for, and usefulness of, a carefully designed and clearly labeled set of work sheets. Without them, the chances of missing an important cost element, incorrectly calculating an intermediate result, or costing the competing alternatives inconsistently are substantial.

Work papers should be dated and signed so that a clear trail is established as to who did what and when. The best way to tie it all together is to file, with work papers, one copy of the final report which is cross-referenced to significant sections of the work papers.

Adhering to time schedules

Effort should be made to anticipate some of the possible delays, and the time schedule should allow for unforeseen delays. Most complex tasks are harder than originally anticipated and therefore take longer than estimated. In complex studies, detailed schedules for component parts may be necessary. A proposal to expand the scope of the study or to do more work in order to sharpen the results should be carefully justified, particularly if it involves risk of delay in the schedule.

Leading and coordinating the study team

It is essential to maximize the interaction among the study team members. Physical arrangements which inhibit this should be avoided or modified if at all possible. When gathering the first list of alternatives or hypotheses, brainstorming is extremely useful.

The coordinator should take every practicable step to ensure easy access to the decision makers who expect to use the analysis or evaluation. A continuing (but not necessarily continuous) dialogue should help to make the products useful and well accepted. The coordinator also needs to impress on the team the importance of maintaining an open, honest, and amicable relationship with the personnel of the program under analysis or evaluation. It is all too easy for program people to frustrate a study if they have been antagonized or hurt.

Using computer-based models

For most large-scale, but routine, quantitative manipulations (statistical analysis, linear programming, etc.), good "canned" programs are available and should be used. When a program or problem has many complex interrelationships, however, and the effects of altering the assumptions or data are not obvious, a specially designed, computer-based model may facilitate the study. In such cases, creative computer programmers are extremely valuable.

The structure and operation of any model should be reasonably apparent to decision makers who want to use the study: its output and working must be readily understandable to them. Usually, this can be accomplished by carefully diagramming the components of the model and explaining how each component operates and interacts with the others. Users of the study will normally accept the computational competence of the model if the logic makes sense to them and they have confidence in the study team.

COMMUNICATING STUDY RESULTS

Many persons who do studies fail to understand that doing a good piece of work is necessary but hardly sufficient for bringing about a favorable change in the world. At least two major steps beyond the successful completion of a study are required: the results must be clearly, concisely, and cogently communicated to all of those affected, and a policy or program decision must be made which results in some kind of action.

Specifying the nature of reports

There are three general classes of problems involved in reporting appraisals of results and assessments of alternatives: (1) to whom reports should be made, (2) when reports should be made, and (3) what style and content characterize good reports. Each new study will suggest its own individual requirements and should be made a matter of record in the agreed work plan adopted before the study is begun. A few general guidelines can, however, be set down.

Obviously, the final report should be addressed to those who are in a position to take appropriate action—or to assure that it is taken by others. Unless special considerations dictate otherwise (such as security problems), reports should routinely go first to the team supervisor and others as needed to ensure that they meet the organization's professional standards. Even professionally sound studies, however, may result in disagreements with the managers of the programs being studied. In these cases, the study team should reduce the number of areas of disagreement; and, where such areas continue to exist, the issues should be substantial and clearly defined. Although decision makers waiting to use the report should be kept informed of key findings, it will in the end serve them best if the review process is complete before the final report goes to them.

No report other than the final version should be distributed to persons other than those mentioned above without concurrence of those mentioned. The unauthorized release of preliminary, draft, interim, or partial reports can be harmful because, frequently, erroneous information, even though corrected later, becomes widely diffused and a source of further error and confusion. Publicly available reports should be free of such errors.

In planning the study, sufficient time should be allowed for writing the final draft report, gathering comments, editing, and securing the necessary approvals. The report writers, in turn, have an obligation to complete the report within the scheduled time. Report outlines should be prepared early. They can provide indications of the most critical data gathering and interpretation tasks yet to be completed in order to have a useful and timely report. Decision points come and go relentlessly, and a potentially good, decision-affecting report may lose much of its value because it was not available when needed.

Communicating with clarity and conciseness

Writing a good report is an art, and the required skills are probably as scarce as those necessary for evaluation and analysis. The solution is to insist that staff members work at learning to write well. One helpful step is to provide staff members with specific guidance, such as a good style manual, and to insist that they study and use the manual as a part of their regular duties. In addition, someone on the staff can serve as resident editor. It is frequently helpful to have a skilled technical editor or writer join the team when the report is being written. All significant alterations should be discussed with the author—not only to ensure accuracy, but also to assist the author in learning to write shorter and more trenchant reports.

Study reports are typically directed at readers who lack relevant technical training. Therefore, the main body of the report should be written so that it is readily comprehensible to the nonprofessional reader. However, the material included in the report should be sufficient so that a reader can understand the arguments in support of the conclusion. Jargon should be kept to a minimum, and where it is used, it should be defined carefully. Supporting technical material should be presented in appendixes. Graphs and tables included in the main body of the text must be clearly labeled and fully discussed in the text. Short reports are typically self-contained, while long ones ought to be accompanied by an executive summary of the study's general conclusions and recommendations.

There will, of course, be differences in the format and content of a report appraising program or policy results and a report assessing alternatives, or a report that does both. Within each of these types of reports, some variation in format and content is inevitable, depending on the nature of the policy or program issue being studied and the methods used.

Following up

Writing a clear, concise, and informative "final" report is not the end of the "communicating responsibility." Usually, some decision makers will need assistance in (1) interpreting the report, (2) clarifying aspects of it, (3) getting answers to questions raised but not answered by it, and (4) in general, developing a reasoned reaction to it. Briefings, informal question-and-answer sessions, and various kinds of supplementary written materials may be needed. In some cases, the communicating responsibility may even extend to preparing the supporting technical parts of whatever document emerges from the decision-making process.

It is the responsibility of the staff which performed the work to be available to the decision maker for help in understanding and using the study. The staff should also make a diligent effort to find out whether or not the study was useful. Lessons learned in this way can lead to better studies the next time.

Glossary

Adversary process: A debate, legal contest, or other confrontation in which a decision is obtained or sought through the verbal interchanges of proponents of opposing positions in the presence of a neutral decision maker.

Agenda setting: The process of determining the issues that an organization or jurisdiction will address.

Algorithm: A set of stepwise directions for attacking a problem.

Alternative: One of several possible courses of action or programs considered to offer the same approximate outcome or effect.

Appropriation: The process by which Congress approves in statutes (bills) the actual amounts each unit or agency of government can spend.

Audit: The final phase of the budgetary process; a review of the operations of the agency, especially its financial transactions, to determine whether the agency has spent the money in accordance with the law, in the most efficient manner, and with the desired results.

Authorization: Basic substantive legislation enacted by Congress that sets up or continues the legal operation of a federal program or agency. Such legislation is normally a prerequisite for subsequent appropriations but does not usually provide budget authority.

Advocacy policy: The recognition that policymaking is a highly political process, involving severe differences of judgment, in which the most feasible course of action is likely to emerge from the competition produced when each group pleads for the cause it represents.

Base: The point from which most budgetary calculations begin, generally that appropriation which the agency received in the previous fiscal year.

Baseline: A standard. A reference point on some significant parameter against which changes over time can be measured (e.g., analysis of the solute content in a particular stream on a specific day of the year, so that by measuring the solute content on the same day in subsequent years a trend can be established).

Bounded rationality: The type of rationality (or logical thinking) exhibited by decision makers in situations where the complexity of the environment exceeds the computational powers of the human brain (a term coined by Herbert A. Simon).

Break-even point: The point at which a program's total revenues equal its total costs. In economics, the break-even point is the point at which the firm is just making a normal rate of return.

Budget constraint: The constraint that individuals and, indeed, governments face when they decide how much of their income to spend. The budget constraint prevents individuals from spending more income than they actually have.

Capital budgeting: The separation of expenditures that produce long-term benefits, especially those involving the construction of public facilities, from the annual operating costs of government. The process for reviewing expenditure decisions for capital projects and deciding on the methods for financing them, usually through the sale of bonds.

Capital-intensive program: A program in which the capital investment per employee is high. *See* Capital budgeting above.

Citizen participation: Involvement of the public in decision making. At least three different forms of such involvement can be distinguished: (1) participation in the selection of the decision makers (i.e., exercise of the right to vote); (2) involvement in the deliberations of the decision makers by communications and representations of interest in a desired outcome; and (3) public participation in the decision itself (sometimes called "direct democracy") by plebiscite, public convention, or other means.

Concurrent resolution on the budget: A resolution passed by both houses of Congress, but not requiring the signature of the president, setting forth, reaffirming, or revising specified congressional budget totals for the federal government for a fiscal year.

Constraint: A limiting condition to be satisfied in the design or operation of a system. Examples of constraints are total cost ceiling, the percentage of system life consumed in downtime, physical size or weight, and requirements for the compatibility of a system with other systems.

Controllability: The ability of Congress or the president to control outlays during a fiscal year without changing existing law. The concept "relatively uncontrollable" includes outlays for open-ended programs and fixed costs, such as interest on the public debt, social security and veterans benefits, and outlays to liquidate prior-year obligations.

Cooptation: The strategy of bringing an individual into a group by joint action of the members of that group, usually in order to reduce or eliminate the individual's opposition.

Correlational analysis: The analysis of two or more items that involve a mutual relationship; an effort to determine the degree of correspondence between two sets of data.

Cost-benefit analysis: A procedure that can be used to analyze the net benefits accruing from a particular action. In cost-benefit analysis, all costs are laid

672

out from now on into the future, as are all benefits. These costs and benefits are discounted back to the present, and the costs are subtracted from the benefits, thus yielding a net present value benefit figure. If the net benefits turn out to be negative, then the project or action probably is not justifiable. *See* Discounting.

Cost-effectiveness analysis: The ratio, over an explicit and finite time span, of cost in dollars and other tangible values to some effectiveness or performance measure, such as lives saved.

Cost out: In program analysis, an early step in the assigning of monetary costs to the various program inputs required.

Counterintuitive: Contrary to one's natural expectations. The term was popularized by Jay Forrester, professor of management at the Massachusetts Institute of Technology, in a paper entitled "The Counter-Intuitive Behavior of Social Systems." Forrester pointed out that socioeconomic systems generally do not respond in the way that people anticipate and that as a result, programs undertaken to solve a given problem often fail to solve the problem and may even intensify it. For example, a housing project designed to help poor people may actually increase their suffering by concentrating them in a location where they do not have access to jobs, or increasing bus fares to raise the revenues of a public transit system that is losing money will often cause a decrease in ridership and a further loss of revenue.

Critical path method (CPM): A method of scheduling work by means of diagrams that show which jobs must be completed before other jobs can be started. The jobs are indicated by arrows; hence the technique is sometimes called arrow diagraming. *See* PERT.

Cross-impact analysis: An attempt to identify the various effects that developments have on each other. For example, the development of an improved transportation system may reduce the need for better communications— or vice versa. The structure for accomplishing such an analysis, called a cross-impact matrix, lists fields or specific developments along both the horizontal and vertical axes and provides boxes in which the analyst can note the impacts that two variables have on each other.

Current services estimates: Projections of estimated budget authority and outlays for the upcoming fiscal year at the same program level and with the same policies as those of the fiscal year in progress. To the extent mandated by existing law, estimates take into account the budget impact of anticipated changes in economic conditions (such as unemployment or inflation), beneficiary levels, pay increases, and benefit changes. The Congressional Budget and Impoundment Control Act of 1974 requires that the president submit current services estimates to Congress by November 10 of each year.

Decision analysis: By combining aspects of systems analysis and statistical decision theory, this probability technique helps the analyst to build a decision tree. The goal of a "good" decision, under this technique, is to maximize the probability of a favorable outcome.

Decision tree: *See* decision analysis.

Delphi method: A procedure for forecasting future events. The procedure has been most commonly employed to estimate the probable time of achievement of specific technological or social goals. The technique involves the repeated ("iterative") consulting with numbers of informed persons on when a specified event is likely to occur (i.e., when it will occur, not when it should occur), and providing them with systematic reports on the totality of judgments rendered by the group.

Demand curve: A line on a graph showing the relationship between the prices for which a good can be purchased and the respective quantities demanded at those prices.

Diminishing marginal returns: Usually defined as the law of diminishing marginal returns. After some point, successive increases in the variable factor of production, such as labor, added to the fixed factors of production will not cause an equiproportionate increase in output.

Discounting: The procedure used to reduce future monetary values to their present values. Discounting requires the use of a discount rate, which is the interest rate that is decided on as appropriate for each particular case.

Econometric model: A series of mathematical equations which describe the operations of an economy. The equations can be entered into a computer, and a variety of simulations made, using various assumptions (e.g., a corporate tax reduction of four points).

Economies of scale: A situation in which an increase in all of the factors of production brings about a more than proportionate increase in output.

Elite: Those people at the top of a society who exercise a major influence on public decision making.

Empiricism: A method based extensively or entirely on experience, observation, or experiment, with little or no reliance on science or theory.

Employment Act of 1946: Congress declared in this act that it was the federal government's responsibility to maintain full employment. This act commits the federal government to positive monetary and fiscal actions calculated to maintain full employment.

Environmental impact statements: Analysis of the environmental implications of actions engaged in by agencies of the federal government; such analyses are prepared by federal agencies pursuant to Section 102 of the National Environmental Policy Act of 1969 (NEPA) (Public Law 91–190, approved January 1, 1970).

Ethics: The study of the specific moral choices to be made by individuals in their relationships with others.

Evaluation: The use of research techniques to measure the past performance of a specific program—in particular, the program's impact on the conditions it seeks to modify—for the purpose of changing the operation of the program so as to improve its effectiveness in achieving its objectives.

Externalities: Economically speaking, externalities are costs or benefits not taken into account in a transaction or a system of transactions. In this usage, the right of an industry to pollute a stream (i.e., a "free good") when such pollution is not charged against the cost of doing business would be an externality.

Extrapolation: Extending a curve into the future simply by assuming that the variable will continue to change at the same rate and in the same direction. For example, if the population of a city has increased 2 percent a year and the number of its inhabitants is now 1,000,000, one can extrapolate the trend into the future. Such extrapolation would indicate that the city's population one year from now would be 1,020,000.

Feedback: Broadly, any information about the results of a policy intervention that may be used to adjust that policy.

Fiscal year: The yearly accounting period for the federal government. Beginning with fiscal year 1977, fiscal years for the federal government begin on October 1 and end on September 30. Prior to fiscal year 1977, the fiscal year began on July 1 and ended on June 30. The fiscal year is designated by the calendar year in which it ends (e.g., fiscal year 1979 is the fiscal year ending September 30, 1979).

Forecast: Loosely, a forecast is synonymous with a prediction. However, a forecast is properly distinguished from it in that a forecast is a probabilistic statement at a relatively high confidence level that a specified event will occur by a specified future point in time or within some specified time period. Methodological types of forecasting include probabilistic forecasting, Delphi techniques, gaming, cross-impact analysis, scenario building, extrapolation techniques, contextual mapping, precursive analysis, brainstorming, statistical models, expert panels, relevance trees, network analysis, historical analogy, operation models, individual "expert" forecasting, simulation, and causal modeling.

Free rider problem: Public goods often have the free rider problem, in which an individual, when asked, will claim that he does not want the good in question because he hopes that in this way he will get the good but that others will pay for it. He attempts to be a free rider. *See* Tragedy of the commons.

Futures research: Futures research encompasses various attempts to develop systemic methodologies to identify future options or alternatives, or to narrow probabilities of time estimates.

Game theory: A theory used in operations research to develop a technique designed to make possible the maximization of gains or the minimization of losses regardless of the countermoves by competitors.

Gaming: The use of a game that simulates a real situation. For example, games have been developed to represent the operations of a city government. Different players may play the parts of the mayor, city council, real estate lobby, tenants' association, and so on. By playing the game, the players begin to understand more clearly the problems and opportunities of city government.

Gantt chart: A chart on which progress in the various parts of a program or project is plotted against time. *See* Critical path method (CPM).

Goals, national: In general, these are outcomes, options, conditions, or relationships of large or national scope, held socially desirable by a consensus of persons or by groups, influential individuals, or political decision makers.

National goals may be formal, informal, or tacit. There are many mechanisms by which national goals are proposed, considered, and promulgated as well as many ways by which they are modified, superseded, abandoned, or reduced in force.

National goals of different scope or character may be formulated. For example, there are philosophical goals that state a nation's values or formal governmental purposes (such as liberty, welfare, tranquillity, and security). There are social goals, expressing aspirations for improvement in a social function (such as literacy, or living standards) or for the correction of social defects (such as crime rates or ill health). Political or legislative goals may take the form of formal statements of desired public objectives issued in legislative form by a lawmaking body (such as the "Finding of the Congress that . . ."). Agency goals are expressed initially in the form of legislation— the organic acts creating departments and agencies of government and defining their missions; these are interpreted administratively as expanded mission statements and communications to the public. Pursuant to agency goals are program goals or objectives, and at a still finer-grain level of specificity, project goals or objectives.

Gross national product (GNP): The monetary value of the goods and services produced in a country in a year, without subtraction of amounts chargeable to depreciation.

Heuristic: An approach that serves to stimulate research or discovery. A number of methods may be used because of their heuristic value, that is, their ability to encourage people to learn a variety of new things. For example, students may be asked to design a model community; in the process, they are led to acquire a wide variety of knowledge about how communities operate, what values are important to the students themselves, and so on.

Holistic: An approach to research or analysis characterized by an emphasis on completeness or wholeness; opposed to the atomistic approach. The holistic approach is related to the synergistic approach, with its emphasis on the whole as being greater than the sum of the parts.

Ideology: The combined doctrines, assertions, and intentions with which a social or political group justifies its behavior.

Impact assessment: *See* technology assessment.

Implementation: The carrying out of a policy; program operations.

Incrementalism: An approach to decision making in government in which executives begin with the current situation, consider a limited number of changes in that situation based on a restricted range of alternatives, and test those changes by instituting them one at a time. A normative theory of government which views policymaking as a process of bargaining and competition involving the participation of different persons with conflicting points of view. Often termed "the art of muddling through."

Input-output analysis: A descriptive model of the economy in which I–O tables are used to trace, predict, or evaluate the effect of changes in the different sectors of the system. *See* Input-output tables.

Input-output tables: These tables show the physical relationships (such as value and flow) among goods and services in an industry, region, or some other entity at a specified point in time.

Labor-intensive industry: An industry requiring small amounts of capital per employee.

Leading indicators: Statistics that generally precede a change in a situation. For example, an increase in economic activity is typically preceded by a rise in the prices of stocks.

Lead: The time required for a development to move from conception to completion. In some cases, lead times are very long: building a new power plant, for example, may take ten years because of the delays occasioned by planning, legal problems, construction, and so on.

Legislative intent: The supposed real meaning of a statute as it can be interpreted from the legislative history.

Lobbying: The strategy in which organized interests seek to influence the passage of legislation by exerting direct pressure on members of the legislature.

Logrolling: A legislative practice wherein reciprocal agreements are made between legislators, usually in voting for or against a bill. In contrast to the parties in bargaining, the parties to logrolling have nothing in common but their desire to exchange support.

Lorenz curve: A graphic representation of the distribution of income. A Lorenz curve which is perfectly straight represents perfect income equality. The more bowed a Lorenz curve, the more unequally income is distributed.

Macroeconomics: The study of aggregates such as Gross National Product.

Management by objectives: A process for clarifying the mission of the agency and the specific areas of responsibility within it, including the methods for planning, measuring, and evaluating the activities of employees in relation to agency goals. The process of joint target setting and periodic performance review conducted between a superior and a subordinate.

Management information system (MIS): A special type of information system, generally computer-based, that collects data about past, present, and projected activities and transforms these data into information that managers can use to plan the future course of the organization and to make decisions about the optimal utilization of resources. Also called Decision support system (DSS).

Marginal cost: The increase in cost due to an increase in production. Marginal costs are defined as the total costs for, say, 1,000 units of production minus the total costs for 999 units.

Marginal cost pricing: A system of pricing in which the price charged is equal to the opportunity cost of producing one more unit of the good or service in question. The opportunity cost is the marginal cost to society.

Marginal return: The returns for employing additional units of a factor of production. For example, the marginal return of employing one worker would equal the increase in output after the worker was hired.

Market: A geographic area within which the price of a good or service tends to be uniform, allowing for transportation costs.

Median: For an odd number of measurements, the median is the middle measurement when the measurements are arranged in order of size. For an even number of measurements, the median is the mean (average) of the two middle observations.

Microeconomics: That part of economics specializing in the study of specific economic units or parts of an economic system. In microeconomic theory, we study individuals, firms, and households and the relationships between them.

Mission: A single large operation or task, or a continuing specific function. Examples of missions might include the construction of a number of housing units, the capture of a hill, the development of a prototype fast breeder reactor, the maintenance of national air superiority, and the achievement of improved pollution control or automobile safety. A distinction may be made between an agency of government performing a continuous or repetitive function, such as budgetary control or revenue administration, and an agency responsible for carrying out one of the missions listed above. The latter might be called a "mission agency," but probably not the former.

Mode: In a set of measurements, the mode is the measurement that occurs most often.

Model: A simplified representation of how the real world works. Models can be expressed by mathematical equations, geometric graphs, or simply stated with words.

Monitoring: An activity that evaluates on a continuous or periodic basis the feedback from an operation against established criteria.

Monopoly: A situation in which there is only a single seller of a product for which there are no good substitutes.

Morphological analysis: Any technique which seeks to identify systematically all of the possible means for achieving a given end. One approach is to create a list of all possible variables so that each can be examined and combinations explored.

Natural monopoly: A monopoly that arises out of the peculiar production characteristics in an industry. Usually a natural monopoly arises when production of a service or product requires extremely large capital investments such that only one firm can be profitably supported by consumers. A natural monopoly usually arises when there are economies of scale.

Normative: This important adjective encompasses all values, value orientations, and value-motivated activities. Unlike the scientific method, which aspires to be value-free, a normative procedure or activity concentrates on the assigning of social values. What we have here, is Hume's distinction between "is" and "ought." Thus, normative forecasting of technology represents an attempt to identify what kinds of innovation will be needed (i.e., what society will desire or ought to have) by some future date, and normative analysis attempts to determine what is good or bad; science, on the other hand, simply states what happens and why.

NIH (not invented here) syndrome: Alleged to be a characteristic of many organizations, its major symptom is a lack of interest by professionals in new ideas which have originated outside their establishment or perhaps even in another division of their establishment. The NIH syndrome may be considered an organizational pathology which impedes communication and innovation. It is caused by a conviction, based on institutional pride or confidence, that "if it were any good, we would have thought of it first.

Obligations: Orders placed, contracts awarded, services rendered, or other commitments made by federal agencies during a given period that will require outlays during the same period or a future period.

Operations research: The application of scientific methods, including mathematical or logical analysis, to fairly well-defined problems involving the operation of systems in order to provide optimal solutions given a predetermined set of objectives and a fixed range of acceptable alternatives.

Opportunity cost: The true cost of choosing one alternative rather than another. Opportunity cost, also called alternative cost, represents the implicit cost to an individual of the highest forgone alternative.

Optimum: The course of action that minimizes overall losses or maximizes overall gains.

Outlays: Checks issued, interest accrued on the public debt, or other payments made, net of refunds and reimbursements.

Overhead: Costs that do not vary with output over a period of time.

Paradigm: A pattern or model representing a situation or condition. As used today, paradigm typically refers to a person's basic conception of a certain aspect of reality. He or she may, for example, view science as the paradigm of knowledge, that is, as the way knowledge is or ought to be. The current usage of the term was stimulated by Thomas Kuhn's *The Structure of Scientific Revolutions*.

Paradox of voting: A minor difficulty in voting, often referred to as Arrow's dilemma, that people with a mathematical turn of mind enjoy toying with. Let A, B, and C be the three alternatives, and 1, 2, and 3 the three individuals. Suppose that individual 1 prefers A to B and B to C (and therefore A to C), that individual 2 prefers B to C and C to A (and therfore B to A), and that individual 3 prefers C to A and A to B (and therefore C to B). Then a majority prefer A to B and a majority prefer B to C. We may therefore say that the community prefers A to B and B to C. If the community is to be regarded as behaving rationally, we are forced to say that A is preferred to C. But in fact a majority of the community prefer C to A. It follows, the argument runs, that in such situations majority rule by voting is deficient for making rational decisions.

Parameter: A quantity or characteristic having fixed values for a particular subject for separately indicated cases or conditions. For example, the strength or resistance to failure of a given material (one parameter) will vary according to temperature (another parameter). The information can be presented in the form of a table or a curve.

Mathematically speaking, parameters are those factors, generally variables, which together represent or approximate the nature, functioning, or behavior of a system. For example, the parameters which completely define a straight line in a Cartesian system are distance along the x-axis, distance along the y-axis, and the point at which the line crosses the y-axis.

Parameters are generally quantifiable and, when quantified, subject to mathematical formulation. However, the term parameter may be loosely applied to factors which are not readily subject to mathematical operations. For example, parameters required to predict the outcomes of elections may include numbers of registered voters, party affiliations, past voter turnouts, voter attitudes, expected impacts of major issues, and expected impacts of major interest groups, several of which are nonexclusive and nonquantifiable.

When parameters are quantifiable, or at least subject to analysis in qualitative form (such as "popular" or "unpopular" candidates and "important" or "unimportant" issues), but not reducible to mathematical formulation (that is, not reducible to a statement of equality or nonequality), they may be analyzed in other ways. Such "parametric" analyses include rank orderings, frequency distributions, graphic analyses, cross-impact matrix analyses, algorithms, Delphi methods, and heuristic modeling.

Pareto optimality: This equilibrium point is reached in a society when resource allocation is most efficient. That is, no further changes in resource allocation can be made that will increase the welfare of one person without decreasing the welfare of other persons.

Peak-load pricing: Pricing which accounts for the fact that during the peak periods of using a resource, such as a toll bridge, a freeway, or streets, the marginal cost for each individual's use is higher because of the congestion that is caused. Peak-load pricing involves a surcharge or an additional charge for use of the resource during a peak period.

PERT: Program evaluation review technique. A more elaborate version of the critical path method which takes more factors into account.

Phillips curve: A curve showing the relationship between unemployment and inflation. The Phillips curve gives the trade-off between unemployment and inflation.

Pluralistic democracy: A system of democracy in which political elites actively compete for leadership, voters choose from among those elites, and new elites can emerge in quest of leadership.

Policy: A general course or method of operation adopted or proposed for the achievement of a condition or goal. The term is customarily employed with respect to social, public, administrative, and business institutions, particularly to characterize the general principles that are used to guide the operational decisions of their principal executives in an effort to achieve coherence and consistency of management. "Policy means . . . intelligently directed action toward consciously determined goals—as distinct from aimless drift and blind faith." An administrative hierarchy of procedure should be identified. It begins with *policy* (as defined above), which leads to a *plan*, then a *program* ("an ordered set of interrelated actions"). Program, in turn, may be further subdivided into *projects* or tasks, each contributing coherently to a program in support of a policy.

Policy analysis: Generally, the analysis of policy calls for an investigation of the effects of policy alternatives in order to identify at the earliest possible time an agency's preferred broad course of action toward its goals.

Viewing policy as the complex of principles that govern action toward given ends, policy analysis includes such matters as the examination of the adjudication of laws, statements of leaders, agency documents, legislation and laws, and position papers from the private sector, for the purposes of evaluating goals, means, processes, objectives, achievements, and intentions. In this way, it seeks to formulate guidance for the management of government programs, the use of resources, and the control of human behavior. The analysis of policy includes: conflicts among policies, internal consistencies, impacts on society and its environment, political consequences, problems of administrative implementation, institutional and organizational aspects, problems of coordination, the determination of relative priorities, timetables for action in programming, and evaluation and overview requirements.

Policy science: This term is relatively new and subject to considerable interpretation. It appears mainly to encompass (1) an understanding of the process by which broad principles useful in institutional problem-solving activities are evolved and (2) the kinds of knowledge—both scientific disciplines and value systems—useful in the application of that process to particular conditions, circumstances, or problems.

Pork barrel legislation: Appropriations made by legislative bodies for local projects which are often not needed but which are created so that local representatives can carry their home district in the next election.

PPBS (planning-programming-budgeting system): First introduced in the Department of Defense in the early 1960s, PPBS integrates planning, programming, and budgeting into an organization's decision-making process. Decisions on programs based on carefully articulated plans are made in light of the required resources. To arrive at these decisions, plans are needed to translate agency goals into specific objectives and programs are framed for each alternative method of achieving those objectives. Budgets must reflect the total cost of each alternative. Decision makers remain cognizant of these phases while judging the effectiveness of performance versus cost.

PPBS is a means, therefore, of analyzing both policy and the implementation of policy, a consideration of the available alternatives and of the resources that would be required by each alternative. It is a means for allocating resources on a national scale by overcoming the problems presented by the fact that requirements for programs are relative, that clear criteria are wanting, and that information as to the costs and benefits of alternatives is rarely available. Any individual program can plausibly demand resources in excess of a reasonable expectation of the capacity to provide them. (See Program budgeting.)

Prediction: Loosely, synonymous with forecast. Properly distinguished from a forecast in that a prediction is a declaration (a nonprobabilistic statement at an absolute confidence level) that some specified event will occur at a specified future point in time or within some time period.

Price elasticity of demand: Formally equal to the percentage change in quantity demanded divided by the percentage change in price. Price elasticity of demand is a measure of the responsiveness of consumers to changes in the price of a good or service.

Price elasticity of supply: Formally defined as the percentage change in the quantity supplied divided by the percentage change in price. Price elasticity of supply is a measure of the responsiveness of suppliers or producers to an increase or a decrease in the price of the product they are producing.

Priorities: Any systematic methodology for putting first things first. The use of priorities is the systematic application of pertinent criteria to a set of options in order to rank the options in a rational order of preference as claimants for a limiting resource. The limiting resource can be, for example, management attention, dollars, or personnel. The implication of a priority system is that not all programs can be undertaken at once, or with the same degree of completeness or the same expenditure of resources, and that therefore resources must be reserved (allocated) in accordance with a set of rationally determined preferences.

Private sector: Industries or activities that are considered the domain of free enterprise.

Probability distribution: A display, which can be presented as a table, graph, or formula, that shows the probability associated with the value y. To illustrate, consider an experiment in tossing two coins, and let the variable y represent the number of heads observed. Then y can take (assume) values 0, 1, or 2. The probability distribution of this example would be:

y	$P(y)$
0	.25
1	.50
2	.25

Production possibilities curve: A curve, sometimes referred to as the production possibilities frontier, depicting the maximum production possibilities for an economy at a given point in time. The curve shows the trade-off between producing one good as opposed to another.

Program: A set of actions to implement an agency's mission, or a major part of the mission. A pattern of instructions to a computer.

Program budgeting: A long-range approach to budgetary decision making that relates future expenditures to the broadly defined purposes or objectives of government, thus providing top executives with information on the distribution of scarce resources between competing objectives and revealing the total program costs required to accomplish any given objective.

Public choice: An approach to political analysis positing that politicians, bureaucrats, and voters all act rationally in their self-interest.

Public interest: Until recently, public interest could be defined as something in which the public, the community at large, has some pecuniary interest or some interest by which their legal rights or liabilities are affected. It did not mean anything so narrow as mere curiosity, or as the interests of the particular localities, which may be affected by the matters in question. Since the early 1960s, however, the concept of the public interest has been given a broader, less well-defined meaning which includes (1) the public's general interest in such things as consumerism and environmentalism, and (2) a rationale for an expansion of the government's influence in business and private affairs, particularly through the quasi-judicial powers of administrative agencies. "Public interest" law firms and such interest groups as Ralph Nader's organizations and John Gardner's Common Cause are an outgrowth of this movement. *See* Citizen participation.

Public goods: Goods whose consumption by one person does not lessen the amount available to other persons, once the good is produced. Examples of public goods are national defense and radio and TV signals.

Public sector: Industries or activities run by the government.

Quality of life: The extent to which a person enjoys a "good" life. As currently used, the expression "quality of life" generally emphasizes the noneconomic aspects of a person's life, such as the purity of the air, security from crime, effective cultural institutions, and general feelings of satisfaction and well-being.

Random sample: From a population of n measurements, a random sample of one measurement is one in which each of the n measurements has an equal probability of being selected.

Range: The difference between the largest and the smallest measurement in a set of measurements.

Relevance tree: A diagrammatic technique for analyzing systems or processes in which distinct levels of complexity or hierarchy can be identified. A relevance tree for a new drug might start with biomedical objectives, under which would be listed prevention, diagnosis, treatment, and so on. Under diagnosis, the tree might branch into structure, function, composition, behavior, and so on. A relevance tree enables an analyst to identify the various aspects of a problem or a proposed solution and thus arrive at a more complete understanding of his subject. This technique is also useful for identifying unintended side effects of innovations.

Resources: In general, resources encompass all of the means or potential means toward ends or potential ends. They can include physical inputs, people (and their levels of training), information, institutional arrangements, available financial assets and credit, and so on.

Risk: The chances of damage, loss, or other unwanted events; often stated in probabilistic terms.

Risk analysis: A probabilistic forecasting method used in dealing with one-time-only operations. The event-free or the fault-free approach used in this method.

Satisficing: Adopting a course that is merely "good enough" from all viewpoints, rather than seeking the best possible course (a term coined by Herbert A. Simon).

Scatter diagram: A plot of all the pairs of data on a coordinate-axis system. The input variable, x, is generally used for the horizontal axis and the output variable, y, for the vertical axis.

Scenario: A description of a sequence of events that might occur in the future. A scenario is normally developed by: (1) studying the facts of a situation, (2) selecting a development that might occur, and (3) imagining the range and sequence of consequences that might follow from its occurrence. For example, a person charged with protecting a city might first seek to identify the various possible threats and the responses that the city's agencies might make to them; he or she could then imagine what would happen if the potential challenges to the city's security actually occurred. In this way, the scenario writer can try to identify potential weaknesses in a city's security system and to suggest ways to eliminate them.

S-curve: A mathematical curve representing a variable which first increases in magnitude at an accelerating rate, decelerates, and eventually grows very little or even declines. Also known as the sigmoid curve, from the Greek letter *sigma*.

Second-order effects (or consequences): Side effects from a program or project.

Sensitivity analysis: An analytical procedure to identify particularly sensitive responses of a system to changes in specific inputs or other factors.

Side effects: The purpose of all public policy is to improve the human condition in some explicit way. But it has been noted that innovative programs invariably produce other effects, unintended and often undesirable. These side effects may be inherent in the programs, or they may result from the misapplication of the programs. They may be immediate or long range, decisively important or minor, discrete or incremental, or perhaps synergistic.

Simulation: The use of a model, generally mathematical, to represent a real system for the purpose of gathering information about how the real system responds to changing conditions. Advantages of simulation are: (1) it is typically faster and cheaper to simulate changes in the real system than it is to actively make those changes; and (2) simulation does not disturb the real system.

   Simulation is usually done on a digital computer because of the computer's speed and its capacity to store information and instructions. However, simulation may be done by hand, with an analog computer, or by means of physical representation, which is normally in miniature, as with a wind tunnel.

Social costs: Costs of an action which include all the costs that society bears. Social costs are different from private costs in some situations where externalities are involved.

Social equity: The normative standard that makes equity, rather than efficiency, the primary criterion for judging the "goodness" of policy. In accordance with this standard, analysts must weigh the impact of their programs upon the welfare of individual human beings in order to promote an equitable distribution of services, to eliminate the injurious effects of programs, and to make certain that any inequities in service are always in the direction of enhancing the power and the well-being of disadvantaged groups.

Social indicator: A statistical variable relating to the state of society. The crime rate, the level of literacy, and the incidence of alcoholism may be viewed as social indicators. The concept of social indicators developed as a social equivalent to that of economic indicators (e.g., unemployment rate).

Spin-off: A shorthand term for a sequence in which technology developed expressly for major (mainly aerospace) governmental purposes is then applied elsewhere with economic benefit.

Standard deviation: This measure of variability is the positive square root of the variance (see Variance). The sample standard deviation is denoted by s and the corresponding population standard deviation by the symbol σ.

Strategic thinking: The art of developing a plan (or set of objectives) for attacking a problem; prioritizing.

Subgovernments: Bureaucrats tend to seek political support for their programs by building these informal alliances outside the official hierarchy. The alliances are formed with groups (primarily legislative committees and organized pressure groups) possessing resources that the bureaucrats lack.

Subjective: Resulting from the preferences and customs of the individual; value-laden. Often contrasted with objective.

Suboptimization: Excessive attention to the quality of one component of a larger system to the detriment of total system performance. Literally, the term means optimization of a subordinate part; but since all systems represent a compromise of component quality in order to maximize total system performance, with limited total resources available for the whole, devoting excessive resources to one part takes away essential resources from other parts. For example, a school system that overemphasized (suboptimized for) automobile repair would degrade the general educational quality of its graduates.

Supply curve: A line showing the various quantities that will be forthcoming from suppliers at different prices. The supply curve, sometimes referred to as the supply schedule, represents the minimum price at which a given quantity will be forthcoming.

Synergy: The combined action of a number of parts so that the result is greater than the sum total of the results produced by the separate action of the parts. The term *synergetics* was originally proposed by Buckminster Fuller to describe the characteristics of metallic alloys or structural forms which are stronger than their constituent parts. Since then the concept has been expanded to apply to situations in which various forces in combination achieve more than might have been expected from the strength of these forces in isolation.

System: An entity made up of a number of interacting variables or components.

Systems analysis: A continuous process of reviewing objectives, designing alternative methods of achieving them, and weighing the effectiveness and costs of the alternatives, largely in economic terms. A much broader concept than operations research and a major part of policy analysis. See also Holistic.

Tax expenditures: Losses of tax revenue attributable to provisions of the federal tax law that allow a special exclusion, exemption, or deduction from gross income or provide a special credit, a preferential tax rate, or a deferral of tax liability.

Technological fix: An innovation devised for the purpose of correcting a social defect—for example, a drug taken orally to prevent unwanted conception as a means of population control.

Technology assessment: The evaluation of a technology in terms of both its long-range and its immediate impacts. Technology assessment advocates have stressed that a technology has many impacts that are ordinarily not considered adequately by its designers and propagators. These advocates contend that a proper assessment would evaluate the long-range, far-reaching, and hidden social and economic impacts of a new or proposed technology.

Technology forecasting: The use of special techniques, such as systematic surveys of experts in a field or the assessment of future demand, to anticipate new technological developments that will change the management of an organization or the character of the environment in which it will operate.

Time horizon: The farthest distance into the future that one considers in forecasting and planning. An agency may be viewed as having a "short time horizon" if it rarely gives serious consideration to events that are forecast to occur in more than two years.

Trade-off: Forgoing some portion of one benefit in order to achieve an increased portion of another benefit; or forgoing some portion of a benefit in order to achieve a reduction in a cost; or accepting an increase in one cost in order to achieve a decrease in another cost.

Tragedy of the commons: The principle that the maximization of private gain will not, as Adam Smith argued, result in the maximization of social benefit. More specifically, the tragedy of the commons alludes to a situation in which each of several herdsmen seeks to maximize his gain by adding cattle to a common pasture. A herdsman could rationalize his action in adding one animal to the commons on the basis that he would receive all of the benefit of grazing the additional animal while the detrimental effects of overgrazing caused by his action would be shared equally by all of the herdsmen. In this type of situation, some form of governmental regulation might be required to prevent the economic ruin of the herdsmen who share the commons. The same principal applies to many societal problems (for example, environmental pollution and overpopulation).

Transfer payments: Payments made to individuals for which no goods or services are provided in exchange. The government makes many transfer payments, as in public assistance.

Trend: A change in a variable that takes place over an extended period of time. A trend is normally distinguished from a fluctuation, which is a change that occurs over a brief period of time and is often of no long-term significance. For example, since the beginning of the twentieth century the United States has experienced a trend toward greater frequency of divorce; in 1946, when soldiers returned from overseas, there was a brief upward fluctuation in the divorce rate, which reached a level that did not recur until the 1970s, when the long-term trend reached and surpassed the 1946 level.

Trust funds: Funds collected and used by the federal government for carrying out specific purposes and programs according to the terms of a trust agreement or statute, such as the social security and unemployment trust funds. Trust funds are not available for the general purposes of the government. Trust fund receipts that are not expected to be used in the immediate future are generally invested in interest-bearing government securities and earn interest for the trust fund.

Validity: In policy evaluation, validity refers to the extent to which a test measures what it is designed to measure.

Value analysis: A systematic analysis of each component of a product, and of the operations performed on each component, in order to determine whether the value contributed by each component is great enough to justify the component's cost.

Variance: The variance, s^2, of a sample or set of n measures is the sum of the squared deviations of the measurements from their mean (x) divided by $(n - 1)$. For example, given the five measures 6, 3, 8, 5, and 3, the variance would be calculated as follows:

$x - \bar{x}$	$(x - \bar{x})^2$
1	1
-2	4
3	9
0	0
-2	4

Welfare economies: The branch of economic theory concerned with the social desirability of alternative economic states. The theory helps analysts distinguish those circumstances under which markets can be expected to perform well from those circumstances under which markets will fail to produce desirable results.

Zero-based budgeting: A procedure for forcing a review of an agency's entire budget by assuming that the minimum funding level for the agency is zero, thereby requiring agency administrators and analysts to justify all expenditures by the same standards of review that are normally applied only to new programs or to increments above the base.

Index

A

Abortion, 443, 608, 645, 646–47
Acid rain, 81–82, 370
Action levers, 498–500
Adams, Henry, 435
Administrative Procedures Act (APA), 47
Affirmative action, 645, 647
Agenda: setting, 13–14, 62
  systemic and institutional, 68
Agricultural mechanization, 420–21
Agricultural policy; see Farm policy
AIDS, 620
Alcoholism, 203
Allende, Salvador, 271
Allison, Grahaw T., 456
Alternatives
  checking, 341–48
  classification of, 296–313
  developing a range of, 280–81
  how to generate, 313–41
  ordering, 284
  range of, 290–96
  screening, 281–82
American Enterprise Institute, 57
Analogy, 328–31
Analysis, 6–7, 30
  limits to, 430–32
Appalachian Regional Development Act, 572
Aristotle, 638–39, 643, 644, 645
Arms control; see National security policy
Asbestos, 615–16
Asian-Americans, 340
Automation, consequences of, 421
Automobile emissions, 12

Automobile safety, 405, 411, 412, 465, 500;
  see also Fifty-five mph speed limit and
  National Highway Traffic and Safety
  Administration
Avoidance, 100

B

B-1 bomber, 354
Bargaining, 459–66
Bay of Pigs, 14
Beethoven, Ludwig, 336
Behavioral approach to politics, 438–56
Bellwethers, 217
Benefits, 352–64, distribution of, 364–66
  total and marginal social, 395–98
Bentham, Jeremy, 622
Bilingual education, 473, 475
Black family
  median income, 127
  structure, 101
Blacks, discrimination against, 339–40
Boards, 65–67
Boston Housing Authority, 527
Bounded rationality, 317–19
Brookings Institution, 57
Buchanan, James M., 483
Bureau of Labor Statistics (BLS), 114

C

Cancer, 411, 413–16, 615
Cannae, Battle of, 225–26
Carter, Jimmy, 14, 58, 77, 93, 223, 233,
  244, 259, 266, 269, 504

687

Case study, use in evaluation of public policies, 588, 594–96
Castro, Fidel, 14
Catastrophe theory, 157
Causation, 137, 143–47
Center for Disease Control (CDC), 458
Central America, 256–57, 279; see also Nicaragua
Chamberlain, Neville, 270
Churchill, Winston, 241
City councils, 64–65
Civil rights, 233, 271
Civil servants, 45
Clausewitz, Karl Von, 227, 521
Claybrook, Joan, 219–20, 254
Client politics, 466, 469
Coalition building, 484–86, 494–95
Cobb, Roger W., 67
Code of Federal Regulations, 506, 511–12
Cognitive dissonance (Festinger's), 94
Cognitive psychology, 266, 313–41 passim, 444
Commissions, 48–50
Computers
  consequences of, 429
  use in policy analysis, 562–70
Comparable worth, 90
Compound interest formula, 194, 566
Congress, 30, 36, 45, 46
  budgeting, 55–57
  committee system, 53–55
  intellectual origins, 50–52
  reform, 559–60
  resources, 52–53
  role, 50
Congressional Budget Office, 53, 57
Congressional roles, 448–50
Congressional staff, 52–53
Constraints, 283–84
Contingency decisions, 521–25
Control group, 586
Consumer analysis, 130–33
Contracting, 454, 527, 531, 550–52, 582–83
Coolidge, Calvin, 183
Cooptation, 454, 477
Correlation, 137–47
Cost-benefit analysis, 282–83, 362–63, 398–410
  applied to welfare economics, 631–34
  decision rules, 402–3
  in evaluation, 598–99
  in incentive decisions, 535–36
Cost effectiveness, 282, 410–18
Costs
  capital, 354
  distribution of, 366–69
  indirect, 18
  operating and maintenance, 354
  total and marginal social costs, 395–98

Council of Economic Advisors (CEA), 39
Courts, reform of, 560–61
Crime; see Criminal justice
Criminal justice, 138–39, 152, 196–97, 232, 249–50, 473–74, 621, 650–51
Crisis-mongering, 155
Cronkite, Walter, 63
Cross-impact matrix, 157
Cyclic change, 189–90, 195–97

D

Darwin, Charles, 278
Davis, Jefferson, 227
Day care, 420
Decision analysis, 378–85
Decision tree, 21; see also Decision analysis
Defense policy; see National security policy
Defense spending, 22–23
Deficits, 109–10
Deinstitutionalization, 501–4
Delphic technique, 128, 210
Depression, 272, 489
Deregulation, 186
  airline, 371
  banking, 371
  energy, 446–48
Desegregation, evaluating effects of, 593–94
Design, see Policy, design of
Diagnosis, 87–153
Discounting, 24, 399–402
Displacement, 442
Distributive policies, 6
Doctrine, 247
Domestic Policy Council, 40
Douglas, William O., 313
Downs, Anthony, 72–73, 442
Draft, 371; see also Selective Service System
Drug addiction, 242–43
Dukakis, Michael, 592
Dynamic feedback, 15–16
Dyson, Freeman, 269

E

Easton, David, 5
Econometric models, 157
Economic history, 272–74
Economic policy; see Economic history; Economic Policy Council; Monetary policy; Reaganomics; and Tax policy
Economic Policy Council, 39
Economics of scale, 535, 552
Education policy, 221, 364–65, 392, 404–5, 552–53, 575, 582; see also Bilingual education

Efficiency, 577–79
  and equality, 625
Elasticity
  demand, 547
  income, 181–83
Elderly, as big economic winners, 98
Energy policy, 3, 155, 213–14, 216–17, 249,
  260–61, 328–29, 362–63, 368–69, 373–
  74, 387–92, 406, 446–98
Entrepreneurial politics, 467, 469
Environmental policy, 85, 88, 95, 161, 204,
  260–61, 355–59, 368, 393, 527, 534–35,
  578–79, 581–82, 649
Environmental Protection Agency (EPA),
  47, 58, 534
Ethics, 29, 606
  economic, 621–34
  ubiquity in policy studies, 607–21
Eudaernonia, 638
Evaluation, 9
  methods, 587–601
Executive Office of the President, 39–40
Expected monitary value (EMV), 21, 378–
  81
Experiment design, 588, 590
Exponential growth, 193–94
Experts, 209–12
Expert systems, 568–70
Externalities, 17–18, 175, 575–77; *see also*
  Costs, indirect

F

Family, changing forms, 203
Famine relief, 27, 104, 154
Farm policy, 175–86, 257, 259
Federal Communications Commission
  (FCC), 46
Federalist, 51, 319
Federal Register, 47, 509
Federal Reserve Board, 274, 555
Federal Trade Commission (FTC), 99, 508,
  510
Field experiment, 588, 591–94
Fifty-five mph speed limit, 407–10, 585–86
Fiscal year, 56
Flood protection, 533, 649
Ford, Gerald R., 14
Foreign policy; *see* National security policy
Founding Fathers, 229
Free market transactions, 17
Freeze-frame statistics, 127–28

G

Gambling, 354
Game theory, 486–88
Gamma score, 125
Garbage can model, 75–82

General Accounting Office (GAO), 53–54,
  578
Generational learning, 266
Gettysburg, Battle of, 350–51
Global Report 2000, 58, 199, 217
Goals, 2–3, 220–23, 501–2
Gorbachev, Mikhail, 63
Granada, 271, 476, 493
Grant, Ulysses S., 227
Groupthink, 340–41

H

Handicapped, 350
Hannibal, 223–26
Hart, B. H. Liddell, 224–26
Head Start programs, 532, 598–99, 603
Health care policy, 70, 87–89, 129, 151,
  153, 187–88, 242, 324–25, 337–38, 411,
  413–18, 446, 528–31, 633
Health insurance
  catastrophic, 239–41
  market, 651
Heuristic search, 319–40
History, 14–15, 264–80
Holmes, Sherlock, 227, 332–33
Homeless, 148; *see also* Deinstitutionaliza-
  tion
Housing policy, 70, 125, 131
  low income, 645
Humanities, 12
Human rights, 640–41

I

Ideology, 94
Ignorance, as source of error, 95
Illegal immigration, 105, 249
Illiteracy, 105–6
Impact assessment, 418–30
Implementation, 8–9, 498–554
Imports; *see* Trade, foreign
Incrementalism, 25
Indifference curve, 628–29
Indirect assessment, 133–37
Indirect costs; *see* Costs, indirect
Industrial development, 580–81
Industrial policy, 80–81, 505
Information, imperfect, 174–75
Input, 29
Input-output matrix, 157
Institutional approach to politics, 438,
  456–58
Insurance, unisex, 371
Integrated Political Analysis Technique
  (INPAT), 450–56
Interdependence, 25, 460
Interest group analysis, 537–40
Interest group politics, 468–69

Interstate Commerce Commission, 582
Intervention effect, 585–87
Iran, 244
Iron triangles, 53–54
Issues networks, 41, 45

J–K

Jacobs, Jane, 579
Johnson, Lyndon B., 14, 19, 38, 62–63, 101, 233, 270, 572, 617
Johnson, Samuel, 64, 95
Justice, 583–84
Keats, John, 642
Kennedy, John F., 14, 19, 223, 233, 332, 340, 617
Kennon, George, 230–32, 259, 330, 643–44
Kingdon, John W., 77
KISS (Keep It Simple, Stupid), 156
Kissinger, Henry A., 61, 109
Khomeini, Ayatollah, 14
King, Martin Luther, 643
Knee Deep in the Big Muddy Phenomenon, 599
Koch, Edward I., 222

L

Lag, 98–100
La Guardia, Fiorello, 222
Learning curve, 510, 513–14
Lee, Robert E., 223, 227–28
Legislatures, state, 64
Liability law, 204
Life cycle of an issue, 84–85
Lincoln, Abraham, 19, 227
  debates with Stephen A. Douglas, 634–36, 642–43
Lindblom, Charles E., 219, 455
Linear programming, 566
Lippmann, Walter, 96–98
Lobbying, 36, 53, 578
Locke, John, 50–51
Logrolling, 462
Lowi, Theodore, 5

M

MacArthur, Douglas, 14
McClellan, George B., 504
MacIntyre, Alasdair, 637–45 passim
Madison, James, 51
Majoritarian politics, 466, 469
Malthus, Thomas, 155, 164
Marginal analysis, 21–22, 395–98
Marginal cost pricing, 541–46
Marine Mammals Protection Act, 27
Market, 170–75
Marshall, George C., 230, 279, 330

Masking problems, 103–5
Massachusetts Institute of Technology, 262–64
Mass media, 62–64, 203
Means-ends analysis, 332–34
Medicare; see Health care policy
Mergers, 99
Microcomputers, 205
Mill, John Stuart, 128, 624
Minneapolis domestic violence, experiment, 589–91
Minority owned business, 365
Modeling; see also Economic models
  model defined, 158–59
  use, 159–60
Monetary policy, 274
Monitoring, 201–9
Monopoly, 172–73
Monroe Doctrine, 247
Motorcycle safety, 597
Moynihan, Daniel P., 101, 364
Mozart, Wolfgang Amadeus, 335–36
Murphy's Law, 521–22
Murray, Charles, 146
Mutual Assured Destruction (MAD), 80, 101

N

National Aeronautics and Space Administration (NASA), 3, 246, 248, 250–51
National Highway Traffic and Safety Administration (NHTSA), 219, 505, 586
National security policy, 100, 104, 112–14, 235, 243, 259–60, 269, 274–75, 277, 459, 473, 558, 573–74
Nazis, 96–98
Newton, Isaac, 159–278
Nicaragua, 91, 109, 323
Nixon, Richard M., 233, 440, 617
Noise, 96–98
Nonmarket failures, 26–29, 480–81, 631
Normal distribution, 122
Nozick, Robert, 627
Nuclear energy, 375–76
Nuclear weapons; see National security policy
Nuclear Regulatory Commission, 376

O

Occupational Safety and Health Administration, 505, 527, 596–97
Office of Management and Budget (OMB), 41, 42–44, 56, 526
Office of Special Trade Representative (OSTR), 39
Office of Technology Assessment (OTA), 53, 59, 349, 421, 596

Okun, Arthur M., 611–13
O'Neill, Thomas P., 437
Opportunity costs, 22–24
Options; *see* Alternatives
Organizational structure, as source of
    error, 92–93
Otto test, 600
Output, 29, 571–75

P

Pareto-optimal, 17, 171–75, 628–31
Payment in Kind Program (PIK), 186
pd > c rule, 345
PERT chart, 514–17, 563–65
Peace Corps, 328–29, 332
Pearl Harbor, 14
Pecuniary effects, 352–53
Peters, Thomas J., 222–332
Phased program planning, 246
Photocopying, consequence of, 428
Piston, Walter, 335
Plan, 2–3
Policy, 1–6, 31
    design of, 229–62
    as hypothesis, 601–3
    termination, 599–601
    types, 5–6
Policy agenda, 13
Policy analysis
    corporate, 206–9
    interdisciplinary aspects, 11–13
    use, 58–62
Policy entrepreneurs, 289
Policy intellectuals, 59
Policy issue development, 67–68
Policy making process, 8–11
Political psychology, 440–56
Political resources, 452–53
Politics, 11
    nature of, 435–39
    as symbolic action, 471–78
Popper, Karl, 246, 627
Population studies, 155
Pork barrel, 433–34, 463–64
Post hoc, ergo propter hoc, 146
Poverty, 110–12, 126, 146–47, 234, 251–52,
    326, 455, 586–87, 594–96; *see also*
    Workers
Power
    distribution of, 28
    dynamics, 25
Power of the purse, 54–57
Presidency, 30, 36–39
    appointments, 41, 44–45
    staff, 39–41
Pricing of public goods, 536, 540–49
Privacy, 205
Private goods, 18

Privatization; *see* Contracting
Problems
    how they capture our attention, 87–92
    how to represent, 106–18
    sources of error in diagnosis, 92–106
Productivity, 89
Projection, 442
Proto-problems, 107–10
Pseudo-problems, 105–7
Psychology of choice, 20–21; *see also* Cog-
    nitive psychology *and* Political psy-
    chology
Public choice, 439, 478–88
Public goods, 18
Public participation, 618
Public policy; *see* Policy
Public relations, 518–21

Q–R

Qaddafi, Muammar, 618–19
Quantification, 12, 147–49, 390
Racism, 339
Rational approach, 219; *see also* Bounded
    rationality
Rawls, John, 345, 613, 626–27, 639
Reagan, Ronald, 14, 22, 38, 63, 78–79, 88,
    99, 147, 235, 244, 247, 435, 494
Reaganomics, 574–75
Regression analysis, 139–41
Regulatory policies, 6
Regulatory process, 508–10
Rent control, 28
Reorganization, as symbolic action, 473
Resource buffers, 245
Risk, 369–87
Roosevelt, Franklin D., 93, 331, 334, 489,
    492, 617
Russians; *see* National security policy

S

Sagan, Carl, 615, 646–47
Satisficing, 325
Scenario planning, 524–26
Scheduling, 514–18
Schelling, Thomas C., 361
Schmidt, Helmut, 269–70
Science policy, 287–88, 334–35, 353, 556–
    57, 648
S-curve, 193–94
Selective Service System, 255
Sensitivity analysis, 284
Shadow price, 359–60
Shaw, George Bernard, 344
Significance, statistical, 125, 142
Simon, Herbert A., 12, 247, 318–19, 326
Simulation, 567–68
Small Business Administration, 532

692

Smith, Adam, 169
Social security
  legislation, 47
  trends, 188, 370, 437, 462, 496, 501
Solar energy; see Energy policy
Soviet Union; see National security policy
Space policy, 259; see also National Aero-
  nautics and Space Administration
Stalin, Joseph, 24
Standard deviation, 121
Star wars; see Strategic Defense Initiative
Statistical Package for Social Sciences
  (SPSS), 565
Statistics, 119–23
Stockman, David, 440, 459
Strategic Defense Initiative (SDI), 57, 79–
  80, 277, 353, 374–75, 500, 554, 614
Strategic factors, 235–43
Strategic thinking, 18–20, 218–64
Strategies, 9
Strategy, grand, 224
Stratified sample, 124
Structural approach to politics, 438, 468–
  78
Structural change, 188–89
Survey research, 123–28
Syasa, Thomas, 679
Systems view, 15–16, 255
  counterintuitive native, 255–56

T

Tax policy, 77–78, 367, 370, 372–73, 475
Technology assessment; see Impact assess-
  ment
Telephone, consequences of, 425, 428
Think tanks, 57–62
Third world, 104, 108, 242
Thought experiments, 339–40
Thurow, Lester, 609, 613, 616
Time series, 195
Trade, foreign, 232, 243, 256, 271–72, 372,
  393

Transportation policy, urban, 90, 200–201,
  260–61, 320–23, 343–44, 433
Trend extrapolation, 186–201
  hazards, 197–201
Truman, Harry S., 222, 247, 259
Tullock, Gordon, 481, 483
Type III error, 221

U

Unemployment, 114–18, 205, 242, 249–50,
  260–61, 419–20
Unintended consequences, 419–21, 576–
  77; see also Nonmarket failures
Urban renewal, 419
U.S. Constitution, 55, 319, 460–61, 554–56
Utilitarianism, 622–28, 640

V

Validity, 142
Value, theory of, 632
Veterans Administration (VA), 525–26
Vietnam war, 18, 63, 234, 243, 280
Virtue, 637–44
  and policy, 644–45, 648
Voting paradox, 481–84

W

War, costs of, 350–51
Washington, D.C., 35
Water resources, 205, 403–4, 406, 548
Welfare; see Poverty
Welfare economics, fundamental theorem,
  16–17, 631
Wildavsky, Aaron, 55, 501, 601
Wild Boy of Aveyron, 619–20
Wilensky, Harold L., 92
Wolf, Charles, 26–29, 480, 632
Women, changing role, 202
Workfare, 591–93

ABOUT THE AUTHOR

Grover Starling is Professor of Public Affairs and Management in the School of Business and Public Administration; and Director, Center for the Management of Advanced Technology at the University of Houston–Clear Lake, where he has taught since 1974. Starling is a graduate of the U.S. Military Academy and holds a Ph.D. from the University of Texas at Austin. He is the author of *The Changing Environment of Business; Issues in Business and Society: Capitalism and Public Purpose;* and *Understanding American Politics*. While at UH–CL, he has been Director of Programs in Public Affairs.

Starling has served as a consultant to a number of corporations and federal agencies, including NASA, the Department of Education, and the U.S. Air Force. His research interests include the psychology of thinking, the interrelationship of business and government, and the use of historical analogy in policy analysis.

A NOTE ON THE TYPE

The text of this book was set in 10/12 Palatino using a film version of the face designed by Hermann Zapf that was first released in 1950 by Germany's Stempel Foundry. The face is named after Giovanni Battista Palatino, a famous penman of the 16th century. In its calligraphic quality, Palatino is reminiscent of the Italian Renaissance type designs, yet with its wide, open letters and unique proportions it still retains a modern feel. Palatino is considered one of the most important faces from one of Europe's most influential type designers.

Composed by Arcata Graphics/Kingsport.

Printed and bound by Arcata Graphics/Halliday, West Hanover, Massachusetts.